HUNGARY AND
HER SUCCESSORS
1919 — 1937

D1599048

HUNGARY AND HER SUCCESSORS

THE TREATY OF TRIANON AND ITS CONSEQUENCES
1919 — 1937

By

C. A. MACARTNEY

OXFORD UNIVERSITY PRESS
LONDON   NEW YORK   TORONTO
*Issued under the auspices of the Royal Institute
of International Affairs*

1937

OXFORD UNIVERSITY PRESS
AMEN HOUSE, E.C. 4
London Edinburgh Glasgow New York
Toronto Melbourne Capetown Bombay
Calcutta Madras
HUMPHREY MILFORD
PUBLISHER TO THE UNIVERSITY

PRINTED IN GREAT BRITAIN

FOREWORD

IT is the duty of the author of a book published under the auspices of Chatham House to call attention to the conditions under which Chatham House lends its *imprimatur* to such works: to wit, that the sole responsibility for the correctness of any facts recorded, and the sagacity of any opinions expressed therein, rests with the author alone. It must be his pleasure to acknowledge most gratefully the invaluable help rendered him by the staff of the Library, the Press-cutting and Information sections, and other departments of the Institute.

Many other kindly helpers have given me much assistance both by supplying information, in the first instance, and by reading the draft of all or part of the manuscript, correcting errors of fact, and persuading me to renounce unreasonable judgments. If I insist once again on my sole responsibility for the final result, this is not due to satisfaction with it; but some who helped me most, including in particular certain experts in the countries whose conditions are here described, feared that if I accepted and acknowledged their help, the impression might arise that they had secured the removal of what was objectionable to them in the first draft, and agreed with the residue. I gladly record that this is not the case; nor did I myself expect, or even seek to reach such complete agreement with any one party to questions so complex and controversial. I am, however, deeply indebted to these experts, and also to the officials of their countries, including in particular the staffs of their London Legations for facilitating my journeys, and in some cases my inquiries.

If any person has the patience to read this book right through, he may complain of a certain unevenness of treatment. For example, the negotiations for the settlement of the Austrian and the Slovak frontiers are described in some detail, while the corresponding negotiations with Yugoslavia occupy only a few paragraphs, those with Roumania only a few lines. The economic position in Slovakia-Ruthenia and in Hungary is treated much more fully than that in Transylvania and the Voivodina; almost as much space is devoted to the national feelings of the Bunyevci as to those of the Transylvanian-Roumanians. This is, I fear, due in part to the very unequal wealth of the sources of information, but partly also to purpose. This book was written, not as a history, but as part of a series dealing with the problems of treaty revision, and it therefore dwells most closely on what is most nearly germane to the revision problem: the doubtful and disputed points, or the cases where one argument, e.g. the economic, may be set against another—the strategic or ethnographical.

Many places in what used to be Hungary have two or three national names, and it is a sore problem to decide which should be used. I have attempted in each case to use the name current in the country with which the section in question is dealing, placing the alternative names in brackets after the first use of the name in that section. Thus in the Hungarian section I write 'Pozsóny (Pressburg, Bratislava)' when mentioning that historic city for the first time, thereafter 'Pozsóny' alone; in the Austrian section, 'Pressburg (Pozsóny, Bratislava)', thereafter 'Pressburg'; in the Czechoslovak sections, 'Bratislava (Pozsóny, Pressburg)', then 'Bratislava'. The solution is not ideal, and involves difficulties, in particular in connexion with quotations from historic documents; but I can devise no better.

Finally, I would ask understanding, if not indulgence, for the many mistakes which these pages must contain. To mention one difficulty alone, at least seventeen different languages are indigenous to the area covered; and that is counting the dialects of Ruthene as one.

C. A. MACARTNEY

TABLE OF CONTENTS

LIST OF ABBREVIATIONS

Czech Claims == *The Territorial Claims of the Czecho-Slovak Republic* (Memorandum presented to the Peace Conference, 1919).

H.P.C. = TEMPERLEY (H. W. V.) ed.: *A History of the Peace Conference of Paris.* 6 vols. London, 1920–4.

Hungarian Peace Negotiations == *The Hungarian Peace Negotiations: an account of the work of the Hungarian Peace Delegation at Neuilly s/S. from January to March 1920.* 3 vols. in 4. Budapest, 1921–2.

Hunter Miller, *Diary* == MILLER (David Hunter): *My Diary at the Peace Conference of Paris.* 21 vols. Printed privately, 1924–6.

L.N.O.J. = *League of Nations Official Journal.*

Revision Memorandum == *Memorandum concerning the Situation of the Hungarian Minority in Czechoslovakia.* Budapest, 1934.

BIBLIOGRAPHICAL NOTE

THE following list does not attempt to do more than indicate some of the more important publications on the very wide subject-matter of this book. It is a guide for further reading, rather than an enumeration of my own sources, a large proportion of which do not consist of printed matter at all. On the other hand, I have tried where possible to avoid recommending books which I have not myself read; partly in deference to some scruples expressed to me by some foreign helpers who supplied me with lists of what were in their opinion the best books—for, they said, if I had read those works my conclusions would have been different; and I must beware of pretending to more authority than my elementary studies can justly claim; but partly because I myself have learned from experience that not all works popular among individual nations are either wise or helpful. I have included such works only where the list, without them, seemed one-sided. Many of the titles given below are abbreviated.

Pre-War History. The histories of Hungary before the War, and also those published since in English, French, or German, usually give little help in understanding the causes of Hungary's break-down. The best in this regard is Count P. Teleki, *The Evolution of Hungary and its place in European History* (Williamstown, 1923). There is now a monumental 7-volume history, *Magyar Történet*, by Professors Hóman and Szekfű, of which an abbreviation is to appear in English. J. Kornis, *A Magyar Művelődés Eszményei* (Budapest, 1927, 2 vols.), throws much light on the ideology of the whole modern period; J. Hermant, *La révolution hongroise de 1848* (Paris, 1901), for the first great revolution; I. de Nagy, *A Nemzetiségi Törvény* (Budapest, 1929), for the succeeding period, for which see also the various writings of Baron Eötvös on the national question. For the period after 1867: G. Gratz, *A Dualismus Kora* (Budapest, 1934); J. Szekfű, *Három Nemzedék* (latest edition, Budapest, 1935). See also Count Tisza's speeches in his *Összes Munkái*. Criticism of modern Hungarian policy from the Magyar side: L. Mocsáry, *Nemzetiség* (Vienna, 1858), *Programm a nemzetiség és a nemzetiségek targyában* (Budapest, 1860), *Néhany szó a nemzetiségi kérdésről* (Budapest, 1866), and O. Jászi, *A nemzetiségi kérdés* (Budapest, 1911), *Der Zusammenbruch des Dualismus* (Vienna, 1918), and *The Dissolution of the Habsburg Monarchy* (Chicago, 1929). An important study on the development of the nationalities: A. Balogh, *A népfajok Magyar-*

országon. For a Magyar point of view, I am referred to the works of G. Beksics, *Magyarosodás és Magyarosítás* (Budapest, 1883), *A Magyar politika* (Budapest, 1899). Much material is contained in the three volumes dealing with the work of the Hungarian Peace Delegation (*The Hungarian Peace Negotiations: an account of the Hungarian Peace Delegation at Neuilly s/S. from January to March 1920.* Published by the Royal Hungarian Ministry of Foreign Affairs, Budapest, 1921-2. Quoted here as *Hungarian Peace Negotiations*). The chief non-Magyar critics: A. Popovici (Transylvanian-Roumanian) in *Die Vereinigten Staaten Gross-Oesterreichs* (Leipzig, 1906), and above all R. W. Seton-Watson's works, particularly *Racial Problems in Hungary* (London, 1908). From the Yugoslav side, a work by M. Kirilović is appearing shortly. For the various national movements, general: B. Auerbach, *Les Races et les nationalités en Austro-Hongrie* (Paris, 1917); A. Fischel, *Der Panslawismus* (Berlin, 1919) (very useful account, unsympathetic to the Slavs), and various memoranda in the *Hungarian Peace Negotiations*; Germans (Suabians): R. Kaindl, *Geschichte der Deutschen in den Karpathenländern* (Gotha, 1907, 3 vols.); S. Rádo, *Das Deutschtum in Ungarn* (Berlin, 1913); *Deutschtum und Magyarisierung in Ungarn* (Munich, 1908), and a few other pamphlets.

For the Slovaks, Seton-Watson, *Racial Problems in Hungary*, with bibliography of the earlier literature on both sides, *q.v.*; from the Magyar side I am recommended L. Steier, *A tót kérdés* (Liptószentmiklós, 1912). For Czech-Slovak relations, A. Szána, *Geschichte der Slowakei* (Bratislava, 1930), most useful; much material also in the Czech War-time propaganda on the one hand, and the *Hungarian Peace Negotiations* on the other. For the Ruthenes, Hungarian writers: A. Bonkaló, *Die ungarländischen Ruthenen* (Ungarische Jahrbücher, vol. i, 1922), chiefly historical, and *A Kárpátalja rutén irodalom és művelődés* (Pécs, 1931); Czech thesis, K. Krofta, *Die Podkarpatska Rús und die Tschechoslovakei* (Prague, 1934). The Roumanians, R. W. Seton-Watson, *A History of the Roumanians* (London, 1935), with full bibliography. From the Hungarian side, the chief works are those of B. Jancsó, *A román nemzetiségi törekvések története* (Budapest, 1896, 1899), and *A román irridentista mozgalmak története* (Budapest, 1920); from the Roumanian side, the works of Jorga, notably his *Histoire des roumains de Transylvanie et de Hongrie* (Bucharest, 1915), and of Hasdeu, Xenopol, &c., also A. Popovici, *La Question roumaine en Transylvanie et en Hongrie* (Paris, 1918), G. Moroianu, *La Lutte des roumains transylvains* (Paris, 1933). The Transylvanian Saxons have a monumental 3-volume history of their own: G. and F. Teutsch, *Geschichte der Siebenbürger Sachsen* (4th ed., Hermannstadt, 1925), and a rich literature of 'Volksbücher'.

For the Southern Slav question in the Dual Monarchy the classic works are R. W. Seton-Watson, *The Southern Slav Question and the Habsburg Monarchy* (London, 1911), with bibliography, and 'Südland', *Die südslawische Frage und der Weltkrieg* (Vienna, 1918) (interesting, anti-Serb). Both of these deal more fully with Croatia than with the Voivodina. H. Wendel, *Aus dem südslawischen Risorgimento* (Gotha, 1921), and E. Haumant, *La Formation de la Yougoslavie* (Paris, 1930), have interesting chapters on the Serb movement in the Voivodina. A short work on the Banat, from the Hungarian side, is that of E. Horváth, *The Banat* (Sárkány, 1931). The latest work by a Magyar is B. Nádasdy, *Délszlávok* (Budapest, n.d.). Older literature on the Voivodina: J. H. Schwicker, *Geschichte der oesterreichischen Militärgrenze* (Vienna, 1883), and *Politische Geschichte der Serben in Ungarn* (Budapest, 1880); G. Czirbusz, *Délvidéki németek* (Budapest, 1913).

For the economic development of Hungary: J. Grunzl, *Handelspolitik und Ausgleich in Oesterreich-Ungarn* (Vienna, 1912); K. Mandello, *Rückblicke auf die Entwicklung der ungarischen Volkswirtschaft 1877–1902* (Budapest, 1902); A. von Matlekovits, *Geschichte des ungarischen Staatshaushaltes 1867 bis 1893* (Prague, 1895); id., *Die Zollpolitik der Oesterreichischen-ungarischen Monarchie und des deutschen Reiches* (Leipzig, 1891); W. Offergeld, *Grundlagen und Ursachen der industriellen Entwicklung Ungarns* (Jena, 1914) (an interesting study from outside); R. Sieghart, *Zolltrennung und Zolleinheit* (Vienna, 1915); J. Szterényi, *La Grande Industrie du royaume de Hongrie* (Budapest, 1901) (by the man largely responsible for Hungary's industrial development before the War). Retrospective post-War works, written largely to prove the unwisdom of the Treaty: L. Buday, *Dismembered Hungary* (Budapest, 1922); id., *The Economic Unity of Hungary* (Budapest, 1919); I. A. Edvi, *Hungarian State Policy with Regard to the Position of Industry* (Budapest, 1920); I. Edvi and A. Kalasz, *Magyarország a háboru előtt és után* (Budapest, 1926). There is also much material in *Hungarian Peace Negotiations*, and some in *Justice for Hungary* (Budapest, 1928), a collection of articles by different hands, of very unequal value.

The period of the 'Umsturz' is described as regards Hungary generally, in many works, *inter alia* G. Andrássy, *Diplomacy and War* (London, 1921); E. Glaise-Horstenau, *The Collapse of the Austro-Hungarian Empire* (London, 1930); G. Gratz and R. Schüler, *Der wirtschaftliche Zusammenbruch Oesterreich-Ungarns* (Vienna, 1930); A. Hevesy, *L'Agonie d'un Empire* (Paris, 1923); Th. Batthyány, *Für Ungarn gegen Hohenzollern* (Vienna, 1930); O. Jászi, *Magyariens Schuld, Ungarns Sühne* (Vienna, 1923); M. Károlyi, *Gegen eine ganze Welt* (Munich, 1924). *Justice for*

Hungary contains a valuable chapter (easily the best in the book) by A. Horváth, 'The Diplomatic History of the Treaty of Trianon'. Short summary, C. A. Macartney, 'Hungary', in *The Modern World* series (London, 1934). For the proceedings of the Peace Conference, *A History of the Peace Conference of Paris*, edited by H. W. V. Temperley (6 vols., London, 1920–4), supplemented by the same author's article, 'How the Hungarian Frontiers were drawn' (*Foreign Affairs* (New York), April 1928), and D. Hunter Miller's *My Diary at the Peace Conference of Paris* (21 vols., privately printed, 1924–6), these forming the standard works; H. Nicolson, *Peacemaking* (London, 1933), with details of the work of the Commissions on Hungarian frontiers. Austria, Hungary, Czechoslovakia, and Roumania have published official material relating to the proceedings at the Conference. For the Austrian frontier, see also V. Miltschinsky, *Das Verbrechen von Oedenburg* (Vienna, 1922), and E. Traeger, *Die Volksabstimmung in Sopron* (1921); some details also in O. Bauer, *Die Oesterreichische Revolution* (Vienna, 1923). For Czechoslovakia: Masaryk, *The Making of a State*, and Beneš, *Der Aufstand der Nationen*, are essential, also, for Ruthenia, Žatković's *Exposé* (Homestead, Pa., n.d., roneoed only). General account in J. Opočensky, *The Collapse of the Austro-Hungarian Monarchy and the Rise of the Czechoslovakian State*, and *Umsturz in Mitteleuropa* (Dresden, 1931), also A. Pechány, *Comment les Tchècques ont accaparé la Slovaquie* (1928). Szána, op. cit., gives without comment very valuable contemporary documentary and press material. For the Roumanian and Yugoslav frontiers there are no available accounts on the other side to balance the story told in *Justice for Hungary*. L. Várjássy, *Révolution, Bolchévisme, Réaction* (Paris, 1934), gives a few interesting details on the Banat.

For **Post-War National Conditions in General,** much of the best material is published in periodical form. *Nation und Staat* (Vienna, 1927– , monthly) is the most useful of the periodicals. It is fullest for the German minorities, and reflects chiefly the more *völkisch* point of view, but prints valuable 'Situation Reports' for other minorities also. *Magyar Kisebbség*, in Magyar, with an abbreviated version, *Glasul Minoritaţilor* (Lugoj, Roumania), containing also articles in French, German, and Roumanian, is edited by Magyars and is fullest for the Magyar minorities in Roumania, whose point of view it reflects. *The Danubian Review*, published in Budapest, the *Voix des Peuples— Minorité* of Geneva (1933–)—deal chiefly with injustices perpetrated on the Magyar minorities, but also with other shortcomings of the Successor States. The 'omnibus' volume, *Die*

Nationalitäten in den Staaten Europas, edited by M. Ammende (Vienna, 1931, supplement 1932) contains a very valuable summary of the situation at the time. The point of view is that of the minorities; the sources often identical with those of *Nation und Staat* and *Magyar Kisebbség*. The German *Volk und Reich* (Berlin, monthly) often has interesting, but biased, articles. The periodicals published in English or French by the Governments are usually pretty innocent affairs: the best are those of Prague, *The Central European Observer*, and *L'Europe Centrale*. The *Nouvelle Revue de Hongrie* and *Magyar Szemle* reflect the views of circles connected with Count Bethlen: in another field, the *League of Nations Official Journal* contains a large number of minority petitions, sometimes with the replies of the Governments. Any one making a detailed study of post-War conditions should go through these periodicals, where he will find a wealth of material. See also on the minority problem in general, C. A. Macartney, *National States and National Minorities* (London, 1934), with bibliography.

General Works on the Magyar Minorities. *The Hungarian Minorities in the Successor States* (Budapest, 1929) and the publications of the Hungarian Frontier Readjustment League; see also below under 'Treaty Revision'. General works on the Germans: *Handwörterbuch des Grenz- und Auslandsdeutschtum* (Breslau, 1933); R. Bahr, *Volk jenseits der Grenze*, and *Deutsches Schicksal im Südosten* (Hamburg, 1936); U. C. von Loesch, *Volk unter Völkern* (Breslau, 1935). Special areas: on the Burgenland, see the works quoted in the text, of which that of de Nagy has a bibliography; another bibliography is given in *Magyar Kisebbség*, 1934, no. 13, pp. 389–91. A big Austrian atlas and encyclopaedia of the Burgenland is said to be in preparation. For Slovakia the literature is richer. Official statistics in the *Annuaire Statistique* of the Czechoslovak Republic. For the nationality laws, E. Sobota, *Das tschechische Nationalitätenrecht* (Prague, 1931). For a sketch of the political parties, J. Borovička, *Ten Years of Czechoslovakian Politics* (Prague, 1929). For the land reform, several official accounts have been issued by the Ministry of Agriculture in Prague. For political conditions, the main works friendly to the régime are R. W. Seton-Watson, *The New Slovakia* (1924), and *Slovakia Then and Now* (London, 1931), a collection of articles by various Slovak writers on many aspects of Slovak life, with the most valuable introduction, friendly but critical, by Professor Seton-Watson. In similar vein, C. J. C. Street, *Slovakia Past and Present* (London, 1923). Much material can be found also in *L'Europe Centrale* and *The Central European Observer*, both published in Prague, and in *Le Monde Slave* (Paris). Dr. Beneš, *Discours aux*

Slovaques sur le présent et l'avenir de notre nation (1933), is important both historically and as a statement of policy. On the other side, H. Hassinger, *Die Tschechoslowakei* (Vienna, 1925); L. Steier, *Ungarns Vergewaltigung* (Vienna, 1929); Fr. Jehlička, *Une Étape du calvaire slovaque* (Paris, 1930); R. Donald, *The Tragedy of Trianon* London, 1934) (chiefly material from Magyar sources); O. Tarján, *The Ways of Czechoslovakia and its Magyar Minority* (Budapest, 1934); *Memorandum concerning the Situation of the Hungarian Minority in Czechoslovakia* (Budapest, 1934). For the Germans, the various *Flugschriften* of the *Zipser deutsche Partei*. For industry and commerce, *Jahresberichte der Zentralvereinigung der slowakischen Industrie* (Bratislava, 1925–). A series by A. Fichelle on the economic role of Slovakia in the Czechoslovak State ran through *L'Europe Centrale* in 1934; the material is excellent, although the interpretation seems unduly optimistic. The decay of Slovak industry is vividly illustrated by Edvi and Halász (op. cit.), by A. Halász, *Felső magyarország munkával való ellatása a magyar és cseh uralom alatt* (Budapest, 1927), and by I. B. Kardos and L. Artner, *A Felvidék ipari népességének alakulása a háboru előtt és után*, in *Ipar*. See also L. Pasvolsky, *Economic Nationalism of the Danubian States* (New York, 1928); M. Moritz, *A felvidék gazdasági élete Trianon óta* (Budapest, 1931).

For **Ruthenia**, Žatkovič's *Exposé* is valuable for the early period, which Szána (op. cit.) also covers. For later years, the accessible literature is sparse. There is a semi-official 'omnibus' volume in Czech entitled *Podkarpatská Rus*. R. Martel, *La Ruthénie Sub-Carpathique* (Paris, 1935), while strongly Czechophil, gives a good account of the national imbroglio. F. Gerandó, author of *Le Complot rouge en Ruthénie*, appears from internal evidence to have spent only twenty-four hours in the country, but has collected and reproduced material from the Kutyak party. Similar material (viz. complaints against Czech rule) in M. Yuhasz, *Wilson's Principles in Czechoslovak Practice* (Homestead, Pa., 1929). The best material generally available consists of the Ruthene petitions to the League of Nations and the Czechoslovak Government's replies; the first of these were issued as separate League documents, the later printed in the *League of Nations Official Journal*. Important, for the Government attitude, is Dr. Beneš's long *Discours aux Ruthènes*. For economics, see Slovakia; also J. Brandeis, *La Ruthénie subcarpathique du point de vue agricole* (Paris, 1935).

For **Transylvania since the War**, there is practically nothing on the Roumanian problem. For the minorities, from the Roumanian side, S. Dragomir, *The Ethnical Minorities in Transylvania* (Geneva, 1927), expanded and brought up to date in *La Transylvanie roumaine et ses minorités ethniques* (Bucharest, 1934); 'Transylvanus', *Les minorités ethniques de la Transylvanie* (Paris, 1934); and the *Revue de Transylvanie*, 1933—tendentious, but interesting. From the Hungarian side, a collection of early complaints in *The Grievances of the Hungarian minority in Transylvania*, issued by the Hungarian-Siculian Society (Budapest, 1922); Zs. de Szász, *The Minorities in Roumanian Transylvania* (London, 1927), a full and careful work, excellent for the early period, but polemical; more recent, M. de Eckhardt's speech at the League of Nations Assembly of 1935, and pamphlets issued in connexion therewith. The *Magyar Kisebbség* specializes in Roumanian questions; many of its articles have been reprinted in pamphlet form. The American Committee on the Rights of Religious Minorities produced two volumes, edited by L. Cornish, *Transylvania in 1922* (Boston, 1923), and *The Religious Minorities in Transylvania* (London, 1926), and a third, *Roumania Ten Years After* (Boston, 1929); a 'reply' to the above, from Roumanian (nominally neutral) side, is H. M. Tichner, *Roumania and her Religious Minorities* (London, 1927). J. M. Cabot, *The Racial Conflict in Transylvania* (Boston, 1926), is unfavourable to Roumania, L. S. Rouček, *Contemporary Roumania* (London, 1932), strongly partial to the Government; good bibliography. For the agrarian reform: I. L. Evans, *The Agrarian Revolution in Roumania* (Cambridge, 1924); D. Mitrany, *The Land and the Peasant in Roumania* (London, 1930); and from the Hungarian side, as a reply to Mitrany, M. Móricz, *The Fate of the Transylvanian Soil* (Budapest, 1934); also many polemical articles and pamphlets. I pass over the literature on the optant question. For the Germans, *Siebenbürgen*, edited by K. Bell (Dresden, 1930); also rich material in *Nation und Staat* and in the copious local German Press. For economics: the Chamber of Commerce and Industry of Brașov produces occasional reports; there are also, of course, Government statistics.

There is very little serious literature on **Yugoslavia**. General works on the country include A. Mousset, *Le Royaume Serbe-Croate-Slovène* (Paris, 1926), strongly pro-Yugoslav. For the Croat side of the Croat question, the works of Pavelić and Pribičević—both of them written by embittered enemies of the régime. A series of articles by R. W. Seton-Watson in *International Affairs*, the Journal of the Royal Institute of International Affairs ('Jugoslavia and Croatia', March 1929; 'The Yugoslav Dictatorship', January 1932; 'The Problem of Treaty Revision and the Hungarian Frontiers', July 1933; 'Some Aspects of the Danubian Problem',

September 1934), traces the development of the problem since the War, and especially since the proclamation of the Dictatorship. For the Magyar minority, S. Margitai, *A Horvát-és szlavonországi magyarok sorsa.*

For post-War conditions in the **Voivodina** there is no single book to recommend. The fullest written information on the Magyar minorities is contained in the two sources quoted as '*Hungarian MS.*', and '*Hungarian Petition*', in *Nationalitäten in den Staaten Europas* and in the various numbers of *Glasul Minoritaţilor.* I am referred also to articles in the *Magyar Szemle* by S. Berkes (Jan., May, and Oct. 1928), and by I. Prokopy (1932). For the Germans, *Nationalitäten in den Staaten Europas; Nation und Staat passim;* H. Rudiger, *Die Donauschwaben in der südslawischen Batschka* (Stuttgart, 1931); P. Rühlmann, *Das Schulrecht der deutschen Minderheit in Südslawien* (Berlin, 1932); T. Grentrup, *Das Deutschtum an der mittleren Donau* (Münster, 1930). I know of no detailed work from the Yugoslav side, although stray references occur in various works on Yugoslavia.

For the **Minority Question in Hungary since the War**, Count S. Bethlen, *Beszédei és Irásai* (Budapest, 1933); C. A. Macartney, *Hungary* (London, 1934). The Germans: S. Bleyer (ed.), *Das Deutschtum in Rumpfungarn* (Budapest, 1928) (statistical and historical); Dr. A. Rieth, *Die geographische Verbreitung des Deutschtums in Rumpfungarn in Vergangenheit und Gegenwart* (Stuttgart, 1927); U. Bell, *Das Deutschtum in Ausland: Ungarn* (Dresden, 1935); H. Göttling, *Aus Vergangenheit und Gegenwart des deutschungarischen Volkes* (Budapest, 1930) (popular). Ample material to study every phase of the question will be found in the columns of the *Sonntagsblatt*, the *Pester Lloyd*, and *Nation und Staat*, and in *Nationalitäten in den Staaten Europas.* Many articles by Count Bethlen, Dr. Gusztáv Gratz, M. L. de Ottlik, and others have appeared in the *Magyar Szemle*, the *Nouvelle Revue de Hongrie*, and other periodicals, chiefly in 1929, 1933, and 1934. It is well, however, to compare these measured and statesmanlike utterances with what the jingo Press has to say on the subject at the same time. F. Svojše has written a series of pamphlets against Hungary's policy towards her Slovaks, including *The Racial Minorities in Hungary and Czechoslovakia* (Prague, 1922), and *Le Traitement des minorités en Tschéchoslovaquie et en Hongrie* (Prague, 1927); more modern, J. Chmelař, 'La Minorité slovaque en Hongrie' (in *Le Monde Slave*, July 1933), C. J. C. Street, *Hungary and Democracy* (London, 1923), and J. D. E. Evans, *That Blue Danube* (London, 1935), are also severe on Hungarian policy.

For **Hungarian Economics since the War**, Buday (op. cit.), *Justice for Hungary*, &c., enumerate Hungary's losses under the Treaty. I do not know of any one book which tells in detail the story of her re-adaptation. Pasvolski (op. cit.) was written very early. The Royal Hungarian Statistical Office produces ample material for those able to use it. There is an extremely useful annual series by G. Kemény and I. Vágo, *Die Volkswirtschaft Ungarns im Jahre* — (Budapest, 1926–); further, periodical reports by the League of Nations Commissioners, the National Bank of Hungary, the Ministry of Finance, and various private banks.

General Works on Treaty Revision: an immense amount of revisionist literature exists, but most of it adds up to little more than the repetition of the arguments set forth by the *Hungarian Peace Negotiations* and in *Justice for Hungary*, plus accounts of political abuses and economic decay in the different areas. See, however, for a recent re-statement, Count S. Bethlen, *The Treaty of Trianon and European Peace* (London, 1934) (four lectures delivered in London by the Hungarian ex-Premier). For the difficulties of revision in a nutshell, R. W. Seton-Watson, *Treaty Revision and the Hungarian Frontiers* (London, 1934). R. Dami recommends a modified form of 'lesser revision' in *La Hongrie de demain* (Paris, 1933). Short summary of the conflicting views in C. A. Macartney, *Hungary* (London, 1934).

INTRODUCTION

§ I. THE PROBLEM

NONE of the Peace Treaties was more drastic in its terms than the Treaty of Trianon. By it Hungary was not so much mutilated as dismembered. Even if we exclude Croatia-Slavonia, which had stood only in a federal relationship to the other Lands of the Holy Crown—although one of eight hundred years' standing —Hungary proper was reduced to less than one-third (32·6 per cent.) of her pre-War area, and a little over two-fifths (41·6 per cent.) of her population. Territories and peoples formerly Hungarian were distributed among no less than seven states: the remnant which still called itself Hungary, Austria, Czechoslovakia, Poland, Roumania, Yugoslavia, and Italy; Roumania alone securing at Hungary's expense an area (although not a population) larger than that left to Hungary herself. These losses were proportionately far greater than those inflicted on Germany or Bulgaria. The Austria of 1937 was, indeed, an even smaller fraction of the State which had borne that name in 1918; but the old Austria had not been a unitary state, but only a federation of Kingdoms, Duchies, and provinces, the hereditary estates of a super-national dynasty, the composition of which was seldom the same for two successive generations. The Treaty of St. Germain simply divided this federation into its constituent elements. The real losses suffered by the German-Austrian provinces, in the South Tyrol, along the marches of Styria and Carinthia and on the Bohemian border, were painful, but insignificant compared with those of Hungary. So, too, Turkey retained almost intact the Turkish core of her Empire, losing only outlying portions. The losses of Bulgaria and of Germany itself were, for that matter, nearly all comparatively recent conquests, attained in some cases by sheer spoliation.

The Hungarian State, on the other hand, had existed for a thousand years within frontiers which, if not entirely unchanged, had shown a very remarkable degree of stability. The political State enclosed within those boundaries had been unitary from long before most of the States of to-day. Moreover, its geographical structure had imposed upon it also a very close economic coherence, obviously beneficial to almost all its inhabitants. The unity of Hungary was thus something of an entirely different order from that of the Austrian or the Ottoman Empire; it was even far more firmly established than that of Germany or Bulgaria.

These things were never seriously denied, although historic

counter-claims were, of course, advanced (usually in somewhat half-hearted fashion) in support of the demands made by the beneficiaries of the Treaty, most of whom also found that just the areas which they claimed were precisely those vital to their own economies and unnecessary to Hungary's. But the true reason for the partition of Hungary was, of course, that the racial diversity of its population was at least as undeniable as its historic or geographical unity. The 1910 census, taken at the end of a half-century during which Hungary had done everything in her power to promote knowledge of the Magyar tongue, and taken, moreover, on a basis (that of 'mother-tongue', defined as 'the language which the person speaks best and most readily') and by methods which certainly favoured the appearance of uniformity, yet showed only 9,944,627 persons out of a total population of 18,264,533,[1] or 54·5 per cent. of the whole, who admitted Magyar as their mother language, and of these, well over half a million were Jews. The persons speaking other languages were enumerated as follows: German, 1,903,357 (10·4 per cent.); Slovak, 1,946,357 (10·7 per cent.); Roumanian, 2,948,186 (16·1 per cent.); Croat, 194,808 (1·1 per cent.); Serb, 416,516 (2·5 per cent.); Ruthene, 464,270 (2·5 per cent.); other languages,[2] 464,270 (2·2 per cent.). The number of persons entered in the census as speaking two languages showed that those whose parents, at least, had not really been Magyar-speaking were even more numerous than the figures seemed to show, for the true Magyar would rarely admit to a knowledge of Slovak or Roumanian, and most of the persons speaking those languages as well as Magyar were certainly of recent non-Magyar origin.

Indeed, only the heart of Hungary, its great central plain, was in 1910 indisputedly Magyar, and here, too, there were numerous non-Magyar colonies, which near the southern frontier outnumbered the Magyars substantially. In the mountains which occupied the north, east, and a sliver of the west of the country, the Magyar speakers were represented only by one large compact body, half a million strong (the Székely), in the far east of Transylvania; by a certain number of smaller islands of population, of which the most important were, again, in Transylvania (although in parts of the north they were also not inconsiderable), and finally, by a thin upper caste of landowners and their entourage in the country districts, and in most of the towns a body, often considerable but usually of recent date, of officials, business men, and skilled

[1] Excluding Croatia-Slavonia. Including those lands, the total population was 20,886,487, and the percentage of Magyar speakers 48·1.
[2] These were mostly gipsy, Polish, and varieties of the Southern Slav group of languages, described in the census as Sokaz (Šokci), Bunyevac (Bunyevci), Dalmatian, Bosniak, and Illyrian.

labourers. The majority of the indigenous populations of the periphery[1] was German in the west, Slovak in the north, Ruthene in the north-east, Roumanian in the east; while in the south there was a large contingent of Serbs, mingled with the Magyars and with German and other colonists.

It was, broadly speaking, the principle of 'national self-determination' which was invoked in 1919 to bring about the dismemberment of Hungary. The German area in the west (or rather, a part of it) was assigned to Austria; the north, both Slovak and Ruthene, to Czechoslovakia;[2] the east to Roumania, and the south to Yugoslavia, Italy pouching the port of Fiume; while the centre remained with Hungary. The old State of Hungary was thus replaced, more or less, by a number of national states, either, as Czechoslovakia, new creations or, as Roumania, enlargements of existing states.

The ethnographical boundaries were not, however, followed exactly, and that for various reasons. Firstly, the ethnical line was practically nowhere clear-cut. The broad divisions were fairly plain; but long centuries of interpenetration, assimilation, migration, and internal colonization had left in many places a belt of mixed and often indeterminate population where each national group merged into the next, while there were innumerable islands of one nationality set in seas of another, ranging in size from the half-million of Magyar-speaking Székely in Transylvania through many intermediate groups of fifty or a hundred thousand down to communities of a single village or less; while in the great colonization area of the Banat, the national distribution was such as to defy description. No frontier could be drawn which did not leave national minorities on at least one side of it.

But, further, the line indicated by ethnography tended too often to run counter to other requirements, particularly those of economics. The mountains and the plains of Hungary, and their populations, were to a high degree mutually interdependent. Unhappily, the line between the Magyar and the non-Magyar populations tended frequently to coincide with the line between the foothills of the mountains on the one hand and the plain on the other. It was very difficult to leave this line as the frontier (although it was done in the west). It usually seemed more reasonable either to leave the mountains with the plain, or alternatively to attach to the mountains at least so much of the plain as to allow

[1] By using the word 'indigenous' I do not, as will be seen later, mean that the ancestors of the peoples concerned had been settled from time immemorial where their descendants are now found; but they were firmly established with that settled peasant class which forms the basic substratum of any nationality.
[2] One or two small areas in the extreme north were afterwards obtained by Poland.

their inhabitants transverse communications. Either solution meant increasing still further the number of national minorities.

These economic arguments (to which various strategic considerations and what not were added in some cases) were freely adduced on both sides, the Successor States in the main claiming that the principle of their existence, within their ethnographical frontiers, was intangible, and, where they were not 'viable' without adding parts of the plain, then those parts must be added. Hungary, who fully admitted the difficulties involved, argued, on the contrary, that if the new States needed for their existence nearly as many minorities as Hungary herself had contained, there seemed no advantage in making the change at all. The Allies, however, accepted the contention of the Successor States in principle, and, in most cases, in detail also, being quite clearly actuated in this decision by an unspoken belief that Hungarian national policy had been something quite particularly oppressive, which the Successor States could be trusted not to imitate; the more so as they were being required to sign special treaties with the Principal Allied and Associated Powers for the protection of the national minorities assigned to them. One point after another was conceded; and in the end Roumania was given an area in which the Roumanians formed only 55 per cent. of the total population. The Slovaks in Slovakia were 60 per cent., the Ruthenes in Ruthenia 56 per cent., the Serbs in the Voivodina only 28 per cent., or 33 per cent. counting all the Yugoslavs together; while the Magyar-speaking persons in each area formed close on one-third of all the inhabitants: over one million in the territory assigned to Czechoslovakia, over 1,650,000 in that given to Roumania, 450,000 in Yugoslavia's portion.[1] And many of these were living in compact blocs contiguous to the new frontiers. Hungary herself retained no considerable frontier minorities except in the west, where Austria had not been treated with the same generosity as the other Successor States. The few other non-Magyars left to her were mostly scattered minorities, living far from the frontiers.

It is the existence, in particular, of the Magyar bloc immediately outside her frontiers on which is based that Hungarian claim for revision for which the most sympathy is probably felt abroad; for if we admit the justification of dividing up Hungary on national lines, then at least, one may say, the principle ought to be equally applied. Hungary to-day commonly divides her demands into the so-called 'lesser' or 'narrower' revision and the 'larger' or 'integral' revision; meaning by the latter the restitution of her pre-War

---

[1] These figures are based on the Hungarian census of 1910. As we shall see, they were queried in some cases, and do not always correspond to national conditions to-day.

frontiers (with certain qualifications to be explained later), and by the former a strict and impartial application of the ethnographic principle. In the sections which follow we shall explain in each case to what extent, and on what grounds, the ethnographical principle was modified, and shall venture to suggest how far the demand for the 'lesser revision' seems justified. The question of the 'integral revision' demands more detailed treatment. For this question also has two sides. For the Successor States and their advocates it was, of course, plain. They took their stand on the simple 'right of self-determination of the peoples', which, according to them, automatically justified the non-Magyars in leaving Hungary to form their own national States. This right seemed so obvious that it was hardly argued at Trianon, but it was, in fact, stated to have been proved by certain popular manifestations made and resolutions taken at the end of the War; while, in addition, evidence was brought to show that Magyar rule in Hungary had been unjust, oppressive, and tyrannical. That some of the nationalities concerned were comparatively recent immigrants, that others had lived for many centuries without serious conflict with the State, was regarded as equally irrelevant. In the former case, they had at least been there long enough to make up their minds, in the latter, 'an injustice did not cease to be unjust because it had existed for a thousand years'.

Hungary did not altogether deny the 'right of national self-determination', but she protested very warmly against the conclusions drawn from it. She admitted as valid only the decision taken by the Sabor (Diet) of Croatia-Slavonia. For the rest, she questioned the representative character of the popular meetings referred to above, and maintained stoutly that the nationalities never really wished to separate from her at all. If the point was uncertain, it could be settled by plebiscites, which she requested, vainly, might be held. She was confident that their result would be favourable to her, for, she said, the nationalities had no reason to desire a change. The geographical and economic unity of the country was so marked that every material consideration had always drawn its peoples together, as was proved by the remarkable cohesion shown by the Hungarian State throughout history. And although the Magyar nation had predominated in Hungary, by virtue of its numbers, its central position, and its cultural superiority, yet it had never in any way oppressed the non-Magyars. The only postulate had been the political unity of the State. A non-Magyar had been left entirely free to enjoy his own national culture in private and local affairs; only if he wished to share in the larger life of the State must he transact its business in the language of the State, and observe its unity. Any Hungarian citizen, be he

Magyar, Slovak, German, or Serb, who was ready to conform to these moderate requirements, was not only allowed but encouraged to live the rest of his life in his own way. Therefore, to speak of oppression was absurd, and to parcel up the old historical and economic unit of Hungary was to inflict not merely injustice but also disaster upon the peoples concerned.

Which of these opposite theses was the true one? This is the fundamental question to be answered if we are to pass judgement upon the justification of the major issue or its contrary: on whether Hungary ought to have been dismembered at all. In each of the ensuing sections we shall sketch the national movement among each of the nationalities concerned and try to judge whether it did in reality involve any ambition to separate from Hungary. It will, however, save some duplication, and also possibly help to correct the balance, if we preface these several stories by some account of the national question in Hungary as a whole, and particularly its development during the last crucial century. Only then shall we be able to see the whole question in its true perspective.

§ 2. THE ORIGINS OF THE QUESTION IN HUNGARY

The national conflict in Hungary, which led to the break-up of the ancient kingdom, was the result of the impact of new ideas, new ambitions on a situation which, in its essentials, had existed since time immemorial. For although the Middle Danube Basin forms in many respects a singularly perfect, compact, and self-contained geographical unity, it has always been a meeting-place of many peoples; and peoples, what is more, of particularly diverse origin. The outliers of the Alps which form its western rim have been Germanic for fully 1,500 years; the hills and valleys to its south have been inhabited for almost as long by Southern Slavs; on the north, peoples of different branches of the Slavonic stock penetrated the Carpathians long ago; and a race of quite different origin from any of these inhabited Transylvania two thousand years ago and—whether the occupation has been continuous or not—such a race inhabits it again to-day. The central plain, which from the demographic-geographical point of view constitutes the prolongation and last outlier of the great belt of open plain which runs along the north coast of the Black Sea and thence into the heart of Asia, has harboured a whole succession of invaders of wholly different origin and habits again: nomadic warriors and huntsmen from the east: Scythians, Sarmatians, Huns, Avars. Of these the Magyars, although not the last, as they were not the first, were alone able to establish themselves permanently—an achieve- ment which they owed partly, no doubt, to exceptionally favourable circumstances, and partly also to the presence among them of elements socially and economically more advanced than were found among their predecessors or their successors.

The population which the Magyars found on their arrival (which is usually dated at A.D. 896) was no doubt sparse, but it existed; and they themselves reinforced it thereafter by the admission of elements kindred to themselves, by inviting colonists and by slave-raiding.

Therefore, although almost from the very first Hungary was organized as a unitary political State, only Croatia and, to a lesser extent, Transylvania enjoying separate dispensations,[1] yet racially it was never at any time a unity.

During its first centuries, however, this racial diversity did not constitute a national problem in the form in which we know it to-day. The position is not easy to explain in modern terms, nor even to see with modern eyes; but we must attempt to understand it, for a true understanding of the modern position is incomprehensible without some knowledge of its origins.

The Magyars themselves, when they entered Hungary, were not a homogeneous nation in the modern sense of the word. They were themselves a mixed race in which former Turki overlords had blended with the more numerous Finno-Ugrian stock to form the main body of the nation. Several of their seven tribes were of pure Bulgaro-Turkish stock, and they were accompanied by one Turki tribe whose distinctive origin was still remembered.

Nevertheless, they were already far more nearly a nation than any contemporary western community. Their social and political system had not developed the differentiations which so largely destroyed western nationality in the Middle Ages. Its basis was, and long remained, the body of free men—the *nemesség*—a term somewhat inaccurately rendered by the Latin 'nobilitas' and afterwards known collectively as the 'Hungarian nation'. Among all these freemen, differences in wealth and status notwithstanding, there prevailed a high degree of equality; each one of them, rich or poor, enjoyed 'one and the same liberty', and between them and all others a great gulf was fixed.

The true basis of association between them was thus social rather than racial, but in practice the distinction between them

---

[1] The frontier districts were usually governed on a special system, as much military as political; but as the frontiers were gradually pushed outward, each region, as it ceased to be in the danger-zone, was successively incorporated into the ordinary administrative system. When political conditions became stable, this was extended to the frontier districts also. This happened in the north and the west, but Transylvania really remained a frontier district until the nineteenth century, and the south had to be reconstituted as such against the Turkish danger. Croatia was the only territory which from the first was attached to Hungary on a federal basis.

and the other peoples whom they encountered was very near a
'national' one in the modern sense; for the invaders had achieved
a very substantial degree of unity in many of the modern attributes
of nationality, such as religion and habits, and even language. In
all these respects they differed widely from most of the other inhabitants of the Middle Danube Basin. And the State which they
founded can fairly be described as a primitive national State, for
it was founded by and for the invaders, the local population of other
nationalities being conquered and enslaved or put to tribute.

But its national character was primitive and not modern. Although as a general presumption the Magyars regarded themselves
as overlords and the other peoples as underlings, yet from the first
they admitted certain alien elements to their ranks, in virtue either
of their social status or of their fitness on other grounds (e.g.
military prowess). This was a purely social process. It would
never have occurred to either party that such admission implied an
obligation upon the new-comer to give up his native tongue, alter
his name, or disguise his origin.

Still less was there any question of enforcing uniformity on the
disregarded underlings, who were entirely free to speak their own
tongues, labour, or make merry in their own fashions and even to
settle their small affairs under their own customary law. Larger
groups, in time, had their rights fixed in written charters; and the
same system was adopted in the case of the immigrants or 'guests'
who were invited into the country in large numbers by some of
the Hungarian kings.

Some of these privileges were so important and far-reaching as
to constitute a real derogation from the political unity of the
country; but this was only in the outlying districts. Normally
speaking, the new-comers were simply absorbed into the body of
the people, and where they were admitted to the ranks of the
'nobles' this was on the principle that 'omnis nobilitas Hungarica',
i.e. that the *political* unity of the State was preserved. Croatia, as
we said, was on a different footing; but although there were many
nobles of Slovak origin there was, and could be, no separate,
specifically Slovak nobility—just as there was no specifically
Magyar nobility, but only a Hungarian nobility which was *de facto*
preponderantly Magyar.

And in course of time such distinction as had existed between
the conquering Magyar and the conquered Slav or German ceased
very largely to be real. With the change in the national mode of
life from horse- and cattle-breeding, varied by raids, to agriculture,
an increasing number of Magyars sank into servitude. The social
distinction was as rigidly enforced as ever, but it had largely ceased
to be national. At the same time, a process of natural assimilation

was going on, not only among the nobles, but also among the villeins in all save the more remote corners of Hungary, or those (chiefly in the south and the east) where unorganized immigration was going on on a particularly large scale. Magyar historians estimate that, in 1500, four-fifths of the population of Hungary was Magyar by birth or assimilation.

Most of the remaining fifth were treated just as though they had been Magyars; if nobles, like the Magyar nobles, if villeins, like the Magyar villeins. The chief exceptions were a few chartered communities, most notably the Transylvanian Saxons, who clung to their special privileges. On the other side, there were certain nationalities who were not readily admitted to nobility, or even to equal treatment. Such were the Jews, the gipsies, and, to some extent also, the Roumanians.

Had Hungary's life continued undisturbed for two or three centuries longer she might, like France, have achieved a substantial national unity, in the modern sense, throughout by far the greater part of her territories. Unhappily for her, the position was entirely transformed by the Turkish invasion and by her acceptance of Habsburg rule.

The Turks not only made havoc of Hungary's civilization; but the brunt of their attack and subsequent occupation fell full upon the unprotected central plains which were the stronghold of the Magyar population, the German, Slavonic, and Roumanian areas of the periphery escaping far more lightly. They thus altered the balance of the population very greatly to the disadvantage of the Magyars. The motives of the Habsburgs were different, but the effects of their action very similar. For the Habsburgs were not, as the Árpáds and even the Angevins had been, national Hungarian kings, but rulers of an enormous empire of which Hungary was only a part, and not one of the easiest to deal with. They would defend its territory, which was also their own, against outside enemies; they even refrained from tampering on any large scale with its frontiers for their own benefit (a forbearance which is one of the causes why Hungary's historic case was so very strong in 1918). But they had no personal or family reasons for valuing Magyar nationality higher than German or even Slavonic, while the strong Magyar spirit of national independence was, in their eyes, the very embodiment of truculent rebellion.

The Habsburgs waged a long war against this spirit, by methods which ranged from massacre to flattery. Some went out against them with fire and sword; some forced the Protestants, by terror and persuasion, back into the Catholic fold; some enticed the high nobility to Vienna, loaded them with favours, and estranged them from their people. Nearly all sapped at their constitutional liberties.

By one means and another, they managed to reduce very greatly both those liberties and the will to defend them.

But besides this, when the Turks retreated, the Habsburgs filled up the waste spaces of Hungary with settlers of non-Magyar nationality, while they weakened the political unity of Hungary, not only by keeping Transylvania separate from it, but by detaching further portions along the southern frontier and ruling them directly from Vienna.[1] So there arose a situation entirely different from that before the Turkish invasion: the Magyar population of Hungary had sunk to 45 per cent. after the Turks retreated, and to 39 per cent. by 1778, when the colonization was far advanced. Of the remainder, a substantial fraction felt themselves more Austrian, or Imperial, than Hungarian subjects, and were prepared at any time to seek support for their claims or their wishes in Vienna.

Thus the foundations had been laid for the growth of the modern national problem. Yet even as recently as the eighteenth century the question was still not truly national, but political, social, and economic. Hungary was still struggling, not with Roumania or Serbia, where Turkish pashas still held sway and irredentism was still unborn, but with the Emperor. The Hungarian 'nation' was defending its privileges, the Emperor was attacking them, not because they were of Magyar national character, but because they impeded the exercise of absolute power, hindered the uncontrolled levying of soldiers, and were held also to prevent the economic development of the Imperial possessions; since among the privileges enjoyed by the Hungarian nobles was that of the exemption of their lands from taxation. Even when Joseph II, the most enterprising and autocratic of the Habsburgs, attempted to substitute for the Latin language of Parliament and administration the German which he designed as the *lingua franca* of his empire, this was done purely out of administrative considerations; and the real conflict which broke out between him and the Hungarian estates revolved not round the linguistic problem, but round the social reforms which he desired to introduce.

---

[1] One must, however, be careful not to impute to the Habsburgs exaggeratedly national motives, or even any deep purposefulness at all. Their first object was to fill up the land, in order to increase their own resources and fighting strength. A Magyar peasantry was simply not available for the purpose, owing to the depopulation of the country. German settlers were preferred, being considered the best material. The Magyar landowners were prevented from returning to their estates in order that these might be given to Imperial Generals, &c. The support which the Crown gave to elements such as the Serbs was always most irregular and half-hearted, so much so as to throw them repeatedly into the arms of the Magyars. Finally, much of the colonization of Central and Southern Hungary with non-Magyars was done, not by the Crown, but by the landowners themselves, some of whom were foreigners, but others Magyars. The native landowners, however, drew for their labour less on Germany than on the Slavonic north of Hungary itself.

The true nature of the conflict is shown not less clearly by the composition of the parties resisting it than by the assault. Many of Hungary's most fervent champions during this first phase of her renaissance (as, indeed, to-day) were wholly or partly of non-Magyar origin—Kossuth himself is the crowning example; while Széchenyi, the second great figure of the age, although of good Magyar stock, hardly spoke the national language. Moreover, the Magyars were joined in their struggle very enthusiastically by some of the non-Magyar nationalities, notably by the great majority of the Germans (the Saxons of Transylvania excepted) and the Jews, with a goodly proportion of the Slovaks and Ruthenes: these being in the main the nationalities who enjoyed no special status in Hungary, but lived as an integral part of the nation; so that their social and constitutional status *vis-à-vis* Austria was exactly the same as that of the Magyars themselves.

There was, however, another side to the question. The privileged nationalities of the Military Frontier and the Banat felt no loyalty to a Hungarian State which they had never known—for if the later Habsburgs had paid lip-service to the Hungarian Constitution they had put it aside in dealing with the nationalities. They were the Emperor's men, his faithful servants and his protégés. The Transylvanian Saxons, although they remembered Hungary, preferred a Transylvania which should belong directly to Austria, partly because this offered a better guarantee of their special position, partly for national reasons. The Roumanians hoped to find in Vienna a protection which Kolozsvár had never given them and which they could not hope to find in Pest. Much more the Croats, whose historical rights were well established, and were now endangered by the movement in Hungary.

It is easy, in these circumstances, to see how the question took on, by indefinable but quite inevitable stages, the forms of modern nationalism. Among the Magyars themselves there were two motives. The first regarded their own position. The assault on their constitutional life had taken, in part, the form of an assault on their nationality, as when the attempt was made to Germanize the administration. But this last and supreme effort of autocracy coincided with the spread from Western Europe of that mysterious romantic movement which found expression almost everywhere in Europe in a series of national rebirths. The Magyars, always impetuous and swift to move, felt this strange stirring as strongly as any people in Europe. A great national revival took place. The jejune, almost moribund language was revived, fed, and fattened. Everything that was national in speech, costume, and habit became the mode.

The movement could not confine itself to private life. No less than Joseph II, the Magyars felt the dog-Latin of their Parliament and administration to be a charnel relic; but where the Roman Emperor and German King wished to replace it by living German, they, naturally, desired that their own language should succeed it.

Then came the position of the nationalities. The centrifugal ambitions of some of them were an obvious source of danger. In the past the separate privileges had been resented chiefly by the landowners and Estates, who found their power hampered. But now it was a larger question: a question of uniting Hungary against the foreigner. The separate status of the privileged nationalities was an obstacle which clearly needed to be broken down. But even apart from this consideration, it was natural that the Magyars, identifying their own national movement with the constitutional struggle against Austria, should have quickly and easily persuaded themselves that the salvation of the whole country lay chiefly in the Magyar national language and spirit. Without and against the nationalities, it was quite impossible to defy Austria or, for that matter, to administer an independent Hungary; but either of these things could be done if the nationalities could be brought to re-inforce the Magyar national stock. As early as 1781 the Magyar statesman Bessenyei had formulated the 'fundamental idea of the cultural policy of the Magyar national state of the nineteenth century, that the foreign nationalities inhabiting the Danube Valley must be Magyarized linguistically'.[1] Others of his contemporaries preached the same gospel.[2] True, the Magyars had regarded themselves hitherto as a race superior to the Slovaks or the Vlachs, and from that point of view, the natural policy would rather have been one of exclusiveness. But circumstances alter cases; and, as one writer put it, 'if we take an inferior drink to add to a noble wine, we do not destroy the qualities of the latter, but it mixes with the other'.[3]

And it must not be forgotten that those who preached these doctrines were genuinely convinced that they were not in any way oppressing the nationalities, but, on the contrary, conferring upon them great benefits. Thus Count Zay, Inspector-General of the Lutheran Church (himself of Slovak origin), told an audience of Slovaks that

to impede the Magyarization of our country even indirectly, and to strive for the development of any other language than the Magyar, is equivalent to sapping the vital forces of constitutionalism and even of Protestantism itself, and hence that the Magyar language is the truest

[1] G. Kornis, *A Magyar művelődés eszményei* ('The Ideals of Hungarian Civilization') (Budapest, 1927), vol. i, p. 107.

[2] Ibid., pp. 107, 112, 121-2.

[3] Cit. R. W. Seton-Watson, *Racial Problems in Hungary* (London, 1908), p. 60.

guardian and protector of the liberty of our country, of Europe and of the Protestant cause. Let them therefore convince themselves that the triumph of Magyarization is the victory of reason, liberty and intelligence.[1]

It was not all Magyars who approved of, or believed in, this policy. Count Stephen Széchenyi, known to his own and subsequent generations as 'the greatest Hungarian', held strongly that the policy of Magyarization was mistaken. A speech which he delivered in 1842 as President of the Hungarian Academy of Sciences was devoted almost entirely to this theme, and contained a solemn warning to the nation of the dangers of overstraining the bow. But the general feeling was on the other side; according to a modern Magyar historian, this speech 'finally estranged the opinion of the day' from Széchenyi. The Hungarian Diet pressed on its plans for strengthening and unifying the country. Laws were passed introducing Magyar into the administration and schools, with an almost sublime disregard of the susceptibilities, or the difficulties, of the nationalities. This, at least, ran contrary to no established right; but the laws were extended, although not in quite their full force, to Croatia-Slavonia as well, whose constitutional position was attacked in other ways also. Then the conflict broke out.

§ 3. THE FIRST CRISIS OF THE NINETEENTH CENTURY

We have now reached the beginning of the last stage of Hungary's history—the last, that is, of which a writer can speak in 1937. We are full in the midst of the central question of Magyarization. We have seen how and why it began. To-day, more than a hundred years later, it is extraordinarily difficult to pass judgement on the rights and wrongs of it. For the sense of nationality is of all the great political feelings the most subjective and the most variable. Where an individual is possessed of an active national consciousness, which he is determined to preserve, then any force or pressure exerted to deprive him of it is assuredly dishonouring to those who apply it, as it is also (as experience has proved) futile. On the other hand, not all nationalities possess such a consciousness, and even when it is generally awake in some nation, there will always be individuals and sometimes whole social classes whom it leaves untouched. This was even more widely true a hundred years ago than it is to-day. Europe is full, not only of individuals, but of whole nations which have become assimilated completely and of their own free will.

Moreover, some nations—at least at certain periods in their

[1] Cit. R. W. Seton-Watson, *Racial Problems in Hungary* (London, 1908), p. 67.

histories, for the quality does not seem to be constant—do possess
an active power of attraction which enables them easily to absorb
alien elements, while others are passive, yielding readily to assimilation. The 'Auslandsdeutsche' were until recently conspicuous
examples of the latter type. It is extremely hard to say wherein
this active or passive quality resides. It may be only in the advantage of social status or superior economic strength; but certain
nations seem also to possess a mysterious inherent attraction which
is independent of material considerations. And I think it right to
state here, as my personal opinion, that few, if any, nations in Europe
possess this attraction in so large a measure as the Magyars. When
all their predecessors from the East failed and disappeared, they
alone made good their foothold and survived. Mixed as is the
blood of every nation in Europe, few are of such diverse origin as
they. The tiny original stock of invaders has absorbed many times
its own numbers of foreign elements, and this process has gone on
both in medieval times, when it was unconscious, and in modern
days, when it was done of set purpose. It has been not only
extensive, but intensive also. No other European nation contains
so many recruits who are not at all unwilling prisoners but, on the
contrary, heart and soul for their adopted cause—indeed, its most
intolerant champions. To deny that the 'Magyarization', whether
in older or in more recent times, often met with the full approval
of the persons assimilated would, I believe, be to misunderstand
the position very seriously.

But it is also true that the Magyar is excessively impetuous and
impatient of opposition. Everything with him runs to extremes.
To-day we are more accustomed than our fathers were to violence
of speech and action, and nothing surprises us. But in pre-War
Europe probably few, if any, nations allowed themselves to indulge
in so many intemperate and entirely reprehensible outbursts
against those who thwarted them as these same Magyars. Failure
to accept in entirety their dogmas—general or partial agreement is
not enough—seems to arouse in them a sort of fury. Therefore
those who did not succumb to their attraction were often roused
to a bitter hatred against them.

And finally the Magyars are too headstrong, too instantaneously
convinced of the rightness of their own cause, and too optimistic, to
be good judges of political forces. They invariably underestimate
their enemies. So it was in the first half of the nineteenth century.
Absorbed in the wonders of their own national renaissance, they
hardly noticed the similar movements which had begun among
non-Magyar 'nationalities'; certainly did not regard them of equal
importance with their own, still less even dream of making political
concessions to them. On the contrary, the hint of opposition

(which they seldom admitted to represent the real opinion of the people) only incited them to hurry on with their own programme, with disastrous results.

1848 is commonly regarded as the prototype of 1918, and in fact the events of the two years are closely analogous. In both cases the Hungarian Government found itself in conflict with the outer world; in both, a part of the nationalities stood by Hungary while a part allied themselves with the enemy. In both cases the issue, which would almost certainly have been favourable to the Magyars had the lists been clear, was decided against them by an outside force. If the dismemberment of Hungary dates from 1918 and not from 1848, it is because the impact of that force was different. In 1848 the nationalities enjoyed little help from their kinsmen beyond the frontiers. Certain encouragement and even help came to the Serbs and Roumanians, causing the more far-sighted observers to prophesy difficult times ahead. Then, however, no practical irredentism was possible. Serbia was small, weak, and still semi-dependent; Roumania had not yet even achieved her own independence, the Czechs were still fighting for their own national rights in Bohemia. The forces against Hungary were the Russian Tsar and the Austrian Emperor, the role of the former being purely military, while the Emperor, of course, did not desire such a situation as has arisen to-day, being as much preoccupied as the Magyars themselves to keep the frontiers of Hungary intact against Serbia or Roumania.

The event proved the centripetal forces in Hungary to be far from negligible. There was little division in the ranks of the Magyars themselves, once the peasants had been satisfied by some hurried reforms. Most of the Suabians and Jews supported the Magyars, as did a large part of the Ruthenes and the Slovaks. Some of the latter, however, demanded recognition of themselves (as of the other Hungarian nationalities) as a 'nation' with a separate Diet, national guard, and flag, and various linguistic concessions. The Serbs, after making somewhat similar demands and meeting with a blunt refusal, took up arms against Hungary, allying themselves with the Croats who led the campaign in the Emperor's name. In Transylvania, where the Union with Hungary was proclaimed, most of the Saxons and the Roumanians were undoubtedly against it, preferring the position of Transylvania within a great Austrian state. Although Roumanians took part on both sides in the fighting, the majority were certainly against Hungary.

The alacrity with which so large a fraction of the nationalities had turned against them came, by their own confession, as a complete surprise to the Magyar leaders. When the struggle first began, they had been prepared not only to maintain the political unity of Hungary but even to attack the separate and time-hallowed privileges of Croatia. Only in July 1849, in the last days of its existence, did the Diet make a belated attempt to conciliate the nationalities. It still retained the political unity of the country, rejecting the principle of 'national' autonomy for the different nationalities, and Magyar was still (as it had been proclaimed a few months previously) to be the official language of administration, justice, and the army. Considerable individual concessions were, however, made. Every citizen was allowed the right to use his own language in the Communal and County Assemblies. The language of instruction in the schools was to be that of the locality, and parish registers were also to be drawn up in that language. Petitions might be presented in any language, and appointments to all offices were to be made without distinction of language or religion

But these concessions, which were adopted in the face of considerable opposition from the die-hard minority, came much too late to fulfil their object—if, indeed, they could ever have done so. In any case, the law remained a dead letter, since only a few weeks after its enactment the Russian armies completed the subjugation of Hungary.

The period which followed was a very interesting one. Those of the nationalities who had turned against Hungary had done so in the hope of securing better terms from Austria. Francis Joseph duly reduced the relative advantage formerly enjoyed by the Magyars. Croatia received back Slavonia (which Hungary had proposed to take from her) and the Muraköz (Medjemurje); the union of Transylvania with Hungary was annulled; the Bačka and the Banat were formed into an 'autonomous Serbian Voivodina', and the rest of the country divided on very rough ethnographical lines into five districts, two of which were mainly Slav, two mixed, and one purely Magyar. The bias in favour of the Slavs was unmistakable; besides the Voivodina, Bach, Francis Joseph's Minister of the Interior, seems at one time to have entertained the idea of giving the Slovaks a similar 'national home'. The educational and cultural life of the nationalities made a certain progress. But the object, as soon became clear, was not to encourage Slav national feeling, but to repress every national movement alike. The administration was centralist, its language German, and gradually, but with growing speed, German was made the language of education also. Moreover, the entire system, although in technical efficiency probably superior to anything which Hungary had ever known, was informed by a spirit of reaction and repression.

A very few years of this régime sufficed to bring about a strong reaction among the nationalities in favour of an understanding with Hungary. It became clear that a considerable proportion of them—and not only those who had taken their side in 1848—were now anxious to remain in Hungary, if only they could reach a reasonable settlement of the national question. The Magyars, on their side, had been frightened by 1849; their former leaders, where they had not been executed, were in exile or discredited; and their political thought was at that time strongly influenced by two unusually safe statesmen, Deák and Eötvös, both of whom had constantly opposed intolerance towards the minorities, and Magyarization, as being both inhumane and politically unwise, insisting that such methods would not achieve their object, but would merely drive the nationalities into the enemy camp. Wisdom, toleration, and liberty, on the other hand, would attach them firmly to the Hungarian cause.

Consideration of the national question was resumed in 1861, after the 'October Diploma' of 1860 had again recognized Hungary's historic individuality and restored in part her ancient constitution. On Eötvös' motion, the whole question was referred to a Parliamentary Committee, which on August 1st, 1861, produced a very remarkable report.[1] It began by pointing out the difficulties in the way of territorial autonomy, occasioned by the admixture of races. The old communal, denominational, and municipal autonomy traditional in Hungary offered a better means of protecting 'the just demands of the individual citizen . . . in such manner as to guarantee in free union the possible development of the individual nationalities as corporations'.

Two guiding principles were laid down:

(a) that the citizens of Hungary of every tongue form politically only one nation—the unitary and indivisible Hungarian nation, corresponding to the historic conception of the Hungarian state.

(b) that all peoples dwelling in this country—Magyars, Slovaks, Roumanians, Germans, Serbs, Ruthenes, &c.—are to be regarded as nationalities possessing equal rights, who are free to make valid their special national claims within the limits of the political unity of the country, on a basis of freedom of the person and of association, without any further restriction.

An outline follows of the measures recommended by the Committee. These may be summarized as follows:

Every citizen may employ his mother tongue in addressing the authorities. The Church Communes may choose their own language of instruction in their primary schools. Every denomination and nationality is free to erect secondary and higher schools, the choice of system and language of instruction resting with the bodies founding them, subject to the Government's right of super-

[1] Text in Seton-Watson, op. cit., pp. 421-33.

C

vision. In State schools the Government decides on the language
of instruction, but must take into account the languages spoken in
the district of the school concerned. The language of the State is
Magyar, but its offices and dignities are to be filled in virtue of
capacity and merit, without regard to nationality. The language
of Parliament is Magyar. In local government local languages are
used, provision being made for translations, &c., to ensure the
rights of minorities and mutual comprehension between the local
and central authorities.

The provisions do not apply to Croatia or Transylvania.

One peculiar phrase will be noted in this draft: the reference to
the 'development of the individual nationalities as corporations'.
The subsequent proposals make no provision for implementing the
national corporate life suggested by these words—for the references to 'nationalities' in the clauses relating to education are quite
vague and ambiguous. It is hard not to suppose that we have here
what is a common thing in committees composed of persons of
divergent views: a phrase inserted to placate one party, while the
majority is willing to accept the general phrase but not to admit its
implications. In fact the Magyars and the nationalities had failed
to agree on this point of 'national corporations'. The Serbs, at a
meeting held at Karlovci in the April preceding, had asked for the
revival 'within Hungary, viz. within the Triune Kingdom of
Croatia, Slavonia, and Dalmatia' of the 'Serb Voivodina' with its
own Diet and 'collective representation' at Budapest. The Slovaks,
in June, had also asked for 'national recognition and an autonomous
territory'. Even the Ruthenes desired separate territorial autonomy. Only the Germans had put in no demands.

The Magyars, however, were not prepared to go so far as this;
they stood rigidly by the 'political unity' of Hungary.[1] Thus, on
this one point, there was a complete divergence of views.

Parliament was dissolved before any action could be taken on
it, and the next action of the Magyars was to drive the Slovaks
back to Vienna by threatening their small educational freedom. If
the situation did not change greatly during the next five years or
so, this was because Hungary was again subject *de facto* to Austrian
absolutism, while it was universally recognized that the position
was provisional and must be succeeded by a more comprehensive
solution.

When the Compromise of 1867 was concluded, the Magyars
were already in a stronger position. The Crown had decided to

[1] This was the attitude not merely of the Magyar chauvinists, but of men like
Eötvös, who was prepared to surrender entirely the predominance of the
Magyar nationality and language in favour of complete equality, only retaining
Magyar as the language of Parliament and the central administration, as a matter
of convenience.

make its peace with Hungary on the basis of the historic rights claimed by the national leaders. This meant that it would at least not actively support the nationalities, who had to make what terms they could with the Magyars. These terms were embodied in three main instruments: the Compromise with Croatia, the Union with Transylvania, and the Nationalities Law.

The details of the Compromise need not concern us here. It granted Croatia a status which in the main did full justice to her historic rights, and if a Croatian question still remained, there was henceforward no question of equating this with the ordinary nationalities question in Hungary. Not so Transylvania, which was united with Hungary by a law which also abolished the special privileges of the various nationalities and proclaimed the equality of all citizens, irrespective of race or religion. A promise was given that the rights and privileges of the Saxon University (except its judicial functions) should be maintained. Many of these were, however, subsequently abolished; and, except for this qualification, Transylvania became legislatively and administratively an integral part of Hungary.

For the remaining nationalities, the governing provisions were those of the Nationalities Law of 1868. Consideration of this question had been resumed by a Parliamentary Commission in 1866. The debates had been very prolonged and even embittered.[1] The representatives of the nationalities who spoke[2] (with the exception of the Bunyevci and some of the Slovaks, who took the point of view of the majority) insisted very strongly on the principle of complete equality for all the nationalities of Hungary, with re-grouping of the Counties, &c., as nearly as possible on ethnographical lines, and far-reaching autonomy within these for each nationality. The demand was not always expressed in identical terms, for the nationalities failed signally to adopt a common front, and each had a particular interest which it was anxious to press even at the sacrifice of the desires of the others: the Serbs the revival of their old privileges, the Saxons the maintenance of their 'University', the Roumanians the abolition of all discrimination against them. The general sense of their claims was, however, identical in each case. The Magyars, on the other hand, insisted absolutely on the maintenance of the political unity of Hungary and its predominating Magyar character. Only within these limits were they prepared to grant religious liberty and *individual* linguistic rights to the members of the various nationalities.

In this event the Parliament adopted the point of view of the

---

[1] For an interesting account of the debates see I. de Nagy, *A nemzetiségi törvény a Magyar Parlament előtt 1861-1868* (Budapest, 1930).

[2] No representative of the Suabians or of the Jews appears to have spoken.

majority, in the form of an amendment to the original majority
draft put forward by Deák, the chief difference of which, as compared with the majority draft, lay in the addition of a preamble,
setting forth what Deák held to be the fundamental principles
of Hungarian national policy. The text of this preamble ran as
follows:

Since all citizens of Hungary, both in virtue of the principles of the
Constitution and from a political point of view, form a single nation—
—the indivisible unitary Hungarian nation—to which all citizens of
the country belong, irrespective of their nationality, and enjoy equal
rights: since, moreover, this equality of rights cannot be submitted to
differential regulation except regarding the official use of the various
languages of the country, and that only in so far as is necessitated by
the unity of the country, the demands of administration and the prompt
execution of justice: the equality of rights of all citizens of the country
remains absolute in all other respects, while the following rules will
serve as a basis regarding the official use of the various languages:

The law goes on to lay down provisions which do not differ very
widely from those of the 1861 draft, excluding the ambiguous
mention of 'nationalities' contained in the earlier documents. The
language of State is 'in virtue of the political unity of the nation'
Magyar, which is the language of Parliament, of the University,
and the official language of the administration. In the County
Assemblies the minutes are to be kept in Magyar, but can also be
kept in another tongue if one-fifth of those present desire it; and
any one may speak in those Assemblies either in Magyar or in his
own mother tongue, if that is not Magyar. The communes choose
their own language of business, and in dealing with persons belonging to the commune, must use the language of those persons.
The Counties are to correspond with communes and individuals
as far as possible in the language of the latter. The language
of the higher Courts is Magyar, but reasonable provision is made
for parties of different mother tongue. Individuals, communes,
churches, &c., enjoyed a free right to found, and to collect and
administer funds for, elementary, secondary, and higher schools,
prescribing themselves the language of instruction therein. The
State prescribed the language of instruction in State schools, but
wherever citizens of any nationality were living together in 'considerable numbers' they must be given an opportunity to receive
instruction in their mother tongue 'up to the point where higher
education begins'.

§ 4. HUNGARIAN NATIONAL POLICY, 1867–1918

Every writer, from either camp, who discusses this law gives it
fullest praise. It is certainly one of the best nationality laws that

have ever been drafted; the League of Nations Minority Treaties, which have drawn very largely upon it for inspiration, fall far short of it in generosity. In the opinion of many writers, it could have solved the national question in Hungary. It is interesting and melancholy to consider why it failed to do so.

The first and most obvious reason is that, after the first few years at least, it was never applied by the Magyars themselves. Magyar patriotic writers to-day usually deny with characteristic vehemence this, the reiterated complaint made by the leaders of the nationalities and their friends, and in doing so, render their country a singular disservice; for the inescapable conclusion, if they are right, is that the wisest of laws, scrupulously applied, could not reconcile the nationalities to life within the Hungarian State. If this were true, then Hungary was doomed indeed.

But it is not true. The fact is that the school of Deák and Eötvös exhausted its strength in a few years after the passage of the great law. There existed, indeed, to the last among the Magyars a small group who believed that the application of the law could solve the national question; and some, too, who questioned the policy of Magyarization on moral grounds. But in public life, at least, their voices were completely drowned by the clamour of that rival school of thought which had already made itself heard when the law was being drafted, and within a few years had become the almost unchallenged master of Hungarian national policy.

The central tenet of this school was still really political; it was the maintenance of the old unitary nature of the Hungarian State, of the old doctrine in modernized form, of 'omnis nobilitas Hungarica'. But this doctrine now involved far more Magyarization than in the old days, when all the peoples of Hungary had enjoyed a certain equality through their common use of dog-Latin. Now, when Magyar, not Latin, was made the language of public life, it followed that the whole upper structure of the State must be Magyar. This ideal soon came to be applied not merely to Parliament or to the officials but to all the moneyed classes and the national intellectual life. For a member of the bourgeoisie to insist on his non-Magyar speech or origin was to render him suspect, at least, of non-acceptance of the unitary Hungarian State: of treasons, stratagems, and spoils.

Hungary maintained to the last that she sought no more than political unity; and in fact the peasants were, at least during the first decades, left pretty well to their own devices. But this was due to two causes: firstly, the sheer impossibility of making any great impression on the peasant masses which Hungary had at her disposal until she had trained up a sufficient number of teachers and leaders; and secondly, the traditional mentality of the Hungarian

State, which has always been oligarchical and has never regarded the peasants as a serious political factor. But the feeling was certainly widespread that Hungary would not be really safe until every man, woman, and child within her frontiers had been Magyarized: until she had become, as some enthusiasts dreamed, a 'thirty-million Magyar kingdom'.

Thus the turn of the disregarded social classes came late—in some cases had hardly been reached when the débâcle arrived. But more and more the ideal of complete Magyarization was gaining ground. And successive generations of Hungarian statesmen, strong in their sublime confidence alike in the rightness of their cause and in their ability to achieve their aims, held to this ideal until the very last. Even the obvious disaffection of the Serbs and Roumanians during the War did not lead them to think of concessions, but rather to redouble their efforts. With the world cracking round them they stood unchanged, like the missionary in Stevenson's fable, and hardly to-day will their successors admit ruefully that 'it seems that there was something in it after all'. As late as mid-October 1918, when the King-Emperor issued his famous manifesto promising the transformation of Austria into a federation of national States, the Hungarian Government threatened to cut off food-supplies unless a clause were inserted that 'the integrity of the Lands of the Holy Hungarian Crown is in no way affected by this reorganization'; and on the day when the manifesto appeared, Dr. Wekerle, the Hungarian Minister President, repeated in the Parliament at Budapest, in words which any of his predecessors might have used, that Hungary would at all costs maintain unimpaired her national integrity and unity. 'Within this framework we are willing to give the nationalities, whom we have always treated humanely . . . individual rights.'

The opposition to this policy was practically confined to a few stalwarts of the 1848 party, who had been so embittered by the conduct of the King-Emperor in 1848 and 1849 that they were ready to make far-reaching concessions to the nationalities in order to buy their support against the Crown.[1] But the representatives of this school of thought never came into power until the very end. It was only on October 31st, 1918, that Michael Károlyi took office. Then, indeed, there was a hurried attempt to change the long-set course—an attempt initiated by Károlyi and put into partial practice by the man whom he made his Minister for Nationalities, Oskar Jászi. Jászi, indeed, went so far as to repudiate the idea of Magyar supremacy altogether and to advise 'equal rights for all

---

[1] The few concessions made to the nationalities (especially the Roumanians) by Count Stephen Tisza were purely tactical moves to weaken the Hungarian nationalists, against whom he was ruling for the Crown.

nationalities and the development of national autonomy on the Swiss model'.[1]

The activities of this Ministry form an interesting and little-known chapter of Hungarian history. As told elsewhere,[2] it was able to agree on and actually to put into operation a statute for the Ruthenes which probably satisfied the majority of opinion among that people, in so far as an articulate opinion existed. It also produced a statute for the Germans, which was put into force in West Hungary,[3] and even a Slovak Statute, which might have satisfied the Slovaks if Hungary had had to deal with the Slovaks alone.[4]

But by this time the situation was quite out of the hands of any Hungarian Government, or of the Hungarian nationalities. Jászi himself saw this clearly, and writes himself that he had no hope of saving Hungary's old political integrity; all that he could aim at was saving the plebiscite principle, so as to secure as favourable frontiers as possible for Hungary, preserving the old connexions of economics and communications, and preparing for a future federative *rapprochement* of all the States in the Danube Basin.[5] And in the event even this, as will be seen, proved impossible.

Hungary's real nationality policy was contained, not in Jászi's belated attempts, not in the Nationalities Law of 1868, but in the measures which were taken by successive Hungarian Governments between 1868 and 1918. These are described at length by a writer much better acquainted with the subject than myself, and able to deal with them more fully (although every smallest fact is really relevant to the present theme). Here I can mention only the main features, referring the reader for details to Professor Seton-Watson's numerous and authoritative works.[6]

[1] O. Jászi, *Revolution and Counter-Revolution in Hungary* (London, 1924), p. 57, n. 2. See also his views expressed at length in his later work, *The Dissolution of the Habsburg Monarchy* (Chicago, 1929).
[2] See below, p. 213 f.   [3] See below, pp. 49 ff.
[4] The Slovak Statute was issued on March 12th, 1919, as People's Law No. XXX of 1919 (text in A. Szana, *Die Geschichte der Slowakei* (Bratislava, 1930), pp. 282–4). It follows closely the lines of the Ruthene and German Statutes, creating an autonomous 'Slovenska Krajina' (divided into three Governments) with a National Assembly autonomous for internal administration, justice, education, and religion, proportionate representation for the Slovaks in the Hungarian Parliament for common affairs, a Slovak Minister responsible to both the Slovak National Assembly and the Hungarian Parliament, and protection for the national minorities.
[5] Jászi, *Revolution and Counter-Revolution in Hungary*, p. 57.
[6] *Racial Problems in Hungary* (1908) (general, and the Slovak problem in particular); *Corruption and Reform in Hungary* (1911); *The Southern Slav Question* (1911); *A History of the Roumanians* (1934).
To Magyar writers, Professor Seton-Watson is anathema. They cannot deny the accuracy of his facts, but they hold his outlook to be biased and the picture which he presents to be distorted. It is true that he concentrates chiefly on the conflicts between the Magyars and the active nationalists among the nationalities, and may perhaps under-estimate both the extent and the sincerity of the voluntary assimilation which took place. I can, however, find

The Electoral Law of 1874 kept the nationalities politically impotent. The provisions of this law look paradoxical at first sight, since the constituencies of the nationalities were usually far smaller than those of the true Magyar areas, and in fact the Liberal Party ruled mainly through a majority returned from Transylvania, the Slovak Counties, &c. The explanation is that the Hungarian Governments which stood by the Compromise were opposed also by the partisans of Magyar independence, who were in reality their most dangerous enemies. These were checked by making the constituencies large; while in the periphery, the extremely restricted franchise and open voting left the power in the hands of the Government. Every sort of intimidation was practised on the voters, so that it was the rarest thing, costing the greatest courage and sacrifice, for such a constituency to elect a representative of the nationalities. The nationalist point of view was thus almost unrepresented in Parliament up to 1918.

Justice and administration, down to the Commune, were almost exclusively Magyarized, the reorganization of the judicial system in 1869 failing to renew the rights guaranteed to the nationalities in the old County Courts they abolished, while hardly a pretence was made to observe the linguistic provisions regarding administration. But the most systematic assault was made against the separate educational and other cultural life of the nationalities. In 1874 the three Slovak gymnasia were suddenly closed, and in the following year the Slovak cultural society, the Slovenska Matica, was closed down and its property confiscated—a foretaste of what was to come. In 1879 a new Law on primary education made a knowledge of the language of State compulsory for every teacher, imposed State control on the training colleges in this sense, and gave the Ministry of Education power to decide the number of hours to be devoted to the teaching of Magyar, and to close any institutions which failed to conform with instructions. The nationalities still, it is true, enjoyed a certain protection in the autonomy of their churches, who controlled the denominational schools. They were, however, handicapped by their poverty, and when they were forced or induced to accept a subsidy the price was always a diminution of their freedom. If, moreover, a denominational school failed to come up to the educational requirements laid down by the State (and many of them were primitive indeed) it could be closed and a new State school erected. Great numbers of these new schools

no work from the other side to set against his; since his opponents either ignore or deny the problems of which he treats, instead of explaining them. The reasoned Magyar view has yet to be expounded in any West European language. Meanwhile, Professor Seton-Watson's works remain unsurpassed in any language as collections of the facts and of the utterances of Magyar statesmen and Parliamentarians on the National question.

were built, and mainly in the non-Magyar districts, the Alföld suffering badly by comparison. In these the language of instruction was always exclusively Magyar: in 1906 only a single exception to this rule could be found in all the 2,046 State elementary schools then existing. (It is, of course, true that no compulsion rested on parents to send their children to State schools where denominational schools existed, and this system of 'analysis of names' was unknown in the old Hungary.) In 1883 came a Secondary Education Act. The 14 non-Magyar secondary schools still existing (6 Roumanian, 1 Serb, 7 Transylvanian Saxon) were placed under strict official control and Magyar language and literature made compulsory subjects in them. The language in all State gymnasia now became exclusively Magyar. All secondary schools founded thereafter were purely Magyar, requests by the Slovaks and Roumanians for permission to found further institutions meeting with such official obstruction as to be tantamount to flat rejection. In 1891 came a Kindergarten Law, which also aimed undisguisedly at promoting Magyarization. In 1902 the Minister of Education ruled that from 18 to 24 hours a week should be devoted to Magyar instruction in the primary schools (in which the total number of hours of instruction never exceeded 26). Then in 1907 came the Education Acts associated with the name of Count Apponyi—laws which in practice were never fully applied, but rank in theory with the least liberal of their day. The liberty of teachers in State elementary schools was further restricted. Similar control was applied to the teachers in the denominational schools, who became henceforward State officials. New standards of equipment and salaries were laid down for the denominational schools which made it practically impossible for them to carry on without State grants. These were coupled with conditions: the teacher must be able to read, write, and speak Magyar correctly and must give instruction in the manner and to the extent laid down by the Ministry, which in certain cases acquired a veto on appointments and even a right to make appointments without consulting the school authorities. A special oath of loyalty was exacted from all teachers, and disciplinary inquiries might be instituted against any of them for neglect of Magyar instruction, for a tendency hostile to the State, and for other political offences; they were liable to dismissal unless they could ensure that their pupils of non-Magyar tongue could 'express their thoughts intelligibly in the Magyar language, orally or in writing', by the end of the fourth school year. About eighteen hours weekly of the total twenty-three of instruction had to be devoted to the sole purpose of instruction in Magyar.

Incidentally, the use of non-Magyar languages was widely prohibited in every sphere of public life, and there are many authenticated cases of even little children being severely punished by their teachers for speaking their own language in play. The place-names of Hungary were officially Magyarized, and strong inducements were held out to officials—and indeed, to others—to Magyarize their names—an operation which they could perform for a few pence. Thus an outward appearance, at least, was achieved of a purely Magyar country.

But above all, any public manifestation of any national sentiment other than the Magyar, any protest against the non-fulfilment of the Nationalities Law, met with the most intemperate and insulting reception from the Magyar and Magyar-Jewish press and Parliament. The peoples' representatives vied with each other in finding abusive and even filthy terms to apply to those of their fellow citizens who were unwilling to accept the ideals thrust on them in so uncompromising a fashion.

§ 5. THE ECONOMIC DEVELOPMENT OF HUNGARY UP

TO 1918

The story is not, however, exhausted by the purely linguistic or educational, nor even by the purely political measures. Reference must also be made to the very important changes arising out of Hungary's economic development.

In the eighteenth and early nineteenth centuries Hungary's economic situation had been deplorable. The Turkish invasion had destroyed her old prosperity, and even after the Turks retreated, plague and disorder practically closed the southern and eastern frontiers, while Austria, after acquiring Galicia, surrounded Hungary on all remaining sides and had her in a strangle-hold.

Maria Theresa and Joseph II frankly exploited this position for the benefit of the Austrian Crown lands. Hungary was to be a 'colony', to supply Austrian industry with cheap raw materials and the Austrian consumer with cheap food-stuffs. A tariff barrier was maintained between Austria and Hungary. At first Hungarian agricultural produce was taxed on entering Austria, and Austrian industrial products on entering Hungary. Under Joseph II the latter duties were abolished, so that Austrian industry had free access to the Hungarian market, Hungary being prevented from competing by the heavy dues levied on foreign raw materials, and by the refusal of the State to grant her industries subsidies such as were lavished on Austrian entrepreneurs (a refusal justified by the attitude of the nobility on the tax issue).[1] But even Hungary's main exports, such as wine and even wheat, were allowed into

---

[1] For a description of the position see especially H. Marczali, *Hungary in the Eighteenth Century* (London, 1910), Chapter I.

Austria only in so far as the importation did not conflict with the interests of Austrian producers.

The Diets of the early nineteenth century regularly demanded the abolition or at least the reduction of the Austrian tariff; at this time the land-owning agrarians were all-powerful, the movement for complete independence was weak, and the formation of a free trade area with Austria seemed to offer the best chances for Hungary's economic progress. After the publication in 1840 of Liszt's great work, *Das nationale System der politischen Oekonomie*, ideas suddenly changed. Kossuth and his friends conceived the idea of an autarkic Hungary, with high tariff protection against all the world, Austria included, which should allow the development of an independent Hungarian industry. In 1844 Kossuth founded a society for the development of Hungarian industry; its members had to swear to buy no foreign-made article which was also manufactured in Hungary, for seven years. The demand was strengthened by the consistently deplorable condition of Austrian finances, which involved those of Hungary.

After 1849 the absolutist Government, of course, adopted the very opposite course. The tariff barrier between Austria and Hungary was abolished on October 1st, 1850, the whole system of taxation made as nearly uniform as possible, the tobacco-monopoly introduced, the economical and financial life of the country modernized. Incidentally, the tariffs of the whole Monarchy were lowered very considerably.

These reforms were carried through by the Austrian absolutism; but it is proof of their soundness that they were left almost unaltered in the Compromise of 1867. Hungary recovered, however, the forms and much of the substance of her economic independence, such as the right to pay only an agreed and limited quota to the common expenses of the monarchy, and to refuse her consent to the raising of any future common loan. The great question of the tariff was settled by a characteristic compromise. Hungary maintained her constitutional right to enact her own legislation and establish her own customs barriers. In view, however, of the 'many and important contacts' between the interests of Hungary and the rest of the Monarchy, Hungary was prepared to conclude periodically a commercial and customs alliance, which should cover the whole conduct of trade questions. This was to be worked out in connexion with the establishment of the quota, and of common principles to be adopted in connexion both with indirect taxation and with railway policy.

When this arrangement was reached, the idea of Hungarian autarky had fallen again into disrepute. Deák and his colleagues, the authors of the Compromise, believed that Hungary's interests would best be served by the closest possible relations with Austria: the more so as Hungary possessed only one harbour (her right to which was disputed by Croatia), while Austria straddled across all her lines of communication to the west. It was thus possible without great difficulty to conclude an alliance in 1867 which laid down that for the following ten years the territory of the whole monarchy should form a single customs unit surrounded by a common customs frontier.

For some years this school of thought prevailed. Harvests were good and there were large export surpluses, which were easily placed in Western Europe, and particularly in Germany. There was thus no justification or indeed desire for industrialization, and the few enterprises which had been founded for political reasons soon disappeared. Only the milling industry of the plains developed. Hungary's ambition to modernize herself found its outlet in the expansion and adornment of Budapest, and above all in the construction of her railway system, which was carried through at high speed. First Budapest was linked by rail to all parts of the country, then a beginning was made with certain provincial centres, of which Pozsóny (Pressburg, now Bratislava) and Temesvár (Timişoara) were the first, while large sums were spent on developing Hungary's single port of Fiume.

At the end of the decade the Customs Alliance with Austria was renewed, but each partner now reserved the right to denounce it. The tariff was, incidentally, now autonomous. In 1879, after the imposition by Germany of her high protective tariff, which largely crippled Hungary's export to her of wheat and cattle, thoughts turned back to the possibilities of industrialization; particularly as the railway network, without which an active policy was impossible, was now complete. 1881 saw the first Hungarian law for the furtherance of home industry by various subsidies, loans on easy terms, freight reductions, grants of machinery, exemption from taxation, &c. In the following ten years the population employed in industry increased by 125 per cent.

The tariff policy of the next decade again rather favoured the agrarians, who used their strength, incidentally, to crush their competitors in Roumania and Serbia—a policy which inflicted severe losses, in particular, on Transylvanian industry. Further Acts granting even more extensive advantages to Hungarian industries were, however, passed in 1890 and 1899, while Hungary's legal independence from Austria was made even more apparent. In 1899, the Delegations of the two Parliaments having failed to agree on certain disputed questions, Hungary assumed the 'legal position of an independent tariff area'. After long negotiations the common tariff area was made secure in 1906, *de facto*, for a further period. The Tariff Alliance was replaced by a customs treaty valid for a further ten years. At the same time the negotiations for a separate National Bank—a demand loudly voiced by the nationalists —were carried a step farther.

In the following years the autarkization of Hungary made exceedingly rapid progress. Yet another Law (1907) gave even greater advantages to native industries, with the avowed intention of developing the manufacture of articles hitherto not produced in Hungary, or produced only on a small scale. Almost every party in Hungary was agreed on the final aim of preparing the ground for economic separation from Austria; the only difference between them being that the industrialists wanted to hurry on the process, while the agrarians wished to wait until they could be secure of marketing all their surplus in the country. No government, however, could now return to the old policy of a balanced Austro-Hungarian economy, and the furtherance of industry was pursued by all alike. In particular the textile, iron and steel, and machinery industries received very extensive help and grew with mushroom speed. The number of persons employed in industry in Hungary rose from 818,000 in 1890 to 1,038,000 in 1900 and 1,347,000 in 1910. By 1914 it was certainly already considerably larger. During the World War it was possible for Hungary, if under the most unfavourable conditions imaginable, yet to realize at last her long-cherished dream and to achieve economic separation from Austria.

This story was worth recounting in so much detail, because it is extremely important to understand both what influences were at work, in what direction they were tending, and how recently they had begun to operate. Hungary's motives were undisguisedly political. She wished to turn herself into a compact economic unit, self-reliant if not entirely self-contained, and for this she employed both positive and negative methods. Thus, while cheap and quick connexions were formed between Budapest—the political as well as the natural centre—and the most distant corners of the country, communications between the peripheral districts and the outer world, which might strengthen centrifugal tendencies, were ingeniously thwarted.[1] The industrial policy was similarly designed to strengthen the interdependence of the various parts of Hungary and loosen their ties with the rest of the world.

[1] Cf. Seton-Watson, *The Southern Slav Question and the Hapsburg Monarchy* (London, 1911), pp. 324–34, for particularly glaring instances of how Croatia's communications with Vienna, and more crassly still, with Dalmatia and Bosnia, were hampered, either by simple neglect to build railways at all, or by the manipulation of freight tariffs which forced Croat produce to pass through Budapest (under the Hungarian-Croatian Compromise of 1868, Croatian autonomy did not apply to the railways). The connexions between Western Slovakia and Moravia, West Hungary and Styria, Transylvania and Roumania were little better.

This economic policy was in many respects Hungarian rather than Magyar. There was no question of impoverishing the nationalities, or of placing them at an economic disadvantage compared with the Magyars. Budapest was, indeed, embellished very splendidly and at great cost; but in general, in economic as in educational questions (where far more money was spent on teaching little Slovaks Magyar than on teaching little Magyars arithmetic), the tendency was rather to neglect the purely Magyar districts at the expense of the non-Magyar. As a rule, the development seems to have followed the lines dictated by straightforward economic interests, raw materials and sources of power being utilized where they were found, and factories placed where most suitable. In part, too, efforts were made to give employment to the inhabitants of the most poverty-stricken districts, and thus to guard them against the threat of famine.

The chief industrial development (outside Budapest) was thus precisely in the non-Magyar districts. Hungarian statistics on the support given to industries in money and machinery between 1881 and 1914 show that, reckoning by area, the north-west easily leads the way. All the Counties receiving more than 600 crowns per square kilometre lie in this part of Hungary and more than half in the present Slovakia, about the same proportion being purely Slovak. The Counties receiving 300–600 crowns lie chiefly in Western Slovakia and German West Hungary, with one purely Magyar County in the plain, and one German County in Transylvania. The 100–300 Counties are in Slovakia, a part of Western Hungary, and along the strip which borders on the Transylvanian mountains, while below that mark come the Magyar plain, the Ruthene and Roumanian mountains, the remainder of South-West Hungary, and the Southern Slav districts. Statistics on subsidies received per head of population show even more clearly the absence of national discrimination.

It is, however, quite true that subsidies and even ordinary facilities, such as licences, were refused to the distinctively national enterprises which the leaders of certain of the nationalities attempted to establish with the purpose of keeping alive national sentiment or providing funds for political parties. In such cases the authorities employed every resource to frustrate the plan.

So, too, with the choice of workers. The single case in which national discrimination was sometimes practised was that of the Roumanians. Some factory owners did try to 'keep the Vlachs out' just as the colonists centuries before had banned them from their land.[1] Any discrimination between the other nationalities was

---

[1] Some of my critics have queried this statement, and I wish to repeat that I am quite satisfied of its accuracy.

based on quite different considerations. If the Ruthenes were un-popular in factories on account of their alleged roughness, German workers were often preferred to Magyars for their greater skill and Slovaks for their lack of pretensions.

At the same time the Magyars certainly saw in the industrializa-tion a welcome aid to their policy of Magyarization. To Magyarize the peasants must clearly take many decades; it was, indeed, hardly possible even to begin seriously with the task with the means at Hungary's disposal in the nineteenth century. It did, however, seem possible to make of the towns centres and foci of Magyar life and culture, whose influence would gradually irradiate the country-side; and this policy was deliberately pursued. Special attention was paid to the towns in districts of mixed population, where conditions were favourable for quick results; thus such cities as Sopron (Oedenburg), Kassa (Košice, Kaschau), Temesvár, or Ujvidék (Novi Sad) grew into important administrative, indus-trial, and cultural centres, contrasting advantageously alike with the few impregnable fortresses of the nationalities and with the safe Magyar strongholds of the Alföld.

These developments went a very long way indeed towards giving Hungary the economic unity which her champions claim for her. A hundred years earlier the different Counties could without gross exaggeration have been described as so many mutually independent agrarian republics; while town and country were at perpetual loggerheads. By 1914 the foundations of a real unity had been laid; and with the development of the economic life, and the differentia-tion of production and labour, the different parts of Hungary had become mutually interdependent to a degree never previously achieved in her history.

Moreover, the development was proceeding apace. Hungary was still in many respects a backward country, and this was due in no small degree to the faults of her own ruling classes. The social system was exceedingly reactionary, the façades hurriedly erected in the chief centres screened appalling poverty and ignorance, fostered by a most rigid political class-rule. It is, however, unfair to lay all Hungary's shortcomings to the account of her ruling classes. Many of them were due to her tumultuous past history. She had, after all, only enjoyed some half-century of real de facto independence. Given another equally long period of peace, she might have developed into a strongly consolidated, and, in view of her great natural resources, a highly prosperous, modern state.

This, however, depended ultimately—as the example of Austria before the War and Czechoslovakia since it show—on her ability to solve, in one way or another, her national problem.

§ 6. THE NATIONAL BALANCE-SHEET

It is extremely difficult to assess what progress Hungary was making towards her avowed goal. To the casual traveller, Hungary would have appeared by 1914 as an almost completely Magyar country. On the railway he would have passed only towns and villages bearing Magyar names (since the earlier local appellations had been officially changed), seen only Magyar inscriptions, heard Magyar orders shouted. If he had had any dealings with officialdom, he would have found the Magyar language reigning unchallenged; and, alike in polite society and on business, he would have been given to understand that the use of any language other than Magyar was only a concession to a foreigner.

Some of this was, of course, only what is popularly known as eye-wash. In many villages, for example, the new Magyar name was exclusively official, while the inhabitants never dreamed of using it—perhaps, indeed, did not know it. But it was not all show. Hungary really had, in that short space of time, made Magyar not only the façade of her house, but many of its more important structural elements. It was not merely that the so-called upper classes were Magyar; that administration, justice, and higher education were the same. This would have been important enough, seeing what a large proportion of the country's activities were comprised therein; but further, the great majority of the middle classes, commercial, industrial, and 'intellectual', as well as official, now spoke and felt Magyar. And by 'middle-class' we mean here a large section of society, including even most of the artisans and skilled workmen. Hungarian figures of the joint-stock companies in 1915, based on the language used by the boards or 'the names of the leading men', showed that 97·4 per cent. of these companies with 99·3 per cent. of the share capital, 99·4 per cent. of the preference shares, and 99·5 per cent. of the total assets were in the hands of Magyar-speaking persons (largely, of course, Magyarized Jews). 1·1 per cent. of the companies belonged to Roumanians, 0·9 per cent. to Slovaks, 0·5 per cent. to Transylvanian Saxons, and 0·1 per cent. to Serbs, these representing the few specifically 'national' enterprises of the non-Magyars.[1] The industrially employed population was divided, according to the 1910 figures, into 65·1 per cent. Magyars, 15·2 per cent. Germans, 8·1 per cent. Slovaks, 5·3 per cent. Roumanians, 1·8 per cent. Serbs, 1·0 per cent. Croats, 0·5 per cent. Ruthenes, and 5·0 per cent. others.[2]

[1] Vol. iii A, pp. 410–11, of *The Hungarian Peace Negotiations: an Account of the Work of the Hungarian Peace Delegation at Neuilly s/S. from January to March 1920.* Published by the Royal Hungarian Ministry of Foreign Affairs, 3 vols. in 4, Budapest, 1920–2. Subsequently referred to as *Hungarian Peace Negotiations.*   [2] Ibid., p. 353.

The nationalization of the towns—the first object which the Magyars had set themselves—had made astonishing progress. Thus Budapest, which was three-quarters German in 1848, had become 68 per cent. Magyar by 1890. Arad, which had been half Roumanian and one-third German, had become 65 per cent. Magyar; Pécs (Fünfkirchen) had changed from almost purely German to three-quarters Magyar. The same story could be told of Poszóny, Sopron, Ujvidék (Neusatz, Novi Sad), Szabadka (Subotica, Maria Theresiopol). Between 1880 and 1890 alone, the Magyar population increased in Nagyvárád (Grosswardein, Oradea Mare) by 26 per cent., in Kassa by 39 per cent., in Szabadka by 24 per cent., in Ujvidék by 37 per cent., in Sopron by 66 per cent., in Pancsova (Pančevo) by 76 per cent., in Temesvár by 42 per cent., in Versécz (Werchetz, Vršac) by 25 per cent. In all these towns the population of other languages registered either small increases, or decreases, amounting in the case of Subotica to 15 per cent. In the 25 largest towns of Hungary the Magyar-speaking population grew in this period by 688,000, or 29 per cent., and in the 101 smaller towns by 16 per cent., while the German-speaking population remained almost exactly stationary, with a slight decrease. The two decades after 1890 saw a still further, rapid increase in Magyar-speaking population.

Thus everything that represented the new advanced, growing Hungary seemed to be safely Magyar, while the other languages were confined to the backward peasant communities of the periphery, were becoming more and more subordinate, second-rate, losing their vitality and their power of development.

Counting in these peasant masses, the progress was, of course, far less rapid. The census figures shown below indicate that

	1880		1890		1900		1910	
	Total	Per cent.	Total	Per cent.	Total	Per cent.	Total	Per cent.
Magyars . .	6,403,687	46·65	7,356,874	48·61	8,651,520	51·4	9,944,627	54·5
Germans. .	1,869,877	13·62	1,988,589	13·14	1,999,060	11·9	1,903,357	10·4
Slovaks . .	1,845,442	13·52	1,896,641	12·53	2,002,165	11·9	1,946,357	10·7
Roumanians .	2,463,035	17·50	2,589,066	17·11	2,798,559	16·6	2,948,186	16·1
Serbs and Croats	631,995	4·60	678,747	4·48	629,169	3·7	656,324	3·6
Ruthenes. .	353,226	2·57	379,782	2·51	424,774	2·5	464,270	2·5
Others . .	211,366	1·54	243,795	1·62	333,008	2·0	401,412	2·2

the increase in the Magyar-speaking population was not at all large in the country districts. To take, for example, the decade 1880–90, the growth outside the towns amounted only to some 200,000, showing a rate of increase lower than that of several other nationalities; and that in spite of the fact that both the system and the methods by which the census was taken favoured the appearance of an increase in the Magyar element. It appears, in fact, that while the scattered groups of non-Magyars living in the plain, and

D

surrounded by Magyars, such as the Slovaks and the Ruthenes
out in the open plains, the Germans of the Bakony district, the
Bunyevci round Szabadka, were Magyarizing fairly rapidly, under
what were probably for the most part natural influences, yet the
nationalities living in compact masses round the periphery had
hardly been touched by Magyarization. A good example is the
German linguistic frontier in the west, which has hardly shifted a
kilometre for centuries.

In this connexion it is most interesting to read the verdict of
M. P. Balogh, an ethnologist who investigated the situation for the
Government in 1902 and reached the conclusion—which seems at
first sight curiously at variance with the census figures—that in the
period of Liberal rule (since 1875–1900) the Magyars had lost 465
communes to the nationalities, while gaining only 261 from them.
Their chief gains had been at the expense of the Slovaks, their chief
losses to the Roumanians and Germans. Of all the nationalities
of Hungary, the Ruthenes had been the largest losers, then the
Magyars, then the Serbs. The Roumanians had gained most on
balance; after them the Slovaks, then the Germans.

The great question for Hungary was, then, whether by virtue of
what she had already achieved, by the influence of the foci which she
had established, and by the intensified Magyarization of elementary
education she could make the same impression on these peasant
masses as she had on the urban population. She did not despair,
and, indeed, her previous record entitled her to hope. On the other
hand, there was always the possibility that the resistance would
stiffen in the future. She owed something of her progress to her
own long start, and as wealth and education spread through the
country, reaching one backwater after another, the same causes
which had made possible the great development of the Magyars
might also operate, in turn, in favour of the nationalities. ·

We shall see, in the subsequent sections, how the situation developed with regard to each nationality. It is hardly possible ever
to give a conclusive answer, for in nearly all cases two rival forces
were at work: the attraction of Magyarization, and the national
resistance. The former seemed much the stronger in the case of
the Slovaks, the Ruthenes, the Germans; the latter, in that of the
Roumanians. But the force which each possessed depended largely
on incalculable factors, and the answer to what would have happened if the War had not intervened can never be given with any
assurance to-day. We can only say that by 1918 the whole upper
structure of the State was Magyar, while the peasants were still
much as they had been half a century earlier.

§ 7. THE CROWN AND THE FORCES OUTSIDE HUNGARY

It is, however, necessary to call attention to certain factors outside Hungary itself which assumed a large, perhaps a dominating role in the situation. Magyar historians are fond of emphasizing the part played by the Crown in favour of the nationalities and against the Magyars. This, as we have seen, is true and most important up to 1867. If Hungary had been ruled by national kings in the seventeenth, eighteenth, and nineteenth centuries, she might well have solved her national problem as completely as France did. On the other hand, without foreign help, often forcibly administered, she would not have been rid of the Turks when she was; so that the Crown cannot be counted only as an enemy. In any case, after 1867 it became quite definitely a friend. Having once concluded the Compromise, Francis Joseph left the nationalities to make their own terms with the Hungarian Government. He never again intervened in their favour. None of them even dared to approach him until the Roumanians did so, nearly a generation later; and then they were stonily rebuffed.

In appearance the position of the Crown was one of neutrality; in reality it proved a strong support for the Magyars. The whole conservative power of one of Europe's most conservative states stood behind Hungary's own system, which itself depended so largely for its efficiency on its oligarchic character. More important still, through her partnership in the Dual Monarchy, Hungary belonged to one of the Great Powers of Europe whose might constantly overawed the little Roumanian and Serbian states which were now coming to constitute the real threat to Hungarian integrity, while the position of the Czechs and the Ruthenes in the monarchy made it hardly possible for a Slovak or a Ruthene question in Hungary even to arise. It was largely for this reason that Count Stephen Tisza (and others with him) clung so tenaciously to the Austrian connexion, believing that without it Hungary could not permanently resist the centrifugal pull of Roumania and Serbia. Others believed that without the Crown, and with a thorough democratization of Hungary, the national question could be solved—indeed, that the only solution lay that way. But the bulk of the governing class were certainly not prepared to pay in advance the price of the experiment.

It was their loss of the Crown's support that made the nationalities abate their claims after 1868. We have seen that in 1865 both the Slovaks and the Serbs had desired 'national' autonomy on a territorial basis. The wishes of the Roumanians (not included in the 1865 negotiations) were certainly not less far-reaching. At the worst, all these three nationalities wished for complete equality for all languages of Hungary; the minority draft of the Nationalities Law, signed by the sixteen non-Magyar deputies, contained proposals to this effect. Only when Francis Joseph finally abandoned them did they decide to make do with the Nationalities Law. Later, as Francis Joseph grew old, the situation changed once again. His heir apparent, the Archduke Francis Ferdinand, notoriously believed the national policy of the Magyars—towards whom he felt an almost passionate detestation—to be a danger to the integrity of his future dominions, and he proposed, like Joseph II, to postpone his coronation and to force through some reorganization of Austria-Hungary based on a different system from the German-Magyar hegemony on which the Compromise rested. It was not known exactly what shape his plans would take—indeed, they probably changed more than once. Undoubtedly, however, they involved some sort of support of the non-Magyar nationalities. For a time he appears to have been strongly impressed by a remarkable book, *Die vereinigten Staaten Gross-Oesterreichs*, published in 1906 by a Transylvanian Roumanian, M. Aurel Popovici, who pleaded for a federalization of Austria-Hungary into fifteen states on a federal basis, with German as the *lingua franca*. Afterwards, it was suggested, Roumania and Serbia would enter the federation under Habsburg overlordship. At another period Francis Ferdinand contemplated changing the Dualist form of the Monarchy into Trialism by uniting all the Southern Slav districts of both Austria and Hungary, with Bosnia and Herzegovina, into a third Habsburg state. Later, again, he seems to have entertained less far-reaching ideas. But at all times he kept in close touch with the leaders of the nationalities, particularly the Roumanians (who hailed him almost openly as their destined saviour), but also the Slovaks.

The fact that the dormant political ambitions of the leaders of the nationalities became active again only when they saw once more the prospect of finding a friend outside Hungary may seem to strengthen Hungary's case that, left to herself, she might have solved her problem. But we must remember that the Crown was still, in one respect, a tremendous conservative force. Francis Ferdinand was no less an enemy than Francis Joseph to Serbian and Roumanian irredentism. He proposed to destroy Magyar supremacy, but not Hungary. Whether a truly independent Hungary, under a truly national Hungarian king, could have permanently defied at least the Roumanian and Yugoslav irredentas is a doubtful question indeed. And that, if any, is the real hypothetical question when we review Hungary's last years and ask—could it have been otherwise?

§ 8. THE BREAK-DOWN AND THE TREATY

At all events, the success or the failure of Hungary's experiment could not but depend very largely on factors outside her own frontiers. It is therefore relevant, and will, again, avoid a certain duplication, to record the precise circumstances in which her final tragedy came about. She entered the War, of course, as one of the Central Powers. Her Prime Minister, Count Tisza, had not at first been in favour of the monarchy's projected war against Serbia. He had even threatened to resign if the ultimatum were made impossible for Serbia to accept, as Berchthold planned. Later he withdrew his opposition, stipulating only that the monarchy should receive no acquisitions of territory. Hungary's enemies have attempted to fix theodium of 'war-guilt' on Hungary for his conduct; she has repudiated the charge with equal vigour. We need not here go into the details of this controversy, since the Treaty of Trianon was not avowedly punitive; but it is, of course, germane, although somewhat superfluous, to remark that from July 1914 onward Hungary was committed to the side of the Central Powers, which proved also to be the losing side.

Throughout the War she stood loyally by Austria and her allies, even although, towards the end, she exploited Austria's difficulties somewhat ruthlessly to strengthen her own position as partner in the Dual Monarchy. Her attitude changed only in the very last days. She was then still intact, and her troops stood everywhere on foreign soil, but Austria was disintegrating visibly, and in October 1918 her own integrity seemed once more threatened from Serbia and Roumania. Her troops then began to clamour to be sent home to defend their own frontiers. Simultaneously social unrest was increasing, and a party was proclaiming that Hungary's whole policy had been mistaken; that by dissociating herself from the Central Powers she could make her own peace with the Entente. The leaders of this party believed that by concessions to the nationalities they could persuade all, or practically all, of them to remain within the rejuvenated and reformed Hungary.

On October 31st the king appointed Count Michael Károlyi, the leader of this group, his Minister President. Károlyi formed a Ministry drawn from the Party of Independence and the Parties of the Left. His Minister for War, a Social Democrat, recalled the Magyar troops from the Front, but began to disband many of the units, fearing that they might be used for revolution, or for counter-revolution.

Meanwhile, on November 1st, the Austro-Hungarian Supreme Command concluded an armistice with the Italian Commander-in-Chief at Padua, fixing a line of occupation in the south-west only.

Elsewhere the line was to consist of the existing political frontier, but the Allies were entitled to occupy the interior of the Monarchy if they desired. Croatia-Slavonia had already, two days previously, proclaimed its independence of Hungary; and Fiume was necessarily lost to Hungary also.

The Allies now advanced in the Balkans and reached Belgrade. Károlyi went to meet the French Commander, General Franchet d'Espérey, who was chiefly preoccupied by his anxiety to cut off the retreat of General Mackensen's German Army, then in Roumania. It never occurred to him to treat the new Hungary as a friend; on the contrary, he prescribed a line running across the whole of the south and east of Hungary from Besztercze (Bistriţa, Bistritz) in Eastern Transylvania, southward to the Maros (Mureş), west along the course of that river, and through Szabadka, Baja, and Pécs to the Mur. Allied troops were allowed to occupy the area east and south of this line, but the Hungarian civil administration was to continue functioning there, as elsewhere in Hungary. This agreement was concluded on November 6th and signed on November 13th. Thereupon Serb troops advanced up to the line in the south and Roumanians in the east. The local populations then produced demonstrations, of varying degrees of spontaneity, in favour of the new States, which thereupon took over the civil administration also.

The Belgrade armistice did not touch Northern Hungary; but the Czechoslovaks had obtained from the Allies recognition as an Allied Army and State; a popular assembly of Slovaks had decided in favour of a Czechoslovak State, and Czech troops began early in November to cross the frontier. Subsequently they obtained permission to occupy a line corresponding roughly to their claims and Hungary was forced by the Allied representative in Budapest to withdraw her troops behind that line. Meanwhile the Serbs had advanced in some places beyond the line first laid down by General Franchet d'Espérey, and the Roumanians had moved right out into the Hungarian plain. On March 20th, 1919, Hungary was forced further to withdraw her troops so as to leave a neutral zone between them and the Roumanians.

In the meantime, the Peace Conference had already opened in Paris. The Serbs, Czechs, and Roumanians were all represented there by delegations recognized as Allies. Each of them stated its case before the Principal Allied and Associated Powers. Their statements of claims, together with the other documentary material which had been collected by the Allied experts (including the Hungarian national statistics), were then taken over by Commissions, comprised of American, British, French, and Italian experts. These Commissions worked out frontier lines and recommended them to their chiefs.

So far as Hungary was concerned, most of the work of these Commissions (except as regards a few points of detail) was completed for the northern, eastern, and southern frontiers as early as March or even February 1919. Only the west frontier was undecided; Austria, like Hungary, had not been invited to the Conference, and it was not yet certain whether she would claim any part of Hungary.

While the frontiers were being worked out, Károlyi had been succeeded as Minister President by a government of the extreme Left, whose *spiritus rector* was Béla Kun. Fearing to see Communism spread, the Allies allowed the Roumanian troops to advance as far as the Theiss. Kun now undertook an offensive and drove the Czechs out of Eastern Slovakia, but this only hastened the decision of the Allies. They forced him to withdraw, and issued a declaration (June 13th) that a line closely corresponding with the demarcation lines in the north and east would constitute Hungary's political frontiers with Czechoslovakia and Roumania respectively. The declaration did not apply to the south, where some controversy appears still to have been proceeding over the Yugoslav claims; but the broad decision had been taken there also, and the details were agreed soon after, when the draft Peace Terms were finally approved.

As regards all frontiers except the west, nothing mattered much after that. The Roumanians actually advanced and occupied Budapest in August, but this act brought them no additional concessions. Conversely, when a Hungarian Conservative Government was reestablished and was at last invited to send a delegation to Paris, where it arrived on January 7th, 1920, this was not in order to negotiate but simply to accept the decisions reached. No concession was made nor even any serious discussion entertained on the broad principle of Hungary's dismemberment; nor were the proposed frontiers even altered in detail in any important respect. In reply to Hungary's protests, M. Millerand, speaking for the Peace Conference, agreed that in certain cases where frontiers were found 'not to correspond precisely with ethnical or economic requirements', 'an inquiry held on the spot may, perhaps, make apparent the necessity of a displacement of the limits laid down by the Treaty in certain parts'. No general inquiry was possible, but if the Delimitation Commissions found that the Treaty anywhere 'created an injustice which it would be to the general interest to remove', they might report to the Council of the League, which would offer its services for an amicable rectification. 'The Allied and Associated Powers', said M. Millerand, 'are confident that this procedure will furnish a convenient method for correcting in the delimitation of the frontiers any injustice against which objections not unfounded can be raised.'

In the event, the Delimitation Commissions made only few and trivial alterations, not all of which were even in Hungary's favour.

One frontier alone, that with Austria, was exempted from this summary procedure. Here the two countries were treated as equals, and Hungary obtained certain important concessions.

Hungary signed the Treaty on June 4th, 1920, and ratified it on November 13th, 1920.

THE BURGENLAND

THE Burgenland, as the territory allotted to Austria at Hungary's expense is called,[1] is far the smallest of any of Hungary's losses to her immediate neighbours, its area of 3,967·19 sq. km. being less than one twenty-fifth of that of Transylvania. It consists of a long, narrow strip of territory running the whole length of the Austro-Hungarian frontier, from a point in the north where the boundary between the two countries meets the bridge-head allotted to Czechoslovakia opposite Pressburg on the right bank of the Danube, to the hills south of the Raab, where it joins the frontier of Yugoslavia. Geographically, this strip falls into two very distinct halves, almost cut off from each other by the loop containing the city of Oedenburg, which has been left to Hungary. One salient of this loop leaves a space only about three miles across, and containing only a single road between the old and new frontiers of Austria.

The northern and broader half is in the shape of a right-angled triangle, the hypotenuse of which is formed by the low Leithagebirge, along which the old frontier ran in part. The new line now runs south from the Czechoslovak bridge-head, until reaching the Neusiedlersee–Danube canal, where it turns due west along the canal, crosses the lake near its southern end, and as it does so turns north to form the Oedenburg loop, which fills the greater part of the gap between the Leithagebirge and the Rosaliengebirge, south of Wiener Neustadt. Once the terraced vineyards of the modest range dignified by the name of Leithagebirge are left behind, the whole northern Burgenland is merely a corner, divided from the main part by a barrier, which is purely political, of the Lesser Alföld of Hungary. The country is flat, open, and sandy, and dotted with numerous lakes, many of which are mere pools. The Neusiedlersee itself, although 20 miles long and 6 to 8 miles

[1] The name is a post-War invention, the credit of which appears to belong the Herr Odo Rötig, a Viennese resident in Oedenburg (Sopron), who in 1919 began to issue a paper entitled *Das Vierburgenland*, after the German names of the four West Hungarian Counties regarded as composing German West Hungary (Pressburg (= Pozsóny, Bratislava), Oedenburg, Wieselburg = Moson, Eisenburg = Vásvár). The numeral had to be dropped when Pressburg was assigned in its entirety to the Czechs, but Professor Waldheim of Vienna, an Oedenburger born, and Dr. K. Amon, a lawyer of Neusiedl, urged the retention of the rest of the name, which was in any case appropriate owing to the large number of 'Burgen', or fortified castles, in this old frontier district. Interestingly enough, it was afterwards discovered that the term for the district current among the local Croats was Gradište—an exact translation of the German Burgenland. The name Burgenland rapidly became popular, and was officially adopted by the first Landtag when it met in 1922.

in average width (so that it occupies no mean fraction of the total area of the northern Burgenland) is seldom more than 6 feet deep, and generally only 2 or 3, while in certain annual cycles it shows every symptom of an intention—never resolutely fulfilled—of drying up altogether.

From below the Oedenburg loop, the frontier runs south-west, almost parallel with the old line, but gradually approaching it until the two lines finally meet. This portion of the Burgenland is formed, geographically, by the last outliers of the Styrian Alps, and consists of a series of hill ranges, of considerable height to the west, but sloping rapidly downward, and of intervening and gradually broadening valleys. In the extreme south the valley of the Raab gives the country a more open look; on the other hand, the Günser Gebirge, in the centre, are a substantial range, across which communication is difficult. Broadly speaking, the frontier marks the line between the hills, to-day assigned to Austria, and the plain, which has been left to Hungary. In medieval times the whole of this area must have been densely wooded, and although much has been cleared for pasture and arable land, large forests still remain. The population is sparse, and there are no towns larger than small market centres.

A greater contrast still is afforded by the country to the west of these two areas. Behind the Leithagebirge lies the 'Wiener Becken', containing the important cities of Wiener Neustadt and, farther away, Vienna itself, with Pressburg to the north, Oedenburg on the south. Lying as it does full on the great natural highway between Eastern and Western Europe which is formed by the Danube Valley, the Northern Burgenland has been an immemorial channel both for trade and invasion. The southern half of the area, on the other hand, lies against a wall. In the extreme south, the valley of the Raab forms a gap giving access to Graz and Styria generally, and a railway from Graz links up at Körmend with the main Hungarian system. Apart from this, the steep and densely wooded Styrian Alps are crossed even by few roads, and only a single railway threads its way from Wiener Neustadt, via Aspang and Hartberg, to Fürstenfeld, across the 'Humpy World' (*bucklige Welt*), as the south-eastern corner of Lower Austria is aptly named. Until some years after the transfer, there was no connexion between this line and those of the Hungarian system, all of which stopped short a few miles from the valley mouths.

The population of this area was, according to the Hungarian census of 1910, 285,609, including 26,225 Magyar-speaking persons. The Austrian census of 1923 gave a figure (Burgenland citizens only) of 275,356, of whom 222,417 were Germans, 41,761 Croats, 9,606 Magyars, and 2,702 'others'. The 1934 figures gave a total population of 299,503, of whom 241,326 were Germans, 40,500 Croats, 10,422 Magyars, 6,452 gipsies, and 933 others. The Jews are not listed as a separate nationality in any of these figures. The discrepancies between the Hungarian and Austrian figures are due chiefly to emigration of Magyars, and to the defection of gipsies and Jews.[1]

§ 1. GEOGRAPHY, POPULATION, AND HISTORY

All of this territory, with the Hungarian plain itself, as far as the Danube, belonged to various Germanic tribes after the destruction of the Roman Empire in the Danube Valley, and again formed part of the Frank Empire in the ninth century, after Charlemagne had crushed the Turanian Avars who had themselves succeeded the Germans as masters of the Middle Danube. The Magyars, however, conquered it within a few years of their arrival in Central Europe. The Leitha appears as the Austro-Hungarian frontier as early as A.D. 1043, while in the south the Lafnitz seems to have become the line between Hungary and Styria about the same date. Thereafter the frontier remained remarkably stable, the gains made by each side at various times seldom proving long-lived. Some of the border castles and cities were ceded or pledged by Hungary in the fifteenth century to the Emperor Frederick IV, his brother Duke Albrecht VI, and the Emperor Maximilian, and some of them were administered thereafter by the Estates of Lower Austria. On the strength of these ancient charters, Austria in 1919 claimed some of these estates on grounds of historic right. The Hungarian Estates, however, never agreed that the territories in question had thereby ceased to form a part of Hungary. They gradually recovered possession of the disputed castles in the sixteenth and seventeenth centuries, and although the claims and counter-claims went on, in one case until 1833/4, yet in practice the frontier of 1918 had remained stable, and had been accepted by Austria for many decades before that date.

Historically, therefore, Hungary's claim to most of the Burgenland was unquestioned, and to the few disputed areas it was at least strong. Ethnographically, on the other hand, the Burgenland had been mainly German for quite as long as it had been politically Hungarian. The German tribes who succeeded Rome in Noricum and Pannonia were probably swept aside without a trace by the Avars, who themselves occupied the open country in the north, while if any non-Avar population existed in the forests farther

[1] See de Nagy, 'Westungarn-Burgenland in Oesterreich', in *Glasul Minoritaților*, June 1932, pp. 148 ff. The Hungarian Refugees Office received 1,187 persons as refugees from the Burgenland in 1921–3.

south, it was probably of Slovene stock. When, however, Charlemagne destroyed the Avars at the end of the eighth century, he cleared and colonized part of the land with German settlers. Steinamanger (Szombathély), Oedenburg, and Pinkafeld (Pinkafő) already appear in the records of the ninth century. The Magyars probably swept away these colonists from the open country in the north, which they occupied themselves or settled with the kindred nation of the Petchenegs. Their own kings, however, acting either directly or through the agency of various monastic orders, afterwards recolonized the whole open space on both sides of the Neusiedlersee with German settlers, apparently of the same Bajuvarian stock as most of the Austrians. This colonization lasted through the eleventh, twelfth, and thirteenth centuries and the descendants of the settlers still make up a large proportion of the population of the Wieselburg district, and still preserve their distinctive dialect and habits. The villages between the Neusiedlersee and the Danube were almost wiped out in the Turkish wars of the sixteenth and seventeenth centuries, but the country was again re-colonized, mainly by Germans—in this case, Protestant Suabians, driven from their homes under the Counter-Reformation. These 'Heidebauern' form another distinctive group of the population.

In the Middle Burgenland a few Germans probably survived the first Magyar onslaught. The country was settled more fully in the twelfth and thirteenth centuries, with yet another group of Germans, the so-called 'Heinzen' or 'Heanzen',[1] who appear to be of Frankish stock, and differ widely in dialect and manners from their neighbours in Styria and Lower Austria. In the Raab Valley the colonization was carried out largely by the Cistercian monks, and the population is akin to that of Styria.

The Magyars themselves never coveted the hills and forests, and their settlement stopped short where the plain ends. The line of demarcation between the two peoples had remained practically unchanged for centuries, and astonishingly clear-cut, except for two or three German villages of recent origin in the plain, and a tiny group of Magyar villages in the Pinka Valley. Apart from the latter, the only Magyar element in the country-side, within the German line, consists of a few large landowners and their staffs.

In the towns, on the other hand, important changes in the national composition began some half-century ago. Almost all the towns of West Hungary were of German foundation and preserved their Germanic character, language, and atmosphere quite intact until well past the middle of the nineteenth century. Thus in 1880 Oedenburg had 17,115 Germans and only 4,877 Magyars; Güns (Kőszeg),

---

[1] No satisfactory explanation of this name has yet been given.

5,296 Germans and 1,458 Magyars. Farther east even such towns as Steinamanger, where the surrounding villages were Magyar, stood as German islands in a Magyar sea. From about that date onward, the position changed rapidly. Not only the towns with a Magyar hinterland but also those lying within the German linguistic area were Magyarized, more or less thoroughly; had the process continued the position would have been completely reversed, and such towns as Oedenburg and Eisenstadt would have become Magyar islands in a German sea.

The third element of some importance in the population consists of the Croats. These are comparatively recent arrivals, their ancestors having fled from Croatia and Bosnia (for the most part in the sixteenth century, although a few came earlier and one colony was established as late as 1793) before the Turkish advance. They were settled, partly by the Government, partly by private landowners, on lands laid waste by the Turks, along a line reaching from the Mur in the south as far north as the Marchfeld, and even Moravia and Slovakia. They never formed a compact mass, but rather a sort of archipelago in the German and Magyar sea, and, thanks in part to this isolated position, many of them were rapidly assimilated. The colonies in the Marchfeld have long become German, and many of those farther south also became merged in time with the local Germans or Magyars; although there are also cases where persons of German origin have adopted the Croat language and customs. The survivors in Austrian territory to-day form four fairly compact blocs, in the neighbourhood of Parndorf, Eisenstadt, Hornstein, and Unterpullendorf respectively, and two more scattered groups centring respectively in Podgoria and Güssing.

The Croats, who still speak an antique seventeenth-century dialect (or rather, variety of dialects) of Croatian, heavily interspersed by German and (to a lesser extent) Magyar terms, are practically all Catholics, and are a people of peasants, with a small intelligentsia and modest literature. Their speciality is poultry-keeping and dealing, and the characteristic carts in which they were wont to bring their stock to Vienna were well known in that city before the age of the lorry. Some of them also followed the traditional Slovak calling of besom-binders and hawkers, while many emigrated in the nineteenth century to the U.S.A.

In recent years their distinctive national dress has almost disappeared in favour of the local German costume; but they keep up various specific family and religious ceremonies.

The other elements in the local population are far less numerous. The Jews never penetrated West Hungary in large numbers, but the 'Seven Communes' of the north long enjoyed a reputation extending far across the Hungarian frontier as the homes of strict piety and cultural activity. Eisenstadt, with its picturesque ghetto, Mattersburg, and Deutschkreuz still harbour considerable Jewish communities, and still earn the respect of all interested in the country. The private museum established by Mr. Wolf, of Eisenstadt (Kis Marton), is even to-day one of the best private collections in Europe, and a storehouse of interest for the Burgenland.

The gipsies, who spread over Hungary in the fourteenth century, encamped in considerable numbers on the spacious shores of Neusiedlersee. So far as outward national culture was concerned, they adopted the Magyar in preference to the German.

Finally, a few Slovenes are to be found in the extreme south of the territory.

The connexions between all West Hungary, including the Burgenland, and Austria have naturally been intimate for many centuries. When the Turks held Central Hungary, the western strip which remained under the Habsburgs was at times almost a part of Austria, and it was the stronghold of the big landowners and princes of the church whose spiritual affinities lay far rather with Vienna than with the 'betyárs' of the Alföld. In the nineteenth century a close economic connexion also developed. The central Burgenland, which gravitated naturally towards Steinamanger, formed an exception, and incidentally remained economically the most backward part of the country. The southern districts, on the other hand, tended increasingly to look for their markets in Graz and the industrial towns of Styria, rather than in the small and undeveloped towns of South-Western Hungary, while in the north a similar orientation towards Vienna and Wiener Neustadt was even more clearly marked. Even Hungarian writers admitted that the population of Pressburg, Oedenburg, and the surrounding districts stood economically and culturally far nearer to Vienna than to Budapest. Economically, this tendency was particularly strongly marked. The dairy and garden produce and the wines in which the Counties of Wieselburg and Oedenburg excelled went almost exclusively to Vienna, which again drew a very considerable proportion of its supplies of these commodities from North-Western Hungary (at this time there were no customs duties between Austria and Hungary). The immigration into Austria was, moreover, important. In 1890, out of 221,139 Hungarian citizens domiciled in Austria, 130,905 of whom were in Lower Austria alone,[1] no less than 29,314 came from the County of Pressburg, 30,386 from Oedenburg, 29,500 from Eisenburg, and 7,352 from Wieselburg; the great majority of these were Germans. A large

[1] At this time Vienna formed part of the 'Land' of Lower Austria.

number of the immigrants were gardeners, builders, or domestic servants; but many also rose to eminence.[1]

Very important also for the poorer classes was the rapid development of industry in Wiener Neustadt and other localities in the plain south of Vienna. Many of the workers in the new factories came from the Burgenland, and travelled in by train to their work either daily or for the week, returning on Sundays to their homes.

In spite of this, there was before the War no irredentist movement among the Germans of West Hungary, nor did the Magyarization of the towns awaken any resistance. This may be taken as absolutely certain, since it is agreed both by Austrian writers, who deplore the fact, and by Hungarians, who make the most of it. Perhaps the most striking testimony which I have found is that of a journalist sent by a nationalist paper in German Bohemia in, I think, the 90's, who wrote as follows:

I could never have thought possible such a hot-house culture of renegade feeling as goes on in the little towns of West Hungary, only a few hours' journey from Vienna. The Germans there, especially the so-called educated classes, are in a great hurry to be rid of their German character, and Jews, as well as priests of all cults, especially, of course, the Roman Catholic, hurry on the Magyarization as fast as they can. It is incredible how the members of the German people in West Hungary, who are far superior to the local Magyars in numbers and culture, simply throw themselves on the neck of that little people.[2]

This report is completely corroborated by all that I have heard from other sources.

Nor was there any question in Austria of a West Hungarian irredenta. The Austrians are a modest and incurious people, and to them the land a mile beyond the Hungarian frontier was a *terra incognita*. After the last frontier disputes had died of inanition in 1833, the question was hardly raised again; a couple of speakers in the Austrian Reichsrat, a brochure published in Vienna in 1906 by one S. Patny under the title of *Westungarn in Deutsch-Oesterreich*, an occasional reference to the subject in the literature issued by the Alldeutscher Verein and other Pan-German societies in the Reich, about exhaust the interest taken in it outside Hungary until the autumn of 1918.

[1] The rate of overseas emigration was also high, although lower than that of North Hungary. This was due to the prevalence of large estates, and has continued under Austrian rule.

[2] I copied this quotation out of a book lent me in a foreign land, and regret to say that I have now lost the reference. It was one of a series of reprinted anti-Hungarian articles; the author was a fervent German nationalist.

§ 2. THE MOVEMENT FOR ATTACHMENT TO AUSTRIA

The active German national movement in Hungary, of which
the West Hungarian movement is only a part, began only towards
the end of the War, under the influence of the wave of nationalism
then sweeping over Europe and, in particular, of the personal
contact into which the War brought the German soldiers of West
Hungary, for the first time in their lives, with their German and
Austrian kinsfolk. The national re-awakening came too late to
touch many of the Hungarian Germans at all; a considerable proportion of them, confronted for the first time with a choice of
loyalties, decided in their hearts for the Magyar ideal, and must be
counted, henceforward, as Magyars. The remainder fall into two
groups, which were soon in venomous opposition to each other.[1]
The one was on the whole most strongly represented among the
Transylvanian Saxons, whose leader, Dr. Brandsch, was its spokesman and chairman of the 'Deutscher Volksrat' formed to represent
it. The Deutscher Volksrat started from the postulate of the
German nationality of its members, and was prepared to come
to agreement with whatever State offered it the most favourable
terms from the national point of view. As price for remaining in
Hungary, Dr. Brandsch demanded at least far-reaching autonomy
for the whole German 'nation' in Hungary.

The second group was stronger among the Suabians, and its
leader and chairman of its 'Deutsch-ungarischer Volksrat' was Professor Bleyer, of Budapest University. Professor Bleyer accepted
absolutely the Hungarian State, and was prepared only to accept
the best terms which he could get, within those limits, by negotiation with the Hungarian Government. In no case did he wish for
'national' organization, nor even for so much German education
as would impair the cultural unity of Hungary.

The latter movement counted many adherents among the Germans of Hungary, but at the end of 1918 their voices were not
often heard; the more so as the Deutscher Volksrat was, of the two,
the more strongly represented in the Ministry of Nationalities.
West Hungary had two representatives in the Deutscher Volksrat,
one of whom, the spokesman for the northern districts, supported
the claim of the Volksrat for national autonomy within Hungary;
but the representative of the southern districts advocated separation from Hungary and union with Austria.

In the course of the following weeks, a number of communes in

---

[1] A sketch of these events, from the Austrian side, is given by Dr. H. Kunnert
in *Burgenland, Vierteljahreshefte für Landeskunde*, Folge 2, 2. Jahrg., pp. 127 ff.
See also D. Eitler, 'Der Kampf um Oedenburg', in *Volk und Reich*, 1929,
Heft 1, pp. 69 ff. I have supplemented these sources out of certain private
information.

the centre and the south, including some Croat villages, held meetings or organized plebiscites in favour of union with Austria or with Styria (in one case, in favour of an independent 'Heinzenland Republic', as a prelude to such union). The north, and with it the majority of the special 'Deutscher Volksrat für Westungarn' which had been established to concert policy and watch over the interests of the West Hungarian Counties, still stood by the integrity of Hungary, but grew impatient as the promised autonomy for the Germans failed to appear, although a law for the Ruthene districts was issued on December 25th.[1] When the Czechs occupied Pressburg and the Serbs advanced in the south, the impatience grew even greater, and on January 20th, 1919, a general meeting of the Germans of West Hungary, assembled in the County buildings at Sopron, sent the Government an ultimatum demanding the immediate enactment of the autonomy; failing which, West Hungary would proclaim either its independence or its union with Austria.

The Ministry for Nationalities, through its German representative, now hurriedly drafted an Act, modelled on that already issued for the Ruthenes but adapted to the peculiar circumstances of the Germans.[2] This measure, which was adopted by the Ministerial Council on January 27th as People's Law No. 6 of 1919, recognized all the Germans of Hungary as a single 'nation'. Where the Germans lived in compact masses, districts ('Gauen') were to be formed, in agreement with the non-Germans living in them. Within these districts the German people enjoyed complete legislative and administrative autonomy as regards internal administration, justice, education, and cultural and church questions; the language of communication with the authorities was German, even in 'common' affairs not falling within the sphere of their autonomy. For autonomous questions the German nation possessed a National Assembly of its own; for questions of common interest, they were represented in proportion to their numbers in the Hungarian Parliament. A German Ministry was established under a Minister who was to be equally responsible to the German National Assembly and to the Hungarian Parliament, and to sit as an equal member of the Hungarian Government in all common questions. The different districts each had its Governing Council, composed of departmental specialists, under a governor, and an elected assembly. The work of the districts was controlled by the German Minister. Other provisions safeguarded the rights of national minorities; while a provisional Council was appointed, consisting of four members of each of the two Volkräte and two representatives from each district inhabited by Germans.

[1] See below, p. 213 f.   [2] Text in Szana, op. cit., pp. 265-7.

E

It had been proposed to create five districts: Transylvania, North Hungary, South Hungary, West Hungary, and Central Hungary. In fact, the north, south, and east were by this time all in enemy occupation, and in the centre the resistance of Magyar opinion was too strong to allow the plan to be realized. For West Hungary, however, a Governing Council and Governor (M. Zsombor) were actually established, with a German Minister in Budapest (M. Junker). It was certainly never fully effective, owing to the resistance of the Magyar and Magyarophil officials, but the administration was partially Germanized, and a good deal of work was done as regards the schools, a number of which were turned into genuine German schools with Magyar taught only as a subject. This work went on almost undisturbed during the Communist period, since M. Kalmars, himself a German, who under the Commune succeeded M. Junker as People's Commissary for German affairs, sensibly left the Germans to work out their own salvation and even abstained from placing any Communists in the Ministry. Not many Communists were sent at all into the German districts, which lived a bourgeois existence enough under the Commune.

The People's Law of July 16th re-enacted the law of January 27th without substantial modification, except in one respect: the position of Oedenburg. Here the local Magyar press resisted the January law vehemently, declaring it to be no less of a catastrophe for Hungary than the Serbian occupation of Pécs. An agitation began for exempting Oedenburg from the law, on the ground of its Magyar character and culture, and a 'propaganda office for the maintenance of the integrity of Hungary' was founded to press this claim. Herr Junker refused it, but Kun excluded Oedenburg from the operation of his law and from the competence of the District Council (Gaurat) set up thereunder.

On August 1st the Commune broke down. The counter-revolutionary Government swept away the autonomy, first ignoring it, then definitely cancelling it, with all other legislation of the revolutionary period, under the comprehensive Law I of 1920. Plebiscites were arranged calculated to reverse the impression made by the previous demands for autonomy or for union with Hungary, and troops were garrisoned in the district to fortify the loyal sentiments of its inhabitants.

Meanwhile, a parallel and more open agitation had begun in Vienna in the autumn of 1918, although even among the Austrian politicians not all were agreed on the desirability of annexing German West Hungary. The comparatively small Pan-German Party favoured it; and the Social Democrats, who officially advocated self-determination for all peoples of Austria, saw no reason why they should not benefit from it. Moreover, they entertained small respect for the sanctity of historic frontiers. The Christian Social Party, on the other hand, and particularly its right, or monarchist, wing, was more or less openly opposed to the annexation out of respect for historic rights, consideration for Hungary, and anxiety that no apple of discord should disturb the friendship between Austria and Hungary so necessary to any plan for a restoration.

An active agitation was, however, carried on by some Viennese of West Hungarian origin, who, to awaken interest in the question, founded a 'Verein zur Erhaltung des Deutschtums in Ungarn', and was supported in the old Austrian Reichsrat by two German Bohemian Deputies, Lodgmann and Heilinger, who urged the Reichsrat and later the Austrian National Assembly to plead at least for the Germans of West Hungary to be given an opportunity to exercise the right of free self-determination.

The resistance of the Christian Socials was swept away by the strong feeling among the other parties, and the Austrian Delegation, which left for St. Germain in the spring of 1919, headed by the Social Democrats, Renner and Seitz, acceded to a request from the German West Hungarians in Vienna and attached to their number an expert for the region (Dr. Ernst Beer).

§ 3. PROCEEDINGS AT THE PEACE CONFERENCE

The Conference had already had this question before it in another connexion: it had been urged to grant a strip of West Hungary either to Czechoslovakia or to the Serb-Croat-Slovene State, in the form of a corridor linking up the two States.

The first reference to this plan which I have found is in a draft for a proposed—or perhaps ideal—Slav Empire elaborated by Dr. Kramař, the well-known Czech Slavophil leader, and given by him in June 1914 to the Russian Ambassador in Vienna.[1] This exceedingly generous scheme, which contemplated incorporating in various Slavonic States all territory which could by any stretch of imagination be termed Slavonic, suggested assigning to the enlarged Serbia a strip of West Hungary (comprising, so far as can be judged from the map, most of the County of Zala and the Raab Valley as far as the Danube), the excuse being the existence in this region of the Croat settlements.

This plan was revived in 1915 by no less a person than Professor Masaryk, afterwards first President of Czechoslovakia, who

---

[1] This plan was reprinted in the *Národni Osvobozeni*, of Prague, June 24th and July 5th, 1934, reproduced in translation by the German periodical *Volk und Reich*, Nov. 1934, pp. 819 ff.

submitted to the British Foreign Office a statement of Czech claims, or desires, including the following passage:

The maximum of Czech and Serbo-Croat aspiration would be the connexion of Bohemia and Serbo-Croatia. This can be effected by giving the strip of land at the Hungarian frontier in the west either to Serbia, or the half of it (north) to Bohemia, the other (south) to Serbia. This corridor would be formed of parts of the Counties of Pozsóny, Sopron, Moson, and Vas. The population is German, containing considerable Croatian minorities; the south is Slovene; . . . This Serbo-Bohemian corridor would facilitate the economic interchange of both countries—industrial Bohemia and agricultural Serbo-Croatia—and it would lead from Bohemia to the Serbo-Croatian ports. The corridor would, of course, have great military significance. It must be added that many Serbo-Croatian politicians accept this plan of a corridor just as the Bohemian politicians. By forming this Serbo-Bohemian corridor the Allies would prevent Germany from colonizing the Balkans and Asia Minor, and they would prevent the Magyars from being the obedient advance guard of Berlin.[1]

If such a corridor came into being, it was suggested that Bohemia could be a monarchy, and a personal union could be established between Bohemia and Serbo-Croatia.[2]

According to Dr. Beneš, the plan was the subject of 'repeated negotiation' during the War, but the Czechoslovak National Committee finally dropped it, before the Peace Conference, on account of Italy's sharp opposition.[3]

It was, however, placed before the Peace Conference on February 5th, 1919, by M. Beneš, at the end of his statement on the Czech claims—merely, it is true, as a 'suggestion'. He asked for 'a small territory either under the Czech or Yugoslav Government, or under the League of Nations' to enable Czechoslovakia 'to free itself from the grip of the Germans and Magyars' by establishing 'close relations with the Yugoslavs and Italy'. A railway line alone, with territory on either side of it, would, he thought, be insufficient. He would suggest that this territory should be marked out, as the

[1] Reprinted in C. Nowak, *Chaos* (Munich, 1923), pp. 313 ff.
[2] According to Masaryk himself, the idea was not his own, and indeed seemed 'impracticable' to him. It was suggested to him in the late autumn of 1914 by Dr. Lorković, a Croat Deputy, who also supplied Masaryk with a map and statistical tables of the Croat settlements in the projected corridor. The Plan was 'warmly supported by many of our people and by some Southern Slavs' (Masaryk, *The Making of a State* (London, 1927), p. 41. Masaryk took it up again when he visited Rome in December 1914, and 'interested the Southern Slavs, though I thought that, at best, it should only be mooted as a tactical move. Several Southern Slavs took it up, but Trumbić was reserved and wished it to be left to the Czechs' (ibid., p. 55). The Yugoslavs who advocated the 'corridor' included, by his own account, M. Radić (see his autobiographical notes in *Current History*, October, 1928, pp. 84 ff.).
[3] Beneš, *Der Aufstand der Nationen* (Berlin, 1928), p. 60.

confines of the Germans and the Magyars. It would thus furnish a corridor between Czechoslovakia and Yugoslavia.[1]

The suggestion met with small sympathy from the majority of the Entente representatives,[2] but it might yet have been adopted (since France was inclined to favour the project) had not the Austrian representatives hastily drawn the attention of the Italian delegation to the danger which might threaten Italy from the 'Slav Corridor'.[3] Italy, therefore, interposed her veto on the 'corridor', while the knowledge that their own moderation might not benefit Hungary, but only the Slav States, caused the Austrian Conservatives to drop their opposition to the idea of claiming the Burgenland.

On their own demand being refused, the Czechs suggested dividing the area between Austria and Hungary, hoping by this means to prevent an alliance between Austria and Hungary against Czechoslovakia. They also wished the two railway lines connecting Slovakia with Croatia to belong to different states, since they calculated that they were unlikely to be at war with both Austria and Hungary at the same time.[4]

When the Conference turned to discuss the treaty with Austria, it was at first proposed to leave the frontier with Hungary untouched; but, Mr. Balfour having intimated that the population might wish to join Austria, a Commission was appointed to report. No action was to be taken unless either Austria or Hungary raised the question.[5] The draft terms presented to Austria on June 2nd gave her no gains at Hungary's expense; but Austria in her replies of June 16th and July 10th asked that if the inhabitants, through a plebiscite, declared this to be their wish, she should be given the German-speaking districts of the Counties of Pressburg, Wieselburg, Oedenburg, and Eisenburg: an area of some 5,800 sq. km., with a population of about 495,000, 325,000 of which were Germans. She argued that the majority of the population was ethnographically and linguistically German, and that, while under the old system the frontier had been unimportant, if Hungary became a strange and 'possibly hostile' State the strategic position of Wiener Neustadt, Vienna, and even Graz would be dangerous; a barrier would be interposed between the Neustadt factories and the workmen from Hungary; and the food-supplies of Vienna and Graz would be endangered, while their factories would lose

---

[1] D. Hunter Miller, *My Diary of the Peace Conference* (printed privately, 1924–6—subsequently referred to as Hunter Miller, *Diary*), vol. xiv, p. 224.

[2] Harold Nicolson, *Peacemaking* (London, 1933), pp. 252, 273.

[3] Statement by Dr. Renner in a speech at Eisenstadt, Sept. 12th, 1931.

[4] O. Bauer, *Die österreichische Revolution* (Wien, 1923), p. 155; Renner, loc. cit.

[5] Hunter Miller, op. cit., vol. xvi, pp. 227–9.

important markets. Budapest had ample alternative sources of supply.[1]

The Commission had reported on July 9th recommending by 4 votes to 1 (the Italian) a line substantially identical with that finally adopted, except for the Oedenburg loop.[2] The Supreme Council adopted the report unchanged, and on July 20th informed Austria that she would be assigned a frontier accordingly, without a plebiscite (which was held to be impracticable in the circumstances).[3] Austria renewed her previous request on August 6th, protesting that the line offered her excluded precisely those districts which were economically most valuable to her,[4] but on September 2nd the Allies replied that the frontier offered by them was the best for all concerned. It could not be extended. If Austria decided to take a plebiscite within it, she might; but the will of the population was so clear as to make such a step unnecessary, and the Powers could not help to supervise or organize it.[5]

Hereupon Austria gave up her efforts to obtain further concessions, signed the Treaty on September 10th, 1919, and ratified it on October 17th. She was not, however, allowed to proceed to occupation, in spite of her repeated requests that she might do so to maintain order; but on September 17th the Powers agreed to send an Inter-Allied Military Commission to Oedenburg 'to assist in the maintenance of order in the territories granted to Austria by the Treaty of St. Germain'.[6]

§ 4. THE OEDENBURG (SOPRON) PLEBISCITE

Meanwhile, as we said, the counter-revolutionary government had succeeded the Communists in Hungary, and showed no disposition to reconcile itself in advance with the loss of the Burgenland. It suggested to Austria that a plebiscite should be held to

[1] Austria: Konstituierende Nationalversammlung, *Bericht über die Tätigkeit der deutsch-österreichischen Friedensdelegation in St. Germain en Laye* (Wien, 1919—subsequently referred to as *Bericht*), i. Bd., pp. 130 ff., 135 ff. The document of June 10th is the short 'reply'; that of July 16th the larger official counter-proposals, which contain the same arguments set out in more detail. From Temperley, *A History of the Peace Conference of Paris* (6 vols., London, 1920–4—subsequently referred to as *H.P.C.*), it would appear (vol. iv, p. 382) that the strategic argument proved unexpectedly effective owing, no doubt, to the existence of a Communist régime in Hungary; for the Powers were at the time far from reassured that Western Europe was safe from infection by militant Communism.
[2] Hunter Miller, *Diary*, vol. xix, p. 510. The Italian seems to have wished the whole territory to remain with Hungary, or at all events to keep it undivided. According to Dr. Renner, loc. cit., the true reason for refusing Austria the German-speaking districts of Eastern Wieselburg was the desire to meet Czechoslovakia's wish that the two north–south railway lines should run through different states.
[3] *H.P.C.*, vol. iv, p. 385.
[4] *Bericht*, Bd. ii, pp. 99–100.
[5] Ibid., Bd. ii, p. 307.
[6] Ibid., pp. 315, 320.

determine the fate of the area, and offered her certain commercial advantages as the prize for her consent. Austria, however, now maintained that the area was legally hers, and refused to renounce it, or even to negotiate concerning it.

In January 1920 the Hungarian delegation arrived at Trianon, where it was handed the draft peace terms, including the frontier as fixed with Austria. Hungary refused to take this as final and by her answers of January 14th and 26th and February 12th, 1920, refuted Austria's historic claim, and went on to deny that the Burgenland was economically at all necessary to Austria. It did, indeed, send vegetables to Vienna; but Budapest's own supply was being cut off by the other treaties. The main sources of Vienna's milk and meat supplies were the Magyar districts lying farther east. In this, the Hungarian argument agreed with the Austrian; but it differed in suggesting that if economic factors alone were to be considered, it would be more rational to move the frontier west instead of east, and to incorporate the whole basin of Graz in Hungary. As to Austria's industrial argument, there was no reason why Hungary should be made to pay for the fact that her industry had been repressed in past years, in favour of Austria's, while the annexation would ruin such industries in the annexed territories as had, in spite of all, managed to take root.

In a more detailed annexe the Hungarians argued, mainly from war-time statistics, that the German-speaking areas were economically passive, particularly as regards cereals, and they further affirmed that although the population of the region concerned was German-speaking, it was neither Styrian nor Austrian and had never shown any discontent with its position in Hungary, nor any hostility towards the Hungarians except for a transient phase when they had been alienated by the Communist régime, since destroyed. They therefore asked the Powers to revoke the decision passed by the Austrian Peace Treaty and to leave Hungary the territory 'if necessary by means of an impartial plebiscite'.

A further memorandum by the Magyar population living in the territory claimed by Austria stressed particularly the argument that the industries in the area transferred would be cut off from their sources of raw material, and would be ruined by the competition of Austria.

A promise was given that the population should enjoy the widest freedom in cultural and national matters.[1]

The Allies did not reply in detail to Hungary's objection to this frontier, but on May 6th required Hungary to accept the Peace terms, with such slight modifications as were made in the second draft, while holding out the hope of further rectification if the

[1] *Hungarian Peace Negotiations*, vol. i, pp. 11, 516 ff.

frontier were found particularly oppressive or unjust in any detail. Under pressure Hungary signed the Treaty on June 4th, 1920.

No steps were, however, taken to enforce the transfer, which was to take place only when the Hungarian Treaty came into force. This had not been effected when the elections of October 1920 brought the Christian Social Party into power in Austria. Unlike the Social Democrats, who had sought the friendship of the Czech Socialists, the Christian Socials desired to renew relations with 'Christian Hungary', and negotiations to this effect were opened. Hungary, however, demanded as prize for any rapprochement Austria's renunciation of the whole, or at least the greater part, of the Burgenland; and in view of her attitude the Austrian Government had to return to the Czech orientation of its predecessor.

The ratification of the Hungarian Treaty was still delayed, and when, in April and May 1921, the Tyrol and Salzburg held provincial plebiscites which voted by overwhelming majorities for union with Germany, the Allies actually threatened to cancel the transfer of the Burgenland unless the dangerous movement for Anschluss were stopped. Thereupon a change of government took place in Austria; the Treaty of Trianon was ratified at last (July 26th, 1921) and the transfer became imminent. An Inter-Allied Commission, headed by the Italian, General Ferrario, was sent to Oedenburg to supervise the operation. The Commission arrived in Oedenburg on August 6th and fixed August 29th as the date of the transfer.

Meanwhile, Hungary had not been idle. Official resistance was, indeed, impossible, but for some time past bands had been assembling and drilling on the large estates of the Magyar landowners in the Burgenland. These bands were for the most part in mufti, but armed with rifles, hand-grenades, &c., and often commanded by regular officers or assisted by various officers, notably MM. Pronay, Hejjas, Osztenburg, and some others.

Hungary maintained that this movement represented a spontaneous upheaval of the local population of the Burgenland, determined to resist to the last the transfer to Austria, and that the Government in Budapest was unconnected with it and, indeed, unable to control it; while Austria contended that it was organized, financed, and controlled from Budapest and carried through by elements imported from the interior of the country, who terrorized the genuine local population. As our judgement as to how far the transfer of the Burgenland accorded with the principle of self-determination must clearly depend largely on which of these two theses we believe to be more nearly correct, it is impossible to avoid pronouncing upon the question, delicate as it is. It is therefore necessary to say that the weight of evidence clearly supports the

Austrian contention. The large landed proprietors were undoubtedly against the transfer. They helped to organize and assist
the resistance, of which their estates were the chief centre. The
bands certainly included a proportion of the personnel employed
on these estates, and also a number of the Magyar intelligentsia,
notably the Oedenburg high school students. To this extent the
movement was local.

On the other hand, there is nothing to show that the German or
Croat peasants joined the bands, except in quite isolated instances.
As a rule they seem to have remained quite passive. The bulk of
the armed bands, by the admission of Hungarian speakers themselves, and by the overwhelming evidence of contemporary eye-
witnesses, consisted of elements brought by train from other parts
of Hungary. Most of them were refugees from Slovakia or Transylvania, and they included, in particular, large numbers of
Székely. The main organizers belonged to that group of officers
which had taken a leading part in stamping out the embers of the
Socialist and Communist movements in Hungary, and continued
in later years also to play a leading, if not always an official, part in
Hungarian politics, and their close connexion with high official
circles in Budapest was admitted by some of their number in the
Hungarian Parliament and Press.

While, therefore, the participation of some local elements is not
to be denied, it must be stated categorically that these elements
belonged almost exclusively to the Magyar minority; that the bulk
of the resistance came from inner Hungary; and that to regard it as
a spontaneous resistance on the part of the local population to
Austrian rule would be greatly mistaken.

In view of the prospect of resistance, Austria had returned to the
idea of a plebiscite (to be carried out not only in the area promised
to Austria, but in the larger area claimed by her). On August 27th
proposals on this basis were made to Hungary, but received no
answer. On August 29th Austria began her attempted occupation,
but in such manner as to court disaster.

The Austrian army was at this time a Socialist organization,
deeply unpopular in Conservative circles, and regarded by its
enemies as little better than a band of Bolshevik agitators. It was,
if possible, even less popular among the Austrian Conservatives
than outside the country. When, therefore, the clerical leaders in
Oedenburg requested the Inter-Allied Commission to order that
only gendarmerie should carry out the occupation, the Austrian
Government raised no objections; but the result was that when the
gendarmerie crossed the frontier, it was met by the armed bands
and quickly driven back to the frontier, and across it. The Austrian
army, supported by Socialist armed formations, was hurriedly

brought into action to defend the frontier, and some fighting took place on Austrian soil. A complete deadlock ensued.

The Commission of Generals was quite impotent, and when Osztenburg's bands had successfully expelled the Austrian gendarmerie, it found no other resource than to 'take note of', and acquiesce in, Osztenburg's action. The Conference of Ambassadors, meanwhile, continued to reject Austria's repeated requests to be allowed to send troops into West Hungary, while informing Hungary that they insisted on the maintenance of the Treaty, and the transfer of the whole area. The Hungarian Government temporized, and little real change occurred in the situation. Meanwhile, the Hungarian Government had requested Italy on September 14th to guarantee that Oedenburg and its immediate entourage should be left to Hungary after the rest of the area had been transferred. She made a similar request to the Czechoslovak Foreign Minister, asking him to guarantee that Austria would return Oedenburg. Austria rejected Dr. Beneš' intervention, and protested strongly to Italy; but the Ambassadors, while again calling upon Hungary to evacuate the disputed area within ten days (September 22nd), announced publicly that they would not object to mediation. Italy then renewed her offer (October 2nd), and on the following day it was announced from Budapest that the evacuation had begun, and that all military and civil authorities would have left the area by midnight. In fact, however, the civil officials were not withdrawn, and the Oedenburg police also remained, at the request of the Commission of Generals, who also, surprisingly, asked for the retention of the 'Osztenburg Gendarmerie' to help maintain order. In the rest of the Burgenland the bands remained undisturbed.

France and Great Britain urged Dr. Schober, the Austrian Chancellor, to accept Italy's invitation, and on October 10th the Austrian and Hungarian plenipotentiaries met the Italian Foreign Minister in Venice. On October 13th the so-called 'Venice Protocol' was signed, under which Hungary agreed to compel the irregulars to evacuate the territory, while Austria (who had been threatened by Italy with withdrawal of credits) consented that a plebiscite should be held in Oedenburg and the eight adjoining villages, eight days after the Commission of Generals who were to preside (assisted by one Austrian and one Hungarian delegate) had satisfied itself that the country was completely pacified. If Oedenburg was returned to Hungary, Hungary promised to grant Austria railway facilities.

A further delay was caused by the ex-King Charles's arrival in West Hungary on October 20th; and Austria, who was standing out for guarantees that the plebiscite would be impartial, did not ratify the Protocol until threatened by the Conference of Ambassadors that, unless she did so, they would disinterest themselves in the whole question. On November 14th, however, the Austrian forces began their occupation of the Burgenland outside the plebiscite area, and had completed it by December 3rd, almost without incident.

The plebiscite in Oedenburg and district took place on December 14th and 15th. Many protests were heard at the time against the fairness and reliability of the arrangements. The Commission had issued its regulations on November 18th. These were along normal lines, with the one important exception that the time left for drawing up and revising the register of voters was extremely short. The Austrian delegation only reached Oedenburg on November 29th, and the revision did not begin until December 4th, leaving actually only six days for the lists. Hungary had working for her the entire apparatus of State, County, and municipal officials, assisted by ready volunteers. The issue of the necessary documents was thus entirely in Hungarian hands, while, in addition, the frontier was closed almost hermetically against Austria—the home of many persons born in the plebiscite area—while wide open to Hungary. Further, the area was still under martial law, the gendarmerie active and severe. The Austrian delegates protested many times against alleged abuses, and resigned in a body on December 12th, the Austrian Government declaring that it could not accept the verdict of the voting. The actual voting, however, took place in good order and under conditions of secrecy, under the control of Entente troops, which arrived on December 8th, the Hungarian forces leaving Oedenburg on December 12th.

Eighty-seven per cent. of the persons inscribed on the registers were recorded as having voted, and the polling resulted in 15,334 votes for Hungary and 8,227 for Austria. Six wards of the city and two villages had a majority for Hungary, one ward and six villages for Austria. The Conference of Ambassadors upheld the result, supposing that Austria's grievances related to intimidation of voters, and that the result would therefore have been unaltered even had all the remaining voters voted for Austria. The plebiscite area was therefore handed over to Hungary on January 1st, 1922, and Austria persuaded, on February 25th, to recognize the cession.

Writing so long after the event (although the writer was at the time in fairly close touch with what went on) it is hard to pass judgement on the fairness of this result. It is not to be doubted that many abuses took place; that votes of unqualified persons were registered for Hungary, and that qualified Austrian voters were disfranchised. Whether a completely fair vote would have tipped the scale in favour of Austria it is difficult to say; the fact that, in spite of all the abuses, six out of the eight villages gave a majority for Austria must give rise to doubts whether a fair vote would not still have given a Hungarian majority in Oedenburg.

The final delimitation of the frontier was made after a commission had been over the ground. When this was due to meet, Hungary put forward very far-reaching claims, asking for the cession, in all, of no less than 97,000 hectares, with over 62,000 inhabitants, or nearly one-quarter of the total area and one-fifth of the population. Fears of a fresh *coup* were awakened by the reappearance of some of the armed bands, notably on the Esterházy estates in the north, and Austria hurriedly reinforced her garrisons. Only minor incidents, however, occurred, and the adjustments recommended by the Commission, in accordance with which the final line was laid down, comprised the re-cession of only a few communes to Hungary.

§ 5. ECONOMIC AND ADMINISTRATIVE CONDITIONS SINCE 1920

It will be seen that the cession of the Burgenland was conducted in a manner very different from that of Northern, Eastern, or Southern Hungary. Austria could not count on the indulgence of the Powers. What she received was given her grudgingly, with strict regard for the principle of nationality and with none of the concessions to economic advantage so generously lavished elsewhere. It is hardly probable that Hungary would have retained Oedenburg had the rival claimant been Roumania or Czecho-slovakia, nor that the frontier would, in such a case, have run so closely along the edge of the hills, to the grievous detriment of the transverse communications.[1] The natural result has been to burden Austria with a disproportionate weight of economic problems, but to leave her almost entirely free of the corresponding political difficulties.

The principal problem—and one which no goodwill and no effort can ever completely overcome—is one of communications. As regards the north and centre this has, of course, been immeasurably accentuated by the loss of Oedenburg, the natural centre on which the entire rail and road system converges. The transit agreement with Hungary stipulated in the Protocol of Venice was, indeed, concluded in 1922, when a system of privileged transit traffic between Wiener Neustadt and Parndorf on the one hand and the districts south of Oedenburg on the other was introduced. These arrangements are punctiliously observed,

[1] The effect of the final adjustment had been, for example, that the frontier cuts the course of the Pinka and of the road which follows it eight times in twelve miles.

and give rise to no friction. The possibility of free transit cannot, however, compensate the districts round Oedenburg for the loss of their natural centre and local market.

The Oedenburg loop, moreover, almost cuts the Burgenland in half, only a single road running through the narrow strip between the loop and the Rosaliengebirge. Farther south, the situation is even more difficult. The northern districts have easy access through open country to Wiener Neustadt and Vienna; but the valleys of the centre are the natural complement of the plain, from which they are now cut off, and their natural markets are Güns and Steinamanger. The situation was partially easy for the villages in the Stoob Valley when in 1929, after prolonged negotiations conducted in part through the League of Nations, Austria took over the management of the Oedenburg–Güns railway, including those parts of it which lie on Hungarian soil. This did not remedy the fact that in 1918 there was no railway communication between Austria and Hungary along the whole stretch between Oedenburg and St. Gotthard. With great difficulty, and at heavy cost owing to the nature of the soil, Fürstenfeld and Friedberg were linked up by a new line which thus brought the Central Burgenland into direct rail communication with Vienna via Aspang. The Fürstenfeld–Friedberg–Vienna railway is, however, itself a single line, which winds a slow, laborious, and costly way through mountains of some altitude. Traffic along it can never be either quick or cheap, while the hardly less important construction of a line from Güssing to Fürstenfeld has not yet been undertaken at all, for lack of funds.

There is clearly a much greater future for motor traffic, and, in fact, most of the villages are now linked up by motor omnibus services; but here, too, conditions are unfavourable. The roads when Austria took them over were in a deplorable state. The few which possessed any pretensions were those leading down the valleys into Hungary; transverse communications were poor, roads into Austria almost non-existent. A good deal of spirited work has since been done, including the construction of a through road right down the Burgenland from north to south; but an Austrian map published as recently as 1929 divided the entire system into roads which were respectively impassable, passable with difficulty, and fairly well passable in wet weather; the last-named category being much the smallest—and rightly so, as I can testify. Even if all the roads were put in first-class condition, the difficulty would remain that all traffic from the Central Burgenland must make a long and difficult journey before reaching any market in Austria.

The lack of communications has thus weighed heavily on the

Burgenland, cutting it off from the markets on which it must now depend, and, conversely, preventing access to the country from the rest of Austria. In spite of vigorous propaganda, the Burgenland still remained for many years a closed book to the conservative and incurious Viennese, not to mention foreign tourists, and does not get anything like the share of tourist traffic to which its natural beauties and interest entitle it. In this one respect, the world depression which set in in 1929 proved an unexpected boon to the Burgenland. Owing to the general impoverishment, and to the difficulty of exporting currency out of all Central European countries, foreign travel almost ceased, and the Viennese began to discover this cheap and agreeable land which lay at their doors.

The difficulty of communication does not, however, affect the whole territory in equal measure. For the centre, it must be permanent; not so for the northern districts, which possess alternative lines to Vienna and Wiener Neustadt. The loss of Oedenburg was serious, but its inconveniences to Austria may have been exaggerated at times for obvious political reasons.

That loss had, however, other consequences. The Burgenland, as has been pointed out, is no historic unit, but merely a strip of land cut out of the western edge of four separate Hungarian Counties. All the higher administrative, economic, and educational apparatus was centred in the various county towns, not one of which was allotted to Austria. She was left merely with a number of rural districts, isolated from each other and lacking any apparatus more elaborate than had been required by local needs. It would obviously have been far more economic, when Oedenburg was receded to Hungary, to partition the country between Lower Austria and Styria. The decision to adhere to the original plan of constituting the Burgenland as a separate province seems to have been taken partly out of a desire to spare the political susceptibilities of the Burgenländer, by giving them a status equal to that of the Styrians and Tyrolese, partly as a gesture of defiance and hope that Oedenburg might after all one day come to Austria (some say that an element of caution was present also: the fear that the Burgenland might one day be lost again, and the desire to avoid complications if that day ever came). It was a brave resolve, but an expensive one. To begin with, a new provincial capital had to be chosen. When, after large hesitation, Eisenstadt was selected, on account of its size and accessibility from Vienna, new Government buildings had to be erected and homes provided for the officials. A large number of other administrative buildings, schools, hospitals, gendarmerie, post, customs-stations, &c., were also required.

The federal constitution of Austria being very wide, and leaving many important interests to the sole charge of the 'Länder', much of this necessary work had to be paid for by the Burgenländer themselves. The Federal Government had advanced the funds for current expenditure during the transitional period, but cut off its supplies as soon as the first Diet was constituted in July 1921, and the next year sent in its account for the moneys advanced, with interest. After that the Burgenland had to shift in most things for itself, and it found the task difficult, for the taxable capacity of the peasants was low, and for several years lack of confidence in the stability of the new order was so great that it was unable to obtain any credit whatever. Things improved later, and eventually it was possible to float an internal loan for the most urgent improvements. The Federal government has also helped where it could; but its own resources have, of course, been scanty.

Progress has thus necessarily been slow, and the country still wears a somewhat forlorn and ragged aspect. In respect of public works of all kinds—roads, drainage, public buildings, &c.—the Burgenland is still the most backward of all the Austrian Länder and is likely to remain so for long years to come. The roads are still rough, the countryside poverty-stricken, signs of any life more spacious than the village are rare, except for some few modernized castles and the ancient but tiny 'royal free cities' of Rust and Eisenstadt (the only two places in the whole territory possessing old municipal charters). Nevertheless, the progress has been real, and cannot possibly be denied by any person acquainted with the country as it was in 1920 and as it is to-day. It has also, so far as the writer could judge, been more rapid on the Austrian than on the Hungarian side of the new frontier. Even Hungarian writers admit the praiseworthy efforts made by the Austrian Government.[1]

Moreover, the transfer to Austria has undoubtedly proved of great economic advantage to most of the inhabitants of the Burgenland. The cereals, sugar-beet, wine, fruit, poultry, and fat cattle of the northern districts, in particular, are products of a kind in which Hungary is only too rich, whereas many of them are entirely lacking in the greater part of Austria. They can thus count on a ready market, lying, moreover, at their very door—far nearer than Budapest. Not only is the market secure, but agricultural products of all kinds have ever since the War commanded far higher prices in Austria than in Hungary, so that the independent producers have benefited very largely. Much, too, has been done for the local agriculture, which in 1918 was in a somewhat backward state, the credit system being grievously

[1] de Nagy, op. cit., p. 154.

disorganized, and the average yield per hectare of nearly all crops substantially lower than in neighbouring Lower Austria; in some cases the difference amounted to 70–80 per cent. The credit difficulty proved very obstinate, since the only facilities offered during the first years came from Hungary, and it was thought advisable to reject these for political reasons. It was several years before an Agricultural Mortgage Institute was set up, with the help of the sister institution in Lower Austria, to enable the small-holders to get long-term credits at reasonable rates, while an extensive network of co-operatives (mainly on the Raiffeisen system) has been set up. The technical advance in agriculture has been considerable; the yield of wheat per hectare increased between 1921 and 1927 from 11·5 to 15 zentner, and the total wheat harvest from 362,000 to 487,000 zentner.

Unfortunately, the independent producers with a surplus to market constitute only a minority of the population. Of the 56,000 agricultural properties listed in the Burgenland in 1929, 200 belonged to large landed proprietors, 1,000 to big farmers (these two categories between them owning 44 per cent. of the total cultivable area), 7,500 to smaller independent farmers, while about 42,000 were dwarf holdings of 5 hectares or less. The largest landowners alone owned 24 per cent. of the total, half of this being in the hands of a single family, the Princes Esterházy. Moreover, nine-tenths of these great estates belong to non-Austrians (for the most part to Hungarian nobles), and the revenues from them are spent in Budapest. From the Austrian point of view, the situation has the additional disadvantages that the landowners (who, as remarked, are nearly all Magyar) are able to exert a considerable political influence through the appoint-ment of priests, teachers, and even local officials. Nevertheless, Austria, alone among the Successor States, has carried through no land reform on any large scale, although this was often de-manded by the Social Democrat representatives of the Burgenland. By her restraint Austria avoided many political complications with Hungary, but she certainly increased her economic and social difficulties. There is much misery among the dwarf-holders and landless peasantry of the Burgenland, who still emigrate in much larger numbers than the population of any other Austrian province. Besides the permanent migration, seasonal migration also remains high, and the masons and other seasonal workers are forced to seek a living, not only in other parts of Austria, but much farther afield also: in Germany, Switzerland, and even in Russia and Turkey. The independent farmers themselves suffer from this situation, for the competition for the available land has driven up its price to a quite uneconomic level.

Exactly the same evils, however, exist in Hungary. Austria has not created a difficult situation; she has only failed to remedy one which already existed. Moreover, the Austrian organization for placing the migrants has probably been more efficient than the Hungarian.

The position of the important forestry industry is far less satisfactory than that of agriculture proper. If Austria is poor in cereals, Hungary over-richly endowed, the reverse is true of timber. Moreover, the forests lie for the most part in the centre of precisely that district in which communications are easiest towards Hungary, most difficult and expensive towards Austria.

Partly owing to the shortage of land mentioned above, industry plays a considerable, if still a minor part in the life of the Burgenland. Large-scale industrial establishments are, however, very rare, the overwhelming majority of persons engaged in industry being independent artisans, working alone or employing at the most one apprentice. Many dwarf-holders also work seasonally, or during the week, in factories in and around Wiener Neustadt. Owing to the close relations between the two countries which existed before 1914, the establishment of any frontier which constituted a real barrier was bound to have a disturbing effect, and the present arrangement has admittedly ruined a certain number of establishments. The effects have not, however, been altogether so bad as might have been feared, owing to the very small scale and local importance of most undertakings. The workers would probably have suffered far more severely had they been cut off from Wiener Neustadt; in addition, they reap the benefit of the far more advanced system of social legislation prevailing in Austria.

§ 6. POLITICAL FEELING AMONG THE GERMANS

For the peasant and small labourer, living in that desperate poverty which still reigns throughout Central Europe, where a few pence mean the difference between destitution and something approaching comfort, the economic factor bulks largely in determining political attachment. It may, indeed, easily outweigh all other considerations in a district where national passions do not run high; and they had never been violent on Hungary's western frontier. Thus the Germans of the Burgenland to-day, when asked their opinion on the comparative merits of Austrian and Hungarian rule, generally answer by a reference to markets and prices. The older people, who remember the days before the War, will most usually reply that they were better off in the old days, when not merely Hungary, but the Austro-Hungarian monarchy itself, was intact. If, however, Austria and Hungary

F

were to be divided, then almost all agree that under present conditions they are better off in Austria than in Hungary. This answer will be given both by the farmers, who enjoy better prices and a more secure market, and by the workers, who receive better wages and enjoy a more advanced system of social insurance.[1]

The largest fly in the ointment is the heavier taxation due to the increased cost of administration. Hungary was never a bureaucratic country, and if its administration was less efficient than that of Austria, it had the merit of simplicity and cheapness; virtues much cherished by those fortunate enough to enjoy them. The old system has been in part retained, so that the administration of the Burgenland, even to-day, differs in several respects from that of the rest of Austria. Nevertheless, the modifications which were made involved the introduction of a considerable staff of new officials, some 800 in all, nearly all of whom came from inner Austria. While these included some first-class men, the general level was not quite the highest which Austria has to offer, and the Burgenländer are inclined to regard many of their activities as superfluous. The system of taxation, too, is regarded as unnecessarily complicated. These drawbacks, however, weigh but little in comparison with the advantages. If cultural and political considerations carry less weight than economic, they speak, for the great majority of the population, at least as decisively in favour of Austria. Admittedly, it was only a minority among the Germans of West Hungary which before 1918 felt the Hungarian cultural policy to be aggressive. The Germans of to-day are not, however, the Germans of 1914. In the last twenty years they have become conscious of their 'Deutschtum', and they would no longer tolerate assimilation to Hungarian culture. The educational system in the Burgenland is still unsatisfactory. There is still a plethora of small, ineffective schools (sometimes there are even four in one village, each imperfectly equipped and often consisting only of a single class), relics of the old Hungarian system of denominational education, which could not be altered owing to the resistance of the Catholic Church to any increase of lay influence on education. Nevertheless, improvements have been made; new schools built, new classes opened, and the period of school attendance lengthened from the six years obligatory in Hungary to the eight years general in Austria. Secondary and higher education laboured under a still more severe handicap, owing to the fact that practically all the towns of West Hungary were left to Hungary. Great efforts have, however, been made

---

[1] During the first decade after the transfer, the workers also appreciated the greater political freedom and influence. To-day (1937) they have a choice between two systems of repression.

both by the parents themselves, by the provincial and Federal Governments, and by such organizations as the Südmark, to fill in the gaps. If much still remains to be done, yet the population is conscious that the authorities are working in the same direction as themselves, engaged in a common struggle against material difficulties. If the Burgenland returned to Hungary to-morrow, any attempt to return to the old Hungarian system would meet with violent opposition; and the fear that such an attempt might be made weighs heavily with the local population.

If only on cultural grounds, nearly all the Germans of the Burgenland would to-day oppose a reversal of the decision of 1919; the more so as Austria, alone of all the Successor States, has escaped the reproach of over-centralization and forcible assimilation. The decision to constitute the Burgenland a separate 'Land' entailed heavy economic and financial burdens, but politically it was wise. The Burgenländer have appreciated the opportunities which the decision allowed them of managing their own affairs and of preserving their local characteristics. For their home to be placed on a footing of equality with Styria or the Tyrol was flattering for them, and they are gradually developing a provincial patriotism similar to that which prevails in those territories.

§ 7. THE NATIONAL MINORITIES

The minority problem is comparatively unimportant. All the minorities together comprise only about one-sixth of the total population; and of them, the larger number are at least equally content with Austrian rule, while none, so far as could be ascertained, has any real grounds for complaint. The Magyars number only a few thousand persons, nearly all peasants, with a few officials and a sprinkling of landowners. Austria has treated all categories with great consideration. The landowners have been left undisturbed in possession of their estates, and nearly all the officials who were prepared to do so were allowed to retain their posts (the most irreconcilable, including all the magistrates, left when the transfer took place, and a few were dismissed). Although all the higher education, including even the burger schools, has been Germanized, instruction in Magyar has been retained in the primary schools in the little group of Magyar villages, and no discrimination appears to be practised against the Magyar peasants. While it is to be presumed that most of the Magyars would prefer to return to Hungary, it is admitted even in Budapest that they are well treated and have no cause for complaint.

The Croats, like most minorities in a similar position, probably feel little genuine attachment in their hearts to either party. Some of them voted for the annexation in 1918 and 1919, others remained neutral. Since the event they have conducted themselves as loyal citizens of Austria, and on one occasion (in 1925) protested vigorously against the impertinence when M. Pribičević, then Yugoslav Minister of Instruction, closed some German schools in the Voivodina as a protest against the alleged oppression of the Croats in Austria.

I have not, in fact, found any evidence of oppression. It is true that Austria since the War has considered herself a purely German national state; German is the official language, both of the Federal Government and of the Burgenland. No attempt is, however, made to assimilate the Croats against their will. Every commune is free to determine the language of instruction to be used in its elementary schools, and this applies not only to the denominational schools, which comprise 80 per cent. of the whole, but to the state and communal schools also. There are in the Burgenland to-day twenty-nine purely Croatian schools, where German is only taught as a subject of instruction, and eight 'utraquist' schools, in which instruction is given in Croat in the lower classes, in German in the upper. The number of Croat schools is perhaps rather lower than it ought to be, as there is a shortage of teachers; but in several Croat communes the parents have themselves requested that instruction should be given exclusively in German. A long-felt wish was gratified in 1934 when a Croat school inspector was appointed. There is a flourishing Cultural League, with many local branches, and the local Croat periodical literature, although still scanty, is richer than it was in Hungarian days. There has been in the past complete freedom of cultural association, and although the language of the Courts is German, any person unable to express himself in that language is given full facilities for the use of his mother tongue.

The fact is that the Croat minority is not possessed of an active national consciousness, and is gradually being absorbed by a process of an entirely natural and voluntary assimilation. This is probably proceeding faster under Austrian rule than it did under Hungarian. This may be regretted by the few nationally conscious leaders, one of whom complained to me that the Austrian rule was a greater danger to Croat nationality than the Hungarian had been, precisely because of its higher standards. So long, however, as the assimilation proceeds by the will of the minority itself, there seems no purpose in wishing to check it, although we may, on the score of historical and ethnographical interest, deplore it. Such little active national feeling as exists is artificially fostered by the same circles who desired the formation of a 'Slav Corridor' and have not even to-day altogether given up hope of reviving that project. There seems no valid reason why any one else should support these ambitions.

At the first elections held after the transfer, the Croats put up a national candidate; but he polled only 2,557 votes out of 120,620 cast in the province, and thereafter about one-third of the Croats voted with the Social Democrats, the remainder concluding an electoral pact with the Christian Socials.

I cannot venture to interpret the feeling of the gipsies, beyond remarking that, as a general rule, this race is strongly attached to Hungarian culture. The same remark has usually proved true in the past of the Jews, but most of the West Hungarian Jews undoubtedly welcomed the transfer to Austria, which took place just when the White Terror in Hungary was at its height. To-day that movement has spent its force, and a Nazi Austria, either as part of Austria or merely *gleichgeschaltet*, would hold out far more terrors to the Jews than any régime which seems at all likely to take power in Hungary. Hitherto, however, the Jewish voice, such as it is, has been in favour of Austria.

§ 8. THE POSITION OF OEDENBURG

For Austria, the acquisition of the Northern Burgenland, at least, has been of great advantage. Vienna draws from the Burgenland a considerable proportion of its requirements in garden produce and smaller quantities of dairy produce, live stock, and cereals, and Austria's balance of payments is thus relieved of a burden which it could ill afford to shoulder. The fears expressed by the Hungarian delegates at the Peace Conference that these districts would prove a drain on Austria have fortunately not been justified; neither has Budapest suffered notably from the diminution of its supplies, which the other rural districts of Hungary have easily been able to make good.

It is, however, also true that the relief to Austria's balance of payments, while definite, has not been great. Vienna still depends on Western Hungary for the bulk of her supplies of dairy produce and live stock. The arguments of both parties at the Peace Conference have proved correct.

The Central and Southern Burgenland, on the other hand, have proved of little value to Austria, whereas their timber would have been important for Hungary, and is much more easily transported to Hungary than to Austria.

Of the towns which the Treaty left just within the Hungarian frontier, Oedenburg has been placed in by far the most difficult position. The tiny ring of villages left to it after the plebiscite form no compensation for the far wider field of which it was previously the centre. It has lost much of its position as a market and centre for local traffic, this having been largely captured by Mattersburg; the loss is the more important since the peasant of the present Burgenland has far more purchasing-power than the labourer on the estates in the Hungarian plain. Oedenburg's importance as an administrative centre has declined also. The general decline in prosperity is, however, far less than logic would lead one to suppose. Oedenburg was described to me, even in 1934, as the richest town in Hungary. It is, indeed, suggested that the wealth which it still undoubtedly enjoys is due largely to the solid and careful German qualities of its inhabitants, who have husbanded their resources much more carefully than most Hungarian towns. The city has, however, other resources. It is a considerable centre of tourist traffic, its beautiful old buildings and picturesque surroundings attracting many visitors from Hungary and other countries. It is the Cheltenham of Hungary: retired Generals, Heads of Sections in Ministries, and other Excellencies occupy a whole imposing villa-quarter above the town. It has developed into an educational centre, containing no less than six High Schools and three Teachers' Training Colleges, besides a University Faculty of Evangelical Theology and a Forestry School moved from Pressburg when that city became Czech, and a mining school. It has certain activities as a railway centre and even as a frontier station,[1] and it has developed since the War a medium-scale industry which had been unable to flourish before, owing to the proximity of Vienna. Most of this has been done by local initiative, for the inhabitants repudiate the suggestion that they have received any special concessions from the Government. As a legitimist centre, they allege, they have suffered, if anything, from discrimination against them.

Thus Oedenburg still presents a reasonably flourishing appearance, and has probably suffered less than Güns—a smaller place and also hard against the frontier—or Steinamanger, which lies farther from the frontier but possesses less solid economic foundations.

§ 9. INTERNATIONAL CONSIDERATIONS

As an international problem, the Burgenland stands on a different footing from Slovakia, Transylvania, or the Voivodina. Hungary, it is true, has never renounced her claim to recover it,

---

[1] In this connexion the flourishing smuggling industry deserves special mention. In theory, all towns near frontiers suffer from the separation from their hinterland. In practice, the inhabitants of such places do a roaring trade in smuggled goods—at the expense, indeed, of their own country's legitimate revenues. Smuggling is a major industry both of Oedenburg and of the Burgenland.

although she acknowledged in the Venice Protocols, and by agreement stated publicly, that in her view the solution found under the Protocols represented a 'just compromise'. On a later occasion again, Count Bethlen, then Minister President of Hungary, stated publicly that his country 'had no intention of raising the Burgenland question as a practical issue, not even in connexion with our often-misunderstood policy of revision'.[1] Nevertheless, in the view of Hungary's statesmen, the dogma of the maintenance or recovery of her territorial integrity, within its pre-War frontiers, admits of no exception. In some respects, indeed, Hungary felt the loss of the Burgenland to be an unkinder cut than that of Transylvania, Slovakia, or the Voivodina. The Serbs, Czechs, and Roumanians, she felt, were enemies, from whom hostile conduct was only to be expected; but Austria was a friend and an ally. Therefore, even if any separatist feeling had existed in West Hungary (which she denied), Austria ought not to have taken advantage of it. Her conduct amounted to a treacherous stab in the back. It was even suggested, and is still believed (although the history of the negotiations shows the insinuation to be unfounded) that the Allies only made the transfer in order to throw a bone of contention between Hungary and Austria.

Hungary, then, still maintains her claims, although she has put them for the time into cold storage. Only two days before the speech quoted above, Count Bethlen had told a German audience that he thought that 'the 70 million Germans who had been Hungary's allies would not in the long run refuse to reconsider this question in agreement with Hungary and in accordance with her wishes'.

Austria on her side, once she had made up her mind to claim the Burgenland, fought for it as stubbornly as any other claimant, and has on various occasions stated officially that she had no intention whatever of giving up her rightful property. *A priori*, then, there is the same absolute conflict of interests on Hungary's western frontier as in the north, east, or south. On the other hand, the Burgenland itself is small; the number of Magyars in it is positively insignificant, and their treatment by Austria has, by common consent, been equitable; nor has Hungary lost in the Burgenland any important part of her economic system. Thus her grievance against Austria is so small, by comparison with those which she cherishes against her other neighbours, as not to preclude the possibility of friendly relations, which she has, in fact, maintained with Austria for some years past. Austria, again, is not one of those States whose very existence is bound up with the maintenance of the Peace Treaties. In nearly every other respect

[1] *Frankfurter Zeitung*, December 17th, 1928.

she stands to gain rather than to lose by treaty revision. She
would hardly join an anti-revisionist bloc, like the Little Entente,
merely on account of the Burgenland.

Moreover, in spite of the official utterances of her Chancellors,
from Schober to Dollfuss, she is not wholly opposed in principle
to restitution. As we saw, a party in Austria (in power again in
1930) was reluctant to accept the gift at all. Certain circles long
played with the idea of reversing the decision; at one time there
even existed in Vienna a 'League for the re-cession of the Burgenland'. More important still is the possible influence of Italy. Italy
is at present acting as protector of Austria and Hungary both, but,
at least for some years, she undoubtedly looked on Hungary as
her chief friend. Inspired articles against the Austrian administration were at one time not uncommon in the Italian Press.

Thus the curious situation has arisen that while the Burgenland
is the one area, of all which she has lost, the loss of which has been
the least important to Hungary, the restoration of which would
remove the fewest justified grievances—it is yet the only one
which she has any prospect, however faint, of recovering by
negotiation.

But there is yet another side to the question. Since the Allies
treated Austria with such strict justice, as compared with their
lavish generosity towards the Little Entente, any local revision,
if carried out on either economic or on ethnographical grounds,
would go in Austria's favour and not in Hungary's. The Burgenland remains a torso without Oedenburg, the incorporation of
which would certainly be of great economic and administrative
advantage. More than this: the German population east and south
of the Neusiedlersee has in recent years, despite all official pressure,
awakened to new national life.

If Austria continues to exist as an independent state—independent in the true sense of the word—then Hungary may feel
safe, may even hope for favourable revision by negotiation. But
if Germany should consummate the *Anschluss* with Austria, or
if Austria came wholly under German influence, a different
situation might arise. It might be that Germany would leave
Hungary unmolested, or even cede certain areas to her, calculating,
as Herr Hitler has hitherto done in the case of the South Tyrol,
that a grateful ally was worth the 'Deutschtum' of a few score of
thousands of peasants. On the other hand, she might stretch out
her hand, as some Hungarians fear, over Wieselburg and Altenburg
and as far as the Balaton itself.

What would happen is speculation; but the possibilities are
interesting and various. The little Burgenland may yet become
the scene of great events.

CZECHOSLOVAKIA

SLOVAKIA

§ 1. GEOGRAPHY AND POPULATION

THE territory attributed to Czechoslovakia under the Peace Treaty falls into two parts which, although their problems (especially economic) are usually analogous and often identical, must yet be treated separately. The larger of the two is the territory now known as Slovakia. It has an area of about 49,000 sq. km.,[1] little less than that of Bohemia itself, but differs from that province widely in its natural features. Broadly speaking, it consists of the northern section of the Carpathian mountains with a strip, of varying width, of the plain at their foot. The western frontier, which coincides with the old boundary between Hungary and Moravia, begins at the junction of the Morava (March) and the Dyje, whence it runs north-east along or near the crest of a range of hills until the Polish frontier is reached. The line now runs east, following the crest of the Carpathians, though including the valley of the Poprad, which, although rising south of the High Tatra, empties its waters into the Dunajec, and thence into the Vistula. Thereafter the watershed is regained until reaching the present boundary with Ruthenia, west of the Už (Ungh). This northern frontier is almost identical with the time-hallowed boundary between Hungary and Galicia; but two small areas went to Poland by the decision of the Conference of Ambassadors. The eastern boundary runs down the west side of the Už, and thence southwards across the plain to Čop (Sop). The southern frontier runs westward across a section of plain (the basin of the Upper Tisza and the Bodrog), through some foot-hills, across the valley of the Hernad some miles south of Košice (Kassa, Kaschau), thence through hills until the Ipel is reached south of Lučenec (Losonc). It follows that river down its narrow valley until it joins the Danube at Szob; and thence follows the Danube upward, past Komárno (Komárom) and Bratislava (Pozsóny, Pressburg), to the mouth of the Morava, leaving on its north a broad and fertile plain before the hills commence.

The open land between Szob and Bratislava, and south of Užhorod (Ungvár), forms, geographically, an integral part of the

---

[1] The *Year-book of the Czechoslovak Republic* gives 48,933. The figures there given neither agree entirely with others which I have consulted, including those given on p. 290 of the same volume, nor do they add up to the total given; but let others concern themselves with such niceties.

great Hungarian plain, belonging respectively to the valleys of the Danube and of the Upper Tisza. It presents all the characteristics of the Alföld: a flat and sandy soil, subject in summer to droughts less parching than those of the heart of Hungary—since the adjacent mountains temper the rigours of the climate—but often severe enough. At other seasons of the year floods may appear, rarely in the west, where the Danube is very carefully regulated, but much more frequently in the wilder eastern half of the country. When these disasters hold aloof, the soil bears rich harvests, and it is heavily cultivated with wheat, maize, and other cereals. The great Žitny Ostrava, 'Csalloköz', or 'Schüttinsel', formed by two branches of the Danube which separate just below Bratislava to reunite only at Komárno, is, with the strip adjoining it on the left bank of the lesser arm, the granary of Slovakia.

Above the plain is a line of foot-hills, which in the centre extend down to and across the frontier. Behind them rise the mountains, which occupy the rest of the country. Although nowhere of Alpine dimensions, these often rise to considerable heights, particularly in the imposing massif of the High Tatras, on the Polish frontier, the highest point of which reaches 2,700 metres above sea-level. The remaining mountains are less lofty, not exceeding 2,000 metres, and their lower slopes are often gentle and charming. The climate and soil, however, render them unsuitable for agriculture except of an elementary kind, and they are given over almost entirely to forests and pasture. As a rule, all the mountain flanks except the lowest slopes and the summits are clothed with forests, which cover one-third of the total area of Slovakia and a full half of its highlands, beech, conifers, and oak predominating in the order named. The lower clearings are meadow land, while the summits are used for summer pasture. The central bloc, the Rudohoří (Ore Mountains), contains important deposits of various iron-ores and has for centuries supported a mining population.

The rivers which drain the mountains run, with the single exception of the Poprad, directly or indirectly into the Danube. Many of them (particularly the Váh) are of considerable size, but they are shallow and swift, and unsuitable for navigation, although timber can be, and is, floated down them. Most of the valleys are narrow and precipitous, but here and there they open into wider basins.

It is easy to move up and down the valleys, but difficult and laborious to pass from one to the other; except in the south and again far to the north, there is an easy passage from the headwaters of the Váh to those of the Poprad, and thence to the valley of the Hernad. The country thus falls naturally into three main divisions: the west, including the plain between Bratislava and

Komárno, with the valleys of the Váh and the Nitra; the central uplands, with the Lower Tatra and the Ore Mountains; and the east, where Košice forms the natural capital of the basin of the Hernad.

The only considerable towns lie in the plains, or near the mouths of the valleys. Bratislava, an ancient and historic city, better known under its earlier names of Pressburg and Pozsóny, comes easily first, with a population of some 120,000. Košice, in the east, has rather more than 50,000. The hill-towns, which are dotted about the various upland basins, are only small local centres of ten to fifteen thousand inhabitants apiece, although many are of great historic and artistic importance. The normal habitat is the village, varying from the rich farming centre with several hundred houses, in the plains, to the minute hamlet in some upper mountain valley.

The history of this area is very simple. To the earlier Illyrians, Celts, and Germans in the mountains, and Germanic, Sarmatian, and Turki peoples in the plain there succeeded a Slavonic people which were probably the direct ancestors of the Slovaks of to-day. References are found in medieval literature to two early Slavonic States: one founded by a certain Samo, who revolted against the Avars in the seventh century A.D.; the second, and more important, a kingdom of 'Great Moravia', which certainly existed as early as A.D. 830 and lasted until destroyed by the Magyars soon after their crossing the Carpathians at the end of the ninth century.

'Great Moravia', after many centuries of peaceful burial, was dug up for the benefit of the Peace Conference in 1918, to be paraded as the earliest Czechoslovak State. It may therefore be well to remark that although it was undoubtedly a Slavonic State, which extended over much of what afterwards became Northern Hungary, there is no certain evidence that it reached beyond the Morava in the west. As for Samo's empire, it is not even proved that it was situated in any part of Czechoslovak territory at all; many historians believe it to have lain in the present Carinthia and Styria.

The arrival of the Magyars ended the political vicissitudes of Slovakia; from the end of the ninth or at least of the tenth century[1] to the early twentieth, it formed part of Hungary, with the single exceptions that a robber chief named Csák established himself in a position of semi-independence in the fourteenth century, that in the fifteenth Hussite troops from Bohemia invaded it and their

---

[1] Czech historians claim that Western Slovakia was attached to Bohemia in the tenth century (see K. Krofta, *Tchèques et Slovaques jusqu'à leur union politique*, reprinted from *Le Monde slave*, March–April 1933, pp. 6 ff.). There were also, of course, frontier warfare, invasions, and perhaps transitory conquests.

leader, Ziskra, ruled parts of it for some years, and that thirteen
of the cities of the Spiš (Zips) were pledged to Poland from 1412
until 1772. Apart from these episodes, Slovakia always formed
a part of Hungary and, what is more, an integral part. Unlike
Central Hungary, it was never under Turkish rule; and, unlike
Transylvania or even the Serb districts of the south, it was never
in a position of either *de jure* or *de facto* independence or semi-
independence from the rest of the country. So long as there was
a Hungary, Slovakia formed part of it—and, during the Turkish
period, the larger portion of what at that time could still entitle
itself the Kingdom of Hungary.

The Magyars on their arrival destroyed, dispersed, or assimilated
such Slavonic population as existed in the plains, but although
they conquered and garrisoned the uplands they never themselves
settled in them in large numbers. Consequently, the distribution
of the population seems to have remained fairly stable in its broad
outlines throughout the centuries. When altered by causes such
as the Turkish invasion, it has tended to readjust itself as soon as
those causes were removed.

In the mountains and the smaller valleys, the basic population
is almost everywhere Slavonic: Slovak from the frontier of Moravia
(and indeed beyond it: Eastern Moravia is largely Slovak) as far
as the High Tatra, after which the Slovak linguistic frontier begins
to run south-east, while the higher mountains are occupied by
a wedge of Ruthene settlements. This wedge broadens gradually,
until near Užhorod it reaches the plains, and the Slovaks stop
altogether. On the extreme north, on each side of the High Tatra,
the Slovaks are replaced by Poles, the two nationalities shading into
each other through a host of those intermediate dialectal gradations
which are the politician's delight, but the statistician's despair.

In the uplands the Magyar element is small. In the country
districts it is represented almost exclusively by the land-owning
class, much of which was, indeed, originally of Slovak origin,
but Magyarized in the course of centuries. The towns and some
of the larger villages contain a Magyar population which is in
some cases considerable, this having come about partly through
immigration of officials, workers, &c., partly through the Magyarization of Slovak, German, and Jewish business and other
middle-class elements.

As soon, however, as the valleys open out towards the wider
plain, the country-side becomes overwhelmingly Magyar. It is
true that these Magyars are not all lineal descendants of Arpád's
warriors, for there has naturally been a steady tendency for the
prolific and poverty-stricken population of the uplands to drift
down into the more fertile plains. In particular, when the Turks

left Hungary at the end of the seventeenth century and a general southward shift of the population took place, Slovaks poured into the open, largely deserted spaces as far south as the Danube and beyond it. In the next two centuries, however, they became Magyarized by a process which was for the most part quite natural, and was already far advanced before any methodical Magyarization set in. Conversely, there are villages in the hills, formerly Magyar (relics of the earlier northward flight before the advance of the Turks), which are now purely Slovak.

Apart from Slavs and Magyars, the two main elements in the population are the Germans and the Jews. The Germans were at one time far more important and numerous than they are to-day. German settlers were invited into the country at an early date. They were the founders of all the principal towns in the country, including such centres as Bratislava and Košice. The German cities of the Spiš and Saros, founded, apparently, in the twelfth and thirteenth centuries from Hungary and Poland, long occupied a special position, enjoying a wider degree of corporate autonomy than any other German community in Hungary, except only the Saxons in Transylvania. The important mining area of Central Slovakia, which, so far as is known, has been German since the thirteenth and fourteenth centuries, and may never have known an earlier Slavonic population, also played a great part in affairs in its day.

In the course of time, however, the German element gradually declined. The Spiš cities were greatly weakened when thirteen of them were pledged to Poland, and although Maria Theresa, when she recovered them, united them with three others into a 'Corporation of the sixteen Cities', modelled on the League of the twenty-four Cities which had existed four hundred years earlier and endowed with a degree of self-government exceptional for their age, their spirit was broken. Unlike the Transylvanian Saxons, they showed little energy in defending either their charters or their 'Deutschtum'.

By 1918 most of the towns of Hungary had lost their German character. In some, almost all traces of their past, beyond the architectural, had vanished. In others, the process was half-complete: the inhabitants were conscious of their German origin, but spoke Magyar as fluently as German, and were strongly pro-Magyar in feeling: both in Bratislava and the Spiš cities, attachment to Hungary and the Magyar cause was a deep-rooted tradition. In some of the upland towns, again, where the surrounding population was Slovak, the Germans had assimilated not to the Magyars but to the Slovaks. Only the miners and industrial workers of Central Slovakia, living in their remote valleys, had remained Germans, but without separate national ambitions.

The Jews have always been numerous in Northern Hungary[1] and more so than ever since the great immigration from Galicia set in in the latter half of the nineteenth century. This affected chiefly the eastern half of the country, where the Jews largely replace the Germans as the local middle class. Here they are still Orthodox in appearance and creed, and their habitual language is the Yiddish 'jargon'. As one moves from east to west, the type gradually changes, and in the towns of the western and the southern borders the Magyar-speaking, assimilated type prevails. In 1910 only a few thousands were entered as speaking Czech or Slovak.

Parallel with the Magyarization of the Germans and the Jews was proceeding (as will be explained in more detail hereafter) a similar Magyarization of the Slovaks and Ruthenes. This had hardly affected the peasantry of the mountains, but those of the more open country, and the upper and middle classes everywhere, had, with few exceptions, succumbed to it. Thus we get a social stratification, consisting, in the north, of a Magyar or Magyarized upper and middle class, more or less thinly dispersed among the great mass of Slovaks and Ruthenes, who were peasants or wood-cutters with a tiny intelligentsia; while, where the plains began, all classes of society were predominantly Magyar-speaking and -feeling, even if the process of Magyarization was not yet complete in the towns.

While the general position and distribution of the population is thus clear enough, it is extremely difficult to arrive at anything like an exact estimate of their numbers in 1918. The Hungarian system of taking calculations by maternal language, interpreted in a way approximating to habitual language, naturally allowed of large numbers of persons to be entered as Magyar-speaking who were of non-Magyar origin and not necessarily of Magyar political consciousness. The figures given by the Hungarian census of 1910, and the Czechoslovak of 1921, respectively, are as follows:

	1910 (language)	1921 (nationality)
Slovaks	1,686,696	1,941,942
Czechs	7,468	71,733
Ruthenes, &c.	97,051	85,628
Magyars	893,586	634,827
Germans	196,942	139,880
Jews	..	70,522
Poles	..	2,499
Gipsies	..	7,999
Others	43,508	968
'Foreign Subjects'	..	42,246
	2,925,251	2,998,244

[1] In the seventeenth and eighteenth centuries, North Hungary was popularly known as 'Magyar Israel'.

Between 50,000 and 100,000 Magyars (mainly officials, but also some miners and workmen) emigrated to Hungary after the War.[1] On the other hand, the Czechs of 1921 are almost all immigrants. Thus the genuine movements of population balance roughly, while we may assume the War losses and the natural increase of population to be fairly well proportionate (in so short a space) to all nationalities. We must then fit in the Jews and Gipsies of 1921 under other headings in the 1910 figures, and shall not be far wrong if we take 90,000 of these as having been entered in 1910 as Magyars, and the remainder (Yiddish-speaking 'Ostjuden') as Germans.[2] The 'foreign subjects' are in fact most of them stateless persons— citizens of no country, and many of them were in 1910 Hungarian citizens, who had failed to obtain Czechoslovak nationality by 1921. In 1930, when 75,604 'foreign subjects' were found, these consisted of 27,145 Czechs and Slovaks, 4,280 Russians, 20,344 Magyars, 7,293 Jews, and 7,320 Germans.

Further, the remarkable increase in the Slovak population must be due to a certain number of persons' describing themselves in 1921 as Slovaks who in 1910 were entered either as Magyars or Ruthenes.

One cannot really say more than that there were in 1918, on the territory of the present Slovakia, about three million persons. Of these, very roughly, perhaps 1,900,000 were Slovaks, 700,000 Magyars, 120,000 Germans, 140,000 Jews, 100,000 Ruthenes, 10,000 Gipsies, and the rest Czechs, Poles, &c. Fully half of the Germans and Jews and some 200,000 Slovaks must also have spoken Magyar, and many of these were in a fair way to becoming entirely Magyarized.

§ 2. THE ECONOMIC SITUATION UP TO 1918

As we have said, Slovakia is still largely an agricultural country. The Magyar farmers in the plains and the German wine-growers of the foot-hills have always been a prosperous class, favoured both by the natural wealth of the soil and the proximity of important markets.

In the mountains, on the other hand, communications are

---

[1] I. Sasek, *Les Migrations de la population intéressant le territoire de la Tchécoslovaquie actuelle* (Geneva, 1932), p. 53, gives 56,000; the Hungarian Refugee Office, over 106,000.

[2] In 1910 there were 140,467 persons of Jewish faith in Slovakia, of whom 76,553 were entered as speaking Magyar, 58,355 German (under which term the Hungarian census included Yiddish), 4,956 Czech or Slovak, 274 Ruthene, and 327 other languages. In 1921 the persons of Jewish faith numbered 130,762 (excluding foreign subjects) and their languages were as follows: 29,290 Czech or Slovak, 21,744 Magyar, 9,012 German, 164 Ruthene, 70,480 Yiddish, and 72 'other'. The 'non-Aryan Christians' (to borrow a modern term) numbered only a few thousands, or perhaps hundreds.

difficult, the climate inclement, the land stony, precipitous, and barren. The natural difficulties with which the peasant class has to contend were enhanced before the War by an unfavourable distribution of land. Some 3,000 proprietors owned between them nearly one-third of the whole cultivable land of Slovakia, and three-quarters of the forests were in the hands of a few very large owners. On the other hand, nearly three-quarters of the agriculturists owned only one-fifth of the cultivable land between them, and as many again were altogether landless.[1]

The poverty of most of the Slovak peasants is terrifying. Semi-starvation is almost common, actual starvation by no means rare. It was stated in the eighties that in many of the Slovak counties the population 'only ate bread on Sundays' and 'meat, practically never'; that 'there was no difference in the food between work-days and feast-days'. The staple food was the potato.[2] One result of this has been the great mobility of the Slovak population. There has for many centuries been a constant trend downwards into the plain, whenever conditions have been favourable; hence the large Slovak population (sometimes wholly, sometimes partially Magyarized to-day) of Central Hungary, including its towns. More recently came the emigration to the U.S.A. No statistics of this were kept before 1899, but it is known that the emigration from Hungary began on a large scale about 1870, precisely in the Slovak districts of North Hungary, while between 1899 and 1914 over 300,000 Slovaks migrated to the U.S.A.[3] A considerable

---

[1] According to the Hungarian official statistics of 1895, the agricultural establishments, exclusive of properties consisting solely of forest and pastures, in the Slovak and Ruthene Counties (corresponding roughly to the present Slovakia and Ruthenia) were as follows:

	No. of holdings.	Slovak Counties. Total area.	No. of holdings.	Ruthene Counties. Total area.
Less than 1 hold	93,754	38,028	19,140	7,982
1–5 hold	140,587	389,034	28,292	77,899
5–10 ,,	97,136	699,786	18,776	135,895
10–20 ,,	75,613	1,051,964	15,534	217,515
20–50 ,,	33,573	966,508	8,561	250,562
50–100 ,,	5,299	356,573	1,426	94,143
100–200 ,,	1,609	224,109	375	52,063
200–500 ,,	1,446	461,395	207	62,539
500–1,000 ,,	790	556,969	81	59,027
over 1,000 ,,	842	2,677,797	93	474,084
	450,649	7,422,163	98,485	1,431,709

Some 60 per cent. of the properties in the last category (1,524,518 hold in Slovakia, 334,751 hold in Ruthenia) were composed of forests.

[2] C. Keleti, *Magyarország népességének élelmezési statisztikaja* (Food Statistics of the Population of Hungary), cit. G. Schütz, *La Situation matérielle des classes laborieuses en Hongrie avant la guerre* (Menton, 1930), p. 64.

[3] Sasek, op. cit., p. 48.

number of Slovaks, particularly from the western districts, also migrated to Austria, chiefly to the province of Lower Austria (including Vienna).[1] Many of these were not permanent emigrants; the wandering Slovak tinker, pedlar, or broom-binder was a familiar figure of the old Monarchy as early as the eighteenth century,[2] and in modern times achieved the distinction of becoming the central figure of a charming opera (*Der Rastelbinder*).

Extremely important, also, was the seasonal migration of harvest labourers into the Hungarian plain. This was organized in Hungary under two Government Commissions: the Highland (for what is now Slovakia and Ruthenia) and the Transylvanian. The labourers were registered, found work, and given free, or very cheap transport; the Commission was also intended to assure the workers equitable contracts and decent standards of living. The Highland Commission alone arranged contracts for periods exceeding six months for 44,000 workers in 1909, 71,000 in 1913, and 65,000 in 1914. Most workers, however, arranged their own terms. It is estimated that the annual average from the Highlands was some 200,000.[3]

The question had two sides. The cheap and docile Slovak labourers were undoubtedly exploited in the interests of the great Hungarian landowners, and even used as strike-breakers in the time of the agrarian riots among the Magyars of the Alföld. Nevertheless, this harvest labour formed a traditional and very important part of the Slovak national economy—and, indeed, of the Hungarian. The harvest labourers were paid largely in kind. The wheat and pulse which they took back with them kept the highlands in food through the winter, and helped to assure the plain of a market for its surplus.

In addition, Slovakia, at various times in its history, has been an industrial area of some importance. The iron-workings are the subject of an obscure and laconic reference by Tacitus.[4] Under the Hungarian kings, the mines and ironworks of the Spiš towns and of the district centring in Banska Bystrice (Besztercze Banya, Neusohl) were very important and flourishing. These conditions continued during the period of the Partition, when the Habsburgs gave considerable encouragement to the local industries. The textile industry, in particular, employed large numbers of persons, many of them artisans who had been rendered unemployed by the decay of mining.

The prosperity of North-Western Hungary went down in the late eighteenth and early nineteenth centuries, particularly in relation

---

[1] Sasek, op. cit., p. 43.   [2] Marczali, op. cit., pp. 24, 89.
[3] *Hungarian Peace Negotiations*, vol. i, pp. 474–5.
[4] *Germania*, 43. Cotini, quo magis pudeat, et ferrum effodiunt.

to the central and southern districts, which were developing very rapidly after their liberation from Turkish rule. Austria had every interest in encouraging the production of raw materials in the latter districts, since they afforded welcome sources of supply for her own industries. The mining, textile, and wine industries of the north-west, on the other hand, competed with analogous Austrian products, and were therefore systematically subjected to disadvantages of various kinds.

The position was reversed when, towards the close of the nineteenth century, Hungary initiated her own policy of economic self-sufficiency. Now it was precisely the industries which might compete with those of Austria which were chiefly encouraged. In any case, the presence of abundant resources in the shape of timber, ores of various kinds, and coal, combined with ease of communications and proximity to markets, automatically designated Slovakia as the chief centre for Hungary's primary industry, and as an important secondary centre of her finishing industries.

Of the State subsidies paid out to industry between 1881 and 1914, North Hungary (Slovakia and Ruthenia), with an area of 19·3 per cent. of Hungary and a population of 17·1 per cent., received 33·5 per cent. of the total subsidies, and 40 per cent. of those granted to the textile industries.[1] The highest subsidies went, incidentally, to non-Magyar Counties, such as Liptó, Turóc, and Szepes. Of the 84,169 persons employed in 1910 in the Slovak Counties in enterprises employing 20 persons or more, 40,778 were of Slovak mother tongue, with 1,618 Czechs and 663 Ruthenes, against 11,627 Germans, 26,818 Magyars, and 6,265 'others'.[2]

The progress of industrial development was very rapid. In 1900 there existed in Slovakia 429 undertakings, employing 20 or more workers, with a total number of 46,041 workers. By 1910 these figures had risen to 586 and 75,066 respectively. The number of persons employed in smaller enterprises rose during the same decade from 112,312 to 126,139, and the number of enterprises from 77,220 to 82,965, the increase being the more rapid, the larger the enterprise.[3] The total number of industrial enterprises had risen by 72 per cent. between 1898 and 1906, by 104 per cent. between 1906 and 1910, and probably by another 25 per cent. between 1910 and 1914.[4] Although most of the enterprises, particularly those connected with the clothing industry, were still extremely small, some

[1] A. Halász, *The Providing of Labour for the Population of Upper Hungary under Hungarian and Czech Rule* (Budapest, 1927), p. 5.
[2] *Manuel statistique de la République Tchécoslovaque* (Prague, 1920), p. 57. The figures quoted are Hungarian official figures of 1920.
[3] B. Kardós and C. Arkner, *Ipar; A Felvidék ipari népességének alakulása a háború elött és utan.*
[4] A. Fichelle in *L'Europe centrale*, p. 235.

were considerable. The Krompachy (Krumpach) ironworks, for example, were a very important industry, and the annual production of iron-ore averaged well over 1 million tons, of which about half was exported to Austria, the remainder being worked up on the spot. The average annual value of raw iron produced here was over 15 million gold crowns. The metallurgical industry employed nearly 25,000 persons; stone, clay, asbestos, and glass, another 15,000; timber, as many; textiles, rather fewer.

This industry was important not only for itself but also for Hungary's economy. Slovakia with Ruthenia produced about half Hungary's timber (most of the rest coming from Transylvania), 23·6 per cent. of her iron, 58·3 per cent. of the iron-ore, all the zinc, 54·7 per cent. of the manganese-ore, 25 per cent. of the salt, and contained 26·9 per cent. of the iron and metallurgical industries. Twenty per cent. of the wood and bone, 33·7 per cent. of the textiles, 93·7 per cent. of the paper industry, 19 per cent. of the stone, pottery, and glass, 27·4 per cent. of the wine and beer, 18·6 per cent. of the total mines and factories employing more than 20 employees, 21·1 per cent. of those employing more than 100 workers, and 17·4 per cent. of the total industrial enterprises were in the same area. The primary materials were usually within easy reach of the finishing factories, many of which were situated in or round Budapest, while the deficiencies in food-stuffs could again be made up from sources near at hand. The economic link between Northern and Central Hungary was thus particularly close.

§ 3. THE SLOVAK QUESTION UP TO 1914

The case for including Northern Hungary in Czechoslovakia does not rest on historical rights, although the ghost of Sviatopluk, ruler of Great Moravia, was made to serve his turn.[1] But Sviatopluk's historic claims were obviously less valid than those of Hungary, with her thousand-odd years of uninterrupted possession. He was more important as supporting, by the evidence which he gave of an early connexion between Czechs and Slovaks, the real claim, which was that of self-determination.

Essentially, the case as regards the Slovak areas rests on the theory that the Czechs and Slovaks are so closely akin as to be one people, speaking a single 'Czechoslovak' language; and that the

[1] Cf. *The Territorial Claims of the Czecho-Slovak Republic* (Memorandum presented to the Peace Conference—hereafter quoted as *Czech Claims*), p. 1: 'Slovakia, violently torn away from the Czechs several centuries ago, and artificially separated from Bohemia'. So Dr. Beneš before the Council of Ten (Hunter Miller, *Diary*, vol. xiv, p. 220): 'Slovakia had at one time formed part of the Czecho-Slovak State. It had been overrun by the Magyars at the beginning of the tenth century.'

Slovaks (or Slovak branch of the Czechoslovaks) thus had naturally to be included in the Czechoslovak State; furthermore, that they themselves desired this union, expressing their wish in 1918 by formal declaration of their representatives.[1]

The justification for including Bratislava and the strips of valley and plain south of the Slovak linguistic area was mainly economic and military. The Czech spokesmen at the Conference urged, indeed, that these territories had once belonged to the Kingdom of Great Moravia; also that the population consisted in large part of Magyarized Slovaks; and thirdly, that since a large number of Slovaks must be left in Hungary, it was reasonable to 'compensate' Czechoslovakia by allowing her, in return, an equivalent Magyar minority. It was even suggested that the principle of reparation ought to be applied in tracing the frontier.[2] The economic argument was, however, pressed with more conviction. The Danube frontier in the west, with the port of Bratislava, was declared to be 'of the most vital importance' and to 'admit of no concession, nor yet of being discussed by the Magyars'. Bratislava was traditionally 'the capital of Slovakia' and the Danube 'the only possible natural frontier between Magyaria and Slovakia in those two regions'. Further, it was absolutely necessary for Czechoslovakia to become 'a veritable Danubian State, access to the Danube at one or two points only being quite insufficient'. The frontier demanded in the south-east, which would have run along the southern slopes of the Matra, Bukk, and Hegyalia Hills, was, again, 'the only natural frontier'.

Hungary replied, firstly, that it was contrary to all principles of self-determination to take away from Hungary the compact masses of Magyars which, even when the Czech claims had been reduced, remained beyond the frontier, and along large sections of it,

---

[1] Beneš, loc. cit.: 'The conquerors had attempted without success to Magyarize the country. The population still felt Czech, and wished to belong to the new State. There was never any suggestion of separation in Slovakia. The same language, the same ideas and the same religion prevailed.'

[2] All of these claims were put forward either by Dr. Beneš verbally before the Council of Ten, or in *The Territorial Claims of the Czecho-Slovak Republic* subsequently laid before the Conference, or both. For the claim to 'reparation' see *Czech Claims*, p. 21. In his verbal statement Dr. Beneš said that if his claims were allowed, 650,000 Magyars would be included in Czechoslovakia (350,000 in the west and 250,000 in the east), while 450,000 'Czecho-Slovaks' would be left in Hungary. The *Czech Claims* give 393,692 Magyars in the west and 465,000 in the east, as against 123,702 Czecho-Slovaks on the west bank of the Danube and 486,014 plus 20,000 elsewhere in Hungary (supplement on Slovakia, pp. 22, 23). Considering that the line then claimed ran well to the south of that finally decided, these claims seem to rest on a very narrow basis. Dr. Beneš himself says that he wrote most of his 'memoirs' without proper material and that they thus contained 'many errors of fact', but he denies that these were intentional and argues that they had, in any case, no effect on the final decisions (Beneš, op. cit., p. 688). This last claim hardly seems to be borne out by the actual course of events.

immediately adjacent thereto. Naturally, moreover, she rejected the historical claim; and, as regards economics, argued that the very fact that Czechoslovakia thought it necessary to ask for so large a section of the plain showed that it was disastrous to divide the highlands at all from the lowlands, Northern and Central Hungary forming, according to her contention, a natural and indivisible geographical and economic unity.

But she also contested the correctness of Czechoslovakia's major premiss. She maintained that the Czechs and Slovaks were not one nation but two, closely akin, indeed, but racially and linguistically distinct, and, above all, severed by deep historical and cultural differences. Only a minority of the Slovaks, not truly representative of the people, desired the union, and the nation as a whole, if consulted (she denied the representative character of the meeting which had voted the union), would have desired to remain with Hungary.

The final decision of the Conference, while it rejected the more extravagant of the Czech claims, allowed them Bratislava, on the score that it was destined to play an 'important and indeed essential part as the Danubian Port of Czecho-Slovakia', attributing to it also a small district south of the Danube as a guarantee against hostile raids, and as being the property of the municipality (this area was not allowed to be fortified). Farther east, the main channel of the Danube was taken as 'the only possible frontier', it being considered that the whole economic life of the Magyar inhabitants was 'bound up with the left bank of the Danube'. The argument that the population really consisted of Magyarized Slovaks seems to have carried some weight, and with regard to the Žitny Ostrava it was also thought that 'without it Czech access to the Danube might have been seriously curtailed'. East of this again, the frontier was drawn on something approximating to the ethnographical line, although the railway station of Satoralja-Ujhely was given to Czechoslovakia to assure her communications with Roumania.[1]

It does not appear that the major contention was given any close consideration. In fact, by the time of the Peace Conference, the Allies were already committed to the broad principle of incorporating the Slovak districts in Czechoslovakia; but even before casting the die they seemed to have entertained no real doubts of the justice of the Czech thesis.

To pronounce finally on the exact relationship between the Czechs and the Slovaks would involve giving a verdict *ex cathedra* on many points of ethnography and philology so nice that the native experts have never been able to agree on them. Broadly speaking,

[1] *H.P.C.*, vol. iv, pp. 271 ff.

it seems safe to say that the Czechs and Slovaks, in the homes which they occupied before crossing the Carpathians, must have been next-door neighbours, if not of identical ancestry, and differed absolutely, as such, from the Finno-Ugrians and Turks who formed the original 'Magyars'. If a single dynasty had united both peoples in a permanent, or at least an enduring, union a Czechoslovak nationality would assuredly have been formed, and with it, a Czechoslovak language; any minor dialectal differences which existed would have been smoothed out. This did not happen; and while the Slavs of Bohemia developed the Czech nationality and language, to which the intermediate dialects of Moravia gravitated,[1] the Slovaks, under Hungarian rule, not only developed along different lines from the Czech but were not even able to form a single literary language. As will be seen, as late as the nineteenth and even the twentieth century their language was still fluid; it consisted (and consists to-day, in popular usage) of at least three main dialects, one of which approximates more closely to Czech, another to Polish, while a third is more individual. An ordinary Czech and an ordinary Slovak (not being politicians) understand each other easily enough, but also recognize that they are speaking differently. Whether the differences are large enough to justify speaking of two 'languages' or small enough to allow the term 'dialects' is a matter of sentiment rather than science. The difference is certainly not so great as that between the average two languages which are ordinarily recognized as kindred but different, e.g. German and Dutch, or French and Provençal.

However close the original bonds may have been, the ten centuries during which the Slovaks formed part of the kingdom of Hungary, while the Czechs were subjected to German and Austrian influences, naturally brought about a marked differentiation between the two people. Even the physical stocks cannot be so closely related to-day as they were a thousand years ago, for the Czechs are to-day inextricably mingled with German elements, while the Slovak mountaineers have retained their racial purity to a larger degree; such admixture as they have received is largely Slavonic (Polish and Ruthene), although the present population must also have many German and Magyar ancestors. There is, however, a noticeable difference both in physical appearance and in character between the dour, efficient, but somewhat ungainly Czech, and the

---

[1] The Hungarians still attempt at times to differentiate the Moravians from the Czechs. The day for this is past; but as recently as 1848, in the debates in the Viennese Parliament, the Germans referred to the Moravians as a separate nationality, and the Czech leader Rieger himself said: 'I do not know whether the Moravians consider themselves a nationality of their own!' See Gumplovicz, *Das Recht der Nationalitäten und Sprachen in Oesterreich-Ungarn*, pp. 73, 76.

airy, talkative, happy-go-lucky Slovak. The religious cleft is deep. For the Czechs, Master John Hus was and is not only a religious but essentially a national figure; and, if the nation returned to Catholicism under the pressure of the Counter-Reformation, it is a truism that every Czech is a Hussite at heart—a Hussite in the wider sense of the term, denoting a blend of somewhat self-assertive nationalism with a 'Protestant' attitude towards all authority, social, national, or religious, which is felt to be in any way alien. For the Slovaks, Hussitism was the alien doctrine, Catholicism the natural faith. The Slovak soul has an innate reverence for authority, a natural *penchant* for forms and hierarchies; so that, paradoxical as it may sound, a Hungarian Count is a far more objectionable animal to a Czech than to a Slovak.

It is an interesting and important fact that the Protestant Slovaks, who number about 16 per cent. of their total number, are among the most nationalist and the most Czechophil of their nation. Partly this is due to their having received the Bible in the Czech (not Slovak) translation made in Hussite times, while the Catholics continued to use the Latin version; partly, perhaps, to the admixture of Czech blood which must have entered their veins from Czech Hussites who settled among them in the Jiskra era.

How far the differences of habit and mentality between Czechs and Slovaks are outweighed by the similarities is one of the great points at issue to-day, the Czechs and Centralist Slovaks maintaining that the differences are trivial, while they are emphasized by the autonomist and Magyarone Slovaks.

One thing is indisputable: that in contrast to the stormy Czech history, which is one long story of political and spiritual rebellion, the life of the Slovaks passed for centuries with very few signs of ill feeling between them and the Magyars. In the one really unrestful century—the fifteenth—the leaven in the lump came from Bohemia. The Slovaks—a naturally submissive race—made no particular claims. The chief element of friction in past times was absent, since both Slovaks and Magyars (in Western Hungary) were Catholics. The aristocracy became Magyar. The peasants lived a life of their own, without either national ambitions or national martyrdom. The prevailing economic misery, strange as it may appear, rather reduced than increased national differences, since it gave rise to the habit of seasonal migration to the plains, in the course of which the Slovaks came into contact with Magyar speech and Magyar ways.

The national renaissance which began among the Slovaks towards the end of the eighteenth century thus had difficulties of its own to encounter. Its leaders had to decide, not only what the

Slovaks ought to become, but also what they were; and on these questions the philologists and littérateurs were no more unanimous than the politicians themselves. The first literary movement was, interestingly enough, directed primarily against the Czechs, its father, a Catholic priest named Bernolak, being chiefly concerned in championing the independence of the Slovak language against the 'Hussite tongue' of the Czech ecclesiastical literature used by the Slovak Protestants. Bernolak was supported for political reasons by the Hungarian Government and by the Hungarian Primate of the day, who was himself of Slovak origin. An energetic counter-party maintained the substantial identity of the Czech and Slovak languages. In 1803 this group founded a chair of Slavonic languages and literature in the Lutheran College at Bratislava, and its leader, Palkovič, who held the chair for many years, made of that town the centre of Slovak cultural life. Among his pupils were two of the great figures of Slavonic scholarship of the day, Kollař and Šafařik, who held different views on the Slovak problem. Šafařik recognized a difference between Slovak and Czech, but held that Slovak was the pure, original form, of which Czech was a mere corruption. Kollař recognized only four main branches of the Slavonic language: Russian, Czech, Serb, and Polish. Kollař, and many other Slovaks after him, were strongly influenced by Pan-Slav ideas. The very expression 'Pan-Slavism' was coined by a Slovak, and there has always been a party among the Slovaks tempted by the idea of submerging the whole Czecho-Slovak batrachomuomachy in the vast and comfortable ocean of universal Slavdom.

Meanwhile the Magyars, ably assisted by a very vigorous party of Magyarone Slovaks, were vehemently propagating the complete Magyarization of the country. In 1844 this party succeeded in expelling Palkovič's assistant, Štur, who had become the real leader of the 'Pressburg School'. The consequences were momentous, for Štur now became convinced that it was impossible to maintain Czech as the language of Slovak culture; if Slovak was to exist at all, it must stand on its own feet. Accordingly, with his two friends Hurban and Hodža (both Lutheran priests), he adopted as the language of his movement the purest of the Slovak dialects, that of Central Slovakia. In 1847 a formal agreement was reached with Bernolak's school to adopt this dialect as their common language. The Czechophils resisted vociferously for a while, but came into line in 1851, after the question had been submitted for arbitration to a professor in Prague. Thus Slovak established its right to exist as a separate language just in time, as it transpired, to consolidate its position; for the next ten or fifteen years were the period in which Hungary was ruled by officials from Austria who, if not in principle friendly to the Slovak cause[1] as such (the absolutist era was the enemy of all national aspirations alike), was at least more hostile still to the Magyars. Thus the Slovaks were enabled to found gymnasia in Revoca, Turčiansky Svätý Martin (Thurócz Szent-Mártón), and Klaštor (Kloster) respectively,[2] and, also in Svätý Martin—now established as the recognized national centre—a promising national literary society (the Slovenska Matica) which was supported by Catholics and Protestants alike.

The political movement of the period was no less divided. In 1848 the national party, led by Štur, Hurban, Hodža, and others, attempted to secure from the Hungarian Government certain political and national rights, including equality for all nationalities in Hungary; the recognition of each as a 'nation' (i.e. a corporate body) with its own Diet; a national guard and flag; free use of their language and educational facilities, and social and political reform. But only a fraction of the nation was behind these demands. Just as some of the most prominent figures of the Magyar literary renaissance, e.g. the poet Petöfi, and some of the most enthusiastic champions of Magyarization, e.g. Count Zay, were themselves of Slovak origin, so were not a few of the most vehement supporters of a politically united and independent Hungary, including Kossuth himself. When, later, the exiled Slovak leaders and the Imperial Commissioners tried to raise the Slovak districts against the Magyars, their success was only very partial, and Slovakia witnessed nothing like the racial war which broke out in Transylvania and in the Serb district of South Hungary. Indeed, many Slovaks fought in the Honvéds for Hungary, although some places boycotted, and one refused, the levies, and two units were formed which fought against Hungary. The 'Czecho-Slovak' movement was far less in evidence in the political field than in the literary. Palacký, indeed, proposed to unite the Slovak districts of Hungary with the Czech parts of Austria in his famous plan for the reorganization of the Monarchy; but there was no corresponding movement of any importance among the Slovaks.

After Hungary had been conquered by Austria and Russia, the Slovak nationalists naturally turned to Austria with their request for autonomy; but after they had met with a refusal less brutal but no less decisive than that which they had received from Hungary the political movement 'gradually simmered out'.[3]

[1] A large proportion of the officials sent into the country were, however, Czechs, and many of these were personally friendly to the Slovak movement. The High Commissioner for the north-east, himself a Slav from Galicia, openly encouraged the Slavs in every way, to such an extent that a contemporary historian writes that 'it was clear that he wanted to set up a Slovakia' (Rogge, Oesterreich von Világos bis zur Gegenwart, vol. i, p. 210).

[2] The last-named was founded after the Austro-Hungarian Compromise.

[3] Seton-Watson, Racial Problems in Hungary, p. 107.

Indeed, the era of Austrian absolutism, if it allowed the Slovak cultural and literary movement to put forth some modest shoots, threw the political movement back into the arms of Hungary, and the next request made by the Slovaks for national rights (in 1861, when the Bach régime was *in extremis*) was addressed to Hungary, and was considerably more modest than the programme of 1848. It again asked for freedom of national development and equality of rights for all nationalities of Hungary, for recognition of the Slovaks as a 'nation', and for the creation of an 'Upper Hungarian Slovak Territory', in which Slovak should be the language of administration, religion, and education; but recognized clearly, and even warmly, the unity of Hungary, and agreed that Magyar should be the language of communication with the central authorities.

Refused again by the Magyars, the Slovaks once more approached Austria, and succeeded in laying similar requests before Francis Joseph. Once again their political demands were rejected lock, stock, and barrel, but they received some cultural concessions. In 1867, however, Francis Joseph concluded the 'Compromise' with Hungary, and the Slovaks were left again without allies.

The period which followed marked an absolute retrogression of the Slovak national movement. The Magyars acted with their wonted vigour. All higher state education was already in Magyar; the three private gymnasia were shut down, and their funds confiscated, in 1874, all petitions made subsequently to reopen them being refused. A similar fate overtook the Matica in 1875. Primary education soon followed suit. The number of elementary schools with Slovak language of instruction, after remaining until about 1880 at a figure which ranged between 1,971 (the peak figure reached in 1874) and 1,800, sank steadily to an average of 1,300 in the eighties, 510 in 1900, 241 in 1905. In 1914 the figure was 365 (out of a total of 4,253 elementary schools in the country), but the Slovak character was already little more than nominal since the introduction of the Apponyi school laws.[1] Not only all higher education, even that given in burger schools, was in Magyar, but even all the 448 kindergartens in the country were Magyar. Of the elementary-school teachers in the Slovak districts, only 345 gave Slovak as their language, against 129 with German and 4,257 with Magyar; in the higher elementary schools, the respective figures were 1, 16, and 425; in higher education, 10, 12, and 638.[2]

Of the State functionaries in the Slovak districts, 1,733 were Magyar-speaking, 32 German, 2 Slovak; for the County func-

[1] *Czech Claims*, Section on Slovakia, p. 6. The Hungarian statement to the Peace Conference (vol. ii, p. 264) puts the figure of Slovak-speaking elementary schools still lower: 327, of which 6 were State, 2 communal, 158 Roman Catholic, 2 Calvinist, and 159 Lutheran.
[2] Ibid., pp. 28–9.

tionaries the figures were 920, 11, and 18; for municipal employees 753, 59, and 11; for public and district notaries 1,080, 20, and 33; for magistrates and public prosecutors 461, 3, and 0; for subordinate officials of the courts 805, 13, and 10.

In assessing the real meaning of these figures it must be remembered that the Hungarian statistics, from which they are drawn, refer not to origin or to 'race' but to language. They are evidence, indeed, of the practical extinction of Slovak as a language of administration and justice; but not evidence of the exclusion from employment of persons of Slovak origin. An idea of their meaning would be gained by taking similar figures given for the English-speaking and Gaelic-speaking teachers and civil servants of Scotland.

That the Slovaks were systematically Magyarized, with every sort of pressure and by the help of every device which could suggest itself to a determined and resourceful people, is a fact so patent that the denials of it which a section of Hungarian writers still think fit to issue can only awaken wonder at the degree of credulity which they impute to the foreigner. Quite another question is whether the process really encountered any widespread resistance; for denial of national culture is only oppressive when it is felt to be oppressive. No less certain than the fact that the Magyarization was exercised, and no less fundamental to the present theme, is the fact that it was in no way resented by the great majority of the Slovaks. When a people is conscious of its nationality, and determined to preserve it, nothing short of physical extermination can wipe out that consciousness. The Slovaks were not such a nation. When the pressure was relaxed, as among the emigrants in the U.S.A. (who were to play such a part in 1918), they could remember their national identity; but in Hungary they required little persuasion to forget it. A Magyarone writer, in a famous phrase, described the Magyar secondary school as a machine into which Slovaks were poured at one end to emerge as Magyars at the other. The simile was just. To the dwellers in the poverty-stricken uplands, the life of the smiling plains and the rich cities which dotted them, and above all Budapest, with its rapid growth and spacious opportunities, offered attractions which were both strong and natural. They were few who resisted when the chance offered. Since the road to a wider life lay through Magyarization, they let themselves be Magyarized, easily and even gladly. To be a Magyar was to be a gentleman, to be a Slovak was to be a chaw-bacon. The public services and free professions of Hungary were well stocked with Slovaks who had learnt the Magyar language and with it had fully accepted the Magyar outlook. The Church, in particular, was a favourite resort of the Slovaks, many of whom rose to the highest ranks in it. The fact that most of the Slovaks and most of the Magyars shared a common faith was, indeed, one of the greatest aids to the Magyarization of the former; while, conversely, one of the chief barriers against Magyarization was removed by the fact that the Catholic Slovaks, unlike the Serbs and Roumanians, possessed no national educational system anchored in the autonomous rights of a non-Magyar church. The Lutheran Slovaks maintained themselves better precisely because the Lutheran Church in Hungary was mainly non-Magyar.

The Magyarization of the peasants had not proceeded nearly so far; it had, indeed, not seriously set in until the nineteenth century. The peasants were as a mass not nationally conscious. But they were glad enough to acquire the little accomplishment which allowed them an opportunity of augmenting their incomes.

For a long time there seems to have been no opposition at all to this policy. According to Czech writers themselves, the 'Czecho-Slovak' idea practically died out, in Hungary and in Bohemia alike, after about 1880.[1] Svätý Martin survived as a sort of national centre, but the leaders there contented themselves with literary work and with a sort of mild and misty Russophil Pan-Slavism. It was not until 1895 that certain of the Slovaks, Serbs, and Roumanians of Hungary met and decided on a programme of fulfilment of the Nationalities Law of 1868, delimitation of the Counties on national lines, and political and social reform—modest demands indeed, compared with those of a generation earlier.[2]

Just at the same time the 'Czecho-Slovak' idea was reborn. Its spiritual father was Professor Masaryk, a Slovak, but from Moravia; and among the young men who became the disciples of his new 'realist' school were not only Czechs but also a few nationally-minded young Slovaks, who had come to Prague to study. In 1896 this group founded the 'Czechoslovak Society' (Československá jednota), a very active institution, the aims of which were to work for the national unification of Czechs and Slovaks, to assist Slovak students at the Universities and High Schools of Bohemia and Moravia, and to emancipate the life of Upper Hungary from Magyar influence. It is fair to record that the quarrel between the pro-Czech and anti-Czech Slovaks promptly broke out again, no less violently than before; at a discussion held at Sväty Martin in 1897, 'agreement was reached on hardly any point'.[3] Bad blood was also caused by the free-thinking tendencies of the *Hlas*, the organ founded by the Czechophils. The latter had now definitely

[1] Krofta, op. cit., pp. 61, 62.
[2] There had been a few earlier meetings among students and negotiations for co-operation, but the first decisive step was that of 1895.
[3] *Prager Presse*, March 7th, 1930 (Masaryk-Beilage), cit. Szana, op. cit., p. 124.

abandoned the attempt to supplant the Slovak language by Czech, although they maintained that the two peoples were but branches of one great nation. One member of the other group, on the contrary, set out to prove that Slovak was more closely akin to Southern Slav than to Czech, and called on the Hungarian Government for support against the Czech intruders.

The overt political movement, at least, was not 'Czecho-Slovak'. The programme of the Slovak National Party, which entered the field of active politics in 1901, did not even include a separate Slovak territory or national personality, but only recognition of, and equality for, the Slovak language, with various educational, political, and social desiderata. In their hearts, many of its adherents would doubtless have liked wider concessions; but many, again, would have been genuinely contented with fulfilment of their public programme.

The Magyars were at first inclined to look on the Slovak movement with comparative indifference, so convinced were they of the loyalty of the people. The sentences imposed on Slovak nationalists were notably milder than those inflicted, for similar offences, on Roumanians. After a while, however, this attitude changed, and the various resources at the disposal of the Hungarian Government were ruthlessly applied. Among the many scandalous instances was the particularly detestable 'massacre of Csernova' of October 27th, 1907, when the gendarmerie fired on a crowd outside a church (gathered to protest against what was itself a most oppressive action of the authorities), killing twelve persons and wounding sixteen. The immediate sequel was that severe penalties were imposed on a number, not of the gendarmes, but of the crowd. The ultimate result was an immeasurable strengthening of the Slovak movement.

In spite of all chicanery and terror,[1] the movement maintained itself. The party won 4 seats in 1901. It lost them again in 1905, but in the famous free elections of 1906 it increased the number to 8. It fell again to 3 in 1910; but by this time it had further been reinforced by a small Slovak Socialist party. In 1912 a Slovak National Club was founded, but by 1914 it had not proved possible to bring about any real reconciliation or close co-operation between the various groups.

Owing to the Hungarian electoral system and methods, the voting strength of the parties did not represent, even approximately, their real popularity in the country. Nevertheless, it remains a fact which is not only emphasized by Hungarian writers to-day, but freely admitted by the Slovaks themselves, that the active nationalist

---

[1] Ample and convincing details of these methods will be found in Professor Seton-Watson's works, *Racial Problems in Hungary*, &c.

movement was confined to an almost infinitesimal fraction of the Slovak population and even of the Slovak intelligentsia. The Hungarian Ministry of the Interior itself, in a secret list kept by it for police purposes, had only marked down 526 names as dangerous.[1] Estimates given to me in 1935 by Slovak leaders of all parties have not varied very greatly from this figure; indeed, they have usually been below it.[2] And of the 250, 500, 750, or even 1,000 Slovak nationalists, certainly not all desired union with the Czechs, or would even have preferred the Czechs to the Magyars, given equal political conditions.

It is, moreover, the general opinion among the Slovaks to-day, and among those foreign observers most competent to judge and most sympathetic to the Slovak cause, that the national movement was fighting a losing and not a winning battle.[3] Being myself deeply convinced of the extraordinary innate power of the national idea, I should have expected the evolution to be different, but there were still passive nationalities in Europe before the War, and the Slovak was, it appears, one of them. It is commonly stated by the Slovaks themselves that, had the War not intervened, Slovakia would have been completely Magyarized within a not very distant period: according to some, fifteen years; to others, twenty years; to others, a single generation—it is rarely suggested that more would have been required. This can hardly mean more than the final linguistic Magyarization of the intelligentsia, and the attainment of complete political mastery over the masses, since linguistic assimilation of the mountain villages was clearly impossible in so short a time. It is certain, however, that for the nationally-conscious minority the War came in the nick of time.

§ 4. THE CREATION OF CZECHOSLOVAKIA

Even the outbreak of the War brought no immediate change. A certain wave of rather vague Pan-Slav feeling appears to have touched the people when news of the Russian advance filtered through; but nothing like so strongly as in Bohemia. M. Juriga, leader of the Slovak Deputies in the Budapest Parliament, made two declarations (April 26th and December 9th, 1915) in which he solemnly affirmed the entire devotion of the Slovak people to the Hungarian cause.[4] Any utterance to the opposite effect was, of course, impossible in view of the extremely severe repression exercised by Hungary on any national movement; but there is no

[1] Szana, op. cit., p. 146.
[2] Professor Seton-Watson, in *Slovakia Then and Now* (London, 1931), p. 30, gives an estimate of 750–1,000 'as apart from the uneducated and neglected masses'. This is the highest which I have heard from any source.
[3] So Seton-Watson, op. cit., p. 25.   [4] Szana, op. cit., pp. 161, 166.

evidence that the Slovaks in Hungary were anything more than passive in their attitude until well on in 1918, when every one except the governments of Austria and Hungary knew already that the War was lost.

The active work of preparation for separating the Slovak territories from Hungary and attaching them to Bohemia was done, up to the last moment, from outside. Among the men who took the leading parts in this work, there were some of the young generation of Slovaks which had sat at Masaryk's feet at Prague; but the moving spirits in the whole matter were unquestionably Masaryk himself and his right-hand man, the young Czech, Dr. Beneš, who succeeded in imposing their will, not only on the Allies, but even upon M. Durych, the accredited representative of the Czech 'Maffia' itself. Masaryk tells us that from the first he 'kept the inclusion of Slovakia constantly in view',[1] and in fact the map which he presented to Sir Edward Grey in April 1915 traces a proposed frontier in Northern Hungary which (except that it does not include Ruthenia) does not differ greatly from that adopted four years later. The explanatory memorandum[2] states that

The Slovaks are Bohemians in spite of their using their dialect as their literary language. The Slovaks strive also for independence and accept the programme of union with Bohemia.[3]

The really decisive diplomatic step by which the Allies found themselves committed to the creation of an independent Czechoslovakia was the work of Dr. Beneš, who, with Professor Masaryk, had prepared the ground.[4] This gave international sanction to the

---

[1] Masaryk, op. cit., p. 41.

[2] Text in Nowak, op. cit., pp. 319 ff.

[3] Nowak, op. cit., p. 336. Similarly Beneš begins his pamphlet, *Bohemia's Case for Independence* (published in 1917), with the words: 'The term Czecho-Slovaks, or simply the Czechs, includes two branches of the same nation'. A little later (p. 2) he speaks of a 'separatist' movement of 'certain Slovak patriots' which was

accentuated by the establishment of the Austro-Hungarian dualism of 1867, which made the Slovaks members of another State, and completely separated them from the Czechs. This division of the two branches of the Czecho-Slovak nation has therefore existed only since the second half of the nineteenth century and has produced quite insignificant differences.

[4] In retrospect, there seems little doubt that Czechoslovakia was really created on that day of January 12th, 1917, when the Allies, in their answer to President Wilson's request for a statement of their peace terms, included therein 'the liberation of the Italians, as also of the Slavs, Roumanes, and Czecho-Slovaks from foreign rule'. For accounts of this, see Masaryk, op. cit., p. 127; Beneš, op. cit., pp. 142 ff.; *H.P.C.*, vol. i, pp. 171–3, and vol. iv, p. 254. The Allies had not previously pledged themselves to the dismemberment of the Dual Monarchy. The original phrase had been 'Italians, Roumanes, and Southern Slavs', and probably referred to the promises made to Italy and Roumania under the secret treaties of Rome and Bucharest, and to Serbia. Italy insisted that the word 'Southern' should be omitted, and Beneš then

ideas of the 'Czechoslovak Council' which Masaryk and his supporters had constituted in Paris a few weeks earlier.

On May 30th, 1917, the Czech Deputies in the Austrian Reichsrat, convoked at last after years of silence, followed suit by demanding 'the union of all Czechs and Slovaks in a single Bohemian State[1]'—a demand reiterated in the 'Twelfth Night Declaration' of January 6th, 1918; and thenceforward the destiny of the Slovaks was firmly linked to that of the Czechs. As the latter advanced towards independence, they carried the former with them.

Lacking touch with the Slovak leaders at home, the *émigrés* made what contact they could with the large Slovak colonies abroad who, as we have said, had preserved the spirit of Slovak nationalism in a way which the Slovaks of Hungary had failed to do. In Russia the Czechs and Slovaks appear to have agreed as early as August 28th, 1914, to work together for Slovak autonomy;[2] but whether 'Slovakia' was to be part of Hungary, of a federalized Austria, of a Czecho-Slovak State, of Poland, or even of Greater Russia, was uncertain. Later on the old division of opinion characteristic of Czecho-Slovak relations appeared here also. The extreme Slovak national individualists, led by Dr. Koniček, repudiated the tendency of the opposite party to identify the two nations. Another split was between the 'Westerners' (Masaryk's followers), who were strongest in Petrograd, and the centre in Kiev, where the 'Eastern' tendency and Holy Russia were all the vogue. It was only in 1917 that Masaryk's ideas, expounded with eloquence and conviction by his young Slovak disciple Štefánik, carried the day, and the Slovaks of Russia, in the majority, accepted the programme of the Czecho-Slovak National Council in Paris.

In America the representatives of the Czechs and Slovaks met at Cleveland on October 25th, 1915, and agreed to co-operate. The Slovaks stipulated for a federal form of state, with full

prevailed on the French to allow his own kind of Slavs to be particularized; the French persuaded the other Allies. Even so, Professor Temperley (*H.P.C.*, vol. iii, p. 172) takes the view that the phrase could be interpreted as meaning autonomy within Austria-Hungary and indicated 'no attempt or resolve to break up' the Monarchy. Lord Robert Cecil stated in the House of Commons on January 24th, 1917, that 'we were not pledged to the form of liberation'. The event was, however, to prove that the Allies were henceforward committed in fact, if not in intention, to the dismemberment of the Monarchy.

[1] This was the first public statement to this effect made by the Czech leaders at home; but they seem to have entertained the same ambition much earlier, although they attached less weight than the *émigrés* to the Slovak question. The Archduke Frederick, in arresting Kramař on May 24th, 1915, said in his statement of reasons that 'The object of the above associations is the independence of the Lands of the Bohemian Crown, including Hungarian Slovakia' (*Das Verhalten der Tchechen im Weltkriege*, p. 39).

[2] Szana, op. cit., p. 156.

national autonomy for Slovakia, including a separate Parliament and administration. An agreement to this effect was forwarded to Paris, and Masaryk is said to have confirmed it.[1] The famous and hotly debated 'Pittsburgh Convention' of May 30th, 1918, was along the same lines. The Slovaks of the U.S.A. thereby registered their approval of the programme of union of Czechs and Slovaks in a single state, but stipulated that Slovakia should have its own Parliament, administration, and Courts of Justice, and that Slovak should be the official language of education and public life in Slovakia. The formulation of detailed provisions regarding the constitutional laws was to be left to the accredited representatives of the liberated Czechs and Slovaks.

At the wish of the American Slovaks, this document was shown to Masaryk (who was then in the U.S.A.) and he signed it. Unluckily, the parties concerned failed to make quite clear to each other what they were doing. The American Slovaks imagined that Masaryk was acting as head of the Czecho-Slovak Government, with plenipotentiary powers, and that his signature to the document made of it an obligation binding on the Czecho-Slovak State; particularly as the first Czecho-Slovak Government in Prague, on November 11th, 1918, expressly recognized as valid and binding on the Czecho-Slovak State all Conventions and engagements concluded or undertaken by Masaryk during the revolutionary period. The Slovak autonomists have since adopted the same view regarding what they call the 'Pittsburgh Treaty'. Masaryk, on the other hand, writes that the Convention 'was concluded in order to appease a small Slovak faction which was dreaming of God knows what sort of independence for Slovakia'. He signed it as 'a local understanding between American Czechs and Slovaks upon the policy which they were prepared to advocate'. Further, the document itself agreed that the constitution was to be determined later.[2] The Czechs appear also to have objected to the validity of the document on the ground that the Slovak League was not officially recognized by the American authorities until 1919,[3] although it was good enough for the advocacy of Czecho-Slovak claims in 1917.[4] A great deal of subsequent recrimination would certainly have been averted if all signatories to the document had at the time made it clear, in writing, exactly what their respective signatures meant.

The story of the gradual adoption by the Allies of the theses of

---

[1] Szana, pp. 165 ff.
[2] Masaryk, op. cit., pp. 208, 209.
[3] Szana, op. cit., pp. 176–8.
[4] Masaryk, op. cit., p. 211:

In May 1917 it [viz. the 'National Alliance' and the 'Slovak League'] presented to President Wilson, through Colonel House, a memorandum setting forth our political aspirations.

H

Masaryk and his group cannot and need not be retold here. By patient and indefatigable propaganda they implanted their major postulates—the existence of a 'Czechoslovak nation' and the desire of the Slovak branch of it to form part of a Czechoslovak State—so firmly in the minds of the Allies that they were never seriously questioned at the Peace Conference. The 'Czecho-Slovak' Government had been recognized by all the Principal Allied and Associated Powers even before the peace negotiations began—an act which implied that the Slovak question was in principle already settled—while when the moment arrived for settling all questions of detail, including the drafting of the frontier, it found the Czecho-Slovak Government firmly established as a negotiating party; indeed, in something like a privileged position.

Meanwhile, the Slovaks of Hungary had at last begun to move. Contact with the Czech 'Maffia' had been established at the end of 1917; and on May 1st, 1918, after a preliminary conference had been held in Vienna between Dr. Šámal and the active Slovak politicians, Dr. Šrobár, leader of the Slovak Social Democrats, made an important declaration at Liptovský Svätý Mikuláš (Szent Miklós). After referring to the sufferings undergone in the War by all nations, including 'the Hungarian branch of the Slovak people', the declaration demands a just and speedy peace, with free right of self-determination for all nations 'not only outside the frontiers of the Monarchy but also for all nations of Austria-Hungary, and also, therefore, for the Hungarian branch of the Slovak people'.[1]

On May 24th a number of leaders of the Slovak National Party met to consider 'whether they should intervene in the course of political events or whether they should persist in their attitude of passivity'.[2] There appears to have been considerable disagreement. One party, including particularly some of the older leaders, expressed fears both for the fate of Slovak industry if it became subject to competition from Bohemia, and for the national individuality of the Slovaks, who had so nearly been effaced by the Magyars and might be in even greater danger from the Czechs. But even they, it appears, did not oppose the Czechoslovak union on principle. Their fears were soothed by the younger men, and Father Hlinka declared:

It is the hour for action. We must decide now whether we will, in the future, stand with the Hungarians or with the Czechs. Let us not

[1] Szana, op. cit., pp. 171–2. See also L. Steier, *Ungarns Vergewaltigung* (Wien, 1929), p. 553, which reproduces the original text in facsimile. This shows that the declaration at first referred to 'the Hungarian branch of the Slovak people' (*teda i uhorskej vĕtvi slovenského národa*); but another hand altered the word '*národa*' (nation) to '*kmena*' (stock) and inserted the addition '*česko-*' before '*slovenského*'.

[2] Jan Opočenský, *The Collapse of the Austro-Hungarian Monarchy and the Rise of the Czechoslovak State* (Prague, 1928), p. 194.

beat about the bush. Let us declare definitely that we are for the Czechoslovak orientation. Our thousand-year-old wedlock with the Hungarians has not succeeded; we must divorce them.[1]

The following statement was drawn up (May 29th):

The Slovak National Party adopts the point of view that the Slovak race has the absolute and unconditional right to self-determination, on the basis of which it claims for the Slovak nation a share in the creation of an independent State to consist of Slovakia, Bohemia, Moravia, and Silesia.

Matthew Dula is charged with informing the Czech delegates in Prague of this final decision.

No more of importance is recorded during the summer; but in October a Slovak National Council was formed. Austria was by now fast approaching dissolution, and on October 16th the Emperor issued his famous manifesto promising that Austria should become a federal State on national lines. The Hungarian Premier had, however, secured the insertion of a phrase that 'the integrity of the Lands of the Holy Hungarian Crown is in no way affected' (threatening to cut off food supplies unless this was done). On October 19th Juriga declared in the Hungarian Parliament that the Slovaks demanded the right 'to form our own State as a nation in our own territory'; to be entirely free from any foreign influence; and to be represented at the Peace Conference by Slovaks appointed by the Slovak National Council or National Assembly.[2]

According to Count Károlyi, who had been negotiating privately with the Slovak leaders, the latter had never demanded more than autonomy within Hungary. He was convinced that they were sincere, and would have accepted such autonomy if it had been offered. But Károlyi was not at the time in power, and the Premier, Dr. Wekerle, refused to promise anything more than individual rights.[3] Moreover, the men with whom Károlyi was negotiating were not, as the event proved, those whose voices counted most.

On October 18th the patient work of Masaryk and Beneš bore its fruits. The Emperor-King telegraphed to Washington his willingness to conclude peace on the basis of the Fourteen Points; and Wilson replied that he could no longer accept that basis. Since publishing the Fourteen Points, he had recognized the Czecho-Slovak National Council, and that Czecho-Slovaks must themselves 'be judges of what action on the part of the Austro-Hungarian Government will satisfy their aspirations'. Thereafter,

[1] Ibid., p. 157.
[2] Szana, op. cit., pp. 188-9; Opočenský, op. cit., pp. 157 ff.
[3] M. Károlyi, Gegen eine ganze Welt, pp. 308-9.

events in the west moved fast. The Czech State came nearer to fruition every day. Every day Austria grew more ramshackle. At last, on October 27th, Count Andrássy, the last Foreign Minister of the Dual Monarchy, telegraphed to Wilson that he accepted the President's conditions, including his conception of the rights of the Czecho-Slovaks and Yugoslavs; on the following day the Czech National Committee took over the power from the Austrian authorities in Prague. But these things seemed to pass Hungary by. As late as October 22nd Count Tisza spoke in the Budapest Parliament of the 'phantasmagoria of a Czecho-Slovak State' and insisted that the Slovaks—with exceptions which could almost be counted on the fingers of the hand—felt no sort of community with the Czechs.[1]

Neither Andrássy's message nor the events in Prague were known to the Slovak politicians when they assembled on October 29th at Turčiansky Svätý Martin to consider their future course of action. The leaders of the chief national parties were present; but not the representatives of the Magyarone tendency, nor those of the national minorities.

On the next day[2] the assembly considered its programme. It had before it at least three drafts. One, by Bishop Zoch, which had been approved by various politicians, including Juriga, was based on the Imperial Manifesto. It insisted on the proclamation of one race, one nation, and one Czechoslovak culture, and proclaimed the desire of the Slovaks to be united with the Czechs in a single Czechoslovak State, in accordance with Wilson's principle of self-determination. An alternative motion by Dr. Stodola went nothing like so far. It enumerated the sacrifices made by the Slovaks and the injustices suffered by them, and declared that, 'considering that there is no hope of the Hungarian factions even duly considering the equitable rights of the Slovak nation, the Slovak National Party considers it necessary, in this historic time, to raise its voice, as that of the Slovak people, to the areopagus of the free nations of the world, claiming also the right of the Slovaks to settle their own affairs themselves'. Dr. Pantůček also brought a memorandum on the suggested political organization of the new State, including a section on its administrative autonomy.

The Declaration as adopted on October 30th appears to have been a compromise between Zoch's and Stodola's drafts. It began with a long preamble on the wrongs of Slovakia, and an insistence on the sole right of the Slovak National Council to speak for Slovakia; neither the Hungarian Government nor the

---

[1] Szana, op. cit., pp. 195–6.
[2] For the following, see Szana, op. cit., pp. 148 ff.; Opočenský, op. cit., pp. 159 ff.

so-called 'Representative Committees', which had been elected
on the narrow Hungarian franchise, were conceded any such right.
It went on to make the three following points:

1. The Slovaks form a part of the single Czechoslovak nation.
2. The Slovaks propose to exercise the right of free self-
determination.
3. The Slovaks will be represented at the Peace Conference by
a special Slovak Delegation.

The same night, however, at 11 p.m., Dr. Hodža arrived from
Budapest with the news that revolution had broken out in that
city, Count Tisza had been murdered; and that Andrássy had
recognized Wilson's demands. On seeing the Declaration, which
had already gone to the printers, he objected that it was already
out of date.

It was agreed, therefore, that the Committee should meet again
the next day. Many of its members had already gone home; but
about fifty attended the second meeting. Here Hodža argued that
there was no purpose in sending a Slovak delegation to Paris,
when there already existed there a Czechoslovak Government,
recognized by foreign Powers and by Andrássy himself. From
the moment the Slovaks had accepted the Czechoslovak State,
they had accepted also the Czechoslovak Government, and the
way in which it was organized in Paris. The participation of
Slovaks living outside the historic frontiers was, of course, absolutely necessary, but the Government, he pointed out, already
contained a number of Slovaks; the National Committee in
Prague should also be asked to send some Slovak experts to the
Peace Conference. Further, he proposed that a sentence should
be inserted taking note of the legal situation created by Andrássy's
acceptance of Wilson's proclamation; and that the recriminations
against Hungary might well be cut short.

All these proposals were accepted unanimously, and the draft
altered accordingly. The final version, after the preliminaries
claiming exclusive competence for the National Council to speak
for the Slovaks, went on as follows:

1. The Slovak people is both linguistically and by virtue of its
cultural history a part of the single Czechoslovak people. The Slovak
branch has participated in all the cultural battles which the Czech
people has waged, and which have made it famous.

2. We also claim for this, the Czechoslovak people, the absolute right
to self-determination, on a basis of complete independence.

3. In virtue of this principle, we express our agreement with the
new system of international law formulated on October 18th, 1918, by
President Wilson, and recognized on October 28th by the Austro-
Hungarian Minister of Foreign Affairs.

The important difference in the redrafting lay, then, in the substitution of the new third paragraph for the former paragraph demanding separate representation for the Slovaks at the Peace Conference. According to Dr. Jehlička, a very vehement opponent of the present régime in Czechoslovakia, some further alterations were made: in the first paragraph, the reference to linguistic unity was, he says, inserted by Zoch and Hodža, who also suppressed the reference to Slovak self-determination.[1] These allegations are not supported by the *officieux* accounts of the events in question. Most unfortunately for all, the verbatim text of the draft as it stood before the changes seems never to have been printed. It is the singular misfortune of the Czechs that nearly all the major negotiations which went to the making of their state have about them an appearance of irregularity which provides fuel for malicious insinuations. In the present case, there is no reason to suppose that the full meeting would have refused its approval to the changes agreed by those of its number who saw them; the more so, as the Declaration was subsequently ratified by more than 100 local Councils.

The question of Slovakia's relations with Bohemia was certainly discussed, and according to Dr. Opočenský some of those present were not satisfied that the plans of the Prague 'Maffia' respected sufficiently the autonomy of Slovakia, while others wanted a dictatorship for ten years, after which the position was to be reconsidered. The real reason for this latter suggestion was the belief that the Slovaks might go back to Hungary unless they were given a period in which to 'demagyarize'. Dr. Hodža opposed the claims for autonomy, and said that Slovakia could obtain a certain degree of autonomy on the basis of the plans which he had discussed with Pantůček and Rašín. Opočenský states specifically that no resolution was taken on the point. On the other hand, some of the most extreme nationalist Slovaks have since maintained that an agreement was reached at Turčiansky Svätý Martin whereby the Slovak nation should have the right to declare, after ten years, whether it wished to remain 'within the Czechoslovak union, or whether it desired autonomy or complete independence'. This part of the resolution was, it was alleged, turned into a 'secret clause' and its existence thereafter denied. This alleged 'secret clause' played a great part in the Tuka high-treason trial of 1929,[2] at which its existence was strenuously denied on what appeared to be overwhelming authority. Unluckily, the original of the Declaration had disappeared.

---

[1] Dr. F. Jehlička, *Une Étape du calvaire slovaque* (Paris, 1930), p. 61. Jehlička has for some years been in the service of powers hostile to Czechoslovakia, and his statements must be accepted with particular caution.   [2] See below, p. 132.

The Turčiansky Svätý Martin Declaration proved to be another decisive step in the history of the formation of Czechoslovakia, although it might easily have been otherwise; for many declarations were made in those perturbed days of which little was ever heard again. The purport of the meeting seems to have been entirely misunderstood by Count Károlyi, who had now become Minister President in Hungary, and on October 31st telegraphed to the Slovak National Council a warm message of fraternal greetings. He must have got a rude shock when on November 4th he received an equally cordial reply intimating that Slovakia had separated from Hungary, and that in future 'the free Czechoslovak nation wishes to live in good neighbourly relations and friendship with the free Hungarian nation'. Károlyi obviously had no idea that he would be unable to save the territorial integrity of Hungary, and as recently as October 24th had issued a programme which declared that that integrity could be maintained precisely by granting self-determination to the minorities.[1] Jászi was clearly less optimistic, but even he thinks that he 'should have been able to come to an agreement with the Slovak leaders, at all events until the peace negotiations, if Milan Hodža had not been so definitely disavowed at the last moment by Prague'.[2]

What Jászi was now hoping to do was to postpone a *fait accompli* until he could secure permission to hold a plebiscite under neutral supervision; and he believed firmly that such a plebiscite would end in Hungary's keeping Slovakia. The Czechs, on the contrary, were bent on avoiding any such thing. That they appreciated how precarious their position might, after all, prove to be, is shown by the instructions which their representatives issued 'that no one was to negotiate with Károlyi, as this might endanger the Slovak interests with the Allies and help the Magyars to save the integrity of Hungary'.[3] In reviewing the events which followed, sympathy with the Magyars must blend with admiration for the skill of the Czechs in negotiating successfully so many finesses and finally making a contract which their cards never seemed to justify.

On November 1st Austro-Hungarian delegates met the Italian Military Command at Padua, to arrange an armistice. This was signed at 3 p.m. on November 3rd (to take effect 24 hours later) and laid down a line of demarcation on the south-west front. Elsewhere the line consisted of the old political frontier; but the Allies were entitled to occupy the interior of the monarchy if they desired. Nothing was said about North Hungary, which the Hungarian Government continued to consider as part of Hungary.

---

[1] Károlyi, op. cit., vol. i, pp. 458–9.
[2] Jászi, op. cit., p. 59.   [3] Beneš, op. cit., p. 605.

The Czechs, on the other hand, maintained that the recognition by the Allies of the 'Czecho-Slovak State' implied that Slovakia as a whole was already theirs; only the details of the frontier remained to be settled. They therefore sent in such troops and gendarmerie as they could command, who on November 4th and the succeeding days occupied certain districts of Western Slovakia.

Haste was, indeed, urgent, for already voices opposed to the Turčiansky Svätý Martin policy were making themselves heard. The Magyar districts of the south were solid against it; and the Magyar, Magyarized, or Magyarone towns also repudiated the wish to sever their connexion with Hungary, an example followed by the County Assembly of Trenčín and by other Counties. The franchise for these assemblies was, of course, such that they were entirely unrepresentative of the masses of the country-side; but it was not equally clear that the masses would fail to follow them. Bratislava, after considering and dropping the idea of forming an independent republic, asked Budapest for troops to defend them against the Czechs.[1] The Germans of the Spiš, in a meeting held on November 4th at which all German towns and communes of the Spiš were represented, declared unanimously against Czechoslovakia and, while emphasizing their Germanic character and feelings, announced their spontaneous adhesion to Hungary, whose new legislation would, they believed, safeguard their national rights. If separation from Hungary was inevitable, they voted for an independent republic.[2] Finally, Polish troops occupied Sentra Hora, Jablonka, and the Upper Spiš district on November 6th.

The Magyars, meanwhile, were gradually recovering from the shock, and some of their troops were returning from the front. Károlyi and Jászi, having decided that their first aim must be to 'safeguard the principle of the plebiscite', sent an emissary to

[1] The story of Bratislava was a mixture of comedy and tragedy. The troops sent up from Budapest proved to be 200 naval mutineers from Pola, of exceedingly disorderly character and conduct, who wrought little but havoc in the ancient city, which was glad enough to see their backs. The burghers, however, consistently protested their loyalty to Hungary in dignified terms, and if the only persons who attempted to oppose the advance of the Czechs by force were two unhappy workers, who marched out alone to face the legionaries and by them were beaten to death, the special constabulary continued for weeks to express its protests by the sporting of red, white, and green cockades and, when these were forbidden, by the wearing of white-spotted red toadstools and green leaves. On March 15th, 1919 (a Hungarian national festival), 35,000 of these toadstools (which by that time had also been forbidden) were deposited before the memorial of Petöfi (né Petrović, the Slovak's son and Magyar poet and patriot).
[2] When the Poles occupied the Spiš, they pressed the local leaders to go to Paris and petition for incorporation of the district into Poland. The leaders refused, saying that of the two Slav nations, if they must have one, they preferred the Czechs; but their hearts were still with Hungary.

Prague to demand that Slovakia should be occupied by Slovak regiments, while the administration should be shared between the Slovak National Council and the Hungarian Government, acting through the newly appointed Hungarian Minister of Nationalities. On the Czechs' refusing this suggestion (Nov. 11), Hungary mobilized three divisions of repatriated prisoners of war, with one division returned from the front, and opened a counter-offensive which speedily drove the Czechs out of Slovakia.

The Belgrade Armistice of November 13th made no mention of Northern Hungary. Hungary therefore maintained that any occupation by foreigners of territory beyond the Belgrade line constituted a violation of the armistice. On November 17th she protested to Prague to that effect, maintaining that Czecho-slovakia had no right to anticipate the decisions of the Peace Conference; preparing, meanwhile, to occupy Slovakia with stronger forces.

Kramář, from Prague, replied on November 19th that the Czecho-Slovak State, including the territory inhabited by the Slovaks, had been recognized by the Allies, and that Hungary could not conclude an armistice for Slovakia, as a part of the Czecho-Slovak State. The Conference would only occupy itself with details of the frontier, not with the question of principle. At the same time, he appealed most urgently to Beneš for his intervention.

Beneš, with his usual energy, approached Berthelot, Pichon, Clemenceau, and Marshal Foch. He also tells us that he saw the British and Americans; but he concentrated chiefly on the French, pressing them both for a 'clear interpretation' of the Belgrade Armi-stice and for determination of the frontier with Hungary. To Foch, he sketched a line of demarcation of the areas which he declared it to be most important for the Czechs to occupy, whatever the later decisions of the Conference. This line ran: the Carpathians, the Morava, the Danube as far as the Ipel (Ipoly); the Ipel to Rimav-ská Sobota (Rima Szombat); thence as the crow flies to the junction of the Už and the Bereg; the line of the Už up to the Carpathians. He asked 'that this territory should be attributed to us without prejudice to the Peace negotiations'.[1] Finally, he had the satisfac-tion of receiving a letter from M. Pichon on November 27th, agreeing with his point of view and informing him confidentially that the Magyar troops were being ordered to withdraw from 'the areas illegally occupied by them'.

Meanwhile, the Czechoslovak Government had sent Dr. Hodža

[1] Beneš, op. cit., p. 678. This line resembled closely that proposed by Masa-ryk in his memorandum to Grey of April 1915; although the wording of that document is not altogether unambiguous (text in Nowak, op. cit., pp. 319 ff.).

to Budapest, as minister plenipotentiary, to 'liquidate the conflict with Hungary'. Hodža arrived in Budapest on November 23rd.[1] The French Colonel Vyx, who arrived in Budapest on November 27th as representative of the Allies to supervise the execution of the armistice, at first took the Hungarian view. He told Hodža that he thought the Czech occupation of Slovakia had been a mistake and a violation of the armistice, and he recommended them to withdraw. On Hodža's maintaining the Czech thesis, Vyx promised to refer the question to his chiefs. This he did by sending the Czechs' request to the Commandant of the Army of the Orient, whence it could be forwarded to the Inter-Allied Council at Versailles. Meanwhile, Hodža opened negotiations with Jászi. According to the Hungarians, they had every hope of reaching an acceptable agreement. Hodža himself represents Jászi as saying that 'he had to respect our standpoint, but it was difficult for the Hungarian Government openly to renounce the integrity of Hungary'.[2]

Jászi repeated his earlier proposals that Slovakia (viz. all territory inhabited by more than 50 per cent. Slovaks) should be occupied by Slovak troops, under Hungarian (or perhaps Allied) officers, and should be governed by the Slovak National Council, under the Hungarian Minister of Nationalities. Hungarian enclaves should be accorded autonomy, the Slovak National Council nominating a Government Commissioner, while Hungarian Commissioners should be admitted to the Slovak Council to defend Hungarian interests. The administration was to remain in Hungarian hands, and the railways and finance to be under Hungarian command, the National Council only exercising 'control'.[3]

Hodža could not accept these proposals, but to gain time set aside his main contention, and opened negotiations on November 29th for a provisional *modus vivendi* pending the decision of the Peace Conference. No agreement could be reached, as the Slovaks demanded the surrender to themselves of the administration, which the Hungarians insisted on maintaining.

Meanwhile, Beneš had been suggesting that Hodža should be recalled, on the ground that as the Hungarian Government had not been recognized by the Allies, the Czechoslovak Government could not send a Minister Plenipotentiary to Budapest, and the decision on the new situation in Slovakia would be made in Paris, not in Prague or Budapest. He also urged Kramář confidentially 'to occupy Slovakia *via facti* and create a *fait accompli*; we must command the situation'.[4] On December 1st the Government in

---

[1] Dr. Stodola had held the post for a few days previously.
[2] Szana, op. cit., p. 244.
[3] Opočenský, op. cit., pp. 203–4.   [4] Szana, op. cit., p. 245.

Prague published a communiqué that no one had been authorized by them to treat on questions of a political, economic, or military nature, and that Hodža had been sent to Hungary solely to discuss the liquidation of the Hungarian administration in Slovakia.[1] On the night of December 3rd Beneš's activities were crowned with success; Vyx informed the Hungarians that Czecho-Slovakia had been recognized by the Allies and was entitled to occupy the Slovak territories. He therefore called on the Hungarians to withdraw their troops immediately from the 'Slovak Territories'.[2]

The Czechs had now won their main battle; but the 'Vyx Note' laid down no line of demarcation. Hodža urged Beneš to ask for immediate authority to occupy the line Bratislava–the railway through Galanta and Nové Zámky (Ersek Ujvár)–Komárno–the Danube to the Ipola–Ipolské Šahy (Ipoly-Sagh)–Balašské Ďarmoty (Balassa Gyarmat)–Lučenec–Šalgotarján–Rimavská Sobota–Revúca–Rožnava–Košice–Čop and Užhorod. This line was rather more favourable to Slovakia in the east than that proposed by Beneš, although less advantageous in the west (it excluded the Žitny Ostrava Island), but Beneš asked the Allies in Paris to accept it. At the same time, Hodža on December 6th agreed with the Hungarian Government on a provisional line of demarcation (to be effective only until fresh instructions arrived from Paris) which left Bratislava, the Island and Košice also with the Hungarians.

The Hungarian troops immediately began to retire. The Czechs advanced, and within the next fortnight had reached the line laid down in the provisional agreement in most places except the far east.

The Hodža–Bartha agreement was so far advantageous to the Czechs that, as their own publicists claim, it 'prevented the Hungarians' organizing a plebiscite in Slovakia and allowed the Czechoslovak Republic to start to organize it'.[3] At the same time, it gave the Hungarians an opportunity of which they were quick to take advantage. They argued that the Hodža–Bartha line was that duly agreed between the accredited representatives of the two nations, that it answered the real needs of the situation, and that the Czech demands in Paris were far too exigent. The resultant confusion took all M. Beneš's diplomacy to straighten out. He got the Government in Prague to declare officially

that the occupation of Slovakia had not been the subject of negotiations between the Czechoslovak and the Hungarian Governments, that the

[1] Opočenský, op. cit., p. 206.
[2] Text in *Documents concernant l'exécution de l'armistice en Hongrie* (subsequently referred to as *Documents*), p. 95.
[3] Opočenský, op. cit., p. 211.

Czechoslovak Government had never empowered any one to conduct such negotiations and that our representatives Tusar and Hodža had been sent to Vienna and Budapest exclusively to deal with questions of liquidation.[1]

The Allies accepted this declaration, and did not inquire for what reason the Hungarian troops had retired. Beneš returned to the assault in favour of his own original line, as agreed in November, and 'after wearisome and nerve-racking negotiations at the Quai d'Orsay, received an assurance in the middle of December that his line would be respected'.[2] Colonel Vyx was instructed accordingly. On previous occasions when he had referred to the historic frontiers of Slovakia, the Hungarians had made the embarrassingly truthful reply that no such things existed. Colonel Vyx, in his new Note on December 23rd, said firmly that:

> The limits claimed by the Czecho-Slovak State as the historic limits of the Slovak country are as follows:
> [There followed the line demanded by Beneš.]

The Colonel added that the definitive boundaries would only be fixed at the Peace Treaty, by agreement between the Allies; and requested the Hungarian Government to withdraw its troops south of the line.[3]

Hungary protested vehemently,[4] but obeyed. The Czechs continued their advance, and by the middle of January had occupied the territory subsequently allotted to them, incidentally establishing therein a civil government, and as early as December 10th ordering such State, ecclesiastical, and municipal officials as were not dismissed to take the oath to the new State (the decree was published December 24th). The Government was established first in Žilina (Zsolna, Sillein), and moved to Bratislava at the beginning of February.[5] To Hungary's protests, Colonel Vyx on January 10th, 1919, returned the remarkable answer that the Belgrade Armistice did not prejudice decisions taken subsequently by the Allies on other fronts and that

consequently, the Czecho-Slovak State, recognized by the Allies, has the right of absolute sovereignty on the territories which it has re-occupied within the limits of the provisional frontiers fixed for it.[6]

With the Czech advance in the east there disappeared yet another of the short-lived independent republics of Central Europe—an 'East Slovak Republic' which had been founded at Prešov in December by a journalist named Dvorcsák, and seems to have maintained itself for a fortnight or so.[7]

---

[1] Beneš, op. cit., p. 68.   [2] Ibid.   [3] Documents, pp. 95–6.
[4] Ibid., pp. 96–8.   [5] Szana, op. cit., p. 250.
[6] Documents, p. 98.   [7] Szana, op. cit., p. 246.

Meanwhile the Peace Conference had assembled. On February 5th, Dr. Beneš put his case to the Council of Ten, which immediately consented to the general principle of including the Slovak territories in Czechoslovakia, while referring the tracing of the southern frontier to a Committee. There appears to have been some disagreement in this body, the Americans wishing to trace a frontier as near as possible to the ethnographical line, while the French and, in the main, the British, were prepared to disregard the ethnographical principle in so far as was thought necessary for Czechoslovakia's lateral communications. The south-eastern frontier was a compromise between these two points of view.[1] In the west, all parties agreed to give Czechoslovakia the port of Bratislava, but there was much divergence of opinion over the Island. The French wished to give it to Czechoslovakia, the Americans to Hungary. The British member of the committee, Mr. Nicolson, although not sympathetic to the Magyars as a nation,[2] sided on this question with the Americans. He was overruled, but remained unhappy about it,[3] and when in March he accompanied General Smuts to Prague, Smuts, at his request, asked Masaryk to abandon his claim to the island in return for a bridge-head at Bratislava. Masaryk hesitated, and Nicolson believed that he had agreed; but when the point was raised at the Conference the Czechs maintained their claim, saying Nicolson had 'completely misunderstood' Masaryk; and in the end they got both island and bridge-head.[4] Mr. Lansing cross-questioned the rapporteur of the Committee, M. Laroche, who informed him that the island was 'partly German and partly Hungarian',[5] but that it was closely connected economically with the Czecho-Slovak hinterland, and that the population desired to maintain this connexion on economic grounds. In any case, the frontier as proposed gave only 855,000 Magyars to Czechoslovakia, while leaving no less than 638,000 Slovaks in Hungary.[6]

The Council adopted the Committee's report on May 8th. This was really the end of the battle for the Czechoslovak negotiators. They had won their case in broad outline and in detail. There were, however, one or two more alarums and excursions before the Treaty was signed. While the negotiations described above were proceeding, the Czech troops in Slovakia had occupied some territory beyond the demarcation-line. On coming into power, the energetic Bela Kun reorganized the Red Army, opened an offensive, and within a few days' fighting in early June had cleared a considerable portion of South-Eastern Slovakia. This success,

[1] Nicolson, op. cit., p. 275. [2] Ibid., p. 34.
[3] Ibid., p. 279. [4] Ibid., p. 324.
[5] According to the 1910 statistics, the population consisted of 108,000 Magyars, 3,030 Germans, and 1,170 Slovaks.
[6] Hunter Miller, *Diary*, vol. xvi, p. 230.

according to Dr. Beneš, 'affected our prestige and position in Paris for a while very considerably',[1] and he must have appealed for help. On June 10th, Clemenceau sent Kun a remarkable telegram[2] saying that the Allies were 'just about to call the representatives of the Hungarian Government to the Peace Conference to inform them of the Allies' views on the just frontiers for Hungary. At that precise moment the Hungarians directed violent, unjustified attacks against the Czechoslovaks and overran Slovakia.' He called on Kun to stop his attack immediately, failing which, 'extreme measures' would be taken. Kun replied that he was prepared to stop hostilities and to negotiate a just peace; he did not insist on the territorial integrity of Hungary. He suggested negotiations in Vienna. Clemenceau answered on June 13th, communicating the frontier which had been settled in Paris and stating that this would be definitive. The Hungarian troops were to withdraw behind this line immediately. Kun protested vehemently, but the overwhelming majority of the Communist Party Executive, whom he consulted, advised acceptance (among the few dissidents was the extremely able Chief of Staff, Stromfeld),[3] and Kun obeyed, at the same time informing his country that the evacuation was not to be regarded as definitive. By the beginning of July, Slovakia had been cleared; the Czechs re-entered it, and soon liquidated the Soviet Republic of Slovakia which had reigned for a fortnight in Košice.

The accession to power of the Archduke Josef in August 1919 caused another crisis, described by Beneš as being 'as severe or more severe' than the above;[4] but it passed over.

§ 5. THE SLOVAK QUESTION SINCE THE WAR (1)

Slovakian history since 1918 had had its full share of complexities and difficulties, many of which must have appeared inexplicable to those who took at their full face value all the optimistic statements made at the Peace Conference. It all seemed so simple then. A nation, united in itself, and identical in race and language with the Czechs, was only awaiting the hour to cast off the yoke of Magyar oppression and join hands with its fellow Czechoslovaks in the Historic Lands. Nothing was simpler than to fulfil this ambition; and such a nation could face with equanimity the inclusion within its frontiers of nearly a million Magyars and Germans, even though 95 per cent. of the minorities in normal times and 70 per cent. during either the Red or the White Terror would probably have remained loyal to Hungary.

[1] Beneš, op. cit., p. 213.
[2] Text of these notes in Szana, op. cit., pp. 299 ff.
[3] W. Böhm, *Im Kreuzfeuer zweier Revolutionen* (Munich, 1924), p. 472.
[4] Beneš, op. cit., p. 684.

But, as the event proved, the minority question was not the only political problem in Slovakia. That of the Slovaks themselves was perhaps less intractable but even more delicate, besides being absolutely fundamental to the existence of the State. The key to the problem lay in the position, not of the Magyars, but of the Magyarones. The Magyar elements in the administrative, judicial, and educational systems could have been removed without too much difficulty, or, where retained, could have been rendered harmless, had nationally conscious Slovaks been there to take their places. But even apart from the fact that the mass of the Slovak peasantry, although harbouring deep and justified grievances against the former ruling caste, was conservative and docile, and showed small inclination to revolt actively—far more important— the great majority of the middle-class elements which might have led the country, and for whose sake the whole change had largely been made, were in the enemy camp. The active Slovak nationalists, even when reinforced by the inevitable band of turn-coats, re- mained a mere handful, consisting only of a few hundreds of men, totally insufficient in numbers and sometimes in training or even capacity to undertake the complex task of ruling the country. The remainder of the intelligentsia, who might have given a lead to the masses, had become Magyarized both in language and mentality.

The central task was thus to build up a national sentiment favourable to the new régime round what was only a tiny nucleus in the sea of apathy blended with much actual hostility. And while this was being done—and it was clearly to be a long and not an easy task—the administration and business of the country had to be carried on.

It is from this initial weakness in the position—which could never be openly avowed, since to admit it would have been to acknowledge a large part of Hungary's case for keeping Slovakia— that much of the subsequent friction between Czechs and Slovaks arose. To a large extent, the Czechs have been unfairly blamed. The accusation so frequently levelled at them, once the first rap- ture was over, of having intended from the first to treat Slovakia as a conquered country or as a 'colony' for exploitation, is probably untrue. If we except the motives of business interests, which are notoriously superior to national prejudices (and were in any case as much German or Jewish as Czech), the Czechs were undoubtedly most sincerely anxious to give the Slovaks their full due in every respect. The weakness of their friends in Slovakia, when it became apparent, must have been not only a source of great embarrassment but also a dismal surprise. Given the original position, however, and given also the natural determination to keep what had been won, what followed was inevitable. It was possible, indeed, to watch the Czechs being forced, step by step, along the unpopular path which they took.

In the first days of the Republic, the Czechs apparently hoped and believed it possible to govern the country through the Czecho-phil Slovaks, without themselves intervening directly. They did not, indeed, leave the National Assembly of Turčiansky Svätý Martin, nor the numerous local Slovak Councils which had sprung up. They organized, as has been described, a 'Government Office', which had its seat first at Žilina and then in Bratislava. The head of this office was nominated from Prague, the choice falling on Dr. Šrobár, one of the leaders of the Centralist wing. Thus, from the first, care was taken that the particularist wing—still more the Magyarophils—should not exercise undue influence. On the other hand, Dr. Šrobár was invested with practically plenipotentiary powers. The very largest issues of policy were decided from Prague, but in all else the Government Office enjoyed practical autonomy.

An analogous arrangement was made as regards political repre-sentation. Immediately on the constitution of the Republic, a National Assembly was convoked in Prague. For the Historic Lands, the various Czech parties were represented in as accurate a proportion to their known strengths as could be estimated, the results of the latest Austrian election being taken as the key for making the calculations. For Slovakia, on the other hand, the results of the Hungarian elections (which would, of course, have given an almost purely Magyar list) were set aside as unrepresenta-tive—as indeed they were—and at first 40, afterwards 54, Slovak Deputies were nominated from among the more active members of the local Councils, with the addition of 4 Czech champions of the Slovak cause and of Dr. Alice Masaryk. As in the Historic Lands, the national minorities were entirely unrepresented, and among the Slovaks, although the main leaders of the various tendencies were included, the representation was undeniably weighted in favour of the Centralist wing.

The Government Office rapidly expanded into an elaborate organization, with thirteen departments, each under a 'Referent' and concerned respectively with the interior, agriculture, trade, railways and posts, justice, militia, education, Catholic affairs, Protestant affairs, social welfare, and public works. All thirteen 'Referents' were Slovaks. Once these departments got to work, the Czech legionaries who had first occupied the country were withdrawn.

The Government Office undertook with energy the task of reorganizing the administration of the country. Under an emer-gency law, all municipal and commercial assemblies were dissolved, as having been elected on an undemocratic and anti-social basis, and replaced by commissions nominated by the Government. Slovak was proclaimed the official language of the State. The law authorized former officials to be retained if properly qualified, and if they took the oath of allegiance. The two highest officials in each county—the 'Főispán' (Lord Lieutenant) and 'Alispán' (Deputy Lieutenant), who were the chief props of the Hungarian system—were, however, immediately replaced by Slovak 'Župáns', and many other higher officials either left voluntarily or were dismissed as unqualified, or as refusing to take the oath. In this connexion, it is frequently claimed as a grievance that the new régime often exacted the oath before it was entitled to do so, and in fact, as our earlier narrative has shown, the position in the early days rested rather on *faits accomplis* than on *droits acquis*. It would appear that no very scrupulous consideration was observed towards officials who were at once influential and notoriously Magyarophil. The smaller fry, who might otherwise have been left undisturbed, played into the hands of the new régime when, in December, a general strike broke out among the post office and railway employees, notoriously organized from Budapest with the object of cutting communications between Slovakia and Bohemia and preventing their ultimate union. In consequence of this strike a large number of lower State employees were dismissed, and their places filled very largely by Czech volunteers who had come in, in response to appeals from Bratislava, to maintain an emergency service.

The treatment of the teachers in the State schools was perhaps even more drastic than that of the administrative employees. The 'Referent' for education, Dr. Štefánek, reorganized the whole system on national lines, leaving to the minorities a quota of schools proportionate to their numbers, but taking over the rest for the use of the Slovaks. In a question of such importance, he did not think it safe—nor, indeed, would it have been safe—to give the former Magyar teachers a chance to learn the new language of instruction, but dismissed the lot with gratuities, at a considerable cost both in human suffering and in hard cash. He even went farther, and placed under State control the Catholic 'gymnasia', thus violating, in the interests of de-Magyarization, a principle which Hungary had always strictly observed.[1] Similarly, the University in Bratislava

[1] No legal right was disregarded by this action, since the Catholic Church, alone among the more important religious denominations in Hungary, did not (and still does not) enjoy internal autonomy; the reason lying in the peculiar relationship of the State and the Apostolic Crown to the Holy See. The Catholic Church is therefore actually less well protected in law against a hostile Government than the Lutheran, Orthodox, or even the Jewish faith. The principle of freedom of denominational education was, however, always observed. Dr. Štefánek writes of his own action that 'the only alternatives

I

was taken over, in the face of very vehement protests from the
Hungarian Government, which finally withdrew the staff bodily to
Inner Hungary.

Even the Church was affected by the reorganization, if less immediately than other branches of public life. The change-over was
not too difficult for the Lutheran Church, where a Slovak, even a
Czecho-Slovak, national spirit had always managed to survive. The
seats of all three Bishops lay in Inner Hungary, and it was thought
impossible 'alike for political and practical reasons' to maintain
their authority over the Slovak parishes,[1] while several of the next
senior Church officials—Seniors and Inspectors—also retired, for
'purely political reasons'. Following an appeal by the remainder,
the Government established a provisional Church authority, which
obtained from the Government recognition of all obligations of the
former Hungarian State towards the Church, with certain additional
subsidies. In 1922 a new Church constitution was approved under
which the Lutheran Church was guaranteed internal autonomy
and liberal financial endowments from the State. Almost all the
Bishops, Seniors, and Inspectors provisionally appointed in 1919
were confirmed in their offices; these being, for the most part,
Slovaks by origin and sympathies.

The question of the Catholic Church was far more difficult.
Here, most of the episcopal seats lay within Slovakia itself, but
some of the bishops and other higher dignitaries withdrew to
Hungary, while others, owing to the strength of Slovak sentiment,
'had to yield to the unanimous pressure of public opinion and
hurriedly abandon their positions in Slovakia'.[2] The substitutes
left behind by the bishops were, however, themselves usually
Magyars or Magyarophil, as were the great majorities of the
chapters. Owing to the difficult relations between Prague and the
Vatican, little could be done for several years towards Slovakizing
the Catholic Church, and even after fifteen years the process was
far from complete.

With this exception, the liquidation of the old régime proceeded
with unexpected rapidity; but a gap was left which the nationalist
Slovaks themselves were frankly unable to fill. The difficulties
were, of course, tremendous, especially in Eastern Slovakia, where
under the Hungarian régime a Slovak intelligentsia had simply
not been tolerated. Here it was difficult even to find candidates for
office. But neither for the upper ranks of the administration nor
(after the strike) for the lower ranks, nor for education, was it

would have been to close them [the gymnasia] altogether or to leave them in
Magyar hands' (Seton-Watson, ed., *Slovakia Then and Now*, p. 121). The action
was, as it proved, deeply resented not only by Magyars but also by Slovaks.
    [1] The Rev. F. Ruppeldt in *Slovakia Then and Now*, p. 193.
    [2] The Rev. K. Medvecky in *Slovakia Then and Now*, p. 177.

possible to find nearly enough qualified and reliable Slovaks to do even the most urgently necessary work. The vacancies had therefore, quite inevitably, to be filled from the only available reservoir: the Czech districts of the Historic Lands. This was done, largely on the invitation of the Slovak Government Office and its Referents themselves; and that great influx began of Czech officials, teachers, and employees whose presence has to this day so deeply affected Czecho-Slovak relations.

Simultaneously, a reaction, prompted in part by the centralist theories of the parties in power in Prague, partly by recognition of the weakness of the 'Czechoslovak' element in Slovakia, and partly by considerations relating to conditions in the Historic Lands, set in against the initial trend towards autonomy. Before dissolving itself, the Constituent Assembly enacted a most important Law of February 29th, 1920, under which it was proposed to abolish the old Lands of Bohemia, Moravia, and Silesia, and the *de facto* Land of Slovakia, and to reorganize the whole territory of the Republic (except Ruthenia) into twenty-one 'Župy' or administrative districts, six of which were to be in Slovak territory.

The Župy and their subdivisions, the Districts, were invested with elected assemblies competent to deal with local affairs. The administration, however, was mainly in the hands of the nominated officials, while the Župán, who was also a Government nominee, presided over the meetings of the Assembly. Further, a certain number of 'official experts' nominated by the Government took part in the meetings and voted at them. Thus the local autonomy allowed for by the Župa system was fairly restricted; and it must be remembered that the Župy themselves were replacing the old Hungarian Vármegyek, or Counties, which enjoyed far wider liberty of action, although owing to the restricted franchise (whereas that of the new bodies was very wide) its benefits were reaped by a narrow circle. Finally, the special status of all the former Free Boroughs in Slovakia, with the sole exceptions of Bratislava and Košice, were abolished, the administration of the cities being brought within the scope of the general Župa scheme.

This Law, as a matter of fact, never came into force at all in the Historic Lands. It was brought into force, for Slovakia alone, on January 1st, 1923. It had always been intended to form the Župy into territorial groups with a certain community of action. The separate treatment of Slovakia was thus in accordance with the intentions of the measure itself, while, further to meet the wishes of the Slovak Deputies, the Minister for Slovakia was retained. His powers were, however, gradually restricted. The Department of Finance was replaced by a general Finance Office for all Slovakia, in Bratislava, and the functions of the Departments of Justice, War, and Railways transferred to similar bodies. The remaining Departments of the old Government Office were formed into separate offices, which, while remaining in touch with the Minister for Slovakia, and acting subject to his approval, especially in political questions, were directly subordinate to the respective Ministers in Prague.

Meanwhile, the political situation had been gradually clarifying. The Slovak Deputies in Prague had at first formed a single political club, but soon had begun to sort themselves out according to the broad divisions of political opinion. On the one side, the more active representatives of the pronounced 'Czecho-Slovak' tendency, led by Dr. Šrobár and Dr. Hodža, formed a 'National Party' which, besides its national programme of support for the Czechoslovak idea and State, adopted a strongly agrarian programme, as that best answering to the needs of the majority of the Slovaks. From the first this party co-operated closely with the Czech Agrarians, and ended by combining with them in a single party.

Shortly after, the Social Democrats—a tiny party before the War, but swollen immediately after it to almost unrecognizable dimensions by a flood of recruits from among the landless peasants and dwarf-holders, who were now for the first time allowed, and even encouraged, to express themselves politically—followed suit, also fusing with the sister party in the Historic Lands, which at this time stood very far to the Left, wavering in allegiance between the Second and the Third Internationals.

On the other side, the anti-centralists gathered round the veteran leader, Monsignor Hlinka, who on December 18th, 1918, founded the Slovak People's Party, with a programme the keynote of which was Slovak nationalism, while its dominant was clericalism. Few months of the Republic's existence had elapsed before this party was in very active opposition to the National Party, owing in some degree to an unhappy personal rivalry between Dr. Šrobár and Monsignor Hlinka. It is now known that Dr. Šrobár himself behaved very generously towards his veteran rival;[1] but the People's Party undoubtedly had a grievance from the first in the manner in which its members were generally excluded from power and office, and its opinion and advice consistently disregarded in Prague in favour of those of the National Party.

The differences, however, soon became deeper than a mere personal rivalry for power, although a happier handling of the personal question might possibly have removed them. The autonomists believed that they had a right to receive full and immediate self-government, and they held this right to be theirs not merely on general grounds but in virtue of quite specific under-

[1] See Seton-Watson, *The New Slovakia* (Prague, 1924), p. 24, footnote.

takings. It has already been mentioned that the signatories to the 'Pittsburgh Convention' do not seem to have made quite clear to one another what they were doing, or what were their respective powers. Many Slovaks were left under the impression that the 'Pittsburgh Convention' constituted a binding agreement between Czechs and Slovaks, which laid the former under an international obligation to grant Slovak autonomy. The Czech nation, they argued, assumed this obligation when the Constituent Assembly, on November 12th, 1918, approved and ratified all agreements and undertakings made by Masaryk during his struggle to achieve Czech freedom.

While the Peace Conference was still sitting, Monsignor Hlinka and his then right-hand man, Father Jehlička (who was afterwards to go over openly into the Magyarone camp) actually travelled to Paris, where, with Polish help, they printed a petition asking, on the basis of the Convention, for either autonomy or a plebiscite for Slovakia. Their efforts were frustrated by the Czech delegates to the Conference, with the help of the French police, and the treaties concluded at the Peace Conference made no reference to Slovak autonomy;[1] but after this episode the rift between the Centralists and the Autonomists was very deep.

After the dissolution of the Constituent Assembly, elections were held (April 1920). The result, as will be seen from the table on p. 118, was fairly even as between the National and the People's Party (which had voted on a single list with the Czech Clericals, under the common title of the Czechoslovak People's Party), with a very large vote, as big as that of the other two parties together, going to the as yet undifferentiated Left. Most of the remaining votes went to the parties of the national minorities. The Agrarians and Socialists were at first both in power, but only a few months later occurred the great split in the Czechoslovak Social Democratic Party, following which most of those in Slovakia who still supported the Left (a smaller number than in the months immediately after the War) went into opposition as Communists. In 1922 the People's Party also seceded from the Government coalition and from the united Clerical Club. In practice, therefore, Slovakia was ruled by the two main centralist parties—the Agrarians and the Social Democrats—with the support of the Czechs; and this continued to be the case even after the 1925 elections had shown the People's Party to be, at that time, much the strongest single Slovak party.[2]

[1] See the account by Jehlička in *Pesti Hirlap*, November 4th, 1930, cit. Szana, op. cit., pp. 320-2.

[2] For the votes cast for the various parties in the 1925 and subsequent elections, see the table on p. 118. The position was complicated after 1920 by the action of many of the Czech parties which at various dates extended their

POLITICAL PARTIES IN SLOVAKIA, 1920–1935

Party.	1920.	1925.	1929.	1935.
1. Republican Party of Agrarians	..	248,034	278,979	286,739
2. Slovak National Party (Peasants' Party up to 1925) .	242,045	35,435	..	..
3. Small-holders and Traders' Party	..	..	6,901	..
4. Magyar Peasants' Party .	26,520	..	..	..
5. Czechoslovak Traders' and Middle-class Party. .	..	11,576	30,134	41,996
6. Czechoslovak People's Party	235,389	18,036	36,548	37,489
7. Slovak People's Party (Hlinka) . . .	..	489,111	403,683	489,641
8. Slovak People's Party (Juriga) . . .	..	..	5,395	..
9. Autonomous Provincial Union	..	6,894	..	..
10. Czechoslovak Social Democratic Party . . .	510,341	60,635	135,506	184,389
11. Magyar Social Democratic Party	108,546	..	..	..
12. German Social Democratic Party	..	5,137	4,824	5,409
13. Czechoslovak National Socialist Party . .	29,564	36,909	43,968	51,930
14. National Labour Party .	..	13,608	..	..
15. Communist Party (Czechoslovak Section of Third International) . .	..	189,111	152,242	210,785
16. Independent Czechoslovak Communist Party . .	..	356	..	..
17. Czechoslovak National Democratic Party (in 1935 included in No. 18) .	..	24,954	53,745	..
18. National Union Party (1935)	..	..	..	25,490
19. League against tied candidates (in 1935, No. 18) .	..	..	1,810	..
20. National group of Fascists (Gajda) . . .	..	..	..	32,609
21. Unified Magyar Parties .	..	..	..	230,713
22. Magyar National Party .	4,214	Voted with no. 30	104,106	..
23. Regional Christian Socialist Party	139,355	98,337	122,801 (incl. German section)	..
24. Western Slovakia Christian Socialist Party .	..	17,285	..	..
25. Regional Peasants' Party .	..	4,546	..	..
26. German Electoral Community. . . .	..	..	13,704	..
27. German National Party .	..	3,410	..	..
28. German National Socialist Party	..	..	..	..
29. Sudetendeutsche Party (Henlein) . . .	..	..	..	27,558
30. Bund der Landwirte Party (including Party No. 22 after 1925) . . .	..	109,635 (incl. votes) of no. 22)	Voted with no. 23	255
31. Provincial Parties of small farmers, traders, and workmen . . .	..	..	6,901	No separate list; voted chiefly with Social Democrats or Middle-class parties, especially no. 5.
32. Associated Jewish Parties in Slovakia . . .	45,217	..	..	
33. Jewish Parties . . .	..	38,442	..	
34. Electoral Associations of Polish and Jewish Parties	..	..	33,679	
35. Jewish Economic Parties .	..	5,144	..	..
36. Two other Parties . .	..	..	..	546
Total of valid votes recorded	1,341,191	1,425,595	1,434,926	1,625,549

This not unnaturally aroused considerable discontent. At this period the Slovak People's Party was largely under the influence of M. Tuka, a man of somewhat extreme views, who was unconcealedly anti-Czech and strongly suspected of being pro-Magyar. Relations between Slovakia and the Historic Lands became so strained that every one saw the impossibility of keeping in force the Župa system. It was therefore remodelled, largely in accordance with the proposals of the more centralist Slovaks, who acted as intermediaries. A new Act was passed on July 14th, 1927, which came into force in Slovakia on June 28th, 1928. Slovakia now became one of the four 'Lands' into which the Republic was divided (Bohemia, Moravia with Silesia, Slovakia, and Ruthenia). Each of these is provided with a President and Vice-President, and an Assembly, with a smaller Executive Committee. In the latter bodies, two-thirds of the members are elected, while the other third consists of 'experts nominated by the Government, regard being paid to the economic, cultural, national, and social conditions'. They deal (subject in practice to far-reaching limitations and control from Prague) with humanitarian, sanitary, economic, and cultural questions, and questions of communications, affecting the Land as a whole, being assigned a limited budget for the purpose. The Župy were abolished; the District Councils remained, being composed on the same principle of part election and part nomination, and dealing with similar questions on a smaller scale. Below these again come the Parish Councils. This organization has remained unaltered till to-day. In connexion with this reorganization, the Slovak People's Party entered the Government and received two portfolios.

§ 6. THE SLOVAK QUESTION SINCE THE WAR (2)

As has been said, the steps by which the Czechs assumed so large a measure of control over Slovakia were practically inevitable. If Slovakia was not to be allowed to return to Hungary, it had to be governed mainly by Czech officials, and it could not be granted full autonomy, or even full self-expression. The phrase so often heard, and so deeply resented, that the Slovaks are 'not ripe for self-government' certainly was, for many years, true both in the literal sense that sufficient trained Slovak administrators were not available, and in the further unacknowledged but equally apparent

party organization into Slovakia—an operation facilitated and made almost inevitable by the adoption in the Constitution of the principles of proportional representation and single-list voting for the entire Republic. These parties depend, of course, in part on the votes of the Czech officials and settlers in Slovakia, but some of them, particularly the National Democrats and National Socialists, secure a fair number of Slovak votes also.

meaning, that a Slovak parliament could not be trusted not to fall under Magyar and Magyarone influence and, during the early years, even to vote its own return to Hungary.

Moreover, the Czech rule (this is what it amounted to) brought the Slovaks many benefits. First and foremost, it put a full stop to the Magyarization under which the Slovaks were so rapidly losing their national identity. Naturally, every measure, legitimate or otherwise, directed towards Magyarization was repealed and every effort made, on the contrary, to emphasize the Slavonic character of the population. The whole educational system was entirely re-cast, the Magyar establishments being reduced to the strict needs of the Magyar minority, while in the Slovak districts all traces of Magyar were abolished. In 1934 the Slovaks possessed a hundred or so kindergartens and crèches; 3,362 elementary schools, with 8,949 teachers and 448,445 pupils;[1] and 160 secondary establishments, some two-thirds of which were burger schools, the remainder being various types of higher schools, including teachers' training colleges. There were considerable numbers of apprentices' schools, technical, commercial, agricultural, and industrial schools and colleges, and some provision for higher education, including the University of Bratislava. Even to compare these figures with those of pre-War years will not fully reveal the extent of the change, for the average number of classes to each school has been substantially increased (it is now little under three, while most of the pre-War denominational schools consisted only of one class each), the length of the elementary-school course has been increased by two years, and in many cases the school buildings have been greatly improved and enlarged. Theatres, libraries, and reading-rooms have sprung up; the Matice has been revived, and other similar cultural societies founded in private and commercial life; and in the Press the use of the Slovak language has been freed from all restrictions. The process has not been merely negative— an elimination of Magyar influence—but also positive—a fostering of culture and education generally, especially among the poorer classes. It has borne good fruits, both in a great diminution of ignorance and illiteracy among the peasants and in a rapid development of art and literature in the middle classes.

Next, within certain very well-defined limits, the Slovaks have been introduced to the blessings of political liberty. The Czechoslovak franchise is far more liberal than the Hungarian, which completely deprived the great majority of the Slovaks of the opportunity of voting altogether, and ensured that the votes of the remainder, as a rule, should be ineffectual unless cast for the

---

[1] These figures were kindly supplied to me by the Department of Education in Bratislava.

Government. The Czechoslovak franchise is wide, and the ballot is genuinely secret. Further, Czechoslovakia (if not Slovakia) possesses a Parliament, even to-day, which is able freely to debate the condition of the country, and whose opinions and votes mean something. What is probably far more important for the ordinary Slovak peasant and worker is the genuine democratic spirit which pervades all Czech institutions, and is emphasized almost ostentatiously in Slovakia to mark the contrast with Magyar 'feudalism'.

It is true that this democracy does not extend so far as to give the Slovaks any real self-government, except in minor questions. The last word rests with the bureaucracy, which, at least in its higher ranks, is still mainly Czech. The Czech bureaucracy is, however, probably the best in Europe, east of Germany. The wayward character which the Czechs presumably inherited from their Slavonic ancestors has been profoundly modified by long contact with German methods and also by a very strong admixture of German blood. The Czech is to-day the bureaucrat *par excellence*, and if he lacks experience in the highest spheres he performs minor administrative duties, without particular grace, but with diligence, accuracy, and a standard of honesty above the local average. If the Slovaks have to be administered from outside their own narrow walls, they are probably better off, from the purely technical standpoint, under the Czechs than under most other nations; particularly since the Czechs are, after all, by far their nearest relations.

Certain very important reforms have been introduced, which benefit especially the poorer classes. The workers have profited by the Czech industrial and social legislation, which is far more advanced, not only than that of pre-War Hungary (that comparison, although frequently made, would be quite unfair), but also than that of Hungary to-day. It includes the 8-hour day in industry, provision for Works Councils and industrial arbitration, the prohibition of child labour, and a comprehensive system of old-age, sickness, and invalidity insurance. Since Socialist parties have been in the Czechoslovak Government during a substantial part of the State's existence, a worker is quite free to call himself a Socialist, or even a Communist, and freedom of association and expression, in purely industrial and social matters, is wide.

Similarly, the poorer peasants and agricultural workers enjoy immeasurably more freedom and political influence than they ever dreamed of in the old days. Such of them as belong to the Agrarian Party, which has been in office almost without intermission since the Republic was founded, are a power in the land. But even the supporters of the Opposition, in so far as they belong to Slovak parties at all, have gained greatly, not only through the establishment of the new political system, but also through the agrarian reform which was carried through in the first years after the War. So long as the big estates remained, their owners, thanks to the extraordinary candour of the Hungarian ballot, wielded over their tenants and labourers an almost unlimited influence. The political effects of the distribution of these estates has been immense. It is, indeed, probable that this reform was due at least as much to national and political considerations as to purely social and economic. The desire to weaken the power of the landowners was reinforced by the wish to stop the drainage of national forces through emigration, for which the current system of land tenure was blamed.[1]

The reform itself was carried out on much more conservative lines than the corresponding measures in many other states. Existing proprietors were allowed to retain minima of 150 hectares of arable land, or 250 hectares in all, which might be increased to 500 hectares if necessary to preserve natural beauties or historic or artistic treasures. Buildings, installations, &c., unconnected with the exploitation of the estate, as also State and communal property, were exempted. Other land above these minima was placed under sequester, the owner being forbidden to sell, lease, or transfer it without permission of a special Land Office. The Office was entitled, although not obliged, to take over all sequestrated land; if it exercised its right, it was obliged to pay compensation (in cash, 4 per cent. bonds, or a mixture of the two) calculated on the average price in the open market in the years 1913–15, with a graduated reduction in the compensation for estates above 1,000 hectares, and a further reduction based on the date of expropriation. For this purpose, a Czech crown was taken as equal to a pre-War gold crown. The Land Office was also empowered to exchange sequestrated land against free or State land, if to do so facilitated its task of distribution.

The land thus acquired was distributed in the following ways:

(*a*) It might be retained by the State for reasons of public utility.

(*b*) Tenants enjoying long leases had, under certain conditions, the right to buy their holdings.

(*c*) A large number of building-plots were allotted, chiefly by an urgency procedure introduced immediately after the War, to individuals, associations, communes, or towns.

(*d*) Holdings might be leased or sold to small-holders, artisans, or landless persons, preference being given to Czechoslovak ex-soldiers and legionaries (who must, however, be capable

[1] C. Viskovsky and A. Pavel, *La Réforme foncière* (Extrait de *L'Encyclopédie tchécoslovaque*, Prague, 1928), p. 3.

of farming), co-operatives, communes, public utility corporations, or scientific or humanitarian associations. The
size of a peasant holding was fixed at 6, 10, or 15 hectares
according to the quality of the soil. Provision was also
made, however, for larger holdings in two forms: so-called
'residual estates' and other larger estates (the latter being
usually properties of forest or pasture, and generally assigned to communes or corporations). These might be
attributed either to individuals or corporations. Existing
tenants or former employees were entitled to first consideration in allotting these estates, legionaries coming next in
order of preference.

Recipients purchasing their holdings might get credits up to a
maximum of 90 per cent. of the price of the land and 50 per cent.
of that of the buildings, or of the cost of constructing such buildings. Disabled legionaries, or their widows and orphans, were
entitled to even more generous treatment.

Former employees on estates acquired for distribution, if not
taken over by the recipients of residual estates, might be (a) given
land, (b) found suitable work, (c) allotted a compensation in cash,
(d) given an old age or invalidity pension.

The total results for Slovakia are as follows[1] (areas in hectares):

	Arable Land.	Total.	Number of Persons concerned.
1. Total area . . .	2,436,902	4,896,563	..
2. Area sequestrated . .	498,693	1,396,135	873
Percentage of 1 to 2 .	20·46	28·50	
3. Land acquired by exchange	5,282	10,207	..
4. Total of 2 and 3 . .	503,975	1,406,341	..
Purchased by tenants on long lease	..	7,497	9,800
Building lots . . .	..	4,361	20,341
Purchased by small-holders .	..	203,435	152,762
Leased to small-holders .	..	4,737	3,971
Colonies	..	24,490	1,850 (app.)
Residual estates . . .	..	55,202	455
Other estates of over 30 ha. .	..	87,478	797
Acquired by State . .	..	129,448	..
Exempted or released from sequester . . .	157,667	309,785	..
Still at disposal of Land Office	71,739	579,256	..

These results were, as will be seen, modest compared with those
achieved in some other countries. The average size of the lots distributed was, in particular, very small, being only 0·22 hectares
for the building-plots and 1·41 for the ordinary small-holdings. A
colonist's lot averaged 15·98 hectares, and a residual estate 115·97;

[1] Dr. J. Voženílek, *Résumé des résultats acquis de la réforme foncière dans les
pays de Slovaque et de Russie Subcarpathique* (Prague, 1932).

but the native agricultural populations were not the sole or even the chief beneficiaries from these more favourable arrangements. The fact, however, remains that in Slovakia 5·15 per cent. of the total population, and 19·6 per cent. of the active agricultural population, benefited to a greater or less extent by the reform. The beneficiaries have had their troubles, as we shall see; and certain other factors in the question, to be described later, have aroused much discontent. Nevertheless, the reform must be counted as a solid piece of work for which the Slovak peasantry have to thank their change of national status.

Against those benefits, many of which are solid and enduring, must be set a number of factors which are often intangible and difficult to describe. At their head should be placed, perhaps, the intelligible disillusionment when the Slovaks discovered that they were not, after all, going to be masters in their own house—or, at any rate, not until they had been adjudged by Prague 'ripe for self-government'. They had not been given to understand during the War, or when it was a question of soliciting their suffrages against Hungary, that they were so immature as they now discovered themselves to be—in Czech estimation.

As we have said, the failure to grant autonomy was probably due far less than is commonly supposed to deliberate treachery on the part of the Czechs, and far more to their own miscalculation of the strength of their supporters. One may agree that the 'Czech invasion' was unavoidable, yet it is not to be expected that all Slovaks should be readily alive to its necessity, and the suspicion of double-dealing in the past still does much to poison Czecho-Slovak relations.

This might matter less if the suspicion was all on one side; but the Czechs have at times been all too ready to look on most Slovaks as 'Magyarones' and potential traitors, and have employed battalions of censors, police agents, and other customary instruments of unpopular Governments, which always end by making the situation worse than before.

Further, it is admitted even by indulgent critics that the scale of the invasion was much more extensive than it need have been. The Slovaks were accustomed to Hungarian methods, which were often slap-dash and left much undone, but worked, at least, with a great economy of personnel. The Czechs had been through a very different training. In the latter years of the Austrian Empire, the possession by a given nationality of any post in the Government service, however small, had become a precious political objective, for which the parties struggled with extraordinary tenacity. This system was imported into Slovakia, and even posts of complete unimportance, which could perfectly well have been filled by Slovaks—often, indeed, far better by Slovaks than by Czechs, when the post was one involving constant intercourse with the public—were yet allotted, for purely party reasons, to Czechs from some remote corner of Bohemia. As, moreover, the Czech scale of administration is far more extensive than the Hungarian, the new bureaucracy would have appeared to the Slovak taxpayers redundant even if their own men had been filling it; far more so, when the beneficiaries of the system were mainly 'outsiders'. And the influx was really considerable. In 1910 only 7,468 persons of Czech mother tongue had been counted in the territory of the present Slovakia. In 1921 this figure had risen to 71,733, and in 1930 to 120,926, a considerable proportion of whom were engaged in Government service.[1]

This was a far less important factor in the situation in the early days, when there were not many Slovaks who could possibly have aspired to the civil service. In the first year or two there was, indeed, a shortage of candidates even for those posts which were vacant. The few possible applicants preferred easier, if more speculative livelihoods. Soon, however, the position became quite different. A large number of students passed through the High Schools and qualified for Government employment; and in an age in which unemployment was rife the thoughts of most of them turned longingly to the safe haven of a State career. But the vacancies had been filled—and filled with persons whom they regarded as foreigners: and discontent waxed high at what was regarded as exploitation.

But, apart from this, neither the policy of Prague nor the attitude of the Czech officials in Slovakia was always either wise or tactful. Much harm was done in the beginning by a certain section of the legionaries, who formed a large contingent of the troops which then occupied Slovakia. The exploits of the legionaries have achieved in Czechoslovakia the proportions of a heroic saga; and many of the men concerned were very fine. There was, however, a section among them that was neither the most orderly nor the most desirable material. Deserters from the old Austrian army, they had passed through a rough schooling in Russia before returning to Europe. Their nationalist enthusiasms, their extreme social ideas, their deep-rooted Hussitism had all been strengthened by their experiences. They returned to find themselves fêted in Prague as the pillars of Czech society. They marched into Slovakia determined to stand no nonsense either from Magyars or from Slovak

[1] Of the 120,926 Czechs of 1930, 20,652 were military. Of the remainder 49,094 were gainfully employed, 19,524 of whom were employed in the public services, making over 40,000 persons dependent on those services (counting families).

Magyarones who were no better than Magyars. And from the
latter, indeed, they stood no nonsense, and left behind them a
heritage of bitterness not mitigated by the fact that they were
soundly thrashed by the former.

The Czech officials were less rough-hewn than the legionaries,
but something of the same aroma clung about them. It soon appeared that the profound differences between Czech and Slovak
national mentality were no mere invention of the Magyars. Above
all, the Czech Socialists, who played such a large part in the
Government of the first years, incorporated all those Czech characteristics most obnoxious to the Slovaks. They were crude, they
were ill mannered, they were aggressively egalitarian, and they were
almost fanatically anti-clerical, seeing in the Churches in Slovakia
a twofold enemy, social and national. A great many very unfortunate mistakes were undeniably made, particularly during the
first years, and especially in connexion with religious affairs.

In the struggle that went on for several years between Prague
and the Vatican—culminating in the painful incident of 1926 when
the Papal Nuncio left Prague as a protest against the official
celebrations in favour of Jan Hus—Slovak sympathies were almost
entirely on the side of the Holy See. They were deeply alienated
by a number of acts committed by the Czech authorities: the
assumption of State control over the Catholic gymnasia, the
gradual replacement of the Confessional primary schools by State
establishments, the restriction of religious instruction, the novelties
introduced into the curricula—there can be no doubt that in many
cases children were taught in the schools doctrines which, whatever their merits or accuracy, were deeply repugnant to the
children's parents and to the traditional Slovak spirit—the seizure
or arbitrary administration of Church lands, the order making
clergy liable for military service, the propaganda made, with official
support, in favour of the newly established 'Czechoslovak Church.'

In a more general way, the Czechs have done much to arouse the
resentment even of Slovaks naturally favourable towards them,
and have grievously damaged their own cause, by overstressing the
'Czechoslovak' idea, and by certain measures regarded by the
Slovaks as attempts to deprive them of their own nationality. It is
paradoxical, but natural, that the weakness of the foundations on
which the 'Czechoslovak' idea rested became most apparent the
moment that the idea received official recognition. Such phrases
as 'Czechoslovak nationality' and 'Czechoslovak language' might
be used for the benefit of the outside world, and in constitutional
and other State documents, but the fact remains that to the vast
majority of both peoples the idea remained a pure fiction, and the
languages, like the peoples, were, in solid fact, two and not one.

The practical solution was to use both languages on an equal footing in matters of common concern, while giving Czech priority in the western half of the Republic and Slovak in the east. In fact, however, Czech was employed almost exclusively in common affairs, and exclusively in Bohemia, and a great many of the Czech officials and teachers in Slovakia thought that the problem of the existing duality could most easily be solved by eliminating Slovak as a literary language altogether. Much of the teaching in the new schools, up to and including the University, was carried out in Czech, not all the teachers troubling to make themselves acquainted with the language of their pupils. Much resentment was aroused by the methods in this respect of the Czech professors at Bratislava University, who should, it was felt, have taken the lead in fostering and developing the Slovak national language and culture, whereas they worked actively, on the contrary, to destroy it. Similarly, a group of Czechs and extreme centralist Slovaks gained control for a time of the 'linguistic committee' in the resuscitated 'Matice Slovenska', which was designed to form the centre of Slovak national life and had in fact secured the united co-operation of nearly all groups of Slovaks—Catholics, Protestants, and even Jews. The Czechophils worked industriously to reverse the decision of eighty years previously, and to secure acceptance of the West Slovak dialect as the literary language of Slovakia. A climax was reached in 1932, when a new Slovak grammar, drawn up by Czechs with this end in view, was presented to the Matice. Protests poured in from nearly all the leading figures in Slovak literature, journalism, and cultural life; the Czechophils were ousted from the committees, and a new and purely Slovak body entrusted with preparing a different and more acceptable grammar. A similar revolt has been in progress for some years against the Czech teaching in the schools and universities.

Finally, the economic history of Slovakia, especially in the first years, confirmed only too exactly the dismal prophecies which the Hungarian delegates had made. It is true that Hungary had done her best to make it so. The Hungarian Red Army, when it retired from Slovakia in the summer of 1919, either destroyed or carried off a large amount of machinery and other equipment. For this the Czechs could not fairly be blamed; at the same time, it set many Slovaks reflecting very early that the economic price of their liberation was likely to prove higher than they expected. Another circumstance arising directly out of the War caused very deep ill feeling. Hungary had suffered far less than Austria during the War from privations due to army requisitioning and the Allied blockade. Indeed, she had increasingly husbanded her own resources and let her sister kingdom stew in her own juice. In 1918 food was comparatively plentiful in Slovakia, when Bohemia was on the verge of starvation. The new frontier at once cut Slovakia off from her normal and traditional source of supplies, and threw down the barrier which had sheltered her from the impoverished west. During the first few weeks the Historic Lands drew on Slovak resources with a thoroughness which gravely increased the distress among the local population, and left an impression which the later efforts of the Czech authorities to send in supplies quite failed to efface.

But far more durable were the difficulties arising out of the necessity, which soon became apparent, of reorganizing afresh the entire economic life of the country. Agriculture was, at first, comparatively prosperous, since the depreciation of the currency had freed the landowners, big and small, from much of the burden of their indebtedness, while the prospect of receiving land under the agrarian reform kept the small-holders in good humour. The labourers, on the other hand, who, as we said, formed a large class of the agricultural population, began to suffer immediately from the impassable barrier now erected between them and their former harvest work in the plains. The efforts made by the Government to find alternative harvest labour, although sustained, were only partially successful. Thanks to the generous frontier-line adopted, a fair number of labourers could find work in the plains of Slovakia itself; but outlets in foreign countries proved hard to find.[1] One result was a renewed rush of emigration to the U.S.A., which continued until the Immigration Restriction Acts restricted this outlet also. Even after that date, the number of emigrants per 10,000 inhabitants continued to be some five times as high for Slovakia as for the Historic Lands.

Industry suffered more immediately and more severely. The industry of Northern Hungary had, as has been said, been deliberately fostered by the Hungarian Government in execution of its programme of national autarky. Its proximity to the Budapest market gave it great natural advantages in this respect; but, even so, much of it had still to consolidate its position by 1918, and could hardly have maintained itself without the special protection and help which it received. The Krompachy ironworks, large and important as they were, had never actually paid their way. A corollary of this position was that much of the Slovak industry was under-capitalized for normal conditions. In certain respects it was, also, still somewhat primitive; some of the blast furnaces, for example, were still fuelled with charcoal instead of coke.

The situation changed entirely when the frontiers were altered. The natural advantages enjoyed by most of the establishments

[1] See Table opposite.

PLACING OF AGRICULTURAL LABOUR FROM SLOVAKIA
1919–1934

The following figures were kindly supplied to me by the Labour Exchange for Agricultural Workers, Bratislava.

Year.	Seasonal Workers.									Single Labourers.			Total.
	Slovakia.	Bohemia.	Moravia.	Silesia.	Austria.	France.	Germany.	Yugo-slavia.	Latvia.	Bohemia.	Moravia.	Silesia.	
1919	36,823	2,274	7,354	106	4,104			585					51,246
1920	58,386	3,468	7,410	694	4,371								74,329
1921	52,936	3,346	7,200	895	5,916		8,466						78,759
1922	36,175	4,018	5,751	831	5,487		4,045	1,855					58,162
1923	32,587	5,249	4,707	869	5,653	3,137		187					52,389
1924	36,535	6,525	4,863	1,009	7,300	5,634	155			343	10	8	62,383
1925	38,262	7,393	5,532	932	9,431	2,524	1,607			874	24	36	66,615
1926	31,162	10,303	5,347	1,011	10,387	1,505	1,603			935	56	12	62,321
1927	29,876	10,607	5,013	995	10,859	392	1,836			594	59	12	60,242
1928	25,156	10,755	4,954	1,196	11,601	1,194	3,807		26	758	107	1	59,566
1929	23,993	12,151	6,433		12,730	3,218	4,119			702	82		63,429
1930	20,943	12,923	6,604		13,832	5,930	5,257			629	70		66,188
1931	19,434	10,451	5,544		14,483	2,192	2,180			686	71		55,031
1932	12,977	9,046	4,084		11,931	1,186				973	136		40,333
1933	10,756	8,302	3,182		7,284	1,763				1,505	154		32,946
1934	11,389	7,445	2,719		5,059	1,471				1,695	110		29,888
Total	477,390	124,257	86,697	8,538	140,428	30,136	33,075	2,627	26	9,694	879	80	913,827

K

applied only when they were working for the Budapest market. For serving the Historic Lands, or for exporting to the west, they were extremely badly placed. The waterways could not be used for this purpose, while the Hungarian railway system, both by nature and design, centred on Budapest. Only one important railway in Slovakia ran east and west; and, in any case, freights were bound to be high when the railways had not only to traverse long distances but to wind through intricate valleys and climb forbidding ridges. On top of this came the circumstance that the Slovak railways were of old construction, with out-of-date rolling stock and bad permanent way; and nearly half of them were in private hands. The freightage normally charged on them was 30 per cent. higher for light traffic, and 50 per cent. higher for heavy traffic, than in the Historic Lands. The State was anxious to unify tariffs throughout the Republic, but the owners of the private companies vigorously resisted expropriation, and the unification could not be begun until 1920, and was not completed until November 1st, 1932. Even then the result was very unsatisfactory to the Slovaks, who have not ceased to complain of the meagre concessions allowed on the long distances which Slovak materials have to travel.

In this difficult situation, the Slovak industry had to face the competition of the great and old-established Bohemian and Silesian concerns. The richer firms bought up, or obtained control through holding-banks (notably the Živnostenská Banka) over, the greater part of the Slovak establishments. The latter were thus left at the mercy of the owners in the Historic Lands, who worked them or closed them down as they pleased. Probably nearly one-third of all the Slovak industries disappeared in this way during the immediate post-War period, the heavy industries and textile factories being chiefly affected. The production of iron-ore, after reaching a maximum output of about 1,300,000 tons in 1917, during the War (an abnormal year, of course), sank to 487,132 tons in 1919. It then recovered to some extent, but never reached its pre-War figure, and the last of the eight important Slovak blast-furnaces was blown out in 1931. The metallurgical industry which depended on the local ores declined disastrously. The Krompachy works were closed down in 1922; those in Zvolen in 1924; those in Trnava (Tyrnau, Nagy-Szombat) reduced production radically. The Podrežova works were taken over by the State, which, however, worked them at a loss. The textile factories, which were much farther than those of the west both from their overseas supplies of raw materials and from the chemicals of Germany, were hardly less severely hit. Breweries, fairly numerous before the War, were quite unable to stand up to the competition of Pilsen, and the glass-works to that of the old Bohemian firms. In Lučenec, near the frontier, only a single factory remained working out of thirteen, many old and important concerns, such as the enamel-works, which formerly employed 900 workers, having to close down.

Slovakian industry undoubtedly did not receive from the Czecho-slovak Government the help which it urgently needed to carry it over this difficult period. On the contrary, it was placed in many respects under quite unnecessary disadvantages. Until taxation was unified throughout the Republic (which was not until 1929) it was much more heavily taxed in many respects than the Historic Lands. The tax on earnings, as imposed by the old Hungarian kingdom and maintained unaltered for ten years, was 10 per cent. in Slovakia, while in Bohemia it was only 3 per cent.; the tax on alcohol was 23 per cent. per hectolitre in Slovakia, 10 per cent. in Bohemia. The rates paid by professional and business men were, on an average, three times as high in Slovakia as in Bohemia.

In other respects, also, there were many complaints that the Czechs were using their superior economic and political strength to place the Slovaks at an economic disadvantage. It is an old and widely voiced complaint that Slovakia has received much below her fair share of Government orders, particularly, although not only, during the first years. Thus in 1924, when the Ministry of Defence gave out orders for 1,314,000,000 Czech crowns, Slovakia got only 49,819,500 (3·78 per cent.) of these; in 1925, 61,000,000 (6·45 per cent.) out of 935,000,000. According to its ratio of taxation (if that is really any criterion), it should have received 15–18 per cent.; the general average of orders seems to have been about 5 per cent. A special concession was established in 1923, by which Slovak enterprises were to receive prior consideration for State contracts if their tenders were anything up to 5 per cent. above those of their competitors in the Historic Lands (the qualities being equal). This did not, however, show any great results.

The question of officials, again, had a very big economic aspect, since it meant that the Slovaks were taxed to provide Czechs with incomes. Even in the agrarian reform, a number of the colonists, who were easily the chief beneficiaries of the process, were Czechs.

At the same time it was clear that Slovakia needed much more to be done for her than before; for under the Hungarian régime many services, e.g. specialist hospital facilities or higher educational establishments, had quite legitimately been concentrated in near-by Budapest. Obviously Prague could not fulfil the same role, and a very large amount of expenditure was needed to create adequate local institutions in Slovakia itself.

Thus, one way and another, the first years of the union brought about many economic difficulties, which fed the resentment occasioned by political maladjustments.

§ 7. THE SLOVAK QUESTION SINCE THE WAR (3)

The partial decentralization ushered in by the Act of July 14th, 1927, did not put an end to the differences between Czechs and Slovaks. Indeed, the actual intervening period between the passage of that Act and its coming into force was marked by the most serious crisis in all the relations since the War between the two peoples. The atmosphere had already been heated by Lord Rothermere's abrupt assumption in the summer of 1927 of the Hungarian cause, and the consequent revival of Hungary's hopes of revision. On January 1st, 1928, M. Tuka, then Vice-President of the Slovak People's Party, published in the party organ an article entitled 'Vacuum Juris', in which he argued that the Declaration of Turčiansky Svätý Martin contained a secret clause limiting to ten years the operation of the union effected in virtue of the Declaration. After that period, the Slovaks would be free to reconsider their position.

No official action was at first taken, but a Slovak advocate, Dr. Ivanka, published a pamphlet accusing Tuka of being a traitor in the service of Hungary. Tuka did not answer the charges, and Ivanka then brought an action against him in his own name. The authorities gradually decided to move. In the following winter Tuka's Parliamentary immunity was suspended; in January 1929 he was arrested, with the secretary of the party and a third person. In the summer they were tried, and Tuka was eventually convicted of espionage, communicating military secrets to a foreign power, planning the separation of Slovakia from the Republic, and forming armed bands for the purpose. He was sentenced to fifteen years' imprisonment. The actual evidence was flimsy, and the charges were hardly proved so thoroughly as to justify the savage sentence, but it was made reasonably clear that Tuka had been in receipt of foreign funds. The whole trial was, however, singularly unedifying, and the defendant was not the only person to emerge from it with grievously damaged credit. Czecho-Slovak relations were deeply poisoned. The People's Party refused to disavow Tuka, even after his conviction. On the contrary, it took up and repeated in its Press, with the utmost virulence, all the most vehement accusations which he had launched against the Czechs. Thus anti-Czech feeling was intensified, while the Czechs were no less estranged by the attitude of the Slovaks.

Yet, once the first excitement was past, the trial cleared the air. General elections were held again shortly after Tuka's condemnation, and the People's Party lost five seats and a very substantial number of votes. They withdrew, indeed, into opposition once more, but for the time, at least, they seemed to enjoy less popular support than before for their policy, and Czecho-Slovak relations began once more gradually to improve.

In political and cultural questions, at least, a great change has come about in the last few years, and many of the grievances described in earlier pages have been removed or at least attenuated. The decentralization of 1927/8 was a step forward, even though it did not mean that Prague had relinquished the real control of any important question. In what is really the central question, the attempt to 'Czechize' the Slovaks and their language has been practically abandoned. The official language of the State is still described as 'Czechoslovak', but in practice Slovak counts as the official language in Slovakia, while Czech holds that position in the Historic Lands. Czech officials stationed in Slovakia learn and use Slovak. No attempt whatever is made to restrict the use of Slovak in non-official use. Education is growing more and more genuinely Slovak, both as regards the language of instruction and the spirit. From this point of view, at any rate, it is fortunate that extreme left-wing influences have lost so much of their weight in Prague. The general political atmosphere of Czechoslovakia, and indeed of Central Europe as a whole, is much less alien to the Slovak mind to-day than it was in 1919.

In practice, too, the vexed question of officials is progressing towards a solution. The journey is a tedious one, since reasons of humanity and justice, as well as policy, have prevented the dismissal of the Czech officials who took service in 1919 in Slovakia. Hitherto room has been found for the Slovaks chiefly at the expense of the national minorities, but in practice to-day vacancies are nearly always filled by Slovaks. The following figures,[1] which are of interest also as showing the position of the minorities, give an idea of how the situation has developed.

Administrative Services

	1921		1930	
	Number.	Per cent.	Number.	Per cent.
Czechs	8,654	39·4	9,874	41·3
Slovaks	8,258	37·5	11,363	47·5
Magyars	3,661	16·7	1,486	6·2
Germans	860	3·9	642	2·7
Ruthenes	92	0·4	118	0·5
Jews	215	0·9	65	0·3
Others	26	0·1	25	0·1
Foreign subjects	220	1·1	338	1·4
	21,986	100	23,911	100

[1] These figures are taken from a study by Dr. A. Boháč, *Statistický Obzor*, 1935, nos. 4–5, pp. 183–90.

The population of Slovak employees has probably increased considerably since the 1930 figures. It is a question whether it will not again be adversely affected by the promises made to the minorities in 1937.

Railways

(a) Railway Clerks, &c.

	1921		1930		1935[1]
	Number.	Per cent.	Number.	Per cent.	Number.
Czechs	3,042	50·6	2,916	50·5	6,384
Slovaks	1,903	31·6	2,436	42·2	14,562
Magyars	622	10·3	164	2·8	248
Germans	304	5·1	192	3·3	1,362
Others .	150	2·4	66	1·2	..
	6,021	100	5,774	100	

(b) Railway Labourers, &c.

	Number.	Per cent.	Number.	Per cent.
Czechs	2,694	11·5	2,356	11·4
Slovaks	16,802	71·6	16,302	79·2
Magyars	2,853	12·2	1,370	6·7
Germans	543	2·3	309	1·5
Others .	581	2·4	266	1·2
	23,473	100	20,603	100

Postal Employees

	Number.	Per cent.	Number.	Per cent.	Number.
Czechs	1,788	33·4	1,980	29·3	1,161
Slovaks	2,623	49·0	4,321	63·9	3,274
Magyars	686	12·8	295	4·4	251
Germans	148	2·8	108	1·6	61
Others .	105	2·0	57	0·8	..
	5,350	100	6,761	100	

Total services and free professions

	Number.	Per cent.	Number.	Per cent.
Czechs	18,815	23·1	21,828	22·9
Slovaks	39,622	48·6	54,555	57·2
Magyars	14,876	18·3	9,868	10·3
Germans	3,762	4·6	4,183	4·4
Others .	4,472	5·4	4,926	5·2
	81,447	100	95,360	100

In 1935 the more important political, &c., positions were filled as follows:

	Czechs.	Slovaks.	Magyars.	Germans.	Ruthenes.
Heads of districts	13	62·	..	1	1
Communal notaries	40	1,002	151	24	17
Local administration .	1,581	3,191	267	82	61
Magistrature	225	147	79	55	47
Sub-magistrates .	40	89	9	2	14
Magistrate's clerks, &c.	355	836	100	..	86

[1] The figures for 1935 are taken as a whole and cover both (a) and (b) under the heading *Railways*.

Most important of all is the striking success achieved by the Czechs in making their peace with the Holy See. The first important step forward was the conclusion of the 'modus vivendi' of February 2nd, 1928.[1] This very important document laid down the principle that no part of the Czechoslovak Republic should thereafter be subject to an 'Ordinarius' whose seat lay outside the frontiers of the Republic, nor should Orders and Congregations whose houses were situated in the Republic be subject to such of their provincials as were in foreign countries. Before nominating archbishops, bishops, &c., the Holy See agreed to intimate the name of the candidate to the Government, so that the latter might assure itself whether there was any political objection to him; on appointment, the dignitary should take an oath of loyalty to the Czechoslovak State. Other provisions dealt with the administration of Church property pending the re-delimitation of dioceses provided for above.

By this agreement, Czechoslovakia was for the first time enabled to put up a successful resistance to Magyar and Polish influence exercised through the Catholic Church; while the Vatican benefited by the gradual relaxation of the anti-clerical legislation which had marked the early years of the Republic. Relations between the two contracting parties continued thereafter slowly to improve. The Franciscans and the Barmherzige Brüder of Slovakia (although not the Jesuits or the Capucins) formed single Conventions with the corresponding Orders in Prague. The 'Catholic Day' held in Prague in July 1935 was another landmark, the significance of which was emphasized, a few months later, by the great activity shown by the representatives of the Holy See in supporting Dr. Beneš's candidature to the Presidency of the Republic.

§ 8. POLITICAL FEELING AMONG THE SLOVAKS

The central political fact which emerges from the consideration of this history is the definite and, for the purposes of our present age, final crystallization of a Slovak national consciousness. On the one hand, there is no longer any danger—or hope—that the Slovaks will merge their nationality in that of the Magyars. The older generation still numbers many who, faced with the decisive question in 1918, felt old political loyalties to be more compelling than new national ones. Sometimes their children feel as they. But such families should be counted as Magyars, with recognition of the

[1] See the chapter: 'The Modus Vivendi with the Holy See, and its effects', by Monsignor Bishop Karel Kmeťko, in *Slovakia Then and Now*, pp. 183–90.

fact that centuries of common history have so intermingled the two stocks as to make analysis along 'racial' lines a hopeless task (there are also good Slovaks with Magyar names). But, the great sorting-out once accomplished, there has been an end to the gradual submergence which was so far advanced in 1918.

No less certain, in the writer's opinion, is the bankruptcy of the extreme 'Czechoslovak' idea. The genuine and uncompromising believers in a single, indivisible Czechoslovak language and people were certainly never so large, at least in Slovakia, as they were made to appear. To-day they have dwindled to a mere handful, under the influence of actual experience of the considerable differences which exist between Czechs and Slovaks. In the Historic Lands the partisans of the theory are probably stronger (while, of course, the great mass of the ignorant accept the official view without further thought); but the very enthusiasm with which these zealots have attempted to impose their views in Slovakia has defeated its own object.

In effect, the battle of the hyphen, which was joined with such *élan* on both sides,[1] has ended with a nominal win for the Czecho-slovaks, but a real, decisive, and permanent victory for the Slovaks. We have already mentioned the literary revolt against the attempt to impose upon the Slovaks a language which they did not recog-nize as their own. There are some who believe that this revolt itself carried the pendulum too far; that it will swing back, and the two languages, in the course, maybe, of a couple of generations, will imperceptibly assimilate. It seems, however, more likely that Slovak has now passed beyond the indeterminate and malleable stage, and has definitely established itself as an adult, individual language. At present it is, in practice, recognized by the Czechs themselves as the official language of Slovakia. The political and national resistance has been no less tenacious, and to-day the name of 'Czechoslovak' is practically confined to official documents and to literature issued for the benefit of foreigners. During many weeks in the country, I only remember hearing one person use the term of herself; this was a half-German, half-Hungarian girl, who used it in a purely political sense, meaning that she thought irredentism futile. No Czech and no Slovak feels or calls himself, when speaking naturally, anything but a Czech or a Slovak as the case may be.

The development of political opinion is not quite so clear. The cardinal question to be decided is whether political attachment to Hungary has diminished with the decrease of the trend towards national assimilation; and how far, even if a Czechoslovak *nationality*

---

[1] i.e. the question whether the name of the new State should be written as 'Czechoslovak' or as 'Czecho-Slovak',

has failed to establish itself, a Czechoslovak *political* loyalty has managed to take root. It is not easy to deliver a true verdict, owing to the multiplicity of witnesses and the great variety of their testimony. The official accounts, which include the vast bulk of the material available on the subject in English, naturally paint the situation between Czechs and Slovaks in the rosiest colours, denying explicitly, or, more frequently still, by the implication of their omissions, the very existence of any discontent. On the other hand, a survey of the Slovak press (assigning their due value to the numerous white spaces left at the request of the censor) or a few personal interviews with local politicians, either Magyar or Slovak, would probably lead the inquirer, at the end of the first day or so of his investigations, to the conclusion that the whole country was smarting under an intolerable tyranny and eagerly awaiting the day to throw it off.

Caution is needed in either case. On the one hand, the Czechs are past masters in the art of propaganda, which they carry out with infinitely greater skill than the Serbs or the Roumanians, never perpetrating crude falsehoods, as the latter do, never denying flatly the existence of some inconvenient fact which protrudes itself under the traveller's nose, but subtly influencing him by persuasion, suggestion, and that highest art which conceals so much art. It is, however, equally easy to be misled by the intemperate violence of the opposition. The Slovaks, like the Croats and the Magyars themselves, have breathed for generations an atmosphere of what is locally and expressively known as 'Gravaminalpolitik'— a policy of grievances. Opposition has become second nature to them, and if they did not keep up a good running fire of complaints they would be no true politicians in their own eyes or those of their constituents. But who shall be the target of their darts? The local minorities are poor devils struggling for their own existence, while the Czechs are the *beati possidentes* of to-day. It is they who rule the country, dictate policy, fix the railway tariffs, man the administration, collect the taxes. They are the natural butt for attacks, the acerbity of which must not always be taken at its full face value.

Finally, it is important to note that feeling varies very greatly in different parts of Slovakia. The central valleys round Ružomberok and Turčiansky Svätý Martin are traditional strongholds of Slovak nationalism, and as such threw off most easily the Magyar influences. The west is comparatively prosperous under the new conditions and is establishing economic contacts with the Historic Lands. The east was Magyarized far more thoroughly before the War, and has suffered far more grievously from the economic effects of the change-over. Here Magyar sympathies have lingered on

much more tenaciously. Thus the whole process of gradual transformation which we shall describe can only be taken as complete,
perhaps, in the centre; as far advanced in the west; as comparatively embryonic in the east.

On a broad view, and averaging out sentiment through the
country, Magyar influence over the Slovaks, and Slovak sympathies
for Hungary, have beyond any doubt waned steadily during the past
eighteen years. The older generation, with its memories of what
was after all a comparatively peaceful and spacious existence, is
dying out. The young men who are growing up to-day take the
existence of Czechoslovakia for granted. They are no longer under
the influence of the Magyar landlords; the weight of the administrative system has long been thrown on the side of Czechoslovakia,
and even that of the Churches has now become, on balance, Czechoslovak rather than Magyar. Above all, the new educational system
is bearing its fruits. The younger Slovaks have received a purely
Slav education. Except in a few of the towns, they do not understand a word of Magyar. Hungarian history is represented to them
as a tale of unmitigated oppression of the Slavs by the Magyars,
the long record of co-operation between the two nations being
carefully glossed over, while the most possible is made of such
instances as the past can show of *rapprochement* between Czech
and Slovak. The Hungary of to-day is painted as a country of
tyrannical squireens, with which no one in his senses would have
any truck.

Moreover, if few of the Slovak intelligentsia have yet got posts
in the administration, they still enjoy a reasonable prospect that
this situation will improve; above all, they can hope to expand at
the expense of the local minorities. If Slovakia were returned to
Hungary, the most for which they could hope would be some
degree of autonomy for the purely Slovak districts. Hungary
would never extend Slovak autonomy to the Magyar districts of
what is now South Slovakia. And do the history of Hungary and
the Magyar character provide guarantees that that autonomy would
prove enduring?

In every respect the nation which is now, after all, the more
favourably situated of the two has no interest in seeing the positions
reversed, and the Slovaks of to-day are both less willing and less
able to take the way out of Magyarization.

This view of the diminution of Magyar influence and of Hungarian sympathies among the Slovaks is borne out by the electoral
figures. If we compare these figures with those of population, we
find, when allowance is made for the Communist vote, which is not
on a national basis, that the political alinement now corresponds
closely enough with the national. Some Slovaks, particularly in

mixed districts with a Magyar majority, certainly vote for Magyar candidates; rather more Magyars vote for Slovak or Czechoslovak parties, but the numbers are not large in either case. They would probably be more favourable still to the Slovaks if some of the returning officers taking the 1930 census had been less restrictive in their interpretation of what is a Magyar.

On the other hand, the strength of pro-Hungarian feeling is not to be gauged merely by the votes cast for the Magyar parties alone. It must be remembered that although the ballot in Slovakia is genuinely secret, and the elections conducted on quite another plane from that usual in Central Europe, yet there are very material advantages in being known or reputed to belong to one of the great parties in whose hands lie the distribution of favours so varied as a residual estate for oneself, a job in the post office for one's nephew, or a tobacco-kiosk for one's widowed aunt.

These desirable things can be obtained by support in particular of the Agrarians, who are the real masters of Slovakia, and are, moreover, promoting a policy which is in the direct material interest of most of the Magyar voters. A vote for a Magyar party (which will, inevitably, always be in the opposition) can never be anything more than a gesture—a declaration of national loyalty. It would be different if the issue of an election were the choice between Hungary or Czechoslovakia; but no election has ever been fought on that line, nor any plebiscite held. Furthermore, during the first years of the Republic in particular, there were large elements within the Slovak parties themselves whose sympathies lay with Hungary rather than with Czechoslovakia. In the first period, before elections were held, only the more nationalist trend of opinion was represented at all in Parliament, and it was frankly admitted on more than one occasion that to allow free expression of opinion in Slovakia would simply be unsafe for the future existence of the Republic. The Slovak People's Party, whose members are an extraordinarily heterogeneous collection, has undoubtedly always contained a strong Magyarophil element. At certain times, particularly during the early years of the Republic, these Magyarophils probably exercised the predominant influence in the party and might, given a favourable foreign political situation, have carried most of it clean over into the Hungarian camp. Father Jehlička, who, as recounted, accompanied Monsignor Hlinka to Paris in 1919 in the cause of Slovak autonomy, afterwards went over openly to the Hungarian cause, attacked the Czechs most violently by the written and the spoken word, and associated himself with Hungarian politicians when they toured Europe preaching revision. He now openly demanded the return of Slovakia to Hungary—not, indeed, under the old system, but with generous cultural autonomy for Slovakia; but, in any case, with severance of the political tie between Czechs and Slovaks. It is true that by this time he had long been dissociated from and disavowed by his party. Professor Tuka, however, who for several years occupied the most influential position, after Monsignor Hlinka himself, in the People's Party (in which he probably wielded more real influence than his chief), was not only virulently anti-Czech (the 'Žilina Memorandum' issued by the party, under his auspices, in 1922 attacked the Czechs as vigorously as any publication of the Hungarian Revision League) but also at heart almost certainly in favour of the restoration of Slovakia to Hungary. So much appeared plainly enough from his trial, even if the specific charges brought against him were none too satisfactorily proved. And even if many of his colleagues in the party did not share all his views, their refusal to disavow them showed that they were not profoundly shocked by them.

Since Tuka's condemnation, the People's Party seems to have acquired a certain belated sense of the value of discretion, and has not again given such a handle to its enemies as it did in 1929. While it still contains Magyarone elements, and notoriously still keeps regular, if cautious, touch with Budapest (besides a cautious pontoon more recently thrown out in the direction of Warsaw), its intrigues to-day should be regarded less as serious indications of separatist ambitions than as typical manifestations of peasant slyness—in fact, political blackmail on the Czechs. Father Hlinka himself has frequently and strongly repudiated any separatist ambitions. A very impressive incident occurred in December 1933. Father Jehlička had gone to England at the same time as the Hungarian statesmen, Count Bethlen and Dr. Eckhardt, who were pleading Hungary's cause in a series of speeches. Father Jehlička associated himself with these statesmen and their wishes, and in doing so claimed to be speaking in the name of the Slovak people; accrediting himself as the representative of the so-called Slovak Council of Geneva. All the Slovak Senators and Deputies in the Parliament of Prague, from all the Slovak parties except the Communists, then united to issue a joint declaration[1] in which they stated categorically that Father Jehlička possessed no mandate from any Slovak party, corporation, or cultural association and had no right to speak in the name of the Slovak people. The Geneva 'Council' was, they said, a mere instrument of Magyar revisionist propaganda, directed and financed from Budapest and serving

---

[1] The text of this may be found in Seton-Watson, *Treaty Revision and the Hungarian Frontiers* (London, 1934), pp. 22–4, and at the end of Beneš's 'Discours aux Slovaques sur le présent et l'avenir de notre nation' (*Le Monde slave*, March 1934); *not* in the *Daily Mail*, which had printed Father Jehlička's writings (cf. Seton-Watson, op. cit., p. 75).

Hungarian and not Slovak ends. Slovakia had left Hungary and joined Czechoslovakia of her free will, and, if she had her difficulties, she would resolve these herself in the framework of the Czechoslovak State. She would energetically and resolutely oppose any attempt to force her to return to Hungary and was 'irreconcilable to any policy which wishes to destroy the Czechoslovak Republic and thus to plunge the Slovak nation again into its ancient dependency and its ancient slavery'.

The Slovak autonomists have more than once been willing to enter the Czechoslovak Government, while they have on no single occasion formed a firm Parliamentary coalition with the parties of the national minorities.[1] Such minor and local agreements as have been reached have usually been between the minorities and the Centralist parties, notably the Social Democrats, who possess a Magyar and a German faction in Slovakia, and the Agrarians. The attitude which we have described does not apply only to the broad question of Slovak-Magyar relations. On the point of local frontier revision, also, the Slovaks are more intransigent than the Czechs themselves. There is reason to believe that some very highly-placed Czechs would have been willing to consider the return to Hungary of the Žitny Ostrava: it was opposition from Slovakia which made this impossible. Slovaks in general regard every inch of Slovakia to-day as holy ground;[2] and among the most chauvinistic—I use the word deliberately—are the Slovak so-called Socialists. The Communists themselves, although true in theory to their principles, wilt at the prospect of revision, since their position in Czechoslovakia is far more secure than it would be in Hungary. Thus it seems safe to say that a substantial majority of Slovak opinion is to-day opposed to the idea of a return to Hungary.

It follows from this that most of the Slovaks regard the relationship between Slovakia and the Czechoslovak State as settled, in the broad sense that they propose to continue in the future to remain part of that State.

The exact position of Slovakia within the State, and the relation-

[1] Monsignor Hlinka said to me that he would like to do this but it would 'split the party'. Protracted negotiations went on in 1930, but they were admittedly begun on the initiative of the Magyars, who found the Slovaks 'very difficult and hesitating'; and in the end they came to naught. In 1925 some of the Magyar Christian Socials voted for the Slovak People's Party; but after Tuka's fall they revised their hopes and their policy.

[2] In one of his speeches Hlinka regretted publicly that 'there were persons in high places in Czechoslovakia who did not hesitate to speak of revision and rectification of frontiers'. He declared solemnly that 'no one might touch the frontiers of Slovakia without the consent of the Slovaks, and that the Slovaks would never allow the smallest strip of land to be separated from Slovakia'. (*Pester Lloyd*, October 22nd, 1930, quoting the *Slovak* (Hlinka's organ).)

ship between the Slovaks and the Czechs, are more debatable questions.

The usual division of parties and of public opinion is into 'centralists' and 'autonomists'. These terms are roughly, but not exactly, true. They need particularly to be qualified in the case of the centralists. As a large number of the so-called autonomists were probably separatists at heart during the first years, but have now become more or less reconciled to the State, so the 'centralists' in their turn have shed their extreme wing. There are hardly any of them now who either wish for the submergence of the Slovak nationality or believe it to be possible. Indeed, most of the centralists are as good Slovaks at heart as the autonomists. There are, of course, differences in the degree of national feeling. The one party is more conscious of what the Slovaks have in common with the Czechs, the other more keenly aware of the divergences. Even to-day the old distinction largely holds good, and the Protestants are much more generally centralist, the Catholics autonomist. But, in the main, the difference is much rather one of method and of tactics than of ultimate aim. The autonomists are intensely conservative, and strongly subject to local influences. With the utmost sympathy for their feelings, and full recognition of the many mistakes which the Czechs have made, one must still describe their attitude as rather parochial, and rather unrealistic. They are 'Gravaminalpolitiker' through and through, obsessed to-day by the grievances inflicted upon them by the Czechs, as twenty years ago they were in eternal opposition to the Magyars. They spend an inordinate proportion of their energies in reiterating the rights which they claim to possess under those two ill-fated documents, the Pittsburgh Agreement and the Declaration of Turčiansky Svätý Martin. They have undoubtedly a strong moral case under both, even if the letter of the law may be on the side of the Czechs; it is difficult not to believe that impressions were given—perhaps deliberately given—which led to natural hopes which were afterwards disappointed. It is often more annoying to feel that one has been cheated, and to be unable to prove it, than it is to be treated with more open cynicism.

But the constructive policy of the autonomists is far less convincing. Their only remedy for their grievances is to withdraw into their own little world, and to slam and barricade the door against all outsiders. They express their ambitions in the simple formula *suum cuique*. Let the Czechs keep out of Slovakia and they in their turn will not trouble the Historic Lands. The concrete form which their demands take is for at least a Ministry in Bratislava, with full control of the internal administration of Slovakia and the exclusive power of appointing officials. Sometimes they seem to want a separate legislature.[1] At any rate, they ask for wide autonomy in cultural, religious, and linguistic questions, and for all government posts in Slovakia to be reserved for Slovaks.

It is a programme which, looked at in one light, is curiously unambitious, since it necessarily involves renouncing for the Slovaks the opportunities of a far wider and richer existence which a closer participation in the general life of the Republic would afford. One must, however, admit that, as the weaker partner in the Republic, Slovakia has needed a good deal of protection, and that the stronger brother has sometimes used the opportunity given by the centralist régime rather to exploit than to help. Moreover, whether from traditionalism or whatever the reason, the Slovaks have in fact hitherto made little use of what opportunities they have been offered.[2] Also, whatever the legal validity of the famous Pittsburgh Agreement and similar instruments, the Slovaks were certainly given to understand in 1918 that if they wanted autonomy they would have it.

By contrast, the autonomist programme is almost arrogant in its assumption that Slovak nationalism is strong enough—and would have been strong enough at any time since 1918—to hold its own against the national minorities and the Magyarones in its own ranks. 'There is no danger any more', said one of their leaders to me, with sublime confidence.[3]

For the autonomists, so far as I understand them, mean their autonomy to apply to the whole of Slovakia, including the minority districts. One of the objections raised from the other side is that, if the Slovaks were to be given Slovakia as their own preserve, the Germans of the Historic Lands could claim the same status in their own area of settlement, and even the Magyars in Southern Slovakia would have to receive a similar concession.[4] It is difficult to decide whether this argument is advanced seriously, or only to frighten the Slovaks. Certainly the prospect of such a system would in no way allure them.

The centralists are much more realistic. As we have said, the vast majority are just as good Slovaks at heart as the autonomists. The real difference lies, perhaps, less in their estimate of the

[1] Cf. the interview given by Monsignor Hlinka to the *Montag*, summarized in the *Journal des nations*, December 12th, 1935.
[2] In spite of the far higher Slovak birth-rate and the difference in the standards of living, there are many fewer Slovaks in the Historic Lands to-day than Czechs in Slovakia.
[3] It appears, however, that Hlinka himself at one time admitted to Masaryk that 'he wanted autonomy, but not yet, only when the Slovaks had become politically ripe for it' (*Reichspost*, February 28th, 1930).
[4] Cf. Beneš, 'Discours aux Slovaques sur le présent et l'avenir de notre nation', p. 49.

Czechs than in their estimate of the Magyars. It was because they feared above all other things that Slovakia without the Czechs would revert to Hungary that they welcomed the Czech teachers, officials, and soldiers. Many of them would be glad to see Slovakia enjoy, at least cultural autonomy, as soon as the Hungarian danger is definitely banished; but until they are certain of this—and they are not yet fully reassured—they resist autonomy more vigorously than the Czechs themselves (many of whom would be glad to let the Slovaks have what they want and be done with it). But, besides this, they feel that Slovakia is too weak in every way, and particularly in her economic position, to stand alone. In spite of the difficulties which have occurred, they still believe that the Slovaks would on the whole lose more than they would gain by cutting themselves off from the wider opportunities and higher standard of living of the Historic Lands. They count on the genuine sensitiveness of the Czechs to criticism of their Slovak policy, and on their real desire and need to meet the Slovaks' wishes, to secure ultimately a position in the Republic at least equal to that to which their natural resources seem to entitle them. And even if in some respects they have hitherto got less from the Czechs than they hoped, it is still, they believe, more than they would have obtained from the Magyars.

It is not easy to judge which of the two tendencies is gaining ground among the Slovaks. If we take the party figures given on p. 118, we may reckon as Czechoslovak Centralist parties those numbered 1, 2, 3, 5, 6, 10, 13, 14, 17, 18, 19, and 20. The totals of votes given for these in 1925, 1929, and 1935 respectively (1920 may be treated as abnormal) were, in round figures, 449,000, 588,000, and 659,000. From the last figure, some 40,000 should be deducted for the Jewish vote, and from each of the three perhaps 20,000 for the Magyar peasant vote. The local Czech vote also naturally goes to the centralist parties; 35,000 might be deducted from the 1925 figure, 45,000 from that of 1929, and 50,000 from that of 1935. This would give, for our three figures, 394,000, 523,000, and 549,000, a substantial and regular rise, while the Autonomist vote has remained practically stationary (496,000 in 1925, 409,000 in 1929, 490,000 in 1935). The Communist Party can hardly be called centralist, but it is certainly anti-autonomist.

A gradual advance of centralist feeling is what would naturally be anticipated from the political evolution which we have sketched, with its slow diminution of the important initial grievances. There have been occasions on which the battle seemed as good as won. In 1935 the Slovak People's Party voted solidly for the election of Dr. Beneš to the Presidency of the Republic; and with a President who enjoyed the confidence of the Slovak autonomists, and a Slovak centralist, in the person of Dr. Hodža, as Prime Minister, it seemed as though Slovakia was united as never before in support of the Czechoslovak State, and even of its Government.

Nevertheless, it would be a mistake to assume too hurriedly that the autonomist feeling is losing ground. Not all the so-called 'centralist' parties are governmental, and the fact remains that the Government has been obliged more often than not to rule Slovakia against the wishes of most of its inhabitants, maintaining itself only by the expedients of restricting the powers of the self-governing bodies to within the narrowest possible limits, of filling the seats designated for 'experts' with its own nominees, and utilizing freely the weapons of censorship and police supervision. Moreover, what was said above about the reliability of election-figures as a guide to Magyar feeling, applies to Slovak feeling also. No election has ever been held on the issue of centralism versus autonomy, and a vote for the autonomist party is little less of a gesture than a vote for the Magyars; while the sweets obtainable through known membership of the Agrarian Party are even more easily plucked by a Slovak than by a Magyar. Moreover, the 1929 elections were held in the shadow of the Tuka trial, and were thus themselves somewhat abnormal.

The end of the political and cultural difficulties has not yet been reached. They lie very deep, and new occasions of stumbling are continually arising. Thus in 1935 and 1936 very great offence was given in Slovakia by the Government's Russophil policy, which culminated in the Czechoslovak–U.S.S.R. treaty. The vehemence of the autonomists has certainly not diminished. In 1932 there were vigorous demonstrations against the attempts to 'Czechize' the language and people; on August 13th, 1933, there was a very sensational mass meeting at Nyitra, attended by some 80,000 persons, at which Czech ministers were shouted down and Monsignor Hlinka made a fiery speech, crying, 'There are no Czechoslovaks. We want to remain just Slovaks—out with the Czechs!' There followed collisions with the gendarmerie, the censorship was tightened up, and tempers for a time were ugly. It is also significant that the Slovak émigrés in the U.S.A. have, in the great majority, adopted an extreme Slovak attitude and have even founded a 'Revision League' with a programme of complete independence (which, it is said, has nothing in common with Hungarian revision, and is not to be confounded with frontier-rectification in favour of Hungary).

Things might—indeed, they probably would—have been different if the economic crisis had not supervened after 1929. It is true that Slovak autonomy would prove no cure for the economic misery of Slovakia; but neither is Czechoslovak autarky the remedy for the woes of Czechoslovakia, and yet she has sought for her salvation therein. So, too, the crisis has undoubtedly poured water on Father Hlinka's mills. Both those who rejoice in the fact, and those who deplore it, are agreed that Slovak autonomist feeling has made rapid progress since its nadir after the Tuka trial, and particularly among the younger men and women.

One hears various estimates, but the most common, with which I incline to agree, is that about one-third of the younger generation of Slovaks is 'centralist', two-thirds 'autonomist'. Another estimate (which came to about the same thing) was that 80 per cent. of the Protestants were centralist and 80 per cent. of the Catholics autonomist. The latter are perhaps more truly described, as one observer put it to me, as 'not so much autonomist as radically nationalist'. Most of the younger intellectuals—as they must be described for want of a better word—have probably not at all thought out all the implications of autonomy; they simply wish to have the running of their own country, and above all to man its Government services.

It is not easy to prophesy how the situation will develop. Should the Czechoslovak Republic be granted a long period of political stability and economic prosperity, the political attachment to it of the Slovaks will probably grow. Cultural grievances are gradually being removed, and the coveted posts in Slovakia are bound to be given to Slovaks as they fall vacant. In the fullness of time the Slovaks may even emerge from their native haunts (which they have hitherto singularly failed to do), invade the Historic Lands, and come eventually to occupy a position something like that held by the Scots in the United Kingdom.

At the same time, Czech influence will automatically diminish as the Czech officials are withdrawn, and the national incalculability will have scope to reassert itself.

One is bound to consider what the attitude of the Slovaks would be if Central Europe were to be thrown once again into the melting-pot. Supposing the present solution lost its attraction of safety and respectability; supposing, even, it became physically impossible?

It has been said that few Slovaks to-day would willingly return to the Hungary of 1918. More would be prepared, in the above eventuality, but not otherwise, to consider some sort of federal system under which Slovakia would form an economic unity with Hungary while enjoying cultural autonomy. But it is a measure of the secret uncertainty with which the situation is still judged that other possibilities are also seriously considered. Somewhat surprisingly, complete independence is not among their number. It would, indeed, be quite impracticable; if confined within its ethnographical boundaries, such a State would perish of sheer poverty, while if extended far enough south to prove viable it could not long resist the magnetic attraction of Hungary.

In older days, as we saw, many Slovaks dreamed of incorporation in Russia, or in some Pan-Slav federation. The idea has become altogether impracticable to-day, owing to the geographical barrier interposed by resurrected Poland. It is, however, significant that something like one-seventh of the electorate votes regularly for the Communist Party, which, although preferring Czech to Hungarian rule at the present day, is fundamentally opposed to either, and looks forward to some reconstruction of Central Europe on a different basis altogether from that of nationality. A certain proportion of the younger intellectuals (too few, indeed, to sway the country) also believe the only solution to lie in some United States of Europe, or of Central Europe.

These are dreams at the time of writing, but they may be nearer to experimental realization, at least, than is commonly supposed. Meanwhile, there is one other existing State which cherishes very practical and realistic designs in Slovakia. That is Poland. The Polish claim—'pretext' would, perhaps, be a better word—rests partly on very vague historical arguments which apply only to the Spiš district, partly on the fact that some of the dialects of Northern Slovakia differ little from the local Polish spoken across the frontier (and, indeed, certain customs of the two peoples indicate a common origin), and partly on the suggestion that Poland, as an irreproachable Catholic Power and chosen bulwark of the Vatican, is less alien to the Slovak Clericals than are the Hussite Czechs.

Poland possesses as yet no strong following in Slovakia. Some of the extreme anti-Czech émigrés are established in Cracow, and a certain limited contact is maintained with the People's Party; but the intrigues which go on are probably conducted, on the Slovak side, less with any serious intention of coming to terms with Poland than as a bug-a-boo to frighten the Czechs.

On the Polish side, the intentions are more serious. It is notorious that Poland is anxious to establish a common frontier with Hungary, and that since the conclusion of the German-Polish Pact she has been taking every opportunity to undermine the position of her southern neighbour. What is less certain is how she conceives the future if her plans succeed. She certainly covets Czech Silesia for herself, and as certainly she could not rest content to leave all the rest of her Carpathian frontier unmodified. How much she would hand back to Hungary and how much she would keep for herself, the present writer does not venture to conjecture.

§ 9. CZECHOSLOVAK MINORITY POLICY

The minority problem in Slovakia is of an importance second only to that of the Slovaks themselves. The national minorities in Slovakia number nearly one-third of the total population, and on that score alone the ensuring of their happiness and welfare must be among the foremost preoccupations of any government. But more: not only their numbers, but their social and political situation are such that the very existence of Slovakia can hardly, in the long run, be assured without a satisfactory adjustment of the relations between the majority, the minorities, and the State.

The whole question turns, of course, on the position of the local Magyars. Twice as numerous as the Jews, Germans, and Ruthenes together, they exercise, by virtue of the historical achievements of the old Hungary and the geographical proximity of the new, an influence disproportionate even to their numbers. The compact bloc of Magyar population which, in spite of the recent colonization, still composes the overwhelming majority both in the towns and the country along the southern frontier, separated from 'Mutilated Hungary' only by the turbid but shallow waters of the Danube, invites all too readily consideration of the possibilities of local frontier revision; while the wider influence which the Magyars exercise through the country as a whole might easily keep alive or resuscitate the feelings which in 1918 so nearly prevented Czechoslovakia from coming into existence at all.

The other minorities are by comparison almost negligible. Not only are they far weaker numerically, but their geographical position is such that only the Ruthenes and that handful of Poles or half-Poles on the northern frontier could in any circumstances themselves become irredentist. The Germans, Jews, and gipsies are 'Schicksalsminderheiten': whether in Czechoslovakia, Hungary, or Poland, they would still be minorities. It is true that the position of the Germans is slightly complicated by the existence of the great German minority in the Historic Lands, since the Carpathian Germans, even although themselves necessarily non-irredentist, yet provide their little contingent to the army of the Sudetic Germans, so long as Czechoslovakia exists, and their position is inevitably affected by that of the larger body. Similarly the Ruthene question is influenced by the problem of Carpatho-Ruthenia, to be described in the next section of this work. Broadly speaking, however, Czechoslovakia is faced in Slovakia with one political problem only: the danger of Hungarian irredentism.

The methods which Czechoslovakia has adopted towards her minorities differ greatly, and in a way which does her great credit, from those followed by Roumania and Yugoslavia. In this connexion, it is important to emphasize how strongly the situation has been governed by factors lying outside Slovakia itself. Had the whole history been played out within Slovakia only, the Slovaks (if they had ever won their independence at all) might have been less gentle and less cautious. Control, however, has not lain in their hands, but in that of the Czechs. And the training and outlook of the Czechs, and particularly of their political leaders, are thoroughly European. Centuries of existence within the Austrian State, and of contact with its more advanced elements, have imbued them with a respect for legality, an aversion from extreme methods, a civilized attitude which their worst enemies must acknowledge.

And even if the Czechs had been naturally inclined to brutal methods, a large measure of restraint would have been imposed on them by their own position. In Slovakia they powerfully reinforce the Slovaks in their struggle against the Magyars— indeed, as we have shown, without their aid the Slovaks would never have been able, perhaps would never in majority have desired, to 'cast off the Magyar yoke'. But they are themselves faced in the Historic Lands with a most formidable minority problem. For ethnographically Czechoslovakia, as her enemies are never tired of repeating, is the old Austria writ small. Of a total population, according to the 1930 census, of some 14,300,000, the Czechs, with 7,200,000, constituted only a fraction over 50 per cent. By including the 2,000,000 or so Slovaks, the numbers of the 'Staatsvolk' could be brought up to about two-thirds of the total; but this still leaves some 5,000,000 national minorities, including in the 3,300,000 Germans the largest and most powerful single minority, relative to the State as a whole, of any country in Europe.

The mere existence of this huge minority in the Historic Lands has been of great benefit to all the minorities in Slovakia—with the exception, possibly, of the local Germans. The nationality legislation of the Republic was primarily devised by the Czechs with an eye on the position of the Sudetic Germans, to whom comparatively favourable terms had to be granted. As it was not possible to lay down one law for the western half of the Republic and another for the east, without special reason adduced, and not always easy to make such reason plausible (although it has been done on some occasions), the minorities in Slovakia have in general received the same privileges as have been accorded to the Germans.[1]

---

[1] The equality is not absolute. For example, in the Historic Lands, but not in Slovakia, the school boards are formed with separate sections (Czech and German) which enjoy a certain autonomy. There are also certain other differences.

And, while the Germans have shown small interest in Slovakia, yet they are sufficiently aware of the virtues of analogy to keep a watchful eye on the general minorities policy of the Republic. The Germans are, moreover, even more powerful than their numbers would indicate; for the Germans of the Reich are alert to seize upon and stigmatize any act of oppression committed against their brothers within the Czechoslovak frontiers. So, of course, are the Magyars; but while Magyar complaints can sometimes be discounted abroad, in dealing with Germans any Government has to watch its step. To counteract this national pressure, Czechoslovakia can rely only on the far less solid foundations of Slavonic sympathies (which are apt to prove more of a quicksand than a rock), on purely political alliances, or on the general esteem which a wise and liberal policy may win them in the councils of Europe.

These combined considerations have partly led, partly driven Czechoslovakia to adopt towards her minorities a policy which is in many respects admirable. There is an excellent system of laws, and, what is far more important, the law is decently observed. The unholy trio of the colonel, the gendarme, and the police spy who do what they will in the Balkans are kept in their proper places in Slovakia (which is not to say that the political informer is less effective there than elsewhere; but he is servant and not master). A member even of the Magyar minority, if he keeps out of politics, can live unmolested, and if wrong is done to him he will obtain due redress. So much gentler are Czechoslovak methods than Roumanian or Yugoslav that the essential identity of all three policies is sometimes difficult to discern. Yet in their fundamentals they are identical, since Czechoslovakia, like Roumania and Yugoslavia, is a national State. Dr. Beneš, indeed, in a famous and much-quoted memorandum to the Peace Conference indicated that Czechoslovakia was to become a 'second Switzerland', by which was meant, if the words meant anything, that all the nationalities in it should enjoy equal rights. In fact, however, Czechoslovakia has never attempted to follow this course, had repudiated it even before Dr. Beneš spoke, by the decision of the Constituent Assembly which proclaimed the Republic to be the national State of the Czechs and Slovaks. It may well be that the experiment (which, had it succeeded, would have ranked among the happiest of modern times) was too hazardous; that equality would not have satisfied the Magyars and Germans, accustomed so long to domination. But rightly or wrongly it was not tried. Czechoslovakia's policy, like that of her Allies, is one of national imperialism, which is even more successful than the more violent methods fashionable elsewhere, because its discretion and subtlety disguise the pertinacious and implacable nature of its pressure. For the same Austrian schooling which taught the Czechs mildness in method trained them also in an iron purposefulness and an unrivalled ingenuity in achieving their ends. The Czechs do not storm the gate; they sap under the walls, slowly but surely undermining the political, social, and economic strength of their adversaries. They seldom take a step which cannot be explained or justified—only—there remains an uneasy feeling that something—it is never quite clear what—is wrong somewhere. One reads the explanation again; one dismisses the unworthy suspicion. But a year later one looks at the situation once more; and somewhere or other, imperceptibly, the Czechs have become a little stronger, the minorities a little weaker yet.

These statements require qualification in one respect. The encouragement given to the national cultures of the Germans and the Jews is a tactical move only, due to the well-grounded belief that they can more easily be detached from the real adversary—the Magyars—by this means than by attempts at Czechization, which might fail and drive them into the enemy camp. But the Czechs have reached such a stage of economic and social development as to make it possible for other considerations than those of pure nationalism to play their part. They themselves, in their relations with other nationalities, have always been ready to put aside social differences and form a common front in the hour of danger; both in the old Austria and the present Czechoslovakia, the Czech bourgeois and the Czech socialist have always stood shoulder to shoulder in any national question. They are, however, capable of appealing to social differentiations among others. As we shall see, the Magyar and German peasants and workers have received many advantages, which might lead them (and have led some of them) to accept their position as not merely tolerable but desirable. This again might be regarded as a tactical move, although one which in its effects is very advantageous for the people concerned. But here and there it is something better; it is no mere move to sap the solidarity of the national enemy, but a genuine manifestation of a super-national outlook.

§ 10. THE MINORITIES: POLITICAL RIGHTS

The advantages and the limitations of the Czech system are excellently indicated in the political position of the minorities. To-day Czechoslovakia, almost alone among European countries east of Switzerland, enjoys a genuine parliamentary system of government. There is a franchise which is equal for all nationalities, a ballot which is genuinely secret, reasonable liberty of agitation and propaganda, and, what is equally important, a Parliament whose decisions really count. The minorities of Czechoslovakia (unlike those of Hungary or Yugoslavia) are allowed to form political parties, the conditions regarding which do not discriminate between the different nationalities,[1] and all of them have, in fact, availed themselves of this privilege. Their leaders, including those of the Magyar nationalist party, can travel freely about the country, and even abroad; can make electoral propaganda, and when they speak in the Parliament or Senate at Prague will be heard with due decorum, and not greeted, as they might be in neighbouring capitals, with ink-pots, rotten eggs, or revolver-bullets. Their remarks will elicit a courteous response, and if the matter in question is not one which touches the national hegemony of the Czechs and Slovaks their wishes will probably be met.

But let them once try to exert a real influence, and they will come up against that impenetrable wall of national solidarity which the Czech bourgeois and workman form when danger threatens. They are not necessarily excluded because of their nationality; the Magyar and German sections of the Social Democrats and Agrarians work entirely unhampered and are allowed both to influence policy, in proportion to their numbers, and to enjoy the varied and often succulent sweets of power. Where they are willing not merely to dissociate themselves from the national front of their own peoples but to attack it actively, they enjoy a liberty amounting to licence, and the censor takes a holiday when their publications come before him.

A national party, on the other hand, may enjoy freedom of movement, but never freedom of action. Even their present liberty was not accorded until it appeared safe. In the earliest stages they were excluded from any parliamentary participation whatever by the simple expedient (already described) of nominating only Slovaks to the Constituent Assembly, and of holding no elections at all in Slovakia. Afterwards, great difficulties were put in the way of the formation of the Hungarian National Party;

[1] Law 201 of October 25th, 1933, which authorizes the dissolution of a party if its activities 'endanger to an increased extent the independence, constitutional unity, integrity, democratic republican structure or security of the Czechoslovak Republic', was directed chiefly against certain Czech parties, and of the minority parties only the German National Socialists had by 1936 fallen under its ban. (Extracts from this law are printed on pp. 91 ff. of the *Memorandum concerning the Situation of the Hungarian Minority in Czechoslovakia*, published by the Hungarian Revision League, Budapest, 1934, and quoted henceforward as *Revision Memorandum*. This book is, of course, one-sided in character and should be used for facts rather than opinions as, indeed, should almost all literature on both sides.) In 1937 the Magyars had 11 Deputies and 7 Senators at Prague. In the Provincial Council of Slovakia they possessed 5 representatives, as compared with 49 Slovaks.

the old Hungarian system was retained, for a considerable time, under which ten times as many signatures as in the Historic Lands were required for a nomination. Even at the 1925 elections great pressure was undoubtedly exercised, many of the leaders being molested and even arrested. If these things have ceased to occur, yet some of the electoral districts have been remodelled to ensure that the Magyars shall be regularly outvoted (the map of the Bratislava district is a real curiosity) and others with a clear Magyar majority are excessively large, so that the number of votes required to elect a Deputy or a Senator is substantially higher than in the purely Czech districts (in Ruthenia, it is true, it is higher still).

Of still greater practical importance are the measures which have been taken in the sphere of local government. We have already mentioned the system under which the so-called self-governing bodies are weighted with a proportion of so-called 'experts' who are in fact nearly always nominees of the central Government. The present constitution in any case allows much less local initiative than the old Hungarian system of counties and municipalities with extensive autonomous rights. This system had, of course, been manipulated by the Hungarian authorities to eliminate the influence of the non-Magyar national-ities, and the local Magyars had certainly wielded through it a power out of all proportion to their numbers. Now, however, the minorities have been deprived of any effective power whatever except in matters of smallest local importance. The towns, in which the Magyar element was the strongest, have, with a few exceptions, lost their autonomous rights. For some time after the War, both the counties (then still retained) and the towns and even the villages were ruled very largely by Government Com-missaries, often assisted by nominated councils. It was frankly admitted that the purpose of these measures was to keep Slovakia for the Republic. The electoral system has now been restored, but the Government controls strictly the appointments (in Ruthenia alone it recently refused its sanction in forty-four Magyar com-munes) and has often dissolved the councils in Magyar towns and villages; while in the four most important centres of Magyar life in Slovakia and Ruthenia—Bratislava, Košice, Užhorod, and Mukačevo (Munkácz)—the burgomaster is not elected at all, but nominated by the Government. Thus the minorities in Slovakia enjoy little more political power than they do in Roumania or Yugoslavia, and much less than was exercised, for example, by the Poles in pre-War Germany; for no Czech party will ever ally itself with a minority on a national issue. The Parliamentary régime in Czechoslovakia, however, does allow the minorities opportunities, not accorded elsewhere, of ventilating their grievances and even getting them removed, where the larger questions of power politics are not involved.

§ 11. THE MINORITIES: LINGUISTIC AND ADMINISTRATIVE CONDITIONS

The law concerning the official use of languages in the Republic is very complicated, but liberal enough. It is contained in two main instruments: the Language Law of February 29th, 1920,[1] which forms a part of the Constitution, and a later Government Decree,[2] which regulates and interprets the application of the earlier law. A large number of decisions of the Supreme Legislative and Administrative Courts also bear on the question. Broadly speaking, those instruments lay down that 'Czechoslovak' (in practice, either Czech or Slovak) is the official language of the Republic and of its central offices, of the National Bank, and of command in the army. The use of this language can never be out of order, even in a district inhabited by an overwhelming local majority of Germans, Magyars, or Ruthenes. Where, however, the sphere or authority of a Court of Justice, office, or State administrative department extends over a judicial district in which at least 20 per cent. of the citizens speak the same minority language, the authorities are bound to accept all legal documents regarding matters pertaining to their jurisdiction and lodged by persons belonging to the minority concerned, in the minority language, and to reply to them in that language as well as Czechoslovak.[3] In effect, then, a linguistic minority of 20 per cent. strong in any given district is entitled to the official use of its language in that district.

Similarly, self-governing authorities, municipal councils, and public corporations are bound to accept and dispatch all matter, lodged orally or in writing, in Czechoslovak, and the Czechoslovak language may always be used at their meetings, but here, too, the '20 per cent. rule' applies. Where there is a linguistic minority 20 per cent. strong, its language may be used, and if the minority numbers more than 50 per cent. its language will be that in which the business is conducted—(in such a case Czecho-

[1] Law No. 122 of February 29th, 1920. Text in Sobota, *Das Tschechoslovakische Nationalitätenrecht* (Prague, 1931), pp. 215-43.
[2] Governmental Decree No. 17 of February 3rd, 1926. Text, ibid., pp. 361-427.
[3] Under the agreement of February 20th, 1937, between the Czechoslovak Government and the German Activist Parties, the terms of which are to be extended to all minorities, higher authority will henceforward attach gratis a translation of all documents sent to a commune in which the great majority of the population belongs to a single linguistic minority.

slovak may also be used, but must be translated). Where the minority numbers over 66·6 per cent. certain transactions, relating solely to members of the minority, may be carried out in the minority language only.

Communal offices are not bound to conduct business with the public in any language but that in which the business of the commune is conducted, but are enjoined where possible to use a language understood by the public. In Courts of Justice the regulations go rather farther; thus the indictment against a defendant must be drawn up in his own language.

These laws, where admitted to be applicable, seem to be fairly well, although not perfectly, applied. Their scope is, indeed, more restricted than might reasonably be expected, since by a peculiarly irritating subterfuge it has been laid down that the postal and railway services, although in State hands, are 'commercialized undertakings', to which the Language Law does not apply. Thus notices and regulations for these two services are put up in Czecho-slovak only.[1] Those who have attempted to send off anything more complex than an inland picture postcard from a Central European post office will appreciate the devastating effect of this trick, which may have serious consequences in commercial life. In practice, the officials of these departments in Slovakia are more humane than in Prague.

Public notices, not affecting these two services, are usually put up in the minority language, as well as the language of State, in predominantly minority areas. The local officials in such areas are not always, but usually, able to speak the minority language, and not all, but many, of them are good-natured and conscientious fellows enough, prepared to do their best with the local population. I have myself more than once been spontaneously invited to speak Magyar when my Slovak broke down, as it did after some two words. I should say that, in about a third of the cases, the use of the minority language in official intercourse was allowed and accepted without demur. More often it is allowed, because the law so enjoins, but it is not encouraged. Peasants are not harassed, but lawyers or other members of the bourgeoisie transacting business with the officials find it better not to stand on their rights, since the authorities are better humoured and things go more easily if they use Czech or Slovak. The districts in which the law is simply disregarded, owing either to the chauvinism of the local authorities or the simple lack of any person with sufficient linguistic qualifications, are comparatively few, and where such

[1] This statement has been queried by a Czech gentleman to whom I made it; but my own recollection accords with the statements made to this effect by the minorities. There may be exceptions in some localities.

conditions are found it is owing to the former reason more often than the latter. Correspondence relating to the gathering of taxes is scrupulously conducted in all local languages. Of the higher offices still one hears mixed accounts. A German told me that the Minister President's Office and the Foreign Office were usually willing to answer him in German (and he emphasized that those of the authorities who were able to appreciate the international situation were genuinely anxious to conciliate the minorities) while the others replied only in the language of State. This gentleman, like nearly every one whom I questioned on the point, found the Czechs less difficult in this respect than the Slovaks. Moreover, sundry ingenious devices have been adopted which in practice reduce still farther the value of the safeguards provided by the law. When the administrative, judicial, &c., districts of Slovakia were reorganized in 1926, the boundaries of five judicial districts in which the Magyars were particularly strong (Bratislava, Nitra (Nyitra, Neutra), Rimavská Sobota, Košice, and Sečevo) were so remodelled as to bring the Magyar percentage below the statutory 20.[1] Czechoslovak writers maintain, indeed, that the reorganization was undertaken for quite other purposes, to eliminate anomalies (which certainly existed in plenty), and that 'a transfer affecting language rights was a mere secondary occurrence'.[2] Yet it is difficult, when one looks at the administrative map of Slovakia and its curious contours, to regard the reorganization, in this respect, as otherwise than deliberate and artificial.

The same manipulation was effected with the municipalities of Bratislava and Košice, Slovak villages being included and Magyar suburbs cut out. In Bratislava the desired result was achieved only in 1930, after the census (the results of which were used against the minorities in many places). Here the Magyar's loss of his rights has been emphasized in a singularly childish manner, since some one has taken the trouble to go round the central streets and draw a line through the Magyar version of the names, which, for the rest, remain visible and even legible. Thus we read at the corner of a certain square:

MASARYKOVO NÁMĚSTÍ

MASARYKPLATZ

~~MASARYK-TÉR~~

More undignified and humourless still was the removal from the public baths of the notices which informed the Magyars in which part of the waters it was safe for them to bathe, or into which

---

[1] The six 'Župys' introduced in 1921 and abolished in 1926 were similarly arranged.

[2] For this view, see Dr. M. Ivanka in the *Central European Observer*, December 18th, 1933, pp. 476 ff.

lavatory each sex might enter with decorum. But the trick is not merely silly but serious, and the more irritating since it is so obviously a trick. In all the places where it has been practised the municipal and local elections regularly give the Magyars a far higher voting strength than they might expect from the official figures of population; the streets and cafés are thronged with persons speaking Magyar, and in one of the places to which I have referred I never heard a word of Czech or Slovak spoken in the course of a fortnight's sedulous bathing.

In acting thus, the authorities have not even followed their own laws, since the Language Law is designed for *linguistic* minorities, but it is applied as though it referred to *national* minorities. Thus when Magyar-speaking Jews or gipsies enter their nationality as such they are not allowed to count among the speakers of Magyar or German for the purposes of the Language Law.

To-day some 15 per cent. of the Magyar minority (even assuming the accuracy of the census figures) is excluded from even the nominal protection of the law. This considerable figure, amounting according to one Hungarian calculation to 133,662 persons,[1] includes some 20,000 Magyars in Bratislava alone, while the numbers excluded from effective protection must be substantially larger.

The Germans have suffered in the same way. General administrative policy towards them is probably less strict than towards the Magyars, and the application of the Language Law less strict, if only because it is easier to find a Czechoslovak officer who knows German than one who understands Magyar. On the other hand, they have suffered relatively far more than the Magyars by the defection of the Jews,[2] and to-day there are only five judicial districts (Kezmarok = Kesmark, Kremniça = Kremnitz, Gelnice = Gölnitz, Bratislava, and Priwitz) which still show the statutory minimum of 20 per cent. 61,750 or 41·88 per cent. of all the local Germans are deprived of the benefit of the Language Law although the reorganization of 1926, if it had really aimed at facilitating the position instead of making it more difficult, could easily have reduced these numbers very largely.[3]

Not the least sufferers, incidentally, are the German- and Magyar-speaking Jews, whose defection in the census made many of these restrictions possible.

The Language Law is thus less good than it looks. At the same

---

[1] *Pester Lloyd*, September 10th, 1935.
[2] Cf. above, p. 79 n., for the disastrous defalcation of the Jews from the 'German' language.
[3] *Nation und Staat*, April 1934, p. 439.

time it is fair to emphasize that even where the 20 per cent. is not reached, this does not mean that the persons concerned will be unable to transact any official business in their mother tongue. They may still enjoy the right in their communes; they may even, at least in oral communications, use their language where a strict application of the law would forbid it; and, of course, their freedom to speak as they will in non-official intercourse remains unaffected. And even despite these chicaneries the law is far more liberal than that of any Central European State except Hungary; and in Hungary, although the law allows linguistic minorities practically the same rights as Czechoslovakia, it is far less generously applied in practice.

As regards justice, the linguistic provisions designed to safeguard defendants not speaking the language of State are, so far as I could tell, scrupulously observed. More important, the equality before the law which the Constitution guarantees seems to be a reality, at least as regards criminal offences. I have heard of no complaints of national prejudice against the ordinary Courts of Justice.

In the public services, the Magyars lost most of their representatives very soon after the War, owing to the events previously described—events in which neither side was blameless. Many of the persons affected were so frankly hostile to the State that they could not possibly have been retained in their posts. It seems certain, however, that the oath of allegiance was demanded in many cases before it could legitimately be required, and that some officials who were perfectly willing to take it were dismissed on very flimsy pretexts. It is difficult to determine to-day how many persons were affected. A Czech source puts the number of Magyars leaving the country in 1919–20 at 56,000, and, while agreeing that most of them were officials or teachers with their families, adds that some miners and workmen were among them.[1] The figure given by the Hungarian General Board for Refugee Questions is much higher: 106,841.[2] The thoroughness of the clear-out may be judged by the fact that as early as 1920, according to semi-official data, only 153, 184, and 410 Magyar officials were employed in the Ministry of Interior, the Ministry of Finance (which includes the Customs and Excise Services), and the Post Office, respectively.[3] Since then the numbers have further declined.

According to statistics supplied to me from Magyar sources in Czechoslovakia there were, in or about 1935, 7,644 Magyars employed in the public services of the Republic—about one-third of the number to which their numerical proportion would entitle

[1] Sasek, op. cit., p. 53.   [2] *Revision Memorandum*, p. 29.   [3] Ibid.

them, if that were taken as guide. Recent figures for Slovakia have been given in a previous section.[1] They show that both Magyars and Germans are seriously under-represented in the public services. They show, too, that the process of reduction is steady. Thus the number of Magyars in the administrative services decreased between 1921 and 1930 by 59·41 per cent.; in the railways by 55·86 per cent.; and in the postal services by 57 per cent. In every case the decrease was larger, and usually much larger, as regards the more responsible posts. The decreases in the case of the Germans were 25·35 per cent. in the administrative services, 36·84 per cent. railway clerks, 43·06 per cent. railway labourers, and 27·03 per cent. postal employees. Taking all government services and free professions together, the Germans registered a small absolute increase of but 421 persons, but the Magyar figure declined by 5,008, or 33·66 per cent.[2] Practically all those of either nationality still retained in the public services are the old hands. It is very difficult to-day for a member of a minority, especially a Magyar, to enter the State service, and it is growing increasingly difficult as the pressure of the younger generation of Slovaks grows stronger. Admission is practically confined to persons who have passed through Czechoslovak schools, and have affiliations with one of the important Czecho-slovak political parties, preferably the Agrarians or Social Democrats. A serious feature of the continued preference, first of Czechs and latterly of Slovaks, is that the new officials, who seldom or never learn Magyar, and not much German or Ruthene, are not really qualified for positions in minority districts. This is beginning to affect the proper application of the Language Law. Professor Seton-Watson suggests that, owing to this refusal of the younger Slovaks to learn Magyar, the Magyars who make them-selves bi-lingual will 'enjoy a practical advantage over their Slovak contemporaries in the competition for posts'.[3] More usually, in practice, the Slovak gets the post and the law goes by the board.

While the State clearly cannot be expected to employ in its service persons of doubtful loyalty to itself, the continued ex-clusion of the minorities to-day is certainly perpetuating a feeling of inequality and preventing the growth of genuine loyalty. There are plenty of young men to-day who would be prepared to give perfectly correct service, but their national origin raises an insur-mountable barrier. The Germans feel this perhaps more strongly than the Magyars: for, they say, in the old days they could, and

---

[1] See above, pp. 133–4.
[2] In part, of course, this is nominal, owing to different registration in the census.   [3] *Slovakia Then and Now*, p. 60.

would, have Magyarized, and then would have been accepted without further question; to-day, even if they learn Slovak, they will hardly get a post.

It is possible, indeed, that this situation may be about to change. The agreement of February 1937, between the Government and the German Activists, mentioned above,[1] contains, indeed, a promise that, 'subject to the *conditio sine qua non* of loyalty to the State, an endeavour will be made in admitting members of minorities to State service, to consider not merely general and regional interests, but also the interests of the minorities in the sense of a just proportion'. This would seem to mean cautious recognition of the rights of the minorities to a number of State posts proportionate to their numbers. It is far too early to judge, at the time of writing, what the practical effects of this promise will be, but they should be considerable.

Closely connected in practice with the question of State employment is the miserable problem of statelessness. We shall have to refer to this again in other connexions, since Czechoslovakia, although she has a bad record, is not the only offender (nor, indeed, are the Magyars the only sufferers); but an explanation of the problem must be given sooner or later, so may appear here.

The condition of statelessness arising out of conflict of treaties[2] arose mainly out of the unwise drafting of the Peace Treaties which relate to Central Europe. It was the intention so to draft the Treaties that every person formerly possessed of Austro-Hungarian nationality should acquire the nationality of one or another of the Successor States. The criterion originally proposed was that of 'habitual residence', but when the Treaty of St. Germain was being drafted this was dropped, at the instance of the Czechoslovak delegation and with the consent of the Austrian, for that of *Heimatsrecht* or citizenship of a commune, it being alleged that the latter was the basis of the administrative law of the Dual Monarchy, and that every Austrian citizen possessed *Heimatsrecht* in some Austrian commune or other.

The Czechoslovak Minorities Treaty accordingly provided that all Hungarian nationals possessing *Heimatsrecht* in former Hungarian territory assigned to Czechoslovakia at the date of coming into force of the Treaty should automatically become Czechoslovak citizens unless they opted to the contrary. The same applied to children born in territory now Czechoslovak of persons possessing such *Heimatsrecht*, even if they themselves did not possess the same right. Further, all persons born on Czecho-

---

[1] P. 154, note 3.
[2] There are also certain much less numerous cases, not confined to Central Europe, of statelessness arising out of conflict of laws.

slovak territory, and not born nationals of any other State, became Czechoslovak nationals.

The first of these clauses was subject to any special provisions in the Peace Treaties. In fact, the corresponding clause (Art. 61) in the Hungarian Peace Treaty, while laying down that every person possessing *Heimatsrecht* in territory which formed part of the old Monarchy automatically obtained the nationality of the State exercising sovereignty over the territory concerned, to the exclusion of Hungarian nationality, made a further restriction by providing that if the *Heimatsrecht* was acquired after January 1st, 1910, Czechoslovakia was entitled to refuse citizenship to the person concerned. In that case, he automatically obtained the nationality of the State exercising sovereignty over the territory in which he had previously possessed *Heimatsrecht*.

There were further complicated arrangements for exercising a right of option.

In accordance with these provisions, the Czechoslovak Constitutional Law[1] lays down that Czechoslovak citizenship is acquired automatically by 'persons who acquired *Heimatsrecht* in those parts of the former Austro-Hungarian Monarchy, which now belong to Czechoslovakia, on January 1st, 1910, at the latest, and have possessed it since without interruption', together with the other categories named in the Minorities Treaty. Czechoslovak citizenship was further acquired automatically by other nationals of the former Monarchy who became regular officials of the Czechoslovak State or employees of its State undertakings.

These provisions would have been reasonable enough, although in the case of Czechoslovakia there was no particular justification for setting the date back to 1910,[2] if *Heimatsrecht* in the Dual Monarchy had been what it was represented to be: a working administrative institution which covered the entire population. Unfortunately, this had long ceased to be the case. *Heimatsrecht* was really a survival of a much earlier age. Its chief use had been for purposes of poor law, every commune being bound to maintain its own members in case of destitution, and unable to expel them. It had actually been acquired originally through *jus sanguinis*—a feasible enough arrangement in days when nine-tenths of the population lived, worked, idled, or died in the parishes of their birth.

[1] No. 236 of April 9th, 1920; text in Sobota, op. cit., pp. 247–8.
[2] The idea of advancing the date had originated in connexion with the Treaty between Poland and Germany, it being urged that Poland ought not to be forced to accept as her nationals persons recently settled on her soil with the deliberate purpose of strengthening the German element. It had some sense also as applied to Serbian Macedonia, where Bulgarian soldiers and officials had entered after the Balkan Wars. There was no similar reason operating in the case of Czechoslovakia.

M

When, however, modern industry developed, large movements of population took place, and it was obviously impossible, in the case, say, of a bad industrial crisis, with widespread resultant unemployment, in a big town like Vienna or Budapest, to return all the workers to the forsaken villages which their grandparents had left to seek their fortunes. Some kind of 'naturalization' had to be introduced. In Austria a law was enacted in 1896 providing that *Heimatsrecht* could be acquired in a new commune by any person who had resided in it uninterruptedly for ten years without coming on to the rates. In Hungary the law was much simpler. Any person having resided for four years in a commune and having 'participated in its charges' was deemed to have acquired citizenship therein automatically and 'tacitly' if no complaint was raised against him. Even participation in the charges was not required of public officials, including teachers and the clergy, of whatever denomination, they being exempted from such payments. Moreover, no registers were kept, and a certificate of *Heimatsrecht* was issued only on demand.

Naturally, in the old Hungary there were many thousands of persons who did not know, and probably did not care, in what commune, if any, they possessed rights of citizenship. Well-to-do families had probably not bothered to inquire for generations where, if anywhere, they were entitled to poor relief. In countless other cases the relevant papers were lost, or had never existed, or the position was being languidly disputed between two village notaries.

Thus very many inhabitants of Slovakia could not in any case have proved their communal citizenship; but the number was further inordinately swollen by two very extraordinary and, to the lay mind, quite indefensible decisions of the Czechoslovak Supreme Court, which applied elements of the Austrian practice to the ex-Hungarian territories.[1] It was subsequently slightly reduced by a law passed in 1926, in the face of strong opposition from Prague, at the instance of a courageous Slovak Deputy, M. Derer. This law allowed, in principle, all persons settled before January 1st, 1906, in those parts of Czechoslovakia which were formerly Hungarian to claim Czechoslovak nationality. It contained, however, many exceptions; others were made in applying it; and in any case its validity lasted only until August 1st, 1931.

A stateless person suffers at best under great disabilities, and may easily be plunged into abject misery. He has no papers of

---

[1] One of these decisions laid down that the contribution to the communal charges, as well as the residence, must have been uninterrupted, whereas Hungarian practice had required only a single contribution; the second made acquisition of *Heimatsrecht* conditional upon production of a certificate from the new commune.

legitimation to enable him either to enter or leave his country of residence, or to enter any other. He is liable to arbitrary expulsion —a situation aggravated by the fact that if he is expelled from one country no other is bound to take him in, so that he finds himself, often from no fault of his own, or a very trivial one, an offender against the law and liable to imprisonment for being anywhere at all. He is not entitled to poor relief, and often not to employment benefit or other social services. He is not eligible for Government employment, and in many cases, where restrictive laws exist for protecting the national labour market, he cannot legitimately engage in any gainful occupation whatever. Yet he is not entitled to a pension for past services. He has no Parliamentary or local suffrage; and yet, by common usage, he is liable to military service.

It would require a volume to tell the misery to which many of these unfortunates—who abound in nearly all the Successor States of the old Dual Monarchy—have been reduced. Perhaps it may be illustrated by a single authenticated case of a man arrested on the banks of the Danube who was repeatedly making the motions of flying. He told the police that he was trying to fly to the sky to find a country there. Ten years of continued expulsion and imprisonment had driven him mad.

A large number of stateless persons belong to precisely those social classes which have deserved best of their fellows, and are the most helpless in their hands. These are the persons entitled to pensions, by virtue either of past State service, or as war invalids. They are not, however, confined to these categories, but include persons drawn from all classes of society, ranging from Senators, former Lord Lieutenants, and at least one bishop, to illiterate peasants who probably lost their chance of regularizing their position through sheer ignorance of the laws.

The Magyars, in particular, have a just grievance against the Czechoslovak Government over this question; not only on account of the great misery into which many of their members have been plunged, but for the way in which advantage has undoubtedly been taken of the situation for political purposes, e.g. by refusing, or threatening to refuse, papers of nationality to voters just before elections and, still more drastically, by refusing citizenship to inconvenient political leaders, as in some of the cases quoted above. Similarly, nationality papers have been refused to a large number of priests, school-teachers, and other persons capable of influencing public opinion.

It is very difficult to say how many people have been, or still are, affected by this condition. Some years past the common estimate given by unofficial societies interesting themselves in the question (e.g. the local League of Nations Societies) was 90,000–100,000 in Slovakia and Ruthenia alone. The 1921 census gave 42,246 'foreigners' in Slovakia and 6,862 in Ruthenia. The figures for 1930 were 75,604 and 16,228 respectively. These were officially shown to include in Slovakia 27,122 Polish, 25,023 Hungarian, 4,737 Austrian, 3,424 Roumanian, 3,171 Yugoslav subjects, and 7,354 stateless persons or persons of undeclared nationality, while in Ruthenia there were shown 4,670 Polish, 4,747 Hungarian, 2,965 Roumanian nationals, and 2,579 stateless persons, &c.[1] The Magyar minority itself, however, places the number of Magyar stateless persons in Slovakia and Ruthenia together as high as 15,000–20,000,[2] and it seems pretty certain that the Hungarian, Polish, and other 'subjects' are in many cases persons who are not recognized by Hungary and Poland respectively as their nationals, and thus, in fact, stateless.

A certain improvement is probably now in progress. The Czechoslovak Statistical Year-book shows that between 1929 and 1935 18,996 persons of former Hungarian nationality acquired Czechoslovak nationality, while 2,698 Czechoslovak subjects acquired Hungarian nationality.[3] Probably the situation will soon cease to exist as a mass phenomenon; but not before it has caused indescribable suffering (apart from all political consequences), while the last cases of individual hardship are not likely to disappear before the death of the last unfortunate concerned.

One very severe grievance in connexion with the dismissal of officials and the refusal of citizenship is that of the payment of pensions. The whole question is too complex to be described in detail here. It turned, in part, round the administration of certain central pension funds in Budapest, for the distribution of which agreement was necessary between the Hungarian and Czechoslovak Governments. Pending the failure of such agreement, many hundreds of individuals were reduced to destitution, sometimes to actual starvation, while the pensions which they had lawfully earned were withheld from them. I have heard, further, a great many complaints regarding pensions being withheld on various pretexts, and, at the best, they are calculated on an ungenerous scale, so that the wholesale pensioning of officials in 1919 caused a great deal of hardship.

Stateless persons receive no pensions at all; and one of the

---

[1] *Annuaire statistique de la République Tchécoslovaque*, 1934, p. 11, Table II, 8.
[2] *Revision Memorandum*, p. 26. Others place it far higher still. As recently as January 1937 one informant gave it at over 100,000. In the census of 1930 some 200,000 persons originally entered their nationality as 'unknown', 'uncertain', &c., and the whole matter had to be sent back to the district authorities for further investigation.
[3] *Annuaire statistique de la République Tchécoslovaque*, 1934, p. 30, Table III, 18.

commonest reasons for denying citizenship is the wish to escape the consequent obligation of paying out some pension due to the individual. It is the same consideration which has made Hungary (and Austria) refuse to grant citizenship to a large number of Magyars (Austrians) whom they would have been glad enough to receive when the other Successor States rejected them. Hungary has, in fact, burdened her budget very heavily by making such payments to many thousands of refugees; but her resources and her goodwill alike are limited.

§ 12. THE MINORITIES: EDUCATIONAL AND CULTURAL QUESTIONS

As regards education, the Language Law lays down that instruction in all schools erected for members of national minorities must be given in their mother tongue; the internal administration of the cultural institutions of the minorities is also conducted in their own language. The language of instruction must be taught as a subject in all elementary and burger schools.[1] Czechoslovak may be taught as a subject in elementary and burger schools, and, in the latter, pupils are to be 'given the opportunity of acquiring it', while in all secondary schools it is a compulsory subject.[2]

Under a general law,[3] enacted in the first year of the Republic and designed to apply equally to all languages, a public elementary school with instruction in a given language may be erected in any commune, not possessing a public school with instruction in that language, which possesses a minimum (calculated on a three years' average) of 40 school children of school age of the mother tongue in question. For a burger school the requisite minimum is 400 children. Lower minima may be allowed, exceptionally, for 'important reasons'. The law provides, however, the principle on which the authorities work throughout the Republic.

The law relating to private schools, which also applies equally throughout the country,[4] lays down no limitation or restriction beyond the normal safeguards required in every country as to qualification of teachers, healthiness of premises, &c. Minorities are given, under the constitution (which here reproduces the terms of the Minorities Treaty), an equal right with other Czechoslovak nationals to found, maintain, and manage, at their own expense, charitable, religious, social, and educational establishments and,

[1] Law 226 of July 13th, 1922; Sobota, op. cit., p. 333.
[2] Decree 137 of June 8th, 1923; Sobota, op. cit., p. 343.
[3] Law No. 189 of April 3rd, 1919; Sobota, op. cit., pp. 183 ff.
[4] This law is, technically speaking, not in force in Slovakia, since, while it came into force in the Historic Lands immediately on promulgation, its application in Slovakia was made contingent on a special decree which has never been issued.

where they form a 'considerable proportion' of the population, to receive an equitable share of any public funds allotted to educational, religious, or charitable purposes.

It is in this field, and in the cultural sphere generally, that the difference in the treatment of the various minorities is most marked, the obvious tendency being to reduce Magyar cultural influence, if necessary by fostering the culture of the other minorities. The Czechs can argue that the treatment is not differential; they are simply applying the principle, disregarded in pre-War days, of *suum cuique*. The fact remains that the application has involved grievous losses to the Magyars, who have thereby seen disappear practically all their higher education, a large part of their secondary education, and two-thirds of the elementary schools which they maintained before the War;[1] whereas the Germans now enjoy for the first time for decades an elementary school system of their own.

The position for all the minorities is most satisfactory as regards elementary education, where a genuine effort seems to be made to ensure that every child is instructed in its mother tongue. The Magyars were left in 1934 with 741 elementary schools, with 1,820 classes, and 91,592 pupils.[2] The number, compared with that of the Slovak schools, is slightly below what the ratio of populations would require, since, whereas the 1930 census showed 1 Magyar to every 3·89 Slovaks, the ratio of elementary schools was 1 : 4·54, and, of both classes and pupils, little under 1 : 5.[3] The position appears to be better in the villages than in the towns of mixed population. In the former, there is alleged to be a total shortage of some 70 schools.

The Magyar *Revision Memorandum* quotes official statistics to the effect that 86·4 per cent. of the Magyar children in the Republic enjoy elementary education in their own language, compared with 99 per cent. of Czechoslovak children.[4] Other figures given to me officially showed that out of 116,615 children, 95,322 attended purely Magyar schools, 11,377 mixed schools with parallel classes in Magyar and other languages, and only 8,392 Czechoslovak schools. It is also maintained that the latter number includes many whose parents have deliberately chosen, by their own free act, to send their children to Czech or Slovak schools, this applying particularly to Jews who, although describing themselves as

[1] No less than 1,456 Magyar elementary schools out of a total of 2,223 had been converted to other languages by the end of 1924.
[2] Figures kindly supplied to me by the Department of Education, Bratislava.
[3] The *Revision Memorandum* draws a more unfavourable comparison still by taking the ratios between Magyars' schools and population and those of the whole Republic. It seems to me fairer to confine the comparison to Slovakia, where local conditions are similar.
[4] *Revision Memorandum*, p. 107.

Magyar-speaking, are willing for their children to learn differently. I myself met many such cases, and not among Jews only, but also among true Magyars; and I agree that the choice was free, i.e. not made under administrative pressure. It was, however, prompted in nearly every case by the consideration that only a child who had been to a Czechoslovak school could hope for a decent job in his after life.

The Germans have 116 elementary schools, a number which corresponds well enough to their needs. They have, indeed, encountered no difficulty in this respect, since German schools were founded after the War wherever the population was German-speaking or the parents could be induced to make the necessary request. The Ruthenes had, in 1934, 103 elementary schools, with 175 classes and 11,919 pupils. Here, again, the figures compare unfavourably with those of the Slovak schools, and it is possible that, in some places, Slovak education is being forced on the Ruthenes (who in any case maintain their real numbers to be higher than the census shows). The position is, however, much better than before the War, and if the Ruthenes are being Slovakized in places, this is at least in part a natural process, which was proceeding even before the War.[1] So far as the villages are concerned, the danger to the minorities comes less from the direct action of the authorities than from the 'Slovenska Liga', an unofficial body which enjoys, however, the active support of the authorities. Its aim is to protect the Slovak minorities in non-Slovak, especially Magyar, districts, and to prevent them from being denationalized or, in its own words, to 'work for the complete national reconquest of Slovakia'.[2] It devotes special attention to the Czech and Slovak colonies established on the southern frontier under the Agrarian Reform Act. Up to 1935 it had built 239 'minority schools', i.e. schools for Czechoslovak minorities, consisting of 213 elementary schools, 9 burger schools, and 17 kindergartens. The League itself declares that it works only where there is a Czechoslovak minority, in order to avoid even the appearance of denationalization, and has refused requests from Magyar communes to build schools. In some districts, however, the minorities which it protects are very small, and both Magyars and, even more, in recent years, Germans, have complained of its encroachments.[3]

The number of burger schools is already far less satisfactory. The Magyars have only 15 such schools (in 1937, indeed, according to official figures, only 13), compared with 160 Slovak, and only

[1] See below, p. 186.
[2] Report on 'The spread of Slovak Minority Schools in South-West Slovakia', cit. *Revision Memorandum*, p. 109.
[3] A. L. Erben, *Sterbende Wirtschaft, hungerndes Volk* (*Flugschriften der Zipser deutschen Partei*, No. 6), Kesmark, n.d. (1932), pp. 31 ff.

31·58 per cent. of the Magyar pupils in burger schools receive instruction in their own language. The Germans, with 8 burger schools, and the Ruthenes with 2, also complain of a shortage. For secondary education the position is better. The Germans have 3 gymnasia and a Handelsakademie, while further facilities are, of course, available in the Historic Lands. The German desiderata do not go beyond better accommodation for the gymnasium in Bratislava, a German training college, and some German school inspectors.[1] The Ruthenes have no secondary education, but this is no hardship to them, since, if they want it (which is doubtful), they can find it in Ruthenia. The Magyars have 1 gymnasium, 4 Real-gymnasia, 1 training college, and parallel classes in 1 Real-gymnasium, 1 'reformed Realgymnasium', and a girls' training college. 72·52 per cent. of the Magyar pupils of this class attend their own schools. There is, however, a grievous shortage of technical education, in which the Magyars have only 2 agricultural colleges, 1 Handelsakademie, and 1 apprentices' school—figures which are genuinely insufficient for the needs of the Magyar and Magyar-speaking Jewish population. The agreement of February 1937 may possibly bring about an improvement in this field also.

Certain more general grievances are alleged by all the minorities, headed by the Magyars. It is said that the minority school buildings are of old and inferior types and that the denominational schools, which still compose the bulk of the Magyar schools, are technically inferior to the new Czechoslovak state schools. It is, however, fair to recall that the Magyar minority itself has clung firmly to the principle of denominational education and resisted proposals to etatize the whole educational structure on the ground that they would thereby lose the last vestiges of their cultural autonomy.[2] I have not heard it suggested that the minorities schools received less than their fair share of public endowments. The higher administration of the educational system, both in Prague and Bratislava, is almost exclusively in Czechoslovak hands, and there is a shortage of minority school inspectors. As regards the genuineness of the minority instruction, both in curriculum and in spirit, the chief complaints affect secondary education. In 1932, 52 of the 138 teachers in Magyar secondary schools were non-Magyars, and the heads of the establishments where the Magyars possessed only parallel classes were, of course, Slovaks. Some of the 52 must, however, have been Magyar-

---

[1] *Staatshaushalt und nationale Minderheiten* (*Flugschriften der Zipser deutschen Partei*, No. 2), Kesmark, 1928, p. 20.
[2] *Revision Memorandum*, pp. 40–1. In 1931–2 42 per cent. of the Czecho-slovak schools were State, 5 per cent. communal, and 53 per cent. denominational, while of the Magyar schools 11 per cent. were State, 9 per cent. communal, and 80 per cent. denominational.

speaking Jews. The position is better as regards elementary schools.[1]
Here, according to the same source, 215, or 12 per cent. of the total
teachers in Magyar schools, declared themselves non-Magyars.[2]

It is often said that instruction is given 'in the Czechoslovak and
not the minority spirit', and although there do not seem to have
been such scandalous incidents as have occurred in some other
countries, it appears to be true that the light in which, for example,
Hungarian history is presented is very different from what a
Hungarian, or even a neutral person, might think fair.

To Czechoslovakia's credit must be booked the fact that the period
of school attendance is longer than in pre-War days, so that Magyar
children actually get a longer Magyar schooling than they did in
Hungary. Moreover, most of the minority schools genuinely deserve
that name; they are not, as in Yugoslavia and Hungary, bi-lingual
schools with a preponderance in favour of the language of State.

There is no higher education whatever in Magyar, although the
numbers of the Magyars would fairly entitle them to a Faculty of
their own at Bratislava, with chairs and lectureships held by
Magyars. Hitherto there has only been a single Readership, held
by a Slovak. Czechoslovakia does not object so strongly as her
allies to the scions of Magyar families attending Hungarian universities. It is possible, although not easy, for them to obtain the
necessary passports (a difficulty which has arisen since 1931 is that
of getting sufficient foreign currency). They and their parents will,
however, inevitably be *mal vus* by the authorities if they do so; and,
in any case, any degrees which they may obtain will be of no
practical value to them as regards a career in Czechoslovakia, since
the Republic withdrew its recognition from the degrees of Hungarian universities. The decision was taken in answer to Hungarian
revisionist propaganda and actually only imitated the practice
adopted by Hungary before the War towards the Austrian universities. The effects have, however, been most unhappy for the
local minority.

The shortage of higher educational facilities for the Magyars is
the more painful to them because Slovakia has not even been able
to utilize fully all the establishments of which the Magyars have
been deprived.

The other minorities are also without higher education in Slovakia; but their numbers hardly justify giving it to them, and the
Germans, at least, have ample facilities in the Historic Lands.

The full use of any language in private intercourse, commerce,

[1] Ibid., p. 30.
[2] According to other official figures supplied to me, the nationality of the
teachers in the Magyar elementary schools in 1934 was: 1,521 Magyars, 119
Czechs or Slovaks, 8 Russians, 21 Germans, and 32 others.

religion, the press, and publications is guaranteed by the Constitution, the provisions of which are perfectly observed. Czechoslovakia has not descended to the evasions or frank violations of this principle so common in certain other states. The use, for example, of Magyar in the streets does not seem even to cause unpopularity in the chief centres (in which respect Bratislava can set an example to Prague, as regards German) although the Slovenska Liga has begun an agitation in some smaller towns—not against the Magyars, but against some Slovaks who are alleged still to prefer to talk Magyar as the 'gentleman's' language (an interesting comment on the political situation).

The law provides, and the Germans and Jews have from the first enjoyed, the utmost freedom and encouragement to cultivate their genius in as many 'Vereine', &c., as they wish. Even the Magyars enjoy more freedom than most minorities in Central Europe, if they have had to struggle hard less against the Czechs than the Slovaks. In the first years, many Magyar cultural societies were suspended on political grounds, some of which were justified, others not. In two cases suspensions were quashed by the Supreme Court, and yet means were found locally to prevent the societies in question from reopening.

The Magyar Cultural Association for Slovakia only succeeded in 1927 in getting its statutes approved, and is said to have been refused permission to open many local branches in districts where the Magyar population numbers less than 20 per cent.[1]—an interpretation of the Language Law which appears entirely unjustified. The Hungarian Academy of Literature, Science, and Art, founded by President Masaryk in Bratislava in 1930, is an institution which does all honour to its founder and performs some useful cultural work, and it is no fault of his that it has largely failed to achieve its purpose, those men who take advantage of it being regarded contemptuously by their co-nationals as renegades. Some of them are, in fact, refugees from the days of 1918/19.

The same interpretation of the Language Law has been used to prevent Hungarian plays from being given in towns with a Magyar population of less than 20 per cent. The law on public libraries, which allows minorities to possess independent libraries wherever they number 400 persons in a commune, or can claim an elementary school, seems to be fairly well observed. There is no restriction on the appearance of minority literature, periodical or other, as such. The censorship on local productions is severe, but not exercised more drastically, even against the Magyars, than against the Slovaks. It is very strict on works entering the country from Hungary. Of all the Budapest newspapers, only the Socialist

[1] *Revision Memorandum*, p. 58.

organ, the *Népszáva*, is allowed into Slovakia. Many perfectly non-political works are denied entry. There can be no doubt that the censor has often acted in a foolish and even oppressive manner. At the same time he is a gentleman to whom all one's sympathy must go out in a difficult task, which is rendered doubly disagreeable by the fact that highly inflammatory political matter is often included in the advertisements or on the wrappings of non-political works.

Here, again, the assault is not directed against the Magyar language or culture as such, but against their political traditions. Writers in Magyar on purely technical or literary subjects are not discouraged if the authorities can satisfy themselves that they are, in fact, politically neutral. If they are hostile to the present Hungarian régime they are even treated with an extreme liberality.

We have already touched on the religious question. Religious toleration, as such, has been admirably maintained in Slovakia. I have heard no allegations to the contrary from either the Jews or the Ruthenes—the two national minorities which are also religious minorities—nor any suggestion of unequal treatment as regards state subsidies, &c. Within the Catholic and Protestant Churches, to which the Slovaks, Magyars, and Germans alike belong, the latter type of question does not arise, but a long struggle, already described, has gone on to replace Magyar influence by Slovak. The Magyars have their complaints. Many of their leaders have been forced into retirement or exile. The 'congrua' paid by the State to supplement the stipends of the clergy have in some cases been withheld permanently, or for longer or shorter periods, on various pretexts. The Hungarian Lutherans, numbering 30,000, were not allowed to form a separate diocese, while the 15,000 Slovak adherents of the Reformed Church were separately organized.[1] All of these are, however, clearly political rather than religious grievances.

§ 13. THE MINORITIES: ECONOMIC POSITION

In economics, equality before the law is guaranteed and observed; there is no discriminatory taxation or legislation as between majority and minorities.[2] In this respect Czechoslovakia's record compares favourably indeed with that of Yugoslavia and Roumania, and equals that of Hungary. A certain number of official measures have, however, been enacted which have reacted unfavourably on the minorities.

[1] Ibid., pp. 21–2.
[2] In spite of repeated inquiries, I only once heard a suggestion to the contrary; in one place I was told that land belonging to Magyars was being assessed too highly, so that they became liable to an unduly heavy scale of taxation. Apart from this one instance, I was agreeably surprised at the unanimity of the replies which I received.

Chief among these is the land reform already described. The vast majority of the persons expropriated under it were members of minorities (nearly all Magyars or Magyarone Jews),[1] and their losses were heavy, since, although compensation was paid, it was calculated on a price in pre-War Austro-Hungarian crowns, the value of which was at least five times that of the present Czechoslovak crowns. Hungarian sources estimate the loss incurred by Magyar landowners in this way at 3,500 million č. kr.[2]

Scant sympathy ever appears to be wasted in this century on the large landed proprietor; but the peasant has more friends, and the question whether the Magyar peasantry has received its fair share in the distribution has therefore been very warmly canvassed on all sides.

The following official figures, kindly supplied to me by the Ministry of Agriculture in Prague, show the position on January 1st, 1931.

	Number of Beneficiaries.		Area in Hectares.	
	Total.	To Magyars.	Total.	To Magyars.
Small estates . .	175,111	17,756	244,673	17,622
Residual, &c., estates .	1,252	102	132,680	9,918

These figures show to be untrue the statement, often made by Hungarian sources, that the Magyars received nothing at all from the reform.[3] It is also true that the distress and need of the Slovak

[1] According to statistics supplied to me from a Hungarian source, based on Czech official statistics and on private inquiries, 79·8 per cent. of the land expropriated under the reform had belonged to Magyars, 4·5 per cent. to Germans, 1·6 per cent. to Slovaks, 0·1 per cent. to Ruthenes, 11·2 per cent. to the Church, and 2·8 per cent. to other owners.

[2] *Revision Memorandum*, p. 4.

[3] A less sweeping statement is given in an article on 'Die Lage der ungarischen Minderheiten in den Nachfolgestaaten' reprinted from *Glasul Minorităţilor*, 1930, pp. 18 ff. This gives a total based on 'semi-official information' of 11,502 Magyar recipients and an area of 24,364 hectares. The figure quoted is 'up to the end of 1928'. I have since received further details of this total. They are clearly incomplete, but there is no reason to suppose that the proportion between Magyar and other recipients has changed since. They are as follows:

	No. of Beneficiaries.	Per cent.	Area (cadastral yokes).	Per cent.
Allotted for small-holdings .	160,311	100	390,215	100 }
To Magyars .	10,729	6·7	34,242	8·7 }
„ to colonists . .	2,257	100	68,049	100 }
To Magyars .	4	0·0	43	0·0 }
„ as building sites .	21,749	100	8,229	100 }
To Magyars .	749	3·4	345	4·1 }
Residual estates, &c. . .	479	100	100,745	100 }
To Magyars .	22	4·6	7,690	7·6 }
Total . . .	184,806	100	567,237	100 }
To Magyars . .	11,502	6·2	42,320	7·4 }

mountaineers was on the whole greater than that of the Magyar peasantry of the plains (a remark which does not at all apply to the residual estates, which were too often allotted on a basis which had nothing to do with need). Further, in Slovakia, as in other parts of the Successor States, a certain number of Magyars were deterred from applying for estates by the almost criminal propaganda of the Magyar landowning class and their satellites of the White Terror. Nevertheless, when all allowances are made, the distribution has clearly not been just. There were many more Magyar applicants than those who were satisfied, and the share of the Magyars is clearly too low, whether reckoned by the number of beneficiaries or by area distributed. It is further stated that the Magyar beneficiaries were much less generously treated as regards quality of land and in the matter of credits and other facilities than the Slovaks, much more the Czechs. This is a statement which cannot easily be checked; but it has been made to me repeatedly by Magyar peasants in tones which carried conviction, and also by persons of neutral standpoint.

For many of the Magyar peasants, indeed, the reform has been much more of a curse than a blessing. The new small-holders have no need of hired labour, and the landless Magyars who formerly got their living by working on the large estates have now been reduced to great destitution. I have found this to be one of the most deeply felt grievances of the Magyar peasantry.

The whole subject of the Land Reform is, in fact, unpopular among the Magyars, for the above reasons and even more, on account of the so-called 'colonies'—the new villages or village suburbs which have sprung up in large numbers in the plain. M. Voženilek gives a total of 15 of these in Slovakia, comprising 1,319 farms with an area of 37,607 hectares. Hungarian calculations put the figure higher (91 in Slovakia and Ruthenia).[1] Practically all of these are situated in areas which were formerly purely Magyar,[2] whereas the colonists are exclusively Slovaks or Czechs (in the proportion, it would appear, of 40 : 60),[3] the latter being partly ordinary landless peasants, partly legionaries, occasionally returned emigrants from the U.S.A. The colonists have undoubtedly been generously treated, as a glance at their homesteads will show, although experience has proved the experiment to be a costly one; many of them have failed to make good, despite all

[1] *Revision Memorandum*, p. 43.

[2] See the map at the end of the *Revision Memorandum*, which shows that only 11 of the 91 colonies marked were in areas not containing a Magyar minority.

[3] Ibid. This statement is said to be made on the basis of Czechoslovak official statistics. I should judge from my own observations that it is roughly correct. The high number of Czech colonists is a stumbling-block to the Slovaks as well as the Magyars.

concessions, and had to leave their holdings. The grant of land to
these outsiders where the local peasantry, if not destitute, could
well have done with larger holdings, has created much local ill
feeling. Even deeper is the resentment of the minority leaders, who
see in the colonization an attempt to destroy the unity of the
Magyar territory and to stake out an ethnographical claim against
frontier revision. In this they are certainly right; the purpose is
hardly concealed, and the existence of the colonies has in fact been
used to me as an argument against restoring the Schütt to Hungary.

Apart from this, the Magyar producing peasants have done well;
it is, indeed, one of the most curious anomalies of Czechoslovakia's
recent autarkic agricultural policy that the largest of all the beneficiaries have been the wheat-producing areas on the frontier which
are still mainly inhabited by Magyars. As a class they are materially
better off than before the War, and better off than their fellow
Magyars across the frontier.

The financial institutions of the minorities were dealt a hard
initial blow by the unfavourable terms on which the War Loan, to
which the Magyar banks had been the chief subscribers, was
redeemed.[1] Further measures followed.

Between 1919 and 1930 the number of Magyar banking houses
in Slovakia sank from 177 to 37, that of their local branches from
52 to 27, and that of their agencies from 29 to 7, while their capital
sank from 61·5 million to 20·7 million gold crowns, and their
reserves from 30·5 million to 12·2 million. In the same period the
number of Slovak banking establishments also sank from 121 to 50,
but the number of their branches rose from 63 to 135. Much more
important is the invasion of Slovakia by Czech banks, which have
taken over 69 branches from Magyar or Slovak establishments, and
founded 48 new branches. By 1933 the Czech banks already
possessed 44 per cent. of all the capital in Slovakia; the Slovak
banks owned 37 per cent., the Magyar and German banks only
18 per cent. Throughout Central Europe banking is invariably
used as an instrument of national policy, and it would be childish
to suppose that the hold which Czech establishments are thus
gaining over the local economic life would not be used to further
Czech and Slovak interests to the detriment of Magyar. The
Legio Bank, in particular, which enjoys the special favour of the
authorities, is quite outspokenly national in its policy. It is widely
alleged that even ordinary commercial credit facilities are much
less readily granted to minority concerns than to national. It is

---

[1] It is also credibly reported that some of the Magyar leaders advised their
followers not to have their banknotes stamped—an extraordinarily unhappy
counsel, seeing the sound footing on which the Czech currency was soon placed
by Dr. Rašin.

also said that, whereas the Magyar banks were compelled under the banking laws to contribute their quota to the 'reconstruction fund', they have received no assistance from that fund when themselves in difficulties.[1]

In trade and industry the pressure was, until recently, less severe. Czech firms, except that of Baťa, have not as a rule attempted to penetrate the Slovak country-side very deeply, and its local business has remained in the hands of the former owners, most of whom belonged to the minorities. They suffered, indeed, from the difficulties already described, which all industry in Slovakia has encountered, but they suffered in company with the Slovak firms, except in the one respect that they found Government contracts more difficult, if not impossible, to obtain. The Slovak firms themselves, however, obtained little enough from this source.

The Magyar and German workers, until recently, probably enjoyed a decided advantage over the Slovaks, owing to their better training and superior technical skill; particularly as their employers were still largely of their own nationality, or Jewish.

But here also a certain change is coming about. Until recently, the Slovaks themselves were little interested in the creation of their own non-official middle class. The western observer must always wonder at the equanimity with which the Slovaks have hitherto accepted, as some law of God, that their local doctor, dentist, vet., attorney, horse-coper, corn-broker, and money-lender should be a Magyar or a Magyarized Jew—should accept it placidly and happily, while resenting with such passion the presence of a Czech postman, schoolmaster, or tax-collector. Partly this may be due to the incurable traditionalism of the Slovak soul, and may thus not readily alter. But partly it has been due to causes which are passing: to the small number of Slovaks who have either the capital to start in business or the time and money to pass through the University and take the degree necessary for a 'learned profession'.[2]

A revolt is bound to come, as it has already come, with such violence as to dominate the whole situation, in Transylvania. The creation of a non-official Slovak middle class already forms one of the points in the programme of the Slovenska Liga, and is already largely taking the form of attacks on the minorities.

The Czechs and Slovaks have taken the first step in gaining control, to a large extent, of the banks and the big businesses, and signs are apparent of a gradual sapping of the position left to the minorities. Employers find credit difficult and costly, workers find

[1] *Revision Memorandum*, p. 49.
[2] A secondary-school certificate suffices for admission to ordinary State employment.

Slovaks preferred to them, not only by Slovak employers, but also in public works.

Thus, in spite of the legality with which the whole process is surrounded, the national economic life of the minorities is beginning to crumble. It rested before the War on four main pillars: the large estates, the banks, the industries, and the income drawn by the middle classes from the State services. The official class has almost disappeared; the landowners have been impoverished by the agrarian reform; the banks and the industries have both been seriously weakened. The turn of the free professions and perhaps of the skilled industrial workers seems likely to come soon.

§ 14. THE FUTURE OF THE MINORITY PROBLEM

So much for the present state of the minority problem in Slovakia. Unhappily, nearly all my informants are agreed that its most difficult phase is still to come. If till to-day anti-minority feeling has been comparatively mild, this has been due to certain quite specific reasons which will not necessarily operate in the future. Apart from the fact that in the earliest days the new masters, uncertain whether their rule would endure, practised a certain discretion, with an eye to acquiring merit later if positions were reversed—the majority of the older generation of Slovaks (as distinguished from the few who reacted violently) were tolerant of, and even attached to, Hungarian institutions and the Magyar people. More important still has been the restraining influence exercised on minority policy by the Czechs, who have, after all, hitherto been in command. By common consent—this point has been confirmed to me from many sources, including particularly the minorities themselves—the relations of the minorities are much better with the Czechs than with the Slovaks. The Czech official still feels a certain impartiality as between the different races, all strange and all exasperating, of Slovaks, Magyars, Jews, and Germans. He has no traditional quarrel with the Magyar (his historical enemy is the 'Deutschböhme') and he has also considerably more political experience and wisdom than the Slovak. I have heard of many cases in which the Magyar minority found in the Czech official a protection against the local Slovaks. Partly for this reason, the parties of the national minorities have rarely welcomed the idea of Slovak autonomy. The Magyar parties have seemed at times to favour it, but this has been mainly a tactical move, prompted by the hope that the Slovaks without the Czechs would be too weak to withstand the pull of Budapest.

The question is, of course, complicated by the fact that the minority parties stand to gain substantially if some of the economic demands of the autonomists are granted, e.g. a reduction in railway tariffs, a larger percentage of government contracts, and more lavish State grants for public works. But they frankly dread the cultural position if the Slovaks get their heads.

As the Czech finds it easier than the Slovak to be fair to the Magyar, so the average Magyar finds Czech rule, as such, less intolerable than Slovak. Here we have to do with deep traditional national outlooks. The average Magyar dislikes the Czech heartily, but he does not despise him. He regards him as a nasty man, but a man, not *nem ember*. Towards the Slovak he still feels the old sovereign contempt, and a great and bitter humiliation at being placed underneath the despised underling of yesterday. This feeling makes him more than ordinarily unwilling to learn Slovak, whereas a certain number of Magyars, even in Slovakia (and many Jews), have learnt Czech.

To-day, however, a younger generation of Slovaks is growing up which is militantly nationalist in a way unknown to its fathers. Hitherto, as we have shown, this nationalism has found expression largely in anti-Czech feeling: it has not been directed against the minorities, whom the Slovaks have tended to regard as poor devils like themselves. But this attitude is beginning to alter with the birth, which we have described, of an agitation against the economic position of the minorities. Anti-Czech feeling is bound to decline as the Czechs withdraw from the coveted administrative posts; but since the State cannot absorb all the applicants for posts the envious glances will be turned elsewhere, and will inevitably light on the non-Slovak middle classes. The same process is bound to come about as is now in full swing (as we shall describe) in Transylvania: a vehement agitation against all the minorities alike, based on economic motives. Quite possibly, as in Roumania, the Jews (who hitherto have escaped so lightly) will be the first and chief sufferers, while the Magyars, whose turn came years ago, and the Germans, with their self-contained economy, will get off more lightly. But none of the minorities can look forward with much confidence to the future.

At the same time, although we may reasonably expect the future to be more sombre than the past, there is no reason to anticipate for it a Balkanic blackness. The western atmosphere, introduced by the Czechs, may be expected to endure so long as Czechoslovakia itself. But even the Czechs may find themselves forced into ruder measures if international conditions continue to deteriorate as they have done so steadily in recent years. The geographical situation of Czechoslovakia imposes precautions on her, and some of these are bound to affect the liberties of the minorities. A foretaste of the future was given in the Law for the Defence of the State, promulgated on May 13th, 1936.[1] This colossal Act, which contains 201 paragraphs and covers, in the German text, more than 80 closely printed pages, lays down the measures to be taken to defend the State against any attack, or threat of an attack, on its sovereignty, independence, integrity, constitutional unity, democratic, republican structure, and security. Much of it deals with fairly obvious, although far-reaching, measures to be taken on the proclamation of a state of emergency, but it also provides for the constitution of a Supreme Defence Council, with very wide powers, which has 'to carry through the necessary measures for the preparation of the defence of the State *even in peace time*' (para. 6). Two of these measures may affect the minorities very greatly.

Firstly, Chapter III (paras. 18 ff. of the Act) empowers the State to schedule undertakings, &c., as 'of importance for the defence of the State'. An undertaking so scheduled is practically placed at the disposal of the authorities when they require it. It can be compelled to give full details of all its machinery, stocks, &c. (para. 24); to preserve complete secrecy regarding operations entrusted to it (ibid.); to equip itself and to draw up detailed plans for carrying out work entrusted to it (para. 29); and to submit to military inspection and control even in peace (para. 28).

As a rule, before the proclamation of a state of emergency, an undertaking is not to be scheduled without the consent of the owner, but the Government can override this provision (para. 27, sub-para. 2). After the proclamation of a state of emergency, the consent of the owner is no longer required (ibid., sub-para. 3).

Before deciding whether a licence may be granted to an undertaking of importance for the defence of the State, the authorities must decide whether the person to be granted the licence is 'reliable from the point of view of the State' (*staatlich verlässlich*) (para. 19, sub-para. 1). An owner who is adjudged by the authorities to be unreliable has a right of appeal; but if this fails he must appoint a 'suitable manager' in his place (ibid., sub-para. 4). If he fails to do so, the authorities can either withdraw his licence or themselves administer the undertaking as long as they think necessary (sub-para. 9). They are not bound to give their reasons for describing a person as unreliable (sub-para. 6), but a person's language, religion, or race can never constitute a reason for the description.

Those persons, in particular, are to be regarded as unreliable of whom it may be assumed with reason that they would abuse their position in a manner detrimental to the State, and particularly persons

[1] Text in *Sammlung der Gesetze und Verordnungen des Tschechoslovakischen Staates*, 1936, 35. Stück, no. 131 (23.5.1936).

who have engaged in, or engage in activities directed against the sovereignty, independence, integrity, constitutional unity or democratic-republican structure and security of the Republic, who seek to abet or encourage other persons to such activity, or praise, approve or support it, belong to a political party dissolved by the authorities, after the entry into force of the present law, on account of anti-State activities, entertain suspicious relations with other unreliable persons or with foreign countries, &c. (sub-para. 9).

Similarly, under para. 20, directors, managers, controllers, &c., have to be replaced if described as unreliable. Under para. 21, only 'reliable' workers may be employed in undertakings of importance for the defence of the State. 'Unreliable' workers must be dismissed. Foreigners may not be employed without special permission.

A Government Decree interpreting the above provisions was issued on July 11th, 1936. This gave a long list of industries regarded as 'of importance', including the glass, leather, paper, and textile industries, the metallurgical industry in all its branches, many branches of the wood industry, coal-mines and other mines, gas- and water-works, bakeries, the jam industry, cold storage, clothing and shoe factories, sugar-refineries and raw-sugar factories, the chemical and photographic industries, and many others.

It will readily be imagined what a sword of Damocles these provisions constitute, with their almost unlimited licence to the authorities to dismiss or replace both employers and workers in almost every important industry. The safeguard provided in the first sentence of para. 19, sub-para. 9, is merely nominal in view of the provisions of the rest of the sub-paragraph and the discretion allowed to the authorities in interpreting it.

Para. 34 of the Law for the Defence of the State contains measures no less alarming, in establishing 'Frontier Zones' (the exact dimensions to be defined by a later Government decree) along the frontiers of the Republic. In these zones no buildings of any kind may be erected, communications constructed, or industries or mines opened without permission of the military authorities, who are entitled to lay down their conditions before the permission is granted. Their permission is also required for afforestation or deforestation. They may order any alteration or addition to be made to existing buildings or mines, and may cut off and remove electric-power cables. If the interests of the State urgently require it, real property in the frontier zones can be expropriated for the State (sub-para. 8). Foreigners may not reside in a frontier zone without permission of the military authorities; and foreign individuals or juridical persons owning real property or rights of any kind in land in the frontier zones or near places of military importance have to report this to the authorities, which may enact any necessary restrictions, or compel them to transfer the property or rights to Czechoslovak citizens; failing which, the property may be compulsorily sold (para. 49).

Other restrictions on the frontier zones include a facultative ban on photography, &c.

A Government decree of June 24th defined the frontier zones, which consist of a belt of varying width, running round the entire frontiers of the Republic. This belt includes 48 out of the 79 administrative districts in Slovakia, and 12 of the 14 in Ruthenia. Thus the whole of Ruthenia, except a single tiny islet in the centre, is scheduled, and the greater part of Slovakia.

The decree prohibits the construction in this zone, without a permit from the Ministry of Defence, of churches, theatres, gymnasia, warehouses, meteorological observatories, roads, water-works, power stations, gas-works, chemical works, metallurgical factories, hotels, and tourist huts. The military also take over the supervision of the management of the forests. Certain trades, which include printing, bookselling, passenger, transport, and tourist agencies, are also subject to a special permit from the military.

These provisions also are already in force; and since the frontier zone round at least half the Republic is *de facto* mainly inhabited by minorities, and as conversely a very large proportion of the minorities, particularly the Magyars, inhabit the frontier zone, the effects of the decree can clearly be very serious for them. I pass over the provisions for conscription of labour contained in later chapters of the Law for the Defence of the State, although these are very far-reaching and can also be put into force without the proclamation of a state of emergency, by decree of the President of the Republic; also the very severe edicts against espionage issued in a separate law on the same day as the larger Act. No doubt these are justified by the situation of the Czechoslovak Republic. At the same time, we are not concerned only with motives, but also with effects. Even if these restrictions and precautions are abso-lutely necessary, the fact of their existence must be taken into account when we try to estimate the degree of happiness and well-being of the minorities. A State forced by outside pressure to qualify its democratic institutions by military control is not much more tolerable to live in than one which enjoys sabre-rattling for its own sake.

§ 15. POLITICAL FEELING AMONG THE MINORITIES

It is not at all easy to assess the political feelings of the Magyar minority in Slovakia. The inquirer arriving in any town and asking for the local representatives of the Magyars will soon find himself in conversation with the familiar trio: the Magyar land-owner, the Magyarized priest (very likely a Slovak by origin), and the Magyarone Jewish lawyer. He will find them, broadly speak-ing, unreconciled to Czechoslovak rule, and irreconcilable. The degree of leniency or severity with which they are treated is, to them, really irrelevant, and the fact that the régime is milder in Slovakia than in Transylvania or the Voivodina does not affect their resentment against it, since that resentment is directed less against the character of Czechoslovak rule than against its very existence. Officially, of course, they must protest their loyalty to Czechoslovakia; but no one is deceived. What they really want is a *restitutio in integrum*—a return of the whole country to the old sovereignty and the old political and social system. Slovakia is too near Budapest, too intimately connected by the bonds of the past with Hungary, for any regionalist feeling, such as we find in Transylvania, to be able to strike root. Nor have the Magyar leaders found occasion to modify in any way their social and political outlook. Honourably convinced that *extra Hungariam non est vita et si est vita non est ita*, they even cling all the more tenaciously to the old ideas, because of the contrast which these afford to the new-founded Czechoslovak ways.

In doing so, they have managed to retain the loyalty of most of the upper and middle classes, and of a considerable proportion of their humbler followers. Nevertheless, one may question whether their position would not have been stronger if they had spent less time and energy in striving to save, or lamenting the disappearance of, conditions which many of the Magyars them-selves would have rejoiced to see disappear, if the retention of them had not been made into a point of national honour. For among the social classes to which this attitude fails to appeal, the Czechs have scored considerable successes. The Social Democrats are, officially, entirely pro-Czechoslovak, as they have every reason to be, since both their material, and above all their political, conditions are far better in Czechoslovakia than they would be in Hungary. The Communists, who form a larger fraction of the working classes than the Socialists, until recently rejected both States—bourgeois Czechoslovakia and bourgeois Hungary; but, if they had to live in one of the two, they infinitely preferred Czechoslovakia, which allows them to exist and even to carry on a certain activity, whereas in Hungary Communism is a crime punishable with long years of imprisonment. Since the conclusion of the Czechoslovak-Soviet Pact, they have officially supported the Czechoslovak State, bourgeois as it is and remains. Far more important, in view of their far greater numbers, are the peasants.

The peasant is nationally resistant, but passive, and is everywhere strongly influenced by material considerations. These speak in favour of Czechoslovakia. The land reform, it is true, did not give the peasants nearly all for which they had hoped, and proved a curse rather than a blessing to many of the landless class. On the other hand, the Magyar farmers have enjoyed great prosperity since Czechoslovakia introduced her policy of extreme agrarian protectionism and are now in a position which contrasts most favourably with that of the corresponding class across the frontier. Even among the intellectuals there are deserters from the Hungarian cause—young men who revolt against the extreme stability of the Hungarian system, as contrasted with the comparative liberty of thought and expression which still prevail in Czechoslovakia. Some of these men, having achieved intellectual detachment, definitely prefer the new state to the old. And far wider than the circle of active supporters of the new order is that of those who accept it passively, content to let things alone if they are in their turn let alone—which itself pays no small tribute to the Czech régime; for in Roumania or Yugoslavia a Magyar is hardly ever left alone. But in Slovakia this attitude is possible, and even widespread. I think of a girl in a shop, a mechanic in a garage, a boots in an hotel, all of whom told me, in practically identical words, that they could not be bothered with politics and agitation, which only led them into trouble. I remember a Hungarian leader who complained to me that the youth were being brought up in 'a quite un-Hungarian spirit', and another—more revealing still—a most charming and courteous old gentleman who said that he went out Sunday by Sunday to speak to the young people and keep up the old spirit among them, but found it increasingly difficult to get them to come and listen to him.

But while it is safe and easy to record this crumbling of the Magyar national front, it is very difficult indeed to determine its extent. Cases of genuine enthusiasm for Czechoslovakia are to be found, particularly among political refugees from Hungary; but they are rare. More often the mood is one of acquiescence which sometimes approaches resignation. Not all of those who nominally support the new State, not even all who go so far as to declare themselves Slovaks and send their children to Slovak schools, have changed their allegiance in their hearts. Among the workers, it is the leaders who are actively pro-Czech; the masses are only indifferent; and the whole class numbers only a few thousands. The peasants are simply inscrutable. True, they appreciate the advantages which they enjoy to-day, but they do so in a spirit of almost cynical detachment. I spent some days among them, beyond reach of control, and must record that both

I and my companion were surprised at the warmth of pro-Hungarian feeling which we found among them. There was much mistrust of Czechs and Czech methods, and widespread cynicism regarding Czech democracy. 'Democracy and liberty may exist,' I heard more than once, 'but not for us.' I believe this opinion to be unjust, but register it here as sincerely held. And often again I heard the sentiment: 'We are better off under the Czechs than we should be in Hungary, but if a vote came, I should still choose for Hungary. It would be as in the Saar.'

The electoral figures for the political parties cannot tell us much, for, even leaving aside the question of pressure (and this does exist to a certain degree, although it is less than in Hungary or Roumania, not to speak of Yugoslavia), elections are not held on the revisionist issue. A man may be an excellent Magyar, and yet vote for the Agrarians or the Social Democrats.

I believe it safe to say that the active agitation against the Czechoslovak State—even the active resentment against it—is confined to a small fraction of the population. Perhaps the majority would rather that the question of revision was not raised at all at present, since, whenever it has been raised, it has only brought trouble for the minorities. They are like people of straitened means who prefer not to gamble, or not even to undertake any laborious work, to supplement their incomes. But if a sudden change came over the world and a plebiscite was, after all, held under conditions of secrecy, I think it probable that under normal circumstances 70 per cent. of the Magyar population of Slovakia would vote for a return to Hungary. Much would depend on world conditions at the time, and on the character of the régime in Hungary. The figure might rise to 80 or even to 90 per cent.; I do not believe that it would ever fall under 50 per cent.

The position of the other nationalities is somewhat different. The tactics adopted by the Czechs to estrange the non-Magyars from their former Allies have met with considerable success. In the undoubted drift away from the Magyars, the Jews have led the way. As we have said, the Czechs have adopted a liberal cultural policy towards their Jewish subjects, and in other respects also have shown themselves both sage and tolerant. When they first entered Slovakia, indeed, they proclaimed that they were coming 'to free the Slovaks from the Magyar-Jewish yoke', and during this early period some local excesses were not prevented—were even fostered—by some of the legionaries and civilian officials. The White Terror in Hungary, however, had a deep influence on Jewish opinion, which was confirmed after 1933 by the very wise and liberal policy towards the Jews, which was adopted by the Czechs in the Historic Lands, as contrasted with

the attitude of the Germans, particularly in the Reich but also
in the Sudetic Lands. The Jews now regard Czechoslovakia as
one of their principal bulwarks, and even if they preferred Hungarian to Czech rule in Slovakia, they would not make any move
which might endanger the position of the Republic or help German
ambitions. The Czechs in their turn have abjured their early
excesses, and have consistently behaved towards the Jews with
the utmost moderation; a course dictated no less by natural
inclination than by policy. It is, perhaps, more of a *mariage de
convenance* than *de cœur*, for in the west, at least, where the Jews
and the Magyars are most closely identified, the old attitude
towards the former is not dead, while the Jews themselves probably feel towards Czechoslovakia rather solid esteem than the
romantic affection which Budapest seemed able to inspire. As
a matter of policy, however, the authorities have always protected
the Jews against their enemies, not least against the Slovaks, among
whom radical anti-semitism is beginning to grow rather prevalent:
among the older generation on religious grounds, among the
younger, on economic. The autonomists complain with some
acerbity that they are ruled by a 'Judaeo-Czech alliance', and they
have a certain prima facie justification in the economic history of
their country since 1919. The result of the situation is, at any
rate, that the Jews are strong supporters of the Centralist system
and firm allies of the Czechs in the Czecho-Slovak controversy.

At the present moment the Slovak Jews are passing through
a period of transition which has left them scattered in half a
dozen camps. Among the older generation, especially in Eastern
Slovakia, still lingers what may be called pre-modern Judaism—
the humble traditionalism of the ghetto, in which most of the race
was still sunk in the nineteenth century. The practical, middle-
aged Jews of the cities and the west, prospering, or at least cherish-
ing the memory of prosperity, are still Magyarone—often almost
passionately so. Their children are still brought up to speak
Magyar, but they cannot cherish with equal fervour their fathers'
attachment to a country which they themselves have never known.
The Magyarone Jews are probably already outnumbered to-day
by the business men of the younger generation, who were sufficiently practical and elastic-minded in 1918 to adapt their affections.
They are excellent patriots, vote with the Government, send their
sons to Czech and to Slovak schools (more often to the former,
in which they see greater possibilities), and, in some cases, even
subscribe to the Slovenska Liga.

Finally, there is the rest of the younger generation, who have
grown up in a hard school and have seen something of the underside
of both régimes. Many of them will, perhaps, achieve prosperity

in the end, will become bourgeois and patriotic. At present they
hold one of two faiths, or both at once (since the two are not
incompatible): they are fanatic Jewish nationalists, Zionist or
otherwise; and they are international revolutionary Communists.
Both beliefs have this in common, that they are fundamentally
negative to all existing forms of state in Central Europe.

The position of the gipsies is that of the Jews *in petto*. They are
proclaimed before the world a separate race; they are treated in
a decent and enlightened fashion, and efforts have even been made
to provide them with schools of their own. They are, perhaps,
even harder than the Jews to wean from their spiritual allegiance
to Hungary, if only because there is less place for them in the
economic system, as understood by the Czechs, which is based on
organization, industry, and tariff, than in the happy-go-lucky and
spendthrift atmosphere of the departed Hungary.

With the Germans, the same local considerations apply as with
the Jews and gipsies, but the shadow of the Historic Lands falls
much more darkly across them. As we said, Czechoslovakia began
by encouraging the national feeling of the Germans by every
possible means, with a view to weaning them from the Magyars.
The scholastic and, in general, the cultural régime introduced
was very liberal, comparing in this respect extremely favourably
with that which existed in Hungarian days. While not universally
successful—for the attachment to Hungary had been very deep-
rooted—this had its effects, particularly among the younger
generation, who are undoubtedly far more truly conscious of their
nationality than their fathers were. Moreover, growing up ignorant
of the Magyar language, they have necessarily lost touch with
Hungary and with the local Magyars.

But it was easier to wither pro-Hungarian feeling than to im-
plant pro-Czechoslovak. There was, in 1918, just as great a shortage
of educated Germans in Slovakia as of educated Slovaks, and the
deficiency had again to be made up from the Historic Lands.
The teachers for the new schools were Germans from Bohemia
and Moravia. These were anti-Magyar enough, but they were
also by long tradition hostile to the Czechs and all their ways.

Thus the German movement in Slovakia began to get drawn
into the larger German movement of the Historic Lands, which
is even more dangerous to Czechoslovakia than Magyar irredentism. It was a question whether King Log had not been turned
out for King Stork. The Czechs, not unnaturally, took alarm, and
their cultural policy grew less generous; recent years have shown
a reduction, rather than an increase, of German schools. Incidentally the Germans, who were largely employed in mining and
heavy industry (in part also in the transit trade from Hungary to

Galicia, which has now ceased), suffered very heavily indeed in the economic depression which set in about 1930.[1]

These unhappy circumstances have naturally affected the political feelings of the German minority. Like the Jews, they are to-day in a state of transition. The older generation in general, particularly in districts where they are in close contact with the Magyars (e.g. in Bratislava and other southern cities), are still very strongly Magyarophil. The Deputy of the 'Zipser deutsche Partei' has sat, since 1930, with the Magyar Club in Parliament, while the German Christian Socials form a wing of the Magyar party and share premises with it. Officially a *staatserhaltendes Element*, and correct enough in its attitude towards Czechoslovakia, this older generation hardly disguises its real preference for Hungary.

Most of the younger men feel differently. They have no memories of Hungary and are not interested in her. If anything, they feel ill disposed towards her, on account of her illiberal attitude towards the cultural demands of her own German population. I have not, however, found this feeling nearly so strong among the Germans of Slovakia as among those of the Banat, &c.— simply because the former are not looking southward and eastward at all.

Their thoughts are with the Germans of the Historic Lands, and much the strongest party among them is to-day the 'Carpathendeutsche Partei', the counterpart of Herr Henlein's group.

They are not actively irredentist—an attitude which the geographical situation of Slovakia precludes; but they are definitely negative in their general outlook towards the State.

One group—the Social Democrats, who form a section of the Czechoslovak Social Democratic Party—is pronouncedly Czechophil; but, of the four German parties in Slovakia, it polled the fewest votes at the last elections. Even the German industrial workers tend rather to Nazi ideas (or, in some cases, to Communism) than to the old, orthodox social democracy. Thus the Germans have come to occupy a sort of neutral position, largely dissociated from Hungary, but not attached to Czechoslovakia.

The situation of the Slavonic minorities is governed by different considerations again. The most numerous of them, the Ruthenes, were in a curious position before the War. Their intelligentsia and the peasants on the southern fringe were being Magyarized, while, where the peasants came into contact with Slovaks, they were beginning to lose their nationality to the latter. As is

---

[1] Cf. the two *Flugschriften der Zipser deutschen Partei*, quoted above, also No. 7 of the same series: *Im Notstandsgebiet der Zips*, by Dr. W. Neméný (1934). The statements made in these brochures of the prevailing desolation in the German districts did not seem to me exaggerated in 1935, although I am informed that some improvement has taken place since.

explained in the next section, the ancestry of these Slavs is most easily told from their religion, the Ruthenes being Uniates, the Poles Catholics, the Slovaks Catholics or Protestants. Even in 1910 a considerable number were entered in the census as Uniate by religion and Slovak by language—a clear indication of the gradual advance of Slovak nationality at the expense of Ruthene.

Under the Hungarian rule it mattered little which of these two unimportant nationalities predominated. Now, however, that Ruthenia is supposed to form an autonomous area within Czechoslovakia, the position of the ethnographical dividing line has become a matter of acute controversy between the two nationalities, and the fact that the present political frontier favours the Slovaks unduly has excited a fraction of Ruthene opinion. Partly on account of this specific dispute, partly, no doubt out of old attachment, many of the Ruthenes voted at the last elections with the Hungarian or German parties, or with the Communists.

Others, however, voted for the Government, and it seems likely that the assimilation to Slovak nationality is still going on. The 1921 census showed 196,540 Greek Orthodox and Greek Catholics in Slovakia, of whom 85,628 were given as Ruthenes. In 1930 the members of the two confessions together numbered 222,797, of whom 91,079 were Ruthenes. Thus only about 20 per cent. of the increase in the religious membership was booked to the Ruthene nationality; and the Ruthenes in Slovakia were credited with an increase of only 6·37 per cent., while in Ruthenia, in the same period, it was no less than 19·98 per cent. Some of this disparity may be due to undue pressure, as the Ruthenes loudly allege; but since the same process was already going on before the War it cannot be dismissed as wholly unnatural, and points, I think, to a natural tendency to assimilate with the Slovaks. Thus the Ruthenes also may be counted as divided between support of and antagonism to the State.

For completeness' sake we must add the Guruls on the Polish border. These are not admitted to constitute a minority, and have only Slovak schools, but they speak a dialect strongly mixed with Polish elements, and many of their habits betray an origin more nearly akin to that of the people on the Polish side of the frontier than to the Slovaks. They are, in fact, an intermediate people. Had their homes been adjudicated to Poland, they would probably have become Poles. As it is, they are destined to become Slovaks, and appear to acquiesce in their lot.

Thus, even if the defections from the ranks of the Magyars themselves may not be very serious, they have been left isolated by the desertion of their former allies among the other minorities; while far more important still is the transformed political attitude, already described, of the Slovaks. One way and another, the forces actively in favour of a restoration of Slovakia to Hungary have been reduced to, let us say, 75 per cent. of the Magyars, half of the Germans, one-quarter of the Jews, and a small fraction of the Slovaks and of the remaining minorities. This change was reflected, albeit dimly and not without distortion, in the 1930 census, which gave the following results: Slovaks, 2,224,983; Czechs, 120,926; Ruthenes, &c., 91,079; Magyars, 571,988; Germans, 147,501; Jews, 65,385;[1] Poles, 933; Gipsies, 30,626; others, 768; 'foreign subjects', 75,604. When the results of this census became known, the greatest possible consternation reigned both among the Magyars in Slovakia, and in Hungary. At least one petition was submitted to the League of Nations, alleging that undue pressure had been exerted on the population to declare themselves Slovaks, or at any rate not Magyars, and that some places where the persuasion of the commissioners had proved ineffectual had been omitted altogether from the results.

The Czechoslovak Government naturally repudiated these suggestions, and the Committee of Three charged with investigating the case for the League Council accepted its explanations and dismissed the case.[2] Since both parties had recognized that the census constituted a political issue of the first importance, in view of the possible bearing of its results on the question of treaty revision; since the Czechoslovak Government had been made aware of preparations on the other side to secure for the Magyars as large an apparent figure as possible, and had admittedly taken precautions to counteract the assault;[3] and since some of the methods employed were of a type which could be perfectly justified, but might also be misinterpreted[4]—in view of all these things, it would not have been surprising if the commissioners had in some few instances succumbed to human frailty. The decrease in the number of Magyars, amounting to 62,839 persons, or 9·9 per cent., seems, indeed, too good to be true, when it is

---

[1] i.e. persons declaring themselves of Jewish nationality; the total number of persons of Jewish faith was 136,768.

[2] *League of Nations Official Journal* (subsequently referred to as *L.N.O.J.*), June 1932, pp. 1111–13.

[3] Accused of having employed too few census commissioners belonging to the minorities, the Government replied that, of 8,311 commissioners, 407 had been Magyars, 109 Germans, and 60 Ruthenes, and said that it had been obliged to select for these duties persons with a knowledge of the Czechoslovak official language and well-disposed towards the State, as the government had discovered the existence of a vast secret movement, extending even abroad, which aimed at securing as many persons as possible for Magyar nationality, in defiance of all the principles laid down with a view to establishing the real facts.

[4] The entries were made in one of two alternative ways: either by the parties, or by the commissioners, who were entitled to give the parties certain explanations. The latter method was usually employed in Slovakia, and was obviously necessary in the case of some illiterate peasants, but no less clearly might be abused.

considered that the 1921 census was already taken by Czechoslovaks and that, by the time it was taken, the great emigration of
Magyar officials and the first great defection of the nationalities
had already taken place. Moreover, the vital statistics of the
Magyars in Slovakia over a very slightly longer period showed,
not a decrease, but a natural increase of 74,159, while emigration
(1922–30) accounted for a loss of only 12,164,[1] and internal
emigration to the Historic Lands was admittedly insignificant.
Obviously the decrease of the Magyars can only be explained by
defections to other nationalities (chiefly, it would appear from the
statistics, to the Slovaks and the gipsies);[2] and it is difficult to
believe that some of this was not due to pressure.

On the other hand, it is unlikely that any pressure exerted by
the Czechs, whose methods are never entirely forcible, would
have had such large results if the resistance to it had been whole-
hearted. The figures quoted above may—probably do—under-
estimate the number of persons who in their hearts regard themselves as Magyars, and even those who speak Magyar; but they
assuredly reflect also the continued progress of that natural
assimilation of the minority to the majority which goes on in every
country where no great gulf separates the different nationalities,
and in none more rapidly than in Hungary itself. Striking as are
the differences between the figures of 1930 and those of 1910, it
is probable that neither of them distorted very grossly the feelings
of the population at that time. We cannot safely reckon the number
of nationally conscious Magyars much higher than the figures seem
to show it. True, those of the Magyars, Jews, &c., who have
deserted completely into the Czechoslovak camp probably entered
themselves in 1930 as Czechs or Slovaks, and can thus be ignored
in any guesses at the proportions of the different minorities who
would vote for a return to Hungary. Perhaps, therefore, the
estimated percentage of Hungarian loyalists which we have given
above is too low; but in any case it is quite certain that Czechoslovakia has scored an important political victory during the past
fifteen years in bringing over to her side the great majority of the
Slovaks, a fair part of the non-Magyar minorities, and a certain
fraction of the Magyars themselves. And those who remain loyal
to Hungary are not only diminished in numbers, but impoverished
and shorn of much of their old prestige and influence.

---

[1] A. Molnár, 'Das Ergebnis der Volkszählung von 1930 in der Slovakei und
in Karpathoruthenien', in *Nation und Staat*, April 1934, pp. 429 ff.
[2] The Slovak increase on the previous census amounted to 283,041 persons
(14·58 per cent.); that of the gipsies to 22,627 (282·87 per cent.). Apart from
the Czechs, whose increase is due to immigration, the other nationalities showed
only moderate percentage increases, while the Jews registered a decline of 5,137
persons, or 7·28 per cent.

Thus, taking the population as a whole, its feelings have clearly changed very much since 1918. If a plebiscite could be held to-day, and under existing conditions (i.e. with a choice between Czechoslovakia and Hungary), a substantial majority would vote for the former. The party in favour of Hungary is probably only slightly larger, in proportion to the whole population, than the figures shown as Magyars in the 1930 census; the non-Magyars favouring Hungary outnumbering by no very great amount the Magyars who preferred the *status quo*.

§ 16. THE ECONOMIC PROBLEM

There remains the economic problem, which has proved, unfortunately, far more obstinate than the political.

The economic history of Slovakia since the War falls into three main divisions. The first comprises the immediate post-War period already described, which was undoubtedly disastrous for Slovakia. It was followed, however, by some years of comparative recovery. It was greatly to Slovakia's advantage during these years that Czechoslovakia—thanks partly to the industry inherited by the Historic Lands from the Dual Monarchy, partly to her very sound financial policy—was by far the most prosperous of the Successor States. Although the heavy and textile industries, and some others which had been unable to adapt themselves, continued to decline, a certain number of new industries were introduced, and others—particularly those dealing with food and drink—developed. By 1926 industrial production had reached approximately the level of 1914.[1]

Increasingly, however, Slovak economy was tending to concentrate round two main sources of wealth: forestry and agriculture. The two interests may be said to be almost equally balanced, for although the nominal figure of persons affected by the former is much the smaller (in 1926 it was calculated at 55,475 directly employed in the forests and 57,444 in the derivative industries)[2] a much larger number of cottagers and labourers, nominally listed as agriculturalists, depend for their existence on being able to do occasional work in the forests. The forest districts are also poorer in alternative resources than the plains; and for Northern and Eastern Slovakia the prosperity of the timber trade is just as essential as is that of agriculture for the south and west.

Both forestry and agriculture enjoyed reasonable prosperity for several years. The former even developed considerably, for, strangely enough, large-scale exploitation of the Slovak forests had

[1] See figures quoted by A. Fichelle, 'L'Industrie slovaque', in *L'Europe Centrale*, August 4th, 1934. Most of these are based on calculations by M. Karvas, of Bratislava, to whom I am also indebted for oral information.

[2] A. Fichelle, 'L'Exploitation forestière en Slovaquie', in *L'Europe Centrale*, May 12th, 1934.

hardly set in before the War. Between 1918 and 1926 the number of workers employed in the larger saw-mills almost doubled, and much timber was exported into the Historic Lands, where the building trade was very active for some years.

Concentration on the home market led to a certain neglect of foreign markets, with a single exception: Hungary. Here, in spite of the frontier, the old and traditional economic connexion between the mountains and the adjacent plains reasserted itself, and a brisk trade developed, which increased steadily and rapidly. In 1929 Slovakia exported to Hungary goods to the value of no less than 81,451,000 pengö, 57·85 per. cent. of the total being formed by timber in various shapes, while paper—a direct product of the same industry—accounted for another 10·73 per cent. The only other large item was iron ore (7·50 per cent.).

Hungary in return sent into Slovakia goods to a slightly lower value (74,288,000 pengö in 1929), nearly all of which were agricultural. Wheat headed the list with 27·38 per cent.; the value of the main agricultural products imported (wheat, flour, pigs, cattle, wool, raw hides, maize, bacon, and lard) equalled almost exactly that of the timber exported. The total trade between Hungary and Slovakia comprised almost half of the entire trade between Hungary and the whole Republic, in spite of the fact that Czechoslovakia also sold large quantities of coal to Hungary.

In the meantime, agriculture also passed through a succession of fat years. Much was done for it in the way of the provision of cheap credit, the reorganization of co-operatives, &c., and every effort was made to smooth the path of the beneficiaries of the agrarian reform. In some directions, very satisfactory results were achieved. The area under cultivation increased in the case of nearly every crop (potatoes and maize alone excepted), the increase in the case of the area under wheat between 1920 and 1929 being no less than 39·6 per cent.[1] The average yield per hectare also rose remarkably, as shown by the following figures:

	Quintals per hectare.		
	1913	Average 1925–9	Average for C.S.R. (1929)
Winter wheat . . .	12·5	14·9	18·6
Winter rye . . .	11·6	13·3	17·7
Spring barley . . .	13·8	15·1	19·5
Oats	11·0	11·9	17·0
Maize	15·4	19·6	..
Potatoes	78·7	102·9	118·1
Beet	246·1	219·1	242·3

[1] For the following figures, see A. Fichelle, 'Agriculture et Économie Rurale Slovaque' (L'Europe Centrale, June 9th, 1934) and 'La Slovaquie et le Ravitaillement en Denrées agricoles des Pays Historiques', in ibid., November 11th, 1935.

As regards live stock, the position was less satisfactory. The quantities, still below those of pre-War, are as follows:

	1911	1933
Cattle	1,100,800	928,204
Horses . . .	237,800	251,488
Pigs	675,880	574,430
Goats	38,000	75,627
Sheep	993,700	349,847

Moreover, the quality also has deteriorated owing to the difficulty in persuading the peasants to take sufficient pains in breeding and selecting stock—an unfortunate but probably inevitable result of the land reform.

These products, again, found a ready market in the Historic Lands for some years. The importance of this market may be seen from the following table:[1]

Production and Marketing of Slovak Agricultural Produce

1928

	Production (tons).	Sales to Historic Lands (tons).	Per cent.
Cereals and leguminous plants .	2,043,221	187,764	9·10
Potatoes	3,037,998	13,242	0·43
Sugar-beet	1,078,650	49,897	4·62
Milling products and by-products	..	78,372	..

1929

Cereals and leguminous plants .	1,881,172	132,875	7·21
Potatoes	2,285,530	23,357	1·02
Sugar-beet	1,232,915	52,405	4·25
Milling products and by-products	494,355	76,472	15·90

Slovakia does little foreign trade in any of the above products, except barley; nearly all her exports, as also her exports of live stock, are to the Historic Lands. On the other hand, her surpluses are valuable to the Historic Lands, which have an export-surplus of rye and barley, but a deficit of wheat and maize.

These fairly happy conditions continued until the great agricultural depression set in in 1927. It was not long in affecting Slovakia, where, in spite of all improvements, the position had many weak points. Above all, the beneficiaries of the agrarian reform, who had bought their land at a moment of high prices and were often still heavily indebted, found themselves in great difficulties. Even with the action taken, many of them had to give up their

[1] *Die Slovakische Industrie*, Jahresbericht der Zentralvereinigung der Slovakischen Industrie (Bratislava, 1930).

holdings; and their distress was particularly disagreeable to the Government, both for reasons of internal party politics and on national grounds. It can hardly be doubted that political reasons were among those which prompted the Government when, faced with the imminent collapse of the whole class of small-holders, it embarked on a policy of autarky and ushered in the third period of Slovakia's economic history by denouncing the trade agreement with Hungary (December 15th, 1930). In consequence, the two countries entered a 'treatyless state' and each armed against the other. While Czechoslovakia introduced what amounted to little short of a prohibition on Hungarian agricultural imports, the Hungarian autonomous tariff was made applicable to textiles, paper, leather, glass, and metallurgical products, among the articles which had previously figured among Slovakia's exports; tariffs were placed on milk and fuel-wood, and the duties on hops and malt multiplied almost ten times.

The result of this was, of course, practically to kill the Slovak-Hungarian trade. The figures for the years immediately before and after the denunciation of the trade agreement are as follows (in thousands of pengö):

	Exports from Slovakia to Hungary.	Imports from Hungary to Slovakia.
1929	81,451	74,288
1930	62,836	68,862
1931	16,502	13,826
1932	14,779	11,036
1933	12,169	12,678

A quota agreement was, indeed, subsequently made with Hungary which provided for an exchange of Slovak timber against Hungarian pigs; but this has worked with appropriate stubbornness, and has not nearly compensated for the losses caused by the interruption of normal relations.

Controversy has raged ever since on the wisdom or unwisdom of this step. On the one hand, the diminution of foreign supplies undoubtedly saved the producing farmers of Czechoslovakia from ruin. Among these, some of the chief beneficiaries have been the farmers of Slovakia; prominent among them—a piquant thought—the Magyars of the corn-producing southern strip. The higher prices for food-stuffs which have obtained recently have been of the greatest benefit to this class, which to-day enjoys a certain prosperity, although it has not proved possible to reduce their indebtedness at all substantially.[1] Still further measures of control

[1] Prospects of a conversion of agrarian debts have been held out by the Agrarians, but the response made showed that the situation was beyond their powers to cope with.

O

are now being worked out, with the object of establishing a cereals monopoly, and possibly a cattle monopoly also, which is meant to ensure the farmers stable prices and a fair return for their outlay. The ideal appears to be a sort of balanced economy in which Slovakia is to act as purveyor of food-stuffs to the Historic Lands, taking in return the manufactured articles of the latter; the agrarian influence in Parliament ensuring that the 'price-scissors' shall keep duly closed.

Since more than half of the population of Slovakia (1,822,144 persons out of 3,329,793) is still listed as living from agriculture (including cattle-breeding and market-gardening) this idea presents obvious attractions. Against it, however, must be set several facts. The figure of 'agriculturalists' quoted above includes a very large number of agricultural labourers and dwarf-holders who actually stand to lose more than they gain by the raising of prices. These include the considerable number of persons for whom the land reform has brought actual privation; for, in spite of the provision made under the law for labourers formerly employed on the estates divided up, there seems no doubt that many of them were actually deprived of their livelihood by the process. Further, as was remarked above, the problem of the harvest-workers has only been solved in part. The landless agricultural proletariat remains a large and very necessitous class in Slovakia. And when one comes to consider the question more closely, it seems very doubtful whether Slovakia ought really to be described as an agricultural country at all. It is true that she has in the past exported considerable quantities of food-stuffs to the Historic Lands, and that her productive capacity might easily be further improved by more rational methods, more extensive use of fertilizers, &c.[1] On the other hand, even the present surpluses are made possible only by the present phenomenally low standard of living of the population: the annual consumption of beef per head is only 6·52 kg., of pork 8·41 kg., of rye 16 kg. The respective figures for the Historic Lands are 16·52 kg., 14·81 kg., and over 50 kg.; and even those, as regards meat, are exceedingly low measured by the standards of Western Europe.

Further, the continued high birth-rate, combined with the

[1] Fichelle quotes the figures for kilograms of fertilizers used per hectare sown with rye:

Size of Holding.	Historic Lands.	Slovakia and Ruthenia.
2–5 ha.	239	27
5–20 ha.	264	52
20–50 ha.	318	128
over 50 ha.	311	235

difficulties of emigration, are resulting in an increasing pressure of population which must lead to a still further diminution of the agricultural surpluses. It is an interesting and perhaps a significant fact that the introduction of protection did not result in any increase of the imports to the Historic Lands.

This last fact is presumably due to Slovakia's now herself consuming food-stuffs which she formerly imported from Hungary, in exchange for her timber. These imports were, as has been said, on a large scale; in 1929 they amounted to 781,608 quintals of wheat, 129,659 of flour, and 204,439 of maize; 15,841 pigs, 8,476 head of cattle, and large quantities of fruit, vegetables, wine, &c. They were paid for, almost exactly, with the export of Slovak timber.

The cessation of the Hungarian imports has had to be paid by an equal cessation of Slovak exports. It has proved quite impossible to fill adequately the gap left by the Hungarian market, since, for nearly every other, Slovak timber, owing to its high freight-charges if it has to be carried by rail, is at a crushing disadvantage compared with the rival products of the Polish, Austrian, Russian, or overseas forests. Since 1930 the Slovak timber industry has therefore been in a state of permanent crisis, and the population dependent on it has been reduced to almost unrelieved misery. It has, in fact, been doubly hit: not only has its earning-power gone, but it has had to pay more dearly for its food-supplies. It is difficult to resist the conclusion that the pre-War exchange of products, which had reasserted itself between 1919 and 1929, was far more natural and far more advantageous, at least to the population of Northern and Eastern Slovakia, than any other. It seems at least as well established that the timber-supplies of Slovakia are complementary to the economy of Hungary, as her food-supplies to that of the Historic Lands.

The unfortunate economic results of the change-over are even more apparent when we come to mining and industry. The production of lignite and of the rarer ores (most of which are not found elsewhere in the Republic) held its own even after the great depression set in. There is, however, no reason to suppose that they would not have worked equally well under Hungary. The production of copper ore stopped altogether, and that of iron ore fell in 1933 to only about 20 per cent. of its 1929 figure. In that year (the worst recorded) only a single mine was working in the northern mine-field, and a second in the southern field—the latter on a contract for Hungary. But while Slovakia thus continued to serve to some extent as a useful source of raw materials for the Historic Lands[1] the local industry which had depended on those

[1] From 1925 to 1928 inclusive about half the ore produced in Slovakia

resources simply ceased to exist. The Bohemian and Silesian industrials who had acquired control of the industry after the War simply closed it down when the restriction of their export trade forced them to reduce their output.

Since 1933—the blackest year of all—a certain improvement has set in once more, to be attributed partly to the general world recovery, and partly to internal factors, including the devaluation of the Czechoslovak currency. Czech capital, which has few profitable outlets to-day in the Historic Lands, has shown a tendency to seek out Slovakia, while Czech entrepreneurs have discovered the advantages offered to them by the lower wages and weaker workers' organizations of Slovakia. Further, the difficulty of communications is less than it used to be, particularly as regards the west, where two new railways have been built to link the Váh Valley with Moravia (a third is now under construction).[1] Railway tariffs have been further revised, in such fashion that West Slovakia is now almost on an equal footing with East Moravia. Finally, the rapid growth of Bratislava, which, besides carrying on at least ten times as much trade as in pre-War days, has become a large administrative centre, has turned that city and its immediate surroundings into something like an island of prosperity.[2]

The situation is very different as regards Central and Eastern Slovakia. Here, too, both railways and roads have been greatly improved, and the handicap of communications reduced. It remains, however, crushingly heavy and these districts have not shared the revival enjoyed by the west. The following figures, which relate to 1934,[3] may show the relative prosperity of the districts lying near the Moravian frontier, and the unrelieved misery of

was exported to Moravia, and about one-third sent abroad (mainly to Hungary).

[1] A certain number of Slovaks also spend the week working in the industrial area of Ostrava in Moravia (cf. International Labour Office, *The Rural Exodus in Czechoslovakia*, p. 115).

[2] The population has grown from 61,537 in 1900 to 123,832 in 1930. The real growth is rather less, as some outlying villages have been brought within the city boundaries, in order to reduce the percentages of the national minorities. The harbour has been modernized and expanded. Figures for the movement of traffic are as follows (in tons):

	Outward.	Inward.
1913	12,280	29,090
1919	13,723	7,634
1921	177,250	
1925	446,943	
1927	544,768	
1931	136,646	649,471

The chief exports are textiles, machinery, paper, and glass; the chief imports wheat, maize, flour, and mineral oils.

[3] *Die Slovakische Industrie, 1934*, p. 60.

those which depend on forestry, mining, and heavy industries:

Inspectorate of Industry.	New Enterprises.		Existing Enterprises Enlarged.	Former Enterprises Reopened.	Enterprises Closed Down.
South-west .	Bratislava . . 11		11	..	4
	Nitra . . . 3		6	..	5
North-west .	Trenčín		3	2	26
Centre . .	Zvolen . . 1		4	4	16
East . .	Spisská Nová Ves 3		2	4	21
	Košice . . 3		6	1	37

The larger part of the country has simply been reduced to a reservoir of raw materials for the industry of others; and even those materials are not particularly favourably situated for what in an age of economic autarky must be their chief market. It is hard, therefore, to foresee even a tolerably prosperous future for Eastern Slovakia; and even when we include in our survey the more prosperous west, the question, already suggested, arises whether any good can really come for Slovakia out of the policy of treating her as a purely agricultural and primary-producing country. For, as we said, it is true only of half the country to call it agricultural; the rest is simply non-industrialized—a very different thing. Industrialization would undoubtedly benefit the mountain population —would give it, indeed, almost its only chance of subsistence; and since Hungary found it worth while to industrialize the country and Czechoslovakia does not, it seems clear that, economically, its transference from the former to the latter was disadvantageous to the population, at least as regards Central and Eastern Slovakia.

When we come to consider the other parties concerned, Hungary has clearly lost heavily. She has no alternative sources of supply within her own frontiers to replace the Slovak ore and timber. She has since the War created an alternative textile industry—an effort which has cost her large sums. Whether Czechoslovakia has gained as much as Hungary has lost is very doubtful. She has certainly been able to supplement usefully her agricultural supplies, and the Historic Lands have acquired an abundant source of certain raw materials for their factories and a certain market for their finished goods. If Hungary is now, by the loss of Slovakia, less near an autarkic condition than she was before the War, Czechoslovakia, by its acquisition, is near to such a condition. Autarky is, however, much less naturally feasible for her, owing to her geographical configuration. The possession of such a long, poverty-stricken tail imposes considerable burdens on the plumper body. It is difficult to say just how heavy that burden is. On the one hand, the Slovak budget is invariably passive, and the cost of State subsidies to public works, &c., is heavy. On the other hand, various circumstances connected with the accounting of indirect and company taxation make it likely that the adverse balance is much smaller than it appears. If, however, the Historic Lands are ever going to pull Slovakia up to their own level of prosperity (an intention which is often announced) they will have to pay extremely heavily in doing so.

§ 17. POSSIBILITIES OF LOCAL REVISION

Slovakia offers greater possibilities of local revision than almost any other part of the territory with which we are concerned. There are two main areas in which such revision might be contemplated. The first and more obvious is in the south-western corner. Given existing conditions, it is difficult to see how Bratislava could be restored to Hungary under any scheme which stopped short of the complete dismemberment of Czechoslovakia. The area lying east of that city is in different case. The arguments for assigning it to Slovakia were never strong. There seems no particular reason why Czechoslovakia should claim to be a Danubian power, or why she should need more than an outlet on the river. That portion of the left bank which stretches as far as the junction of the greater and less arms of the Danube is amply large enough to provide Bratislava with all the room for the expansion of its harbour which it is ever likely to need. What lies beyond was purely Magyar in 1919, and is still overwhelmingly Magyar to-day. Some colonists of Czechs and Slovaks have, indeed, since been planted there, but the colonists are still few by comparison with the indigenous inhabitants, and it would be surely unfair to allow the interests of this artificially created minority to outweigh those of the great majority. Moreover, although a great deal of money has been spent on those colonies, they have not on the whole prospered. Very many of the colonists gave up their holdings and returned whence they came. On many farms the present tenants are the third, fourth, or even fifth since 1919.

The economic argument is stronger. These lowlands are undoubtedly of more value to Czechoslovakia than they would be to Hungary. Without them, Czechoslovakia's autarkic agrarian policy might well have proved impossible altogether. It might, however, easily be argued that both Hungary and Czechoslovakia itself would have fared better if more economic co-operation had been forced on them.

If local revision were undertaken in this area, it need not be confined to the great Island. The lesser arm of the Danube is no very significant waterway, and the country lying immediately north of it is just as purely Magyar as the Island itself. There is much to be said in favour of a rectification here which should bring the political frontier nearer to the ethnographical line. If this frontier proved geographically artificial, it would at least err in good company.

There seems no reason why Komárno should lose its trade through this rectification. The timber floated down the Váh could not go by any other route. Komárno's second principal article of commerce is Silesian coal, which is in any case bound for destinations outside the Republic, and can surely be as well shipped in Hungary as in Czechoslovakia.

In the central section, the opportunities for local revision grow fewer, although it is probable that a Frontier Commission, working in an unprejudiced atmosphere, might make certain corrections in favour of Hungary. In the east, the situation is different again. It is complicated in the first place by the question of the Ruthenes, which will be treated fully in the next section of this work. Here we need only recall that the higher mountain areas, from a point lying slightly to the east of the High Tatras, and extending thence in a gradually broadening wedge, are inhabited mainly not by Slovaks but by Ruthenes. These Ruthenes were never strongly anti-Magyar and harbour to-day a certain grievance in not having been incorporated in the Autonomous Territory of Ruthenia. South of them, in the Lower Spiš, are some Germans, with Magyars in and around Košice itself.

The Slovaks are, of course, in a majority, but in 1919 they were very largely Magyarized, and even to-day they are nothing like so nationalist as their brothers in Central and Western Slovakia. Moreover, this area has suffered terribly from the economic depression, and has been ruined rather than helped by the recent trend towards autarky. It might still be found that a majority among the local Slovaks themselves favoured return to Hungary. A few years ago this would have been probable. To-day it is much more doubtful, but the possibility is not to be dismissed.

RUTHENIA

THE remaining territory allotted to Czechoslovakia under the
Treaty of Trianon is the Autonomous Territory of Ruthenia.[1]
Politically, it differs from Slovakia, and indeed from any other
area with which this volume is concerned, in that it possesses a
right, guaranteed by international treaty, to a wide degree of
autonomy: a condition imposed by the Powers in 1919 in recognition of the fact that the Hungarian Ruthenes, for whom it was
intended to constitute a sort of 'national home', are racially and
linguistically a distinct nationality. It possesses, therefore, a
whole series of political problems of its own, although many of
these bear very close analogies to those of Slovakia, while its
economic problems differ from those of Slovakia, as a rule, only
in degree—being nearly always more acute—but not in kind.
Geographically, Ruthenia is a pendant of Slovakia; if the one
forms an elongated tail attached to the body of the Historic Lands,
the other forms the tail's tip. Such, indeed, is its shape. Like
Slovakia, it consists of a section of the inner slopes of the Carpathians, with a small strip of the adjacent plain. On the west,
the boundary (in theory still provisional) with Slovakia forms a
simple cross-section of mountain and plain. Of the two longer
sides, the upper, which coincides with the old boundary between
Hungary and Galicia, runs along the watershed of the Carpathians,
curving gradually from an easterly to a southerly direction as
those mountains reach and pass their extreme north-eastern
extremity. At the apex of the arch, where Poland, Ruthenia, and
Roumania meet in wild and lofty mountains, the frontier (hereafter dividing Ruthenia and Roumania) curves back westward, at
first cutting across mountains, then following the course of the
Tisza, which at this part of its journey is a turbulent and fast-
running mountain stream. When the Tisza emerges from the
foot-hills, the latter draw sharply back, so that the line of them
runs from south-east to north-west, while the river takes an

---

[1] The name 'Ruthenia' will be used here for the sake of brevity, and as being
unambiguous enough for our purposes. The official title to-day is 'Podkarpatska
Rus', usually translated 'Sub-Carpathian Russia' or 'Sub-Carpathian Ruthenia',
or 'Carpatho-Ruthenia'. It is well, however, to remark that the question of
nomenclature is the centre of one of those political controversies so exciting to
Central Europe and so difficult for Western Europe to appreciate. See below,
p. 207.

irregular course, full of loops and meanderings, although westward in its general trend. The political frontier follows a fairly straight line westward, cutting the river in two places, and leaving on its right a widening triangle of plain. The whole forms an area of 12,639 square kilometres (4,886 sq. m.), of which mountains occupy some three-quarters.

There is no need to describe in detail either the plain—a typical stretch of the Hungarian Alföld, the haunt of storks, buffaloes, and the Fata Morgana—or the mountains which, with their forest-clad slopes, open, pastoral summits, and narrow intervening valleys, are own brothers to those of Slovakia, while lacking any of the grander peaks of the Tatra. It is, however, worth while emphasizing the close geographical and economic connexion of mountain and plain, which is even more marked than in Slovakia. In the western third of the country only one road which is practicable even by the most modest standards traverses the mountains from west to east. In the centre there are two; in the east none at all, and all traffic must descend to the plain to pass from the valley of the Rika to that of the Tisza. Across the plain, on the other hand, runs an important railway which forms the link between the Slovak system and that of North-Eastern Hungary and Northern Transylvania. Branch lines run up the main valleys. The passage across the mountains into Galicia is not difficult, and two railways and five main roads invite the traveller to attempt it, when political conditions are favourable.

The chief towns—Užhorod (Ungvár), Mukačevo (Munkácz), Sevljuš (Nagy Szöllös), and Chust (Huszt)—lie at the valley mouths, while a few market centres, the largest of which is Berehovo (Bereg Sžasz), lie out in the plain. The mountain centres of population, although sometimes strung for miles along the valleys, are all small.

The natural resources of the Ruthene mountains are smaller than those of Slovakia. The only mineral deposit of value is salt. The Ruthene districts of Hungary formerly produced nearly 40 per cent. of the country's total output in quantity, and over 50 per cent. in value. The frontier now runs through the salt-field, leaving Akna Slatina, the largest and most valuable of the three mines, in Ruthenia, while the other two are in Roumania. After this, by far the most important of the country's resources is the timber, which covers 48·80 per cent. of the total area. A considerable number of men and women find employment, in good seasons, in the forests and sawmills, and a few factories existed before the War for by-products of the timber industry, such as furniture-making and the distillation of wood alcohol. The industrial establishments employing more than 20 persons, however, only numbered 50 in 1910, with a total of 4,943 employees, while another 16,622 persons were employed in smaller enterprises. The increase, as compared with 1900, had been rapid (63·4 per cent. for the larger industries, 33·4 per cent. for the smaller), but the development still lagged far behind that of the Slovak counties.

Apart from the forests, and the few quarries or salt-mines, the mountains are suited only for a little stock-raising and dairy-farming, and for the cultivation of meagre crops of rye, oats, maize, and potatoes, of which only the potato is produced in quantities nearly sufficient for the needs of the population. For their other essential supplies, the mountaineers of pre-War Ruthenia resorted largely to the seasonal migration to the plains at harvest time which has been noted in the chapter dealing with the Slovaks. A large fraction of the 'Verchovina' (as the poverty-stricken mountain district is known) depended for a large part of its annual supplies on this seasonal work. In some years the emigration organized by the Highland Commission alone rose to 15,000; usually it varied between 8,000–10,000.

Overseas migration was high, although not so high as from Slovakia, or even from the German districts of Hungary. Between 1899 and 1914 some 50,000 Ruthenes emigrated from Hungary (44,000 of them permanently), and the Ruthene colony in the U.S.A. amounts to-day to nearly 300,000. Emigrants' remittances formed an important item in the pre-War budgets of many families. Some of them also earned certain sums as ghillies and beaters on the big estates—Ruthenia was really treated by the Magyars as a great deer-forest—although the population as a whole undoubtedly lost far more by the ravages of the game than it gained by this work.

In 1898 the Hungarian Government instituted a special action for relieving the poverty of the mountaineers. This was in the hands of the so-called 'Highlands Commission', which, besides organizing the harvest labour, introduced the beginnings of a co-operative movement and spent sums which were considerable for that time on the purchase of land for settlement, the distribution of agricultural machinery, the introduction of improved strains of live stock, crops, and fruit-trees, and even such varied objects as the establishment and maintenance of osier-beds and the breeding of crayfish. The founder of the Highlands Commission was a Hungarian Government official of Irish origin, named Egan, whose sympathies had been stirred by the miseries of the people. He was assassinated in a lonely spot by persons unknown, and it is still locally believed that he was made away with by Jewish middlemen, whose profits he was undermining.

Some of the local estate-owners helped with this activity, but it cannot be said to have made any very deep impression on the conditions, particularly in view of the constant and rapid increase of the population. Still, a certain *modus vivendi* had been established, based on the natural interdependence of mountain and plain, which assured a living of sorts to most of the mountaineers. Very much more, however, remained to be done before the position could be regarded as at all satisfactory.

By contrast, the plains, with their rich harvests of wheat and maize, and the foot-hills, with their excellent vineyards, which deserve to be more widely known, hold great natural wealth and were able to support a prosperous population.

The censuses of 1910 (Hungarian) and 1921 and 1930 (Czecho-slovak) give the following figures for the population of Ruthenia:

	1910 (maternal language).		1921	1930 (nationality).
Ruthenes . .	319,361	Ruthenes, Russians, and Ukrainians .	372,500	446,911
Magyars . .	169,434	. . . .	103,690	109,472
Germans . .	62,187	. . . .	10,326	13,249
Roumanians .	15,387	. . . .	10,810	12,641
Slovaks .	4,057	Czechs and Slovaks .	19,775	33,961
Others . .	1,062	Jews	79,715	91,259
		Poles	298	..
		Gipsies . . .	..	1,357
		Others . . .	..	278
	571,488		595,114	709,128

While the 1930 figures show a normal development from those of 1921, comparison of the latter with those of 1910 must be made subject to the same reserves as in the case of Slovakia. The figures are particularly affected by the fact that the Hungarian census of 1910 officially reckoned the Yiddish 'jargon' as German; no less than 53,942 persons entered in that year as 'German-speaking' (besides 30,680 listed as Magyar-speaking) were of Jewish origin.[1] The general distribution of the two main nationalities is, *mutatis mutandis*, the same as in Slovakia, viz. a Slavonic peasant mass in the mountains and a Magyar peasant mass in the plains, with a small Magyar population of landowners, officials, railway employees, and industrial workers scattered among the Ruthenes; but the border-line is no more clear-cut in Ruthenia than in the Western Carpathians. Here, too, as a result of past migrations (chiefly connected with the advance and subsequent retreat of the Turks), Magyar villagers had settled in Ruthene territory and Ruthenes in Magyar. Nearly all the former are

[1] Cf. Molnár, op. cit. The figures quoted by Molnár for the 1910 census are slightly higher than those reproduced in the official Czechoslovak publications.

Ruthenized to-day. Most of the Ruthenes in the plains, who were substantially the more numerous, Magyarized very quickly, but the process was not yet quite complete in 1918, and there are still Ruthene and partly Ruthene villages south of Užhorod and Mukačevo, including a few even south of the present frontier. There were also many villages which had lost their Ruthene language but betrayed their ancestry by their membership of the Uniate Greek Catholic Church, which was practically a local speciality of the Ruthenes, shared, among their neighbours, by the Roumanians alone, while the true Magyars, the Germans, and the Slovaks were either Roman Catholics or Protestants. Ninety-seven per cent. of the Ruthenes were Uniate in 1918.

On this ground, both Czechs and Ruthenes attacked the Hungarian statistics in 1919 as showing too low a number of Ruthenes, since the religious statistics gave 567,867 Uniates in North-Eastern Hungary, after deducting the Roumanians of that creed. All these, according to the Ruthenes, ought to be reckoned as Ruthenes; and if nationality is to be reckoned by ancestry, their contention was undoubtedly correct. In some cases, however, the process of Magyarization had been completed generations back.

Broadly speaking, then, the Ruthenes are the mountaineers, the Magyars the plain-dwellers of Ruthenia; but before leaving the question of distribution it should be recalled that the Ruthene area of settlement extends both westward and eastward of the present frontiers of Ruthenia. The eastern outliers consist only of a few thousand souls in the valleys of the Black Tisza and the Visa, now under Roumanian rule. In Slovakia, on the other hand, the Ruthene area of settlement reaches in a gradually diminishing wedge as far westward as the foot of the High Tatras. The Czechoslovak census registered 85,628 Ruthenes in Slovakia in 1921, and 91,079 in 1930, while the Ruthene claims (partly, here also, based on religion) put the figure considerably higher.

Of all the nationalities of pre-War Hungary the Ruthenes, who are now, in theory, the dominant nationality of the Autonomous Territory, were perhaps the poorest and most neglected. The prosperity which they are said to have enjoyed in the seventeenth and eighteenth centuries had given place to a long decadence. The outer world hardly knew them, save when they descended in their droves at harvest-time and stood about the market-places of Debreczen or Nyiregyháza for hiring. In their very mountain homes they were disregarded. Such industry as existed was exclusively in Magyar, German, or Jewish hands and employed workmen of the same nationalities; the Ruthenes were not thought fit for any better employment than lumbering, acting as ghillies

on the huge deer forests which covered most of the country, or
scratching a miserable livelihood out of the tiny plots left to them
under the shadow of the trees. Only the nobleman or his bailiff
driving to the castle passed between long rows of cabins built of
log or clay, with floors of beaten earth and chimneyless roofs of
decaying thatch; the smoke, eddying through the single room,
revealed dim outlines of a promiscuous crowd of cows and children, geese and grandparents. In the muddy lane, half-naked
infants fled from under his wheels, or grown men avoided them
with greater difficulty as they strove to master the fiery brandy
which formed their chief solace and a large proportion—and
perhaps the most sustaining part—of their diet.

Their mental poverty equalled their material destitution. Not
that the Ruthenes are fools, for they have a clear enough natural
intelligence, and a fund of imagination and even poetry, as evi-
denced in their beautiful native ballads, which were largely used
as a source by the creators of the Ukrainian literary movement
across the Carpathians, embroidery, domestic and church architecture, and housecraft, as well as in the remarkable level of technical efficiency attained by their numerous witches. But their
natural aversion from sustained effort of any kind, for which they
are justly renowned, was indulged to the full by the customs of
their church, which allowed the pious among them to celebrate
the saints' days of two separate and exceedingly hagiophilous, not
to say hagiodoulous, calendars.[1] The scattered nature of their
habitations made it difficult for the authorities, with the best
will in the world, to enforce school regulations in the face of the
ingenious and persistent resistance of parents and children combined, nor were the authorities particularly anxious to overcome
that resistance. If they did not, as their enemies to-day aver, leave
the Ruthenes in ignorance of set purpose, in order to keep them
docile and loyal, they were at least in no hurry to take up the
problems of this remote corner of their kingdom. One way and
another the percentage of illiteracy stood as high as 92·8 in 1880,
and at 77·1 as recently as 1910.

How this people remained for so long without any national
consciousness to deserve the name, and how, when the awakening
came, it brought with it a confusion of hopes and beliefs easily
surpassing even that of the Slovaks, is a story which involves a
brief glance at their history.

The Hungarian Ruthenes were long held, on the strength of

[1] Before the War some villages in Galicia kept nearly 200 holidays in the
year. Even to-day the workers in the State forests of Jasina observe, I am told,
an average of 13½ holidays in the month. I can confirm from personal experience
that the office of His Excellency the Governor in Užhorod is little, if at all, less
punctilious.

certain passages in the sprightly but unreliable 'Anonymous Chronicler of King Bela', to be the autochthonous inhabitants of their present homes, and were, indeed, one of the few peoples of Hungary to whom the Magyars were willing to concede historic priority. Modern Hungarian historians, however, now hold that when the Magyars entered Hungary (which they did, according to tradition, by the valleys which lead through Ruthenia to the plain of the Upper Tisza) this remote and savage territory was entirely, or almost entirely, uninhabited. For a long period thereafter the Magyars left it in this virgin state, according to their usual custom, as a barrier against invasion, using it, at most, as a royal hunting-forest, and it was not until the advent of less turbulent times that the land was granted to various lords, lay and spiritual, under whose auspices the ancestors of the present population were settled as colonists, or squatted uninvited in unoccupied areas.[1] In either case, the Ruthenes must have been the first actual inhabitants of the mountains (the first settlements in the plains, all traces of which were swept away in later wars, were German), but can make no claim to a pre-Magyar State; nor, to do them justice, have they attempted to do so.[2]

Many districts have certainly been settled quite recently. The earliest colonies are recorded towards the end of the thirteenth century, while new arrivals were still coming in 400 and even 500 years later. The local origin of the different groups of settlers also varies considerably. The Hutzuls round Jasina (Vereczke) are identical with the mountaineers of the same name who inhabit the highlands of Galicia and the Bukovina, immediately across the frontier. The ancestors of the Boiki and Lemki, who now live a little farther south, seem to have come from the plains of Galicia; while the 'Dolišani' or lowlanders immigrated from what is now the Soviet Ukraine, via Moldavia and Transylvania.

In every case the country of origin appears to have been some part of the enormous Ukrainian linguistic area, and the various local dialects, of which there are great numbers,[3] appear in every case to be at bottom variants, strongly and diversely corrupted by local elements—Polish, Slovak, or Magyar—and by Russian and Old Slavonic terms, of the Ukrainian language. In this sense it is correct to classify the Ruthenes as Ukrainians.

It may reasonably be asked why, if this be so, they are not

[1] See on this especially 'Die Ungarländischen Ruthenen', by A. Bonkáló (*Ungarische Jahrbücher*, vol. i, 1922, pp. 215 ff.—with full bibliography).

[2] No such claim was ever put forward at the Peace Conference, except in the single, and completely disregarded, intervention of the West Ukrainian Government.

[3] A recent philologist has counted 14 dialectal groups, while even the most modest calculations allow 3 main groups with intermediate sub-groups, cf. R. Martel, *La Ruthénie sub-carpathique* (Paris, 1935), p. 26.

universally called by that name. To answer this question (which is of far more than academic interest) a short digression is necessary.

The name of 'Ukraine' in itself simply means 'frontier', and refers to the southern frontier of the old 'Russian land', the district from which the Ruthenes came. At the date, however, when they left their homes, no separate national consciousness had developed among these 'frontier-men', and the inhabitants of the entire 'Russian land', whether coming from the north (the present Great Russia) or from the south (the present Ukraine), described themselves equally as 'Russians'. The Ruthenes thus brought with them the name of Russian (in their dialect, 'Russin'), which name was translated by the scribes of Central Europe with the dog-Latin 'Ruthenus'. The north Russian variant of the same original word 'Russian' is 'Russkia', and when relations between Central Europe and Russia grew closer, a pragmatic distinction was made: the subjects of the Tsar were described as 'Russians', while the men of the same stock who had gone under the rule of Central Powers—the group in Hungary with which we are now concerned, and the much larger body inhabiting Volhynia, Eastern Galicia, and the Bukovina which was incorporated first in Poland, later in Austria—continued to be entitled 'Ruthenes' by their rulers. The adjective formed from 'Russin' is 'ruskij', and when the Ruthenes wished to distinguish between themselves and the subjects of the Tsar they did so by adopting for the latter the name 'russkij' with two s's. It will be seen that the distinction is a nice one, particularly so when applied by a people some 90 per cent. of which was totally illiterate and the remaining 10 per cent. not much better.

It is a commonplace that nations of identical stock may develop quite distinct national consciousnesses if subjected to different historic and cultural influences. The Russians and the Ruthenes had, of course, different histories, and an important cultural distinction arose between them when the latter were converted in 1598 to the Uniate creed, which combines Orthodox ritual with spiritual allegiance to the Holy See. When the importance to the spiritual life of the Slavonic nations of their national churches is remembered, it will be seen that in the nineteenth century there was some ground for expecting that the Ruthenes would develop an entirely separate national consciousness, such as has evolved, for example, in the U.S.A. or in the Spanish-speaking countries of Latin America. On the other hand, the differentiation had not been carried so far as to eliminate all possibility of reversing the process. The most simple and effective method of doing this was by re-conversion to the Orthodox Church, and whenever Russia saw her opportunity to bring about such re-conversion she seized

it with an energy which was often crowned with considerable
success. The Governments of Poland, Austria, and Hungary, on
the other hand, emphasized by all means in their power the distinctive 'Ruthene' characteristics of their subjects.

As though this Ruthene-Russian imbroglio were not enough,
when Moscow attempted in the seventeenth and eighteenth centuries to impose a uniform 'Russian', i.e. Great Russian, nationality,
the inhabitants of the Ukraine, injured in their particularist
feelings, began to insist that they were not Russians at all, but
'Ukrainians'—a thesis strongly opposed by the Great Russians,
who at the most allowed their southern neighbours the status of
a national variant and their language that of a dialect, 'Little
Russian'. The dispute did not remain confined to the subjects
of the Tsar, but spread to the Ruthenes, who had now three
possible national identities between which to choose: Ruthene,
Russian, or Ukrainian.

The struggle began to grow acute only towards the latter half
of the nineteenth century, and was working up towards a climax
in the years before the War. In East Galicia it seemed likely to
end in the elimination of the Ruthene tendency and the predominance of the Ukrainian, which the Austrian authorities had been
obliged, unwillingly enough, to tolerate and even to foster in order
to counter the more urgent danger threatening from a political
and pseudo-religious Great Russian and Orthodox propaganda
liberally financed and energetically propagated from Petersburg,
through the so-called 'Galician Benevolent Society'.

All this manœuvring and counter-manœuvring, however, passed
over the heads of the little group of Hungarian Ruthenes who, ever
since they crossed the Carpathians, had lived a life of extraordinary
isolation. Partly owing to the influence of geographical conditions,
partly by the set policy of the Hungarian Government, they had
had little commerce even with the inhabitants of East Galicia,
immediately behind the passes at their backs. They had not,
indeed, even any great consciousness of their own national individuality or unity, as among themselves. The average Hutzul,
for example, even to-day habitually describes himself under that
name, looking down on the Lemki and the Dolišani as 'foreigners'
and inferior creatures; as will be seen, the Hutzul interpretation
in 1919 of the doctrine of self-determination was to set up neither
a Ruthene nor a Russian nor a Ukrainian State, but a Hutzul
Republic. The natural tendency towards disunity was, of course,
enhanced by the Hungarian political system. There was no unified
Ruthene territory, the highest organization, under Budapest,
being the County, and the different Counties had little connexion
with each other.

On the other hand, the relations of the Ruthenes with Hungary had always been of the closest. As the mountains at their back shut them off from their kinsfolk in the north, so the easy valleys drew their life constantly down to the plains at their feet. In medieval times their attachment to the Hungarian Crown earned them the name of 'gens fidelissima'; and this was fortified during the seventeenth and eighteenth centuries, when, in their sheltered position, they enjoyed considerable economic prosperity. The armies of Rákóczi, the great Hungarian national hero of the struggle against Austria, were largely composed of Ruthene peasants. Of all the Hungarian 'nationalities' they seem, after the Suabians and the Jews, to have taken least part in the anti-Magyar movement of 1848–9, and if some faint strivings of national life, some flickers of a desire for autonomy, showed themselves during the 'Bach' era, they were soon extinguished again after 1867.[1]

In this connexion the role of the Uniate clergy was very important. Unlike the Uniate priests of Eastern Galicia, who led the local Ukrainian movement, or the Roumanian Uniates of Transylvania, who, after a doubtful beginning, had become once more excellent Roumanians, the Ruthene clergy eagerly absorbed Magyar culture for themselves, and from the genteel heights thus attained looked down on their flocks, too often, with indifference or contempt. Far from leading any national movement, they were among the chief obstacles which prevented such a movement from arising.

In these circumstances it was not surprising that the political evolution of the Hungarian Ruthenes proceeded along quite different lines from that of the Galicians. The Ukrainian movement left them practically untouched. One or two writers before the War had attempted to substitute in their works the purer Ukrainian for the usual local vernacular; but this hardly scratched the surface of the local life, and there was certainly no Ukrainian national movement up to 1914.

The Great Russian movement was hardly more active, since its first stirrings in 1848, after which Great Russian had for a while been adopted as the local literary language. The 'rolling rouble',

[1] According to M. Krofta ('Die Podkarpatska Rus und die Tschechoslovakei', *Prager Rundschau*, 1934, pp. 410 ff.) they welcomed Paskievitch's Russian armies when the latter entered Hungary in 1849, and both M. Krofta and M. Beneš, in his speech to the Ruthenes (*Prager Tagblatt*, May 4th, 1934), lay stress on the importance of the 'Messianic Russophilism' of those days. The movement cannot, however, have been very widespread. It is specifically denied by the earlier geographer, Reclus, writing in 1878, and I have found no mention of it in the contemporary histories. Under Bach, a Ruthene named Dobrjanskij was appointed Imperial Commissary for North-Eastern Hungary, residing at Košice, and introduced Ukrainian into the schools and administration. In 1861 the Ruthenes asked for territorial autonomy within Hungary, but they do not seem to have pressed the point, and the movement died away after 1868.

which circulated so freely in Galicia and the Bukovina in the opening years of the twentieth century was slow to cross the Carpathians. Eventually, however, it made its appearance there also, if in diminished quantities, and a few thousand persons were converted to the Greek Orthodox Church. The agitation, nominally religious, was in reality purely political, and culminated in a famous 'monster trial' at Sighet (Máramaros Sziget) in 1914, when thirty-two peasants were condemned to a total sum of $39\frac{1}{2}$ years of imprisonment for treasonable activity. It is quite certain that the agitation was introduced and financed from Russia, had sprung from no spontaneous feeling in the population, and had awakened no perceptible response among it. Most of the defendants in the famous trial were peasants who had obviously been actuated by the simplest and oldest of all motives.[1]

Unmoved by the rival blandishments of Russian and Ukrainian, the Ruthene peasants continued to be Ruthenes, and hardly even that. There was no Ruthene national party and little desire for one. The intelligentsia and middle-class, so far as such existed, not only did not resist, but welcomed actively, the opportunities offered it after 1867 to Magyarize itself.

'They Magyarized with enthusiasm', I was told by one informant, himself a Ruthene. 'They were ashamed of being Ruthenes', said another. It is a fact that one nationalist leader of to-day sued a newspaper for libel during the War for calling him a 'Rusnyak'; and Count Károlyi, when in 1919 he honestly sought for an educated Ruthene to become Minister for Ruthene Affairs in Budapest, could not find one speaking his mother tongue. With the full consent of the persons concerned (some of whom took the opportunity thus offered to rise to high positions in Hungary), all higher education had been completely Magyarized, with the sole exception that instruction was given in Great Russian, two hours weekly, in the 'gymnasia' of Užhorod and Prešov, where the Uniate priests received their training.

The Magyarization of the elementary schools began later, but this also was far on its way towards completion by 1914.

In the first years after 1867 there were still some hundreds of purely Ruthene schools; but by the outbreak of war only a handful was left in which a few subjects were taught in Ruthene, the rest in Magyar, while in all the others the language of instruction was purely Magyar.[2]

[1] One of the agitators who escaped to Russia before the trial lived there until the revolution, when he returned to Ruthenia and settled there. I had the pleasure of meeting him in 1934.

[2] The general situation is clear, although the statistics vary. A memoir from Hungarian sources sent to the League in 1923 (*La Situation des minorités en Slovaquie et en Russie sub-carpathique*) says (p. 51) that there were 285 elementary

Administration and justice were entirely Magyarized. The county administrations and assemblies were Magyar, or run by Magyars, in Magyar. The position to which the Ruthene language (or languages) was relegated may be judged from the fact that in 1910, according to Hungarian official statistics, there were only 542 persons of Ruthene mother tongue in all Hungary practising 'intellectual professions'. Even this unpretentious figure may give rise to exaggerated ideas unless closely analysed. Scrutiny reveals that of the 137 persons employed in the service of the Church, 44 were choristers and sacristans, and of the 244 persons concerned with 'public health', no less than 243 were village midwives. A single Ruthene-speaking person practised literature and the arts.[1] The Ruthene-speaking contingent of the 64,797 public employees and State school teachers in Hungary numbered only 21.[2]

Here we may leave the Ruthenes, as they were in 1914; a poor, remote, and backward people of dwarf-holders and woodcutters, scattered about the hills and valleys of one of Europe's remotest corners; their intelligentsia estranged from them, their affairs ordered for them by others, themselves, it appeared, destined in another half-century or so to lose their own nationality in the Hungarian.

Of the other local nationalities the Magyars need no special description. The Roumanians are a tiny linguistic island of three villages, separated from their kinsfolk in Roumania only by the Tisza, which forms the local frontier. The Germans inhabit several villages near Mukačevo, where their ancestors settled in the eighteenth century. The 'Czechoslovaks' were represented before the War only by one or two Slovak villages near Užhorod; the present large increase is due to the immigration under the new régime of Czech officials. The Jews are a larger and more important element—so large as to give the casual observer the impression, on first sight, that they outnumber all the other local nationalities put together. It is hard to believe that a century ago

schools in which the language of instruction was exclusively Ruthene; also 3 training colleges. *The Hungarian Peace Negotiations*, vol. iii, p. 264, give, on the contrary, only 45 elementary schools in Ruthene, and 771 Greek Catholic (Uniate) elementary schools, 570 of them in the territory claimed by the Czechs, with Magyar language of instruction. A private informant tells me that in these schools Russian was taught for two hours a week, all other instruction being in Magyar; the teachers received a special award of 100 crowns if the inspectors found that the children had a good knowledge of Magyar. The Czech documentation to the Peace Conference and the League says that there were 353 Ruthene schools in Ruthenia in 1871, which number sank to 45 in 1910, 18 in 1914, and o in 1915 (*Mémoire concernant la Russie sub-carpathique*, presented by the Czechoslovak Government to the League of Nations, n.d. [1922]). Another version gives 479 Ruthene schools in 1868, 571 in 1874, 23 in 1906, and in 1913 only 34 Church communal schools in which Ruthene was used for teaching religion, singing, and language (*L.N.O.J.*, March 1934, p. 355).
[1] *Hungarian Peace Negotiations*, vol. iii. A, p. 143.   [2] Ibid., p. 286.

things were quite otherwise; but in fact the large-scale Jewish immigration into Ruthenia began only after 1867, when a great wave from Galicia first overtopped the mountains, while quite a large contingent arrived only during the World War. By now they are firmly ensconced not only in all the towns—in Mukačevo, particularly, they form over 50 per cent. of the whole population— but even in the centre of every considerable village. They are, indeed, so numerous as to have overflowed all the traditional Jewish occupations. Besides controlling most of the economic and much of the intellectual life of the country, they also work in the factories, the vineyards, the forests, and even on the roads, where, contrary to general anticipation, they make excellent labourers; while even more live a wretched existence without any discernible means of support whatever.[1] Only a small fraction of them belong to the 'neologs'—that fraction of Hungarian Jewry which seceded from the main body in 1906, and favours the most complete assimilation to Christian habits and appearances, short of religious conversion—although in such towns as Užhorod the commercial classes are largely Neolog Jews. Most of the Ruthene Jews are strictly Orthodox, preserving the traditional Jewish tenets, habits, and appearance, and speaking among themselves either Yiddish or Ashkenazi Hebrew. A few even belong to the strange Podolian sect of the Chassidim, with its weird, semi-oriental rites and its wonder-working Rabbis. It should be added that although Ruthenia can boast a few rich Jews, especially among the corn-brokers of Berehovo, the community as a whole is not wealthy, and actual destitution is by no means rare; further, that in pre-War days almost all the Ruthene Jews were excellent Hungarian patriots—the Neologs by inclination, the Orthodox in obedience to the injunctions of the Talmud to respect the temporal power. In practice the Jewish innkeeper, the Magyar local magistrate, and the Magyarone priest formed a slightly incongruous but quite harmonious trio, who directed the affairs of their Ruthene village with a despotism which did not altogether lack benevolence.

§ 2. UNION WITH CZECHOSLOVAKIA

Even as late as 1918, few could have foreseen that the following year would find Ruthenia a component of Czechoslovakia. Throughout the early part of the War, at least, the 'gens fidelissima' fairly preserved its repute, although the contact of the

---

[1] According to the Czechoslovak Statistical Office, in 1921, 40 per cent. of the entire Jewish population of Ruthenia had no regular profession whatever; they were what is expressively known in German as 'Luftmenschen'.

soldiers with other Ruthenes, and of the civilian population with the Russian armies, which penetrated the northern fringe of the country, seem to have led to some vague Pan-Slav or Russophil manifestations. The movement does not appear to have been extensive; the Government interned three priests in all for subversive activities.[1] At this time (1917) the Hungarian Government thought it worth while to found a Ukrainian newspaper with centralist tendencies in Budapest. The movement was not, however, strong, and Czech official documents themselves admit that few of the Ruthenes possessed enough energy or national feeling even to dream of liberation. 'Their liberation came from without, from their Czech and Slovak brothers, from the Ruthenians of America, and from the Entente.'[2]

The first step towards any national movement seems to have been taken on November 8th, 1918, when a Ruthene National Council constituted itself at Lubovna, on the Slovak border, and demanded self-determination for the Ruthenes and dissolution of the connexion with Hungary. A resolution to this effect was forwarded to the Slovak National Council. The ideas of this meeting seem to have been somewhat vague, but they are said to have inclined to union with Galicia. On November 19th the council moved to Prešov and extended its membership.[3]

On November 9th a second council constituted itself in Užhorod.[4] This body, on the contrary, declared its loyalty to Hungary (it is fair to point out that just as Prešov (Eperjes) was half Slovak, so Užhorod, or Ungvár, was mainly a Magyar and Jewish town, and a centre of Hungarian administration), greeted with enthusiasm the new Hungarian People's Republic, repudiated all separatist tendencies, but demanded for the Ruthenes 'the same rights as the Republic would be granting to the other non-Magyar nationalities of Hungary': autonomy for the Uniate Church; and social, political, and cultural reforms.[5] These demands were afterwards worked out in greater detail and sent to Budapest. The idea in the minds of the council was to give the Ruthenes a status similar to that enjoyed by Croatia-Slavonia in the old Hungary. The Hungarian Ministry of Nationalities attempted to meet these wishes, and on December 25th issued

---

[1] Martel, op. cit., p. 47, says 100; the figure of 3, with details of their cases, has been supplied to me officially by the Hungarian Government.

[2] League of Nations Document, C. 608 H. 281 (1923) I.

[3] Szana, op. cit., p. 232.

[4] There was also a third (Hutzul) Council in Jasina, which set up what amounted to an independent republic. Repressed by the Užhorod Council, it re-established itself in January and continued in power until dispersed by the Roumanians on June 11th. The Hutzuls confined themselves strictly to their own business, and made no attempt to settle any one else's fate.

[5] Szana, op. cit., p. 232.

an Autonomy Statute (People's Law No. X of 1918) to the following effect:

The Ruthene districts of the counties of Máramaros, Ugocsa, Bereg, and Ung to be united in an Autonomous Territory, to be known as Russka Kraina, which should enjoy complete autonomy in religious, educational, and cultural questions, and in internal administration and justice. 'Common affairs' were to be regulated in common with the Hungarian Republic; these comprised foreign affairs, war, finance, private and criminal law, economic questions, communications, and social policy. The legislative organs were the Ruthene National Assembly and the common Parliament. The head of the administration was the minister for Russka Kraina, who was responsible to both legislative organs, while a governor resided in Russka Kraina.[1] The Act was brought into force immediately, and a minister was actually discovered (not without difficulty) and appointed in the person of Dr. Oreszt Szabo, a gentleman of Ruthene origin who, although speaking not a word of Ruthene, was prepared to act in the interests of his countrymen. On January 8th, 1919, he issued a proclamation reassuring the Magyar population in North-Eastern Hungary, promising that no districts with Magyar majorities should be included in the Russka Kraina, and that the rights of minorities should be respected.[2]

Meanwhile, however, events had been taking a very different turn in the west. The Allies as such do not seem to have occupied themselves with the question, for although Tsarist Russia seems to have entertained plans of annexing all the 'Little Russian' territories of the Dual Monarchy, these came to nought when the Tsardom fell.[3] Knowledge of those plans may have influenced the Czechs, from whom the decisive initiative seems to have come. Professor Masaryk relates that while in Russia (in 1918) he discussed with Ukrainians then the question of incorporating the Hungarian Ruthenes in his future State,[4] and when he reached the U.S.A., in May 1918, he was 'soon in touch' with the Ruthene colonies there, particularly with one M. Žatkovič, a local leader. On July 23rd, 1918, those colonies held a meeting at Homestead, U.S.A.,[5] where they decided in favour of complete independence if possible, failing which the Hungarian Ruthenes should endeavour to unite with their brothers in Galicia and the Bukovina; failing that again they should demand autonomy, 'though under what State', says Masaryk in his narrative, 'they did not say'.[6]

[1] Szana, op. cit., p. 251.   [2] Ibid., p. 257.
[3] Martel, op. cit., pp. 39–44.   [4] *The Making of a State*, p. 239.
[5] There appears to have been a preliminary meeting ten days earlier at McKlensport.
[6] Masaryk, op. cit., p. 240.

M. Žatkovič, with a few friends, formed a 'National Council of the American Ruthenes', which on October 21st, 1918, approached President Wilson with its three alternative desiderata. The President informed them that the first two were not practicable and would certainly not be favoured by the Allies, and referred them to Masaryk to negotiate on the third.[1] On October 23rd the Ruthenes were received as a separate nationality, entitled to self-determination, into the 'Central European Union', a polyethnic body of which Masaryk was President,[2] and the negotiations began on October 25th. The next day the so-called 'Philadelphia Agreement' was signed by Masaryk and Žatkovič, guaranteeing the Ruthenes autonomy if they would join Czechoslovakia, while Masaryk also promised that 'the boundaries will be so established that the Rusins will be satisfied'.[3] On November 12th the National Council met again at Scranton, U.S.A., and adopted a resolution in favour of union with the Czechoslovak State on a federative basis, on condition that the Ruthene State should include 'the now partly Slovakized, but originally purely Ruthene Hungarian Counties of Spiš, Saris, Zemplén, Abauj, Gömör, Borsod, Ung, Ugocsa, Bereg, and Máramaros'. This resolution was shown to Masaryk, who expressed his satisfaction, while warning the authors that the Peace Conference would have the last word.[4] A referendum was then taken among the Ruthene parishes of the U.S.A. Sixty-seven per cent. voted in favour of the resolution, 28 per cent. for union with the Ukraine, less than 1 per cent. each for union with Galicia, Hungary, and Russia respectively, and less than 2 per cent. for independence. The result of the plebiscite was cabled to Beneš in Paris.

Copies of the agreement and resolution were sent to President Wilson, Žatkovič retaining the originals. Žatkovič afterwards set out for Paris, where he arrived on February 13th, 1919.

It is evident that the American delegation to the Peace Conference, at least, was fully initiated into the result of these negotiations, for the 'Outline of tentative Reports and Recommendations, prepared by the Intelligence Section, in accordance with Instructions, for the President and the Plenipotentiaries', as early as January 21st, 1919, already recommended the union of the Hungarian Ruthenes with Czechoslovakia, either as a protectorate or (preferably) as part of the State, with exactly the same arguments as used by Dr. Beneš a few days later: the 'intense hatred' of the Ruthenes for the oppressive Magyar rule; the undesirability of

[1] Krofta, 'Ruthenes, Czechs and Slovaks', in *Slavonic Review*, vol. xiii, p. 622.
[2] The other nationalities represented on this body were the Czechoslovaks, Poles, Yugoslavs, Ukrainians, Lithuanians, Roumanians, Greeks, Italian irredentists, Armenians, Albanians, and Jerusalem Jews.
[3] Žatkovič, *Exposé*. [4] Ibid.

allowing Russia to get a footing across the Carpathians or Hungary to thrust a wedge between Czechoslovakia and Roumania; and the general advantages of Czechoslovak rule for the Ruthenes.[1] Dr. Beneš then restated this case to the Supreme Council on February 5th.

An official memorandum forwarded about this time to the Peace Conference develops these arguments, criticizes the Hungarian population statistics, and suggests a frontier with Hungary which would leave within Ruthenia the important lateral railway line (a concession which had not, incidentally, been claimed by the Ruthenes themselves). The Ruthene-Slovak frontier, it was stated, had been

fixed provisionally, in conformity with the frontiers of the Czecho-Slovak State, whose limits are those of the Užhorod and Bereg Comitats. This could be altered and improved, if so desired, by a special treaty between the Czecho-Slovak State and Carpathian Russia.[2]

The Supreme Council referred the fate of the Ruthenes to the Commission for the study of Czechoslovak questions, which decided to advocate in principle the formation of an autonomous Ruthenia, guarantees being given for freedom of transit between Hungary and Poland, as well as between Czechoslovakia and Roumania. The final decision was referred back to the Supreme Council. There the matter rested for the moment, the Committees being engaged on other work.

Throughout these negotiations Dr. Beneš regularly declared that Czechoslovakia was not claiming this area—which would be a burden to her—but was putting its inhabitants' case for them.[3] It is clear, however, that he was keener than he allowed it to appear.[4] The strategic consideration which in fact lies at the root of most of Czechoslovakia's interest in Ruthenia was probably already present in his mind; for Czechoslovakia and Roumania had already reached a close understanding, while Poland and Hungary were equally already showing signs of making common front with regard to Czechoslovak questions.

At any rate, he was taking all necessary steps to lend weight to his arguments. Czech troops had occupied Prešov on December 28th, 1918, Užhorod on January 13th, 1919, and the valley of the Už during the following days. On January 20th the Inter-

---

[1] Hunter Miller, *Diary*, vol. iv, pp. 231–2.
[2] *Problem of the Ruthenes in Hungary*. This undated document seems to be identical with the 'Memoir No. 6' presented by the Czech Delegation to the Conference.
[3] Hunter Miller, op. cit., loc. cit.
[4] See the rather obscure note in Nicolson's *Peacemaking*, p. 239. Particularly intriguing is the remark that 'the Galician Ruthenes being mostly Jews do not want to go to Russia, still less to Roumania'.

Allied Commission recognized all territory west of the Už as lying within the Czech sphere of occupation. On February 13th a courier from Paris, one Captain Pisecky, arrived in Užhorod, bringing Masaryk's copies of the Philadelphia Agreement and the Scranton Resolution, in order to show the Council the feelings of the American Ruthenes and the advantages of the Czech solution. The Užhorod Council rejected the overture and declared its wish to remain with Hungary; in fact, the autonomous Government had already begun functioning, if somewhat uncertainly, with its Governor in Mukačevo. The Prešov Council proved more accommodating and its Chairman, M. Beškid, left for Paris, where he, with Žatkovič and the Secretary-Treasurer of the American Council, M. Gardos, established a General Commission representing all Carpatho-Ruthenes. Through the intervention of Dr. Beneš, this Commission obtained interviews on February 17th with Colonel House and on February 24th with M. Tardieu, on whom they pressed the advantages of the Czecho-Slovak solution. On March 3rd they were informed that the Council of Five had decided in favour of their proposals. They then drew up a further set of demands, known as the 'Fourteen Points', which they handed to Kramář and Beneš, and on March 4th Žatkovič and Gardos set out for Prague, leaving Beškid in Paris. On March 10th Žatkovič conferred with Masaryk, handing him all the documentation of the case. He then set out for Užhorod, breaking his journey at Bratislava, where he interviewed Dr. Srobár, and at Prešov, where the local representative of the Prešov Council approved all they had done and authorized them to try to unite the nation in favour of their proposals.[1]

Meanwhile the situation had been still further complicated by the appearance of a fresh foreign claimant, backed by another National Council. The Roumanians were showing signs of meaning to advance into Ruthene territory. Hereupon Ukrainian detachments from East Galicia arrived, first in the person of a lieutenant and three soldiers, who entered Máramaros Sziget on a locomotive on January 9th, but seem to have returned by the same route.[2] On January 17th a larger detachment appeared, to protect their brothers against the Czechs and Roumanians and to assure them freedom of self-determination.[3] Four days later they also retired, being expelled by the Roumanians and by bands of the local inhabitants, but not before they had organized the constitution of yet a third Ruthene National Council in Chust.[4] This declared for union with the Ukraine, and requested the Ukrainian Government in Stanislawów to represent it in Paris and to secure fulfilment of its wishes. M. Sidorenko, head of the Ukrainian

---

[1] Žatkovič, op. cit.   [2] Szana, op. cit., p. 259.   [3] Ibid., p. 262.
[4] It was at this time that the Chust Council, referred to above, reasserted itself.

delegation in Paris, in fact asked the Peace Conference to incorporate Ruthenia in the Ukrainian State on ethnographical and historical grounds (the latter being entirely baseless) and on the strength of the request of the Chust Council.[1] In these circumstances an American officer, Col. Goodwin, was sent down, in early March, to inquire into the situation, but his report had no influence on the Conference, which had, indeed, already made up its mind.[2]

In March the Hungarian Governor of Russka Kraina actually managed to carry through elections, which gave a large majority for the 'autonomist party', i.e. that party which desired autonomy within the Hungarian State. A few days later the Ruthene Diet was convoked, and the Minister addressed it in glowing terms. The deputies, however, with rare good sense, decided that their deliberations would, in the circumstances, serve little purpose. They sent an ultimatum to Budapest declaring that the frontiers must be laid down definitively, and in a manner satisfactory to themselves (a rumour had gained ground that the Hungarians proposed not to include the Sevljuš basin in the Kraina). Otherwise they would claim a free hand. They then adjourned, never, as the event proved, to reassemble.

The last thing that the unfortunate Hungarian Government was in a position to do was to determine any frontiers whatever. On March 31st it fell. A People's Commissary succeeded the bourgeois Governor in Mukačevo. The Bolshevik Government preserved its predecessor's work to this extent, that it ordered the constitution of a separate Ruthene Council; but the activities of Council and Commissaries did not last for long. The Roumanians (acting, it appears, at least in part on the request of some of the local bourgeoisie) advanced, and by May had occupied the whole eastern half of the country, as far as the town of Mukačevo, where they were met by Czechs coming from the west, the latter having received permission to advance east of the Už through the personal intervention of Žatkovič, who went to Paris for the purpose.[3] Each of the future allies administered half the town.

This was the situation when Žatkovič arrived in Užhorod to inform the local leaders of the emigrants' decision, and of the course which events had been taking in Paris. On May 8th a new Central National Council, purporting to represent all three earlier Councils, met in Užhorod under the chairmanship of M. Vološin. The Hungarian solution had lost much of its popularity under Kun's régime; no one wanted union with Roumania; and it was agreed that a Ukrainian solution was impossible. The meeting, therefore, voted unanimously to accept the *fait accompli* of the Czech

[1] Szana, op. cit., p. 263; also private information.
[2] Hunter Miller, *Diary*, vol. xvii, p. 161.   [3] Žatkovič, op. cit.

solution (perhaps all the less reluctantly since Czech troops were occupying the town and Czech police actually keeping order in the hall). A delegate asked what was the guarantee that Czechoslovakia would really grant autonomy; Žatkovič replied that the guarantee was given by 'the fraternal relations between the Czech nation and Ruthenia'. The resolution adopted by the meeting stipulated, however, that although foreign, military, and financial affairs should be common, Ruthenia should enjoy internal autonomy with its own government and administration, Ruthene regiments and their own officers, and use of Ruthene in the local schools and religion. The Council held five further meetings to discuss its demands in detail. Finally, on May 22nd, a deputation of 112 persons went to Prague to present Masaryk with a resolution in favour of union. It was stipulated that Ruthenia should remain 'an independent State within the Czecho-Slovak Republic' and that pending the final delimitation of the frontiers (which was to take place by negotiation and be embodied in a treaty) it should include not only the mainly Ruthene counties of Máramaros, Bereg, Ung, Ugocsa, and Gömör, but also the portions inhabited by Ruthenes of the four counties of Abauj, Zemplén, Šároš, and Sepeš. Pending final arrangements the government was to be in the hands of a Ruthene Minister appointed by the President of the Republic (the deputation asked that Žatkovič should be given thi spost), and a draft Statute of Autonomy was appended, which was based closely on the Hungarian Law X.

These demands were forwarded to Paris, where Dr. Beneš had already on May 15th been interviewed by the Committee on New States, to which the question of Ruthenia had been referred. Beneš said that any decentralization would have to be gradual, and that the Central Government would have to remain in charge for some years; but within these limits he was anxious to give Ruthenia 'all possible autonomy'. He submitted a draft, which was closely modelled on the Hungarian Law X, providing for a Governor, a Minister without Portfolio in the Central Government, and a local Diet competent in linguistic, educational, and Church questions and in any other questions which might be attributed to it by the laws of the Republic. Ruthene Deputies were to sit in the Prague Parliament, but not to vote on matters dealt with in their own Diet.[1]

The Czechoslovak Committee unanimously approved this plan in its entirety.[2] The New States Committee afterwards recast it to harmonize with the form of the other Minorities Treaties, and in doing so omitted some of the details of Beneš's draft. Strangely enough, it does not appear (so far as the records show) to have

[1] Hunter Miller, *Diary*, vol. xvi, pp. 360–2.
[2] Ibid., vol. xvi, p. 359.

considered the resolution of the National Council, although it is clear from the similarity of all the documents that Dr. Beneš's own draft had been based on the wishes of the Ruthenes, as understood by him at that date. Žatkovič, however, accepted it as satisfactory, on the understanding that 'local autonomy' meant full internal autonomy.[1] In its final form it was signed on September 10th, 1919, as a special chapter of the Czechoslovak Minorities Treaty.

The old Hungaro-Galician frontier was adopted unchanged on the north. The line with Roumania was only fixed finally by treaty between the two Powers on June 30th, 1921. It left three Roumanian villages, which lie on the right bank of the Tisza, in Ruthenia, and a somewhat larger number of Ruthenes in Roumania. The line approximates fairly closely to the ethnographical boundary, although it would probably have been more advantageous to the Ruthenes themselves had Ruthenia received the whole basin of the Upper Tisza, for, remote as Ruthenia is from Prague, Roumanian Maramureş is even more effectively cut off from Bucharest. It is stated that Czechoslovakia could have obtained better terms had she been willing to make a payment, which was not in all respects regular, and declined to do so. The line with Hungary was drawn far enough south to include in Ruthenia the railway line with Čop eastward.

The Hungarian protest against these decisions may be summarized in the following contentions:

The Ruthenes had always been loyal to Hungary and would wish to return to her. They were, moreover, mixed with other elements which would also remain irredentist. Hungary's historic right to the territory was, moreover, incontrovertible.[2] Further, stress was laid on the economic independence of the mountains and the plains, and on the misery which would be inflicted on the Ruthenes if deprived of the possibility of seasonal labour in the plains.[3] Further, the salt, timber, and stone of Ruthenia were essential to the Hungarian lowlands, while the proposed frontier would cut across the complicated system which had been devised for regulating the waters of the Tisza and its tributaries. As to the part of the plain destined for Ruthenia, it was almost purely Hungarian.[4]

These protests had no effect, and the territory was duly assigned to Czechoslovakia.

As regards the western frontier, Žatkovič was still negotiating fruitlessly with Masaryk, when news arrived from Paris that the Allies had decided to fix the river Už as the definitive boundary. Žatkovič hurried to Paris to interview Beneš, who confirmed the report. Beneš refused to consider the alternative line proposed by

[1] Žatkovič, op. cit.
[3] Ibid., p. 43.
[2] *Hungarian Peace Negotiations*, vol. ii, p. 39.
[4] Ibid., pp. 54-7.

Žatkovič, saying that the Slovaks would never accept it; but agreed, on Zatkovič's request, to ask the Conference to leave the question open, to be settled by later negotiation between the two parties.

§ 3. POLITICAL DEVELOPMENTS, 1919–27

Meanwhile, that portion of Ruthenia which was under Czech control (the Roumanians did not retire until July 1920) was in practice administered through the machinery of the old Hungarian Counties, and by the several, rather than the combined, efforts of the military, of some Czech officials who had been hurriedly sent down, and of such of the former staffs as had not resigned or been expelled. Returning from Paris on July 25th, Žatkovič resumed his efforts to get a settlement of the whole question, including the boundary, with Slovakia.[1] He proposed to Masaryk a 'temporary contract', under which all territory east of the Už ceded by Hungary to Czechoslovakia should be definitely assigned to Ruthenia, while that territory west of the Už claimed by the Ruthenes and marked as Ruthene on Tomašev's ethnographical map should be called 'disputed territory'. In this area a census should be taken by a mixed commission, between May and August 1920, and a final boundary laid down on the basis of ethnographical, economic, geographical, and administrative considerations. Masaryk objected to the form of the 'contract' but consented to conclude an agreement. Žatkovič wanted to return for a short time to the U.S.A., and therefore, failing to conclude the agreement in time, drafted a 'Proclamation', dated August 12th, 1919, to the effect that he had himself been appointed head of an Autonomous Directorate of five members who would administer Ruthenia temporarily, in conjunction with General Hennocque, who was in command of the local military. When the Peace Conference had reached its final decisions, the Ruthene State would be established with full internal autonomy, and the final boundary settled. All the Counties of Bereg, Máramaros, and Ugocsa and parts of the Counties of Spiš, Šároš, Zemplén, and Užhorod would definitely belong to Ruthenia. The other areas desired by the Ruthenes would remain neutral until a census was taken by a mixed Ruthene-Czechoslovak Commission.

This proclamation was viséd as correct and in order by Masaryk's secretary. Žatkovič then left for America, where he informed the Ruthene emigrants of his work, and received their approval of it. Returning in October, he found that no steps had been taken in

[1] The following account of Žatkovič's resignation (except the paragraphs relating to the Czechoslovak Constitution, which is based on the published text of that document) is drawn from the ex-Governor's own *exposé*.

his absence either to settle the boundary question or to appoint the Directorate. The wearisome negotiations recommenced. On November 18th a 'general Statute for the Organization and Administration of Ruthenia' was issued, providing for a Provisional Administrator, who appointed and controlled all officials, and a Provisional Directorate, of which Žatkovič was to be head, with advisory powers in cultural, educational, and linguistic questions, and in questions of local administration. Differences between the Administrator and the Directorate were settled by the President of the Republic; and both acted only until the entry into force of the autonomy. Elections were to be held not later than ninety days after the elections to the Czechoslovak National Assembly.

Armed with this document, Žatkovič proceeded to Užhorod; but the appointments to the Directorate hung fire, the boundary question was left unsolved, and in other respects also the General Statutes were not carried into effect. Meanwhile, the Czecho-slovak Constitutional Law, promulgated on February 29th, 1920, modified the provisions of the Minorities Treaty in certain important respects. The Governor was made responsible 'to the Ruthene Diet *also*', and the President of the Republic was allowed a veto over the legislation passed by the Ruthene Diet which was more absolute than that which he enjoyed against the Parliament of Prague. The distinction between the Deputies from Ruthenia and the other members of the Prague Parliament was reduced by omitting the provisions under which the former were not allowed to vote on certain questions. It was provided that the law fixing the boundaries of Ruthenia should, when enacted, form part of the Constitution.

After renewed negotiations, in the course of which Žatkovič and the appointed members of the Directorate offered their resignations, the General Statute was revised on April 26th. The Government now consisted of a Governor, a Vice-Governor, and a Governing Council. The Governor represented Ruthenia in negotiations with Prague, acted as Chairman of the Governing Council, and signed all administrative decrees and orders, including the appointment of such officials as were not appointed by the central authorities. The Vice-Governor was the immediate head of all the civilian administration, acted as intermediary between the officials and the Government, and countersigned all documents signed by the Governor. The Governor could veto any unconstitutional actions committed by his second in command, but any point on which the two could not agree was referred to the Central Government.

The Governing Council was planned to consist, besides the Governor and Vice-Governor, of ten members elected by the local constituencies and four nominated by the Government. The Central Government had the right to dissolve the council, or to dismiss individual members of it for neglect of duty.

Žatkovič was reappointed 'Provisional Governor', while the all-important post of Vice-Governor was entrusted to a Czech, Dr. Ehrenfeld. It was agreed that the delimitation of the boundary should be left to the Czechoslovak Parliament and the Ruthene Diet. Meanwhile, the higher (and many of the subordinate) posts in the Government service were filled by Czechs (and, to a lesser degree, Slovaks).

Žatkovič set to work at once on drafting an electoral law and a Constitution for Ruthenia. After three months he reported to Prague on the situation and received a promise that elections to the Ruthene Diet should be held in January 1921. It proved, however, impossible to reach agreement on various points, including the delimitation of the frontier between Ruthenia and Slovakia: the Slovak representatives strongly resisting Žatkovič's territorial claims. Moreover, the officials in charge of the census which was taken in Slovakia in January 1921 (without the participation of Ruthene representatives) issued circulars informing the population that the boundaries had already been settled by the Peace Conference and that the 'Rusin agitation was only Hungarian revisionist propaganda'. After vainly endeavouring to secure the adoption of his proposals, Žatkovič resigned his post on March 16th, 1921. His resignation was accepted on May 13th, and he returned to America. No successor was appointed, the administration being carried on by Dr. Ehrenfeld. The Central National Council meanwhile continued in being, and has, indeed, not yet been officially dissolved; but it has long since died of inanition. The question of the frontier was never taken up again.

During the next two years, the process of centralization continued. The fragments of Counties were drawn together into three units, with their head-quarters in Užhorod, Mukačevo, and Sevljuš respectively; but the old Hungarian system of a Lord Lieutenant (Föispán) nominated by the Government, a Deputy Lieutenant (Alispán) elected by the County, and an elected County Assembly was abolished, the powers of these organs being transferred to the Vice-Governor and to a Government-appointed Lord Lieutenant (Župán) in each County. The Hungarian municipal system was replaced by the Czech; Berehovo lost its municipal autonomy, while that of Užhorod and Mukačevo was greatly restricted. In 1926 the counties were abolished altogether, all Ruthenia being constituted as a single unit.

Several petitions were addressed during this period to the League of Nations. The regular reply was that all preparations were being made for introducing autonomy as soon as possible, but that various circumstances made it impossible to grant it immediately. One of these circumstances was the absence of a definitive frontier with Slovakia, lacking which, it was stated, the elections to the Diet could not be held, nor the Autonomy Act promulgated.[1] The dilemma of the Prague Government was serious, since, on another occasion, it stated that the frontier could not be fixed until the Diet was convoked. Stress was also laid on the lack of general and political education among the Ruthenes, and it was frankly pointed out that the mass of politically influential opinion in Ruthenia was still Magyar.

In 1924, after the Communal elections had been held, a new Ruthene Governor was appointed in the shape of M. Beskid, who had been President of the National Council of Prešov which had first voted for union with Czechoslovakia. The Vice-Governor was again a Czech, M. Rozsypal. In the same year elections to the National Assembly were held in Ruthenia for the first time, with the somewhat disconcerting result that the Communists obtained 40 per cent. of the total poll, and more than three times as many votes as the next largest party—and that was a Magyar party. The 1925 elections, however, saw a considerable diminution in the Communist vote.

The last stage (up to the time of writing) in the political development of Ruthenia was ushered in by the Law of July 14th, 1927, described above.[2] Under that Act, Ruthenia was placed in precisely the same situation as the other three provinces of the Republic, with the sole differences that its position is still in theory provisional, and that it still sports a gentleman bearing the honorific title of Governor, who is housed, appropriately enough, in the local museum.

§ 4. THE RUTHENE QUESTION: POLITICAL AND ADMINISTRATIVE

It is quite impossible to deny that Czechoslovakia is under a twofold obligation to grant autonomy to Ruthenia: a treaty obligation towards the Powers, and an obligation of honour to the Ruthenes. It is no less clear that these obligations have not been honoured—the breach of faith being, indeed, a compound fracture, for considerable areas which are preponderantly Ruthene in population are still included—if only 'provisionally'—in Slovakia. These do not enjoy even the shadowy pretence of autonomy enjoyed by the province of Ruthenia; but even in that province it is no more than a pretence, and one which is not kept up with any great conviction by anybody. In fact, as every one knows and almost every

---

[1] *Mémoire concernant la Russie sub-carpathique*, cit. supra.   [2] p. 118.

one admits, Ruthenia is not ruled by its Governor, nor by its Diet, with its twelve elected members and six Government nominees, nor by its local councils, with their strictly limited functions. It is ruled most efficiently by its Czech President, assisted by a bureaucracy in which all the important and responsible posts are exclusively in the hands of Czechs, or, in rare instances, of entirely trustworthy local personalities or émigrés. In the middle ranks of the hierarchy, the local population is admitted cautiously, and not in such proportions as to affect its essential character; in the lower ranks, which entail neither responsibility nor power, local elements, including members of the national minorities, are strongly represented, although even here the lump is leavened with Czechs.[1] This is the system established by Czechoslovakia to safeguard its hold upon Ruthenia; and although her leaders have from time to time, either spontaneously or in response to polite inquiries from the Council of the League of Nations, made declarations that they will one day put into force the autonomy guaranteed by the Treaty,

[1] The following figures were kindly supplied to me by the Zemski Urad in 1935:

Figures for the Central Administration in 1935

	Czechs.	Ukrainian Emigrants.	Russian Emigrants.	Ruthenes.	Magyars.
Heads of the provincial administration	7	1	..	..	..
Heads of districts	7	1	2	2	..
Chief notaries	1	..	..	1	..
Notaries and assistant notaries	163	11	3	42	29
Assistants to heads of administration	21	4	1	3	..
Clerks	497	20	12	85	54
Servants	24	..	1	6	5

In 1921 the figures for the notaries were: 104 Czechs and Slovaks, 69 Ruthenes, 65 Magyars, 4 Jews, 1 Roumanian, 1 German. Thus the proportion of Czechs has actually risen substantially since that date.

	Czechs.	Ruthenes.	Magyars.	Jews.	Germans.
Employees in provincial and district head offices	352	126	11	15	4
In notaries' offices	142	85	17	2	2
Panel doctors	2	36	2	29	1
Financial administration (includes customs and excise)	455	181	99	11	33
Roadmenders	13	202	19	..	..
Employees in hospitals	48	73	8	4	..

In the 3 highest administrative grades in the Zemski Urad were 6 Czechoslovaks, 2 locals; in the 4th, 10 Czechoslovaks, 7 locals; 5th, 2 Czechoslovaks, 17 locals; 6th, 5 Czechoslovaks, 10 locals; 'concipists', 2 Czechoslovaks, 6 locals. In this junior grade only locals are now employed.

Q

these promises have grown less rather than more concrete as the years have gone on.[1]

In many respects the position of the Czechs in Ruthenia reminds the traveller strongly of that of the British in India. Užhorod's prosaic but efficient looking new quarter of Galago, built by the Czechs since the War to house the new army of civilian and military authorities, recalls the European compounds on the fringes of so many Asiatic cities; and the analogy goes much deeper. The Czechs are not only a ruling class, but also a foreign one. They have their own clubs and coffee-houses, patronize, to a large extent, their own shops, and mingle little with the natives, except to order their destinies. They are paid on a scale which is modest enough in itself, but still high by comparison with the excessively low local standard of living. They are well lodged, their children are more than amply provided with schools; and there is a grain of truth in the saying that the 'public works' under-taken by the Republic in Ruthenia consist largely of offices into which the Ruthenes penetrate no farther than the waiting-rooms,[2] or motor roads along which only Czech cars circulate. It is true also that most of the Czech officials feel that they are living in a foreign land. They regard the Ruthenes as 'natives', and many of them sigh frankly enough for the day of retirement when they will be enabled to leave 'Asia' behind and settle down on their pen-sions at home, viz. in the Historic Lands.

The further charges sometimes made against the Czech officials seem to the writer, on the other hand, to be almost entirely un-founded. It is often said that Ruthenia is for the Czechs a sort of Siberia, to which the least desirable of their officials can con-veniently be banished. There were, it is true, a few regrettable scandals during the early period, but, in the main, the Czech officials in Ruthenia to-day are certainly an intelligent, honest, and

[1] A bill is now (end of 1936) before the Prague Parliament, submitted by the Coalition parties, which, if it becomes law, will abolish the office of President. The head of the administration will be the Governor, who will be appointed by the President of the Republic on the proposal of the Government, will be responsible to the Government (pending the Constitution of the Diet), and will represent Ruthenia in negotiations between the Government and the President of the Republic. He will have the power of final decision in all linguistic, religious, and local administrative questions. Pending the constitution of the Diet, he will be assisted by a Governing Council, which will be an advisory body, consisting of the members of the Provincial Council and of six members nominated by the Government on the proposal of the Governor.

[2] I cannot resist quoting here the following story: a new prison had been built, and a very high Czech official came to attend its inauguration. Seeing an old Ruthene peasant regarding the building with awe, he said to him jocularly: 'Well, bácsì (uncle), how would you like a spell in there?' The old man did not realize that the building was a jail, but took it for another housing estate for Czech officials, and replied in his humility and innocence: 'Ah, panitsa (little master), that is no place for a poor old peasant like me; it is rich gentlemen like yourself who should be in there.'

even devoted set of men. Here and there one of them may occasionally try to make a good thing out of the natives in this remote corner where the eye of supervision does not penetrate easily. Many more of them, however, are living a life of service genuinely devoted to the welfare of the people entrusted to their care. From the purely administrative point of view, it is unlikely that Ruthenia would have been as well governed by any other set of men— Ruthenes, Magyars, Poles, or Roumanians—who might possibly have sat in their places had the Peace Conference taken less on trust in 1919. This is a point on which the writer has taken pains to satisfy himself, and which he desires to emphasize. The paradoxical result is that the Ruthenes, whilst denied anything more than the merest shadow of self-government, yet certainly enjoy more political liberty than the inhabitants of many national States in Europe. In particular, the censor must—to judge from the tenor of the local press—be about the most liberal in Europe. And when all allowances are made, the Czechs have done a great deal for Ruthenia, and at a considerable cost to themselves. The total annual revenue from the country has never amounted to much more than 50 per cent. of its expenditure, and in making up the remainder, the Central Government has spent very substantial sums—amounting up to 1933 to no less than 1,600,000,000 č kr. Thus even if the Czech officials are rather numerous, the Ruthenes have not had to pay more than a fraction of their maintenance, and they have enjoyed in return very substantial benefits. Public security is adequate, and yet maintained without such a show of force as to make the country appear police-ridden. The judicial system inspires confidence. Communications have improved considerably, with the construction of a great arterial road across the plain, from east to west of the country, and of numerous bridges; the posts, telegraphs, and telephones have multiplied. The Tisza has been regulated, and drainage and reclamation works carried out. Attempts have been made, which deserve all recognition, to raise economic standards by starting handicrafts, introducing improved methods of cultivation, &c. The public health services have been reorganized and largely expanded, with results plainly to be seen in the rapid diminution (one cannot yet speak of the disappearance) of epidemic disease. Much of this work has only been rendered possible by the utmost devotion on the part of the Czechs and Russians who have carried it out.[1] But the subject to which more attention has been paid than any other has been that of education. Of the total sums spent by the State in Ruthenia

[1] An account of the public works carried out in Ruthenia is given in *Technická Práce v Zemi Podkarpatoruske 1919–1933* (Užhorod, Czechoslovak Chamber of Engineers, 1933 (in Czech)).

since 1919 (excluding the budgets of those ministries not locally administered, e.g. railways, posts, and telegraphs, national defence, justice, and social welfare) about 40 per cent. was devoted to education, being ten times as much as the amount spent on health and five times that spent on agriculture. A great part of the former leeway has now been made up. By 1931[1] the Ruthenes already possessed 45 kindergartens, 425 elementary schools, 16 burger schools (13 of them 'mixed'), 4 higher schools, and 3 teachers' training colleges, with a certain number of vocational and specialist establishments. Illiteracy among the Ruthenes has been very largely reduced, and is rare to-day in the younger generation. There are even the beginnings of a vigorous, if somewhat shallow, intellectual life, chiefly expressed (as is usual in such cases) in the existence of a multitudinous and scurrilous local press. Culturally, as a neutral observer said to me, the country has advanced fifty years since the Czechs came to it. But here we are passing already from the domain of pure administration into that of politics. Not that the Czech zeal for educating the people is prompted solely by political motives; the Czech has always shown a singular enthusiasm for an appreciation of the value of education, and it is perfectly true that even the economic progress of the Ruthenes must be slow and doubtful until education has cleared away the innumerable superstitions which at present clog its wheels.[2] Nevertheless, just as Hungary pursued her own national policy, before the War, by installing a very extensive system of secondary education in Magyar, while leaving primary education in a rudimentary state, so Czechoslovakia has found it her interest to reverse this system and to provide a primary system capable of checking the old tendency to Magyarization. In doing so, however, they have involved themselves in complications which demand a chapter to themselves; for the educational question raises not merely scholastic issues, but the whole problem of the national identity of the Ruthenes.

§ 5. THE RUTHENE QUESTION: CULTURAL, LINGUISTIC, AND NATIONAL

While before 1918 Ruthenia possessed anything between a dozen and a score of peasant dialects, and such written literature as existed hovered uncertainly between Great Russian, Ukrainian,

[1] These figures are taken from an official publication, issued in 1933: *Školství na Podkarpatské Rusi v přítomnosti*. They are probably too low for the present date, especially as regards Czech and Ruthene establishments. The figures quoted above take no account of the 22 mixed elementary schools.

[2] For example, the Ruthenes cannot be persuaded to build chimneys to their cottages, because they take the whistling of the wind in the chimneys for the voice of a particularly malignant ghost.

and a local idiom, this confusion of tongues was almost irrelevant when the exclusive language of administration and of genteel society was none of these, but Magyar.

The position became very different when the problem facing the authorities was to reverse the process and replace Magyar by some other idiom. Which of the various claimants to choose? Each, of course, maintained itself, with passion, to be the only true and natural language of the people, while denouncing all others as the artificial importations of foreign intrigue. But in fact, the linguistic position, viewed from a purely philological point of view, was amazingly indeterminate. It seemed that it should be possible to impose on the population, without real violence, any one of three languages: literary Russian, literary Ukrainian, or some development of their own local dialect. This being so, political considerations were bound to obtrude themselves. National feeling must be expected to follow language, and according as to which idiom was chosen, the Ruthenes might be expected to develop a Russian, a Ukrainian, or a local national consciousness. Neither the Ruthenes themselves, nor the Czechs, could fail, being human, to ask themselves which of these possible developments would be politically most agreeable to them.

The incredibly complicated system which has arisen is due to the competition of purely philological with political considerations; the latter again being exceedingly various and often mutually contradictory. To begin with, the different Czech parties (and Czechoslovakia has invariably been governed since the War by coalitions of several parties) have inclined to take up different views, according to their feelings towards Russia. Most of the Czech bourgeois parties, and notably the National Democrats, who have an old Russophil tradition, have naturally inclined to foster all things Russian. The Social Democrats and Communists have been pro-Ukrainian; the Agrarians have been divided.

But Russia has not been the only country on which the Czechs have naturally been impelled to keep an eye. There has also been Poland—Czechoslovakia's neighbour, herself possessing a large Ruthene, or Ukrainian population. Poland for years was at loggerheads with her own Ukrainians. When Polish-Czech relations have been strained, an obvious and easy way for Czechoslovakia to score off Poland has been to encourage the Ukrainian movement in Ruthenia. If, on the other hand, Czechoslovakia wished to cultivate Poland's friendship, she would naturally repress any exuberant Ukrainophily in her own population; while if, again, Poland made her peace with her own Ruthenes, but quarrelled with Czechoslovakia, the situation might be different once more.

Again, it could hardly fail to occur to the minds of authority that either the Russian or the Ukrainian movement, if allowed to develop, would probably, in the end, give rise to separatist ambitions. From this point of view, the Ruthenian would be the safest solution of all. The danger in this, during the earlier years, was that this had been the policy of Hungary, who had carried it through with so much success that local feeling had become almost identified with pro-Magyar feeling. Finally, it would be easy and not very cynical to say that the greatest safety would probably be in numbers, and to allow no one movement to get too strong, but to play each off against the other.

It will be seen that the possible factors, linguistic, religious, or political, which might determine the national policy to be adopted in Ruthenia, are almost innumerable. It is, therefore, not surprising that the course followed should have proved somewhat wavering. It has in fact resulted in provoking a glorious confusion of tongues and sentiments, such as could hardly have been more effectively achieved by an absolutely consistent policy of *divide et impera*; but this is probably due only in part to intention, and more to the interaction of conflicting policies.

President Masaryk, when first discussing the question with Žatkovič, seems to have favoured developing the local dialects gradually into Ukrainian, which should be used in the schools and public offices, with minority schools in Great Russian for those who preferred it.[1] Žatkovič seems also to have been pro-Ukrainian; and as the Academy of Sciences in Prague, on being consulted, pronounced the Ruthenes to be a branch of Ukrainians, it seemed likely at first that the course would be Ukrainian. On the other hand, few Czechs knew Ukrainian, while it was possible to find and dispatch to Ruthenia a certain number who understood Russian; and since the people called themselves 'Russin' and had pronounced in May 1919 for the 'Ruskij jazyk', and since the language of higher education in Hungarian days, in so far as it existed at all, was a sort of Great Russian, most of these officials seem to have assumed that the Ruthenes, even though admittedly of Ukrainian origin, would wish to speak Russian. Another factor which certainly influenced the situation at the time was the strong belief then current among the Czechoslovak bourgeoisie that the Russian revolution would not endure, and that an intellectual class must be maintained among the émigrés to take over the leadership of Russia when the counter-revolution came. Largely for this reason, Russian émigrés were welcomed very hospitably in Czechoslovakia, and many of them found their way to Ruthenia.

Thus, from the very first, two different tendencies seem to have been at work, each of them straightforward enough in its own way.

[1] Masaryk, op. cit., p. 240.

The situation became far more acute in the spring of 1921, when the Russian contingent was suddenly reinforced by several hundred members of the Church Militant, Orthodox priests evacuated in the previous November with General Wrangel's army from the Crimea to Constantinople, thence dispatched to Serbia and forwarded by the Serbian Patriarch to Ruthenia. In this case it is hard to believe that some wish was not present to weaken the Uniate Church, which, up to that time, had proved obstinately Hungarophil. At all events, no shrewder blow could have been struck at that institution. The Russians at once began to propagate their faith with great fervour and with a sweeping success which owed something to material considerations; for the Uniate priests had been in the habit of demanding tithes in kind, which were most irksome to Ruthene pockets. The Russians were less exacting in their demands, both material and moral, and were also in no way identified with foreign rule. A robust schism occurred. Whole villages went Orthodox overnight, often violently ejecting their previous spiritual pastors. The Czechs, true to the principle of religious liberty, cheerfully handed over the Uniate Churches and Church property to the converts wherever they could show themselves to be in the majority. A religious war (not wholly metaphorical or bloodless) went on for some years, until the Government, confronted with an endless series of lawsuits, solved the immediate question by compelling the return to the Uniate Church of such of its property as had been seized, paying out of State funds the dues to the Uniate clergy formerly paid by their parishioners, and granting the Orthodox communities subsidies to build their own churches. But the unity of the people had been broken. Whereas in 1918 97 per cent. of the Ruthenes belonged to the Uniate Church, the figure was now only some 80 per cent.[1]

With the advent of the Russian priests, the Great Russian movement took a long stride forward; for it goes without saying (since the Church is the veritable bulwark of national life among the Slavonic peoples) that the dispute did not remain confined to theological issues. On the contrary, the Russian priests propagated vigorously not only the Orthodox creed, but also the Russian language and the Russian national idea; denouncing Ukrainianism, as Russians will, as a mere heresy, fallacy, and delusion. But their triumph (to continue the story) was short-lived. Hard on their heels came a fresh wave of immigrants, even more numerous and no less determined. These were Ukrainian-minded Ruthenes from East Galicia, whose struggle against Poland for independence had just ended in defeat. Czechoslovakia, whose relations with Poland

[1] In 1910 386,812 inhabitants of Ruthenia were Uniate and only 577 Orthodox; in 1930 the figures were 359,166 and 112,034 respectively.

were at that period thoroughly unfriendly, welcomed these new
arrivals no less warmly than she had the Russians, and even
founded universities for them in Prague and Podiebrad. Very
considerable numbers of these Ukrainians found their way to
Ruthenia, where they were largely employed in the schools and,
in part, in the administrative services also.

Under the influence of these Ukrainian immigrants, who were no
less energetic than the Russians in spreading their ideas, cultural,
religious, and national, a Ukrainian movement arose in its turn,
equally opposed to the Russian and the local 'Ruthene'. Both
Ukrainian and Russian movements organized actively, their centres
being the cultural societies known respectively as the Prosvita
(Ukrainian) and the Duchnovica (Russian). From these fastnesses
they issued books and pamphlets, arranged for theatrical per-
formances, &c., and attacked each other with unabating energy.

The Czechoslovak Government has generally professed itself
entirely neutral in this question, declaring itself willing to follow
any course on which the parties might agree—if only they would
agree. It has, in fact, made various endeavours to bring them to
terms, being frustrated in each case by the recalcitrance of one or
the other party. It appears, however, to have supported the
Ukrainians the more strongly of the two up to 1930, when a certain
change took place. In that year the National Socialist Party
(Dr. Beneš' former party) sent in a memorandum to the Government urging the necessity of breaking with the Ukrainians in order
to facilitate a rapprochement with Poland, and for that, and other
reasons, asking that Great Russian should be substituted for
Ukrainian in the schools. No radical change in the curricula seems
to have been made, but thereafter the balance was held, perhaps,
rather more evenly, with the result that both parties, instead of
only one as theretofore, thenceforward accused the authorities of
terrorizing their supporters and distorting the natural sentiments
of the nation. More recently still, an attempt was made to revive
the Ruthene tendency, which had now lost most of its dangerous
Magyarone proclivities and which, it was hoped, might develop
into a pronouncedly Czechophil movement, particularly if by sage
and imperceptible degrees the local dialect might be brought to
approximate more closely to the Slovak. Incidentally, it is even
easier to hold the balance between three movements, provided that
they are all mutually irreconcilable, than between two.   .

At present there is no uniform plan. In most of the elementary
schools, the teaching is in the local dialect, with a tendency towards Ukrainianism due to the fact that the present head of the
Ruthene teachers' training college is at this moment a leading
light of the Ukrainians. In the higher schools Ukrainian again

predominates, but not to the exclusion of its rivals. One school teaches in one language, another in another; in some schools, different languages are even taught in different classes.

The Czechs are freely accused by all parties—fraternally united on this one point alone—of having brought about this situation by Machiavellian design, to destroy the unity of the Ruthenes and to thwart their proper national ambitions. These accusations contain some modicum of truth. Yet one must also say that this opportunity was freely, indeed, most lavishly offered, and that the Ruthenes themselves are at least as much to blame for their disunity as the Czechs (not to speak of the other neighbouring nationalities which occasionally drop a hook into these troubled waters).

As regards the second main cultural grievance of the Ruthenes— the Czech schools—Czech policy is less easily defensible, even if, here too, the opportunity and the excuse have been lavishly presented by the dissensions between the various Ruthene groups. Czech schools have been introduced into Ruthenia on a scale unwarranted even by the considerable number of officials. The figures for Czech educational establishments in Ruthenia in 1920/1 and 1931/2 were as follows:

	Kinder-gartens.	Elementary Schools.	Burger Schools.	High Schools.	Teachers' Training Colleges.
1920/1	4	22	1	..	..
1931/2	43	158	14	3[1]	1[1]

Thus the Czechoslovaks, who compose only 4·96 per cent. of the population, possess nearly as many facilities for higher education as the Ruthenes and far more than the Magyars, while there is one Czech elementary school for every 212 Czechs in Ruthenia, the corresponding figures for the Ruthenes, Magyars, and Germans being 997·5, 945, and 779 respectively. This extensive establishment clearly could not be kept up at all if it was expected to confine the Czech schools to Czech pupils. In the burger schools in 1931, for example, there were 61 Czech classes for only 448 Czech pupils.[2] The plethora of Czech schools can, therefore, only be regarded as a measure of attempted Czechization. This is, indeed, carried on much more circumspectly and less extensively than the old Magyarization. Although cases are said to have occurred when the Czechs have taken advantage of quarrels between the Ukrainian and Russian parties, each refusing to learn the rival language, to introduce Czech as a 'neutral' solution, the elements to whom these facilities are chiefly offered, and who take freest advantage

[1] Parallel classes.
[2] L.N.O.J., March 1934, p. 341 (M. Yuhasz's petition).

of them, are not the Ruthenes, but the Jews, who form the chief clientèle of the Czech burger schools and even of the elementary schools.[1] The Czechs justify their action on this ground, arguing that 'no one can refuse the Jews the right to have schools in which the language of the State is taught' and declaring that no elementary school with Czech language of instruction has been set up except at the request of the local population.[2] The procedure seems, however, to be tactless, to say the least of it, and to tend towards the creation of a situation which is certainly not in accordance with the spirit of Ruthene autonomy by its encouragement of a Czech-speaking middle class. It has, moreover, the effect of setting one class of the local population still further against the others. The Jewish authorities themselves have recognized the potential dangers in the situation, and have requested the Jewish parents in the villages to send their children to Ruthene schools rather than to Czech schools. As for the Czechs, while they always deny that their action has really amounted to attempted Czechization, yet they seem to have recognized that it at least gives rise to possible misinterpretation. A party among them has always disapproved, on grounds both of expediency and morality, to the plethora of Czech schools, and some plans for still further developing Czech higher education were recently cancelled by the Government.

§ 6. THE ECONOMIC POSITION

If the Czech cultural policy has been wavering and its results ambiguous, yet one way or another great cultural progress has been achieved. True, some of the Ruthenes to-day learn Ruthene, others Ukrainian, others Russian, others Czech; but nearly all of them learn something, and the general standard of culture and education has undoubtedly risen very greatly. It is otherwise, unfortunately, with the economic situation. No detailed description of the situation in this respect is necessary, since it differs little from that of Slovakia, save in being in almost all respects less favourable still. Ruthenia is even less industrialized than Slovakia, and her industry, such as it was, has suffered even more by the change in frontiers. The salt-mines (which possess almost a monopoly for Czechoslovakia) have kept up their output, but of the larger industrial undertakings proper, existing in 1914, some

---

[1] In 1931, according to M. Fenzig (*Karpatorusskij Golos*, May 8th, 1935), the pupils in the Czech burger schools were composed of 572 Czechs, 66 Ruthenes, 58 Germans, 388 Magyars, 5 Poles, 31 Roumanians, 1,415 Jews, and 3 others. On the other hand, according to the Czechoslovak reply to M. Yuhasz's petition (*L.N.O.J.*, March 1934, p. 358) only 1,266 out of 71,343 Ruthene children were attending Czechoslovak schools on October 31st, 1931, while a considerable number of Czech children were attending Ruthene schools.
[2] *L.N.O.J.*, loc. cit.

70 per cent. (according to an estimate from a reliable source) have been liquidated, in many cases deliberately, without any serious attempt to replace them; the subsidies granted for encouragement of home industries and handicrafts have been a mere drop in the bucket. A considerable amount of building went on for some years, but practically all industrial undertakings now existent work for a strictly local market, and in nearly all of them unemployment is very high.

More even than Slovakia, Ruthenia has been reduced to a purely non-industrial country devoted exclusively to agriculture and forestry, in which no less than 67·78 per cent. of the occupied population, or 66·29 per cent. of the total population, are engaged. It must be noted in this connexion that forestry is even more important for Ruthenia than it is for Slovakia, since nearly 49 per cent. of her total area is covered by forests, while only 18·33 per cent. consists of arable land. The welfare of her timber industry is thus vital to her prosperity, and the only reasonable market for her timber is Hungary, since on the home market she cannot compete even with Slovakia.

It might, therefore, still be possible to maintain a modest level of prosperity by cultivating close commercial relations with Hungary, on the old basis of exchange between mountain and plain; to which would have to be added resumption of the seasonal harvest migration. Unfortunately, the migration has been at a standstill since the War, and the timber trade was cut off in 1930 when trade relations between Hungary and Czechoslovakia were severed. The effect of this, serious for Slovakia, has been simply disastrous for Ruthenia. Many of the saw-mills have had to close down, while others have been kept at work only by drastic wage reductions. At the same time, the rise in the price of food-stuffs has struck a further severe blow to the population.

Thus forestry has gone the way of industry; not dead, but almost moribund and with little hope at present of reviving. There remains agriculture. Can this be so developed as to afford the population a reasonable standard of living?

As we have said, the Government has made considerable efforts to improve local standards of production, and with a success which deserves recognition. There is room for much further improvement still, for methods in Ruthenia are still exceedingly backward, and the production of nearly all crops, even on the existing acreage, can, and doubtless will, be raised substantially. More drastic methods do not seem, however, likely to be very effective. Much was hoped, for example, from the agrarian reform, and at the Peace Conference the misery of the Ruthenes was attributed very largely to the unsound distribution of land. In practice, however, it was found impossible to effect any very large reform. 230,908 hectares (18·83 per cent. of the total) were put under sequester, but only 45,379 of these were arable land, the rest consisting mainly of forests. A small further area was acquired by exchange. A total of 21,191 hectares was distributed to 9,216 small proprietors; 24 residual estates were created, with an area of 2,773 hectares, and 80 other larger estates with an area of 9,147 hectares (1,903 arable); most of these were co-properties or communes. 10,159 hectares (2,203 arable) were taken over by the State. In 1929 29,084 hectares had been restored to their former proprietors; thus no less than 170,434, or 70·2 per cent. of the total area sequestered, still remained at the disposal of the Land Office.

The attempts to relieve the land hunger by colonization in the plains proved exceedingly disappointing. Few applicants came forward, still fewer satisfied the conditions imposed by the authorities, and only a mere handful succeeded in establishing themselves. Indeed, the Ruthenes were so laggard that the authorities committed the extraordinary political blunder—even less excusable here than in Slovakia—of settling Czech colonists in the plains. There were in 1929 a total of 11 colonies in Ruthenia, with 249 undertakings.

These measures, however well meant and well conducted, have so patently failed to solve the problem, or even substantially to alter the relation between large and small holdings,[1] that a plan is now on foot for carrying through a second agrarian reform, which would involve clearing portions of the forests for agricultural settlement. Given the present situation, this measure may prove inevitable, but it is a bitter commentary on the conflict between politics and economics that valuable timber should be destroyed for the purpose of growing crops which cannot (given

[1] The figures for land tenure in 1930 were as follows:

Size of Holding.	Number Absolute.	Per cent.	Total Area.
Up to 0·1 ha.	2,416	2·1	238·14
0·1 ,, 0·5 ,,	10,424	9·2	3,365·72
0·5 ,, 1 ,,	11,939	10·6	8,892·19
1 ,, 2 ,,	25,575	22·6	37,982·82
2 ,, 5 ,,	34,465	30·5	114,955·33
5 ,, 10 ,,	18,486	16·4	128,480·79
10 ,, 20 ,,	6,790	6·0	91,006·53
20 ,, 30 ,,	1,215	1·1	29,262·62
30 ,, 50 ,,	596	0·5	22,721·98
50 ,, 100 ,,	346	0·3	24,085·18
100 ,, 200 ,,	289	0·3	40,678·87
200 ,, 500 ,,	244	0·2	76,507·76
Over 500 ,,	175	0·2	653,692,08
Total. . .	112,960	100	1,231,870·01

the climatic conditions) be other than second-rate, literally within sight of the Hungarian plain, with its treeless stretches teeming with super-abundance of corn. Hungary, meanwhile, is afforesting the Alföld.

Over all these endeavours lies the shadow of the population problem. The Ruthene is incredibly prolific. The density of population has risen from 31 per square kilometre in 1880 to 57 in 1930, rising from 48 in the decade 1920–30 alone. The birth-rate has fallen slightly from the figure of 44·5 per thousand which it reached in 1901–5, but it still stood at 40·4 in 1930. As the death-rate has fallen much more strongly (from 28·8 in 1901–5 to 18·4 in 1930 and 1931) the annual natural increase still amounts to about 20 per thousand.

Emigration provided a certain outlet before the War, but the restrictions since introduced have, of course, largely blocked this safety-valve. During the years 1922–32, 10,182 passports were issued to natives of Ruthenia for overseas emigration, and 6,287 for European countries. During the same period, about 4,500 persons re-immigrated.[1] The net relief given by emigration amounted, therefore, to only some 10 per cent. of the total increase of population. Internal immigration within the Republic is small. Of all the provinces of Czechoslovakia, Ruthenia is that with the least mobile population; in 1921 78·1 per cent. of the population were residing in the commune of their birth.[2] Conditions are extremely unfavourable for the Ruthene to emigrate to the Historic Lands, in which unemployment is already very high. Even were there a demand for workers, the Slovak would stand a far better chance of engagement than the Ruthene, who labours under the twofold handicap of his foreign language and his non-industrial habits (including his propensities to drink and holidays). Thus only a few Ruthenes have taken the plunge, and they have found only the roughest and worst-paid work. In this respect, the situation of the Ruthenes seems to be worse than it was before the War, when there was a small but steady drift into the towns of the plain, followed by Magyarization.

Thus the economic outlook for Ruthenia is gloomy indeed. Terrible as was the poverty reigning in the mountains before the War, even sources highly favourable to the Government admit that the general standard of living has sunk considerably since that date. It is true that part of this deterioration may be put down to the general economic crisis which has hit all parts of Central

[1] I.L.O., *The Rural Exodus in Czechoslovakia*, pp. 105, 107. Of a total of 66,323 re-immigrants for the whole Republic, 3,822 gave Ruthenia as their destination and 6,459 did not specify the province.
[2] Ibid., pp. 84–5.

Europe in varying degrees; but the evil in Ruthenia seems to be more than merely cyclical, and though a certain improvement may be anticipated, it is hard to see a basis for real prosperity so long as the existing political frontiers are coped by the present commercial policies.

§ 7. POLITICAL FEELING AMONG THE RUTHENES

Political life in Ruthenia before the War was engagingly lucid. It was the simple habit of the authorities to present the populace with the choice between two candidates, one representing the Government and the other the Opposition, but both Magyar gentlemen and in most respects indistinguishable. The populace, in so far as it was enfranchised at all, would take the line of least resistance and greatest safety, and register its votes for the Government.

After the War the Hungarian parties retained their organization but deftly transmuted themselves into the so-called 'Political Party of the Ruthenes in Hungary'. Although denounced by the Czechs as a pure sham and totally unrepresentative of the Ruthenes this party undoubtedly commanded, at the time, the allegiance of a large fraction of the Ruthenes (who, as has been said, were far on the road to Magyarization).

Those Ruthenes who had accepted the Czech solution then organized two parties which, they hoped, would prove representative of the real Ruthene nation: a Social Democrat Party to represent the workers, and an Agrarian Party to represent the peasants. This was done in anticipation of the grant of autonomy, which was then confidently expected to occur in a few months. When, however, this receded into the future, faster than the passage of time, the leader of the peasant party, Dr. Kaminski,[1] founded a so-called Agrarian Union, which besides its peasant interest was principally devoted to the struggle for autonomy, and thus definitely oppositional.

Such was the situation for some three years. During that time no elections of any kind had been held, the Czechs frankly admitting to the League of Nations, when questioned on the subject, that the electorate as a whole was still too strongly under Magyar influence to be consulted without disconcerting results.[2] In 1922, then, the Czechs introduced their own party system into Ruthenia, with favourable results. Many of the Ruthenes, including even many who felt quite strongly on the question of autonomy, yet

---

[1] Dr. Kaminski had held a post in the Government of the Russka Kraina, and afterwards served under the Czechs as first Župán in Užhorod, but resigned when autonomy was delayed.

[2] See in particular League of Nations Document C. 608 M. 231, 1923, I, where this is stated with an engaging candour and obvious (and in fact well justified) confidence that the Powers would appreciate this point of view.

thought it more practical, in view of the *de facto* situation, to throw in their lot with the bigger parties in the rest of the Republic. The Agrarian Union came to terms with the Czechoslovak Agrarians, and many of the other parties, including those of the national minorities, followed suit, fusing or striking bargains with the main parties. There remained, of course, a certain number of Ruthenes who felt that the question of autonomy must take precedence of all others. These founded separate parties, the oldest and most important of which is the group formed at the end of 1923 by secession from the Agrarian Union when the latter joined the Czechoslovak Agrarians and known as the Agrarian Opposition, or more usually, from the name of its founder, as the Kurtyak Party. This has roughly the same objects as M. Kaminski's earlier group, namely autonomy as guaranteed in the Treaty, with support of peasant interests.[1] A second specifically autonomist party, that of M. Fenzig, combines the advocacy of autonomy with the propagation of what are often vaguely described as Fascist ideas: strong methods, the principle of 'leadership' and a dash of anti-Semitism. The minor parties, which are exuberantly numerous, particularly at local and municipal elections, need not be described in detail here.[2]

After the agreement had been concluded between the Ruthene and the Czech Agrarians, municipal elections were held (late in 1923) with a result of some 40,000 votes to the Ruthene parties, 15,000 to the Communists, 55,000 to the Magyar and Jewish parties, and 21,000 to 'middle-class groups and local groups of a non-political character'.[3] General elections, held on March 16th, 1924, gave the Communists 100,000 votes, the Magyar and

[1] In the 1935 elections this party co-operated with the Slovak People's Party.
[2] The following table, which shows the parties contesting the municipal elections at Užhorod in 1931, and the votes cast for them, will give some idea of the complexity of local political life in Ruthenia.

United Magyar Parties	. 2,123	Socialist Party of Trade and Industry	. 252
Communists . .	. 2,059		
Jewish Party . .	. 830	Economic Party . .	. 256
Jewish People's Party	. 250	Two small parties whose names have escaped me .	67 and 85
Orthodox Jewish Party	512		
Czechoslovak Social Democrats . . .	588	Republican Party of Trade and Industry . . .	. 338
Russian Bloc . .	. 261	Christian People's Party .	. 340
National Socialists .	. 662	Czechoslovak National Democrats	228
Magyar Social Democrats .	186	Czechoslovak Economic Party	. 234
Czechoslovak Agrarians	. 589	Czechoslovak Labour Community	360

Total, 10,220 votes among 19 parties, two of which are coalitions.

The Czechs are sometimes accused of fostering this state of things in order to break the unity of the Ruthene front, and with this purpose, of founding small parties before each election, but it would be unfair to consider them as doing more than aid and abet a natural tendency.

[3] League of Nations Document, C. 221 M. 310, 1923, I.

Jewish parties 55,000, the Agrarian Opposition 21,000, and the remaining Ruthene parties 60,000.[1] The Parliamentary elections of 1925, 1929, and 1935, respectively, gave the following results:

	1925	1929	1935
Communists	75,669	40,582	78,994
Czechoslovak Agrarians . . .	34,916	77,419	60,747
,, Social Democrats .	18,183	22,925	30,729
,, National Socialists .	15,571	10,025	11,272
,, People's Party . .	7,402	8,779	7,321
Minor pro-Government Parties	5,168	..	..
Minor Oppositional Parties .	13,812	..	..
Agrarian Opposition (Kurtyak). .	28,799	48,609	44,982
Fenzig Party	..	..	28,956
Magyar Parties	29,102	30,455	34,186
Jewish Party	19,121	..	..
Henlein Party	..	..	1,535
German Social Democrats . .	..	..	1,183
Debtors' Party	..	..	366
	253,743	239,794	300,271

These figures, like those for Slovakia, can give only a very rough indication of the development of political feeling in Ruthenia since the War; a feeling which, in the case of the Ruthenes themselves, is doubly difficult to estimate on account of the vast complexity of the national question. The position of the Ruthenes is so far parallel to that of the Slovaks in that they have ceased to regard Magyarization as the natural corollary of advancement in life. While in 1914 it seemed possible to foresee a not distant day when the whole nation would have become Magyar speaking and thinking, this process has now been definitely arrested. On the other hand, the most complete uncertainty reigns as to what is to take its place. The idea of Czechization may probably be dismissed. The attempts made by the authorities to bring it about were never more than sporadic and half-hearted, and were always discountenanced by a large section among the Czechs themselves. They seem to have aroused little but resentment among the Ruthenes.

There remain, then, the three rival national tendencies: the Ruthene, the Great Russian, and the Ukrainian. None of these has yet gained a decisive advantage over the others. If a census of the whole population were taken to-day, probably the vast majority of the peasants, above whose heads the whole controversy has really passed, would still describe themselves, either by some local appellation such as 'Hutzul', or as 'Rusins', meaning thereby their own local brand of Carpatho-Ruthenes.

[1] League of Nations Document, C. 331 M. 107, 1924, I. The above are votes for the Chamber; the votes for the Senate are slightly lower in each case, but the proportions are much the same.

If, however, we look to the future, the Ruthene cause is probably the least hopeful of the three. A Ruthene nationality was possible within the great Austro-Hungarian Empire, when it could have numbered several million adherents. But Czechoslovakia is not Austria-Hungary, and cannot do things on this spacious scale. A Carpatho-Ruthene nationality of, at the most, a million souls is impracticable. A very important factor is that the population of Eastern Galicia has strongly repudiated 'Ruthenism', and now includes among its national demands the complete substitution of the name 'Ukrainian' for that of 'Ruthene'. Scant as are the relations between Galicia and Ruthenia, they do exist, and the influence of the Church in particular, as represented notably by Monsignor Szeptickij, the able archbishop of Lvov, is not inconsiderable.

The intelligentsia, with few exceptions, have rejected the Ruthene solution altogether (a recent attempt by a small group to revive it has met with little success, the more so as Czech pressure is suspected behind it). Their younger members are Ukrainian or Russian to a man. Of these two parties, the Ukrainian seems the stronger, although, oddly enough, both the main autonomist parties, the Kurtyak and Fenzig parties, are Russo-phil. Neither of them is, however, solely interested in this particular question, over which many of the followers of both probably take a different view from their leaders. M. Fenzig has recently been somewhat discredited by his too open attachment to the Polish cause, while the other Great Russian groups, which centre chiefly round small bands of émigrés, represent for the most part an ultra-conservative point of view which no longer appeals to youth.

The Ukrainian movement was admittedly the work of the Galician immigrants, but they have shown extraordinary energy and perseverance which has met its reward. The Prosvita is a much larger organization than its Russian rival and its 'National House' in Užhorod contains a museum, a library, and even a theatre. Vigorous propaganda is conducted, even in the remotest villages, and the press is well organized. The Ukrainians are strongly represented in the educational system. In June 1934, according to their bulletin, there were 1,874 Ukrainian school-teachers in Ruthenia, of whom 1,318 belonged to the association, i.e. were active workers in the Ukrainian cause.[1] M. Vološin, the head of the Greek Catholic Teachers' Training College in Užhorod, has, after sundry vagaries, ended as an Ukrainophil, and the great majority of the young priests who pass through his college, as (so far as can be judged) of the lay students, are fervent adherents of the same cause.

The outcome of this national dispute, if an outcome is ever

---

[1] Martel, op. cit., p. 139.

R

reached, will clearly affect political feeling among the Ruthenes very deeply. If, for example, the Ukrainian movement definitely wins the day, and if the future should bring the establishment of an independent Ukraine comprising all Ukrainian territories beyond the Carpathians (including East Galicia) then the national urge to join that State may become so strong as to drown all other considerations. Under the present circumstances, however, the national dispute is largely academic, and does little more than confuse the immediate political issue. It should be emphasized that the political ambitions of a given group are not to be deduced from its attitude on the national question. The Czechs have favoured all three tendencies at one period or another. Both of the two main autonomist parties to-day are Great Russian on the national question; but one is reputed to enjoy the sympathies of Budapest (which before the War would have put down any such movement with great decision), the other of Warsaw. Most of the Communists are Ukrainian rather than Russian.

The chief question which the present work must try to answer is whether the populations taken from Hungary under the Treaty of Trianon prefer their new situation to their old. Clearly, this question cannot be answered on the basis of the negotiations which took place in 1918 and 1919. The bulk of the population was never consulted; it is, indeed, unlikely that most of them knew that Czechoslovakia existed at the time when their ambition to join that State was being interpreted for them to the Conference. In 1919 the simple peasants of the Verchovina came flocking down the valleys as usual, scythe on shoulder, and remarkable scenes are said to have been enacted when the authorities tried to explain to them that they had now been liberated. They listened politely, but impatiently; it was kind of the noble gentlemen to make them such long speeches, but they were in haste to reach the hiring-fair at Nyiregyháza, and they entirely failed to understand why they were being held up by people in strange uniforms. . . .

To-day their attitude towards the Magyars has, of course, changed; they regard them as fellow beings rather than as natural masters and social ideals. Friendliness and even attachment to Hungary remain, however, very strong. This is due partly to material considerations, for the fall in the standard of living is unmistakable and even the most ignorant peasant understands that the change has been economically disastrous. Partly it is due to natural conservatism and to the extraordinary persistence of social ideals—feelings which will die with time, but not quickly. The Kurtyak Party is well known to have strong sympathies with Budapest, and these are certainly to be found in circles far wider than that of this single party. Many persons in Ruthenia (not

Magyars) have expressed to me their belief that a plebiscite to-day would still give a majority among the Ruthenes for a return to Hungary; at any rate, if this could be accompanied by a guarantee of autonomy similar to that proposed under the 1919 Law. The Czechs, in their hearts, probably share this view. It is fairly clear that the chief quality which keeps the Ruthenes, like the Slovaks, 'unripe for autonomy' is their unfortunate tendency to prefer Hungary to Czechoslovakia.

Yet one cannot speak of a strong pro-Hungarian movement among the Ruthenes, nor of a strong anti-Czech movement. The Czechs point to the fact that more Ruthene electors vote for the centralist parties than for the autonomists as evidence that most of the population has now accepted the Czechoslovak State. This, while true of the Slovaks, is much less certainly true of the Ruthenes. It certainly does not mean that only the autonomists resent the denial of autonomy. There is, on the contrary, very general indignation over the Czech dual breach of faith in reducing Ruthenia to its present limits, and in withholding the promised autonomy, as well as such auxiliary offences as the introduction of Czech as official language (equal with Ruthene), the multiplication of Czech schools and, above all, the monopoly of the higher posts by Czech officials. The last-named grievance is increasing rather than diminishing as the younger generation of Ruthene-speaking intelligentsia grows up. Few outside the little circle of direct beneficiaries of the new order do not share this resentment, which may easily become intense in a few years' time. If most of the electors do in fact vote for the Centralist parties, this is because elections are not held on the question of autonomy versus centralism, and because many believe that they can do better for themselves by hanging on to the skirts of the Government than by persisting in a struggle which, given the relative strength of the parties involved, must be futile and might involve unpleasing personal consequences. Some indication of the disillusionment which has come to many, even of those who welcomed the change in 1919, may be found in the change of attitude of those American Ruthenes whose voice was really decisive in bringing about the original union. To-day these same communities openly express regret for what they did.[1] True, they are only foreigners; but they are in far closer touch with their homeland to-day than they were in 1918. The feelings which they have expressed are shared by many in Ruthenia.

[1] See the pamphlet, *Wilson's Principles in Czechoslovak Practice*, issued by the Rusin Council of National Defence in U.S.A. (Homestead, Pa., 1929), especially p. 59, which contains a strong protest against Czech methods. As in 1918, the Ruthene communes were consulted on this document; 94 per cent. voted in favour of it, and none against it.

But this feeling, again, must not be exaggerated. The attitude of the Ruthenes to the Czechs is generally one of opposition, but it is a resigned, philosophical, and even half-humorous exasperation rather than anything more active. The Czechs and Ruthenes live separate lives, but as different rather than hostile communities. The country does not require large garrisons to keep it quiet, nor even a very large force (measured by local standards) of police and spies. The average Ruthene will freely acknowledge the more obvious merits of the Czech rule; he will, at any rate, not hesitate to admit that he is better off under the Czechs than his brothers in Poland or Roumania. Honest fulfilment of the pledge of autonomy, with rectification of the Slovak frontier, would probably content a large number of the Ruthenes, at least as a temporary measure, although few would regard it in their hearts as a final solution.

§ 8. THE MINORITY QUESTION

Little need be said on the minority question in Ruthenia, since it differs in hardly any respect from the similar problem in Slovakia. There is the same small Magyar ex-ruling class throughout the country and larger towns, the same Magyar peasantry along the southern fringe; more Jews than in Slovakia, but fewer Germans; relatively rather more gipsies, and a tiny frontier minority in the shape of three Roumanian villages on the right bank of the Tisza.

The laws governing minority questions are the same as in other parts of the Republic, and are similarly applied. There is the same circumscribed, but considerable, freedom in non-political matters, and the same indirect but effective methods are adopted to paralyse the political influence of the Magyars. By a strange parallelism, the Magyar-speaking population in Užhorod, just like that of Bratislava and Košice, has dipped slightly but quite effectively below the 20 per cent. mark. The non-Magyar minorities, and particularly the Jews—far the most important minority in Ruthenia after the Magyars themselves—are enlisted as allies of the authority against the Magyars, special efforts being made to equip them with a separate cultural life of their own. The culture of the Jews, in particular, has been encouraged by every possible means. The Orthodox Jewish community (which comprises the bulk of the local Jews) possesses complete autonomy in its cultural and religious affairs[1] and maintains a complex organization, with 27 principle communes, 16 branches, and 45 rabbis. The larger communes levy substantial budgets for charitable and educational

[1] This is the old Hungarian system, which has been maintained unchanged, except that the Ruthene community is now autocephalous.

purposes. There are two Hebrew secondary schools and seven primary schools, while Talmud schools for religious instruction are maintained where no complete Jewish school is available. The Germans and Roumanians have sufficient primary schools, and even the gipsies have a school of their own—said to be the only specimen of its kind in the world.

As in Slovakia, the Magyars now have to content themselves with the schools to which their numbers strictly entitle them. The 5 kindergartens and 101 elementary schools which they possess seem to meet their needs adequately, as regards primary education. Beyond this, however, they have only 5 burger schools and parallel classes in a single gymnasium, and are said to have been refused permission to collect money and build a purely Magyar gymnasium for themselves.

The political effects of Czech policy have been the same in Ruthenia as in Slovakia. The Magyars are in every way weaker than they were in 1918. Their influence over the other nationalities, both Ruthenes and minorities, has diminished, and they themselves have been reduced to a state which ranges from the active support of the Czechoslovak régime of a small fraction to the vigorous opposition of a somewhat larger body, through the more or less resigned acquiescence of the majority. As regards the other minorities, the Germans are, for the most part, playing at Nazis; the Roumanians are too few to count;[1] nobody bothers about the gipsies. The position of the Jews, however, requires a special word.

Being nearly all Orthodox or Chassidim, the Jews of Ruthenia were far more easily detached from the Magyar body than the Magyarized Jews of Western Slovakia, or of South-Eastern and Southern Hungary. Appreciation of Czechoslovakia's encouragement of their national feeling, gratitude for her liberal policy, respect for the Talmudic precept which enjoins obedience to the local authority, worldly wisdom ('we Jews always take the most practical course', said one of them to me) all combined to bring about a very speedy and complete reorientation of their policy. By 1930, 88·3 per cent. of them already described themselves as Jews, and not all of the remainder called themselves Magyars; a certain number preferred to be known as Czechs. The Magyar-ones were reduced to a very small minority, and most of the remainder were vociferous upholders of the Czech régime. They are usually reckoned to-day, by all parties, as a sure pro-Czech element if and when the question of Ruthenia's future is ever

---

[1] I am informed that in the 1935 elections the Roumanians voted with the Magyar parties, but they have since formed a party of their own which has affiliated with the Czechoslovak National Socialists.

raised. And yet the question cannot, one feels, be left there. The Jews form so large an element in the population as to raise a multitude of further problems, besides that of their relations with the Magyars. Firstly, while the true Magyar is, or was, content to reserve for himself positions of social advantage, leaving industry, commerce, and finance to the Jew, the Czech is himself a business man, and Czech business has entered into serious rivalry with Jewish Ruthenia. Hitherto, indeed, most of the Czech business men, except M. Baťa, have burnt their fingers, but they are likely to try again, and a rivalry will spring up which can hardly fail to result in mutual ill feeling.

But much more important is the relation of the Jews to the Ruthenes. One is impressed by the serious fashion in which the Czech officials regard the Jewish question, not in their own interest, but in that of the Ruthenes. The Jews at present form a class of middle-men which is far too large for the capacity of the country, and sooner or later this problem will have to be attacked far more seriously than either Magyar or Czech has ever yet attacked it. It is also safe to prophesy that the anti-Semitism of which there are at present only faint signs (the Ruthenes joke about Jews, rather as the English do; they do not hate them as the Roumanians or the Germans do) will grow stronger as the Ruthenes swing into line with modern cultural fashions. Then the Czechs will have to choose to some degree between the Jews and the Ruthenes, and it will prove an unenviable choice. If they choose the latter, the Jews will swing back towards Hungary; the conversion is, after all, only skin-deep—according to many Czechs, who complain bitterly that in the towns even the Jewish children still speak Magyar, not even that—and the Talmud would be obeyed with just as good a grace if Ruthenia were returned to Hungary, as it was when it was assigned to Czechoslovakia. Should the Czechs prefer the support of the Jews, this would add mightily to the present discontent among the Ruthenes. It is a dilemma which is none of the Czechs' making, but may prove serious for them.

§ 9. CONSIDERATIONS FOR AND AGAINST REVISION

What chiefly distinguishes the problem of Ruthenia from that of all other districts affected by the Treaty of Trianon, is the relatively greater importance which can reasonably and indeed must be attached to considerations other than those of nationality. In 1918 national feeling among the Ruthenes was so faint that no great violence was done to it by assigning them to Czechoslovakia (although the same argument might equally well have been used

for leaving them with Hungary). To-day, the sense of nationality
is, indeed, awake among the intelligentsia, who are now numerous
enough to give a lead to the masses, but it is neither uniform nor
coherent. Moreover, even if all the Ruthenes were to agree on
one single national objective (and nothing is less likely than that
they will ever do anything so sensible), it will certainly be one
which will prove difficult to satisfy. Are they Carpatho-Ruthenes?
Then they will hardly prove able to stand alone in the hurly-
burly of modern political life. They will become too easily the
pawns of intriguing neighbours. Are they Russians? A solid bloc
of Ukrainians will cut them off from their kinsfolk. Are they
Ukrainians? Then, indeed, they will be contiguous with the mass
of that great people, a solid bloc of some 40 million people,
reaching from the Už to the Don, and their situation will call for
serious consideration, since it will form a part of the great
Ukrainian problem—perhaps the biggest unsolved political question of Europe to-day. They might, indeed, be regarded to-day
as preserving in some sort the nucleus of a future Ukrainian culture,
and especially worthy of consideration for that reason.

Yet they will never be quite an integral part of any Ukrainian
State. They will still be an extreme outpost of their people,
divided from their brothers by a formidable natural barrier, with
quite other cultural and historical traditions, and altogether
different economic interests. Even if all the other Ukrainians now
under Soviet, Polish, and Roumanian rule were to be united in
a single national state, there would still be a case for hesitating
before including the Carpatho-Ruthenes in it, if other considerations were present which might weigh against such a decision.
And it is likely that such considerations would be advanced. To
give either the U.S.S.R. or a Ukrainian State, whether Bolshevik
or capitalist in structure, a foothold on the south of the Carpathians
would be so revolutionary an act that one can well imagine the
statesmen of Europe hesitating very long before committing or
sanctioning it.

Thus it appears feasible, and may even prove necessary, to allow
strictly ethnographical considerations to be over-ridden, in this
particular case, by other claims; and the balancing of such claims
is a very difficult and delicate matter.

Excellent as the work of the Czechs has been in Ruthenia since
the War, and greatly as it has benefited the Ruthenes politically,
socially, and culturally, yet it seems to the present writer that in
view of the economic connexions of the country, the course most
advantageous to the Ruthenes themselves, as well as to the
Magyars, at least, among the national minorities, would be to
return the whole district to Hungary on condition that this could

be done under a rigidly enforced statute of autonomy. It would be economically advantageous if the district on the left bank of the Tisza were added to Ruthenia, while on political grounds the frontier with Slovakia should also be corrected. If this solution were adopted, then the purely Magyar districts along the southern frontier could be returned to Hungary proper. Under any other plan, only the most trivial frontier corrections would be possible, since it is imperative to allow transverse communications between the valleys.

If this were done it would be essential, in order to prevent a renewal of Magyarization to which the Ruthenes would no longer submit, to have a resident international commissioner, acting either for the League of Nations or for the Powers, in Ruthenia; and further to conclude arrangements similar to those in force to-day in the Polish Corridor, for allowing Czechoslovakia and Roumania uninterrupted communication across Ruthenia.[1]

The economic advantages of this would not be confined to Ruthenia. Hungary would undoubtedly benefit, and Czecho-slovakia would not be any the poorer—except, indeed, that she would have to buy her salt from abroad: no irreparable loss. Against this she would be relieved of the heavy expenditure now forced upon her in administering Ruthenia, educating its inhabi-tants generally and politically, and keeping them from starvation.

In the present state of national feeling among the Ruthenes, many of them would, I believe, welcome this change, provided that they could get guarantees against a renewal of Magyarization; whole masses of the peasants are still in so primitive a stage that the economic argument far outweighs any other in their eyes.

But in the minds of many, the real and dominant consideration with regard to Ruthenia is neither the national proclivities nor the economic welfare of the Ruthenes, but the strategic position of their habitat. To-day, the only land route by which Czecho-slovakia can communicate with her colleagues of the Little Entente, either by road or by rail, without touching the potentially unfriendly territory of Germany, Austria, or Hungary, runs through Ruthenia, which, conversely, interposes between Hungary and Poland. And in the chain which binds Czechoslovakia, Roumania, and Yugoslavia, Ruthenia is much the weakest link. It is the narrowest point, and it comprises that part of the Car-pathian chain where the passes are easiest and most frequent; it is a traditional route between north and south. Further, it is most remote from the centres of Czechoslovakia and Roumania, who

---

[1] At the Peace Conference it was at first proposed to secure the communica-tions of Poland and Hungary across Ruthenia in the same way, but this idea died away.

cannot possibly send troops thither save at the cost of much time and danger, nor support large armies in it without also occupying the adjacent plain. Small wonder if the Little Entente trembles for it while clinging to it.

This aspect of the problem has never been quite hidden from keen observers. It would be a gross disparagement of Dr. Beneš' intelligence to suppose that it had escaped his notice in 1918 and 1919. Indeed, the more one reads the documents of the period, the clearer it becomes that although never once stated publicly, this was really, even then, the supreme consideration. Dr. Beneš himself put the position exceedingly frankly in the 'speech to the Slovak nation' which he delivered at Nove Zamky on December 7th, 1933.

Without Slovakia and Ruthenia [he said], the Little Entente would have been simply and purely impossible, and so would have been its whole conception of an organization of Central Europe in which our liberated countries have been their own masters, without the predominating influence or domination of any Great Power. This is the great idea which forbids us to renounce anything in Slovakia; the great idea which makes us refuse frontier revision, and never, I affirm and I repeat, never shall we abandon Ruthenia, for it is precisely on Slovakia and Ruthenia that we build up our policy of the Little Entente, our policy in all Central Europe, and in general, our policy of the distribution of nations in the future and of the affirmation of the rights of the small nations of Central Europe in the European battle. . . . As on the one side the Czech lands stretch out a hand to France and Western Europe, so through Slovakia and Ruthenia we join hands with Roumania, Poland, and Russia. . . . It is Slovakia and Ruthenia which have rendered possible the whole conception of our foreign policy in collaboration with Poland, Roumania, and Yugoslavia, and it is that collaboration which makes us, in the eyes of France and of all Western Europe, a force in the whole policy of Central Europe. We shall therefore never allow our territorial link with Roumania to be cut. . . .[1]

One thing has, indeed, altered since Dr. Beneš spoke: his speech was delivered before that strange political reshuffle in Eastern Europe which took place in 1934, before the formation of a revisionist entente between Germany, Poland, and Hungary and the answering Czechoslovak-Soviet Alliance.

These surprising events have brought into the field a new competitor for little Ruthenia's favours, in the shape of Poland, who had been comparatively disinterested so long as her relations were good with Czechoslovakia. Since 1934, however, she has developed a very lively propaganda in the country. It is no secret that she has been the patroness of M. Fenzig, to whose organ, as it was discovered, the Polish Consul in Užhorod contributed a

[1] Reprinted in *Le Monde Slave*, February 1934, pp. 55 ff.

series of articles violently attacking the country to which he was accredited. She has also been working hand in glove with Hungary to foment anti-Czech feeling. The present psychological approach to the problem seems to be to let Poland, as a Slavonic State, occupy the front of the stage, with Hungary in the background; the theory being that if Poland ever obtained Ruthenia, she would hand it back to Hungary. The intricate revolution of wheels within wheels is well shown by the fact that both M. Fenzig's party, with its Polish connexions, and the Kurtyak party with its Hungarian sympathies, are Russian on the intellectual issue. All this has not diminished Czechoslovakia's interest in Ruthenia, which is now an important link in her communications, no longer indeed with Poland, but with the still mightier U.S.S.R. And since Germany thinks it her holy mission to thwart the U.S.S.R. in all things, she, too, has begun to look towards Ruthenia. Thus the importance, real or imagined, of the little country has transcended the bounds of the middle Danube Basin, and this Cinderella of the old Hungary is wooed to-day by more courtiers than any of her better-favoured sisters. Czechoslovakia, Roumania, Hungary, Poland, in the foreground; behind them that Great Ukrainian people, still divided and subjected to alien rule, only recently become conscious of its own soul and still not fully aware of its own strength; behind this again the still more enormous bulk of the Soviet Union, within which three-quarters of the Ukrainian people are organized to-day—truly no part of old Hungary is the plaything of such vast destinies.

Whether such considerations of *Weltpolitik* ought to outweigh the interests of the populations themselves is a question which the present writer hesitates to answer. He can do no more than state his opinion as to where those interests lie, and to indicate the many difficulties in their path.

ROUMANIA

TRANSYLVANIA

§ 1. GEOGRAPHY AND POPULATION

ROUMANIA'S share amounts to no less than 102,787 square kilometres—an area actually larger than that left to Hungary herself. It comprises the entire eastern end of the ancient kingdom, thus taking in the whole of the ancient Principality of Transylvania, the eastern half of the Banat, and to round these off, parts of the mountainous area of Maramureş (Máramaros) in the north, and below it the so-called 'Crişana', viz. the western slopes of the Bihar mountains and a strip of lowland at their foot.

Transylvania, the heart of the whole territory (to which the other areas are mere outlyers), is a natural fortress much in the shape of a capital D, the arch of which is formed by the Carpathians where they take their great sweep southward and then westward (now in their continuation the Transylvanian Alps). The old frontier with the Bukovina, Moldavia, and Wallachia ran roughly along the crest of these mountains, which constitute a sufficiently formidable natural barrier. There are few passes across them, particularly in the north and east. To the south access is slightly easier, the more so as one large river, the Aluta (Alt), instead of taking the natural course westward, most perversely and unexpectedly cuts its way southward through a tremendous gorge to join the lower Danube in Wallachia.

The cross-bar of the D, which formed the old boundary between Transylvania and Hungary proper, is in reality more of a dotted line, consisting of a series of massifs intersected by the valleys of all the main rivers of Transylvania, except only the Aluta. These western mountains are on the whole lower than those of the north, east, and south, but the central massif rises to considerable heights. This is the old Great Forest, whence Transylvania took its Magyar and Latin names.[1]

The slopes of these mountains, which are reinforced in sundry places by spurs running out from the main chains, take up a considerable portion of the area of Transylvania, but by no means all. Within this natural fortress, 'girt, as it were, with a crown of mountains', as a writer of antiquity puts it, lies an open plateau across which numerous large rivers wind their way through open valleys, separated one from the other only by modest hills.

[1] Magyar *Erdö*—a forest, *-elve*—in front of: *Erdély*—the land beyond the forest.

The valleys, spacious and fertile, are excellently adapted for agriculture, and are broad enough to support considerable cities. The lower slopes of the hills between them are covered with fields of corn and maize, while the gentle summits, where too lofty for agriculture, are crowned with woodland. The mountain slopes themselves, beautifully clad with beeches on their lower flanks and conifers on the upper, and with bare, grassy summits, are neither precipitous nor lofty. In summer, sheep pasture on the highest altitudes. Thus Transylvania is no mere poverty-stricken hunger area, dependent on the outer world for its existence, but has a self-centred economic life of its own which, combined with its isolation from the outer world, has made possible its long history of political semi-independence.

The 'partes adnexae' are in different case. The rivers of the Maramureş, the Bihar mountains, and the Banat run down into the plain which is itself, looked at from the east, their continuation and complement, but, to the traveller approaching it from the west, quite indistinguishable from the flat plain which he has been traversing since he quitted Pest. This narrow strip of plain, averaging perhaps twenty miles in width, contains several important towns which guard, from a discreet distance, the various gates of the hills: Satu Mare (Szatmár Németi), Oradea (Nagyvárád, Grosswardein), Arad, Timişoara (Temesvár). Through these towns run the communications which link them with one another, and join Roumania with the west and with her allies. Czechoslovakia cannot be approached at all by rail from Transylvania, except via Satmar, and although a road traverses the mountains between Transylvania and Maramureş, it is, to-day at least, only to be negotiated at the expense of the utmost tedium, discomfort, and mechanical peril.

The population figures given by the Hungarian 1910 census for this area were as follows:

By Language.	Total.	Transylvania only.
Magyar . . .	1,704,851	918,217
German . . .	559,824	234,085
Slovak . . .	30,932	2,405
Roumanian . .	2,800,073	1,472,021
Ruthene . .	16,318	1,759
Croat . . .	2,141 ⎫	944
Serb . . .	54,874 ⎬	
Other languages .	96,431	48,937
Total . . .	5,265,444	2,678,368

The Roumanian census for 1930 (by nationalities) gave the results shown in Table on p. 253.

It will be seen that, as in the case of Czechoslovakia, the census taken under the two different régimes arrive at somewhat different results. The explanation, once again, is to be sought in a variety of factors: change of régime; emigration (chiefly of Magyars)[1] and immigration (chiefly of Roumanians); the introduction of separate rubrics for Jews and gipsies, and the re-awakening, natural or forced, of national feeling among certain elements, notably the Suabians. It is impossible here to judge exactly between the rival claims, but it is necessary to give some explanation of the peculiar

	Transylvania.	Crişana and Maramureş.	Banat.	Total.
Roumanians	1,657,923	1,037,463	570,825	3,206,261
Magyars	826,796[2]	429,076	97,803	1,353,675
Germans	237,266	83,226	223,130	543,622
Czechoslovaks	3,199	29,231	13,731	46,161
Ruthenes, Russians and Ukrainians	4,506	26,148	5,922	36,576
Bulgars	844	524	10,012	11,380
Serbs	616	2,338	40,500	43,454
Jews	65,123	102,042	11,256	178,421
Gipsies	68,567	21,272	17,910	107,749
Others	5,861	1,742	8,348	15,951
Total	2,870,751	1,733,062	939,437	5,543,250[3]

national distribution, which a glance at the map will show to be even more daedal than the average of Central Europe. This involves, unfortunately, reference to some extremely obscure and controversial historical issues; but these loom so large in the polemical literature of to-day that they cannot in any case be burked. We must begin with Transylvania, which has a different history from its present adjuncts.

[1] According to *Die Nationalitäten in den Staaten Europas* (a collection of reports issued by the Europäische Nationalitäten-Kongress), p. 403, 197,000 Magyars were expatriated before the end of 1924.
[2] 540,000 Székely.
[3] These figures are given by S. Dragomir, *La Transylvanie et ses minorités ethniques*. Further (official) figures appeared in the *Buletinul Demograficale Romaniei*, 1936, no. 3, pp. 153–4, and no. 6, pp. 346–7. This gives figures both by nationality and by mother tongue. The tables are as follows (000s omitted):

Language.	Transylvania.	Per cent.	Banat.	Per cent.	Crişana-Maramureş.	Per cent.	Total.	Per cent.
Roumanian	1,876	58·2	521	59·3	840	60·4	3,237	58·3
Magyar	998	31·0	107	11·2	378	27·2	1,483	26·7
German	248	7·7	232	24·6	63	4·5	543	9·8
Russian	2	0·1	1	0·2	1	0·1	4	0·0
Ruthene	1	0·0	5	0·5	19	1·4	25	0·5
Serbo-Croat	..	..	41	4·3	1	0·1	42	0·8
Bulgarian	1	0·0	9	1·1	..	0·0	10	0·2
Czechoslovak	9	0·3	10	1·1	23	1·6	42	0·8
Jewish	52	1·6	1	0·1	58	4·2	111	2·0
Gipsy	30	0·9	9	0·9	7	0·4	46	0·8
Others	1	0·0	6	0·7	..	0·0	7	0·1
	3,218	100	942	100	1,390	100	5,550	100

§ 2. HISTORY OF TRANSYLVANIA UP TO 1867

Transylvania—or the region now bearing that name—first appears in history as the centre of a powerful kingdom of barbarians, the Dacians. Rome conquered Dacia in the first century A.D. and colonized the interior with large numbers of settlers from all parts of her Empire. Two centuries later, under the pressure of continued attacks from Germanic tribes, she withdrew the garrison and 'citizens'; after which all records regarding Transylvania cease for nearly 1,000 years. We know that Germanic, Turki, and Slavonic invaders overran it and at times occupied it, but in what force and with what effects, if any, on the indigenous population (if any survived) we do not know.

At the end of the ninth century the Magyars entered Hungary, and a century or so later achieved the conquest (or occupation) of Transylvania. They pressed up the valleys of the large rivers, notably the Someş, and established themselves in the more fertile portions of the western half of the 'land beyond the forest'. They did not, however, attempt to occupy themselves the whole country, or even the whole of what was in those days its habitable areas. They themselves remained in the west, while leaving the frontiers to other national groups. The first of these were numerous German settlers, known to this day as the 'Transylvanian Saxons' (although most of them seem to have come in reality from the Rhineland and Luxemburg) whom various early kings of Hungary invited to Transylvania and assigned to them a goodly portion of the land: the whole cultivable area lying within the southern mountains and bordered roughly by the Mureş (Maros) and the Târnava Mica (Kis Küküllő) on the north and west of the Aluta on the south-east. Other 'Saxon' settlements centred round Braşov (Brassó, Kronstadt) in the far south-east and Bistriţa (Bistritz, Besztercze) in the north-east. There was also an outlying settlement round Reghinul Săsesc (Sächsisch Reen, Szász Regen), south of Bistriţa, which although not forming part of the Saxon organization proper, has preserved much of its national character to this day, while even in the west, the towns such as Cluj (Kolozsvár, Klausenburg), were originally German, although they became Magyarized after a few centuries.

It was the normal practice of the time to grant such peoples who were assigned the dangerous position of frontier guards, special privileges which should hearten them in their task and ensure their loyalty. The Saxons, thanks to their importance (they were relatively far more numerous in the Middle Ages than they are to-day) were able to make exceptionally good terms. In 1224 they were granted a remarkable charter which constituted them a single 'nation' under their own elected Count, who held office directly under the king, allowed them almost complete self-government in their internal affairs, and made of their territory, the 'Sachsenboden', a strict national preserve, on which no other nationality was allowed to encroach.

The second great group was that of the Székely—a people of mysterious origin, who have been variously claimed as true Magyars, as Dacians, Bulgars, Avars, Goths, and Roumanians, while medieval Hungarian tradition, which still lives on among them, made of them the descendants of a group of Huns under Attila's youngest son, Chaba, who is alleged to have remained behind in Hungary when the remaining Huns fled eastward after Attila's death. As the Magyars themselves, by the same learned tradition, claimed descent from Attila's hordes, this tradition made of the Székely the senior branch of the family. Old documents, however, distinguish them quite clearly from the Magyars. The original Székely were almost certainly a people of Turki origin, at least closely akin to the Magyars. Whether they preceded the latter, or were settled in their present homes by them, really does not matter. At all events, we find them, many centuries ago, occupying in compact masses the head-waters of the Mureş, the Aluta, and the Târnava Mare (Nagy Küküllő), in the extreme east of Transylvania; and there we find their descendants to-day, doubtless reinforced, as the Roumanians claim, by a certain Roumanian element which they have assimilated, but equally certainly wholly Magyarized (if they were not always Magyar) in their speech and national sentiment. They retain, indeed, a strong local and 'tribal' patriotism; but this takes the form of somewhat despising the other Magyars as a mere bastard stock, and latecomers. They differ, in their own eyes, from the other Magyars only in being more Magyar than they.

The Székely enjoyed privileges somewhat similar to those of the Saxons, although rather less extensive. They were, however, all 'free men' and elected their own Count, who held office direct from the king. Their social organization long preserved many traces of the early 'tribal' system followed by the Magyars themselves before their settlement and political reorganization. Thus all their land was held in common, private property being vested chiefly in cattle.

The Magyars, the Saxons, and the Székely had thus occupied, by the twelfth century or so, practically all the agricultural, and, by their standards, habitable area of Transylvania. The question so ferociously disputed to-day is—where were the Roumanians at that time?

This question involves the whole problem of the origin of the

Roumanians, concerning which they and the Magyars hold theories which are diametrically opposed. The Magyars assert that when they entered it, Transylvania was still uninhabited, unless the Székely were there, or a few Bulgars and Slavs. The Roumanians, they say, are of Balkan origin, and entered Transylvania only after the twelfth century as refugees, vagabonds, and wandering shepherds. The Roumanians claim with passion that their ancestors have, on the contrary, inhabited Transylvania, in unbroken continuity, since its days of Roman greatness, having been merely ousted from their heritage by the barbaric, Asiatic Magyar intruders.

I have no intention of attempting to judge between these rival views. It would take volumes to describe the arguments and counter-arguments, and the truth of the matter is that neither party has proved its case with complete certainty. The only result of so many efforts to bridge this yawning historical abyss has been the engulfment therein of many a promising academic reputation. We do not know for certain that Roumanians were in Transylvania in the year A.D. 1000; and we do not know that they were not. And I cannot see that it matters, except to this extent, that their belief in their autochthony has given the Roumanians an added sentimental stimulus to press their claims to it to-day, while the conviction that the pretention is false has made the Magyars demand restitution more boldly. But when Transylvania was assigned to Roumania in 1919, this was not because any 1,000-year-old historic right was admitted as valid to-day; and if it is ever handed back, I hope it will not be because the statesmen have decided that the Magyar controversialists were right after all.

Whether, in any case, there were no Roumanians in Transylvania in the tenth century, or one, or thousands: whether they constituted a quorum within the meaning of the act or no, they cannot have been either numerous or important, neither can they have possessed any ordered social or political society, for the organization which Hungary adopted for her new possession took small account of them; at most, perhaps, accepting the allegiance of certain mountain chieftains, who were, presumably, held responsible for the conduct of their followers. They were not, however, granted any status as a 'nation' nor do we find any record even of isolated groups possessing 'privileges' in the interior of the country.

This does not mean, as their historians are apt to suggest, that they were set aside, under a sort of national anti-privilege, as a race of serfs. They were excluded from the Saxon and Székely areas; but so were the Magyars themselves. The interior of the country had meanwhile been organized on the ordinary Hungarian

County system, with its division of the population into freemen, or 'nobiles', and villeins. Like the other less important or desirable non-Magyar populations of Hungary, the Roumanians were merged in this organization. Any individuals who might be ennobled formed part of the unitary Hungarian nation, on an equal footing with the Magyar-born nobles, while the remainder were in the same position as the Magyar serfs.

There certainly were such Roumanian-born nobles. One of the greatest figures of all Transylvanian, and indeed, of all Hungarian history—John Hunyadi—belonged to this class. They were, however, not numerous, and when they rose in the world they duly joined the ranks of the Hungarian nobility; they did not attempt to raise the status of their fellow Roumanians.

A further consequence of their lateness in arriving, if they did arrive late, or of their weakness in resisting the Hungarian conquest, if they were there to resist it, was that they were excluded from the fertile valleys and had to exist as best they could in the mountains.

We must now turn for a moment to the political history of Transylvania, since it had the effect of perpetuating the national distribution and relationships of the Middle Ages, preserving them like a fly in amber into modern times, and setting the present century a dire problem in liquidating them.

As we have said, the grant of special privileges to frontier populations was a normal Hungarian practice. It was also usual for frontier districts to be placed under a special governor. Usually, this office was abolished, and the ordinary County system introduced, as soon as Hungary's hold on the area in question became more secure. In the course of this process, the privileges usually went the way of all things. In Transylvania, however, the privileged peoples were too powerful for such cavalier treatment; moreover, the country was so large, so remote, and so dangerously placed as to postpone indefinitely the normal constitutional assimilation. Until about 1260 it was treated separately as an appanage of some junior member of the reigning Hungarian dynasty. After that date the office of 'Voivode', or governor, came to be held by some great Hungarian noble, but it could not be abolished. Transylvania remained a semi-independent state, within which the representatives of the Hungarian 'nation' (viz. the nobles of the Counties) were obliged to concede equality of status to the powerful privileged nationalities. Gradually there developed a separate Transylvanian constitutional life. In 1437, after a great peasant jacquerie, the three 'nations' formed a 'brotherly union', which was really a sort of defensive alliance against all social, political, and foreign enemies: peasants, Turks,

s

and royal encroachments. This 'union' developed into a sort of Federal Diet for settling the common affairs of Transylvania (each of the partners continuing to enjoy self-government in its internal affairs).

This national development was carried a stage farther after the Turks had defeated the Hungarian arms in 1526 and occupied all Central Hungary. Thereafter Transylvania was *de facto* independent for nearly two hundred years, although its princes at times owed a nominal allegiance, now to the Sultan, now to the Emperor. Its constitution continued to be based on the division of power (under the Prince) between the three 'received nations'. At the end of the seventeenth century it came again under the Habsburgs with the rest of Hungary, but retained both its separate status and, in part, its constitution. The Habsburgs, while recognizing it as *de jure* part of Hungary, yet in practice governed it as a separate unit through imperial lieutenants, Maria Theresa creating it a Grand Principality, with herself as Grand Prince. The union with Hungary was proclaimed in 1848 but cancelled in the following year. It was only consummated in 1867, when its separate constitution was finally abolished. Thus although Transylvania formed part of Hungary for some eight hundred years, it was integrally united with the rest of the country only for the last half-century of that period.

It is fair to mention, at this point, that this long separate history has left profound marks on the entire population, the Magyars included. Up to 1918 a Magyar of Transylvania would refer to the land 'west of the forest' as 'Hungary'. This particularist Transylvanian feeling is both strong and real: no invention of Roumanian propagandists. It was, perhaps, stronger still among the Saxons who, from the hour of their settlement, had to fight not only against wild Cumans, Turks, and Tatars from over the passes, but also against the encroachments of the Hungarian nobility. Only the separate position of Transylvania enabled them to keep their privileges and their Germanic character alive, and the preservation of the latter, at least, was far easier when their sovereign resided in Vienna and not in Budapest. During the last two hundred years they were, therefore, on the whole (although there were, it is true, two parties among them) far more 'Austrian' than 'Hungarian': in 1848 they voted for the union with Hungary only dubiously and under pressure, and took sides with Austria in the subsequent fighting, and they were never 'Magyar-one', preserving throughout their history (in striking contrast to the Suabians) a strong Germanic national feeling.

It would, however, be mistaken to draw exaggerated conclusions from what has been said in the preceding paragraph. There have always been spiritual and historical differences between Transylvania and Hungary proper. Some of these have even grown stronger in modern times than they were in antiquity. The fact is of great importance that when the Counter-Reformation passed over 'Royal Hungary' Transylvania remained very largely Protestant. At the same time, even when Hungary was partitioned between the Turks, the Habsburgs, and the Princes of Transylvania respectively, there was no genuine separation between Transylvania and that true Hungary which was at the time more of an ideal than a reality. The Princes of Transylvania were themselves Magyars, and the preponderance of the Magyar element among their subjects was accentuated by two important facts: one, that the Székely at this period lost most of their ancient privileges and became entirely assimilated to the Magyars, except for a few local peculiarities; the other, that the Transylvanian Princes held during long periods large tracts of predominantly Magyar territory outside the western frontiers of Transylvania proper. They regarded themselves, indeed, and were regarded, as the bulwark of Hungarian national liberties; laid claim, when opportunity offered, to the Crown of Hungary, intervened frequently on behalf of their fellow countrymen in 'Royal Hungary', and made of their courts the centres of such Hungarian culture as survived. Amid all the changes of the time, Transylvania was ruled only once by a Roumanian prince from beyond the Carpathians, and he held it only for a year; and at that, he proclaimed himself the Lieutenant of the Emperor, showered favours on the Magyar nobility and swore fealty to the peculiar Transylvanian constitution, which had come to be largely based on the exclusion of the Roumanian element.

For the organization which may have been applicable in the twelfth century soon ceased to be so. The Roumanians may have been few in the twelfth and thirteenth centuries; but whether by natural increase, by immigration, by the fact that in their mountain fastnesses they suffered relatively little from the Turkish and Tatar inroads, or, what is most probable, through a combination of all these causes, they increased very rapidly. By the fifteenth century they were certainly already numerous; by the eighteenth, during which there was much immigration from across the Carpathians, they were probably the largest single element in the population, if not in an absolute majority against all others combined. Gradually they had filtered in, filling the mountainous areas on the frontier, the western mountains and the high-lying parts of the central table-land, so that the Saxon and Székely settlements, and even some of the Magyar groups in the west, had become islands in a Roumanian sea—a singularly unfortunate matter for the Székely in particular, who, being by now, at least, true Magyars, found themselves isolated from their kinsfolk. By the nineteenth century the Roumanians had become almost the sole inhabitants of nearly all the highlands; had encroached considerably on the old Saxon and Székely lands in the plain, and were even beginning to penetrate the suburbs of the towns. But in the eyes of the rigid old constitution they were still as naught. There was no question of giving them 'national' status. Unless they could become nobles, they remained 'misera contribuens plebs'.

As such they were still, in theory, no worse off than the Magyar serfs of the Counties. Indeed, the great peasant revolt of 1437 had been the work of Magyars at least as much as Roumanians; the downtrodden of both nationalities joining hands in a brotherly union of their own against their common oppressors. There were, however, certain special factors which made the position of the Roumanians peculiarly hard. The first was their religion. All Roumanians belonged to the Orthodox Church, while, under St. Stephen, Roman Catholicism became the dominant religion of Hungary. Now Transylvania has had a very peculiar and interesting religious history. Like the rest of Hungary it became largely Protestant at the Reformation, but it was spared the full force of the Counter-Reformation. The result of some centuries of religious vicissitudes was to leave the Saxons Lutheran to a man; the Magyars divided between Roman Catholicism and Calvinism; the Székely partly Catholic, partly Protestant, partly Unitarian.[1] In 1571 a compromise was concluded between these four religions, whereby all four were admitted as 'received', i.e. as enjoying official status, mutual toleration being practised between them. To the three 'recognized nations' were now added four 'recognized religions', the whole forming what a Magyar writer once described, in a burst of candour, as the 'Seven Deadly Sins of Transylvania'. The Orthodox faith was specifically and firmly excluded from the benefits of this compromise. Thus a Magyar serf, if he counted for nothing politically, was at least 'recognized' in the House of God. The Roumanian was merely 'tolerated' in either case. And even this 'tolerance' was political rather than spiritual. It is necessary to record that a peculiar national hatred appears to have reigned between the Roumanians and the other nationalities of Transylvania. Old documents and literature abound in scathing

---

[1] The Székely have always been addicted to queer religions. At one time many of them became converts to Sabbatarianism, and two of their villages still practise that unusual creed to-day. There are also among the Székely a certain number of Magyar-speaking persons of the Orthodox or Uniate religion. These are almost certainly Magyarized Roumanians. They are to-day the object of violent controversy—see below, p. 286.

and venomous references to the Vlach vagabonds, thieves, and whores. They were regarded as an alien element and, if in theory membership of the Hungarian 'nation' was open to them as to every Hungarian subject, in practice the vast majority of them remained outcasts, an element deliberately excluded from the body politic.

Nor did the Roumanians, on the whole, seek assimilation. Notably unsedentary in their habits, and practically unencumbered by the ownership of things, they seem only to have lived with one foot in Hungary. Many of them were shepherds, whose periodical migrations took them regularly across the frontiers; but even the agriculturalists decamped readily across the Carpathians if times were hard—just as they immigrated, as casually, when conditions were unusually severe in Wallachia or Moldavia. Of all the nationalities of Austria-Hungary, the gipsies only excepted, the Roumanians seemed to be the least firmly linked with the Monarchy.

Thus whatever its original justification or purpose, the system in Transylvania had come to rest on a basis of national inequality, in which the largest single element was treated as inferior in every way to the privileged minorities. In the eyes of the haughty Magyar noble and the honest but smug Saxon bourgeois, the 'Vlach' was a mere savage, hardly distinguishable from the gipsy. It is true that most of them were, as they are to-day, desperately poor; for a legacy of the colonization era was that the Saxon, Székely, and Magyar agriculturalists possessed between them nearly all the best land, the Roumanians being relegated to the less fertile hills or mountain slopes. Measured by the standards of Western Europe, which regarded only the squalor of their wooden hovels, the semi-starvation of their diet, their illiteracy, and their superstition, the Vlachs remained to the last among the most backward races of the notoriously backward Dual Monarchy (although their percentage of literacy was still superior to that of their kinsfolk in the Regat). It would take a more sympathetic observer than old Transylvania could produce to appreciate their impeccable colour sense in costume and pottery, the plaintive sweetness of their melodies, the extraordinary physical beauty of their children, and the perfect manners of their old people, and to conclude that, measured by a different scale of values, the Vlach might possess something that both German and Magyar lacked.

Their position improved a little when the Act of Union between the Catholic and Orthodox Churches was passed in 1699. The Orthodox priests who accepted the Union (and these were the overwhelming majority) received a certain status with exemption from serfdom. The Act of Union was not, however, a conspicuous success in Transylvania from the point of view of its authors. Unlike the Ruthene, the Roumanian Uniate priests remained obstinately nationalist, and made of their church a centre of the Roumanian national movement, working in disappointing harmony with their Orthodox brothers. The inadequacy of the concession, either to improve the conditions of the Roumanians or to conciliate them, was shown by Horia's savage rebellion of 1784, which was still more savagely repressed. This occurred during the reign of Joseph II, who pitied the Roumanians' deplorable condition and wished to remedy it. Joseph actually abolished the Transylvanian Constitution, but his successor Leopold promptly restored the old order of things, with the single exception that the Orthodox religion became 'received' in Hungary (although left under the control of the Serbian ecclesiastical authorities). Things remained unchanged until 1848 when the Union of Transylvania with Hungary was voted, first in Hungary, then in Transylvania, where the Magyars possessed an overwhelming majority in the Diet.

In the fighting of the following year, both Saxons and Roumanians took the Austrian side against the Magyars, the Roumanians being encouraged by promises of self-government. These were never fulfilled, since, after the fighting had ended, Transylvania was indeed again separated from Hungary, but ruled from Vienna on absolutist lines. In the brief semi-constitutional era of the sixties, however, during which the Magyars abstained from co-operating, the Saxons and Roumanians, left alone together, established the Roumanian 'nation' and its two churches on a footing of equality with the other 'received' nations and churches, and proclaimed the equality of the Magyar, German, and Roumanian languages in official business. The Compromise of 1867, however, re-united Transylvania with Hungary and, while retaining the autonomy of the received Churches (among which the Roumanian Orthodox Church now at last found a place), abolished all special national privileges and proclaimed the equality of all Hungarian citizens, irrespective of their race or language. The last phase before the War had opened.

§ 3. THE NATIONAL MOVEMENTS, 1867–1914

This last half-century is entirely dominated by the clash of two advancing and aggressive national movements: the Magyar and the Roumanian. The Saxons had ceased to count. Canny and non-prolific, they had for centuries been steadily losing ground both in numbers and importance. Magyars and Roumanians nibbled away the fringes of their old national preserve, and even invaded its cities; and what the Hungarian nobles left to them of the substance of political power the Imperial Commissioners took away. They retained the shadow until 1867, and the Act of Union itself laid down that account should be taken of ancient rights. The Hungarian Government, however, reduced the powers of the 'University' to the control of its property, made the office of Saxon Count a government appointment and then abolished it, and even deliberately weakened the Saxon voting-strength by redistributing the Counties. The Saxons had laid the foundations of their communal life too truly for the edifice to crumble easily. The autonomy of their church, round which their life centred henceforward, was buttressed by a solid income derived from foundations and from self-imposed taxation, and, with the help of this, they were able to keep up a remarkably high cultural standard. Economically, too, they prospered. If great wealth was unknown among them, this was because so very large a proportion of all their gains was devoted to communal purposes. Their sedate, old-world city streets, their cosy farms and well-stocked yards told of the conscientious practice of every Victorian virtue, the successful achievement of every Victorian ideal. But they had become purely self-regarding, save that they watched, as in a mirror, the progress of events in the far-off German countries of which they always felt themselves the outpost. In 1919 they were destined once more to play a part as the tongue which sways the balance, but in the Hungary of 1867–1918 they had lost both the ability and the desire to count in politics. They had become interesting.

The Magyars, on the other hand, were bursting with new energies. The Union had deprived them of the special position which they had held in Transylvania, where they had wielded a power out of all proportion to their numbers. It had placed the whole population, the Roumanians included, on a nominally equal footing. On the other hand, it had removed the danger of interference from the Crown and it had given to the local Magyars the whole weight of the Hungarian State, which stood solidly behind them. It was therefore with a good courage that they attacked the gigantic task of moulding Transylvania in the Magyar image. Justice and administration, in its higher grades, were to an overwhelming degree in Magyar hands, except for such local concessions as were still allowed the Saxons. An ingeniously devised franchise practically excluded the Roumanians from parliamentary representation, while all the forces of the courts and the police were mobilized to repress any local political activity.

Thus a super-structure was erected. The ultimate goal could, of course, only be reached through the schools. As usual, higher education was taken in hand first, and by 1914 the Government had built up a very imposing organization, crowned by the University of Cluj. The Magyarization of primary schools, which in 1867 were entirely denominational, and thus benefited by the autonomy of the churches, lagged behind, but even here the various measures and devices described in an earlier chapter were applied, so that the non-Magyar schools dwindled steadily, besides being forced to devote an ever-increasing fraction of their curriculum to Magyar instruction, while a large number of Magyar State schools invaded the non-Magyar as well as the Magyar regions. In 1914 the educational establishments in Transylvania were divided as follows:[1]

	Magyar.	German.	Roumanian.	Total.
Primary schools	1,265	254	1,145	2,664
Apprentice schools	61	13	1	75
Burger schools	55	7	3	65
Training colleges	8	3	3	14
Secondary schools	30	9	5	44
Special schools	23	3	1	27
High schools	7	..	3	10

It is worth mentioning that all these Roumanian High schools were theological academies. All the Roumanian schools, without exception, were denominational. When a State school was founded in a minority district, it was always purely Magyar.

Among the further measures taken to strengthen the Magyar element, two must be mentioned. Colonization was practised, but only on a very small scale (much more extensive schemes were promulgated during the closing years of the War). The development of industry was used much more systematically as a means of Magyarization. As the figures quoted above show, apprentices were Magyarized as carefully as young intellectuals, so that industrial and commercial life should be as Magyar in their upper ranks as the free professions and the administration itself.

These labours were not entirely unsuccessful, as the census figures show. Taking only the main nationalities, the numbers and percentages of the Magyars, Roumanians, and Germans developed as follows:

	1846 (Fényes).		1857 (Ficker).		1880	
	Number.	Per cent.	Number.	Per cent.	Number.	Per cent.
Magyars	368,540	24·35	569,742	26·21	630,477	30·25
Germans	222,159	14·68	202,114	9·30	211,748	10·16
Roumanians	916,015	60·53	1,287,712	59·24	1,184,883	56·86
Others	6,601	0·44	114,096	5·25	56,940	2·73
	1,513,315	100·00	2,173,704	100·00	2,084,048	100·00

[1] *Hungarian Peace Negotiations*, vol. iii A, p. 91.

	1890		1900		1910	
	Number.	Per cent.	Number.	Per cent.	Number.	Per cent.
Magyars	697,945	31·00	814,994	32·90	918,217	34·28
Germans	217,670	9·67	233,019	9·40	234,085	8·80
Roumanians	1,276,890	56·72	1,397,282	56·40	1,472,021	54·92
Others	58,711	2·61	30,703	1·30	54,044	2·00
	2,257,216	100·00	2,476,998	100.00	2,678,367	100·00

These figures show a small but steady increase in the percentage of Magyars. They show, however, that this gain was rather at the expense of the Germans and the minor nationalities than of the Roumanians. Moreover, the gains were almost exclusively registered in the towns,[1] many of which showed during the last decades before the War a large increase, mainly booked to the account of the Magyar element. The following figures are taken at random from a long list:[2]

	1880		1910	
	Total Population.	Magyars.	Total Population.	Magyars.
Cluj	30,363	24,199	60,808	50,704
Braşov	29,584	9,827	41,056	17,831
Bistriţa	8,063	574	13,236	2,824
Făgărăş	5,307	1,734	6,579	3,357

The total urban population rose from 217,926 in 1880 to 350,268 in 1910. The Magyar element rose from 105,824 (48·6 per cent.) to 205,728 (58·7 per cent.). The Germans sank from 23·8 per cent. to 16·1 per cent.; the Roumanians from 24·0 per cent. to 23·4 per cent.

Hungary had succeeded in giving the towns of Transylvania (except, to some degree, the ancient Saxon centres) her own characteristic impress. She had imposed on Transylvania a Magyar or Magyarized upper and middle class, including under the latter designation not only the officials, tradesmen, industrials, and members of the free professions, but also even the artisans and skilled workmen in the factories. But she had not conquered Transylvania.

For the Roumanians had simultaneously been making most remarkable progress: less apparent than that of the Magyars, but more solid. The Magyars were advancing (slightly) with the help of assimilation and immigration; for their later figures included not only many assimilated Jews, Germans, gipsies, and Armenians, but also Magyar officials from Central Hungary, but the Roumanians

[1] The Székely Counties, however, have enjoyed a relatively high birth-rate, both before and since the War.
[2] Hungarian Peace Negotiations, vol. iii A, pp. 74 ff.

were increasing their absolute numbers, and maintaining their
percentage almost intact, in spite of assimilation and emigration.[1]
Withal, they showed a remarkable resistance even to the forms
of Magyarization, and much more to the spirit. The proportion of
Magyarones among them was probably lower than that of any
other nationality in Hungary.

Far from allowing themselves to be assimilated, they both
extended their area of settlement and developed their social structure. A Magyar writer, Dr. A. Balogh, who investigated demo-
graphic questions for the Hungarian Government at the beginning
of the nineteenth century, concluded that, of all the nationalities of
Hungary, the Roumanians were the largest gainers on balance,
and were responsible for more of the Hungarian losses than any
other race.[2] Another writer complained in 1913 that, while the
Hungarian colonization schemes had only affected 67,000 yokes in
twenty years in all Hungary, the Roumanians had in ten years, in
Transylvania alone, bought 160,394 yokes, counting only purchases of properties exceeding 50 yokes.[3] Count Stephen Bethlen
himself wrote in 1912 that 'the Magyarization of the towns is a
temporary phenomenon which will last only so long as the Vlach
leaders do not carry the struggle into the towns as they have
hitherto in the villages'.[4]

And the invasion of the towns was already beginning. If the
Roumanians had few higher schools of their own, they were not
excluded from the Magyar establishments which, indeed, largely
existed to Magyarize them. They attended them, absorbed their
lessons, and rejected their spirit. Others went to Bucharest where,
of course, they learned lessons far more dangerous to Hungary
than they would have absorbed in any Transylvanian school. As
lately as 1910, 72 per cent. of their population was illiterate, and
the vast majority (1,246,639 persons out of 1,472,021 whose profession was recorded) were still peasants or herdsmen. The
members of the 'public services and liberal professions' (which
included posts in the railways, &c., as unskilled as that of the
famous man who tapped wheels with a hammer for 30 years without knowing why he did so) were listed as 22,153 persons only, the
'professional people' as 6,683, of which only 6,093 were 'intellectuals
proper', compared with 15,000 Magyars.[5] Nevertheless, the

---

[1] Between 1901 and 1914 inclusive 209,786 persons emigrated from Transylvania. Of these, 143,325 were Roumanians, 30,386 Germans, 35,546 Magyars,
and 529 other nationalities.

[2] Cit. A. Popovici, *Die Vereinigten Staaten von Gross-Oesterreich*, p. 110.

[3] D. L. Tokay in *Eladó Orszdg*, cit. V. Jinga, 'La Transylvanie économique
et la thèse révisionniste hongroise', in *Revue de Transylvanie*, vol. i, no. 3,
Nov.–Dec. 1934, p. 314.

[4] Cit. Jinga, loc. cit.

[5] *Hungarian Peace Negotiations*, vol. iii, pp. 108, 111.

development was already sufficiently far advanced to alarm Hungarian observers; and it was only in its beginnings.

It is necessary to stress the importance of this social struggle, for in its new phase it has, as we shall see, largely dominated the history of Transylvania since the War. Three of the cardinal factors in the whole Transylvanian situation for a century past, but particularly during the years immediately before and after the War, have been the immense arrears which the Roumanians have had to make up in the social and economic field; their determination to do so; and the resentment which their efforts have aroused among the other nationalities.

This social struggle has deeply coloured and at times dominated the more purely political movement, which began its modern phase a few years after Horia's revolt, when the Uniate bishops of Transylvania petitioned Leopold in the famous 'Supplex libellus Valachorum' for political and civil rights for their 'nation'. Interestingly enough, they justified this demand by their alleged historic priority, thus light-heartedly introducing into Transylvanian politics the horrid spectre of the 'Vlach controversy' which has haunted them ever since. The request was referred by Leopold to the Transylvanian Diet, which rejected it out of hand; but, from that day onward, the Roumanian national movement grew steadily stronger, and, if we need not describe it here in detail, this is because it is so simple and clear-cut. A deep hostility to Magyar policy dominated it. Up to 1867 the Roumanian principalities hardly counted as a factor in politics, the two protagonists being the Austrian Emperor and the Hungarian nation. The Roumanians naturally supported the Emperor, and their demands were such as he might be expected to grant. Thus in 1848 they petitioned for recognition as a 'nation', proportionate representation in the Diet, and the extension to Transylvania of the Austrian Constitution. Disappointed in 1867, when Francis Joseph, in effect, handed them over to the mercies of Hungary, they were not at first sure of their course, and a party among them at first favoured 'activism', i.e. collaboration with the Hungarian State. Soon, however, their experiences convinced them that this policy was futile. The activists, denounced as national renegades, soon dwindled away. Thereafter practically the entire Roumanian population of Transylvania was in fundamental opposition, not merely to the ruling Magyar system, but to the Hungarian state. The only question was whether a solution could still be found within the Austro-Hungarian monarchy, or whether it must be sought elsewhere. It was natural that so long as Austria-Hungary remained one of the world's Great Powers, while Roumania was still a young, struggling, and none too reputable half-Balkan kingdom, the former solution should count its convinced adherents. Most of the public demands made by the Roumanian leaders were for some such solution. They varied from the restoration of Transylvanian autonomy, with political and national rights for the Roumanians (the programme drawn up by the national party in 1881), to the plan put forward by M. Popovici in 1906, in his famous book, for a federalization of 'Great-Austria' on national lines. In the last decade before the World War the hopes which the Roumanians placed in Vienna were strengthened by the obvious sympathy with which the Archduke Francis Ferdinand regarded them. They saw in him a possible saviour; and, that being so, it is true to say that 'in 1906, as in 1848 and 1892, the "Pan-Slavs" and "Daco-Romans" still looked to Vienna'.[1]

This attitude was imposed on them, moreover, by the official policy of Roumania herself. In the late sixties Roumania had undoubtedly intrigued busily in Transylvania. Afterwards, however, King Charles adhered to the Triple Alliance, and all official activities directed against the integrity of her ally were naturally abandoned. Public opinion in Roumania, however (led in part by émigrés from Transylvania), became increasingly conscious of the national unity of all Roumanians and increasingly desirous of translating this into political union. The chief element of uncertainty was whether this should be accomplished within the Monarchy or outside it; there were parties both in Austria and in Roumania itself prepared to attempt the former. In any case, it would involve the separation of Transylvania from Hungary and its union with the Principalities; and it is enough for our purpose to say that the great majority of Roumanian opinion in both countries was at heart in favour of such a readjustment.

A word must be said on the other nationalities of Transylvania, unimportant as they are by comparison with the three protagonists. There are a few thousand Ruthenes in the far north, a few Slovaks, even fewer Bulgarian market-gardeners. There is a gipsy quarter in every town, gipsy fiddlers in every village; for Roumania and Hungary are the classic lands of the gipsies.

> 'Now, in your land Gipsies reach you, only
> After reaching all lands beside . . .
> But with us, I believe they rise out of the ground,
> And nowhere else, I take it, are found
> With the earth-tint yet so freshly embrowned.'[2]

[1] Seton-Watson, *History of the Roumanians*, p. 419. See, however, the criticism of this book by Z. Szász in the *Nouvelle Revue de Hongrie*, Nov. 1934, with quotations from Roumanian public men boasting that their real and ultimate object was always irredentist.

[2] I once tried to date and place 'The Flight of the Duchess' by tracking down the local allusions. Alas, these are so contradictory that no one solution fits them all, but I have no doubt that, generally speaking, Browning was thinking of Transylvania (which he never visited).

The Jews, almost exactly as numerous as the gipsies (according to the figures, some 70,000 in each case) are far more localized. They have never penetrated the Saxon districts of the south, and are rare among the Székely. In each of the three northernmost departments there are some thousands, forming about 4 per cent. of the population in each case. Most of these are recent arrivals from Moldavia or Galicia, and Orthodox in tenets and garb. In the Department of Cluj there are some 15,000, mostly in the capital itself, and other colonies in the other Hungarian towns of the west. These are mainly neologs, and most of them had become completely and even enthusiastically Magyarized by 1918. In Alba Julia (Gyule Fehérvár, Karlsburg) there was a tiny colony of Karaites.

The Armenians, who played a large part in the commercial life of Transylvania in past centuries, and still exist in considerable numbers in a few centres (notably Someş = Szamos Ujvár) had become completely Magyarized in all respects except their religion.

§ 4. THE ECONOMIC POSITION OF TRANSYLVANIA UP TO 1914

Economically, Transylvania is a land of considerable resources. It is less well adapted for extensive agriculture than the plains either of the Hungarian Alföld, or of Wallachia. The soil is, however, fertile in the valleys, and the ordinary peasant proprietor is able to maintain a higher standard of living than the average Slovak or inhabitant of the Western Balkans. The hills are well adapted for the pasturing of sheep and cattle. The forests, which cover 35 per cent. of the total area, constitute an important source of wealth. The mineral resources include gold and salt (both of which have been worked from early times), coal, iron, methane gas, and mercury.

We are concerned here, not with the economics of Transylvania as such, but rather with its place in relation to Hungary on the one hand and the Danubian Principalities on the other. Of this, it must be said that the relative ease of the communications to the west was largely neutralized by the very long distances to be traversed. The Saxon merchants, who enjoyed extensive privileges in medieval Hungary, traded, not without success, as far as Budapest, and even Vienna, but this trade was never a very important element in the national economy. The trade to the south-east, running via Wallachia to the ports of the lower Danube, has, on the other hand, always been considerable, from the days when Dacia purveyed abundant and excellent slaves for the Roman and Athenian markets, through the later age when the merchants of Kronstadt acquired the choice collection of Turkey carpets which still adorns the interior of their beautiful Black Church, down to modern times. The close traditional connexion between the mountains of Southern Transylvania and the Wallachian plain is shown also by the frequent movements of population, both seasonal and more permanent. There is ample record in the past of big movements in either direction, affecting not only the Roumanians but also the Székely: the population tending to retreat into the mountains when the plains were unsafe and to flow down again when conditions improved. The seasonal migration was also important, and again affected the Székely as well as the Roumanians; many of the former regularly spent a part of the year beyond the Carpathians.

As a matter of fact, Transylvania, until recent times, when the growing population began to press on the means of subsistence, probably flourished best as an autarky. The days of its glory were the days of its independence, when its princes kept their court in Kolozsvár, and the city contained no less than twenty-three craftsmen's guilds. Its prosperity declined markedly when it came under direct Austrian rule and was treated, like the rest of Hungary, as a colony to receive Austria's products and supply her with raw materials. The Saxons, who were favoured for national reasons by the Austrian officials and received a share of state and army contracts, retained a certain modest prosperity, but generally speaking the country was relatively far less prosperous in the eighteenth and early nineteenth centuries than in the sixteenth and seventeenth.

In the modern era, industry began to develop on a larger scale than previously. The forests were exploited extensively for timber. The coal-mines and methane gas deposits of the south were opened up, and certain industries, notably the woollen, made appreciable progress. At the same time, the railway system was developed, as usual, in such manner as to facilitate communications with Budapest. In 1867 Transylvania had not a single railway; but in the following decade the main lines were laid, passing chiefly through the Magyar and Saxon areas. Railway communications with Roumania remained scanty.

Nevertheless, the industrial development of Transylvania lagged far behind that of Northern and Western Hungary, and its turn had not come by 1914 for full incorporation in the planned autarkic Hungarian system. The importance which its eastern trade still retained is shown by the vigorous protests lodged by the Saxon towns against the tariff war waged from 1886 to 1892 between Hungary and Roumania in the interests of the Hungarian landed proprietors. Thus the position acquired in earlier centuries had not altered appreciably. Transylvania stood with one hand stretched out to Hungary, the other to Roumania; but her two feet were firmly planted on her own soil.

§ 5. CRIŞANA, MARAMUREŞ, AND THE BANAT IN THE PAST

Crişana and Maramureş have a comparatively simple political history. During the partition of Hungary, the Princes of Transylvania persistently endeavoured, often successfully, to enlarge their possessions to the west. Thus large parts of the areas under consideration, and even regions lying much farther to the west, were often attached to Transylvania as 'partes', and some of these were only restored to Hungary proper in the nineteenth century. It must, however, be remembered that in laying claim to these territories the Princes of Transylvania were always acting as Hungarians. Hungary's historic claim cannot be questioned.

The racial history is more controversial. During the first centuries after the arrival of the Magyars, the population of the plains seems, to judge by the place-names which have survived in documents, to have been overwhelmingly Magyar, with here and there a German town. The mountains were probably at this time almost uninhabited: they constituted the Great Forest beyond which Transylvania began. Gradually, however, they filled up, although the population was probably exceedingly sparse at first. Except for a few Ruthenes in the far north-east, on the extreme eastern limit of their national area, the Roumanians had the entire mountain area practically to themselves. Thus, apart from the small Magyar or German colonies, they were sole occupants of both flanks of the chain of mountains which form the cross-bar of the Transylvanian D.

Then came the Turkish advance, the depopulation of the plain, the subsequent retreat and the influx into the recovered areas. The Magyars, who had remained in a majority on the plain of the Tisza, expanded eastward; the Ruthenes came down to meet them from the north, the Roumanians from the east. The advancing floods met and mingled along a line which in the latter half of the eighteenth century (the first period, after the Turkish retirement, for which we have any reliable data) probably did not differ very greatly from the political frontier of to-day,[1] although it was not at all clearly marked. There were Magyar villages well to the east of this line, and there were certainly substantial Roumanian and Ruthene populations far west of it.

To add to the confusion, certain Hungarian landlords settled large colonies of other nationalities on their estates. There was a big Slovak colony centring round Békéscsaba, and a German settlement, comprising no less than 32 communes, in the County of Szatmár, in and round Careii Mare (Nagy Károly), with smaller

---

[1] See E. Manciulea, 'La Frontière occidentale de la Roumanie à la lumière des études statistiques hongroises', in *Revue de Transylvanie*, vol. ii, no. 3, pp. 344 ff.

German, Slovak, Czech, Armenian, &c., colonies. The large towns, such as Arad and Oradea, were chiefly German. There was the usual sprinkling of gipsies, and of Jews. The latter, comparatively few in the eighteenth century, multiplied vastly in the nineteenth in the Maramureş and Szatmár districts, where conditions were (and are) very similar to those in Ruthenia, the local Jewish population being gaberdined, ringletted, Yiddish-speaking, and Orthodox, with a sprinkling of Chassidim. The present department of Maramureş contained in 1931 33·798 Jews (20·9 per cent.) of the total, and Szatmár 23,907 (8·1 per cent.). Farther south, the towns contained important Jewish colonies, these being of the neolog and Magyarone type.

This position had probably not altered very substantially before 1869. The Magyar statistician Fényes calculated for the County of Szatmár, 76 purely Roumanian communes, 112 purely Magyar, and 72 mixed; for Bihor, 318 Roumanian, 115 Magyar, 36 mixed; for Arad, 150 Roumanian, 6 Magyar, 32 mixed.[1] This shows a compact Roumanian mass in the hills, a Magyar mass in the west (part of which belongs to-day to Hungary), and a mixed race in the middle. After 1880 a change set in. First and foremost, the main towns, which Hungary designated for industrial, cultural, and national centres, expanded rapidly and became almost entirely Magyar, the German and Jewish populations easily surrendering their individuality.

In the country-side the progress achieved was far smaller, but still considerable, particularly among the Catholic population of the plains, and most notably of all among the Szatmár Germans, most of whom, while still remembering their Suabian origin, had become entirely Magyarized in speech.

The Uniate population of the plains was far more resistant. There can be no doubt that all or nearly all of the local Uniate and Orthodox populations were originally either Ruthene, Roumanian, Serb, or gipsy,[2] and the charge of it was divided between the Ruthene Uniate bishopric of Mukačevo and the Roumanian Uniate bishopric of Oradea. Here, too, the local language gradually changed by what was probably an entirely natural process, since

---

[1] *Magyarország Geographiai Szotára*, cit. Manciulea, op. cit., pp. 345 ff.

[2] The Hungarian delegation to the Peace Conference recalled that some Magyars had embraced the Greek faith when the nation was first converted to Christianity. This is true. Greek missionaries were active in Eastern Hungary in the tenth century, and it was a near thing whether the whole nation would not adopt the Byzantine creed. St. Stephen, however, opted for Rome and, although we have record of Orthodox monasteries, &c., existing even after this great event, it is extremely doubtful whether the claim put forward by the Peace Delegation (*Hungarian Peace Negotiations*, vol. i, p. 153) that the present Magyar Uniates and Orthodox are descendants of this ancient population could be substantiated historically.

the influence of the Roumanian priests at least must have been rather on the other side. There thus grew up a considerable Magyar-speaking population. According to the Hungarian Peace Delegation[1] these 'Greek Orthodox Magyars' numbered 304,000, and the majority of them (99·1 per cent. in the County of Hajdu, 82·1 per cent. in Debreczen, 77·4 per cent. in the County of Szatmár, &c.) spoke no language except Magyar. In 1912 the Hungarian Government obtained from the Holy See permission to establish for this population a Greek Catholic Bishopric in Hajdudorog, with a Magyar Vicar-General and Magyar language of liturgy. 184,000 'Magyar Uniates', including some 12,000 from the Székely districts (where there existed also a small Magyar-speaking Ortho-dox and Uniate population), were transferred to the jurisdiction of this new see, with 32,000 Uniate Ruthenes or Roumanians. The Roumanians protested violently, even to the extent of sending an infernal machine to Hajdudorog by post, but Hungary was not deterred, and the activities of the new See, if the War had not interrupted them, would certainly have continued the Magyariza-tion of the Uniate population of the plains.

One way and another, the lowland population of the Counties of Máramaros, Szatmár, and Bihar (round Arad the Roumanian line ran farther out and into the plain, perhaps owing to the proximity of the Banat) were being very rapidly Magyarized, and even the non-Magyarized population contained many elements which were politically Magyarone, as the remaining Szatmár Suabians, and the Orthodox Jews of Máramaros and Szatmár.

The Magyar line ran also up the chief valleys leading into Transylvania, but the population of the hills remained purely Roumanian. It is, however, quite true that these Roumanians had little connexion, economic or spiritual, with their kinsfolk in Tran-sylvania. National feeling was much weaker among them and, although they tagged after the national movement, they would never have initiated it.

Moreover, the chief economic connexions of this area, mountain and plain alike, were with the west. In the north, conditions were much as we have described them in Ruthenia and Eastern Slovakia. There was the same timber industry, depending on the floating of logs down the rivers, the same seasonal migration to the plains. There was a similar seasonal movement from the Bihar mountains, while the inhabitants of the lowlands drove their swine up into the hills in winter to fatten on the acorns. The local life of the hills depended on the markets of the plains, and these again were intimately connected with the lowlands farther west, and with the general economic life of Hungary. They contained several large

[1] *Hungarian Peace Negotiations*, loc. cit.

T

factories of great importance both for themselves and for Hungary at large: the asphalt works at Tataros, which supplied the needs of Budapest, the railway and carriage works at Arad, the mills of Satu Mare, the salt-mines of Sighet, and many others.

The history of the Banat is sketched in the section dealing with Yugoslavia, and need not be recapitulated here. Roumania's share consists of the mountainous hinterland (the frontier in the south running right through the foothills) and the north-eastern portion of the plain. She thus salvaged the majority of her own kinsfolk and also acquired, as the figures quoted above show, very substantial minorities. The mountains are chiefly Roumanian, with a few German and Magyar islands, and the Craşovan villages round Reşiţa. The Department of Timiş-Torontal, on the other hand, contains in its population of 500,000, 180,000 Germans, over 70,000 Magyars, nearly 30,000 Serbs, and 30,000 'others', against little over 192,000 Roumanians. In Timişoara itself the Germans number 30,000, the Roumanians and Magyars close on 24,000 each, the Jews nearly 10,000.

The minorities, particularly the Germans, thus constituted a large and important part of the population: particularly as nearly all the local wealth was in their hands up to 1918. It is necessary to emphasize the very strong difference which then existed between the Suabians of the Banat and the Transylvanian Saxons. The Suabians were not pioneers, but late-comers to a land already inhabited, and with a long history behind it. They had no national 'privilege' to shelter them, and their religion—they are all Catholics —was different from that of the Saxons, but the same as that of the local Magyars. So long as the Banat preserved its separate status, the Suabians were, of course, in no danger of losing their national characteristics, and even up to 1918, not only Temesvár itself but much of the country-side was thoroughly German. A rapid change had, however, begun. The bourgeoisie and intellectuals were Magyarized with extraordinary speed and enthusiasm. It is credibly, and with relish, reported of one of their national leaders of to-day that shortly before the change of sovereignty he had declared in a public meeting that 'if, by opening his veins, he could let out every drop of accursed German blood, he would do so'. Thus the people had already lost its potential national leaders, and, if the peasants still kept their old tongue and customs, the rapid Magyarization of even the primary schools was beginning to affect them also.[1] Politically, they were as good Hungarians as any in

---

[1] In 1879/80 they had possessed in what is to-day the Roumanian Banat, 106 purely German primary schools and 111 bilingual: by 1913/14 the bilingual schools had disappeared and the purely German had dwindled to 34.

the country, and seem always to have allied themselves with the Magyar element against the Roumanians and Serbs.

Like the Crişana, the Roumanian Banat possessed a flourishing industry. The Reşiţa iron and steelworks (which belonged to Viennese banks) were among the largest in the country, and Timişoara, one of the towns on which Hungary had lavished most attention, possessed a large variety of industries. All of the economic life of the Banat gravitated towards Budapest, on whose markets it depended and which, in return, had assigned it an important place in the national economy.

§ 6. THE UNION WITH ROUMANIA AND THE DETERMINATION OF THE FRONTIERS

We need not concern ourselves closely with the intrigues and agreements of the World War because, although numerous, they had little ultimate effect. Every one except Hungary seemed agreed that Transylvania must be the price of Roumania's adherence to either side, but while the Central Powers were prevented from offering this by the stubborn refusal of the Hungarian Government, the Allies were able to buy her over at a perfectly scandalous price, which included Transylvania, the whole Banat, and a line in the west reaching far out into the Hungarian plain, to within a few miles of Szeged and Debreczen. The Treaty stipulated, however, that Roumania should not conclude a separate peace, and this she did in January 1918, thus absolving the Allies in their own eyes of any legal obligation towards Roumania. The get-out was a dirty one, but so was the deal.

Some of the Roumanian leaders in Transylvania had sat on the fence during the War, and most of the troops had fought like dutiful cannon-fodder, but there is no doubt that the leaders were really only waiting their chance. Incidentally, events occurred during the War which raised the mutual national animosity to a very high pitch. When the imminent collapse of the Monarchy became apparent to all, the Roumanians of Hungary constituted a National Council, first at Oradea (October 12th, 1918) then at Arad (October 27th), which claimed the right of self-determination. On November 10th, during the final collapse, this Council notified Budapest that it had taken over control in the twenty-three Counties of Hungary inhabited by the Roumanians, and parts of three others. Count Károlyi recognized this Council as representing the Roumanians of Hungary, and sent Jászi, his Minister of Nationalities, to negotiate with it. Roumania subsequently claimed that by this action Hungary had recognized Transylvanian independence. The Hungarian Government denied this strenuously, and, in fact,

Jászi's whole aim was precisely to save the integrity of Hungary by concessions to the nationalities. The Roumanian leaders were, however, far more obdurate than any of the similar Councils with which he negotiated[1] and Maniu, who presided over the Roumanian Council, had a unanimous party behind him in demanding complete separation.[2]

Meanwhile, Károlyi had on November 8th negotiated the Belgrade armistice (signed on November 13th) which provided an extraordinary line of military occupation, running along the upper valley of the Someş (Szamos), then south-west via Bistriţa and Marosfalu to the Mureş, which it followed till that river's confluence with the Tisza. This line was purely military. It did not prejudice the final political settlement, and left the Hungarian administration in charge of the areas behind it. Moreover, it was clearly dictated by one interest only. General Franchet d'Espérey, who laid it down, cared nothing for Roumanians or Magyars, but he wished to ensure that General Mackensen's army, which was in Roumania, should not return to Germany as a fighting force. With the same object, France instigated Roumania to declare war again on the Central Powers (November 9th). At the same time, Serbian troops were authorized to occupy the entire Banat.

On December 1st a great meeting at Alba Julia proclaimed the union of all Roumanians in a single state. A number of resolutions called for a purely democratic régime, general suffrage, liberty of press, radical agrarian reform, and advanced social legislation. Article 3 of the resolutions laid down:

The National Assembly declares as fundamental principles of the Roumanian State the following:

(1) Complete national liberty for all the peoples which inhabit Transylvania. Each people to educate, govern, and judge itself in its own language through the medium of persons from its own midst. Every people to have the right of legislative representation and of participation in the administration of the country in proportion to the number of the individuals of whom it is composed.

(2) Equality and complete autonomous liberty for every denomination in the State.

The Assembly then established a 'Directing Council' composed of leading Transylvanian politicians, telegraphed to the King and Queen of Roumania announcing union with the Regat as an accomplished fact, and sent a deputation to Bucharest.

The Alba Julia meeting seems to have been a clear enough expression of the will of the Roumanians of Transylvania. Its

---

[1] See Károlyi, *Gegen eine ganze Welt*, p. 391, and Jászi, op. cit., p. 62.
[2] Seton-Watson, *History of the Roumanians*, p. 432.

representative character is not seriously questioned. Of the other nationalities, the Magyars seem to have been opposed, almost to a man, to the union with Roumania. There was not even the bait of superior social conditions which attracted some peasants and workers to Austria and Czechoslovakia, while the old hatred between Magyar and Roumanian played its part. The only Magyars who had any truck with the Roumanians were the reactionaries who afterwards organized the White Army under their shelter.

The Saxons had formed a National Council of their own at the same time as the Roumanians, but did no more at first than raise a civil guard, keep order in their own districts, and watch the situation. They saw, quite correctly, that they would be unable to influence the course of events, and as they have never thought very much about any one but themselves, their obvious course was to wait and see which way the cat would jump. They soon perceived that the animal in question was leaping eastwards[1] and their leaders favoured joining Roumania at once, on the best terms obtainable. In private negotiation, the Roumanians promised them complete national autonomy, with minority rights where they formed 20 per cent. of the population. On the strength of this they decided, by a majority, to join Roumania, but a delay was caused by their very prudent desire to get the promises put into writing. The Roumanian leaders put them off with vague words, and at last said that the Alba Julia Resolutions were so generous as to make further promises unnecessary. On January 21st, 1919, the Saxons accordingly voted for union with Roumania on the basis of the Alba Julia Resolutions.

No other group of the population seems to have expressed an opinion. The Suabians of the Banat, as we have said, also waited to see how the situation would develop, being, in fact, not at all anxious to leave Hungary, but unwilling to antagonize their new masters, whoever those should prove to be. The Roumanian Delegation to the Peace Conference produced a manifesto from the Suabians to say that if there must be any change, they would prefer the Roumanians to the Serbs. The sentiment does not sound enthusiastic, and I am informed that the manifesto was not authoritative (although it may well have expressed popular opinion).

In terms of voting, then, one may say that the Roumanian population (roughly 55 per cent. of the total) was actively in favour of the union; the Magyars (25 per cent.) actively against, while the remaining 20 per cent. was unwilling to commit itself either way, although given a straight plebiscite under normal conditions the majority would probably have voted for Hungary, giving to Roumania roughly 60 per cent. of the total votes.

[1] It is said that one of their leaders was shown the draft peace terms in Paris.

Meanwhile, Roumanian troops from the Regat had entered Transylvania. In the middle of December, alleging danger to the lives and properties of Roumanians west of the demarcation line, they crossed it in several places, and presently obtained from Paris permission to occupy the line Satu Mare, Careii Mare, Oradea Mare, Békescsába, while French troops occupied the Banat, to avert conflicts between Roumanians and Serbs. The Roumanians were thus in occupation of the territory subsequently allotted them when their frontiers were being discussed in Paris and had, indeed, already installed their administration there. Afterwards, as is well known, they occupied Budapest and indeed, practically all Hungary.

The details of these movements can, however, be passed over here, and so can the minutiae of the negotiations in Paris, for the reason that they had little effect on the final settlement. M. Bratianŭ began by claiming the entire territory as far as the Tisza, on the grounds both of the Treaty of 1916, and of ethnography. He renounced only the Debreczen area. In the territory claimed (excluding the Banat) there were, he said, 1,000,000 Magyars and 2,500,000 Roumanians, according to Hungarian figures; but in reality, 2,900,000 Roumanians and 687,000 Magyars, besides 'a race related to the Hungarians' near the Moldavian frontier numbering 450,000 and 260,000 Saxons.[1]

M. Bratianŭ, however, was not so persuasive as M. Beneš. Indeed, his personal unpopularity was so intense as seriously to prejudice the cause of his nation. Mr. Lloyd George declared that the 1916 Treaty no longer held, and emphasized that the Powers were impartial in the Hungarian-Roumanian question. The matter was referred to a Committee, whose line was subsequently adopted.[2] It was based broadly on ethnography, but gave Roumania the main line of communications running north-west to south-east through Szatmár and Arad, in order to allow her access to her north-western territories. It was admitted that this involved a certain sacrifice of the strict ethnographic principle, since a truer ethnographic line 'might in perhaps some cases have been 20 kilometres east'. M. Tardieu, rapporteur to the Committee, admitted that about 600,000 Magyars would be left in Roumania, against 25,000 Roumanians in Hungary.[3] But to move the line would have cut the communications, and if the frontier suggested favoured Roumania unduly, any other possible line would have been 'all in favour of the Hungarians and correspondingly to the detriment of the Roumanians'.

[1] Hunter Miller, *Diary*, vol. xiv, pp. 168 ff.
[2] Ibid., vol. xvi, pp. 225–6.
[3] This seems a remarkable understatement, but the reference is presumably to the Magyar population of the western fringe only.

This decision was early taken. The arguments of M. Bratianŭ had little effect on it. Hungary was, of course, not consulted at the time, and when Bela Kun started an offensive against the Roumanians in the spring of 1919, the only effect was to frighten the Allies into announcing on June 13th that the frontier had been in substance already fixed. The protests of the Hungarian Delegation, when it arrived at last in Trianon, were thus mere wasted breath.

The frontier in the Banat was an issue which lay rather between Roumania and Yugoslavia than between Roumania and Hungary, and is discussed elsewhere.[1]

§ 7. THE ROUMANIAN QUESTION SINCE 1918

The political development of Transylvania has proved, in one great respect, very much simpler than that of Slovakia. There has been no question of carefully nursing (perhaps, even, of delivering) the national consciousness of the local majority. The relations between the Transylvanian Roumanians and the State have been strained, but never to the point of affecting the real and deep solidarity of the Roumanian people. They have been, as it were, a violent toothache, causing intense exasperation and misery, but not a cancer threatening the life of the body politic.

This has proved a deep disappointment to the minorities, particularly the Magyars, who had been fond of stressing the considerable historical, cultural, and moral differences which existed in 1918 between the Roumanians of Transylvania and those of the Regat. They had believed that these differences were fundamental and would soon reassert themselves, once the first intoxication had passed over. The Transylvanians would then come to feel that they had more in common with the Magyars and Saxons whose destinies they had shared for so long than with the Balkanized and Phanariot 'Regatler', and if not actually wishing to reverse their decision of 1918, they would at least combine with their fellow Transylvanians to set up a state which may be linked almost as closely with Hungary as with Roumania.

According to the official Roumanian thesis, of course, the truth lay in just the other direction. They admitted the existence of local differences, but held them to be superficial and fugitive compared with the underlying unity of race, character and, in its broadest sense, culture. The whole movement of the future, they said, would be towards strengthening this unity; local differences would vanish, and if any regional feeling continued to exist, it would stop far short of separatism.

There can be no doubt whatever that on this issue, which is

[1] See below, p. 355.

clearly one of the first importance, the Roumanian prophets
proved the wiser. The distinctions on which Hungary based such
high hopes proved not to be fundamental, nor even to go very deep.
The reason is quite simple. The culture of Transylvania up to
1918 was Magyar and Saxon. The deposed Wallach had had no
hand in creating it and was not even willingly admitted to the
enjoyment of it. In modern times, the Roumanians had naturally
emerged to some extent from their former isolation. Their small
bourgeois class, and even those of their peasants who had penetrated into the old strongholds of the other nationalities, had
adopted some of their ways. But they were always told, brutally
enough, that they were simply enjoying what others had created,
and they themselves probably felt that they were simply wearing
borrowed plumes. They themselves possessed absolutely no indigenous, specifically Transylvanian, higher culture.

This statement needs qualification in one respect only. The
Uniate Church was a genuine Transylvanian Roumanian speciality.
But as a bridge between the local Roumanians and the west, a gate
between them and the east, it proved a failure. The population
never took kindly to it in their secret hearts. They seem to have
sniffed the political purpose which lay behind its creation.
Although the clergy had accepted the union, when it was first
introduced, almost to a man (naturally enough, since they gained
considerably thereby), yet nearly a century later, when Joseph II
proclaimed his Edict of Toleration, the people celebrated it (quite
contrary to the intentions of its author) by returning in masses
to the Orthodox fold. And in spite of every persuasion, in 1910
the adherents of the Orthodox creed were nearly twice as numerous
in Transylvania and the Banat as the Uniates.

Politically, the Roumanian Uniate clergy, in sharp distinction to
the Ruthene, remained nationalist; the best proof is that many of
the War-time measures taken by the Hungarian Government were
directed quite impartially against the two Churches.[1] Since the
War, Orthodox and Uniate have had their differences, which have
at times been acute, but they have not affected the common solidarity
against the non-Roumanians. No member of a minority whom I
have questioned on the subject has drawn any distinction between
the attitude of the two hierarchies in national-political questions.

Thus the spiritual life of the people remained purely Roumanian.
Such westernization as could be found at all was chiefly in the
habits of the bourgeoisie, among whom even to-day one may detect
certain characteristics which differentiate them somewhat from
the Regatler: more solidity and less ornament; more of the
German aura, less of the Latin and Oriental.

[1] Cf. Seton-Watson, *History of the Roumanians*, p. 523.

But the bourgeoisie were, after all, only a small minority. As regards the peasants, who form the great mass of the Roumanian population in Transylvania and the Regat alike, there is practically no difference to be remarked on the two slopes of the Carpathians. The physical type is the same, the architecture of the houses, the costume, pottery, and peasant arts, the customs, folk-songs, and way of living; also, so far as I could judge, the character. The dialectical differences are small. All these things are, indeed, remarkably homogeneous throughout Transylvania. Such contrasts as exist are rather between the mountaineers as a whole and the people of the plain, who are strongly mixed with Slavonic and Turkish elements.[1]

Even among the bourgeoisie, such differences as did exist vanished with unexpected rapidity after 1918—not altogether to the general advantage. The Regat and Transylvania have exercised a mutual influence, but that of the Regat, which is in many ways the less admirable, has proved the stronger. The great boast of the older generation of Transylvanian politicians was their incorruptibility. The old guard can still pride itself on its purity, but the new generation cannot. The financial political scandals which are all too characteristic of Roumanian political life are now no longer a Regat speciality. They are one sign (not a happy one) of the rapid development throughout Roumania of a singularly homogeneous national character.

Who can say how different things might have been if the past policy of the masters of Transylvania had been more generous? Perhaps careful and plentiful dieting, instead of a few crumbs dropped from the table, might have produced a new breed. But the time for this has gone by. The political development has followed the same lines. Not that Hungary's prophecies of discord between Transylvania and the Regat have proved entirely unfounded; but that discord has never led to any disagreement on fundamental national questions, and even the desire for regional autonomy seems to be growing less. The development of the parties had been interesting. In the first years after the War, the Transylvanian Roumanians combined quite solidly in the old National Party which had tried to defend their interests in Hungary. The astonishing degree of unity which they achieved was facilitated by the small degree of social differentiation among them, and forced upon them by their need to defend themselves, not against the Regat, but against the minorities in Transylvania, who

[1] There are also certain variations in costume, &c., between the Wallachians and South Transylvanians on the one hand, and the Moldavians, Bukovinians, and North Transylvanians on the other. The latter group seems to have much in common with the Hutzuls; but whether Hutzul has influenced Vlach or vice versa, I could not say.

were numerically only a little weaker than they, and socially and economically far stronger. The party was federalist second, but nationalist first. As a matter of fact, it entered the Government in 1919, in coalition with the Peasant Party of the Regat.

Unfortunately, although this Government was popular at home and abroad, it held office only for three months, after which the King appointed General Averescu Premier. Under Averescu and the Liberal Premiers who succeeded him, a policy of rigid centralization was introduced. The National Councils of Transylvania, Bessarabia, and the Bukovina were dissolved, and the whole country divided into Departments, under Prefects appointed directly from Bucharest. The situation which now arose was something like that which we have described in Slovakia, with similar causes and similar effects. The special wishes and susceptibilities of the Transylvanians were disregarded. Officials from the Regat, mostly camp-followers of the Liberal Party and not always circumspect or admirable in their ways, filled the Government posts; Transylvania was forced to bear the brunt of the national taxation, while financial cliques in Bucharest monopolized the pickings.

The Transylvanians denounced all these abuses with an acerbity which seemed to justify every prophecy of Budapest. They have never been reconciled to many aspects of Liberal policy, particularly to its extreme centralism, and in fact, when they at last returned to power in 1928, they introduced a large measure of decentralization, remodelling Roumania into seven large Directorates, based on the historic units, and each enjoying wide local autonomy. All the time, however, things had been changing. The party divisions of the immediate post-War period, with their historic and regional bases, had been breaking up. The Liberals introduced their party organization into Transylvania, and the National Party itself fused in 1926 with the Peasant Party of the Regat. The two wings retained something of their distinct characters; nevertheless, this was a very important sign that the country was feeling its way back to the two-party system, based on social and economic interests, which Roumania had striven on the whole with success to maintain before the War. Broadly speaking, it has now returned to that position. There is a multiplicity of minor groups, but the great voting mass of the country is divided between the Liberals and the National Peasants, and these are tending more and more to represent social rather than regional interests. It is true that the former still regard the Regat, and the latter Transylvania, as their strongholds, but each has many adherents in the other's camp, and the National Peasants, which are no longer a regional party, certainly cannot be said to be specifically decentralist. They still officially advocate devolution, but have taken no steps to reintroduce it since their reform of 1928 was cancelled by the Government which succeeded them. Their first interest to-day lies elsewhere.[1]

There remains a small Old Guard of very violent regionalists, their leader being M. Boila, Dr. Maniu's nephew. On the other hand, the newer political parties which have pullulated in recent years seem quite to have outgrown such feelings. The Communists (who exist secretly) stand for the equality of all nationalities in all parts of Roumania. The other groups, which between them command the allegiance of most of the Roumanian youth, are all 'Fascist' in one form or another. They are all intensely nationalist, and although some of them favour decentralization for purely administrative reasons, not one of them seems to make, or indeed to feel, any distinction between one brand of Roumanian and another. Whether their 'Leaders' are from Transylvania or from the Regat (and there are some from each) seems to mean no more to their followers than it would matter to an Englishman whether his chosen leader came from Devonshire or Essex. Among the intellectuals of Roumania, the true line of cleavage is not regional, but one between the new generation and the old. The young men, all over the country, are struggling to form a new Roumania, more national, more united than the old. Moreover, some of the previous causes of dissatisfaction are disappearing; not that the Regat has greatly altered its ways, but that the Transylvanians have shown themselves able to counter-attack. If there are still many officials from the Regat in Transylvania, the Transylvanians are now beginning to fill the posts in the Regat. I have heard no complaints of unfair discrimination against them. Transylvanians are beginning, too, to take their full share in the business life of Bucharest. As time goes on, they will doubtless play a larger part still.

Other grievances remain: most notably, the marked decline in the general standards both of technical efficiency and of honesty in the administration. For there is no doubt that in these respects the annexation has meant a distinct change for the worse; and the older generation remembers and regrets the higher standards that used to prevail. The younger men, however, take the present state of things for granted, or if they revolt against it, their reaction takes the form of an increased nationalism, since, quite mistakenly, they delude themselves into the belief that the foreigner (usually the Jew) is to blame for any scandal which may arise.

[1] In the foregoing account I deliberately abstain from giving any electoral figures in support of my statements, since the Roumanian electoral practices are such as to deprive such statistics of any meaning.

In all this there is little room for any irredentist feeling; and it
will not probably be disputed by any observer acquainted with
the facts that feeling in favour of a return to Hungary is as good
as non-existent among the Roumanians of Transylvania. I remember one politician of the old school who regaled me in private with
anecdotes of the Regat with which I may not, alas! sully these
pages, but declared with unmistakable sincerity that 'better the
most miserable Regat cess-pool than to come again under the
heel of a Bethlen or an Apponyi!' This would certainly be the
general feeling among all classes of Roumanians; the Magyars
themselves hardly dispute it to-day.

Nor have I been able to find any greater sympathy in Roumanian
circles for the alternative plan now popular among many Magyars,
both in Transylvania and in Hungary, for an independent Transylvania. Whatever their differences among themselves, Regatlers
and Transylvanians make common cause against Hungary. The
members of the minorities whom I have questioned whether a
political feeling of 'Transylvanian solidarity' exists have invariably
admitted, frankly and ruefully, that they can find no trace of it.
Most of them, indeed, have said that the Regatlers on the whole
respect the liberties of the minorities better than the Transylvanians. True, it was the National Party which adopted the
statesmanlike Alba Julia Resolutions, and the Regatler who refused
to ratify them; but things have changed since then. I have talked
with many members of every possible minority on their experiences at the hands of Transylvanian and Regat Roumanians
respectively, and the answer has, more often than not, been more
favourable to the latter. The Transylvanians used to be praised
as more honest; they have certain familiar ways, understand local
feelings and problems better—'But,' many have said, 'by that very
fact, they understand better how to find the joints in our armour.'
Dr. Maniu himself has always been popular with the minorities,
who hoped great things of his term of office as Premier, but they
complained at its close that they had been disappointed, although
still conceding that his comparatively negative record was not all
his fault. The two Roumanian Premiers since the War of whom
I have heard most praise from the minorities are Professor Jorga
and M. Duca, who paid for his principles with his life.

§ 8. ROUMANIAN MINORITY POLICY

The national problem in Transylvania has thus been relieved
of one of the great complexities which burden the situation in
Slovakia. The further situation is the same in its essential elements
as the Slovak. Like the Czechoslovaks, the Roumanians have a

purely national conception of their State—termed in their Constitution the 'unitary national Roumanian State'. Their problem, as M. Maniu put it in a speech soon after the Armistice, is to 'Roumanize Transylvania'—that is, to secure for the Roumanian element a position of unquestioned superiority. And, as in Slovakia, the political enemy in chief consists of the Magyar minority, whose power, influence, and numbers must be weakened by all possible means.

The Roumanians have, rightly enough, never considered that they had any serious chance of conciliating the Magyars—and it is worth noting, also, that unlike the Czechs, they have not even thought it worth while to attempt to detach from them any particular social element, such as the workers or the peasants. Their chief attacks have, of course, been directed against the politically active classes, and they have even allowed the Magyar peasants a share in the benefits of the agrarian reform; but generally, speaking, they have regarded the Magyar minority as an irreconcilable enemy, towards which no other policy is possible than one of restraint, if not repression.

Not so the non-Magyar minorities, to whom Roumania, like Czechoslovakia, has adopted a liberal enough cultural policy, with the object, of course, of detaching them from the Magyar cause, but aiming rather at dissolving the Magyar and Magyarized bloc into its component elements than at simply substituting Roumanization for Magyarization. In choosing this policy she has been guided, no doubt, by a sage realization that the suddenly awakened national feeling of the smaller minorities was a force which could not be ignored, and that the attempt to repress it would only defeat its own ends. In any case, however, national distinction between Roumanian and non-Roumanian is very clearly marked, not only by language, but by religion also. Creed, in Transylvania, is a national mark as distinctive and by tradition almost as immutable as colour might be, and there is in the eyes of every one something unnatural about a person whose language or other national attributes are at variance with the creed with which those attributes are usually identified. The Roumanian churches and Roumanian public opinion accept as an unalterable natural phenomenon the non-Roumanian character of the Catholic, Protestant, and Jewish population. Moreover, the very idea of the feasibility—even the desirability—of assimilation is somewhat foreign to the Roumanian mind, especially to the Regat. It is essentially a Central European conception, which was born in Germany and developed to its highest point, perhaps, in Hungary. Roumania, with her lingering Oriental tradition, has never been equally affected by it.

In general, then, Roumania has sought to recover for herself only that proportion of the population which she claims, either on the evidence of surnames (still Roumanian or recently Magyarized) or of religion (in the case of Magyar-speaking adherents of the Orthodox or Uniate churches) to be Magyarized Roumanians. It is true that, as the views of the local politico-savants on their national past are something really grotesque, the share which she has claimed on these grounds is inordinately large. This applies not only to the case of families which, even if their Roumanian origin is indisputable, have yet been Magyarized for generations past so that 're-Roumanization' is now a real act of violence. Still more it applies to the campaign which has recently been opened against the Székely. To enter the Székely in the census and other official lists as a separate nationality is perhaps defensible, so long as the outer world is not deceived as to the true nature of their national feeling. Some Roumanian scientists, however, not content with arguing that there must be Roumanian blood among the Székely—who have lived for centuries as an island in a Roumanian sea, and must, to some extent, have intermarried with Roumanians in the past[1]—now seek to ascribe to them a purely Roumanian origin.[2]

The only law yet passed on the Roumanization of names is comparatively mild. As originally brought forward by its author (in 1934) it provided that all alterations of names which had occurred in the last ninety years should be cancelled. The Government, however, allowed the persons concerned to appeal against the decision. In practice, both census officials and educational authorities have been far more arbitrary, often constructing the most grotesque etymologies to prove that a Magyar name was originally Roumanian. The whole question is, however, somewhat less important in Roumania than in the Slav districts, owing

[1] These mixed marriages have, however, not been frequent in modern times. In 1909–12 in historic Transylvania, only 1,059 out of 34,407 Magyar bridegrooms married Roumanian brides, and only 990 out of 34,642 Magyar brides married Roumanians. The proportion was lower still in the Székely Counties, where it did not amount to 0·5 per cent. of the total number of marriages. It may well be that intercourse was less restricted centuries ago; but this cannot be proved.

[2] The zeal with which this campaign is prosecuted is due to a very unfortunate circumstance. The suggestion was negligently thrown out a few years ago by Professor Jorga, the Grand Old Man of Roumanian learning. Now Professor Jorga is perhaps the most voluminous writer now living, certainly easily the most voluminous historian. He is also possessed of a singularly fertile and errant imagination, and there is practically no conceivable hypothesis connected with the obscure past of Eastern Europe with which he has not toyed, often to lay it aside in his next volume. As, however, he possesses immense authority, his lightest *obiter dicta*, which coming from any other writer would be scattered like dry leaves, bore their way into Roumanian politics like armour-piercing shells; and it is now an article of faith among many Roumanians that the Székely are lost sheep from the Roumanian fold.

to the fact that the Roumanians had Magyarized much less extensively. In any case Roumania, as we said, has aimed, at least nominally, solely at 'Re-Roumanizing', not at Roumanizing nominally non-Roumanian material.

Among the Germans and Jews are no Roumanized elements of any importance. Instead, therefore, of seeking to Roumanize them, Roumania has adopted the wiser and certainly more successful policy of encouraging their own national cultures; since the gains which they may record are solely at the expense of the Magyars. Her purely cultural policy towards these nationalities has been very liberal. The praise to be accorded to it must be qualified only by the fact that it is negative rather than positive, and the liberality is moral and not material. The nationalities, that is, are dissuaded from being Magyars and encouraged to be Germans or Jews; but they have had to pay for themselves, since the material resources of the State have been devoted in overwhelming proportion to developing Roumanian education; this being done on the plea that the Roumanian nation was in the past the poorest and the most neglected and has the farthest lee-way to make up.

This brings us to the second aspect of the national problem in Transylvania, which is, in some ways, even more important than the first: the social and economic aspect. We have seen how, thanks to its very peculiar past history, the social stratification of Transylvania coincided closely with its national divisions. In a sentence, the Roumanians formed the national proletariat, and now that they have the power of the State behind them, they are bent on creating for themselves a national middle and upper class—an ambition which can be achieved only, or most easily, at the expense of the Magyar, German, and Jewish national aristocracy and bourgeoisie. The history of Transylvania since 1918 has consisted very largely of the efforts to carry through what amounts to a complete social revolution on national lines; and the struggle has been a very bitter one. It has, indeed, been conducted in more or less legal forms, since the proletariat has been in a position to lay down the law (whether the laws have been either equitable or compatible with Roumania's international obligations is another question), but it has often been very intense—not less so, we may be sure, because of its dual character. The acres of the Magyar Council or the Saxon Chapter, the director's fees of the Jewish banker, the magistrate's or panel doctor's or railway porter's job are prizes desirable enough, in any case, to eyes grown sore and belts grown slack with long waiting; how much more desirable when the acquisition of them can be hallowed by the name of national policy!

Under this assault the minorities have suffered simply in proportion to what they had to contribute. Political considerations
have, indeed, intervened to some small extent; thus where there
has been a question of sparing Germans or Magyars, the Germans
have usually received the benefit of the doubt. Essentially,
however, the aim has been to take what the minorities had to give,
and none which stood between the Roumanians and their desired
goal has been spared. The most vigorous assault of all has,
indeed, been made not against the Magyars but against the Jews—
in consequence of the influence of the Regat Roumanians, who
cherish no particular animosity against the Magyars, but have
for decades been at loggerheads with their own Jewish population.

In her treatment of the national problem, and, indeed, in her
whole policy, and above all, in the execution of it, Roumania has
proved herself much less 'western' in her methods than Czechoslovakia. The influence of the Regat has been dismally apparent.
Not, indeed, that the Regatlers have been, on the whole, more
hostile to the minorities (except the Jews) than have the Transylvanian Roumanians. As we said, the idea of assimilation is
perhaps less natural to them. But the Regat has, unhappily,
preserved other traditions of its Turkish and Phanariot past
besides that of national indifference. While in Czechoslovakia or
in Austria, even where individual measures are oppressive, the
whole picture is always lightened by a general atmosphere of
western methods, so in Roumania everything is darkened by the
shadow of Levantinism—as when a photograph, which may be
good in itself, is taken on a bad negative, dirtily developed, and
smudgily printed. The heaviest burden on all the nationalities
of Transylvania (the Roumanians themselves not excepted) is not
imposed by the laws themselves. Like all Latin and Latinized
races, Roumanians excel in enacting the most idealistic general
measures, which they can roll on their tongues when quoting
them in Geneva as a true picture of the general situation. Their
laws are usually better than the Czech, infinitely better than the
British. But while the Briton does not usually enact a law unless
he means to keep it in the letter and the spirit, and the Czech
unless, while evading its spirit, he can yet prove that he has kept
its letter, to the Roumanian the law and its execution stand in no
discernible relationship. 'The Roumanians', said a Saxon to me
mournfully, 'have no legal sense (*Rechtsgefühl*) whatever,' adding,
since he was a just man, that the Magyars had too much. But he
was right. There reigns among the Roumanian officials and
politicians (who are all too intimately connected) a contempt for
their own laws which is positively startling. From the Prefect to
the Gendarme, the official does in practice exactly what he likes.

It is an everyday occurrence for some local despot to inflict upon
his subjects some perfectly arbitrary decree or prohibition which
is in flat contradiction to the express law of his country. And his
victims are at his mercy. Redress can occasionally be obtained
from the Courts, but these are so overburdened that it may take
years before the order comes for some quite illegal measure to
be cancelled; and years more, or eternity, before the order can
be reversed. In such cases there is no practical way out but
bribery.

To be fair, this very lawlessness has its silver lining. If the
good laws are often not enforced, neither are the bad ones, for
while the general measures are nearly all good, the enacting
legislation is sometimes almost comically unjust. In particular,
bribery can secure a very great deal. 'The corruption of the
Roumanians', said an old Jew to me, cynically, 'is our Geneva.'
Moreover, the average Roumanian is an easy-going fellow. He is
not brutal by nature; he does not even require very heavy bribing.
It is astonishing what a long way a few lei will go. Even unbribed,
he will often waive the strict application of some burdensome
regulation, especially if it would cause him trouble to enforce. He
lacks altogether the iron tenacity and national purposefulness of
the Czech, or the brutal forcefulness of the Serb. Give him enough
to live on, let a dash of eye-wash be added, and no actual trouble,
and he is content for people to go their own way. One is often
struck in Transylvania by the cynical and good-natured way in
which local Roumanians refer, for example, to rabid Magyar
nationalists in their midst. It is largely slackness, but the fact
remains that in some respects, at least during the first years after
the War, life was more tolerable for the minorities in Transylvania
than in the far better conducted Slovakia.

It is interesting and symptomatic that the younger generation
of Roumanian nationalists are in open revolt against this very
tolerance. 'The minorities', they are fond of saying, 'are much too
well off with us. They snap their fingers at their laws, and do in
practice exactly what they please.' The growing desire for national
regeneration in Roumania, for more legality and less corruption,
thus works in, most unhappily, with the increasing anti-minority
feeling and brings much evil out of what is in itself largely an
idealistic movement.

The growth of this anti-minority movement, particularly of
anti-Semitism, has been very marked in recent years. Things
have become in every way worse since about 1931 or 1932. One
may argue about the reason and indeed I have heard many
different causes adduced. Many say that during the first years
after the War, Roumania never really believed that she could keep

Transylvania, and was reluctant either to provoke later reprisals or to create a situation the inevitable reversal of which would leave its beneficiaries in a worse position than before. Others lay the blame on the Rothermere campaign. My own belief, which is shared by many, is that the change is due to the appearance on the scene of the young Roumanian 'intellectual' class, which hardly existed before the War, and is now being turned out by the thousand from the High schools. The peasant has his own economic situation, which is humble but comparatively secure, and he is little interested in national politics. Even to-day the Transylvanian peasant is quite tolerant towards other nationalities, including the Jews. Not so the young students, nurtured on an intellectual pap which consists very largely of national self-gratification, and then thrown on the world without an assured future, never taught the harder lesson that places in the sun can be created by honest work, and always the easier one, that they are the original and rightful owners of Transylvania, whose fruits would fall into their laps if they were not filched by a gang of Jacobs. The influence of this new element is growing stronger, almost month by month. Many concessions have been made to it; others will certainly follow. Thus, unfortunately, any sketch of the minority situation, even if true when written, will probably prove too rosy by the time it is read.[1]

[1] Startling examples of the lengths to which this agitation now goes are to be found in certain articles which appeared in the Roumanian press in the autumn of 1936, threatening the Magyar minority with a 'Saint Bartholomew's night' if the campaign for revision continued. One article, passed and stamped by the censor, ran as follows (translation from the *Danubian Review*, December 1936):

'While the Hungarian revisionist jackals contented themselves with howling at the moon, the Rumanians were content to spit in contempt. But to-day this concert of mangy curs has been joined by one whom, until now, we had considered as our brother.

'While the jackals howl, Mussolini increases their appetite by playing the barrel-organ. Mussolini has become a revisionist; but only an opportunist revisionist. Otherwise he would have started his revision at home. Budapest will strike on the face of Mussolini that match which is to set Europe on fire and Mussolini may then kiss with his full force the prominent posterior which Hungary will then turn towards him.

'The howling jackals of the plains who turn their muzzles towards us may know that we shall nevermore be their serfs, that we shall nevermore populate their prisons. The worms may draw marrow from their bones and the spirits may make soap from the rotten fat of these fools of the plains.

'God help the Hungarians on that day when the Rumanians consent to revision; because they will kick up the frontiers with the points of their boots and will wipe from the face of the earth that dirt which a fly blew unto the map of Europe and which vitiates the air.

'We shall sit down in the Royal Palace of Budapest and stay there.

'The mangy curs of the plain may know the Rumanians are not intimidated by Mussolini's barrel-organ or by anything else. The Hungarians will get their land, not for the purpose of ruling over it but to be buried in it.

'Let the Hungarian packs of the plains know that the Transylvanian Rumanians will delay the crossing of the Tisza by one night, by a St. Bartholomew night, in which they will extirpate every single Hungarian.'

In this book I have as a rule refrained from pillorying the extreme brutalities and vulgarities of any national press. I make an exception here, reluctantly, partly because the articles aroused such a sensation, partly also because they are, unfortunately, typical of the language in which many young pseudo-educated Roumanians are beginning to indulge.

§ 9. THE MINORITIES: POLITICAL AND ADMINISTRATIVE CONDITIONS

No Roumanian Government has considered giving any minority an effective share of political power. During the first few months the Transylvanian Roumanian 'Directing Council', backed by the Regat troops, exercised a national dictatorship, leaving the Saxons, within limits, to manage their own affairs, but keeping a tight hold over the Magyars. The Parliamentary system was then introduced, but with a single Parliament in Bucharest, in which the Roumanian parties have always formed an overwhelming majority. The unitary and national character of the State is emphasized by the Constitution, which also states specifically that minorities, as such, are not recognized as forming corporate bodies. They are, however, permitted to form associations, and Roumania, like Czechoslovakia but unlike Yugoslavia since 1929, has allowed the minorities to form political parties on a national basis. All the chief minorities have done so. The Germans led the way, simply carrying on with their old organization from Hungarian days. The Magyars, with few exceptions, refused to recognize the existence of enlarged Roumania until after Hungary had ratified the Treaty of Trianon. They then formed two parties which in 1922 fused into a single body, the 'Magyar National Party'. The Jews followed suit some years later; even the Serbs founded a tiny party in 1932.

The Magyars suffered considerable obstruction, intimidation, and even violence in the early years. At the first elections, for example, 30 of the 33 candidates which they put up were disqualified and only one elected. Their claim to represent the Moldavian Csángós has also been consistently rejected. Apart from this, the minority parties have enjoyed a reasonable degree of freedom, measured by local standards, in drawing up their programmes, establishing their organization, and conducting their propaganda.[1] The surveillance exercised over them by the political police has probably been no stricter than that from which the Roumanian opposition parties have suffered (and far less effective, owing to the inability of the honest Roumanian gendarmes to understand what the Magyars are talking about). In elections, they have usually held their own and returned to both Chambers in Bucharest a certain number of representatives, partly because the Germans always, the other parties occasionally, have formed cartels with the Roumanian parties before the

---

[1] The dissolution of the German National Socialist Party in 1934 was certainly not disagreeable to the other Germans, and the party was allowed to reconstitute itself soon after, with very mild modifications of its published aims. Certain elections, notably in 1931, have also been cynically unfair, but not to the minorities parties alone.

elections. These arrangements, however, have related to elections only, and no minority party has ever been represented in the Government.[1] It is worth noting that the minorities only once (in 1927) formed a cartel between themselves. The constituencies are not 'weighted' against the minorities, although the system (lists by Departments) is unfavourable to the scattered Germans and Jews. It is favourable enough to the Magyars, with their solid blocs of population.

The meagre representation which the centralized Parliamentary system allows them is naturally regretted by the minorities, and all of them wish for decentralization, which would give them proportionately a much larger voice in affairs. What weighs on them more heavily still is the curtailment of their rights and powers in local government. Under the Roumanian system the old autonomy of the County (Departmental) and Municipal Councils has, in any case, been very largely reduced, since the real power in the Departments rests in the hands of the Prefects, who are appointed by the Government and are, without exception, Roumanians. The burgomasters of the larger towns with 'municipal rights' are also Government nominees, while the Prefects appoint the notaries who, in practice, are the autocrats of the villages. I have been in villages where the entire population belonged solidly to one single minority, except the notary, his clerk, and the gendarme. In others, these three lonely Roumanian officials are reinforced by the Roumanian teacher of a State school (whose pupils all belong to minorities) and the Orthodox priest of a church without a congregation.

The elected Councils are also reinforced by nominated members who, again, are nearly always Roumanian. In Sighisoara, for example, the municipal elections of 1934 gave 14 elected members to the Saxons and 14 to the combined Roumanian-Magyar list. There were 9 nominated members; 8 of these were Roumanians, and 1 a Saxon. On top of this, Transylvania has passed much of its time since the War under a species of martial law, during which the elected Councils have been suspended and local affairs have been conducted by so-called 'Interim Commissions', nominated by the Government, which has always ensured a Roumanian majority.[2] In the Magyar-Jewish city of Arad, for example, the Council in 1934 was composed of 8 Roumanians, 2 Magyars, and 1 Zionist Jew, the Burgomaster being a Roumanian. Târgu Mureş (Máros Vasárhély), which is 75 per cent. Magyar, had only

---

[1] The only Cabinet post ever held by a member of a minority has been that of Under-Secretary of State for Minority Questions.

[2] Under the latest (1936) administrative reform, the term of office of the Interim Commissions is to be limited to four months.

2 Magyars against 6 Roumanians; in the Department of Tréi Scaune (Haromszék) (87·6 per cent. Magyar) 5 Roumanians and no Magyars were appointed, &c.

The Saxons were for some years more indulgently treated, but they, too, have been gradually driven out of the municipal government of their ancient cities. One Saxon burgomaster after another has been replaced by a Roumanian. In 1933 there were still three left; in 1934 the last survivor (the burgomaster of Bistriţa) disappeared. The loss was very bitterly felt, for the Saxons have always taken a keen interest in their local self-government, and Hungary had respected their rights. To be without a single burgomaster of their own nationality was an experience which the Saxons had not undergone during their 800-year history, and many of their cities, such as Sibiu (Hermannstadt, Nagy-Szeben) had been ruled by Saxons uninterruptedly since their foundation. And the grievance is not only sentimental, for the Roumanian régime is not only one-sided in its national policy, but in many cases quite patently less efficient and less honest than that which it has replaced. Thus the abolition of the system of Interim Commissions and the restoration of a wider measure of departmental, municipal, and communal self-government are among the demands most commonly voiced by the minorities, and with the greatest justification.

The national question in the administration has become very acute in recent years, and is at the time of writing one of the foremost problems. The higher political grades of the administration were Roumanized quickly and thoroughly, the old county and communal bodies being dissolved, and the old Hungarian Föispáns removed, as early as January 14th, 1919. I know of no higher political officer of non-Roumanian stock holding office in Roumania to-day, although one or two may possibly be tucked away in some remote corner of the Dobrudja or Bessarabia. With the subordinate officials, State and local, Roumania behaved at first more generously than either Yugoslavia or Czechoslovakia. Like both those countries, she exacted from them an oath of fidelity to the new régime before it had any legal existence, and expelled many of those who refused to take it, as also those who put up any sort of resistance (there was a certain amount of sabotage, although no such widespread movement as the Slovak postal and railway strike). There were also, undoubtedly, excesses and acts of individual injustice. Generally speaking, however, those officials who wished to remain and who took the oath were allowed to remain in the State service. Some were transferred to the Regat, but most simply carried on in their old posts. Incidentally, Roumania behaved comparatively generously over the vexed question of pensions to the retired ex-Hungarian officials who had refused to take the oath of allegiance. After dragging on for several years the question was regulated in 1928 by M. Maniu, who accepted the argument that the oath had been required before this was legally justified, and even allowed pensions to officials who took the oath some years later.

The reason for this comparative leniency need not perhaps concern us. The Roumanians ascribe it to their own sense of justice; the minorities suggested that they never expected the annexation to be permanent and were afraid of provoking retaliation. But the most reasonable explanation seems to be that there were simply no alternative candidates for the jobs; for the Roumanian, unlike the Czech, is no born *rond-de-cuir*, and the Regat had no stock of ex-Austrian officials flocking back from Vienna and looking for re-employment. Thus, until the educational system had been Roumanized and reorganized, and the first generation of students passed through it, there was no alternative but to carry on with the old personnel.

In any case, for ten or twelve years (about the time required to train up the new generation) the position did not change in any important respect. As minority officials died, retired, or were 'hinausgeekelt' (this expressive German word has no exact English equivalent)[1] their places were quietly filled by Roumanians, but the survivors were left in peace. About 1932, however, a systematic drive against them set in, in consequence of which large numbers of them were dismissed with more or less of formality and their places filled by Roumanians. The pretext given was political. It was alleged that the Magyar officials, in particular, were behaving as though the annexation had never taken place, openly deriding the Roumanian State as a flimsy contraption bound to fall to pieces sooner or later—and the sooner the better; treating the Roumanians in the old style as an inferior race and bidding them, with oaths, to speak Magyar; and themselves refusing to take the trouble to learn Roumanian.

The minority officials had already (in 1929) been examined in the Roumanian language, but consequent on this agitation, an order was issued in 1934 to re-examine all non-Roumanian officials, the order applying not only to officials in the strict sense, but to technical and auxiliary personnel. After each examination, which, for the higher officials at least, includes questions on Roumanian history, geography, and institutions, a proportion of unfortunates is ploughed and dismissed the service.

This question has caused intense feeling on both sides. The Roumanians argue that the question is a political one: that the

---

[1] Literally 'disgusted out'.

State has a right and a duty to require of a person claiming to receive from it a salary and a pension that he shall, in the course of 12 or 14 years, have mastered the elements of the official language; particularly as that language is an easy one, which every waiter, hotel porter, prostitute, or other person whose work brings him or her into professional contact with different nationalities, speaks fluently as a matter of course. The examination, they say, is not at all searching, every consideration being shown to elderly or uneducated persons. Persons who do not pass the examination, they say, are either so stupid or so hostile to the Roumanian State as to be no fit servants of it.

The minorities reply that the question is not political at all, but economic. The examinees of to-day have been doing their duty faithfully enough for many years, and are being thrown out now simply because a horde of hungry ex-students of the Universities want their jobs. The examination, they say, is a mere pretext and a farce, any person being foredoomed to failure whose job a Roumanian happens to want.

It is difficult to judge between the two theses, for each side can substantiate its argument with some irrefutable examples. There have certainly been some cases (although not, I think, many) in which minority officials have behaved with singular disregard of the altered map of Europe, and some where the examination has been lenient enough. Nor can the justice of Roumania's general argument be denied. On the other hand, there have also been many cases of great individual hardship and injustice. Men who have done their duty for years, without giving cause for complaint, and have perhaps already passed an examination, have been called up again and deprived of their work. In other cases, searching tests have been applied in cases where no more than an elementary knowledge of Roumanian seems necessary, e.g. for employees in railway workshops.

Since the process of elimination of minority officials is now in full swing, there seems little point in giving statistics of the relative proportion of Roumanian and minority officials, particularly as these are extremely hard to obtain, and any figures given by either side are immediately queried by the other. A recent writer from the Roumanian side gave some 1934 figures which seemed to show that at that time the proportion of minority officials was still above their percentage of the population: thus, in the postal and telegraphic services in 14 towns, the percentage of Roumanians was never higher than 44, and in 5 towns 25 or under. In the three chief Székely Counties, 470 Magyars were still employed in the administrative services, against 98 Roumanians, &c.[1] These figures

[1] A. Gociman, 'Les Fonctionnaires hongrois de l'état roumain', in *Revue de Transylvanie*, vol. i, no. 3, Nov.–Dec. 1934, pp. 375–81.

are, however, attacked by the minorities as misleading if not inaccurate.[1] I myself have heard innumerable generalities from both sides, but have only very occasionally obtained figures which I could regard as accurate. I obtained, however, the religious statistics for the city of Arad, which show a much less favourable picture than the above figures. In the city administration, 273 officials were Roumanian Orthodox and 10 Uniates (283 Roumanians), 11 Serbian Orthodox, 70 Catholics, 9 Protestants, and 2 Baptists (81 Magyars and Germans), and 2 Jews. In the upper judicature the senior judges were all Roumanians; of the junior magistrates, about two-thirds Roumanians; of the lower staff, all Roumanians. The only service with at all a high proportion of minority officials was the financial administration, where all the senior officials after the two heads, and about half the clerks, were Magyars or Germans. In another office I saw a framed photograph of the cadets who had passed through the gendarmerie college in a certain year (I think 1927). Four of these bore German names, 2 Bulgarian, 1 a Magyar, the remaining 40 odd were all Roumanian. This was in the summer of 1934, when the new examinations were just beginning. In January 1936 the German leader, Dr. Roth, stated that over 580 German officials had lost their jobs through the examinations. The losses of the Magyars must have been far greater.

In any case, there seems to be no question that it is next door to impossible for a member of a minority to enter the Roumanian public services to-day. Here and there there may be an exception: a skilled workman might get some technical post for which no Roumanian could be found—a Bulgarian might get into the gendarmerie, a Saxon might be given a small post in a purely Saxon district. Family influence might even place a Magyar in some corner where the Roumanian nationalist press did not notice him. But broadly speaking, the younger generation of the minorities must renounce all hope of a State career.

The Roumanians usually contend that the present exclusive preference given to Roumanians will go on only until the balance is reduced and the Roumanians represented in the public services in proportion to their numbers. It seems more likely that the end will be the establishment of an administrative service exclusively Roumanian, with only a few very rare exceptions.

Roumania has no comprehensive legislation regulating the use of the different local languages in local government and administration. The Constitution lays down simply that Roumanian is the official language of the State, but provides that the existing law in the different provinces, where it does not directly conflict with the

[1] *Nation und Staat*, April 1935, pp. 464-5.

Constitution, should remain in force until harmonized therewith. Occasional attempts have since been made to draft more detailed laws, but with small effect. In 1928 M. Maniu, when he took office, sent M. Popp, one of his followers, abroad to study minority questions with a view, it was understood, to drawing up an up-to-date comprehensive law. If, however, M. Popp's foreign studies bore any fruit, it rotted ungathered. Again, in 1931, when Professor Jorga created the post of Under-Secretary for Minorities and appointed Dr. Brandsch, the Saxon leader, to it, a general Minorities Statute was expected, but again the expectations were disappointed. Dr. Brandsch passed from office spiritually intestate, and under his successors the post seems to have lost much of its significance. Its present occupant is a Roumanian.[1] Meanwhile, the position remained vague. Characteristically, the Roumanians attached more importance to putting a lick of paint on the outside of the building than to making laborious alterations in its structure. Thus all the names of towns and villages were Roumanized and all street names laboriously adapted to the Roumanian Valhalla, medieval or modern—a measure, it may be remarked, which has entirely failed to alter the habits of the local population. If you ask the way in a Magyar town, you are invariably told to cross the Kossuth Tér, go down the Vörösmarty utca and turn left into the Szabadság Ut, and it is left to your native genius (if any) to divine these time-honoured names under their present guises of the Piața Uniriei, the Strada Carmen Sylva, and the Calea lui Vîntila Bratianŭ. Letters are, however, only delivered (if at all) to Roumanian addresses. Government notices and communications are almost always issued in Roumanian only, even in solidly minority districts, and the population, in its written communications with the authorities, has to use Roumanian, paying, if necessary, for translations. The oral use of minority languages in local administration and self-government depended, however, largely on the whim or the linguistic acquirements of the local officials, and oscillated madly from one extreme to another. During the short-lived period of decentralization in 1930, the Governor of Transylvania forbade the use of any minority language in Departmental or Communal Councils, and in 1931 the Director of State Railways forbade his employees to answer travellers in minority languages, even if they understood them. All railway stations and post offices are plastered with notices enjoining the public to

[1] Dr. Brandsch's failure seems to have been due partly to dissensions among the minorities themselves. Dr. Brandsch favoured the principle—which would naturally, perhaps, appeal to a scholar and to a member of that particular minority which has always done best for itself—that each minority should be treated differently, according to its special circumstances. The Magyars, in just the opposite position, wanted one law to apply to all.

'speak only Roumanian'. On the other hand, the minorities officials, of course, gladly spoke to the public in their own language, and some knew no other. In one town which I visited, although the official notices were all in Roumanian, the town crier went about the streets chanting German and Magyar translations. During the first years, at least, it was usual for members of minorities to be able to use their own languages in all Councils, Departmental, Municipal, &c., Roumanian being the exclusive language of Parliament.

Only as we write, preparations are being made to regulate the use of minority languages in local government. The first draft of the Bill provided that in all Departmental, town, and communal Councils, Roumanian should be used exclusively in discussion and the keeping of records; that only persons able to speak, read, and write Roumanian should be eligible for election to such Councils; and that if any person used a language other than Roumanian, the body in question should be immediately dissolved. In response to protests from the German minority leaders, some of these Draconian provisions were modified. Minority languages may be used in the rural communes, and persons able to read and write their own mother tongue are eligible for election. Even so, the provisions are ungenerous, the Czech legislation being far superior. No steps have yet been taken to give any minority language an official status in administration; this is clearly a considerable hardship. It must not, indeed, be assumed that no Magyar or German will ever be able to speak his mother tongue to an official, but the practice is certainly growing more strict and serious grievances may easily develop. The facilities provided in the Courts of Law are also inadequate. A defendant has no legal right that any part of the proceedings shall be conducted in his mother tongue. I was informed that interpreters were usually provided, but this question seems one of those where legislation, on liberal lines, is most to be desired.

The use of minority languages in unofficial intercourse has never been restricted, with the sole exception that the Roumanian names of towns must be used in newspapers, &c., the local name being added, if desired, in brackets. Recently, too, a surtax of 12 per cent. on the tax on trade and industry has been imposed on firms keeping their books in any other language than Roumanian, the pretext being that the books are to some extent official documents, since they are subject to the control of the Inland Revenue Authorities. In general, however, Roumania is right when she claims that she does not interfere, directly or indirectly, with the use by the minorities of their own language among themselves, i.e. outside official intercourse, and outside the schools which, as will be seen, are not always what they should be.

§ 10. THE MINORITIES: GENERAL CULTURAL AND ECCLESIASTICAL QUESTIONS

The general principles guiding Roumanian cultural policy have already been discussed. It remains to consider their application, and in doing so one must emphasize once again the overwhelming importance of the Churches in the national-cultural life of Roumania. The separate existence of each local nationality is very largely bound up with that of its particular Church or Churches, and even identified therewith. 'Lutheran' and 'Saxon' are, for example, almost interchangeable terms. Such exceptions as still existed in 1918 were of the sort which proved the rule, for the Serbians—the one important national minority which had no Church of their own—were fast losing their nationality for that very reason. Moreover, the Church is not merely the symbol of each nation's existence, but also its most important cultural institution. Up to the middle of the nineteenth century, all education had been exclusively denominational. After that date the State began to intervene, in increasing measure as time went on. The State institutions were always purely Magyar; and thus the situation arose that, while such education as the minorities still retained was solely denominational, Magyar education was about equally divided between State and denominational establishments.[1] The latter were, for the most part, those situated in Magyar districts, rural or urban; the former existed as much, or more, for the benefit of the non-Magyars as of the Magyars. They comprised the higher establishments which served the needs of the country at large, and the primary or burger schools established in non-Magyar districts for purposes of Magyarization. They included, however, also a number of Magyar schools, formerly denominational, which the State had taken over under various complicated arrangements. A high proportion of the social and charitable activities of each nationality is also traditionally conducted by its national Church, the freedom and security of which is thus vital to the nationality in question. On the other hand, the vast political power which lies in the hands of the ecclesiastical leaders must cause the State concern, if it is not sure whether that power will be loyally used.

The Roumanian legislation on the Churches represents a compromise, which each party thinks unduly favourable to the other side, between the claims of the Churches and the State. Roughly

---

[1] Of the total Magyar establishments in 1918, 1,497 out of 2,588 primary schools, 66 of the 109 burger schools, 25 of the 52 lycées and gymnasia, 12 of the 22 commercial colleges, 10 of the 24 training colleges, and all the High schools belonged to the State.

speaking, the position obtaining up to 1918 is reversed. Under the Roumanian Constitution, the Orthodox Church becomes 'the predominant Church in the Roumanian State', while the Uniate Church, as the second Roumanian Church, 'takes precedence over the other Churches'. The special privileges of the Orthodox Church are not very numerous, except that the Royal Family must belong to it. The two Roumanian Churches, however, enjoy an important political advantage over all others in that all their bishops sit, *ex officio*, in the Senate, while only the heads of the other denominations enjoy that privilege, and then only if their congregations number at least 200,000 adherents.

The Constitution guarantees liberty of conscience, and equal freedom and protection for all cults consistent with public order and morals. The position of the minority Churches is regulated in detail by the Law on Cults of 1928, which repeats these guarantees, but also lays down a number of restrictions limiting, not liberty of conscience, but the freedom of action of the Churches. Religious belief cannot exempt any person from the obligations imposed upon him by the law. Political organizations may not be formed on confessional bases, nor may political questions be discussed within ecclesiastical corporations or institutions. A Church may not be subordinated to any authority or ecclesiastical organization outside Roumania, except in so far as its dogmatic or canonical principles require. Churches and religious associations are forbidden to receive any subsidies from abroad, directly or indirectly, without informing the State. Members of the clergy and ecclesiastical authorities must be Roumanian citizens and must not have received any sentence involving the loss of civil rights. The heads of the Churches must be approved by the Crown and take an oath of loyalty to the Crown and obedience to the Constitution and the law. All instructions and orders from ecclesiastical authorities to their subordinates must be communicated to the Ministry of Cults, which can veto them if they are contrary to public order, morality, or the law, or endanger the security of the State.

The Statutes of each Church, again, must be submitted to Parliament, to see that they contain nothing contrary to the Law on Cults. The State retains a control over the expenditure of the subsidies granted by it, and the education given by the Churches in their schools must fulfil certain requirements, notably, the curriculum must include instruction in the Roumanian language, literature, history, and constitution. The limits of dioceses may not be altered, nor new ones created, without legal authority.

Within these limits the Churches enjoy considerable freedom. A Church as such has no legal personality, but its constituent bodies (metropolitan and episcopal Sees, Chapters, Orders, Communities, &c.) have such personality. The Churches administer their internal affairs and their property of all kinds in accordance with their own Statutes. They have the right to found and maintain schools, charitable institutions, &c., subject to their compliance with the general requirements of the Law. They can collect from their congregations the sums necessary for their expenses. It is the members of each Church who are responsible in the first instance for its maintenance, the State furnishing only certain subsidies.

The Law adopts the old Hungarian idea of 'received religions', and enumerates the following cults as 'received' or 'historic', besides the Greek Orthodox:

The Greek Catholic (Roumanian Uniate).
Catholic (of Latin, Greek, Ruthene, and Armenian rites).
Reformed (Calvinist).
Evangelical (Lutheran).
Unitarian.
Armeno-Gregorian.
Mosaic (various rites).
Mohammedan.

Other cults can only become 'received' after fulfilling certain conditions. The Baptists have now become 'received'.

The position of a minority 'cult' is thus not wholly unfavourable, although it suffers by comparison with the autonomy enjoyed by the various Churches in Hungary before the War.

The various minority Churches have gradually succeeded in drawing up their Statutes and agreeing them with the Government. The Lutheran Church (i.e. the Saxons) remodelled their previous Statute without much difficulty. The Church now includes the German Lutheran communities from the other parts of Roumania. The tiny number of Magyar Lutherans have organized themselves separately. The Calvinists, Unitarians, Serbian Orthodox, Baptists, and Armenians have all established their own organizations, while the Jews have three bodies: Orthodox, Neologs, and Sephardim. The chief difficulties arose, naturally, with the Catholic Church, the hierarchy of which was purely Magyar, or Magyarized, in 1918, and which from the first adopted an extremely militant attitude towards Roumania. The position of this Church was very peculiar, for the Catholic Church in Hungary, unlike any other important Church in the country, was not autonomous, its position in the State being too commanding, its relations with the State and the Apostolic Crown too close, to make autonomy either practicable or, in the eyes of many of its adherents, desirable. In Transylvania, however, there existed a special body, partly clerical, partly lay, the 'Status Catholicus', which enjoyed a sort of *de facto* autonomy and administered the local Church property. Neither the Hungarian Government nor the Vatican was ever willing to grant it full autonomy. The Status has not had a smooth passage since the War, having been involved in conflicts both with the Roumanian Government and with the Holy See. By an agreement of 1932 between the Government and the Vatican supplementing and interpreting the Concordat, it has now been recognized as 'Council of the Catholic Diocese of the Latin Rite of Alba Julia', and has been allowed to administer all the property formerly belonging to the Status.[1] The Roman Catholics of Transylvania are further protected by the Concordat concluded in 1927 and ratified after the adoption of the Law of Cults in 1929. The Concordat, incidentally, regulated in a manner favourable to the Catholics a question which had been hotly disputed: the indemnity for the large estates of which the Hungarian Government had assigned the usufruct to the Catholic Church, while retaining the ownership. These lands have been expropriated, but the Government consented to pay the indemnity to the Church, and the fund thus constituted is now administered, under the name of 'patrimonium sanctum', by the Council of diocesan bishops. The Government has also ceded to the Church its rights of property in the buildings, &c., owned by the Hungarian Crown in its capacity of Patron. In both these cases the Roumanian State renounced important funds to which it could probably have made good its legal claim.

Although the minority spokesmen opposed the Law on Cults as a 'retrograde step', on account of the control which it allowed the State over the Churches, the application of it seems to have given rise to few well-grounded complaints. Were it possible to separate genuinely religious questions from national, and national from political,[2] it would probably be found that the minorities had to-day few genuine and purely religious grievances. The Roumanian is naturally indifferent in religious matters, and the Orthodox Church, as such, is not a proselytizing body. Unhappily, since every Church regards itself, and is regarded, as a national institution, political quarrels over apparently religious questions have been frequent, and the minority Churches and their representatives have had to undergo assaults which are in reality part of the national struggle,

---

[1] Cf. 'Der katholische "Status" von Siebenbürgen und seine Kämpfe', by Senator N. E. von Gyárfás, in *Nation und Staat*, May 1935, pp. 513 ff.

[2] As an example of the difficulty of drawing the dividing line may be quoted the cases of SS. Stephen and Ladislaus, duly canonized Catholic Saints of special local repute, and at the same time great figures in Hungarian national history and obnoxious to Roumania owing to their military operations in Transylvania.

but which have made their position less favourable than that of any other religious minority with which this work deals. In the early years there were numerous cases[1] in which Catholic, Calvinist, and Unitarian pastors were maltreated and their congregations hindered in the exercise of their devotions. Some of these outrages were assuredly not unprovoked, since the Catholic clergy, in particular, was openly hostile to the Roumanian State and refused to take the oath of allegiance to it until 1931. After this had been regulated, 'the systematic personal persecutions ceased'.[2] Membership of a Roumanian Church is, however, a strong advantage to any one desiring governmental favour, and there have been a considerable number of cases in which the Orthodox or Uniate religion has been forced on members of minorities. The mission sent to Roumania in 1927 by the American Committee on the Rights of Religious Minorities reported a number of such cases, particularly in connexion with orphanages,[3] and in recent years there have been a good many cases of conversion under duress among persons of supposedly Roumanian ancestry. The chief sufferers have been the Székely, and the Church chiefly affected has been the Unitarian (which has lost some hundreds of 'converts'); the Calvinist Church comes next, the Catholic Church being little affected, the Lutheran not at all. The victims are usually Government employees, who are blackmailed into apostasy by the threat of losing their posts.

In certain cases, also, official pressure has been used (contrary to the law) to ensure that the children of mixed marriages shall be brought up only in the Greek Orthodox faith.

Another edict against which the minorities have protested is one passed in September 1936, that no lay person shall give religious instruction. It is claimed that this law, although in appearance equal for all religions, in effect bears much more heavily on the non-Roumanian Churches. Reference is made elsewhere to the compulsory training of juveniles on Sundays which hampers their religious instruction.

Perhaps more serious, at any rate more systematic, have been the encroachments on the material position of the minority Churches, which have suffered enormous losses. The agrarian reform deprived the Lutheran Church alone of 35,000 yokes, the Hungarian Protestant Churches of 36,000, the Roman Catholic Church of 277,000 yokes, not counting the estates of parish priests

---

[1] Cf. de Szász, *The Minorities in Roumanian Transylvania* (London, 1927), chs. xi and xii.

[2] Ibid., p. 209. There was, however, a strong recrudescence of agitation after the conclusion of the Concordat.

[3] *Roumania Ten Years After*, issued by the American Committee on the Rights of Religious Minorities (Boston, 1928), pp. 96–7

and the school endowments.[1] In each case the losses amounted to by far the greater part of the wealth of the Church in question. According to the law, 32 yokes should have been left to each parish, but of the 240 Saxon parishes only 42 received their full quota.[2] One hundred and nineteen Catholic parishes were left without any land at all.[3]

The Orthodox Church which, by contrast with the vast endowments of the minority Churches, had only owned 1,012 yokes of real property in Transylvania before the War,[4] naturally escaped almost scot-free under the agrarian reform. Even though the endowments of the minority Churches had come, not from the Hungarian State, but from the piety and self-sacrifice of their own members throughout past generations, a certain equalization of this vast difference in the material position of the different Churches was inevitable and perhaps desirable, and even to-day the minority Churches are still richer than the Roumanian. On the other hand, both in the application of the land reform and in other ways, the Roumanian Churches, particularly the Orthodox, have been forced upon the people in a way which has caused much dissatisfaction. There have been several cases in which the parish endowment of a minority Church has been given, in whole or in part, to a Roumanian community with a smaller number of adherents than its previous owners. The commonest and most conspicuous grievance has been in connexion with the building of Orthodox churches. In towns and villages in which the overwhelming majority of the population belongs to minorities, building-sites have been allotted to the Orthodox Church from requisitioned land, or in public parks, &c., and churches erected on them. Thus a huge Orthodox Cathedral has been built at Cluj, which had in 1910 only 1,359 Orthodox inhabitants (it is true that the number has greatly increased with the influx of officials from the Regat).

Târgu Mureș, again, where the Roumanian population numbered under 10 per cent. of the total in 1910, is now dominated by an enormous Orthodox church, which clashes hideously with the surrounding architecture. These are not isolated instances; I have myself passed dozens of new Orthodox churches, many of them in purely minority districts. The minority population has a double grievance in such cases, for, apart from the national-political-religious aspect of the question, the churches are usually erected

[1] Memorandum from the Hungarian Party to the Under-Secretary of State for Minorities, 1933. The figures for the Catholic and Calvinist Churches are estimated in the *Erdélyi Magyar évkönyv*, 1930, vol. i, p. 72; those for the Lutheran Church are given in various Saxon publications.

[2] *Die Nationalitäten in den Staaten Europas*, p. 416.

[3] *Roumania Ten Years After*, p. 100.

[4] V. Nistor, 'Les Cultes minoritaires et l'église orthodoxe roumaine', in *Revue de Transylvanie*, vol. ii, no. 1, Aug.–Sept. 1935, pp. 7–40.

either out of taxation, of which the minorities pay the lion's share, or else by 'private' subscription, which is collected under strong official pressure.

In 1935, then, the Government decided to introduce a new method of calculation and to take into account the 'private resources' of the clergy. As the minority Churches still possess larger endowments than the Roumanian, this meant that very large cuts were made in their subsidies. But the point which evoked the chief complaints was that among these 'private resources' was reckoned the special tax which each Church is entitled to levy on its adherents, and which the State, if required, collects for it. The minorities complained that this method of calculation penalized those Churches which imposed sacrifices on their own members for the benefit of those which allowed the State to do everything. The argument will probably go on for some years.

As regards the State subsidies to the various Churches, each side declares the other to be unduly favoured, but the budget figures seem to show that in fact, during the earlier years, the Orthodox Church received smaller subsidies per head of the population than either the Uniate or the minority Churches (except the Jewish, which has always been left almost entirely to its own resources).[1] The proportions have, however, steadily been changing in favour of the Roumanian Churches. Thus, taking Transylvania alone, the share going to the Orthodox Church rose between 1930 and 1933 from 30·1 per cent. to 38·8 per cent., that of the Uniate Church from 31·3 per cent. to 33·46 per cent., while that of the Magyar Churches sank from 33·9 per cent. to 24·5 per cent., chiefly owing to drastic cuts in the Calvinist grant.[2] This is the more painful to the Magyars because the subsidies granted by the Hungarian Government before the War to the various Churches were very fairly apportioned. Thus in the fiscal year, 1914/15, the 'Magyar Churches' of Transylvania, with a membership of 1,665,805 persons, received subsidies (excluding school subsidies) of 1,748,603 gold crowns (1·05 gold crowns per head), while the 'non-Magyar Churches', 3,446,327 strong, received 3,552,349 gold crowns (1·03 per head).[3]

As an interesting sidelight on Roumanian cultural policy, it may be mentioned that of the three Roman Catholic dioceses in the ex-Hungarian territories, only that of Alba Julia, whose See consists of historic Transylvania, still possesses a Magyar as bishop, and his coadjutor, appointed 'cum jure successionis', is a German. The

[1] Nistor, loc. cit. The Jews, incidentally, only received land under the reform in one commune.
[2] A. R. Szeben, 'Die Staatssubventionen', in *Glasul Minorității*, September 1933, p. 220.
[3] See *Magyar Kisebbség*, 1933, p. 315.

dioceses both of Timişoara and of Oradea-Satu Mare are in the hands of German bishops, and in the lower grades of their hierarchies, particularly in the Banat, the Magyar priests are being gradually replaced by Suabians. The little Armenian Catholic community has also been removed from the jurisdiction of the Bishop of Alba Julia and given its own spiritual chief.

§ 11. THE MINORITIES: EDUCATIONAL QUESTIONS

The educational system again represents a compromise, which each party considers to be too advantageous to the other. Roumania, whose own educational system in the Regat had been (and is) exclusively State-owned, took over for the State all the Roumanian confessional schools in Transylvania, and also, in her capacity of legal successor to the Hungarian State, all the establishments maintained by that body. The higher educational system was made as completely Roumanian as it had formerly been Magyar; for the elementary schools, the Directing Council at first adopted the principle of allowing the population concerned to choose the language of instruction for itself. Thus some of these schools became Roumanian, some were left Magyar, others were taken over by the Suabians or by smaller minorities. The non-Roumanian confessional schools were left, for the time, untouched.

The State elementary educational system was reorganized under the Primary Education Act of 1924. This provides that a State school shall be established wherever there are 60 children of age to attend classes 1–4, with a second room and teachers for 40 children of classes 5–7. The language of instruction is, in principle, the mother tongue of the children, and where the numbers of children of any one language are insufficient to justify the maintenance of a whole school, mixed schools may be set up with parallel classes for the different nationalities. There is, however, one very important qualification to the equality which the minorities enjoy under this law: under Article 8 of the Act, 'citizens of Roumanian origin who have lost their mother tongue may not send their children to any school, public or private, other than a school in which instruction is given exclusively in Roumanian'. A second qualification provides that special treatment is to be accorded to a so-called 'cultural zone', which comprises the Székely districts and some of the mixed Departments on the western frontier. In this zone, in which many new Roumanian schools have been created, the teachers are given additional pay and other inducements to encourage them in their uncomfortable task.

In State schools, the State contributes the teacher's salary, the commune being responsible for all other expenditure.

In non-Roumanian schools, the Roumanian language is taught as a subject for at least one hour a week during the first two school years, and at least two hours a week thereafter. Instruction in Roumanian history and geography is given in Roumanian.

The diplomas issued by training colleges existing in 1918 have been recognized and the colleges allowed to continue, but all teachers in State schools have to pass an examination in Roumanian, and those teaching Roumanian history, geography, and institutions must also qualify in those subjects.[1] The teachers' examinations have acquired a dismal notoriety comparable to that enjoyed by the examinations of officials, and, as in the latter case, a tragically large number of examinees has fallen by the wayside—sometimes, no doubt, by their own fault, but assuredly not always.

By what Roumania regards as a considerable concession, State education was not made compulsory. The status of the former Confessional schools was regulated in 1925 by a further Act which lays down that children may be educated, if their parents prefer, in 'private schools', or at home. 'Private schools' may be established either by individuals, who must be Roumanian citizens, or by juridical personalities, which must not be dependent on foreign organizations. The right of the Catholic Church to found and maintain schools out of its own resources is specifically guaranteed under the Concordat, and the same right is enjoyed by the Lutheran, Calvinist, and Unitarian Churches. The minimum number of pupils required is 20 for a primary school or an average of 10 pupils per class for higher establishments.

The authorities establishing a 'private school' are free to determine what its language of instruction shall be, but Roumanian history, geography, and institutions must always be taught in the Roumanian language. Pupils may only be admitted whose mother language is the language of instruction in the school in question. Thus, not only 'persons of Roumanian origin who have lost their mother tongue' are excluded from minority private schools, under the 1924 Act, but a German or Jewish child is debarred from attending a Magyar school. If he cannot find a school of his own language, he must attend a Roumanian State school.

For primary schools, the State syllabus is obligatory. Secondary schools may draw up their own syllabus, but if they wish to rank as 'public schools', i.e. to have their certificates and diplomas recognized by the State, they must, besides fulfilling certain other requirements, adopt the State syllabus. At the end of the school year the children are examined by a State inspector, and before

[1] In 1935, however, complaint was made that the German teachers for the State schools in the Banat had to attend the Roumanian State Training College, making up the necessary German instruction in their spare time.

obtaining the higher certificate for admission to a High school they have to pass the 'baccalauréat', an examination re-instituted in 1925 in imitation of the French model. The subjects required for this examination have been changed several times, but they always include an oral examination, conducted in Roumanian, in the language, history, and geography of Roumania. This examination is particularly dreaded by the minorities, and there have been many complaints that it has been made a simple pretext for excluding the minority students from the Universities, and thus damaging their chances of State and professional careers. In fact, the examination seems to have varied greatly in severity in different years, although it is safe to say that a Roumanian student stands the rosier chance of satisfying the examiners. In any case, however, under present conditions, the value of a university degree is less than it was, since a member of a minority, whatever his degree, can hardly hope to enter Government service.

In 1934 the minorities in Transylvania possessed the following educational establishments.[1]

	Confessional.	State.
Magyars		
Primary schools .	783	210 schools plus 232 sections
Lycées . . .	7 ⎫	
Gymnasia . .	18 ⎬	7
Commercial classes .	4 ⎭	
Training colleges .	7	0
Germans (Sa. = Saxon, Su. = Suabian)		
Primary schools .	345 (260 Sa., 85 Su.)	54 schools plus 75 sections (all Su.)
Lycées . . .	7 (6 Sa., 1 Su.) ⎫	
Gymnasia . .	18 (9 Sa., 9 Su.) ⎬	6 (all Su.)
Commercial schools	1 (Sa.) ⎭	
Training colleges .	5 (3 Sa., 2 Su.)	
Serbs		
Primary schools .	42	0
Craşovani		
Primary schools .	5	0
Poles		
Primary schools .	1	0
Czechs and Slovaks		
Primary schools .	2	3 plus 1 section
Ruthenes		
Primary schools .	1	0
Croats		
Primary schools .	0	1 section
Armenians		
Primary schools .	0	1 section

[1] A. Caliani, 'L'Enseignement minoritaire en Roumanie', in *Revue de Transylvanie*, vol. i, no. 3, Nov.–Dec. 1934, pp. 300–8.

The Roumanians in 1926 possessed 3,611 elementary schools, 44 burger schools, 40 lycées and gymnasia, and 10 commercial schools, besides the University of Cluj.[1] In 1932 these figures had risen to 675 kindergartens, 4,100 elementary schools, and 199 middle schools.[2]

The difficulties of drawing reasonable conclusions from school statistics is notorious. To compare the number of Magyar establishments in 1918 with those of to-day would be misleading, since many of the former were pure instruments of Magyarization. One should not even quote the number of confessional schools which have been closed without remembering that as soon as Roumania took over the State schools, the Magyars created an enormous number of new Confessional schools, often in districts where there were hardly any Magyar pupils, and many of these afterwards faded away without any official pressure, simply from lack of money and pupils.

In favour of Roumania, one must grant her ungrudging retention of the Confessional school system as the general rule in the annexed territories,[3] and also the comparatively high degree of liberty which those schools enjoy. The amount of compulsory instruction in Roumanian required is not unreasonable, and is less than the Magyar instruction which Hungary introduced under the Apponyi Act of 1907.[4]

On the other hand, it would be easy to draw over-optimistic conclusions from the statistics of the numbers of minority schools, both State and private. Quite a high proportion of the Confessional Secondary schools have either never received, or have gradually lost their public status. All of them are carrying on under much harder material conditions than before the War, owing to the impoverishment of the Churches under the land reform, and the currency devaluation and the increased taxation. The State subsidies do not even begin to make up for these losses.[5] Moreover,

[1] S. Dragomir, *The Ethnical Minorities in Transylvania* (Geneva, 1927), p. 93.
[2] *Annarul Statistic al Romaniei, 1933.*
[3] Under her Minorities Treaty she was, of course, obliged to allow members of her minorities an equal right with the majorities to found and maintain their own schools. Yugoslavia, however, although subject to a similar obligation, disregarded it completely.
[4] The subjects to be taught in the State language are practically the same under the Apponyi law and the Roumanian law. Each side, of course, maintains that the other is the more oppressive in the application. My judgement is based on what has been said to me by local Germans, who are the persons most likely to speak impartially on the subject.
[5] According to minority sources (*Die Nationalitäten in den Staaten Europas*, p. 392) the German schools received only 55 million lei in subsidies in ten years, whereas the average annual cost of maintaining the schools, all the rest of which was borne by the population, was about 108 million lei. The Magyars in the same period received only 14 million lei from the State. In 1932 it was stated that the Magyar Calvinist Church spent 64 million lei annually on its schools, of which the State contributed 3 million only (*Nation und Staat*, Jan. 1932, p. 267). In 1935 and 1936 the subsidy stopped altogether.

many difficulties appear to be placed in the way of the Confessional schools. Apart from the provisions already quoted, forbidding pupils of one language to attend the schools of another, there are restrictive laws and practices. Parents whose children attend Confessional schools have to produce certificates (stamped at a cost of 27 lei) annually that their children have passed the due examinations. Children are forbidden to attend primary Confessional schools outside their own communes; children who have begun to attend State schools may not change over to private schools; Confessional schools are closed or taken over by the State on trivial pretexts, &c.[1]

It is also very often, and I believe very credibly stated, that the State schools of the minorities are only minority in name. They probably vary greatly, but in more than one place I was assured that only religious instruction is given in them in the minority language. In an official complaint from the German Party to the Government in 1935 it was stated that in the State German schools the 5th, 6th, and 7th classes were entirely Roumanized, and, in many Communes, the lower classes also.[2] The teachers are said often to be Roumanians who know little of the minority language; in some cases, nothing at all. Some of them seem to conceive their duties to be simply that of Roumanizing their pupils, by fair means or foul. It seems quite certain, in any case, that these schools are less genuinely 'minority' than the Confessional schools. I have heard many circumstantial tales of pressure being brought to bear on parents to send their children to the State minority school in villages where both State and Confessional schools exist; and of excuses being sought to close the latter. Unless (as seems improbable) the Roumanian Government is actively desirous of spending money rather than saving it, there is no point at all in this, unless the State school is more Roumanian than the Confessional. Certainly the large number of schools which the official statistics allege the Magyars, in particular, to possess, is partly due to the fact that many villages possess both State and Confessional schools, where there is really only room for one; but neither party will leave the field clear for its rival.

The independence of all education, and also the religious instruction of minority children, have further been seriously affected by a recent decree (September 1936) which compels all young people to spend the mornings from 7.30 a.m. to 1 p.m. of twenty-six Sundays in the year in semi-military, semi-religious training (gymnastics, &c.). This training is carried out under State supervision, and the

[1] *Informations sur la situation de la minorité hongroise en Roumanie* (Geneva, 1934), pp. 35–44.
[2] *Nation und Staat*, March 1935, p. 404.

object is to ensure that the children grow up 'good Roumanians'. This further interferes with the Sunday schools of the minority churches, which had already been labouring under difficulties.

If we come to consider the positions of the different nationalities, we find the Magyars, as was to be expected, the chief sufferers, and that even if we discount their 'shrinking pains' and measure their possessions only by their present requirements. Their numbers and social structure would justify them in claiming a considerable amount of higher education, but they have been left only with a single Chair of Hungarian Literature at Cluj. Moreover, Roumania, like the other Successor States, does not recognize the degrees given by Hungarian Universities.

In secondary education they are better placed, but here, too, they have to struggle with great difficulties. In primary education, the western districts seem to have been reasonably well served, at least until recently, but apart from the fact that in the numerous cases of doubtful nationality the benefit of the doubt has always been given to the non-Magyar language, they have genuine grounds for complaint in the way in which the children of many families, which had been completely and honestly Magyarized, have been forced to attend Roumanian schools on the pretext of their real or alleged Roumanian ancestry. The pressure has been particularly strong in the Székely districts.

It is impossible to give accurate statistics; but I have heard it estimated that as many as 20 per cent. of the Magyar children in the 'cultural zone' have recently been obliged to enter purely Roumanian schools. The result, incidentally, is not to Roumanize these unhappy mites, but to leave them complete analphabetes, for they quickly forget their Roumanian and never learn Magyar. Even outside this zone, a not inconsiderable number of Magyar children have to attend Roumanian schools.

An inquiry conducted in 1934/5 by the Magyar minority leaders resulted in the conclusion that instead of 271 State schools and 218 sections with Magyar language of instruction (as shown by the Ministry of Education for 1933) there were in reality only 55 such schools and 57 sections. The remainder 'did not function', had been closed, or were staffed entirely by Roumanian teachers. Some of the last named may perhaps keep up a pretence of giving Magyar instruction, but the reality is clearly far from what the official figures paint it. 211 teachers had died, retired, been dismissed or transferred, and 161 had been appointed, the new appointments having in every case been given to Roumanians.[1]

---

[1] *Magyar Kisebbség*, September 1, 1936, vol. iii, pp. 460, 461 (for summary of results; details are given, school by school, in several numbers of the review in 1936).

The German position is different. The Saxons have to-day almost exactly the same number of establishments as in 1914, and if the upkeep of them has called for far heavier sacrifices from the population itself, this is partially compensated by the more genuinely national character of the instruction which they can now give.

The Suabians, on the other hand, are very large gainers on balance. Under Hungary, their German schools had been melting like snow in spring. In 1879/80 the Germans of the Banat had possessed 124 primary schools with exclusively German language of instruction, and 174 bilingual schools; in 1913/14 the mixed schools had vanished altogether, and the German schools had been reduced to 34. To-day the Banat has 115 German primary schools or sections, 11 kindergarten, 2 lycées, 1 training college, and several other schools.

The case of the 'Szatmár Germans' requires special mention. Their schools had been reduced under Hungary to two, and the population had been almost entirely Magyarized, although many of them, even when speaking no word of German, still described themselves as Suabians. The Magyarization was, moreover, sincere, for when Roumania took the new census, with its rubric of 'ethnic origin', quite a number of them insisted, in the face of all pressure, on putting themselves down as Magyars. Orders given to introduce German into the Confessional schools were boycotted by the local clergy, who carried through three unofficial 'plebiscites', all of which resulted in favour of Magyar. The German local organization protested, and in 1927 German was at last introduced into all the Suabian primary schools of Szatmár and Salai, while in 1929 a German section was opened in the State Lycée at Careii— another 'national gain' for the Germans which they value extremely highly, as they now possess an extra 30,000 sheep which they had thought strayed for ever from the Germanic fold.

Where the issue has lain, not between German and Magyar, but between German and Roumanian, the position of the Germans has been less satisfactory, and certain complaints have been heard from the Banat, especially as regards the kindergartens. As, however, few Roumanian families had become Germanized under Hungary, collisions in this field have been rare. The analysis of names has not, so far as I know, been applied at all against Germans.

In higher education, the greatest loss incurred by the Germans of Roumania has been the Roumanization of the University of Cernauţi (Czernowitz). This does not, however, greatly affect the Germans of the ex-Hungarian districts. No obstacle seems to be placed in the way of Germans receiving higher education abroad.

On the whole, therefore, the German cultural position is much more satisfactory to-day than it was under Hungary.

The Jews have less cause for rejoicing. Like the Germans, they are excluded from the Magyar schools, since they are never allowed to count Magyar as their mother tongue; nor may they give instruction in their own schools in either Magyar or German; these languages may not even be taught as subjects. The Jews are thus thrown back, if they wish to go to schools of their own, on Hebrew, a language which very few of them wish to learn at all, and one which is, in any case, utterly useless to nine-tenths of them. There remains the Roumanian school, which the Jew is in theory free to attend; but owing to the anti-Semitic tendencies of both students and professors, his admission is in practice difficult, especially to a University; and if he does get there, he is subjected to innumerable vexations, if not to actual persecution. Jews thus find it difficult to obtain any higher education whatever, and what they get is of doubtful use to them, or has at best to be supplemented by strenuous private study, since the business life of Transylvania (and a Jew cannot hope for any other career) is still largely transacted in Magyar.

Of the remaining minorities, the Serbs passed through some years during which their educational system practically broke down, owing to the migration of teachers and priests after the disputed Banat frontier with Yugoslavia had been fixed. Only twenty-two teachers remained at one time. Attempts were made as early as 1921 to reach a settlement on the question of educational facilities for Serbs in the Roumanian Banat, and Roumanians in the Yugoslav Banat, but these were many times delayed by political and other difficulties. At last in 1933 a Convention was signed between the two States providing that each of the minorities concerned should receive instruction in its own mother tongue, with certain subjects taught in the language of State, and arranging for a supply of qualified teachers.[1] The Serb schools are Confessional, and seem adequate for the needs of the population.

Another minority which has benefited, rather unexpectedly, is the tiny group of 'Crașovani', who converted their half-dozen schools to the local dialect in 1919 and have since been left undisturbed, perhaps because the Government is unwilling to do either Serbs or Bulgars the favour of endorsing their claims to this little people. The Armenians have got in on the de-Magyarizing programme, the Czechs and Slovaks as allies. The Ruthenes and Bulgars seem, however, to be scantily served.

It will be observed that neither the Saxon nor the Székely 'communities' enjoy the autonomy promised them in the Roumanian

[1] See *Revue de Transylvanie*, vol. i, no. 4, pp. 477 ff.

Minorities Treaty. The fault lies partly in the loose wording of the Treaty, for if the Saxon 'University' might fairly claim to represent the Saxon 'community' or 'communities', no corresponding Székely organization has existed for centuries past. The Magyars have from time to time made courageous efforts to convince the world that the whole Magyar population of Transylvania should be included for this purpose under the term Székely. If, however, the authors of the Peace Treaty meant this, they did not say so, and the name Székely has a perfectly definite, although unofficial connotation. By no stretch of imagination can it be stretched to cover the Magyars of Crişana, nor even of the Cluj area. The Roumanians are, therefore, on absolutely sure legal ground in rejecting this claim. They might conceivably grant the Székely, in the strict sense of the name, a certain limited autonomy, but if so, they would certainly use this concession as a means of driving a wedge between the Székely and the remaining Magyars; and being clearsighted enough to see this, and anxious to avoid a national split, the Székely themselves have refrained from pursuing their claim. As for the Saxons, they have on the whole inclined in the past to accept the Roumanian claim that the Statute of the Lutheran Church gives them all the autonomy which they could expect under the Treaty. In recent times they, too, have been unwilling to weaken their new national unity with the other Germans of Roumania by pressing their separate claim.

The general cultural life of nearly all the minorities in Transylvania is lively. Two general points must be said in Roumania's favour: she has been less pedantic than either of her allies in the matter of literary and cultural associations, and she has in theory an extraordinarily liberal Press law, which contrasts very favourably with that in force in Transylvania before the War.[1] This law has often been partially suspended under the martial law which has so long prevailed, but even during these periods, the Press has enjoyed considerable freedom—compared to many countries of the Continent—in its political utterances and almost complete liberty in other fields.

The cultural life of the Germans is probably more active than at any time during their long history. Among the Saxons it has experienced a renaissance, after its visible decline during the last decades of Hungarian rule, while among the Suabians it is almost a new birth. The importance of this very vigorous movement, which has found its expression in a host of literary, educational and social publications, societies, &c., can hardly be exaggerated, and it should be emphasized that Roumania has encouraged it strongly,

---

[1] The Transylvanian Press Law was until shortly before the War different from, and stricter than, that in force in the rest of Hungary.

only intervening very occasionally against extreme manifestations of Nazi ideas.

The Magyars have not been encouraged like the Germans, but they have, on the whole, been allowed pretty well to go their own way. Roumanian authors are able to point to some impressive figures. Thus the Magyars of Transylvania possess to-day a large number of periodicals, most of which are new since the annexation.[1] It is true that this pullulation of local growths is due largely to the fact that the great Budapest dailies, with very few exceptions, can no longer enter Transylvania; nevertheless, the figures are quite impressive, the more so when it is recalled that they represent the genuine voice of the Magyars themselves, since none of them are subsidized Government publications. The Magyars have 255 bookshops, 147 printing-presses, and 6 regular theatrical companies, and between 1919 and 1933, 5,000 literary and scientific works appeared in Magyar—more than were produced during the whole period 1807–1918. Most of the big literary and cultural societies date from before the War, but one extremely interesting society, the 'Helikon', has been founded since the War, and has become the rallying-point of the new Magyar Cultural movement, reflecting the new political outlook to which we shall return, which is turning more and more to a specifically Transylvanian outlook not necessarily hostile to the local Roumanians.

Roumania has also been the most generous of the Successor States in allowing Magyar literature to cross her frontier. Up to 1926 the restrictions were severe, but they were then greatly relaxed. Thereafter, on an average, Roumania received over 50 per cent. of Hungary's total exports of printed literature, while between 80 per cent. and 90 per cent. of her own total imports of books and newspapers came from Hungary.[2]

§ 12. THE MINORITIES: THE ECONOMIC AND SOCIAL STRUGGLE

But although Roumania's first attention has necessarily been devoted to securing her political control over Transylvania, and although this involves also far-reaching cultural measures, yet the centre of gravity of the Transylvanian problem has lain rather in the readjustment of the social and economic relationships of the different nationalities—a readjustment to which political and even cultural measures are really no more than the essential

[1] Transylvanus, *The Ethnical Minorities of Transylvania*, p. 36, gives 312 periodicals, 53 of which are dailies, 250 of them, including 38 dailies, being new since the annexation. Another source, however (*Transilvanie, Banatul, Crişana, Maramureş*, p. 1307), gives the figure at only 221 periodicals, including 25 dailies.
[2] *Revue de Transylvanie*, vol. i, no. 4, pp. 505 ff.

preliminaries. The national-social revolution which has been carried through since the annexation, partly by legislative action, partly outside the law, has affected the lives of all the peoples concerned far more profoundly than the mere change of sovereignty.

Of the legislative measures, the earliest and, in many ways, still the most important, is the agrarian reform, which was enacted almost immediately after the War. It must be remembered that in any case, Roumania could hardly have avoided carrying through a measure of this kind, owing to the deplorable agrarian conditions in the Regat, which had led in 1907 to perhaps the most savage peasant revolt of modern history.[1] The Roumanian Parliament had decided as early as 1917 to undertake a large-scale redistribution in the Regat. This was duly carried through under an Act of 1921, the sufferers being almost exclusively Roumanian individuals and corporations, and the Roumanian State.

On political grounds alone, therefore, it would hardly have proved possible to exempt Transylvania from the application of the reform, even if it had been considered socially desirable to maintain the existing distribution of land. If, however, a reform were carried through at all, most of the sufferers were bound to be members of the minorities, and most of the beneficiaries must be Roumanians; since, while the majority of the population (say 55 per cent.) was Roumanian, they owned only about 24 per cent. of the land, the large estates were overwhelmingly in non-Roumanian hands.[2]

[1] It has been estimated that 10,000 Roumanian peasants were killed in the repression of this revolt.

[2] I have purposely left my figures approximate, as exactitude seems impossible to achieve. According to official figures (cit. Dragomir, op. cit., pp. 246 ff.) there were in Transylvania, in 1919, 14,933,841 yokes (1 yoke = 0·575 ha.), 7,613,555 of which were arable land. 61·05 per cent. of this belonged to private individuals, 39·5 per cent. to the State, communes, societies, co-possessorates, &c. There were 8,435 owners of property of 100 yokes or over, owning a total area of 5,926,734 yokes. Of these, 209 Roumanians held in all 150,067 yokes, while 8,226 members of minorities held 5,876,667 yokes. Of the small properties under 100 yokes, according to M. Dragomir, 'the Roumanians, although numbering 3,316,345, held only 3,448,602 yokes, while the minorities, numbering 1,891,933, possessed 5,407,141 yokes. In all, then, Roumanians held 3,598,669 yokes and the present minorities 11,233,819.'

The attentive reader will observe: (a) that the last two figures do not, as they should, equal the first; (b) that the first figure (total area of Transylvania) is nearly 4 million yokes too low; (c) that the numbers given for the Roumanian population are larger than the figures given by the Roumanian census of 1930 for that population, while the figures for the minorities are smaller; (d) that State lands are apparently counted as minority-owned. In any case, according to Hungarian critics, no exact figures are or ever have been available for the land distribution in 1919 in the total area annexed by Roumania; nor was the number of Roumanians so low as would appear from these figures. Thus N. Móricz, *The Fate of the Transylvanian Soil* (Budapest, 1934), quotes the following figures for those Counties transferred in their entirety to Roumania (omitting,

Whether the measure was carried out in such manner as to involve national injustice seems therefore to depend chiefly on three points: whether the Transylvanian law was more severe on the landowners than the corresponding measure in the Regat: whether, within Transylvania itself, the Roumanian landowners were treated more indulgently than the minorities; and whether the minority claimants participated equally.

As regards the first point, the Transylvanian law was undoubtedly more drastic than that of the Regat. The fact that the compensation given was slightly lower in Transylvania (an average of 2,181 lei per hectare, against 2,215 lei in the Regat) is comparatively unimportant, since the prices in either case were so low as to amount to confiscation, particularly as they were paid, not in cash, but in 5 per cent. bonds which sank swiftly below par; but other differences are more serious.

In the Regat the expropriation applies to the property, so that a single owner of several estates can keep a part of each; in Transylvania, to the proprietor. In the Regat, only arable land and pasture are subject to expropriation; in Transylvania, forests also. In the Regat, the minimum left to the proprietor is 100 hectares in the mountains, 150–250 hectares in the plains, according to the local demand for land, while 200, 300, or even 500 hectares may be retained in certain cases. In Transylvania the minima are 50 yokes (29 hectares) in the mountains, 100 yokes (57 hectares), in the foot-hills, and 200, 300, or 500 yokes in the plains, according to demand. It has, however, been very rare for more than 200 yokes (115 hectares) to be left to any one proprietor. In certain cases the minima are reduced to 50 yokes for estates farmed by their owners, and even to 10 yokes where neither the owner nor his parents were agriculturalists.

The law was, therefore, clearly more severe in Transylvania,

therefore, the Counties of Bihor, Csanád, Máramaros, Szatmár, Tiniş-Torontal, and Ugocsa):

	Magyar.	Roumanian.	German.	Total.
Producing population	497,253	965,361	142,766	1,657,843
Estates of over 1,000 yokes	209	19	14	244
,, 100–1,000 ,,	1,832	830	376	3,046
,, 50–100 ,,	3,585	4,195	1,374	9,211
,, 10–50 ,,	63,010	167,861	29,413	264,141
,, 5–10 ,,	42,752	178,963	16,106	242,137
,, 0–5 ,,	49,070	213,602	13,501	279,208
Landless agricultural population.	91,022	229,900	10,197	347,941

Other Hungarian sources, however, admit that 87·12 per cent. of the owners of properties exceeding 100 yokes were Magyar (*Informations sur la situation de la minorité hongroise en Roumanie*, p. 26).

where nearly all the persons expropriated belonged to minorities, than in the Regat, where the big landowners were Roumanians (the fact that the expropriation was more drastic still in Bessarabia does not affect our point). As regards the relative treatment accorded to minority and Roumanian landowners, I myself heard no specific instances of discrimination; but it is quite possible that I never visited any of the few regions where large Roumanian estates existed. Hungarian writers claim that in two Departments (Someş and Turda) the Roumanian properties were left quite untouched, but they do not mention the number or size of the estates.[1]

In all, up to the end of 1929,[2] 2,906,073 yokes of private property had been expropriated, and 212,497 yokes of State land ceded. 935,283 yokes of this were arable land, 563,378 pasture, and 1,516,971 forest. The State retained about one-third of the forest-land; communes received nearly 700,000 yokes of forest and over 900,000 yokes of pasture, and 632,923 yokes were distributed to small proprietors in plots ranging from 1 to 7 yokes; 300,196 in freehold and 332,727 on lease. The whole question had been desperately complicated for years by the famous 'optants dispute', perhaps the most wearisome that ever troubled the League of Nations, as the clause providing for complete expropriation of non-Roumanian citizens conflicted with the provisions of the Peace Treaty safeguarding the rights of optants. A settlement was only reached at the Hague Reparations Conference, when it was agreed that the 'Hungarian Optants' should lose their land, but be compensated out of an obscure Reparations fund.

As regards the distribution, according to Roumanian figures, 454,673 applications were received, 337,082 (74 per cent.) from Roumanians, 117,591 (26 per cent.) from minorities. 310,583 persons actually received land, of whom 227,943 (73 per cent.) were Roumanians, 82,640 (27 per cent.) minorities.[3] Thus a slightly smaller proportion of Roumanian applicants were satisfied than of the minorities. Hungarian writers have cavilled at these figures, but have produced, so far as I know, no alternatives. According to Dr. Móricz's figures for the individual Counties, quoted above, one could have expected a somewhat higher proportion of applicants from the minorities, since Roumanians represented only 68 per cent. of the two categories (landless men and holders of 5 yokes or under) who might expect to benefit from the reform, against 32 per cent. of minorities. Probably, therefore, there was a certain discrepancy in the application of the law, but none in principle. The disproportion might, however, appear

[1] *Informations sur la situation de la minorité hongroise en Roumanie.*
[2] These figures are from Dragomir, op. cit., pp. 247 ff.
[3] Transylvanus, op. cit., pp. 41, 42.

greater if account could be taken of the land respectively taken from and attributed to communes, where much more discrimination seems to have been applied. In the matter of building-plots it seems, unfortunately, well attested that Roumanian officials, army officers, and political hangers-on benefited pretty largely.

57,365 yokes were set aside for 'colonization of refugees', and of these 42,748 yokes were distributed to 4,271 families of colonists.[1] The colonization question has not, however, excited anything like so much ill feeling in Roumania as in Slovakia or the Voivodina. In general, Roumania appears to have stuck sensibly enough to the principle of reserving the land for the local population.

Much more ill feeling was aroused by the question of the ex-Magyar colonists. Some 1,700 families in all had been settled by the Hungarian Government, during the decades before the War, on 40,000 yokes of Crown land, which they themselves had cleared. They were still in 1918 not yet legal owners of their land, and the Roumanian Government, in its capacity of successor to the Hungarian Government, ordered their expropriation down to the limits fixed for applicants under the Agrarian Reform. Legally the Government had a case, but its action bore an unfortunate appearance of vindictiveness, and it did wisely when, after prolonged negotiations before the League of Nations, it consented, 'as an act of grace' to compensate the colonists.

The minority landowners certainly lost very heavily under the reform. For the Saxons, the chief loss fell on their Church and communal property. The 'Saxon University' and 'Seven Sees' lost their entire foundation of 35,000 yokes, with the exception of 100 yokes. The Lutheran Church lost large portions of its estates; over 4,000 yokes of land in the 14 communes of the Braşov district alone. It must be remembered that these losses fall very heavily on the Saxons, who pay large sums for educational and charitable purposes and during the past decades often gave up parts of their individual holdings to form or enlarge foundations out of which these expenses could be met. The loss is particularly heavy, since the minority schools are nearly all Confessional, and depend for their very existence on the Church property. The Roumanian Churches have also been expropriated; but the Roumanians have the State schools to fall back upon.

There were few large estates belonging to individual German proprietors, and the peasants owning medium estates were treated more indulgently than the Magyars, although there are cases enough where both individuals and communes have been deprived

---

[1] J. Rusu, 'Quelques considérations sur la réforme agraire en Transylvanie', in *Revue de Transylvanie*, vol. ii, no. 3, March–April, 1936, p. 378. Colonists were allowed 14 yokes, instead of the usual maximum of 7.

of land for the benefit of Roumanians. There were certainly a
large number of smaller abuses which caused much ill feeling.

The Magyar Churches (under which title we include the Roman
Catholic) and cultural institutions lost even more heavily, while in
addition, a considerable class of individual estate owners suffered
what amounts to confiscation of a large proportion of their estates.
It is true that owing to their greater tenacity and adaptability, the
Magyar landowners of Transylvania, as a class, weathered the
storm better than the boiars of the Regat,[1] so that many of them
still enjoy a certain modest prosperity. Their losses were, however, enormous, and the national gains of either the German or the
Magyar peasant beneficiaries certainly cannot begin to compensate
for the losses of the big landowners and institutions of the same
nationalities. The second big loss which the minorities have incurred has been in the public services. We have already referred to
this question in its political and administrative aspect; but the social
and economic effects of the replacement of minority officials by
Roumanians are at least equally important. It must be remembered
that in most countries of Central and Eastern Europe the State,
which controls not only the strictly administrative services, but
nearly all the transport system as well as the production and sale
of the various Government monopolies, is easily the largest
employer of labour, and not only the political influence and social
standing of any national group, but also its collective income
depend very largely on the extent to which it is able to avail itself
of State employment. Roumania's new national policy in the
question of officials has therefore had devastating effects for the
minorities. These effects are not yet fully apparent, since the new
policy is not of long standing, and the minorities of the older
generation, the bread-earners of to-day, are still reasonably well
represented in the Government services, while the minority
pensioners probably outnumber the Roumanian. The proportions
are, however, changing with every year, and the younger generation of the minorities has to accept the situation that it cannot
possibly look forward to anything except private employment.

It is the question of private employment which to-day holds the
front of the stage. As we have seen, the position of the Transylvanian Roumanians in the non-official life of Hungary was hardly
better than in the official. They were only just beginning by 1914
to develop a small lower middle-class, and that had hardly begun
to influence the economic life of the country. Its activities were
confined almost entirely to the specifically Roumanian national
enterprise: the editing of Roumanian newspapers, the manage-

---

[1] R. Braun, 'Herrenklasse, Vermögen und Beruf in den agrarischen Donau-
ländern', in *Oesterreichischer Volkswirt*, November 11, 1933.

ment of Roumanian local banks and co-operatives, the defence of Roumanian clients. The whole general business life of Transylvania was in the hands of Jews, Magyars, and Germans.

The natural revolt against this inferiority has been carried further since the War, and it has been reinforced, and its direction somewhat modified, by two other movements, both originating outside Transylvania. The first of these is the old anti-foreign movement born of the peculiar economic position of the Regat. For Roumania, which is at once one of the newest, the richest, and the least business-like of all European States, has been more in the position of an 'economic colony' than any other European country. When the Phanariot régime ceased, it was only to give place to another form of foreign exploitation—in the form of the ownership and control by foreign capital of the great natural resources. One of the chief objects of Roumanian policy, ever since the formation of Roumania, has been to prevent this exploitation. The desires of the nation are reflected in the provisions of the Constitution that Roumania may not be colonized by people of an alien race, that only Roumanian citizens may acquire rural landed property, and that the sub-soil and mineral deposits are State property, and in various attempts which have been made to keep the control over the oil-fields in Roumanian hands. The reality has been that while the provisions regarding land are honoured, the execution of the laws in other respects have been continually thwarted by Roumanians themselves, who have lent themselves for a consideration to every kind of evasion. The oil-fields and the rest of the large Roumanian industry is still to an overwhelming extent foreign-owned, and not only the Directors and the administrative and technical staff but even the skilled workers are still to a large extent foreigners. The revolt of the Regat Roumanians against this situation is a second element in the Transylvanian position, since the Roumanian, not altogether unnaturally, fails to distinguish between the 'străini' (foreigners) who are foreign subjects in the Regat, and the 'străini' in Transylvania who are non-Roumanians, and have only become Roumanian subjects since 1919.

Thirdly, there is the purely anti-Semitic movement, which is completely foreign to Transylvania (where, except in Maramureş and Bistriţa, the Jews inhabit almost exclusively non-Roumanian districts) but has been imported, again, from the Regat. Parts of Wallachia, Northern Moldavia, and now the Bukovina and Bessarabia, harbour a Jewish population denser than that of any part of the world, except Poland. These Jews are at once a very powerful element in Roumania, much of whose finance and commerce they control, and a truly exotic one. Orthodox almost to a man, they have remained almost entirely unassimilated, and the people

Y

regard them as 'străini'. Moreover, successive Roumanian Governments have done their best to keep them technically in that position. For decades after Roumania's formation she struggled to refuse them citizenship, and succeeded very largely, in the face of great pressure from the Powers. Thus the anti-foreign tendency works hand in hand with a very strong anti-Semitic movement, which has always existed in the Regat. In its modern form, this movement dates from 1910, when Professor Jorga and M. Cuza founded a 'National-Democratic Party', the central plank in whose programme was contained in its 45th Article: 'Solution of the Jewish question through elimination of the Jews and development of the creative forces of the Roumanian.'

The complaints of the minorities concerning the discrimination practised against their economic life would fill volumes. Government and municipal contracts are placed, wherever possible, with Roumanian firms—a matter of very great importance, in view of the predominant role played by the State as purchaser for heavy industrial products. The minority banks passed through exceedingly difficult periods. Both Hungarian and German sources complain that the cheap rediscount credits granted during the early years by the Roumanian National Bank were given almost entirely to Roumanian banks; thus in 1923 four Bucharest banks received rediscounts amounting to over 200 per cent. of their capital, while 98 Magyar banks could obtain rediscounts only up to 4 per cent. of their collective capital:[1] this on top of the heavy losses which they had already incurred through their subscriptions to the Austro-Hungarian War Loan. The difficulties of the banks affected the whole economic life of the respective minorities, whose business men and farmers have also found it very hard to get credit elsewhere. Thus it was reported in 1930 that the 'Creditul Industrial', founded in 1924 with Government participation, for the purpose of giving cheap long-tenure credits to small industries, had not granted a single credit in the purely Székely departments of Ciuc (Csik) and Odorheiu (Udvárhély).[2]

Taxation has undoubtedly been discriminatory. Certain taxes exist which affect minorities almost exclusively, such as a tax on non-Roumanian shop-signs and a surtax of 12 per cent. on the tax on trade and industry applied to firms keeping their books in any other language than Roumanian. In other cases, it is the levying of taxation which is unequal. I was shown details of a case in which the Roumanian engineers in a certain town were taxed 5 per cent. as professional men, while their Magyar colleagues had

---

[1] *Die Nationalitäten in den Staaten Europas*, p. 410 (German complaint on the same score, ibid., p. 424).

[2] Ibid., p. 409.

to pay 16 per cent. as merchants. This was certainly no unusual occurrence; Hungarian sources report many similar cases.[1] And even where the taxes are equitably distributed, they are collected very differently. The minority taxpayer has to be punctual and complete, or he is sold up unmercifully; the Roumanian can let his arrears drag on for years, and can probably get out of paying many of them altogether. Since import and export restrictions have multiplied, and all, or nearly all, Roumania's foreign trade is subjected to the contingent system, a further means of discrimination has been open to the authorities, who grant the lion's share of all permits to Roumanians.

On top of the innumerable injustices and chicaneries, of which the above are only examples, have come a series of more direct interferences. The Roumanian tendency towards centralization has involved the imposition of a multitude of controls on such institutions as co-operatives, Chambers of Commerce, &c., which formerly worked quite autonomously. Further, the so-called 'Comisia Economica Speciala', which was set up for the purpose of 'nationalizing Roumanian industry' (i.e. turning into Roumanian companies the Roumanian branches of foreign companies), concerned itself in practice with all important minority firms in Transylvania, which were obliged to take Roumanian directors on to their boards, or in some cases to submit to the control of Roumanian Government Commissioners.

Thanks to those various measures, a Roumanian middle class is beginning to grow up side by side with the minorities. There are far more Roumanian banks, Roumanian shops, Roumanian doctors, lawyers, and journalists than there were fifteen years ago. And much of this progress has been made at the expense of the minorities.

The extraordinary feature in the situation is that the agitation against the economic superiority of the minorities, instead of abating as these successes are registered, is growing stronger from year to year. Moreover, while the minorities complain quite truthfully of abuse and injustice, the Roumanian nationalists retort that the stranglehold of the minorities on the economic life of the country is stronger than ever. And it is quite true that all the progress of the minorities has not been downhill. The Saxon banks, for example, have expanded very greatly, extended their operations far beyond Transylvania, and now can rival the most important institutions of Bucharest. Even the Magyar banks, who found the initial period of adaptation much more difficult, have recovered in remarkable fashion.[2] Moreover, the minorities still possess the

---

[1] Ibid., p. 411.
[2] See the figures quoted by Transylvanus, op. cit., pp. 44 ff.

lion's share of the industries of Transylvania, some of which have expanded considerably since the War.[1]

The explanation lies partly in the immense start which the minorities possessed in 1919. They had the capital, the good-will, the experience, and fifteen years have simply not been enough to make up the arrears. But there appears to me to be another and deeper explanation.

Roumania since the War has been controlled by the Liberal Party. They have actually been in power most of the time, while the other parties which have from time to time held office have either, like General Averescu's party, been little more than stop-gaps, or else they have existed more or less on sufferance. Only Dr. Maniu's first Government was able to carry out a truly inde-pendent policy, and most of his work was immediately undone again as soon as the Liberals succeeded him. Now, the Liberals represent the outlook and mentality of the Regat, in which, as we said, the business life has always been in the hands of Jews or foreigners. True, they have revolted against this situation, but they have never seriously attempted to transform it. They have instead adopted a sort of glorified gangster policy, allowing the Jews to do the work while contenting themselves with a substantial rake-off. And, as they are essentially an oligarchical party, this policy has suited them admirably, nor has it been altogether unsatisfactory to the minority. The richer the Jew, the bigger the rake-off.

The 'national' policy which the Liberals have applied to the minorities in Transylvania has been just the same. The 'national-ization' of the minority firms has consisted in the practice of putting in a few Roumanian directors, who are given a packet of free shares, or allowed to buy them at a nominal rate. After this, the average Roumanian director has been perfectly content to fill the role of guinea-pig, his contribution to the business being to protect it against the Government. As most of these directors are Liberal politicians, they have usually been able to do so effectively. The activities of the 'Special Economic Commission' have thus, para-doxically enough, been the strongest defence for the minority firms.

The minorities, meanwhile, have pursued a tenacious and systematic policy, along the lines practised for centuries by the Saxons, which are now being successfully imitated by the Magyars. This policy has not been oligarchic, but national. They have had to sacrifice some of their directors' fees, and to submit to various exactions, but they have seen to it that in all other respects their own nationals should benefit. They have bought from their own producers, sold as advantageously as possible to their own

---

[1] Dragomir, op. cit., pp. 234 ff.

consumers, and above all, they have staffed their businesses with their own men.

Thus, up to the present, they have kept their end up not too badly, and that thanks largely to the protection of the Roumanian Liberals themselves, which partially neutralized the measures taken in the opposite direction. In Transylvania itself, moreover, there was no great revolt against this position for the first ten or twelve years. Some of the leading politicians were unwilling on grounds of principle to move against the minorities beyond what was already being done; others had entered the cosy hutch offered to the guinea-pig director.

About 1931, however, the pressure of the new generation began to grow much stronger. The State could not offer employment to nearly all the ex-students, and most unhappily, the sudden growth of the numbers of persons grimly determined to lead bourgeois lives coincided with a moment when no accumulation of capital was taking place which would have enabled them to find shelter in new or enlarged enterprises, but rather a shrinkage owing to the world depression. Thus a new assault on the economic position of the minorities began, which has certainly not yet reached its climax.

This attitude is far more serious than anything which has yet taken place, for it aims at realities, not appearances; it is national, not oligarchic. The young peasants' sons cannot be bought off like the Liberal politicians; for one thing there are too many of them. What they want is work, and their demands, if granted, would cut at the roots of the minorities' economic life.

The most prominent spokesman of this movement is Dr. Vaida Voivod, one of the leading Transylvanian politicians and twice Premier of his country. It is possible that to the three motive forces directed against the minorities we should add a fourth, for in denouncing the position in which the Roumanians find themselves as compared with the minorities, Dr. Vaida is also castigating his political opponents of the Liberal Party, who have failed to remedy the evils in question. The ideas which Dr. Vaida now advocates are, however, in full accordance with his past.[1] At all events he took up the cause of the unemployed Roumanian youth with great fervour. During his own most recent term of office as Premier (January to November 1933) he made several endeavours to introduce some reforms, but met, according to his own account, with complete non-success;[2] the employers of Roumania, tacitly

[1] Dr. Vaida preceded Hitler by some decades in introducing the term 'Aryan' into politics, although the 'non-Aryans' against whom he tilted in his youth were not Jews but Magyars.

[2] Dr. Vaida himself told me that when Prime Minister, he circularized 550 large enterprises, asking them what proportion of Roumanian and minority labour they employed. Only two even answered, and they were firms of which he was himself a director.

supported by the Liberals, simply boycotted all his endeavours; and it is an open secret that his toleration of other organizations holding similar ideas was what led to his fall from power. Naturally, therefore, he pursued his policy all the more vigorously after his fall, and at the Congress of the National Peasant Party in February 1935 he formally proposed the introduction of the now famous 'numerus Valachicus'.

The 'numerus Valachicus', as its author himself kindly expounded it to me, is intended to apply to State employment and employment closely connected with the State: that is to say, besides the Government services themselves, it would apply to those professions, such as that of medicine, much of whose work is conducted for the State and those industries which are of national importance. In all these branches of life, equally, the Roumanians and the national minorities should be represented in proportion to their numbers. Proper education should be organized accordingly. Intelligent children should be selected from the different nationalities, in the same proportions, and taken into the State secondary schools, whence they would pass automatically into State employment, or into one of the scheduled professions.

Outside these limits, Dr. Vaida would allow the minorities as many schools as they like, and would place no restriction on their economic activities. In some respects, therefore, his plan would seem to promise advantages even to the minorities themselves. It must, however, be remembered that given the dependence of Roumanian industry on the State, there are few branches of economic activity which could reckon with any certainty on not coming within the scope of the 'numerus'; and it is obviously unlikely that if Roumanians replace Magyars and Saxons in minority districts, they will be equally ready to make way for them in the heart of the Regat. Certainly the Roumanian youth which hails Dr. Vaida as its leader does not envisage any sort of reciprocity; all its talk is simply of turning the minorities out.

At the Congress in question, the majority of the Party did not accept Dr. Vaida's programme. He withdrew it, and soon after left the party. The proportion of the party which followed him was not very large, but his supporters increased rapidly when he began an independent agitation in the autumn, and by 1936 he commanded a large following. For his ideas are naturally enormously popular among many Roumanians, whose attitude towards them is exactly the same as that of the manufacturer in a country changing over from free trade to protection. The interest of the consumer does not count; all that matters is that the individual producer should be relieved from the pressure of more efficient competition from outside. Resolutions from various professional organizations in Roumania have poured in on the Government, demanding national protection for this trade or that. Perhaps the most original is the demand of the Roumanian chimney-sweeps that members of minorities should not be admitted to their calling; for, they say, a chimney-sweep 'can see everything, hear everything, go freely anywhere'.[1]

Meanwhile, the anti-Semitic feeling which we have mentioned as endemic in Roumania had been growing rapidly since the War. Its appeal was increased in particular by two factors. Firstly, the unsettled economic conditions after the War enabled the experienced and agile-minded Jews to profit very largely, while the slower-witted Roumanians were helpless in face of them. The land reform in the Regat, in particular, transferred enormous sums from the pockets of the Roumanian landowners into those of the Jews. Secondly, the number of Jews in Roumania itself was greatly increased through the annexation of the Bukovina and Bessarabia—both old Jewish strongholds—while it is also persistently alleged that there has been a great influx into Roumania of Jews who are not Roumanian subjects. It is certainly true that Roumania contains at this moment scores of thousands of Jews who do not hold Roumanian passports. In the majority of cases, the fault is not theirs; they are persons who ought, according to the stipulations of the Minorities Treaty, to have been given Roumanian citizenship, but have been refused it under various quite unjustifiable interpretations of the law. There are, however, also many refugees from other countries, who have stepped into Roumania and established themselves there, generally by bribing the authorities. Roumanian anti-Semitic opinion, of course, lumps both categories together, and uses to the full the cry that 'you are being exploited by the alien Jew'.

Thus, although Professor Jorga abandoned anti-Semitism after the War, M. Cuza found no difficulty in carrying on his movement, which altered its name into the 'Nationalist Democratic Christian Party' and in 1923 to the 'National Christian Defence League', since the Roumanian nationalists, like their confrères elsewhere, regard themselves as a 'movement' rather than a 'party'.

In 1927 the younger and more radical members of the 'League' forsook M. Cuza, who is a philosophical old gentleman, to follow a new and far more 'advanced' leader in the person of M. Codreanu. M. Codreanu is a true and legitimate representative of the line of extreme nationalist leaders, who, for some reason, are nearly always strangers to the race to whose advancement they devote themselves. He is, in hard fact, not a Roumanian, nor even a Codreanu, for his worthy father was a Ukrainian named Zilinski, his excellent

[1] *Danubian Review*, April 1936, p. 4.

mother a German called Launer. From the day, however, when he shot a gendarme in Jaşi for defending two Jews, and was acquitted by a sympathetic jury, his career has never looked back. The 'Iron Guard' which he founded soon became a force in the country, commanded the devoted allegiance of hundreds of students, and perpetrated a series of anti-Semitic acts of violence which have darkened the name of Roumania.[1]

In December 1933 a member of the Iron Guard murdered M. Duca, the Liberal Prime Minister, and the Guard was then dissolved. The measure was, however, hardly more than nominal. The title has been dropped in official parlance, but is currently used, while the organization goes on unchanged, and is probably stronger to-day than ever before. Meanwhile, MM. Cuza and Codreanu have been reinforced by a number of further groups and parties. M. Octavian Goga, the Transylvanian ex-Poet, founded a 'National Agrarian' Party, the programme of which closely resembled that of M. Cuza, with whom he then combined in the summer of 1933, the combined parties taking the title of the Christian National Party. The Iron Guard has also found a large number of imitators whose shirts almost exhausted the spectrum.

The strength of all these parties lies outside Transylvania, into which they only make occasional raids. Most of them were at first almost absorbed in the Jewish question, and if they interested themselves in other minorities, it was from a purely political point of view. Thus the Transylvanian Saxons are almost popular with many of the young nationalists, partly because a reflected glory shines upon them as members of the stock which bred Adolf Hitler, partly because of the common bond of a shared anti-Semitism. Gradually, however, they are moving towards Vaida's ideas, as he towards theirs. In 1935 a member of the Christian National Party explained to me his minority policy as follows:

He divided the minorities of Roumania into three groups: (a) The 'Germans, English, French, &c.' who are 'not dangerous to the Roumanian State or people' are to have the same rights as Roumanians; (b) The 'potential irredentists'—Magyars, Bulgars, &c.—are to have the right to engage in commerce, industry, &c., in proportion to their numbers, and also to enter State service, but not the Army, justice, or State education; (c) Jews born in Roumania are to have the same rights as group (b), while the post-War immigrants are to be expelled.

In November 1935 this *rapprochement* was carried a step farther,

---

[1] The worst of these were at Oradea, Cluj, Huedin, and certain other towns in December 1928. A full description of these is given in 'La Situation de la minorité juive en Roumanie', presented to the League of Nations by various Jewish associations in March 1928.

when Vaida's Parliamentary group and the Christian Nationals formed a single Parliamentary bloc, with a common slogan 'Roumania for the Roumanians' and a common programme, the chief points of which are the following: application of the national principle in all State and private enterprises, in the army, justice, administration, and education; reinstatement of the Roumanian Church in its calling of 'creator and judge'; alteration of the Constitution to 'anchor the national idea in the structure of the life of the State'; abolition of trusts and cartels; securing the predominance of Roumanian labour; removal of 'foreign elements' from economic life by checking lists of Roumanian citizens and expelling foreign skilled labour. A number of social measures are also advocated, particularly measures to improve the economic, intellectual, and physical status of the Roumanian peasantry.

The numbers of these combined parties are still not very great, but they have grown considerably in recent times. In the election of 1934 the Cuza-Goga parties obtained about 300,000 votes out of 2,000,000 votes recorded. In the next elections, if the agreement with Dr. Vaida can be consolidated, the extreme right should be strongly represented even in Parliament. Moreover, they work harmoniously enough, each in its different field, with the Iron Guard. 'Nous sommes enchantés de l'esprit de la Garde', said one of M. Cuza's followers to me; adding that the Guard would assuredly come after them and do the things which they cannot themselves do. Ninety per cent. of the students of Roumania are Fascist after one fashion or another, and the movement seems to be growing stronger every day.

As the nationalist parties have usually been in opposition, the amount of actual anti-minority economic legislation has been small. A law for the protection of national labour, enacted in 1926 and amended and strengthened in 1930, referred only to non-Roumanians, who were forbidden to engage in any gainful occupation in Roumania if an adequate supply of Roumanian labour was available. In fact, these laws remained for some time something of a dead letter, although they were enforced much more severely in 1935, when a very large number of aliens were expelled, and several firms fined heavily for contraventions of the law. The chief sufferers among the minorities (as distinct from the aliens) were large numbers of Jews who should have been Roumanian citizens under the Minorities Treaty, but had been prevented by chicanery in various forms from completing their nationalization papers.

Nevertheless, the Liberal Government, driven on, perhaps, by the pressure of public opinion and constrained by political necessity to take some of the wind out of the Opposition's sails, has been much less indulgent towards the minorities in recent years. In

May 1935 the Liberal Minister, M. Jamandi, announced with some pride that 'while Dr. Vaida was disquieting the public with his "numerus Valachicus", the Government was quietly carrying out a programme which went beyond it'.[1]

A long step in this direction is the Act for the utilization of Roumanian staff in enterprises, adopted on July 3rd, 1934. This law provides that every undertaking carrying on business in Roumania must have Roumanian staff to the extent of at least 80 per cent. in each of the groups into which the Act divides employed persons (responsible administrative staff, responsible technical staff, subordinate administrative staff, subordinate technical staff, skilled workers, unskilled workers). All chairmen of boards of directors, at least 50 per cent. of company boards and committees, and at least 50 per cent. of auditors must be Roumanians. Where an undertaking employs less than twenty persons, the proportion of Roumanians who must be employed will be fixed by the Government. New industries may receive permits to employ a larger number of non-Roumanians for two years.

The proportion of Roumanians and non-Roumanians to be employed in undertakings directly connected with national defence is prescribed annually by the Ministry of Commerce and Industry. A list of these undertakings, including State undertakings and public services, is drawn up by the General Staff of the Army. It includes munitions plants, chemical undertakings, and undertakings generating power. The head of each undertaking has to submit annually a list of his staff, showing their names, nationalities, duties, remuneration, &c.

Technically speaking, this law, again, is directed only against the non-Roumanian citizen. At the same time, that a distinction is intended between Roumanians by race and members of minorities is shown by the fact that the schedule of staff not only distinguishes between Roumanian and non-Roumanian citizens, but also requires the 'ethnic origin' of the former to be stated. The minorities thus complain that the law is used as a further means of evicting them from employment, particularly in the enterprises 'connected with national defence'—a very elastic term, the definition of which depends solely on the pleasure of the War Office. It seems clear that the intention is to exclude from these undertakings the so-called 'elemente de incredere', viz. Magyars, Bulgars, Jews, and Russians.

Parallel with the pressure exerted under this Act by the Ministry of Industry, Commerce, and the War Office, is a further pressure in the same direction by the Ministry of Labour. I have myself seen a circular (marked 'confidential') which was sent to many

[1] *Nation und Staat*, May 1935, p. 541.

firms (I believe, all large firms in Transylvania), asking for a list of their employees, divided as follows:

Cetateni Români, Români:
Cetateni Români, Minoritani:
Cetateni Străini.[1]

How far members of minorities have already lost employment under the above Act, or in response to pressure, I should find it difficult to say. I have heard expressed many more fears for the future than actual grievances. I have no doubt, however, that strong pressure is being put on many firms to replace their minority directors and workers by Roumanians, and the Act clearly gives the authorities a handle which, if they are unscrupulous, they can use unmercifully.

As I write, I am informed that new legislation is being prepared under which heavy penalties are provided for firms not employing the requisite proportion of Roumanian citizens, while the proposal is also being entertained that the employees of all private enterprises shall be made to pass an examination in the Roumanian language before a State Commission.

In the spring of 1937 it became known that the Government was preparing an Emergency Decree on still more drastic lines. According to well-informed sources, it was proposed to enact that in undertakings working with national capital, 50 per cent. of the directors, &c., and 75 per cent. of all other employees must be Roumanians by race; in undertakings with foreign capital, the figures rise to 60 per cent. and 80 per cent. respectively. The threat to all the minorities is grave indeed.

§ 13. THE ECONOMIC PROBLEM

The inhabitants of Transylvania, like those of Slovakia, complain that their country is treated as an 'economic colony'; and, it would appear, with some substance. Taxation has regularly been much heavier in Transylvania than in the Regat. Figures are not easy to obtain, but it seems common ground that not only is taxation higher in Transylvania, but it is collected far more strictly; according to one of my informants, 85 per cent. of all taxes due are collected in Transylvania, and only 30 per cent. in the Regat. Many firms have moved their head-quarters to Bucharest, in the hope of escaping this discrimination.

It is also very freely stated that no money is spent on public works in Transylvania, the yield of taxation going mainly to the

---

[1] Roumanian citizens, Roumanians:
Roumanian citizens, Minorities:
Foreign citizens.

Regat. Here again I can give no figures, but my general impression would be that the statement is quite correct. One seldom sees in Transylvania a public building of post-War construction, except only Orthodox cathedrals and churches, or elementary schools—for most of their other needs, the Roumanians have contented themselves modestly with appropriating the second-hand buildings of the minorities. Both the road and the railway system are almost entirely heritages from the past, much the worse for their post-War experiences. There is in Transylvania only a single modern road—the Oradea–Braşov section of the Transcontinental road—and that is only half finished. Most Transylvanian roads surpass nightmares. An ambitious programme of railway construction was planned, and is badly needed to fill in the gaps in the economic connexion between Transylvania and the Regat which had been purposely left by the Hungarian Government; but so far as I know, not a single kilometre has been constructed. It is fair, of course, to remember that Roumania, under the Liberal régime after the War, was nothing like so lavish in raising loans as most East European countries, and has in general followed a restrictive monetary policy. No part of the country has been generously treated in the matter of public works, and Bessarabia and the Dobrudja have perhaps come off worse even than Transylvania; but the Regat, and Bucharest in particular, have undoubtedly got such pickings as have been going.

It is also true, as we have mentioned before, that financiers and politicians from the Regat have managed, one way and another, to get into their hands a large slice of the natural resources and even of the businesses of the Regat, and have exploited them ruthlessly enough. In this way also much of Transylvania's wealth has flowed into the pockets of Regatler. Nevertheless, one may logically conclude that if this process goes on much longer, the seven devils of Regatler company directors will at least expel the devil of unequal taxation. The extreme disorganization, corruption, and inefficiency of the whole Roumanian system have also made the conduct of any business much harder than it would be in a country with higher commercial standards and greater legal security. If, however, we disregard such considerations and look rather to the natural factors in the position, it is doubtful whether Transylvania has lost by the annexation. Its communications to the west are, indeed, easier than to the east, and so long as the West European market continues to be so much more important than the Russian, it would seem *a priori* that any area must lose which had to adopt an eastern instead of a western orientation. On the other hand, the distances by road from Eastern Transylvania, at least, to the Danubian and Black Sea ports are comparatively short, far shorter than the journey across Hungary to Fiume; and Bucharest is much nearer than Vienna or even Budapest. But in reality, it is impossible to consider the position of Transylvania as a whole. Generally speaking, the western half of the country has lost and the eastern half has gained. The west had in any case been much more closely connected with Budapest, whence it is now divided by the frontier, while Bucharest is a long and expensive journey away. There was, moreover, a close economic connexion between the hills and the lowlands, including seasonal migration similar to that of Slovakia and Ruthenia. In the Maramureş, in particular, conditions are very much the same as we have described them in Ruthenia. The harvest labour has ceased, the timber, under present conditions, is unsellable, and the population in the mountains has been reduced to the greatest misery. In the Crişana the agricultural conditions are somewhat better, but the industry of the whole western strip (except only that of the Reşiţa ironworks, which have been largely occupied in munitions) has gone steadily downhill. The milling industries of the northern towns, and certain other factories which had entertained close relations with the Budapest market, have lost their *raison d'être*. An indication of the serious situation is the large emigration into the Regat which has taken place since the War from these districts, particularly the Department of Bihor.

But perhaps the most grievous blow of all was dealt only in quite recent times. There were still certain large industries which occupied a vital place in Roumania's national economy, notably the great Astra locomotive works at Arad and the similar but smaller Unio works at Satu Mare. In 1935 it was decided, for strategic reasons, to remove both of these to Braşov. The gap which they will leave is one which can hardly be filled.

Central and Eastern Transylvania, on the other hand, have undoubtedly gained on balance. Agriculture has passed through a difficult time. Protected up to 1918 by the Austro-Hungarian tariff, it has now been brought into full competition with the agriculture of the Roumanian plains, where conditions are far more favourable than in Transylvania. The full fall of the blow was mitigated for a time by the fall in production resulting from the land reform in the Regat, but the effects of this have now passed away, and cereal-farming in Transylvania, except for home consumption, is now hardly a paying proposition. On the other hand, Transylvania is well adapted both for cattle-farming and market-gardening, and the Germans, in particular, are adapting themselves with some success to the new conditions.

There is, moreover, a large traditional seasonal migration from the Székely districts into Wallachia. This has been greatly facilitated by the displacement of the frontier, while the Székely also readily seek and find employment in Bucharest as domestic servants, coachmen, and factory-workers.

Transylvania is well placed to become the industrial centre of Roumania. Its industries, with few exceptions, do not compete with those of the Regat, so that even where financiers from the Regat have bought them up, it has not (as in Slovakia) been in order to close them down. In fact, Transylvanian industry has developed more rapidly than that of the Regat since the annexation. Brașov, even before the migration of the factories mentioned above, had swollen to over twice its previous size (to the great detriment of its old-world charm). It is planned to make it the centre of the whole Roumanian munitions industry. Mediaş (Megyes), also, has become an important industrial centre.

Whether Transylvania is more important for the economy of Roumania or of Hungary, is a subject which would require a volume in itself. In the old days, when the present Slovakia and Ruthenia formed part of Hungary, Transylvania was of secondary importance, since most of its raw materials, except mercury and methane gas, are also found in the Northern Carpathians. To-day the position is different, and the timber, coal, and mineral deposits of Transylvania would be invaluable to Hungary. It also, however, rounds off the Roumanian economy very neatly since few of its natural riches, except only timber, are found in large quantities east of the crest of the Carpathians.

§ 14. POLITICAL FEELING AMONG THE NATIONALITIES

When we turn to assessing political feeling, we must count the Roumanians, almost solid, as in favour of their new State. There is, as we have said, much ill feeling between the Transylvanian Roumanians and the Regatler; much discontent, many accusations of exploitation. Nevertheless, the Roumanians would oppose, almost to a man, any question of a return to Hungary. They would not to-day even welcome a resurrection of the old Austro-Hungarian monarchy, remodelled on a federal basis as Francis Ferdinand might have attempted. The Magyar minority is hardly less implacably unreconciled to Roumanian rule. There are in Transylvania none of those little pro-Government grouplets to which the inquirer is so innocently guided in other districts by helpful officials who are anxious that he should 'see both sides for himself'.[1] There is not even any important social differentiation,

---

[1] The parties founded in opposition to the official Magyar Party have never endured for long. The most successful hitherto has been the Magyar Peasant Party, which secured three seats in the Parliament of 1932/3. A 'Union of Magyar peasants and workers of Roumania', formed in the summer of 1934 out

for Roumania, as we said, has made no serious attempt to break up the national solidarity of the minorities by offering any one class of them special social or political advantages—nor, indeed, has her system very many such advantages to offer. The only class which has shown any disposition to think on social rather than national lines (except for a very few landowners who have sought friends in Bucharest to save their estates) has been the small group of workers. Among them, one can hear the relative demerits of Roumanian and Hungarian rule weighed with a certain impartiality based on distaste for either, although possibly with a slight bias in favour of Roumania. The Roumanian reaction, one is told, is less dangerous than the Hungarian, because it is less well organized. The general social and political structure of Transylvania at least is more democratic than the Hungarian, the administration less austerely anti-social. With a little baksheesh, a worker can get a hearing. On the other hand, the present Roumanian national drive is threatening the Magyar workers as much as any class of the whole minority. It has already squeezed many of them out of their humble positions in the Government service, and is now threatening their security in private enterprise also.

An interesting effect is that many of the workers migrate to the Regat, where labour is in demand and no one is rejected for not being Roumanian. Indeed, the Germans and Magyars are very generally preferred as better trained and more trustworthy. If this process continues, the result will be that the Magyar working-class element which could be reconciled to the Roumanian State will have moved bodily to the Regat. There they may possibly be Roumanized, but they will not be able to form a counterweight to the irreconcilables in Transylvania. And even the workers contain a good many irreconcilables.

Many of the skilled workers belong to the Social Democrat Party which exists in a state of suspended animation. More, probably, are secret adherents of the Communist Party, which flourishes underground. In any case, however, the workers form only a small proportion of the total majority. The peasants and agricultural labourers, a much larger body, still think and feel nationally. A considerable number of them benefited, it is true, under the agrarian reform; and it is often suggested that these persons would not desire to return under the feudal Hungarian régime.

of dissentients from the official party, accepts the Roumanian State and advocates an advanced social policy, in collaboration with Roumanian democrats, but insists very strongly on minority rights. I cannot believe either of these two parties to be important, since although I discovered their existence from print (to wit, from a Roumanian year-book), I never heard a single reference to them when visiting the country fairly thoroughly in 1934 and 1935.

If they believed that they risked losing their land in consequence
of revision, this would probably be the case, but I have not once
heard this fear expressed; no one believes in any such possibility.
As things are, the gain was pocketed ten or a dozen years ago,
since when the Magyar peasants have suffered much from a host
of grievances which loom large in their lives; arbitrary decrees,
corrupt notaries, brutal gendarmes, the burden of taxation which,
rightly or wrongly, they believe to be unequally imposed and still
more unequally collected, the strain and expense of having to
conduct every official transaction (or at least all which require
the written word) in an unfamiliar language, probably through
the medium of a paid interpreter. Moreover, the Transylvanian
peasants have been hard hit economically by the great fall in
agricultural prices, for which (unjustly but naturally) the Government is blamed, and the local Magyars have not the great advantage
of their cousins in Slovakia of being purveyors in chief to an
industrial community. Agricultural prices in Roumania are even
lower than in Hungary. Thus, the ownership of the land once
acquired, there has been no economic consideration to set against
national feeling.

The great majority of the Magyar peasants are undoubtedly
nationalist to-day. Some years ago, when great demonstrations
against frontier revision were organized on the frontier, a couple
of Magyar villages joined in them, and this was proclaimed as
a voluntary gesture, showing that the Magyar peasant preferred
Roumania; but the very officials who told me the story did so
without conviction, almost shyly, and there seems no doubt that
the 'voluntary demonstration' was made under strong official
pressure. Unreliable as Roumanian electoral statistics are, they
do not err in favour of the opposition, and when they show, as
they do, that the percentage of votes cast for the Magyar parties
equals or exceeds the proportion of Magyar electors,[1] this is convincing proof that there can be no defalcation of any important
social element. Equally unsuccessful have been Roumania's
attempts to drive a wedge between the Székely and the 'true
Magyars'. The Székely may continue to despise the Magyars as
inferior and later imitations of themselves, but they will never
admit themselves to have anything in common with the Vlachs,
and they have held out against all inducements to make a 'separate
peace' with Roumania. The various minority churches never
carry to the outer world any differences which may exist between
them. Thus practically all sections of the Magyar population

[1] The Roumanians calculate the Magyars at 7·7 per cent. of the total population, and the votes cast for the Magyar parties have ranged between 7·5 per cent.
and 9 per cent. of the whole. Dragomir, op. cit., p. 269.

throughout the transferred territories present a common front
against the Roumanian and all his works.

The positive wishes of the Magyars are less easy to define than
the negative. The programme of the Magyar National Party,
which varies little from year to year, envisages the largest possible
measure of self-government compatible with the unity of the
State. It reverts in fact to the medieval 'privilege' system which
survived so long in Transylvania, demanding the organization of
the country into 'nations'. The Magyar 'nation' is to have the
right of self-government, conducting its own administrative and
judicial system through the medium of its own officials. All
religions are to be free, equal, and autonomous. Education is to
be conducted through the autonomous churches and it is to be
Magyar in all stages, although instruction in Roumanian language,
history, and geography is admitted. The army is to be a militia,
instruction to recruits being given in their mother tongue.
Communes and departments are to have wide powers of self-
government.

This programme is, of course, little more than a gesture. The
Alba Julia Resolutions would have conceded a large part of it,
but no Roumanian government to-day would think of granting
even a tenth of it. It is, however, interesting as showing the fundamental point on which all Magyars are agreed: that they wish for
as little Roumanian control as they can possibly achieve.

If, however, the programme is a maximum one in the sense that
it asks for more than it can ever hope to get from the Roumanian
State, it does not necessarily represent also the real maximum
wishes of the Magyars, since no party could safely put forward
openly irredentist demands. Those real wishes, where revealed,
show an interesting divergence which is indeed on local lines,
but less between Székely and Magyars than between the Magyars
of the western districts and those of Transylvania proper.

The Magyars of the Crişana, Maramureş, and the Banat regard
themselves simply as part of unitary Hungary, cut out of its living
body by an unjust frontier. There is no separate local feeling, no
tradition of co-operation with the other local nationalities. They
spend their time looking wistfully across the adjacent frontier and
complaining (often with reason) of the Roumanians. They do not
even attempt, so far as I could judge, to live on tolerable terms
with the non-Magyars. Even a tennis club which was started in
Timişoara failed because the different nationalities could not play
peaceably together. Their ideal is certainly a return to Hungary
and, what is more, a return to the old national order, in which
the Magyars and the Magyars only should rule and the minorities
be kept in their places. (The Magyarized Jew who expounds these

ideals in Oradea or Arad resembles so exactly both in appearance and mentality the Magyarized Jew who expounded them in Lučenec or Košice, that the traveller wonders wildly whether the man has somehow cut across the frontier and bobbed up again to rub in the points made at the previous interview.) If, like good Magyars, they hold as their ideal the restoration of Hungary's pre-War frontiers, their immediate interest lies in their own position, and it is hardly conceivable that they would refuse local revision which stopped short at the Transylvanian frontier.

Incidentally, there is no discernible difference, over these questions, between the outlook of the older generation and the younger. If there is any development, it follows the lines of the development in Hungary, and does not affect the national outlook. In Transylvania itself there is a marked difference, due in part to altered social conditions. True, in the west the material foundations of the old social order have crumbled, but the social outlook has remained intact. In Transylvania the extreme feudal outlook characteristic of Western Hungary never prevailed. There were a few very large estates, but the average Transylvanian land-owner was always a comparatively poor man, living modestly on an estate which was neither very large nor very fertile. On the other hand, in the Székely districts there were still in 1918 many free peasants with a long tradition of independence behind them. The agrarian reform swept away the big estates—and I was greatly struck, in 1935, by the absence of repining with which this measure was regarded, so far as it affected individuals. As for the 'Hungarian Optants', they enjoyed extraordinarily little sympathy. The reform has created a society far more homogeneous than that of Hungary proper, or even of Slovakia; a community of squires and peasants whose standards of living are not so very far apart, and a small bourgeoisie whose life in the little hill-towns has not estranged them from their country cousins.

Consciously or unconsciously, this society is developing very much on the lines which the Saxons have adopted so successfully. The corporate institutions—the Churches, the political party, the co-operative societies (which have been excellently organized and conducted by a young member of the Bethlen family)—count for more than the individual. Each class seeks to help and understand the other. Very characteristic is the keen interest taken by the younger generation of townspeople, particularly the students, in the villages, where they spend much of their vacations, carrying out social and educational work and themselves learning the problems of rural life. The Churches and the political party carry on similar work. In such modest fashion, renouncing the ambition to rear an imposing super-structure, but laying the foundations very firm and deep, the Transylvanian Magyars hope to shelter from the present storm.

In this atmosphere, the old Transylvanian spirit has revived in remarkable fashion. 'The Magyar youth of Transylvania', said a recent writer, 'is Transylvanist. It wishes to live in Transylvania and for Transylvania.'[1] For them the party programme summarized above approximates to the ideal. They would like to see a modification of the old Transylvanian system, i.e. the cohabitation of three 'nations'—now the Magyar, the Roumanian, and the German—on an equal footing, each enjoying the widest possible self-government. This is by no means a return to the old order, since they genuinely recognize that the *de facto* inferiority of the largest element could no longer be defended. And it is interesting that, for this very reason, few of them would welcome an unconditional return to the Hungary of 1914. I have heard prominent men in the National Party say that no good purpose could be served by restoring Transylvania unconditionally to Hungary because 'the country has, after all, a Roumanian majority. We are now under the Roumanians but it would be no remedy simply to reverse things and put the Roumanians under us.' Moreover, the social and political order in Hungary is severely criticized in Transylvania. There is no more wish to return to the old social system than to the old national system.

Meanwhile, there is perfect willingness to co-operate with the young Roumanians, a willingness frustrated by the consistently intransigent attitude of the latter. It is tragic, although natural, that so long as the Roumanians asked only for equality, Hungary refused it to them; when the Magyars ask it, they encounter only Roumania's will to power and a rapid diminution of Roumanian autonomist feeling which postpones the realization of their dream to the Greek Calends.

The distinctive Transylvanian feeling of the Magyars must by no means be interpreted as treachery to their Magyar nationality. They feel themselves perhaps a rather different kind of Magyar, possibly fated to a different destiny, but not less Magyar than the men of the Alföld. Clearly, if they had to choose between a Magyar and a Roumanian national state, they would prefer the former. They would, however, prefer to either a Transylvania in which they could enjoy genuine national liberty and develop their particular local institutions undisturbed.

Feeling among the other minorities is nothing like so clear-cut as among the Magyars, for the Roumanians have, as we have shown, made considerable efforts to detach them, both nationally and politically, from the Magyar cause, and these efforts have not

[1] G. Zathmeczky, in *Nouvelle Revue de Hongrie*, July 1933, p. 709.

been wholly ineffectual. The most important minority, the German, has received the largest favours. As individuals (although the losses of their Church were, as we have said, very heavy) they suffered less under the land reform than the Magyars, and in almost every other respect they have been far more leniently treated. They have been allowed to retain a considerable number of officials, and where Roumanians have been sent into the Saxon districts, these have usually been picked men. The Saxon businesses have not been required to take on many Roumanian employees, the Lutheran Church has not had to complain of forced conversions, elections have been conducted cleanly in the German districts, and they have been allowed to organize in *Vereine* as many and as various as they desired.

Moreover, their cultural life has not been repressed but, in the case of the Saxons, allowed practically unrestricted freedom, and in the case of the Suabians, actually fostered. The encouragement has been, it is true, more moral than material, but its value is not to be underrated. These are considerations which must weigh heavily with a people which, after all, is in a very different position from the Magyars. For the Germans, it is not a question whether they are to be the under or the upper dogs. They will always be a minority and the most they can look for is to find good masters and to make good terms with them. In this they will always be guided exclusively by their own interests, which will be unaffected by any sentiment of loyalty, gratitude, or affection. That the Saxons voted for the Roumanian State in January 1919, and the Suabians accepted it some months later, is no more proof that they necessarily prefer Roumanian rule to Hungarian than is the fact that at every election since 1919 they have formed electoral pacts with the Government. They have simply adopted the ingenuous but successful role of the Vicar of Bray. As a matter of fact, in several visits to Transylvania since 1919, I have always found the canny Saxons chary of expressing an opinion on the rival merits of Hungarian and Roumanian rule. Even when complaining most bitterly of abuses suffered at the hands of the Roumanian authorities, they have declined to commit themselves to the statement that it was better under Hungary. There were things to be said on both sides. . . . The land reform and consequent impoverishment of the churches and schools had been a grievous blow, the administration was a thing to weep over, but, on the other hand, there was much less cultural pressure; the Roumanians left them pretty well alone. . . . No, it was about fifty-fifty, a choice of two evils.

The Suabians, on the other hand, were, until two years ago, very definitely pro-Roumanian, on cultural grounds. Nationalism took them late, but, like mumps, it raged all the more fiercely when it came, and the worthy Suabians became so enthralled in the delights of building up German Kultur in the far south-east as to become blind to almost any other consideration; particularly as Timişoara enjoyed also a considerable material prosperity, as the centre of a fat little world of its own.

The flourishing German culture, the Church, the primary and secondary schools (crowned by the boarding-school, 'Banatia', which every visitor must inspect), the newspapers, bookshops, libraries, cultural evenings, *Vereine*, *Verbände*, and *Vereinigungen*—all these formed a picture which was contrasted ever and again with the position of the Suabians in Hungary, fighting so vainly for the 'B' and even their 'C' schools. It is impossible to exaggerate the effect of this comparison, and of the incidents which occurred from time to time in Hungary to drive it home; the publication of the Hungarian census of 1930, showing an apparent diminution of over 70,000 in the number of Hungarian Germans; the demonstrations against Professor Bleyer, the German leader, in 1933; the trouble over the elections of 1935, where German candidates with nationalist leanings had a most unhappy time at the hands of the authorities, &c.

The peasants were not, indeed, nearly so entranced as the intellectuals. The cultural question meant less to them than the material and administrative. With regard to the former their position had not improved (in the Banat all the peasants owned their own land) while the latter had deteriorated. Perhaps if each man's opinion had been asked separately, there would always have been a majority which thought Hungarian ways better. But the Suabians, like all Germans, are a disciplined people. They obey their leaders, and their leaders would always have voted unhesitatingly for Roumania. They have, in fact, joined quite spontaneously in anti-revisionist demonstrations. In the last two years the increased pressure of the Roumanians, combined with the economic crisis, has caused a certain cooling off of the first enthusiasm. This had coincided, however, with a fresh and even more violent wave of national feeling among the Germans, causing them to attach even greater weight to the comparative cultural liberty which they still enjoy.

An interesting by-product of the German Magyar cultural struggle is the bitter war waged between the two minorities for the body of the Szatmár Germans,[1] who have thereby acquired an importance quite out of proportion to their numbers. While the unfortunate people itself is in a state of complete confusion about itself (it is not uncommon to find a family in which the grand-

[1] See above, pp. 271, 312.

parents speak only German, the parents only Magyar, the elder children Magyar and the younger children German), Germans and Magyars fight like tiger-cats for the possession of them. A young German leader said to me personally that he was opposed even to any local frontier revision in favour of Hungary because this would expose the Szatmár Suabians to a renewal of Magyarization; a Magyar leader declined to mediate in Hungary in favour of the Suabians there until the Germans ceased trying to filch the Szatmár group from their Magyar allegiance.[1]

But even apart from this, the Germans and Magyars have totally failed to co-operate in the new Roumania. The Saxons in particular have shown not the smallest compunction in sacrificing their fellow minorities wholesale where they could get the smallest advantage for themselves. I remember seeing an electoral proclamation issued by the Magyars of Sighisoara (Schässburg, Segesvár) (a mixed town in which the Magyars number 20 per cent., the Saxons perhaps 50 per cent.) before the local elections of 1934. For ten years, this pathetic document proclaimed, the Magyars had concluded electoral pacts with the Saxons. Not one Magyar had during that time sat on the City Council. When officials had been dismissed after 1918, Magyars had always had to go; when vacancies occurred, Saxons had always been put in. Only one Magyar was still employed by the municipality, and he had been put in by Roumanian influence. Two hundred and fifty thousand lei had been received in subsidies for cultural purposes, and the Saxons had taken every leu for themselves. The Magyars had therefore turned to the Roumanian Liberals, made a coalition with them, and had promptly received their share of subsidy for schools and churches, and a proportion of seats on the Council.

I quote this document, not to pillory the good city fathers of Sighisoara—the most beautiful of all the old Saxon cities—but to emphasize the complete absence of any solidarity between the German and Magyar minorities in Transylvania. As already remarked, the minorities have only once combined at Parliamentary elections; nearly always, they have attached themselves to various Roumanian parties. In recent years, however, the political life of the German minority has developed along lines which makes it impossible to consider it purely under the aspect of specifically Saxon or Suabian, or even exclusively Transylvanian, interests. These new developments, incidentally, make of the German minority a far more important political factor than they were in the old days when the Saxons stood practically alone as representatives of the German spirit. All in all, the Germans of Roumania number certainly not less than 700,000; for besides the 225,000

---

[1] M. Jakábffy in *Nation und Staat*, July–Aug., 1933, p. 650.

Saxons, the 275,000 Suabians of the Banat and the 30,000–
40,000 Szatmár Suabians of the old Hungary, there are some
70,000 Germans in the ex-Austrian Bukovina (a highly organized
community, which under Austrian rule possessed a University
of its own at Czernowitz), 80,000 in Bessarabia, 10,000 in the
Dobrudja, and about 20,000 in Wallachia. These various groups,
living respectively under Hungarian, Austrian, Russian, and
Roumanian rule, naturally had no political relations before the
War, and were indeed hardly conscious of each others' existence.
In 1919, however, when the Saxons put forward their own
national demands at their meeting in Mediaş, they expressed the
hope that the same rights would be accorded to the other German
groups in Roumania, that the national unity of all those groups
would be recognized, and that they would themselves follow the
Saxons' lead. The Sachsentag of November 1919 again spoke in
the name of all the Germans of Roumania, and again asked for
a single national statute. Following this meeting, a 'Verband der
Deutschen Grossrumäniens' was established as a central political
and cultural organ to co-ordinate the work of the various 'Volksräte'.

The Verband, although it met annually, accomplished little for
several years. It discussed policy and suggested candidates before
Parliamentary elections; but it was quite inactive in cultural
matters, and showed neither the ability nor even any keen desire
to foster national unity. Even the 'Volksrat' for Transylvania
failed to maintain itself. The Suabians of the Banat, and even
those of Satu Mare, founded separate 'Volksräte', and each group
made, roughly speaking, its own policy and lived its own life,
mainly under the direction of its ecclesiastical leaders; the
Lutheran Church for the Saxons, the Catholics for the Suabians.
Each made its own terms with the Roumanians; the Saxons, under
their highly accomplished political leader, Hans Otto Roth, the
more successfully. In about 1930 things began to change. The
leader of the new movement was Herr Fabritius, of Sibiu, who
had been prominent as early as 1912, but especially after the War,
in certain social activities. In 1930–1 Fabritius initiated a more
active 'Erneuerungsbewegung', the nature and objects of which are
rather difficult to describe. He himself and his followers describe
it rather as a new 'attitude towards the world' than a new policy.
It includes, at any rate, a strong, if somewhat mystical German
national feeling, with a social outlook strongly sympathetic to the
peasant and the artisan and a general adulation of 'Jugend', the
whole flavoured with a dash of anti-Semitism.

Fabritius was soon joined by a much more radical group under
Herr Gust, who carried his imitation of things in Germany much
farther still, organizing S.A. and S.S. and introducing into the

sedate Transylvanian press tones to which its strings had been
untuned for centuries. Between them, Gust and Fabritius founded
a National Socialist Party of the Germans in Roumania ('Neda')
which, having not much else to do, occupied itself largely with
attacking the old leaders.

The latter regarded the movement with discomfort mingled
with incomprehension, and hardly concealed their satisfaction
when the Roumanians, under the influence of Francophil circles
in Bucharest who disliked any untoward spread of Nazi ideals,
threatened to dissolve the 'Neda' as dangerous to the State. In
the hope, however, of maintaining the national unity, they agreed
to dissolve their own 'Einheitspartei' if the 'Neda' were banned.

The ban duly fell in 1934 (after M. Barthou's visit to Roumania),
but the 'Neda' reappeared soon after under the new title of 'Deutsche
Volkspartei', this time with Gust in charge, and Fabritius as a sort
of honorary Führer. Thereupon the 'Einheitspartei,' which had
never dissolved in more than name, reconstituted itself also, and
an immensely complex struggle ensued—all the winds of Aeolus
in a dessert coffee-cup. To call it a fight between the old and the
new would be a gross over-simplification, for on the one hand,
Gust and Fabritius soon parted company, and on the other, the
Conservatives were themselves rent by personal differences, which
cut right across the division of principle between Suabians and
Saxons. It seems unprofitable to follow the intricacies of manœuvring which went on, reminiscent of nothing so much as the children's game of twos and threes. At the time of writing (September
1936) Herr Fabritius had, rather unexpectedly, emerged as Führer-
in-chief, with the tacit support of Roth, who remained head of
the German Political Party and chief intermediary between the
Germans and the Roumanian Government, and of most of the
Conservatives (who regard him as the lesser evil), with Herr Gust
and Herr Bonfert (the latest pretendant to the radical leadership)
in bizarre alliance with the veteran Saxon leader Brandsch (who
had been deposed from his own position for showing insufficient
activity) constituting the radical opposition. Meanwhile, the
Church retains an immense amount of quiet influence and may
outlive all the Führers yet.

In many ways, the whole thing had been much ado about
nothing; for as one old gentleman, father of a young aspirant to
power, said to me plaintively, the Saxons have for centuries past
already practised all the essential points of the Nazi philosophy.
They have always been strongly Germanic; always placed the
'Volksgemeinschaft' above the individual; have based their power
on the rich peasant and the small bourgeois, not bothered their
heads about Parliament, and had no truck with Jews. The only

essential new point seems to be the determination of the 'Er-neuerer' to subordinate the Church to the political control; and strong as is their argument that in no other way can complete national unity be achieved, the counter-argument is equally valid that Roumania is under no obligation to give a German 'Volks-gemeinschaft' any rights whatever, nor even to recognize its existence, while the Churches do enjoy considerable guaranteed rights and practical autonomy.

Certainly, however, the revitalized 'Verband der Deutschen in Rumänien', over which Herr Fabritius was presiding at the time of writing, represents a new force in East European politics—a very greatly increased feeling of national solidarity which pre-vails among all the Germans in Roumania. They are conscious of kinship and community of interest, both among themselves and with other Germans, particularly the Germans of the Reich, and those of Hungary.

The last-named point is the more important, for even the Germans see the absurdity of claiming Roumania as any part of the German Reich, nor are they numerous enough in Roumania to influence its foreign policy. But in a question of frontier revision, as between Roumania and Hungary, their voices might turn the scale, and it is therefore necessary to state plainly that at present, in any case, they take Roumania's side both publicly and (I believe) in their hearts. They are, of course, opposite to the extreme chauvinistic Roumanian policy, rejecting assimilation and claiming the right to a certain separate position in the State, with a degree of self-government under their own officials. They maintain, however, that the younger generation of Roumanians are themselves moving towards the ideal of the 'Volksgemein-schaft', and regard the German ambitions not unsympathetically. They are not antagonistic to the Roumanian State as such, recognizing the superior numbers of the Roumanians and their right to self-determination. And their leaders have expressed to me their active opposition even to frontier rectification in Hun-gary's favour, on the grounds that the present Roumania makes possible the unification of a large number of scattered German groups, and that frontier revision, even on a local scale, would presumably mean the loss of the Szatmár Suabians and possibly of the Banat Suabians as well. So long as Hungary persists in the policy of Magyarizing her minorities in general, and of refusing even to recognize the German nationality of the Szatmár group in particular, they actively support Roumania's claims against those of Hungary.

There can be no mistaking the sincerity and depth of this feeling. Again and again, inquiring among the younger Germans

of every class and type, I have met with almost identical answers:
'We have nothing to gain by going back to Hungary.' 'The
Germans in Hungary are worse off than we.' Not that they have
any affection for Roumania or Roumanians. No consideration of
gratitude or loyalty would bind them if the choice were theirs to
make again, any more than it bound the Saxons in 1919. They
would, however, never willingly return to Hungary upon any
conditions short of very far-reaching national autonomy, which
they would doubtless insist must be granted to all the Germans of
Hungary. If she wished for their suffrages, Hungary would have
to make very generous offers in this direction, and to bind herself
very strictly to fulfil them.

The position of the Jews is a sort of caricature of that of the
Germans. They have been de-Magyarized and restored to themselves. That is, they are entered in the census as a separate
nationality, allowed and even encouraged to form a political party
of their own, and given the opportunity of having as many Hebrew
schools as they care to pay for. But these gifts are a two-edged
sword. The Hebrew school is useless to any child destined for
a career other than that of a rabbi, and the Jew when he appears
as a Jew is perhaps even more unpopular in Roumania than when
he wears the guise of a Magyar.

Political feeling among them is very mixed. The older generation of the Magyarized Jews in Cluj, Oradea, and Arad still clings
to the memory of Hungary with remarkable loyalty. One of the
opposite party suggested to me, indeed, that his Magyar compatriots expected revision to come and feared to compromise
themselves, but I think that he under-estimated their qualities
both of heart and head. The devotion with which many of them
have stuck to their old protectors has made the sudden *volte-face*
of the Suabians look shabby indeed. Several of them have used
to me really touching language regarding their kindly treatment
by Hungary in the past, and the unbreakable spiritual bond which
still unites them to the fatherland. Not a few have got into
grievous, easily avoidable trouble for their vigorous espousal of
the Magyar cause. But this attitude is getting less and less easy to
keep up. The Magyars themselves do not always encourage it.
If their older generation finds the Jewish alliance natural, the
younger men are so far affected by the ideas of to-day as to look
a little askance at it. The Magyars are not nearly so anti-semitic
as the Germans or the Roumanians, but the Székely, in particular,
do regard the Jew as definitely a different animal from themselves.
Moreover, they get on more easily with the Roumanians without
him. More than one Roumanian has told me that he can reach
a sensible understanding with the local Magyars when they are

represented by their own men, but he simply cannot deal with the limitless ingenuity and exaggerated patriotism of the Magyarized Jew. The Magyars feel this, and are turning a little away from their old allies.

Far more bitter are the complaints which one hears of the attitude of the Hungarian Government. Rightly or wrongly, the Jews declare that Hungary has afforded them no recognition whatever for their devotion. She has used them to swell her statistics, but she has not lifted a finger to help them. 'Why', said one to me, 'should I run after a car which will not take me up as a passenger?' And another, a young man, said, 'I cannot be Hungarian because Hungary has introduced the "numerus clausus".'

The greater part of the younger generation have therefore moved away from Hungary. On the other hand, they cannot conceivably become Roumanians. Their religion enjoins the large Orthodox and Sephardian communities of Szatmár and Maramureş to be good citizens of Roumania, while others who have found comfortable niches in the economic system (and that system offers many opportunities for enrichment, not apparent at first sight; thus the Szatmár Jews are said to make a considerable income by smuggling) have snuggled into them and would doubtless be sorry to leave them. But of any sort of sentimental attachment to Roumania there is no trace, nor could it be expected; the students' excesses, the vicious propaganda of the Right, the systematic refusal to many thousands of the right of citizenship, make it impossible to look for any friendship; at the most there may be what the Germans call an 'Interessengemeinschaft' with certain circles. There is not even, among the Transylvanian Jews, any desire for assimilation to Roumanian ways such as is found commonly enough in Bucharest. On the whole, the Transylvanian Jews have agreed with the Roumanians to regard themselves as — Jews. The non-political 'Union of Roumanian Jews' and the Jewish political party, both of which have their chief strength in the annexed provinces, represent the attitude of most of the Transylvanian Jews to-day. They are correct in their relations to the State, and for the rest they lead their own life. But they are profoundly unhappy. If they can no longer be counted as safe allies of the Magyars, neither are they pro-Roumanian.

The other minorities are unimportant by comparison. The largest of them, the Serb, is the only one which could well present any danger of irredentism, and it is peculiarly situated owing to the existence of the Yugoslav-Roumanian alliance, besides being culturally protected by the special treaty already mentioned. I can only say that the Serbian leaders, cultural and political, with whom I spoke (a Serbian Party was founded in Timişoara in 1934, while the Church provides the real national rallying-point) expressed the most correct of sentiments. As for the other small minorities, whether they find life tolerable or not seems to depend chiefly on the personal character of the village notary and the gendarme.

§ 15. THE POSSIBILITIES OF REVISION

What, then, has been the balance of the last fifteen years of Transylvania? As we have seen, the story of these years has consisted, essentially, of a simple turning of the tables. In 1914, Transylvania was ruled by and for the Magyars, without and largely against the Roumanians, with the Saxons occupying a sort of middle position. To-day, it is ruled by and for the Roumanians, against the Magyars, with the Germans still in the middle—culturally better off, socially and economically worse off. Where the Magyars formerly had the political power, the Roumanians have it to-day. Instead of Magyar and a few German officials, and no Roumanian, there will soon be Roumanian, a few German, and no Magyars. Instead of a State-supported Magyar education, with struggling Roumanian and German schools, there is now State-supported Roumanian education, while the Magyars (and the Germans again) have to struggle to keep their schools in existence. Where Magyar industry and agriculture got easy credits, Roumanians get them now; and so on and so on.

Since, under the old régime, only some 30 per cent. of the population were top dogs and at least 55 per cent. under dogs, whereas the proportions have now been reversed, one may perhaps say that, if one accepts as the most desirable goal the greatest happiness of the greatest number, the last state is at least better than the first. But the contention of the Magyars (with which the Saxons to some extent agree) is that the happiness of the Roumanians themselves, not to speak of the minorities, is not best achieved by handing over to them the exclusive power over the country. The Roumanians, they say, are the largest numerical element, but they are also far the most backward. The culture, the intellectual and civic life of the country is, exclusively, the work of the Saxons and Magyars. The Roumanians have ever been uncreative, incapable of evolving even for themselves any sort of higher existence, and totally unfitted to rule over others. Whatever they possess in Transylvania they owe to the minorities, and when given their full freedom of action, they will simply despoil the minorities and by doing so choke up the wells from which they draw their own sustenance.

Historically, the minorities are perfectly right; and as regards the present, the experience of the last fifteen years has supported their case only too well. The whole life of the country seems, as it were, to have been dropped bodily on to a less civilized plane. Standards all round have been lowered. The administration and even the justice seem less honest, less hard-working, less efficient. The trains are less punctual, the police regulations more tiresome, the officials more brutal and more exorbitant, the streets dirtier, the very bugs in the beds bite more confidently, as though feeling that under the new order people do not mind them so much. Things go to ruin and are not repaired, either because the authorities are accustomed to second-rate, shoddy, patched materials or because some one has pocketed the money voted for repairing the damage.

Hitherto, also, the Roumanians have constructed little in Transylvania. They have simply taken over what the minorities had accumulated in past centuries, and are living on it, and often not even keeping it in its old state. As we said, it is rare to see a new building in Transylvania, except only an Orthodox church or perhaps a barracks; for the rest, all that is beautiful and almost all that is valuable seems to date from a long time ago.

Thus the prophecies of the minorities have hitherto justified themselves with dismal accuracy. Moreover, it is quite possible that the worst may be yet to come, for the Roumanization of the administration is only now being completed. It is only now that the new generation of Roumanians is replacing the survivors of the old system, who had still maintained some of its earlier traditions; only now that Roumanian national feeling is developing its full force.

Nevertheless, it is impossible to maintain that the Roumanians of Transylvania are not happier under the present régime than the old. Their position before the War was neither tolerable nor tenable. The rusty shackles of an earlier age, which they wore on their wrists, had to be snapped. For shackles they were. It is true that in theory the Roumanian citizen of Hungary was equal to any other, and the way to the highest positions in the State lay open to him equally with the true Magyar, the Slovak, or the German. But the conditions which Hungary, rightly or wrongly, laid down were such as the vast majority of Roumanians (unlike the Germans or Slovaks) were, rightly or wrongly, unable to accept. They were thus condemned to the narrowest local life, without hope of advancement. Even the benefits of the superior administration were probably little apparent to them, since in the last years a large part of the Government's efforts had been devoted to the purely political end of securing Magyar supremacy. To the Roumanian, the State was thus simply a machine for thwarting his ambitions, just as the educational system was a machine for altering his language—with the result of leaving him illiterate. It is an immense advantage to the Roumanians to be able to develop freely along their own lines, to be able to look forward to a more spacious existence attained through the cultivation, not the repression of their national instincts. The benefit to those to whom the way now lies open, through the new system of Roumanian education, to a higher career, is too obvious to need emphasizing. But even the Roumanian peasant and woodcutter, who aspires to no other position in life, has acquired a new self-confidence, a new hopefulness which contrasts strongly with the mixture of fear, suspicion, and resentfulness with which he used to regard the world. This is a healthy thing, which will benefit in the long run all the peoples of Transylvania. It will be better for the Magyars and Germans themselves if their Roumanian neighbours achieve a higher standard of civilization and self-respect.

Even the economic measures which we have described have their silver lining. Those who do not dissent from the almost universal prejudice in favour of peasant proprietorship will find the present system of land distribution in Transylvania preferable to the old. The total cultivable area held by proprietors of 10 hectares or under has risen from 2,536,738 ha. (34 per cent.) to 4,200,547 ha. (56·45 per cent.), that held by owners of 100 ha. or more having fallen from 2,751,457 (37 per cent.) to 1,087,648 ha. (14·61 per cent.) (the medium property of 10–100 ha. remaining unchanged at 2,153,117 ha., 29 per cent. of the total).

The landless agricultural class, and the category owning too little for the support of their families, although not wiped out, has been greatly reduced. The new owners have not had a happy time, owing to the terrible agricultural crisis which has hit Roumania as hard as any country in Europe. They have become deeply indebted, and the Government has had to come to their rescue by a large-scale cancellation of debts on small properties and conversion of others. Yet during the period when money was almost non-existent in Roumania, the peasant proprietor, who simply retired into his shell and lived a self-contained life similar to that of his ancestors two thousand years ago, certainly suffered far less than the agricultural proletariat of other countries. If he could not sell his produce, he could at any rate eat it.

The land reform has not, on the whole, resulted in a decrease of production. There was a considerable fall during the years 1920–4, as compared with the pre-War figures; this was due partly to the effects of the reform, partly to those of the War, while in some of these years, especially in 1924, the weather was also unfavourable. Both the area under cultivation of the main crops and the total produce rose thereafter rapidly until 1929, after which the effects of the world agricultural depression began to be felt. Since that date, they seem to have remained at approximately the pre-War level.[1]

In the long run, too, it must benefit the whole country that the Roumanian acquired business experience, even that a class of Roumanian skilled workers is beginning to grow up. The standards are still very low and the customer who is forced to buy Roumanian products is far worse served than he who can buy, say, the produce of experienced Saxon firms. But the broadening of the basis of economic life in Transylvania cannot but benefit the country in the long run.

Thus even allowing the past to have been a Slough of Despond as deep and as quaggy as you will, it was one which had to be traversed before the life of Transylvania could be set on a sounder footing. But is firmer ground really in sight?

In one respect Transylvania holds an advantage over Slovakia or Ruthenia. The economic position is not fundamentally, unalterably unfavourable. There is nothing in its natural situation to prevent a recovery if the world situation improves and if the new masters learn to handle their material.

As to this, there are some small signs of hope. If part of the new generation is of simply excruciating quality—infinitely inferior to their delightful peasant fathers—yet one meets, nowadays, a certain proportion who, after passing through a training entirely Roumanian, which owes nothing to the old traditions, yet manage to combine patriotism with intelligence and decency. Maybe Roumania will breed in time a whole generation which the minorities will learn to respect.

But what then? Respect may come; liking is improbable, reconciliation to the idea of living under Roumanian rule is as far off as ever. And even the non-Magyar minorities, it must be emphasized, do not like Roumanian rule; the farthest that any of them go is to prefer it to Hungarian. The Roumanians, on their side, are farther than ever from admitting any of the other nationalities to a partnership within the State, so that their régime continues, more than ever, to be the domination of slightly more than half the population over slightly less than half. And this, if a sounder situation than the converse, is not satisfactory as a permanent settlement.

It is impossible, then, to regard with any complacency either the present position or the future prospects of Transylvania under Roumanian rule. On the other hand, a return to the past is neither desirable nor practicable; the clock does not move back so easily.

[1] See on this point Rusu, op. cit., pp. 371 ff.; and Transylvanus, op. cit., pp. 42–3.

Hungarian official and *officieux* circles themselves recognize an essential difference between the situation of Transylvania and that of Slovakia or the Voivodina. They admit that the Roumanian population is in a slight but definite numerical preponderance, that it separated from Hungary of its own accord and has not since changed its mind.[1] They seem, therefore, to admit that the Transylvanian problem would not be solved by simply restoring the country *en bloc* to Hungary, as an integral part thereof. It is interesting that, as has been noted, many of the more thoughtful Magyars in Transylvania itself hold the same view, and some of them do not even desire such an integral restitution for their own sakes.

Magyar opinion, both in Hungary and in Transylvania, inclines therefore to the view that the best solution would be the restoration of an independent Transylvania, either entirely independent or very loosely linked in some way with one or both of its neighbours, and constructed on the old model of the Renaissance State of Transylvania, with its constitution remodelled and brought up to date. There would be, as of old, three 'nations', but these would now consist of Magyars, Roumanians, and Saxons. Each would enjoy complete autonomy in its internal affairs, and complete equality with the other two in the common affairs of the country.

This solution has theoretically much in its favour. Transylvania is really a unit with a very strong separate geographical, historical, and cultural identity. It has never been so glorious and probably never so prosperous as during its periods of independence. Moreover, this is the solution best adapted to the ethnographical conditions. The Roumanian majority, although it is absolute, is small, and it seems hardly more equitable that the Roumanian 55 per cent. should rule over the 45 per cent. of the remaining nationalities than it was for the privileged 'nations' of old to rule over the Roumanians. The Constitution would require very careful elaboration, for the success of any such political experiment depends entirely on the just and complete application of the principle of *suum cuique*. Nevertheless, a nearer approach to a just settlement could probably be made along these lines than along any others, and it would be easier to-day than ever in history, owing to the events of the last twenty years. The old inequalities between the different nationalities have largely vanished, and it would be easier now to achieve the genuine equality which would be an essential condition, than it has ever been before. Conditions might be more favourable still in a few years' time, when the Roumanians have

---

[1] See particularly Count Stephen Bethlen's lectures delivered in England in 1933 and collected under the title *The Treaty of Trianon and European Peace*, especially pp. 87–8, 98, and 129 ff.

proceeded farther in their long overdue task of creating a national bourgeoisie.

This solution would be welcomed eagerly by the local Magyars, and it is fairly safe to say that the Saxons would accept it gracefully. The difficulty lies, of course, in the fact that not only would it be rejected out of hand by every Roumanian in the Regat, but not 1 per cent. of the Roumanians of Transylvania themselves would look at it. The number of Transylvanian Roumanians who favour any sort of federalization within Roumania is, as we have said, diminishing rapidly, and the small remnant of federalists, with hardly an exception, envisage only so much devolution as will ensure their retaining the supremacy over the other local nationalities. Equality is, unhappily, never desirable to those who can enjoy mastery.

Further, it must be remembered that when Transylvania was independent, there was no Roumania; only a pair of disorganized provinces under Turkish suzerainty. These exercised no attraction on the Roumanians of Transylvania (who were also far weaker than they are to-day relatively to the rest of the population). The situation would be very different to-day, and it is quite possible that the mutual attraction between the Roumanians of Transylvania and those of the Regat (which seems to outweigh the mutual repulsion) would prove too strong to be resisted. Probably, therefore, the plan is more desirable than feasible.

Either failing this solution, or in conjunction with it, there is a good case for some local revision. It seems to me, unfortunately, quite impracticable to fulfil the wishes of the Hungarian Revision League and to restore to Hungary the Székely districts *en bloc*, with a long narrow corridor (which would have to include Cluj) to join them to the main body of Hungary. This would leave Northern Transylvania completely in the air (since there is practically no communication across the Northern and Eastern Carpathians) and the situation would be an impossible one, economically and administratively, both for the Roumanian districts of the north and for the Székely enclave itself. Transylvania hangs together.

The position of the western fringe is different. The strip of plain containing the towns of Arad, Oradea, Careii, and Satu Mare would probably never have been left to Roumania but for the wish to give her a line of transverse communications by rail. It is true that there is no alternative line leading to North-Western Roumania, and Professor Temperley has suggested that Hungary might offer to construct one.[1] I should myself go further, and say that Roumania should construct her own line. Professor Temperley

[1] Temperley, 'How the Hungarian Frontiers were Drawn', in *Foreign Affairs*, April 1928, p. 445.

also points out that the north-west 'could only be fed from the rich plains of the south, and their sustenance was carried by the railway through the Arad-Szatmár strip'.[1] It seems, however, to have escaped the notice of those responsible for this frontier that the population of Maramureş cannot really be fed at all if it is cut off from the Hungarian plain. Its livelihood depends on this plain, and the present frontier, failing freedom of trade and migration, practically condemns it to starvation, or to charity.

I believe that there would be a good case for including the whole area north of the Rodna mountains in Ruthenia. The population of Maramureş consists at present (Roumanian census of 1930) of 93,200 Roumanians, 11,181 Magyars, 3,239 Germans, 19,305 Ruthenes, 33,798 Jews, and 780 others, most of whom are gipsies. The numbers of Roumanians could probably be reduced by certain readjustments of the frontier, both with the Bukovina (it runs at present some miles eastward of the highest crests) and with the south. Even to-day, it may be remarked, Sighet cannot be reached by rail from Roumania without passing through foreign territory. The real importance of the line through Satu Mare is not that it connects the department of Maramureş with the rest of Roumania, but that it joins Roumania with Czechoslovakia. Like Ruthenia, of which it forms the geographical continuation, this corner of the Carpathians is a dead weight economically on any country possessing it, except perhaps Hungary, but it is strategically important as joining two allies and separating Hungary from Poland.

The population of the four Departments of the Crişana consisted in 1930 of approximately 1,550,000, of whom about 880,000 were Roumanians, 415,000 Magyars, 75,000 Germans, and 65,000 Jews. Broadly speaking, the inhabitants of the mountains are Roumanians, while the plains and the wider valleys running up into the mountains are Magyar. Only round Arad does the Roumanian population spill down into the plain. A frontier could easily be drawn which approximated to the optimum ethnographical line, and would restore to Hungary over 400,000 Magyars, with only about 40,000 Roumanians. Such a line would, however, have to wind its way through the foot-hills, and would create a difficult economic situation in view of the close economic connexion between mountain and plain. On the other hand, I cannot follow the argument that the present frontier is economic, for the economic connexions, not only of the plain but also of the whole western slope of the mountains, are with Hungary as a whole. There seems to me, therefore, to be a good case for restoring to Hungary both the northern strip of plain and the mountains which

[1] Op. cit., p. 440.

rise immediately above it. This would not involve handing back to Hungary all 880,000 Roumanians, for, besides the diminution to be expected from the withdrawal of troops and officials, the boundaries of the Departments themselves reach in places across the water-shed and could be readjusted so as to leave a considerable number of Roumanians within Transylvania; and secondly, the Department of Arad where the Roumanians come down into the plain does not stand quite on the same footing as the territory farther north. Here the frontier would turn west until it reached the present line. It should be possible to draw a line which, while economically much superior to the present, would not sacrifice more Roumanians to Hungary than it restored Magyars, while still leaving in Roumania many more Magyars than there would be Roumanians in Hungary.

In the Banat the position is different again. Here the population of the mountains is still Roumanian, but that of the plains is chiefly Suabian, and under present conditions it is necessary to assume that the Suabians would resist a return to Hungary. In any case, the limits of the Banat were not divinely ordained, and most of the mountains go naturally with Transylvania.

One change in the frontiers of the Banat is desirable in any case. The decision to give Vršac and Bela Črkva to Yugoslavia instead of to Roumania was a last-minute resolve, and an unfortunate one. The local Serbs, it is true, outnumbered the Roumanians;[1] but from an economic point of view the line adopted was quite singularly unhappy. Not only does it sever the mountain from the plain, but it cuts the communications in a way calculated to cause the maximum of inconvenience to both parties. On the one hand, the southward communications from Timișoara are blocked by the westward bend of the frontier north of Vršac; on the other, the line from Vršac and Bela Črkva themselves passes once more into Roumanian territory before reaching the Danube. The construction of an alternative line and port would lay no intolerable burden on Yugoslavia; for that matter, a line from Vršac to Pančevo already exists; but for Roumania the alternative is far more difficult, since the hinterland is rugged and mountainous.

---

[1] According to the 1910 census there were in the towns of Vršac and Bela Črkva 10,653 Serbs and 2,685 Roumanians. The parts of these districts assigned to Yugoslavia contained in all 40,609 Serbs and 24,520 Roumanians. A large part of the local population is German.

YUGOSLAVIA

§ 1. INTRODUCTION

THE only portion of modern Yugoslavia with which this work need concern itself in detail is the area which in 1918 formed an integral part of Hungary proper—a strip of the southern plain, no more than one-third as large as Slovakia-Ruthenia or one-fifth the size of Greater Transylvania. Yugoslavia, however, comprises also certain much more extensive territories over which the Hungarian Crown exercised, or claimed, sovereignty: Croatia-Slavonia, which actually lay within the frontiers of the Lands of the Hungarian Crown; Dalmatia, which was *de facto* a part of Austria, but claimed by Croat and Hungarian jurists on the strength of an ancient constitutional link with Croatia; and even Bosnia and the Herzegovina, of which Hungary insisted on being considered part owner, after the Austrian Emperor and King of Hungary had annexed those two provinces in 1908. To describe the whole past history and present circumstances of all this territory would take us far beyond the dimensions of the present work; but some account of the Croatian question is essential, if only for the understanding of the problems of the Voivodina.

CROATIA

§ 2. GEOGRAPHY AND POPULATION: THE CROAT
MOVEMENT UP TO 1914

Croatia-Slavonia, as it existed in 1918, was a curiously shaped territory, to look at on the map rather like a battle-axe laid, head outward, along the south-western frontier of Hungary. The blade of the axe is composed of wild mountains, bounded in the north-east and south-east respectively by Carniola and Bosnia. In the south-west these mountains fall abruptly to the sea; in the north-east, they slope more gently down to the valley of the Save. The axe's shaft is a long, tapering stretch of land bounded by the Save in the south, the Drave in the north. In the west, those rivers are far apart, and green mountains divide them; in the east, as the rivers draw closer, the mountains flatten out into hills; and after the Drave has mingled with the Danube, the hills have merged into a rich, flat plain.

These frontiers are, however, of comparatively modern date. When the Magyars first entered Hungary they found a kingdom of Croatia already in existence; but its centre was in Bosnia and Dalmatia, and the Save and the Kulpa formed its northern boundary. The union between this kingdom and that of Hungary is usually held to date from 1102, when Coloman I of Hungary ascended the throne of Croatia. Whether he did so in virtue oɩ conquest, of inheritance, or of free election, and whether Croatia was subordinate to Hungary (*partes subjunctae*) or an equal partneɩ (*partes adnexae, regna socia*), the sole link between the two kingdoms being the person of the king, are questions hotly disputed to this day between Hungarian and Croatian historians. Probably, in reality, the original relationship was incapable of definition by modern terms. Certainly it varied greatly from time to time. At some moments Croatia acted as a completely sovereign State; at others she was treated as a vassal. She always, however, retained a large degree of internal independence.

The upper portion of the country between the Save and the Drave—to-day the heart of Croatia—was known at that time as Slavonia, and appears usually to have been regarded as belonging to Hungary (although during some periods a single 'Ban' or governor seems to have ruled both Croatia and Slavonia). It enjoyed, however, considerable privileges, which at times approached those of Croatia itself. Most notably, Magyars were not allowed to settle in it. The lower part of the country between the Save and the Drave, Syrmia, was long disputed between Hungary and the Byzantine Empire, and when finally conquered by the former was incorporated as an integral part of Hungary.

In the fourteenth and fifteenth centuries, Dalmatia and Bosnia passed into the hands of Venice and the Turks respectively. There was a gradual drift of population northward, and 'Upper Slavonia' came to be considered as Croatia. We now find the name Slavonia applied to the old district of Slavonia and Syrmia.

In 1526 Hungary was defeated at Mohács. Croatia, whose army was still intact, hastened to make terms with the Emperor, the more eagerly since Hungary seems to have been pressing hard on Croat independence.[1] In fact the Croatian Estates, who were quickly followed by the Slavonian, recognized Ferdinand of Austria as king before Hungary did so. This, however, although an independent act, was no declaration of separation, since the Emperor was not recognized as King of Croatia, but of Hungary.[2]

The Empire in the event proved just what Hungary had threatened to become—a mother who ate her young. Not only

[1] See the interesting letter written by the Ban of Croatia to the Bishop of Zengg when the news of the battle of Mohács arrived, exulting in Hungary's defeat as the 'lasting salvation' of Croatia. Cit. Seton-Watson, *The Southern Slav Question*, p. 19, n. 2.

[2] Marczali, *Ungarisches Verfassungsrecht* (Tübingen, 1911), p. 32.

were the privileges of the Estates severely limited, but the territory over which they exercised any effective control was greatly reduced. The Turks had already conquered practically all the old Croatia, as far as Zengg, and Slavonia. Under the Empire the whole southern strip of what remained to Croatia was separated off and formed into a special 'Military Frontier', under the direct authority of the Emperor. When, in 1699, the Lika district and Slavonia were recovered from the Turks, they too were formed into frontier districts, although in 1745 most of Slavonia was restored to the civilian administration, albeit on somewhat uncertain terms, being disputed for the next century between the Ban of Croatia and the Hungarian Estates.

The Austrian rule, and in particular the institution of the Frontiers, was of lasting importance for the Croatian question. On the one hand, they introduced considerable national minorities into what had been nationally an almost homogeneous territory. The indigenous Croat population of the frontier districts was largely reinforced by new settlers: a few of these being Germans, but many more being Serbian or Vlach[1] refugees from the Balkans. These formed an element not only racially and religiously different from the Croats, but also with different political ideals, since their loyalty was given not to the Croatian Estates, still less to Hungary, but to the Emperor of Austria. Partly owing to the influence of these 'Grenzer', partly to the religious differences which obtained in the seventeenth century between Croatia—which easily accepted the Counter-Reformation—and Hungary—where the national party resisted it—Croatia took at times, although not always, Austria's side during her struggles with Hungary which filled that century, and a party grew up which favoured severing the constitutional connexion with Hungary and joining Austria.

In the eighteenth century, on the other hand, an active pro-Magyar party grew up, chiefly among the higher nobility, and when the Austrian centralization reached its highest pitch, under Joseph II, some of the Croat nobles actually wished to see Croatia incorporated entirely in Hungary. A third party, of course, understood that in her then position Croatia enjoyed the best of both worlds, and wished for no change at all.

Last of all came the birth of the national movement in the modern sense of the term. This, in its first stages, was rather Yugoslav than Croatian particularist—it termed itself 'Illyrian' and owed much of its first strength, oddly enough, to Napoleon I, who

---

[1] The Vlach element seems to have been particularly strong in the Lika. They were Orthodox by religion, and afterwards assimilated in language also to the Serbs. Many Serbs were brought into Croatia and Slavonia by the Turks in the intervals during which they occupied parts of those territories.

for a few years incorporated most of the South Slav districts of the Habsburg Monarchy in a 'Kingdom of Illyria'. As, however, there was at the time no question of rallying round any particular formation outside the Habsburg Monarchy, the political aims of the 'Illyrians' hardly conflicted with those of the pro-Austrian Party.

In the thirties and forties of the nineteenth century the awakening national feeling of the Croats clashed violently with that of the Magyars, resenting in particular the proposed extension of Magyar as an official language to Croatia; and when, in 1848, the 'March Laws' proposed further violence to Croatia's separate status, Baron Jellačić, in the Emperor's name, led an army against Hungary. He and his friends hoped to realize the Illyrian ideal under Habsburg auspices, by uniting Croatia, Slavonia, and Dalmatia with the Serb districts of South Hungary, in a constitutional State ruled by the Austrian Emperor. The Emperor, however, although he used the Croats against the Magyars, had little more regard for the feelings of the one than the other, placing Croatia and Hungary alike under a centralist and absolute régime. When later events obliged him to make his peace again with Hungary, he sacrificed Croatia to her without scruple, inviting the Croats, when they approached him in 1866, to negotiate with Hungary on the basis of respect for Croatia's own historic rights and of the integrity of the lands of the Historic Crown. Willynilly, the Croats were bound to accept this invitation, and concluded the famous Compromise (Nagoda) of 1868, which declared Hungary and Croatia-Slavonia (including the three disputed Slavonian Counties and the Military Frontiers) an indivisible whole, constituting a single unit in international relations (including their relations with other territories under Habsburg rule) but allowing Croatia a Parliament of her own and a wide degree of Home Rule in her internal affairs.

The Compromise, although not unfavourable to Croatia's historic claims, was nevertheless bitterly unpopular in the country. The majority which accepted was only got together by exceedingly corrupt methods, and if the successive 'Bans' (governors) appointed by Hungary were able to retain their hold on the country and even to gather round them a party of 'Unionists', this was due mainly to the exceedingly restricted franchise,[1] which allowed a quite disproportionate weight to the landowners and officials who formed almost the sole Magyarone Party in the country.

The mass of the people detested the Hungarian connexion. Easily the most popular figure in the country was M. Starčević, who advocated a policy of pure, uncompromising Croat nationalism.

---

[1] In 1910 only 49,000 persons out of a population of 2,622,000 in Croatia-Slavonia were enfranchised.

His party, however, was meagrely represented in the Sabor owing to the narrow franchise; moreover, it had no practicable policy to suggest, since Croatia could not, in practice, defy Hungary and Austria at once. After his death his party split in two, and the Jewish-born Dr. Frank, who became leader of one of the fractions (now known as the 'Party of the Pure Right', or more popularly as the 'Frank Party') advocated attaching Croatia to Austria, instead of Hungary, as the most practical solution compatible with the ideals of Croat nationalism. But this solution again was impracticable during the lifetime of Francis Joseph who, having concluded the Compromise, abode by it.

The possibility of a Croat-Serb union, which seems so obvious to-day, was by no means equally apparent fifty years ago. The Serbs and the Croats seem to have been closely akin by origin, and when first they reached the Balkans they settled side by side. But thereafter their ways diverged. The Croats looked west, the Serbs east. The Croats adopted Roman Catholicism, and came thereafter under western influences; politically associated with Hungary and Austria, economically also with the Italian States. The Serbs accepted the Orthodox faith, were in close relations with Byzantium, and afterwards passed under the Turkish yoke. The close linguistic community of the two nations came to matter to them much less than the religious, historical, and cultural differences. In the 'Illyrian' movement of the early nineteenth century, indeed, the cultural leaders of the two had visions of a greater national unity, and in 1848 there was a good deal of political co-operation, notably between the Croats and the Serbs of Southern Hungary. The idea of Yugoslav unity was, however, only embryonic at the time, if only because Serbia herself was not yet fully independent, while Bosnia was still under *de facto* Turkish rule until 1878. After that date Serbia became independent and the Yugoslavs now at last possessed a 'Piedmont' round which their ambitions could centre; but apart from the fact that for twenty years the King of Serbia was a mere creature of Austria, the strengthening of Serbian national feeling by no means meant a corresponding increase in *Yugoslav* feeling. On the contrary, so soon as Austria had occupied Bosnia, Croatia began to remember her dim historic claims to that country—thereby infuriating the Serbs, who also had designs on it; while more important still were the dissensions which arose over the position of the Serbs in Croatia. Since the incorporation of the Military Frontiers, these numbered something like 25 per cent. of the whole population, the figure rising to 45 per cent. in the County of Syrmia. As their confidence increased, they began to press for 'equality of rights', which the Croats showed no disposition whatever to grant. Ill feeling between the two elements grew rapidly and was skilfully exploited by the Magyars, who supported the Serbs in every way. Count Kuhn Héderváry, who ruled Croatia for twenty years, opened Serbian schools, filled the public offices with Serbs, favoured their economic development, appointed a Serb President of the Sabor, and allowed himself to be fêted in Mitrovica as 'the Serbian Ban'.

As recently, therefore, as the end of the nineteenth century, relations between the Croats and the Serbs of Croatia were strained, nor was there any strong feeling in favour of union with Serbia either among the Croats or among the Serbs themselves. About that period, however, a certain *rapprochement* began between the younger men, largely under the influence of Professor Masaryk (many of the students of both nationalities used to go to Prague to escape the repressive atmosphere of Croatia). Among the youthful apostles of Yugoslav co-operation it is interesting to find the names of Stiepan Radić and Svetozar Pribičević. The hostility was, however, still active enough (there were anti-Serb riots in Zagreb in 1902) when a sudden change came about consequent on the crisis of 1904 between Hungary and the King-Emperor. A number of Croat Deputies, led by M. Supilo and Dr. Trumbić, of Dalmatia, took the momentous decision to ally themselves with Hungary against Austria for the price of certain reforms in the Austro-Hungarian Compromise, and the incorporation of Dalmatia in Croatia. A resolution to this effect was adopted at Fiume on October 2nd, 1905, by 40 Croat Deputies for Croatia, Dalmatia, and Istria, and on October 26th, 26 Serb Deputies agreed to support it. The only dissentients were Dr. Frank's Party, representing extreme Croat Particularism, a few extreme Serbs from the Banat, and the Peasant Party recently founded by Radić. The alliance with Hungary broke down within two years over a dispute regarding the official language on the railways; but the Serbo-Croat alliance remained. The Croat elections of 1908 gave the astonishing result of 57 seats for the Serbo-Croat Federation, 0 for the Magyarophil Party, 24 for the Party of the Right, and 7 for the Peasant Party—each of the two latter having been prepared to compromise with Austria, but not with Hungary.

In the same year came the annexation of Bosnia and with it the disappearance of the last hopes of a reconciliation between Serbia and the Monarchy. Thereafter the idea of Yugoslav unity made rapid progress. The feeling of the masses seems to have been well expressed in a court martial for a desertion when a sergeant of the reserves declared that 'the Croats were always loyal to the Emperor, but he did not love them and delivered them over to the Magyars, so that they were forced to turn to the Serbs, who at least spoke their language'. The superior officer who took down this deposition concluded from it that Croatia would in time be entirely lost to the Monarchy.

It will be convenient to give at this point the population figures of the 1910 census. This gave the total population of Croatia-Slavonia as 2,621,954, of whom 1,630,354 were Croats and 644,955 Serbs, the two nations thus forming together nearly 90 per cent. of the total population.

The most important of the remaining nationalities was the Magyar, whose numbers had risen from a few thousands a half-century earlier to 105,948 in 1910. Only a few of these, however, had their roots in the soil. There were three or four old Magyar villages near the Hungarian frontier, and some thousand more recent colonists who had been settled through the activities of the Budapest banks. There was a certain Magyar or Magyarized upper class, and a Magyar-speaking Jewish business class of some importance in Zagreb. Finally there were the officials: a small number of senior officials and a much larger number of railway employees scattered all over the country (since the railways, under the Compromise, were controlled, not by Croatia but by Hungary). It was through these railwaymen that Hungary was making her chief effort to consolidate the Magyar element in Croatia: schools (known as the 'Julian schools', after the society organizing them) were opened for their children, and inducements held out to the children of other nationalities to attend them. The Germans (134,078) were more numerous than the Magyars, but less influential. In Syrmia they formed a fairly high percentage of the rural population; other villages were round Osjek. Osjek itself and many other Croatian and Slavonian towns had been mainly German a century earlier, but the German bourgeoisie was losing its individuality, some to the Magyars, others to the Croats.

The 21,613 Slovaks, the 846 Roumanians, and the 8,317 Ruthenes were peasant colonists, and the 67,843 'others' included also a substantial quantity of Czech settlers. The remainder were Slovenes on the north-western frontier, some Italians from the coast, and gipsies.

§ 3. THE UNION WITH YUGOSLAVIA

By 1914 the party in favour of Hungary had practically vanished. A proportion of the elder generation, and of the clericals, disliked the idea of making common cause with Orthodox Serbia, but the majority of the active young leaders had become irredentist at heart. There was a certain reaction at the beginning of the War, which both Dr. Frank's and Radić's party applauded, while the Serbo-Croat coalition sat silent; and when Italy joined the Allies and the terms of the Treaty of London leaked out (as they soon did) Croatian opinion set strongly against the Allies and in favour of the Monarchy. None the less, negotiations were set on foot with a view to realizing Yugoslav unity after the War. A 'Yugoslav Committee' of émigré leaders from Croatia and Dalmatia was founded, which opened up negotiations with the Serbian Government. There were innumerable difficulties, but in July 1917 the so-called 'Declaration of Corfu' was signed between Pašić, the Serbian Premier, and Trumbić, representing the 'Yugoslav Committee'. This affirmed categorically the unity of the Serbs, Croats, and Slovenes and their intention to form a constitutional, democratic, and Parliamentary monarchy, called the Kingdom of the Serbs, Croats, and Slovenes, under the Karageorgević dynasty. This was to comprise all the territory inhabited compactly and in territorial contiguity by the three branches of the people, who were to be equal among themselves. The Constitution was to be drawn up by a Constituent Assembly, elected by free, equal, and secret suffrage, and was to allow for the possibility of 'local autonomies delimited by national, social, and economic considerations'. This Pact was signed, as its preamble stated, by 'les représentants autorisés des Serbes, Croates et Slovènes', and the Sabor at Zagreb, asked by Hungary to disavow the Committee, had refused to do so. The Serbo-Croat Coalition refused also to support the 'May Declaration' made by the Yugoslav Club of the Austrian Reichsrat in 1917 for an Austro-Trialist solution of the Yugoslav question. The Slovenes themselves, to whom the May Declaration was chiefly due, were probably being more diplomatic than sincere in enunciating it, and when the imminent collapse of Austria became apparent a 'National Council of Serbs, Croats, and Slovenes' was set up in Zagreb on October 6th. This Council claimed to be the sole responsible and authorized party for the conduct of national policy, and declared its object to be 'the union of the whole people of the Serbs, Croats, and Slovenes on the whole ethnographical territory inhabited by them, irrespective of any political frontiers, in a single entirely sovereign state'. On October 29th the Sabor declared 'all constitutional links dissolved between the Kingdom of Croatia, Slavonia, and Dalmatia on the one hand, the Kingdom of Hungary and the Austrian Empire on the other', and called into being a 'Federal State of the Slovenes, Croats, and Serbs' of the ex-Austrian and Hungarian territories. The Ban thereupon surrendered the executive power into the hands of the Council, and two days later the Emperor handed over the Austrian fleet to it. The local Councils which had sprung up in Ljubljana (Laibach), Split (Spalato), Novi Sad, Sarajevo, &c., recognized the Council as their supreme authority.

§ 4. THE CROAT PROBLEM: 1919–29

The Sabor took its decision of October 29th, 1918 to sever constitutional relations with Austria and Hungary quite freely, and in doing so it undoubtedly expressed the will of the great majority of its representatives. Of the 88 Deputies in the Sabor, only the 9 members of the Party of the Pure Right were against any form of union with Serbia, while no less than 65 belonged to the Serbo-Croat coalition. There is no reason to suppose that feeling in the country was any less strong against the Hungarian connexion.

It remains, however, true that no two peoples since the War have bickered more continuously and more acrimoniously, or have shown a more complete and pig-headed reluctance to meet each other's point of view, than the Serbs and the Croats. The story of their relations cannot, therefore, be broken off at this point—which, indeed, constituted a beginning rather than an end.

We have already mentioned the existence of certain very deeply rooted differences in the historical traditions and the national psychologies of the two peoples. To these must now be added very fundamental differences, which became exceedingly apparent, in their conceptions of the new State. It is important to realize how little either nation was, in reality, spiritually prepared for the union. The Yugoslav ideal meant a readiness on both sides to join hands; it did not mean that either had renounced its own national feeling in favour of a wider 'Yugoslav' feeling. Serb and Croat, indeed, knew very little of each other in 1918. Serbia's national ambitions had for decades past been concentrated on Macedonia, Montenegro, and Bosnia—where, as in Dalmatia, those ambitions had immediately come into conflict with those of the Croats. The Croats genuinely regarded the Serbs as belonging to another world, and potentially, if not actually, hostile to them. For the average Serb, again, the Croat was a man who spoke, indeed, the same language as himself, but was obviously not of the same nationality, if only because his religion was different.

There was no question of simple fusion, such as took place in Roumania, but only of an adjustment of the relations of two kindred but different peoples. Now, unhappily, the ideas of the two as to the proper relationship were, and have remained, incompatible.

To the Serbs the principle of the unitary state was and is fundamental. During their century of gallant and extraordinarily successful national struggles they had increased their territory more and more, but always spreading outward from a central core. The expansion had always taken the form of a greater and an ever greater Serbia, built up firmly round this strong core; and they did not believe any other system durable or even feasible. When, therefore, they were offered the juicy morsels of Croatia-Slavonia and Slovenia they did not spew them out (although one party would have preferred to do so), but they never even thought of treating them as other than newly acquired parts of a Greater Serbia still.

It was not that they necessarily wished to 'Serbize' the Croats and Slovenes. This accusation is regularly levied against them, but the best proof of its falsity is that whereas the chief distinguishing mark between Serb and Croat is the difference of religion, no attempt was made to force the Orthodox religion on the Croats, while the Slovenes have in practice enjoyed complete religious and cultural freedom since 1919. But they felt profoundly that the State belonged to them, the Serbs, and that no one else could be allowed to control it—in which fanatical centralism, it is only fair to say, the Serbs of Serbia were easily out-distanced during the first years by the 'prečani'[1] Serbs of Croatia-Slavonia, led by M. Pribičević.

The Croats, on the other hand, had an equally strong tradition in favour of federalism. They, during all their history, had been on the defensive, not the offensive: building up barriers and sheltering behind them, not breaking them down and expanding over new fields. Theirs was the psychology of the weaker party— a psychology which, it must be said, would have made them excessively difficult to handle, even for a far more tactful people than the Serbs. They are essentially negative: they criticize, they oppose everything, but even if they know what they want, it is practically impossible to get them to say it. A Serbian ex-Minister once said to me: 'For the Serbs, everything is simple; for the Croats, everything is complicated.' He told me, in this connexion, of one cabinet meeting, from the days when Croats were participating in the Government, at which a Croat Minister rose to his feet and in majestic oratorical periods poured forth a long list of grievances. The Prime Minister, who was genuinely anxious to reach an understanding, whispered to my friend, 'You know, the man's right', then aloud to the Croat: 'That's what you want, is it! Well, all right, we grant it.' Whereupon the Croat, in high indignation, replied: 'Not so fast, not so fast—we must talk about all that.'

I will not dwell on their continual and most tactless harping on the superiority of their culture and morals, which, in so far as it is still true, is due to their long association with Western influences, and is in any case rapidly diminishing—Croats have played a part of unenviable prominence in several of the more recent big

---

[1] = beyond the river; a term applied to the newly joined territories beyond the Save and the Danube. It is chiefly used of the Voivodina, but also in the more general sense.

financial scandals in Yugoslavia; but it certainly adds to the difficulty of an understanding, and I have at times admired the patience shown by the Serbs under it.

Thus, from the very first, the points of view of the two parties were not merely different, but contradictory. The clash came at the very outset. The Zagreb National Council had sent their President, Monsignor Korošeć (the Slovene leader), to represent them in Western Europe. The objections of Italy to the existence of the Government which Monsignor Korošeć claimed to represent were no stronger than those of Pašić, the Serbian Premier, who wished Serbia alone to be represented at the Peace Conference. Under pressure from various quarters, including the French Government, he gave way so far as to recognize the National Council as 'the legitimate Government of the Serbs, Croats, and Slovenes living on the territory of the Austro-Hungarian Monarchy'; and on receipt of the telegram to this effect the representatives of the Serbian Government, the Zagreb National Council, and the Yugoslav Committee met at Geneva on November 9th and produced the 'Geneva Declaration', proclaiming the union of the two States on the basis that each should exercise complete sovereignty over its own territory, while a joint Ministry should be established for common affairs.

But although the Ministers of this Government were actually appointed, their term of office only lasted until the evening of the same day. The Serbian Government in Corfu, on learning what had been done, immediately withdrew its ministers. The Zagreb Council was left in the dark; it knew nothing of what had been done at Geneva until November 20th. Meanwhile, the Prince Regent had appealed to Svetozar Pribičević, head of the Serb fraction in the Serbo-Croat coalition and a vice-president of the Zagreb Council, to 'hasten the union with Serbia'; at the same time the Serbs of the Voivodina and Slavonia were being urged to declare for direct union with Serbia,[1] and Serbian troops had occupied Croatia, as though it were enemy territory. These methods triumphed: the Council met on November 24th under Pribičević's presidency, disavowed the Geneva agreement and decided in favour of a unitary state. It then dispatched to Belgrade a Commission of twenty-eight members with full powers to 'realize the national union completely and radically'. On December 1st this Commission handed over the sovereignty over the 'Yugo-

---

[1] For these details see Pribičević's own account in *La Dictature du Roi Alexandre* (Paris, 1933, interesting, but written in a period of great embitterment), pp. 40 ff.; Dr. A. Kosutić, 'The Croatian Problem', in *International Affairs*, Jan.–Feb. 1933 (extreme Croat point of view); and, for a neutral account, Dr. E. Holzer, *Die Entstehung des Jugoslavischen Staates* (Berlin, 1929), pp. 35 ff.

Slav State' in the ex-Austro-Hungarian territories to the Prince Regent, who received it and thereupon proclaimed 'the union of Serbia with the lands of the independent State of Slovenes, Croats and Serbs in a single Kingdom of Serbs, Croats, and Slovenes'. The local administrative services and Councils were to continue to act for the time being, while a provisional National Assembly was to be composed by agreement between the Zagreb National Council and the Serb and Montenegrin political parties. Preparations were to be made for the election of a Constituent Assembly on a basis of universal, direct, secret, and proportional suffrage, and the Prince Regent declared solemnly that he would 'always remain true to the great principles of Constitutionalism, Parliamentarism and the widest democracy based on universal suffrage'.

On the strength of this Declaration, a single Provisional Parliament was got together and a Government chosen, which began work. Serbia had imposed her point of view; but she had overridden opposition, not conciliated it. Even though the decision in the National Council had been taken with only two dissentient voices among the twenty-eight members present, it probably did not represent the considered opinions even of the majority which approved it. It was taken hurriedly, in a moment of extreme national excitement, and was strongly influenced by considerations of international policy, since the conclusion of some sort of agreement was urgent, if Italy was to be prevented from swallowing up the Croatian and Dalmatian coasts.

One of the two dissentients, moreover, was a person of very great importance in the country. This was Radić, leader of the Peasant Party who, although the restrictive franchise limited the number of his followers in the Sabor to three, was already beginning to wield the almost hypnotic influence among the Croat people—the most suggestible in Europe—which caused them to follow him blindly for the next ten years. And as luck would have it, Radić, who in his career championed almost every conceivable idea, was at that moment an ardent Croat particularist and a republican. He was in favour of a Southern Slav State, but he wished only for a formation elastic enough to admit within it a Croatian Republic enjoying almost complete independence.[1]

The real opposition to the unitary State was thus very considerable, and it was not slow to express itself. The decision of December 1st was hardly taken before the Party of the Right was protesting against it, denying the representative character of the mission which had gone to Belgrade and of the decisions reached

---

[1] Extracts from Radić's speech on November 24th, 1918, are reproduced in Pavelić, *Aus dem Kampfe um den selbständigen Staat Kroatien* (Wien, 1931), pp. 40–8.

there.[1] On March 1st, 1919, the same party came out with a pro-gramme of an independent Croatia (with Slovenia), with no more than an irreducible minimum of 'common affairs' with any other State.[2] Radić, having first—so he alleges—escaped an attempt on his life by bravoes hired by M. Pribičević,[3] organized a monster petition to the Peace Conference for a 'neutral Croatian Peasants' Republic' with a Croatian Constituent Assembly of its own.

The Government took no notice whatever of these demonstra-tions, except to throw Radić into prison and to keep him there (with one fleeting interval) until November 28th, 1920—the day before the elections to the Constituent Assembly. Not the smallest relaxation was made of the iron military control, and no concession towards Croat particularism.

It was, indeed, conceivably just possible to argue that the measures taken during these two years were of an emergency nature, that the future form of state would be settled by the Con-stituent Assembly, and that in fact Croatia had been adequately represented in the Government by those who, so far as could be judged, were her proper representatives.[4] The elections to the Constituent Assembly, however, which—surprisingly enough—were held quite fairly in Croatia, showed Radić's party to be much the strongest, and the supporters of a centralist State to be practically confined to Pribičević's Serbs (the majority of the votes not going to either of these two parties were captured by the Com-munists). And Radić lost no time in showing his hand: for he forthwith petitioned the Prince Regent as 'the Regent of the fraternal Serbian State' and *de facto* head of the military power in Croatia, declaring the Address of December 1st, 1918, as 'irre-vocably null and void', since it ran counter both to the letter and spirit of the Sabor's decision of October 29th, 1918, to the peti-tion sent to the Peace Conference in February 1919, and to the 'plebiscite of November 28th, 1920'; and asking him to put an end to the dictatorship of the army in Croatia and to allow the country 'to work for a new national and State life in fraternal and equitable agreement with Serbia and in indivisible community with the other Southern Slavs'.[5]

[1] Text in Pavelić, op. cit., pp. 48–9. [2] Ibid., pp. 52–3.
[3] See Radić's autobiographical notes in *Current History*, October 1928, pp. 104–5.
[4] In the first (Concentration) Cabinet, which took office on December 21st, 1918, the Croat-Serb Coalition was represented by two members and the 'Croat Union', formed by a combination of part of the Coalition with the centralist wing of the Party of the Right, by one. The remainder of the Coalition then fused with the Democrats, and when the latter took office in August 1919 Pribičević continued in his post of Minister of the Interior, which he had filled in the Concentration Cabinet, and Trumbić retained the Portfolio of Foreign Affairs.
[5] Pavelić, op. cit., pp. 53–8.

Thus the Serbs and the Croats had no longer any excuse for not knowing each other's position. Unhappily neither side showed the least sign of wishing to meet the other. The Serbian Radicals, when the Constitution came up for discussion and adoption, rejected a first draft by Protić, which had provided for a large degree of autonomy for the historic units, and passed a rigidly Centralist constitution, after shamelessly buying the votes necessary for their majority (those of the Moslems). M. Davidović, leader of the Democrats, was disavowed by his party when he attempted to negotiate with the Croats. When, four years after the adoption of the 'Vidov Dan Constitution',[1] M. Radić suddenly abandoned his previous intransigent attitude, recognized the dynasty, the frontiers, and the Constitution, and even entered the Government, his new allies made no concession whatever to Croat wishes; and when he returned to the opposition he and other Croat leaders were murdered in the Parliament itself by a Montenegrin desperado, acting in obvious connivance with a considerable number of Serbian Deputies.[2]

The murder was simply an extreme case of the usual Serbian attitude of riding rough-shod over any opposition, without attempting to meet it. On the other hand, it must in fairness be said that the Croat attitude had been very unhelpful. Radić's policy of calling in question the whole basis of the State could not but strengthen the Centralists in their belief that they had been right in not allowing the Croats too much rope; besides estranging hopelessly the King and his entourage of Serbian generals. Moreover, his abstentionist policy was extraordinarily unwise. The Serbs were not the people to be checked by it; they simply took advantage of it. The Vidov Dan Constitution could never have been passed as it was if its opponents had taken part in the deliberations. Radić asked for trouble when in 1924 he went abroad on a false passport, visiting Russia and England, after his party had empowered him 'to initiate diplomatic negotiations with a view to the peaceful realization of Croatia's separate aims'. It was no great wonder that the Government imprisoned him on his return, and a proof of genuine desire to avoid the worst when his recantation was accepted and he himself invited to join the Government. Nor was he a convenient colleague. He dodged in and out of office, attacking his colleagues with as much gusto when in power as when out of it. It was not the fault of the Serbs alone that the 'co-operation' of the two years 1925 and 1926 was hardly better than a farce.

[1] So called because it was adopted on June 28th, 1921, on the Serbian national festival of St. Vitus's Day.
[2] The shots were fired on June 20th, 1928. Radić himself died of his wounds some weeks later. His nephew and another were killed outright, and two other Croat leaders wounded.

But if the faults were not all on one side this does not alter the complete and disastrous failure of the elected representatives of the Serbs and the Croats to come to any sort of agreement, by Parliamentary methods, regarding their mutual relations. The only result of nearly ten years of futile wrangling was to leave the parties at a complete deadlock: the Serbs entirely unprepared to make any concession, the Croats united as perhaps never before in their history, stubbornly denying the validity of any act committed since November 1918; for not only did they insist, after the murders, that they could not continue to sit in the Chamber where such a deed had been committed, but they declared that it had annulled both the Constitution and the declaration of December 1st, 1918.

§ 5. THE CROAT PROBLEM: 1929–36

King Alexander's attempt to solve the Serbo-Croat imbroglio by wiping out Serb and Croat national feeling alike, and welding the whole nation into a single 'Yugoslav' nationality, met with no better results. The idea was not necessarily unsound; a non-party government was clearly called for, and admitted to be necessary by the Croats, and the Parliament which had seen the murders of June 20th, 1928, was really not entitled to much consideration. King Alexander might have carried through his purpose, and have truly earned the name of 'Great' which sycophantic courtiers attributed to him, if he had employed better methods and better servants. Unhappily, however, although he declared when assuming the personal responsibility for the dictatorship that it was to be a temporary measure only until a constitutional government based on the new ideas could be introduced, yet he failed to convince the country that his object was anything else than the establishment of a pure personal absolutism—a belief confirmed, rather than weakened, by the 'Constitution' of 1931.

It is an unhappy truth, but one which needs to be stated, that the King did not succeed in convincing the Croats of his sincerity either as regards the ultimate restoration of democratic liberties, or even on the national question. On the latter point, the Croats probably did him less than justice, for in many respects the tyranny weighed more heavily on the Serbs than the Croats. The Croats, however, could not forget that the King was a Serb, of a dynasty more national than any other in Europe—a dynasty which had risen from the people and had never quite succeeded in standing above parties. Further, he rested his power mainly on the army, which in its highest ranks was exclusively Serb, and on the police. The politicians whom he chose to assist and advise him were nearly all Serbs, and what is more, members of the Radical Party, so that the members of all other parties and groups felt that the new régime was not non-party at all, but simply a disguised dictatorship of the Radical Party—a belief which persisted throughout the whole period of the dictatorship, and did much to frustrate its avowed purpose. Finally, in the long series of political trials undertaken under the new régime, the Serbs of Serbia, unless they were Communists, were, on the whole, spared; the murderer of Radić, although sentenced to twenty years' imprisonment, was rumoured to have been seen taking his ease of an evening in Belgrade cabarets, but the leaders of the Croats (and of those Serbs who had joined hands with them) were persecuted, tortured, and murdered. These things, together with the fact that the majority of the King's creatures were Serbs (including General Živković, the *homo regius*), made the Croats believe that the dictatorship was not in reality an attempt to substitute 'Yugoslavism' for the 'Great Serbia' policy of which they had been complaining ever since the War, but rather an attack on the Croat nationality by new and more effective means.

Moreover, had King Alexander been an angel of light, he could not have carried through his programme in less than a generation, at least, for simple lack of the men through whom to work. There were not enough sincere believers in the Yugoslav ideal in the country. The genuine patriots (with a few exceptions) were still Serb, Croat, or Slovene patriots, and they stood aside. The men who came forward to help the King, Serbs and Croats alike (and the King took pains always to include some Croats among his helpers), enjoyed no sort of personal credit. The King himself was interested almost exclusively in foreign policy and in the army. He intervened little in internal affairs, letting his helpers do as they would. Moreover, he had an unfortunate distrust of real ability and could not abide independence of thought, while he either tolerated, or did not perceive, scandalous self-enrichment and gross brutality. Under the dictatorship, the country was ruled worse than it had been in the palmiest days of the Serb Radicals; probably worse in some respects than Croatia had ever been ruled under the most oppressive Ban whom Budapest ever appointed.

Thus, when King Alexander was murdered, and when it again became possible to glean some indications of the state of public opinion, it was found that Croat national feeling was unaffected. The Croats had rallied round Dr. Maček, Radić's son-in-law and successor, as unanimously as they had round Radić. The few Croat supporters of the dictatorship were detested as renegades and traitors—far more unpopular, indeed, among their fellows than the Serbs themselves. Nor was Maček any whit less uncompromising as regards Croatia's demands for civil liberties and for decentralization than his predecessor had been.

It is true that another result could hardly have been expected in the time. A supporter of the dictatorship (I believe, one of its few honest adherents) had warned me that it was impossible to count with the older generation at all. 'But,' said he, 'we shall hold on, and the younger generation will be ours.' This was clearly the crucial point, as regards the national question, and in 1934 I inquired into it as closely as I was able. So far as I could judge, however, the overwhelming mass of the younger generation of Serbs and Croats alike still held by their old loyalties. The young Croats were Croats first and foremost.

Yet, in spite of all this, Yugoslav feeling is, I believe, waxing rather than waning. I was in Belgrade in 1919, during the early days of the union, and received the impression of a thin crust of fraternal sentiment covering a witches' brew of mutually incompatible elements. In 1934 I felt that the crust had broken into little pieces and the varied juices were bubbling angrily on the surface, but a certain uniform sediment was forming at the bottom of the dish. It had not yet set, but it was only a question of time before it would do so.

Even shared tribulation is a bond, and a strong one. It was the common opposition to the King's autocratic methods which brought together the Croats and the Prečani Serbs in 1927, at which time there seemed a reasonable probability that the Democrat Party would also join the Coalition, giving it a majority in the whole country. The King, by his personal action, prevented this,[1] but the 1935 elections showed a development along the same lines. In these elections Maček was supported by the Prečani Serbs, the Serb Agrarians, and the Democrats, all these parties agreeing to sink their differences on the centralist-federalist issue in order the better to conduct a radical campaign of opposition to the Government.

More striking still is the case of the so-called Communists, who are persecuted in a way which makes the treatment of the Croat nationalists appear almost indulgent, but nevertheless comprise the great majority of the intelligent and decent educated youth of the country, including far more than the orthodox Marxians and Stalinites. For them, the difference between Serb and Croat has ceased to exist. I remember sitting in Zagreb with a young Croat and a Serb. The Croat said something about the Serbs, whereupon the Serb murmured, quite good-humouredly, that he belonged to the detested nation.

'Toi,' said the Croat, 'tu n'es pas serbe; tu es communiste.'

It is impossible to overlook the growing feeling of solidarity between Yugoslavia's various races, and this will assuredly circum-

[1] Pribičević, op. cit., p. 61.

scribe the field within which their future political struggles will be fought out. It must, moreover, be emphasized that neither the Peasant Party nor the Communists are separatist, still less pro-Hungarian. The Communists think in terms of a Federation of the Balkan peoples, including the Bulgars and the Macedonians. Hungary and Italy are for them 'fascist' states, and *a priori* hostile. Nor is the Peasants' Party either separatist or pro-Magyar. Its social ideals—republicanism, decentralization amounting almost to anarchism, enthronement of the free peasant class as the dominant element in the State—are quite incompatible with those on which the Hungarian State has traditionally rested. To charge it with treason to the State is absurd. In 1928, after the Skupština murders, King Alexander himself suggested 'amputating' his country, on the ground that it was impossible to live with the Croats, so that the best thing to do was to separate peacefully. Radić on his death-bed refused the offer, and he and Pribičević made a formal declaration

repudiating with the utmost energy the very idea of being against the State and declaring most categorically that by the historic action of their leaders in bringing about the union of the State and by their activities among the people since its formation they had given more proofs and guarantees of being for the State than those who insinuated that they were against it.[1]

The resolutions passed by the Coalition on October 1st, 1928, equally accepted the Yugoslav State, as did a further series of resolutions adopted in 1932 which, I was informed recently, still hold good.[2]

Finally, it must be remembered that the Croatian question is no longer confined to-day to the inhabitants of pre-War Croatia. These are now united with the Croats in Bosnia and Dalmatia; and the latter, in particular, exercise a very important influence on Croat opinion. But the Dalmatian Croats have not even any common historic memories with Hungary. It is simply impossible to imagine them submitting themselves to Magyar rule, and equally difficult to imagine the Croats of Croatia consenting to a fresh partition of the 'Triune Kingdom' which is at least reunited to-day, after all its centuries of dismemberment.

The genuine opposition among the Croats to the Yugoslav State

---

[1] Pribičević, op. cit., p. 83.

[2] These resolutions are given by Pribičević, op. cit., p. 148. They demanded 'the complete application of the principle of the sovereignty of the people', proclaimed the peasantry to be 'the basis of the organization of Yugoslav national life', denounced the hegemony of Serbia, and announced a decisive struggle against that hegemony, returning to the *status quo ante* December 1st, 1918, as the point of departure, and recognized 'the principle and the necessity of the union in one State of the peoples of the Serbs, Croats, and Slovenes on a basis excluding the hegemony of any one partner'.

to-day is, in fact, confined chiefly to the remnants of the old Frank Party, a group consisting mainly of elderly ex-officials and officers, living, some in Zagreb, others in Vienna. Even these men do not look so much for a restoration of the *status quo ante* 1918 as for the constitution of a sort of federal Catholic Monarchy, to include Austria, Hungary, Croatia, and Bavaria. It is essentially an old-fashioned idea, based largely on impossible premisses, the most obvious criticism against it being that the rest of the proposed 'bloc' simply does not exist. For this reason, if for no other, it need not, in my opinion, be taken seriously, even if it may be admitted that at times of particular exasperation its ideas became popular among fairly wide circles whose members have not taken the trouble to think out their implications.

The activities of this group are, as a rule, Platonic enough. For many years past they have hardly extended beyond coffee-house conspiracy. There exists, of course, also an active terrorist group, whose leaders, MM. Pavelić and Perčeć, were at one time connected with the Frank Party, but have since gone another way. In 1929 these two gentlemen concluded a formal alliance with the Macedonian Revolutionary Organization, then a mighty force in Bulgaria. After 1932 they lived abroad, largely in Italy and Hungary, and were responsible, with the connivance and, in one case at least, the active help of one of those countries, for the organization of a large number of terrorist acts, some childish, others revolting, culminating in the murder of King Alexander at Marseilles in October 1934.

It is important to understand the exact position and significance of this group. On the one hand, to represent them as a few isolated individuals, without support in the country, would be a mistake. The sober bourgeoisie of Zagreb, who wish to feel when they walk along the street that they will not encounter a bomb or a revolver-shot, dislike them; but they enjoy widespread sympathy among the more reckless elements of the population, who regard them as national heroes like the Hajduks and Ustaši of old. On the other hand, the fact that they have freely accepted help from Italy and Hungary does *not* mean that they are at the head of a popular movement in favour of either of those two States. Italy and Hungary have used them, as they would use any instrument to weaken the Yugoslav State; but they have used Italy and Hungary. Although the Marseilles murder was organized quite without the knowledge of the Yugoslav Communists, the real political ideals of the terrorists are much more akin to those of the Communists than to those of Italy or Hungary. They wish to destroy tyranny and to build up a free order in the Balkans.

In fact, nothing has drawn Croats and Serbs together, again and again, so powerfully as any hint of outside interference. The man who above all others prevented serious trouble in the first, tentative period was Signor Gabriele d'Annunzio, to whom, if the Yugoslav Government was properly grateful to its true benefactors, it would erect magnificent statues in Belgrade, Zagreb, and Split. Another if not quite so splendid a monument should with justice be erected to Lord Rothermere. For Yugoslavia is no monstrous birth. It is a seven months' child, and triplets at that, which have had to do with one perambulator and one feeding-bottle. There are sore internal struggles yet to come. The 'Yugoslav problem' will not be solved for many a year to come, but there can be no doubt that it will be solved in the end, and, if the will of the peoples is taken for a basis, within approximately the present frontiers.

§ 6. THE PREČANI SERBS

What has been said of the Croats applies *a fortiori* to the Prečani Serbs. The favours showered on them by Hungary before the War had only kept open the breach between them and the Croats; it had not made them pro-Hungarian. They were the moving spirits in bringing about Serbo-Croat coalition—a policy which, although their leaders managed to rebut the charges of high treason brought in extraordinarily clumsy fashion against them, was most profoundly irredentist.

After the War they represented the most extreme centralist tendencies, and in this connexion Pribičević, their leader, acquired a dismal prominence. Whether as Minister of the Interior, centralizing administration, or as Minister of Education, Serbizing schools (he clung to office in one form or another with unexampled tenacity), this 'reincarnation of old Apponyi', as a minority leader described him to me, far outdid any Serb from the Old Kingdom, and must be counted among the four or five men who have done most since the War to injure the cause of Yugoslav unity. At the same time he provided an excellent stalking-horse for the far wilier Pašić, who was always able to point out, with perfect justice, that the strongest pressure towards a complete unitary state came from outside, not inside Serbia.

The Prečani Serbs, were, however, gradually disillusioned. The Serbs of Serbia, and particularly the Radical Party, made use of them without giving them their reward.

After the War [writes Pribičević], Belgrade always called on the Serbs of Croatia for help when the national unity was alleged to be in danger, when 'Croatian separatism' had to be combated. But as soon as it felt it to be in its interest to conclude an agreement of any kind with the

Croats, Belgrade sacrificed the Serbs of Croatia without qualms or scruples, thus making them a red rag to the Croats.[1]

The fact that Pribičević himself lost office when Radić expressed himself ready to enter the Government probably weighed heavily with him.

But, besides this, the Croatian Serbs were not admitted to their share of the spoils. It was the Radical Party machine which during the first years allotted the offices and the sinecures, the positions of power or advantage; and these went almost exclusively to Serbs of Serbia. Even in the posts where the influence of the King was supreme, it was the same story. In the army all the generals and the vast majority of officers were Serbs of Serbia. Pribičević records how he complained of this fact to the King, who replied simply that he could not take ex-Austrian officers into his army.[2] This policy revealed an attitude of mind very wounding to the Serbs of Croatia, who saw themselves lumped in with the Croats as potential traitors; and it caused quite particular material hardships to the old 'Grenzer' families, from the Lika and elsewhere, who had traditionally been army officers from generation to generation, and knew no other trade.

The Serbs of Croatia suffered also from such local discrimination as was practised, e.g. the higher taxation levied on the newly acquired districts, this hitting in particular the Serbs of Syrmia. And they suffered also under the great deterioration of the administration, which by general consent compared unfavourably with the Austrian and Hungarian rule.

Then came the political disappointment. 'We wanted union with Serbia', said a leader to me in 1934, 'but with the free and democratic Serbia of King Peter.' M. Pribičević in his book makes much of this factor. Now whether King Alexander was forced into the position which he adopted, or whether (as is more commonly believed in the country) he deliberately worked to bring it about, there will at least be no dispute that under his rule the régime in Yugoslavia moved gradually from one of democracy to one of extreme tyranny. And this brought the Prečani Serbs into opposition to the dynasty as well as to the Great Serbian tendencies of the Radical Party.

Thus many causes combined to bring about a change of attitude among them, and in 1927 Pribičević reconciled himself with Radić on a common platform of democratic rule and decentralization.

---

[1] Pribičević, op. cit., p. 192.
[2] It is fair to say that this situation is now being remedied, especially as regards the technical services, which are now largely officered from the ex-Austrian and Hungarian territories; also that what has been said of the army never applied to the navy.

Swinging right round, he declared that the sole issue of the problem of the Yugoslav State lay in federalization, doing full justice to the historical and national claims of the Croats. Some Serbs would then necessarily remain in Croatia, but he now felt that their rights could be safeguarded by guarantees inserted in a new Constitution, and could not in any case be seriously endangered, since they would still form part of a common State with Serbia.[1] This has been his party's attitude ever since.

Thus the Prečani Serbs have gone the full circle, from extreme centralism to federalism, from 'springing on' Croatia a situation which made a unitary state possible, and then collaborating in its construction, to denouncing the whole series of events which they had made possible. Indeed, one hears more genuinely revolutionary talk to-day from Serbs in Croatia than from Croats, and the active revolts and secessionist movements, such as the Lika Rebellion, have been led by Serbs. But the increased bitterness is probably mainly due to the greater disappointment, and the Lika Rebellion and kindred manifestations must be judged in the light of the character of the local inhabitants, born positivists and activists, turbulent and fearless, compared with the negative, hesitant Croats. Incidentally, the Serbs are not inspired by that invincible detestation of all things Italian which is second nature to the Croats.

Thus, if a revolution were ever to break out in Croatia against the prevailing Yugoslav régime, it would most likely be led by the Serbs of the Lika; but there would be even less excuse for regarding them as pro-Magyar than the Croats. They remain invincibly Serb; I personally believe that after such a revolution they would swing round again to centralism. In no case would they wish to sever their connexion with Serbia.

§ 7. THE MEDJUMURJE AND THE PREKOMURJE

The question of the national minorities in Croatia-Slavonia need not be discussed separately. On the one hand, they form too small a percentage of the total population to affect the general situation;[2] on the other hand, there is nothing in their own position to call for special remark. Their attitude and their treatment alike are best dealt with in connexion with the much more important minority

[1] Pribičević, op. cit., pp. 189–90.
[2] The 1921 census gave the following figures for Croatia-Slavonia: Serbs and Croats, 2,445,429; Slovenes, 21,847; other Slavs, 67,051; Germans, 122,836; Magyars, 70,555; Albanians, 660; Roumanians, 1,992; Italians, 5,046; others, 4,177. The diminution in the number of the Magyars must be ascribed chiefly to migration, and to the substitution of Croat for Magyar pressure in certain border cases.

problem of the Voivodina, to which, indeed, the Croatian minority problem forms, in more ways than one, an appendix.

Neither does the frontier call for detailed consideration, as regards the greater part of its course. The Drave formed the historical frontier between Hungary and Croatia-Slavonia, and Hungary accepted it without demur as the new frontier also.[1] Discussion is therefore confined to the three areas acquired by Yugoslavia north of the Drave, and one of these—the Baranya triangle between the Drave and the Danube—belongs rather to the Voivodina than to Croatia, and is discussed under that heading. The other two—the 'Medjumurje' and the 'Prekomurje'—may be mentioned here.

The 'Medjumurje' or Mur Island (Muraköz in Magyar) consists of the triangle, 795 sq. km. in area, between the Mur, the Drave, and the old Austrian frontier. Historically, it regularly formed part of Hungary except only during the period of Austrian absolutism, when it was assigned to Croatia, but restored to Hungary in 1868.

On the other hand, of a population numbering in 1910 93,837 (Hungarian figures), only 8,245 were Magyar-speaking, with 419 Germans and 74 Slovenes, while no less than 84,735 were Croats. These, although contiguous with the population of Croatia, really formed the southern outpost of the line of Croat settlements stretching northward through the modern Burgenland into Moravia: their ancestors had arrived from the Balkans between 1575 and 1584. They are said to-day to speak a dialect resembling that of some islands off the Croatian coast; although another informant told me that they spoke just like the peasants between the Drave and Zagreb. They were tenacious of their Croat customs and little Magyarized, and, although said to have fought for Hungary against Austria in 1848, they seem to have possessed an active national consciousness in 1918.

The 'Prekomurje' (land beyond the Mur) is another small strip, 940 sq. km. in area, immediately to the north of the Medjumurje and running up from the Mur to the Austrian (Burgenland) and Hungarian frontiers where they meet below Szént Gotthárd. It formed an integral part of Hungary from the Magyar conquest to 1919, but the population of 91,436 (1910) is, again, predominantly non-Magyar. In the extreme north there are a few Germans (2,093 in 1910), and when the Mur valley was drained in the nineteenth century some Magyar colonists were brought in and settled on the land newly made cultivable. These, with the usual Magyar land-owners and officials, and Magyarized Jews, made up in 1910 20,346

---

[1] Note concerning the Frontiers of Hungary, *Hungarian Peace Negotiations*, vol. ii, p. 28: 'The Drave is the boundary separating us from Croatia. This frontier will serve the purpose as such; for it is an ethnographical boundary too.'

Magyar-speaking persons, or 22·3 per cent. of the local population. The remaining 66,790 were Slavs, but in this case akin not to the Croats but to the Slovenes.

Hungary has always refused to identify this people with the true Slovenes. She entitles them officially 'Wends' and maintains that they speak a different dialect from the Slovenes proper, have no historical, political, or cultural connexion with that people, never participated in the Slovene national movement, and had no desire to join Yugoslavia. She produced at the Peace Conference a memorial from these 'Wends' protesting against annexation, and asked that they should be given an opportunity of declaring their wishes by plebiscite.

It seems to be certain, in any case, that since the Magyarization campaign started in this corner (which it did about 1890, when the Slovene schools were closed and a Magyar burger school opened) it made considerable progress.

On the other hand, the Yugoslavs, while admitting the existence of certain dialectal variations between the Slovene spoken in this area and that spoken farther west, also certain differences in customs (particularly those relating to marriage), folk-lore, &c., and a separate historical tradition, yet maintain that all these distinctions are trivial, but were deliberately exploited by the Hungarian Government, which refused to allow books and newspapers from Austrian Slovenia to enter the Prekomurje. They say also that a vigorous irredentist movement existed, and that when the débâcle came, a monster meeting of 10,000 persons, representing all the Slovene communes in the neighbourhood, was held at Beltnici, and voted unanimously for union with Yugoslavia.

In any case, the Yugoslav claim to both areas was accepted. The Medjumurje was allocated to Croatia, and afterwards to the Banovina of the Save, the Prekomurje to Slovenia, with its successor the Banovina of the Drave. By to-day, the national question seems to have been settled. In a somewhat hurried visit to the Prekomurje, I could discern no signs of irredentism, and was told on the spot that the dialectal differences were being smoothed out. The Medjumurje seemed to be purely and enthusiastically Croat.

Both areas are, indeed, poverty-stricken. The population is very dense, and migration, both permanent and seasonal, has always been high, the harvest gangs going, before the War, both north into Hungary and south as far as the Balkans. A land reform was carried through (most of the country had belonged to a few great Hungarian families, the Esterházy, Festetics, &c.) but could not nearly satisfy the local land-hunger, so that the economic situation remains serious. I cannot, however, think that a vote in either area would go against Yugoslavia.

THE VOIVODINA

§ I. GEOGRAPHY AND POPULATION

THE main portion of that part of Hungary proper acquired by
Yugoslavia is the so-called 'Voivodina'[1]—a blunt triangular
chunk of 19,221 square kilometres hacked rudely off the southern
end of the great Hungarian plain in such manner as to form an
eastward prolongation of Slavonia and an approach from the
north to Serbia.

On the west and south-west it marches with Slavonia, whence
it is divided successively by the Drave to its junction with the
Danube, and the Danube to its meeting with the Save. On the
south the Danube separates it from Serbia. These great rivers
form well-defined boundaries; but the eastern frontier with
Roumania, which runs north-westward from the Danube to a
point just south of the Mureş (Maros), and the northern, with
Hungary, which runs across the Tisza and the Danube back to
the Drave, are mere conventional lines drawn on a map, which
only occasionally and accidentally coincide with any discernible
natural feature.

Natural features are, it must be admitted, hard to find outside
the rivers, which dominate the landscape. Besides the frontier
rivers of the Danube and the Drave, the Tisza flows through
the very heart of the country to its junction with the Danube
a score of miles above Belgrade. The land is simply a great flat
alluvial plain drained, watered, and at times inundated by these vast
and imposing streams, which are at once its benefactors and its
terrors, but at all times its masters. The fields have to be protected
by great dikes, drained by canals. Left uncared for, they speedily
degenerate into fever-haunted marsh. But, once reclaimed and
protected, they yield fruits in incredible abundance. This is the
famous black-earth belt, the old-time granary of Hungary and
Austria too, the country of the Gipsy Baron, where chickens grow

---

[1] The title of 'Voivodina' or 'duchy' was bestowed by Yugoslavia on the area
after its annexation, was abolished when the new system of Banovinas was
introduced in 1929, but will be used here in default of an alternative, since the
boundaries of the new Banovinas cut across the old frontiers between Hungary,
Slavonia, and Serbia. The name is a reminiscence of the 'Serbian Voivodina'
which at one time existed in Hungary; but this, as will be shown, was a short-
lived creation, to equate which with such an historic unit as, say, Croatia or
Slavonia would give a false impression of the extent to which South Hungary
as such ever enjoyed a separate constitution and status.

as big as turkeys and pigs as big as ponies. Purely agricultural—
for it has no minerals, not even stones for its roads, nor any large
woodlands—the Voivodina supports no industry, except mills,
distilleries, and other processes directly dependent on agriculture;
but, given accessible markets, it is the farmer's dream.

The country falls into three natural subdivisions: the Baránya,
between the Drave and the Danube; the Bačka, between the
Danube and the Tisza; and the Banat, on the left bank of the
Tisza. Each of these has its own character, its own local atmosphere and feeling, and to some extent its own private history,
which differentiate it from the other two, although it must be
remarked that these characteristics are not proper to the three
components of the Voivodina, but to the larger units of which they
form only parts. The Baránya is merely the south-eastern corner of
the Hungarian County of that name; the Bačka, the southern and
central portions of the County of Bács-Bodrog; and the Banat, the
westernmost third of the area once officially, and still commonly,
so designated.

The population of the present Voivodina was given by the
Hungarian census of 1910 and the Yugoslav census of 1921
respectively as follows:

	1910	1921
Serbs	383,198 }	} 514,121
Bunyevci, Šokci, Croats	71,708 }	
Slovenes		7,949
Magyars	441,787	382,070
Germans	311,162	328,173
Roumanians	71,788	74,099
Other Slavs	58,051	67,886
Others	12,783	6,162
	1,350,477	1,380,460

No words can, unfortunately, do justice to the distribution of
the population. The Roumanians are mostly to be found in the
east, the Magyars are strongest in the north, the Serbs in the
south; but the three intermingle hopelessly, a wedge of Serbian
settlements pushing in one place far northward, while Magyar
advanced posts run to its right and left well to the south, and outlying Magyar islets are found, even in the country-side, in the
extreme south, as well as in all the towns. The Šokac and Bunyevac
settlements are near the northern frontier, islands in a non-
Slavonic sea, the Slovaks and Ruthenes rather farther south. The
Germans are everywhere. The distribution can be appreciated,
if at all, only from the map, and the reason for it can be learnt
only from history.

§ 2. HISTORY TO 1914

In early days the Bačka—still the bleakest, least sheltered of the three divisions—formed the camping-ground of nomadic Scythians, Sarmatians, Huns, and Avars, while the Baránya belonged to Roman Pannonia and afterwards to German tribes. The Banat formed part of the Dacian kingdom, then of Roman Dacia— a fact which allowed Roumania to claim it on historic grounds. It passed afterwards to Balkan tribelings, who provided Serbia with a counter-claim (although, whoever they were, they were not Serbs). The Magyars, on arrival, conquered all three areas with great ease, and themselves peopled them. In the thirteenth and fourteenth centuries the population was predominantly Magyar as far south as the Danube opposite Belgrade and the foot-hills of the Carpathians. Then, however, Roumanian and, in particular, Serb refugees began to drift in in large numbers as the Turks advanced in the Balkans, and although the political sovereignty of Hungary remained unaffected, yet by the beginning of the sixteenth century the population of the Western Banat and Southern Bačka seems to have been overwhelmingly Serb.[1] Certain persons were, at various times, allowed to bear the title of 'Voivode of the Hungarian Serbs', and exercised a great degree of authority over their countrymen.

In the sixteenth century followed the Turkish conquest of South Hungary, under which the Magyar population disappeared almost completely. The Roumanians seem to have survived better, and to have pushed down here and there into the plains, but there the Serbs easily outnumbered them and even flourished. A continuous immigration went on, even under Turkish rule, and they possessed four bishoprics in the Vilayet of Temesvár (corresponding to the Banat) and another important centre in Pécs; although neither the density of the population nor its level of culture equalled that of the earlier Magyar period.

These scattered Roumanian and Serbian settlers were reinforced, just before the close of the Turkish rule, by the ancestors of the Šokci and Bunyevci who, arriving at a favourable moment when the country was empty (the Turks had gone off bag and baggage to the siege of Vienna), squatted in the areas which their descendants still occupy: the Bunyevci in the Subotica district, the Šokci on the rivers round Mohács and Baja, and in the Baránya south of Pécs.[2]

---

[1] In 1483 King Matthias Corvinus wrote to the Pope that 200,000 Serbs had settled in South Hungary in four years. In 1538 Cardinal Martinuzzi wrote that Serbs formed half the population of Hungary (E. Haumont, *La Formation de la Yougoslavie* (Paris, 1930), pp. 148, 149).

[2] The Šokci are believed to have originated from Dalmatia, the Bunyevci

This curious little invasion was the forerunner of one much more extensive. When the Austrian armies advanced against the Turks at the end of the seventeenth century, numerous promises were made to the Christian population of the Balkans to induce them to rise against the Turks. As a result of some years of very confused intrigue, the Patriarch of Peč (Ipek), Arsen Crnojević, migrated into Hungary with a considerable body of followers, mostly Serbians.[1] It was agreed that they should be settled either in their own homes, if these were conquered from the Turks, or in such part of the Hungarian territories as might be recovered. Meanwhile, they were promised the full exercise of their religion, the right to elect an archbishop of their own nationality and language and to choose their own Voivode, and the undisturbed practice of their traditional customs under their own magistrates; and the archbishop and vice-Voivode were in fact appointed (the Emperor had already recognized a certain George Branković as Despot of Serbia, but fearing his ambitions had most treacherously had him imprisoned).

Pending the issue of the campaigns, the Serbs were settled in various parts of Hungary, some as far north as Buda, Szént Endre, and even Komárom and Győr, but most of them in a strip of land running across the then *de facto* southern frontier of Hungary, and comprising the land between the Körös and the Maros, the Southern Bačka, Syrmia, and Eastern Slavonia. Branković had at one time been accorded certain rights over these lands, and the Emperor now assigned them to the 'Rascian [i.e. Serbian] nation', and collected Crnojević's followers into them as far as possible. It was not, however, an assignment in perpetuity, since both parties hoped that Serbia would eventually be reconquered, when the Serbs proposed to move back into their old homes. But the Peace of Karlowitz (1699) put an end to these hopes, and the Serbs remained where they had been put, forming thus a girdle across Southern Hungary. They now had to be considered as Imperial subjects and permanent inhabitants of Hungary, and the question of their status took on rather a new aspect. Successive Emperors repeatedly confirmed their charter, but, in practice, only the

from Bosnia. By their own tradition they were 'haiduks' (i.e. more or less brigands), but were converted to Catholicism by Franciscan monks. They arrived in 1682 in style, with their families, their arms, their monks, and their Church banners, their little band (in the case of the Bunyevci, only 3,000 armed men) being reinforced by a contingent of Orthodox Serbs. The Bunyevci afterwards turned to farming, while the Šokci became fishers and lightermen, towing the barges up the rivers in the Volga Boatmen style.

[1] The number traditionally given is 36,000 families; but according to Professor Caravić (*Istorija Yugoslavije*, Belgrade, 1931, p. 361) the Patriarch's followers numbered only 30,000 souls. On the other hand, Professor Caravić shows that a large number of other migrations took place which are often ignored by historians.

religious provisions of it were respected, the Archbishop receiving spiritual authority over all the Orthodox Church in Hungary. No Voivode and no second vice-Voivode was appointed. Their land was, indeed, kept distinct from the Hungarian administration, but it was ruled, not by the Serbs themselves, but by Austrians, being formed into various 'Military Frontier' districts.

While this was taking place the Turks were still in possession of the Vilayet of Temesvár, bounded by the Tisza on the west, the Maros on the north. In 1718 they evacuated also this, the last of their possessions in Hungary. The Emperor returned one County in the north to Hungary, but alleging the country to be 'neo acquisita', with which he could do as he would, he retained the rest of it under his control. This new area, known henceforward (officially, for some sixty-five years, but unofficially to this day) as the 'Banat', was made the scene of the most elaborate colonization scheme which had, perhaps, ever been attempted. Only the Magyars were forbidden to enter, since the Emperor wished to wipe out Hungary's claim to it for good and all. The largest number of colonists were the Germans, for whom the best land was reserved, while they formed the chief urban element, almost as a matter of course. But they were not the only element: the settlers included Frenchmen, Catalans, Italians, Cossacks, Armenians, Bulgars, Crassovans.[1] The Roumanians, who were considered unreliable (*sehr wankelmütig*) were not made welcome and were, indeed, forbidden certain areas, but they were allowed in some parts of the plain, and continued to have the more inaccessible parts of the mountains, whither the colonization did not penetrate, pretty much to themselves. The Serbs, on the other hand, were settled in large numbers, although many of them fled to Russia, or back into the Balkans, not liking the local conditions. Nevertheless, they remained the largest element in the Western Banat after the Germans. These Serbs, it may be remarked, were not regarded as belonging politically to the 'Rascian Nation', although they were under the ecclesiastical jurisdiction of the Serbian Archbishop.

As the Banat filled up, the country behind was gradually

---

[1] The Crassovans inhabit half a dozen villages near Reşiţa, in the Banat mountains, and are held to-day to be a transition people, neither pure Bulgar nor pure Serb; but Czornig, in his *Ethnographie der oesterreichischen Monarchie* (vol. iii, p. 145), describes them as Catholic Bulgars. A modern Yugoslav historian claims for them a Croat origin. There is also one Crassovan village, now Germanized, in the Western Banat. Not many of these freak minorities are to be found to-day. The Bulgars and Crassovans both exist (in the Roumanian Banat). The Cossacks died out, since it was part of their military tenets to eschew the unmanly act of marriage. The Italians and Catalans succumbed to the climate. The French villages ended by becoming Germanized, and are distinguishable to-day only by their surnames, by a few words which have survived in their local dialects, and by a slightly different style of domestic architecture.

restored to the civilian authorities. Parts of Slavonia were re-incorporated in Hungary in 1747, the Military Frontiers of the Tisza and 'Janopol', north of the Banat, were liquidated in 1750, as superfluous. Many of their Serbian inhabitants, especially from the 'Janopol' district north of the Maros, migrated into the Banat when this was done.

Hungary was now again titular owner of the Baránya and the Bačka, but the Crown was in fact the largest and indeed almost the sole landowner, the titles of the old landowning families having vanished or been declared void. In practice, therefore, these areas were colonized in much the same way as the Banat. The existing inhabitants were left undisturbed, but the wide interstices between their settlements were filled with new settlers, most of whom, again, were Germans.[1] Only in the north the Magyars moved down to right and left of Subotica. The private landowners brought in non-Magyar labour as readily as the Crown itself, although they preferred, as a rule, to draw on the reservoir of cheap labour in North Hungary. It is to them that the Ruthene and Slovak colonies are chiefly due.

In 1778 the Banat also was restored to Hungary, except a strip along its southern frontier which had gradually been organized during previous decades into a Military Frontier. A certain Magyar immigration now began; but at first only on a very small scale, since the great colonizing era was almost over and the country filled up.

The Serb privileges, meanwhile, had been steadily dwindling, until practically nothing of them was left. In 1790 Leopold II struck the final blow when he transferred the conduct of all Serb affairs to the Hungarian Government. Only the religious and cultural autonomy remained, to be renewed and confirmed in 1868, when, however, repeated demands by the Serb leaders for the renewal of their old lay privileges were rejected by the Hungarian Parliament.

The Serbs of Hungary, however, still at this time remained a rich and nationally conscious element. Towns such as Novi Sad (Ujvidek, Neusatz), Sombor (Zombor), Pančevo (Pancsova), and Zemun (Semlin) were still mainly Serbian, and actually more important as centres of national culture and feeling than the wild Balkan principality itself. This active national feeling caused the Hungarian Serbs (unlike the local Catholic Slavs and Suabians)

---

[1] This country had been as badly depopulated as the southern frontier itself. In 1692 the total population of the three counties of Baránya, Tolna, and Somogy numbered only 3,221 souls, 1,652 of whom were in the city of Pécs (Marczali, *Hungary in the Eighteenth Century*, p. 199). The Bačka and the Banat contained 30,000 inhabitants apiece at the beginning of the eighteenth century (*Hungarian Peace Negotiations*, vol. i, p. 408).

to take the Austrian side in 1848, when the situation held out a possibility of a revival of their ancient privileges. They fought savagely against the Magyars, and asked for their territories to be incorporated into an autonomous Voivody, which they wished to be affiliated to Croatia-Slavonia. Francis Joseph, to reward them, revived the ancient titles of Patriarch and Voivode, promising them also national autonomy. After the War was over, the Bačka and Banat were in fact separated from Hungary and formed into an 'autonomous Serb Voivodina', with its seat at Temesvár. But the Voivodina, while including the Eastern Banat, which was Roumanian, excluded Eastern Slavonia, which was Serb; and it was ruled from Vienna, through a German administration; so that Serbian opinion began to look again to Hungary. The Voivodina was abolished in 1860. In their subsequent negotiations with the Magyar authorities the Serb representatives, while protesting loyalty to Hungary, consistently and vigorously demanded the restoration of their old 'privileges' and an autonomous Voivodina; but in vain, for in 1867 Hungary regained *de facto* control of the area, which she proceeded to organize on the usual County system, and subjected to the ordinary Hungarian administration with all its implications.[1]

For Hungary, of course, this simply meant that she was entering into her own again; for she never recognized the right of the Habsburgs to exclude her parliament from complete control of all her territory. She was also able to claim with justice that if Leopold and Joseph behaved like Emperors of Austria, they were acting as Kings of Hungary, so that Hungary's constitutional title to the Banat and even to the Military Frontiers remained unimpaired. Lawyers would presumably agree that her historical title is sound; but it is worth mentioning that among the Germans and even the Serbs and Roumanians of the Banat, and especially of the Military Frontier, a strong tradition of local independence lives on, and memories of the old Austrian rule are still fresh. To them the Hungarian rule is an innovation, the Magyars new-comers. 'The Magyars were never here', said a Roumanian to me on the Frontier, 'and no one wants them here'—a remark which, unacceptable to the historian, and exaggerated even in other respects, yet does reflect a certain attitude of mind prevalent among part of the Frontier population. It would have been inconceivable, for example, in Slovakia.

In the succeeding half-century the Magyar and Magyar-speaking elements gained considerable ground. In the north, the southward expansion of the Magyar peasantry of the Alföld continued.

---

[1] The Military Frontier was still exempted from Hungarian control in 1867, but was 'liquidated' a few years later.

The sparsely inhabited spaces of the Northern Bačka filled up with a new population of Magyar cottagers and labourers, while in the south of that district, and in the Banat, some new Magyar villages were founded with government assistance.

In the south ethnographical conditions in the villages did not alter greatly; but the towns, which grew rapidly with the great economic development which now set in, attracted large numbers of new-comers, most of whom were either Magyar or Magyarized. The Jews, who now for the first time entered South Hungary in considerable numbers (in 1910 the Voivodina contained 18,771 persons of Jewish religion, to which number several thousands of baptized Jews must undoubtedly be added), were almost all of the Magyarone type, the Orthodox Jew of the Carpathians not penetrating so far south, while Jews speaking Serb or Roumanian as their mother tongue were almost unknown. Immigration of Magyar officials, railway employees, and industrial workers also accounts for part of the phenomenally rapid increase, revealed by the official statistics, of the Magyar-speaking population. This amounted in the Bačka to no less than 21·58 per cent. in the single decade 1880–90, while between 1900 and 1910 the rate for the Bačka was still 10 per cent., and for the Banat 16 per cent. No other nationality could approach these figures, which were certainly due in some part to natural causes.

In part, again, they reflect the Magyarization to which the local 'nationalities' of the Baránya, the Northern Bačka, and even the North-Western Banat soon began to succumb. By 1914 the process was far advanced, not only among the Suabians and Catholic Slovaks, many of whom had been settled in the Northern Bačka, but also among the Bunyevci who, being largely town-dwellers,[1] as well as Catholics, were more exposed than most of the Slavs of Hungary to Magyarizing influences.[2] A small national revival, led by a few priests, which set in at the end of the nineteenth century was making less headway than the opposite process of Magyarization to which, in the opinion of their own leaders, the

[1] Nearly half the Bunyevci live to-day in the single town of Subotica (Szabadka, Maria Theresiopol), most of the remainder in the country immediately surrounding it, while round that again is a Magyar country-side. This unusual phenomenon is due to the fact that Subotica, like other towns of the Alföld, is really an immense village, the inhabitants of which huddled together for mutual protection, while remaining peasants. The country population lives in isolated farms: these are citizens whose land lay so far from the town that they had to build shelters on it during the busy months in the fields, and ended by living there altogether when times grew quiet. The second main Bunyevac centre, Sombor, is similarly constructed.

[2] In the debates on the Hungarian Nationalities Law, the spokesman for the Bunyevci had opposed the Serb claim for an autonomous Voivodina and declared that he 'abhorred' ('*perhorreskáljàk*') the Minority draft (I. de Nagy, *Nemzetiségi Törvény*, &c., p. 30).

whole of this little ethnographical relic would have succumbed in another generation had the War not intervened.

In the south the position was rather different. There lingered on, especially in the old Frontier, a strong local tradition of independence which fifty years were not nearly enough to wipe out. In these districts the Germans and Serbs, to the last, looked on the Magyars as intruders, combined against them, and during the earlier decades at least, before the Government had put forth its whole strength, managed with some success to keep them out of the local administration. More important still, as a barrier against the advance of the Magyars, was the strongly fortified economic position which both these two nationalities had acquired during the previous century and a half. Besides a rural class consisting largely of prosperous freeholding peasants, and even some very wealthy large landowners, they possessed a rich and old-established middle class in many towns of the Banat. The Serbs and the Roumanians were also protected by their churches—again firmly founded and buttressed in earlier generations—which enjoyed complete freedom and were very strongly organized, the Serbs possessing not only their richly endowed metropolitan see in Karlovci (immediately across the river from Novi Sad), which owned over 26,000 yokes of land, but also three other local episcopal sees.[1] Both the Serb and the Roumanian churches were able to keep up a fairly extensive primary educational system in their confessional schools, while the Serbs possessed also a certain modicum of secondary education. In the Voivodina alone, besides their 179 primary schools, they had a gymnasium, a higher commercial academy, a training college, and three secondary girls' schools; but these were only part of the total organization which they possessed in the Monarchy, the centre of which lay in Syrmia. Here there was a second gymnasium, two more training colleges, and a theological academy. The value of their foundations was estimated at 17·5 million gold crowns. Mention must also be made of their famous cultural society in Novi Sad, the Srpska Matica, which was the mother of modern Serbian culture.

Thus, taken all in all, the national position of the Serbs was at least far superior to that of the Slovaks, and the southern frontier districts of Hungary were slow in assuming a Magyar aspect. Even here, however, the Suabians had, by the beginning of the twentieth century, begun to fall into line with their compatriots farther north. Their political attachment to Hungary was unquestionable, and, while the villages still spoke German, most of the young men who 'bettered themselves' naturally, and willingly,

---

[1] In Novi Sad, Vršac, and Temesvár. There was also a see in Pest and two in Croatia–Slavonia.

Magyarized. The Serbs and Roumanians, differentiated by their religion, did not blend so easily with the Magyars, but while they lost only a small proportion of their numbers to the dominant nationality (the proportion of genuinely Magyarized Serbs or Roumanians never approached that of the Slovaks or Germans), politically they seemed to be rapidly forgetting their old ambitions. The local Roumanians took little part in the national movement which was so powerfully agitating their compatriots in Transylvania. The Serbs, from demanding a federalization of Austria-Hungary with a Voivodina for themselves, as they had done in 1861 and even in 1869, came down to official acceptance of the unitary Hungarian State, in which they asked for no more than educational, ecclesiastical, and linguistic concessions. The proximity of Belgrade, which might have been expected to keep their national ambitions awake, had rather the contrary effect; for, since the young country was expanding and short of leaders, any Serb of initiative and active national feeling had only to migrate to Belgrade to find a welcome and a career. Thus the ranks of the more nationalist of their two parties, the Radicals (founded at the same time as the Serbian Radical Party, with which it was in constant touch), were steadily depleted, while the Liberals, who were chiefly desirous of a good understanding with Hungary, became the leaders of the people.

One little minority which withstood Magyarization with unexpected obstinacy were the Protestant Slovaks, whose stronghold is Petrovac, north-west of Novi Sad. They were, as a community, much richer than the Slovaks of the mountains, and, like the Protestant Slovaks of the north, but to an even higher degree, boasted of possessing a more active national consciousness than the larger body of their countrymen. It is interesting to record that it was they who regularly returned to the Budapest Parliament one of the leading Slovak nationalists of pre-War Hungary in the person of Dr. Hodža, to-day (1937) Minister President of Czechoslovakia. Like many Slovaks, they also possessed a strong feeling of Slavonic solidarity and co-operated politically with the local Serbs.

The political unification of the country was helped by its economic development. The Voivodina remained essentially agricultural, such industries as were founded (the chief centres being Subotica, Novi Sad, and Sombor) being either of purely local character (e.g. brickyards) or else directly concerned with the primary agricultural products of the neighbourhood: brewing, silk-production, flour-milling, sugar-refining. Nevertheless, it flourished greatly. Its products found ready markets both in Hungary and in Austria. Fat swine and other live stock went to

Budapest and to Western Hungary in large quantities. Vienna—
a still more important market—drew a considerable proportion
of its supplies of cattle, wheat, and maize from Southern Hungary,
while vegetables, eggs, and poultry went still farther afield, to
Switzerland and even to Paris. Imports came, again, chiefly from
Budapest, West Hungary, and Vienna.

This northward and westward orientation of the local economic
life was, of course, deliberately encouraged by Budapest, which
developed the communications leading towards the centre of
Hungary, while leaving those to the Balkans as primitive as was
decently possible. There was no bridge over the Danube below
Novi Sad, and only a single railway bridge over the Save to Belgrade. This policy was, however, welcomed in the Voivodina
itself, to which Serbia, viewed from the economic angle, appeared
chiefly as an undesirable competitor.

The few articles imported by Serbia from Hungary—industrial
products, wood, coal, and some wool and horses—were not produced in large quantities in the Voivodina, while Serbia's main
articles of export—swine, maize, and plums—were identical with
those of South Hungary and of Slavonia, but produced more
cheaply owing to the lower standards of living. This competition
was one of the causes of the famous tariff war between Austria-
Hungary and Serbia—a war undertaken largely in the interests of
the producers of South Hungary, among whom it evoked no such
general protests as were voiced in Transylvania against the similar
war between the Monarchy and Roumania.

§ 3. UNION WITH YUGOSLAVIA AND DETERMINATION
OF THE FRONTIERS

Of all the nationalities of the Voivodina, only the Serbs and
perhaps the Roumanians seem at first actively to have resented the
War, and perhaps not quite all of them. Disaffection, however,
grew rapidly among the former, being inflamed by the severe
repressive measures taken by the authorities. By the end of the
War the great majority of them were undoubtedly hostile to
Hungary and desirous of joining Serbia. When the break-down
came, they seized the power wherever they could and formed local
councils, with the object of seceding to Serbia. The chief Bunyevac
centre, Subotica, also declared for a Southern Slav State.[1] The

[1] According to Hungarian contentions (e.g. *Justice for Hungary* (London,
1928), p. 160) the Bunyevci and Šokci declared for Hungary in 1918. I was,
however, informed in Subotica that on November 10th, 1918—at a moment
when Hungarian troops were still in the town—the nationalist leaders decided
in favour of Yugoslavia. A meeting of 6,000 people proclaimed the union and
elected a provisional administration. The local Magyars, who had also formed

Šokci, however, do not seem to have moved; the Magyars were for remaining with Hungary and formed rival Councils, where they could, with this purpose. The Roumanians wished for union with Roumania. As for the Germans, they sat on the fence. Incited by both Magyars and Serbs to adhere to their Councils, they did neither. In fact, as I am informed from perfectly reliable sources, they had, at that time, no idea of exchanging their Hungarian citizenship for Yugoslav: their own ambitions did not go beyond obtaining genuine enforcement of the Hungarian Nationalities Law. In the existing situation, however, they preferred not to commit themselves.

The question was really decided by the arrival of the Serb troops in the early days of November, after General Franchet d'Espérey had given them permission to occupy a line which included Temesvár in the east, Subotica in the west, and Pécs in the south. The Serbs did, indeed, call a 'Congress' at Novi Sad on November 24th, which in 'the sacred name of self-determination' voted for separation from Hungary and union with Yugoslavia; after which the Serbs took over the administration from the Hungarian authorities. But the 'Congress' had no genuinely representative character; its members were drawn from a fraction only of the local population, and it was in effect merely a post-dated and nominal justification for a situation already created.[1] More important, in view of later events in Croatia, than its pronouncement

a Committee, did not resist, knowing the Bunyevci to be more numerous and believing them to be armed (erroneously, since they had failed to secure arms from the arsenal). On November 11th the Bunyevci nationalists took over the administration and formed a guard; soon afterwards the Serb troops arrived and settled the matter. Thus the town certainly declared for Yugoslavia, although this decision was chiefly the work of the younger and more determined men put over by force in a time of confusion and uncertainty; if a plebiscite of the whole Bunyevac population had been taken, I doubt whether it would have gone against Hungary; assuredly not if the local Magyars and Jews had also been allowed to vote. Sombor, according to *The Hungarian Peace Negotiations*, vol. i, p. 538, refused to send delegates to the Novi Sad meeting and affirmed the loyalty of the Šokci and Bunyevci to Hungary. Very soon after, however, as other documents make clear (ibid., p. 366), a 'National Council of Serbs and Bunyevci' was in charge at Sombor, in any case before the arrival of the Serb troops there on November 14th. This Council continued to administer the town under the Serb occupation, so it can hardly have been a pro-Hungarian body. The Bunyevci sent their delegates to the Novi Sad meeting mentioned below; but these, of course, represented only the nationalist wing of the people. As for the Šokci, nearly all of them were agricultural labourers, quite incapable of any political activity. It would be erroneous to think of them as weighing the rival claims of Yugoslavia and Hungary, and 'declaring' for either State.

[1] The delegates to this 'Congress' represented 211 out of the 453 communes of the districts concerned and consisted of 628 Serbs, 62 Slovaks, 34 Bunyevci, 21 Ruthenes, 3 Šokci, 2 Croats, 6 Germans, and 1 Magyar. See the article by E. Prokopy, the former Főispán in Zombor and the Bačka, *Pester Lloyd*, July 16th, 1933. The complete inadmissibility of any claim by the Congress to represent the whole local population may be seen by comparing the above figures with the population figures given on p. 381.

against Hungary (which was a foregone conclusion in view of its composition) was the fact that it demanded the direct adhesion of the Voivodina to Serbia, instead of to the embryonic 'Slovene-Croat-Serb' State of the day, then represented by the Zagreb National Council.

After this, the idea of restoring the Voivodina to Hungary, or of allowing a general plebiscite in it, clearly never occurred to any one. As regards the northern frontier—with Hungary—the only question was whether any of the extreme Serbian claims were to be rejected. Serbia appears to have claimed, against Hungary, a line starting at a point just south of Arad (where, according to her proposals, her own frontier was to meet those of Roumania and Hungary) and running thence almost due westward to the Danube, thus passing just south of Szeged, north of Subotica, and southward again of Baja. West of the Danube, the proposed line ran south-westward along the hills south of Pécs to Point 408 on the Tenkeshegy, and thence roughly parallel with the Drave but some miles north-east of it, until it met the Mur above Murakeresztur. The line was justified partly on ethnographic grounds (it gave to Serbia practically all the Bunyevci and Šokci) but even more, and particularly as regards the sector west of the Danube, on grounds of strategic necessity.[1]

Although the broad outlines of the Serb claim had been admitted from the first, it was at first considered exorbitant in detail. In the area claimed west of the Danube, it was obvious that Magyars and Germans greatly outnumbered all the Yugoslavs put together. As regards the Bačka, although the population was admittedly so mixed as to make a clear-cut division impossible, yet the line proposed was obviously disproportionately favourable to Serbia. It left a few Yugoslavs, of various types, on its north; but it included, immediately inside it, not to speak of the areas farther south, a large number of minorities. Even persons friendly to Yugoslavia, who did not admit the distinction between Serbs and Bunyevci to have any real validity, criticized severely Serbia's claim to Subotica, the *New Europe* writing that 'it is impossible to justify the inclusion of Subotica—a mere Slav island in a Magyar sea'.[2] The American Intelligence Department also, in its original

---

[1] I have been unable to find the official Serb statement of claims. The *H.P.C.*, vol. iv, p. 208, describes it shortly as above. A more detailed claim, which appears to be identical with that laid before the Conference, is contained in a pamphlet entitled *The National Claims of the Serbians, Croats and Slovenes*, presented by the Serbian Brothers to the Brothers of the Allied Countries (Paris, Édition l'Émancipitrice, 1919). This pamphlet lays strong emphasis on the strategic justification of the whole line, including that to be drawn across the Bačka.

[2] *New Europe*, February 23rd, 1919, p. 148; cf. also ibid., January 1st, 1920, p. 18, for a criticism of the decision when taken.

suggestions, proposed a line running much farther to the south, excluding all territory north of the Drave, and in the Bačka, running east and west from the Danube just north of Bezdan, Sombor, Kula, Novi Vrbas, and Stari Becse, thence turning north- ward, east of Ada and Nagy Szentmiklós, to the meeting-point of the three frontiers.[1] Nevertheless, these hesitations seem soon to have been dispelled as regards the Bačka, for on February 28th, 1919, the Committee on Yugoslav Claims reported that 'the American, British, and French representatives found themselves in substantial accord on a line in the north which would follow substantially the line proposed in the Serbian memorandum', while the Italian reserved his decision,[2] but does not seem to have pressed his opposition, for the line was unanimously recommended on May 8th to the Conference of Foreign Ministers, adopted by them in turn, and included in the Peace Treaty. It was stated at the time that the line left considerable masses of Slavs north of it, but not enough to justify further concessions.[3]

It appears that in this case the Allies had been easily convinced by the arguments of the Serbian general staff, for the historian of the Peace Conference, although admitting that the frontier was 'highly favourable' to the Serbs and even 'exceeded their expectations',[4] yet considers that the attribution of Subotica to Yugoslavia had its advantages from the strategic point of view.[5]

The claim to the Baránya was not admitted so easily. The committee on Yugoslav claims referred it to a sub-committee, and the report to the Conference of Foreign Ministers which they, again, adopted unchanged left the whole territory north of the Drave to Hungary.[6] The records at this point are very incomplete; but they contain a message from M. Pašić to M. Clemenceau enumerating the Magyar villages in the Baránya which would fall to Yugoslavia, from which it appears as though Serbia had dropped her request for the western strip above the Drave, but was trying to get French support for her claim to the Drave–Danube triangle.[7] It must be remembered that Serbia was at this time in military occupation of Pécs. Then, after all, the Peace Treaty assigned the triangle to Yugoslavia, the frontier being justified on strategic

[1] Hunter Miller, *Diary*, vol. iv, p. 239.   [2] Ibid., vol. xvii, p. 95.
[3] Ibid., vol. xvi, p. 227.   [4] *H.P.C.*, vol. iv, p. 211.
[5] Temperley, *How the Hungarian Frontiers were Drawn*, p. 439:

The claim here [*sc.* in the Bačka] was primarily strategic and is practically the only instance of such a concession. The old Serbian capital of Belgrade was so near the frontier that in former days any threat of war by a neighbouring power produced an extreme state of nerves in the capital, Belgrade.

[6] Hunter Miller, *Diary*, vol. xvi, p. 227.
[7] Ibid., vol. xviii, p. 358. At the same time, M. Pašić made a gallant effort to get for Yugoslavia Baja and the surrounding district.

grounds and also on the score that the shifting beds of both Drave and Danube made them here 'unsuitable as frontiers'.[1]

Even this decision did not quite settle the question of the Pécs area, for the Serb troops did not evacuate Pécs until August 1921, and before leaving it set up a purely artificial 'Republic of the Baránya', controlled (under Serb officers) by the Magyar miners, reinforced by certain émigrés of the Left from Hungary. The hope was clearly that a puppet state should be established under Yugoslav control. The leaders of the Republic, however, refused to ask for separation from Hungary, although they pressed the Allies and the League (vainly) to grant the Pécs area autonomy within Hungary, with protection against the White Terror.

The real struggle at the Conference, however, was not between Yugoslavia and Hungary, but between Yugoslavia and Roumania, for the possession of the Banat. Both sides showed themselves thoroughly intransigent.[2] Roumania claimed the whole territory, appealing to her Treaty of 1916 with the Allies, and maintaining that the country was indivisible: it was a natural and historic unit, surrounded by natural frontiers, containing a river and canal system which could not be divided up, and forming an economic whole in which mountain and plain could not be divided without damage to both. In this unit, the Roumanians were in an unquestioned majority; in the plains the Serbs were in a minority compared with the Magyars and Germans, and the Germans would 'rally round Roumania in order that their numbers should not be diminished by division'.

The Serbs did not ask for the whole Banat, but only for the western half, or the plains. They asked for a frontier running some 10 or 20 miles east of Temesvár, Vršac, and Bela Črkva, leaving Lugos, Rešiţa, and Steierdorf to Roumania. In this area they were, they said, in a majority over the Germans and Magyars and an absolute majority over the Roumanians. The Germans, moreover, would wish to join them on economic grounds. They denied that the mountains could not be separated from the plain, but agreed that the plain was indivisible. In addition, they advanced strategic arguments and certain fantastic historic claims.

The Hungarian contribution began with a sardonic agreement with both sides as regards the indivisibility of the Banat. They further pointed out their own historic claims, and the close

---

[1] H.P.C., vol. iv, pp. 211, 212. The decision is described here as 'a model of how to draw a just and moderate strategic frontier', cf. How the Hungarian Frontiers were Drawn, loc. cit: 'It [viz. Pécs] was not only returned to Hungary, but the adjacent heights were so divided that no advantage was granted to Yugoslavia.'

[2] For this controversy see Hunter Miller, Diary, vols. iv, pp. 325 ff., and xiv, pp. 138 ff.

economic interconnexion of the Banat with the rest of Hungary; and suggested that the Germans did not really want to go to either Roumania or Yugoslavia, but to remain with Hungary.[1]

The Conference decided in the end to divide the Banat. Yugoslavia's claim to the line of towns in the eastern plain was at first rejected, and a frontier drawn which left those towns, with a small hinterland, to Roumania. The Serb and Roumanian minorities were thus balanced out fairly equally, and a reasonable economic line secured. At the last moment, however, an ill-advised alteration was made, and Yugoslavia was given Vršac and Bela Črkva.[2]

Before turning to present conditions, it will be convenient to enumerate the main events in the political history of the Voivodina since 1919. It was governed provisionally as a unit until the adoption of the Vidov Dan Constitution in 1921, after which it was divided into three departments: the Western Bačka with the Baránya formed one unit, with its capital at Sombor; the Eastern Bačka and Northern Banat were incorporated in the Department of Belgrade, and the Southern Bačka in that of Smederevo. The elections to the Departmental Councils only took place, however, at the beginning of 1927, and the communal elections not until the end of that year. The country then enjoyed a more or less normal political life until 1929, when it was ended by the proclamation of the Dictatorship. With this event, all departmental and communal autonomy vanished once more, all existing parties were dissolved, and the rights of free meeting and association were suspended.

Under the reorganization of the country, the Voivodina, with Syrmia, was joined with North Serbia, these districts forming together the Banat of the Danube. All elected local representatives were replaced by government nominees, both in the Banat Council established in March 1930 at Novi Sad (which became the capital of the Banat) and in the communes.

In 1931 'elections' were held to Parliament, only a single list being presented by the Government. In 1933 communal autonomy was restored in name, and elections held, opposition lists being allowed under the law, although in practice (the ballot being open) the concession was almost valueless. The general elections of 1935 were something more of a reality, as opposition lists were allowed; but up to the time of writing it could not be said that any real liberty had been restored.

§ 4. CONDITIONS SINCE 1919

The general background against which our picture of conditions in the Voivodina must be painted is the most sombre of any in this

[1] *Hungarian Peace Negotiations*, vol. i, p. 406.   [2] See above, p. 355.

book (since it does not cover Italy outside Fiume). Not that the
Serbs are deficient either in ability or in qualities. On the contrary, they are probably better natural administrators than the
Roumanians, more honest and more efficient; and they possess a
certain manliness which endears them to the Magyars in particular.
It is curious but certain that Hungary resents the bludgeon blows
which she receives from the Serbs far less than the pin-pricks of
the Czechs; the two countries have often, ever since the War, been
on the verge of a *rapprochement*.

But the Serbs have passed through a rough schooling under the
Turkish Pashas. Then came seven years of almost uninterrupted
war, in the course of which they lost a great part of their man-
power. Among the survivors, the better men chose the army for
their career; and there came into politics and into the administration, both in Serbia itself and still more in the Voivodina, a new
class of men. The subordinate officials (among whom the local
elements are more strongly represented) still maintain certain
standards of decency, and in some places the inhabitants give them
a good name enough.[1] The higher officials, especially those from
the old kingdom, have proved far less satisfactory. There have
been certain grave financial scandals. But worse than the
venality, which is only occasional, is the habitual brutality of
method, and worse than that again has been the despotic, even
terroristic character of the régime itself. Only a faint idea of the
entire absence of any kind of political liberty is given by the bald
statement that no local or communal elections were held until
1927; that all popular representation was abolished early in 1929
in favour of a naked personal absolutism, and that the few concessions made since that date to popular representation have been
little more than nominal.[2] A dictatorial rule may yet be reconciled
with a fair degree of personal liberty for at least the majority of the
population; but in the Voivodina, even the brief intervals in which
constitutional government of a sort prevailed were darkened by
the sinister shadows of the military commandant and the police
spy. During that year or two they only retired a pace into the
background; for the remaining period their rule has been un-
checked and undisguised. In no other part of Europe with which
I have had any personal acquaintance since the War has the
atmosphere of terrorization been so unrelieved.[3] In these respects,

[1] I was much struck (which I think it only fair to record) by the frequency
with which people said to me that 'in our village the officials are not so bad—
but this is an exception'.
[2] It is fair to say that a certain improvement has recently set in as regards local
administration.
[3] Incidentally, it made my own task of gathering information extraordinarily
difficult. The amount of labour, ingenuity, and money spent on spying upon

the dictatorship has proved no worse, if it has been no better, than the régime during which constitutional government nominally prevailed. The incidence of the terrorism changed slightly; it weighed, perhaps, more heavily on the Serbs, relatively less on the minorities, but its degree remained unaltered. The corruption is said to have improved for a time, but afterwards the old ways were resumed.

Besides political terrorization, all sections of the population have complained, and apparently with some justification (although perhaps less than they think), of economic exploitation. For the first ten years of Yugoslavia's existence, the taxation systems previously in force in her various constituent provinces were maintained, and among the heaviest of all these was that of the Voivodina, while a special, very heavy tax (the so-called *doharnia*) was also levied on those districts of Yugoslavia which had not been ravaged in the War.[1] The taxes were unified throughout the kingdom on January 1st, 1929, after which, according to the official version, taxation has been based solely on capacity to pay. The land-tax— the most important from the peasant's point of view—is admittedly highest in the Voivodina; but the land there is richest. The Voivodinians, on the other hand, say that the differentiation is far more than is justified by the differences in yield. In Serbia it is 70 dinars per yoke, in the Voivodina 320—a huge sum when it is considered that the total rental value of a yoke of land is only 499 dinars.[2]

Not only are the taxes in the Voivodina heavier, but they are also much more punctiliously collected. A statement circulated to the Yugoslav Parliament in 1936 regarding the taxes levied and collected in the Danube Banovina showed some remarkable contrasts. Of the taxes plus instalments of arrears, 103·7 per cent. were collected in Pančevo, 98·3 per cent. in Darda, 94 per cent. in Ruma, 90 per cent. in Subotica, 88 per cent. in Sombor, 84·2 per cent. in Apatin, &c. The general figure for the Voivodina ranged between 75 and 90 per cent., the only two towns with a bad record being Bačka Topoler (32 per cent.) and the Roumanian centre of Alibunar (33 per cent.). Of the towns of Serbia included in the Banovina, only one reached the 70 per cent. mark; most ranged between 45 per cent. and 65 per cent.; Smederevo had only 47·9 per cent., Belgrade (district) only 27 per cent., and Rudnik

my movements and in shutting me off from sources of information would, it often seemed to me, have amply sufficed to remedy so many abuses as to make caution unnecessary.

[1] Although the tax has long been discontinued, its arrears, which are immense, are still being collected. These account for much of the extra payments still being demanded from the Voivodina.

[2] Since the outbreak of the agricultural crisis, this tax has been reduced several times in all parts of the country, including the Voivodina.

only 24·8 per cent. The range of figures for the percentage realized of assessment for the year was wider still; Darda had 134·3 per cent. to the 26 per cent. of Rudnik.

Whether they can afford it or no—and they are at least better off than the inhabitants of many inland areas—the Voivodinians have to pay heavily, and do not feel that they have received corresponding benefits. The money has gone on the army, on building ministries in Belgrade, on strategic roads and railways in Macedonia or towards the coast, and, too often, into the pockets of Belgrade and Zagreb public men. One may doubt whether the Voivodinians are really so much worse off as they believe than the rest of Yugoslavia; but then, the consideration that the whole of their new country is in a rocky condition is not particularly consoling.

Against all these grievances one may possibly set, as an asset to the bulk of the population, the comparatively popular spirit of the Yugoslav State, in which social differentiations as yet hardly exist. Thus the peasant (and most of the Voivodinians are peasants) is not considered, or treated, as a person whose interests must always be subordinated to those of the landowner. In emphasizing the tyranny of the police, one must remember that at least the overwhelming pressure of the landowner has been removed, so that in the settlement of their local affairs the population may in some respects be more free than before the change. Labour conditions are, however, no less primitive than in Hungary, and any form of left-wing political agitation is even more severely repressed. A single important social measure has been carried through, in the shape of the agrarian reform which Yugoslavia, like all the other Successor States, carried through after the War. As we shall have to refer on various occasions to the effects of this measure, a short account of its main provisions may be given here.

Before turning to details, it will be well to emphasize the essentially national and political character of this reform. It is true that the land distribution, as elsewhere in the old Hungary, was very uneven. Three thousand nine hundred and seventy-seven large landowners held 31·2 per cent. of the total area, and there was a large class of landless agricultural labourers and dwarf-holders. These conditions prevailed chiefly in the north, in the Magyar districts; the Germans, and even the Serbs and Roumanians, were far more favourably situated. There was, therefore, much social justification for the reform; but the satisfaction of the land-hunger of the local population was only one of the objects of the reform; another—openly and frequently admitted—was the weakening of the minority landowners and the establishment of a frontier cordon of reliable national elements. For this reason, colonization played a particularly large part in the reform, to the detriment of ordinary social and even economic considerations.

The land reform was initiated (for all Yugoslavia) by a proclamation by the Prince Regent in January 1919, which was followed on February 25th, 1919, by a series of 'preliminary enactments', which laid down the general principles of the reform.[1] A Ministry of Agrarian Reform was established to carry these into effect, and worked hard, although with great confusion, for several years. Various administrative decrees were issued under its auspices. In 1931 ten previous enactments were summarized and partially modified by 'a Law relating to the liquidation of the Agrarian Reform on Large Estates', dated June 19th, 1931. This was again modified by two supplementary Acts of December 5th, 1931, and June 24th, 1933. These Acts rendered subject to expropriation any property held by one landlord (whether consisting of one estate or more) in excess of 521 yokes (300 hectares) of cultivated land or 896 yokes (500 hectares) in all (meadows, forests, and pasture were not counted as 'cultivated'). Flood areas, artificially drained (including swamps which the landlord promised to drain), might be retained above the maximum, and a landlord producing breeding stock or selected seed might also, under certain conditions, retain a 'super-maximum' enabling him to carry on these activities. Under the earlier enactments agricultural industries also gave a claim to exemption, but the 1931 Act did not maintain this concession.

The expropriation applied equally to individual landlords, corporations, &c., but public corporations, especially if formed for religious objects, might be granted super-maximal areas as required for the maintenance of their institutions. Church estates could, however, be appropriated with the consent of the Ministerial Council. The estates liable to expropriation in the Voivodina covered 751,149 hectares (1,302,392 yokes), 435,812 of which were cultivated, out of the total area, for the whole territory, of 3,528,800 yokes. The small number of estates affected is remarkable: in all the northern areas of Yugoslavia (Croatia–Slavonia, Slovenia, and the Voivodina) only 850 estates suffered under the reform. Six hundred and seventy-five of these were private, 29 belonged to the State, 117 to communes, 29 to co-possessorates. In the Voivodina 367 estates were subjected to the reform; 120 of these belonged to minority landowners, 79 to the State or the Serbian Orthodox Church, and 150 to communes.

[1] The best account in English is contained in a series of articles by Dr. von Frangeš in the *International Review of Agriculture*, Year XXV (1934), nos. 3–9 (March–Sept.). Dr. Frangeš is favourable to the national aspects of the reform, but strongly hostile to its economic operation.

Under the preliminary enactments, the owners retained 441,651 yokes, 149,693 of which were cultivated (100,313 narrower maxima, 31,869 super-maxima, 17,511 flood areas), the rest being made up of 44,605 yokes of 'extended maxima' and 247,353 yokes of uncultivated land.[1]

Estates belonging to the Habsburgs, to the dynasties of enemy countries, and to foreigners who had received them for services rendered to the Habsburgs were originally declared expropriated without compensation (these enactments had to be modified later). For the rest, the land was at first simply temporarily leased to the beneficiaries at a rent of five times the cadastral net return, of which the landowners received four-fifths and the State the remaining fifth. The landowner also received a small compensation payment for cultivated arable land. In 1920 this arrangement, originally concluded for one year, was prolonged for another four, the landlord now receiving a rent of six times the cadastral net return. Meanwhile, totally inadequate as this rent was, he paid all taxes, rates, contributions to local drainage societies, &c., on the entire property. After July 1st, 1923, the State collected the taxes and rents from the beneficiaries and paid over a share of the latter to the landlord.

From 1925 onward beneficiaries were enabled to buy the land assigned them at an agreed price, direct from the former owner, the State intervening to protect the purchaser where necessary. In this way some 50,000 yokes of property changed hands in the Voivodina.[2] The 1931 Act then at last regulated the question properly. The land was assessed on the basis of the cadastral net return ascertained some years previously for fiscal purposes, the figure in pre-War crowns being multiplied by 120 for conversion to dinars. Where the land was inferior, a lower rate was taken. The actual valuation is said to have varied from 3,240 dinars per yoke of 'Class I' land in the best district to 768 dinars for 'Class IV' land in the worst, but in fact more than 1,600 dinars was rarely paid, and sometimes as little as 600. The owners were given state bonds bearing 4 per cent. interest and redeemable in 30 years. Compensation was to be paid also, in the same bonds, for expropriated crops, implements, live stock, &c. The owners, however, had to pay 10–20 per cent. of the total received to a Land Compensation Fund.[3] The compensation price was admittedly low

---

[1] Figures in Frangeš, op. cit., April 1934, p. 134.

[2] The total sold in this way was 95,000 yokes in the 'Northern Districts', i.e. the Voivodina, Croatia-Slavonia, Slovenia, and the Prekomurje. As the total area expropriated in the Voivodina was slightly over half the total expropriated in the whole Northern Districts, I put 50,000 at a guess.

[3] The 'optants', including the Habsburgs, who made good their claim to compensation after years of negotiation, were to be repaid out of a separate fund, but little of this has been received, as one part, at least, of the contributions ceased when reparations payments were suspended.

at the time it was fixed. The purchase price of arable land in the Voivodina varied between 10,000 and 8,600 dinars per yoke, having at one time stood as high as 30,000 dinars or more. In addition, the bonds soon sank to about 50 per cent. of their nominal value, thus making the actual sums received lower still.[1] It is true that the previous valuation of the land had been well below its real value.

The low rate of compensation did not, of course, nearly exhaust all the losses of the landlords. In the early days the tenants often neglected to pay any rent whatever, and the State afterwards was neither punctual nor scrupulous in handing over the sums due. The rates and taxes thus amounted in some cases to many times the landlord's actual receipts. Finally, only a fraction of either the bonds or the compensation had been paid by 1937. Generally speaking, the reform amounted to ruin for most of the ex-landlords.

The beneficiaries were of three categories: local applicants holding either no land at all, or less than they could work themselves, the latter amount being calculated at 1 yoke per member of the family, without distinction of age or sex; the so-called *dobrovoljci* or war volunteers (i.e. persons who deserted during the War to the Serbian or Montenegrin armies or legions); optants, refugees, and other colonists from the interior of Yugoslavia. The *dobrovoljci* and colonists were normally allowed to receive 8·5 yokes apiece. The *dobrovoljci* received their land free; other beneficiaries, so far as they did not buy their land under the 1925 Act, had to pay the price passed on to the ex-owner in compensation in 30 annual instalments at 5 per cent. interest.

In the Voivodina, by the end of 1928, 12,265 families of *dobrovoljci* had received 100,689 yokes; 4,730 families of colonists, optants, &c., had received 30,088 yokes, and 58,193 families of local applicants, 171,950 yokes. Further, 12,862 families had received small building-sites. Thus a total of about 88,000 families, 70,000 of whom were local, received some benefit under the reform. Sixty-one thousand six hundred and twenty new dwarf-holdings (1–5 yokes) were created with a total area of 163,554 yokes, and 16,541 medium holdings (5–20 yokes) with a total area of 135,442 yokes, the remainder of the land going to enlarge existing holdings.

The land granted to the local applicants certainly represents an assuagement of land-hunger and a real advantage to the beneficiaries. This result was not, however, achieved without much mortification and suffering due to the rough and ready methods employed, the haste with which the distribution was begun, and the long delays before it was made definitive. In the early years

---

[1] I am informed that they have risen since this was written.

grotesque situations arose. Sometimes the land had been so notoriously apportioned among the supporters of a single political party that the beneficiaries did not care to maintain or improve it, or sometimes even to cultivate it at all, as they felt that at the next elections it might be taken from them and given to members of a rival party. In other cases applicants received land but no implements or capital, so that they could not work it if they would.[1] Sometimes the parcels lay too far from the applicants' homes to be workable; they were usually much smaller than had been expected. It was only after some years that matters were put on a rather better footing by the organization of credit and the operation of the various 'Land Settlement Offices'. In the meantime, many high hopes had suffered shipwreck.

But the greatest cause of dissatisfaction was the favour shown to the *dobrovoljci* and other colonists, who, although far fewer in numbers, received almost as much land as the local applicants, and on far more favourable terms. Most of the land assigned to the *dobrovoljci*—130,000 yokes out of the 170,000 in the northern territories—was, indeed, the property of the Hungarian optants; but this land itself was coveted by the local population, while in quite a number of cases they were also settled on the communal land belonging to villages and towns. Many communes had in the past divided up all or part of their lands, some of which were very extensive, and leased them to their own members as orchards, market gardens, &c. The colonization thus approximated to the expropriation of the local peasantry. Magyar communes were the chief sufferers, but Bunyevac and even some Serb communes were also affected. In spite of all complaints, the Act of 1931 sanctioned the situation, leaving the communes only with a maximum of 100 acres of arable land, and such pasture-land as had not been appropriated under the reform. The losses of some of the larger communes have been enormous.

The *dobrovoljci* themselves, and particularly the colonists from such mountainous areas as Montenegro, passed through an exceedingly difficult time. Many of them gave up their land in disappointment and returned to their homes. Great efforts were, however, made, and considerable expense incurred, to get them established on a sound footing. Particular pains have been taken with the new villages established in the frontier zone. There are probably about seventy or eighty of these,[2] chiefly on the northern

---

[1] It was not at all uncommon, in the first years, for the beneficiaries to approach the old landowner and ask him to work the land as their tenant.

[2] The head of the Novi Sad Agricultural Office, who looks after colonists in 130 communes, told me that 40 of these were new villages (the remainder are suburbs of existing towns or villages). There are 12 in the neighbourhood of Vršac, and I have guessed the odd 20 for the Petrovgrad (Veliki Bečkerek) office.

frontier round Subotica, but some also in the east of the Banat. After long years of struggle, helped by every sort of concession, including large-scale remission of debts, they are beginning at last to make some headway.

This, in itself, is satisfactory, but not to the local population, whose discontent at the preferential treatment of the strangers is enhanced by the fact that the latter form a decidedly turbulent element in the population. Many of them come from the more lawless districts of Yugoslavia, such as the Lika; and as they are secure, within limits, of the support of the authorities, they have often behaved with scant regard for the feelings, or even the rights, of their neighbours.

Against the eighty or ninety thousand families who have ultimately benefited by the reform must be set a considerable number who have undeniably lost by it. Apart from the direct losses to the expropriated landlords, which are heavy enough, the dissolution of the big estates also dealt a severe blow, at least for a time, at the agricultural industry, which again had its repercussions on agriculture.[1] The reform was also definitely disadvantageous to the dwarf-holders in the neighbourhood of the large estates and to the labourers formerly employed upon them. Of the reform in Croatia, Dr. Frangeš writes that where they received any land at all, the income which they earned from it was nearly always considerably smaller than what they had earned by supplementary work on the large estates. The supply of surplus agricultural labour was so greatly increased by the reform that wages fell to one-third and one-fourth of their former level, and the Government, to prevent further falls, had actually to prohibit the use of machinery for harvesting.[2] Conditions in the Voivodina, if not quite so bad, were yet analogous. There are still to-day at least 90,000 landless agricultural labourers in the Voivodina, and their condition presents a very serious problem. Finally, we must not forget the considerable costs in which the whole operation involved the State— costs which must ultimately be met out of taxation.

§ 5. THE SLAV PEOPLES SINCE 1919

The lack of political and personal freedom, and above all the sense of economic exploitation, combined with a feeling of disappointment at what they felt to be the insufficient recognition afforded them in the matter of appointments and other perquisites,

[1] Details of the estimated losses incurred in this way by individuals and the State (through falling off in receipts from taxation) are given by Frangeš, op. cit., April 1934, pp. 134, 135. I have not reproduced the figures, as calculations made in 1919 and 1920 in crowns have little meaning to us to-day.

[2] Frangeš, op. cit., April 1934, p. 132.

have had their effect even upon the most favoured class of the local population—the Serbs. They began as centralists of the centralists —'bigger Serbizers than the Serbs themselves', as one writer puts it;[1] sided with Belgrade against Zagreb even in November 1918; protested in 1925 when Pašić concluded an agreement with the Croat leader, Radić; and were mainly responsible for the non-introduction of elections in the Voivodina until 1927.

These feelings have undergone a very notable transformation. The Voivodinian Serbs have a little ditty which is immensely popular wherever it can be sung with safety:

> 'I gave four horses
> To bring the Serbians here—
> I would give eight
> To take them away.'

They have swung right away from centralism. In the summer of 1932 their principal leaders, at a secret meeting in Sombor, proclaimed the principle of 'the Voivodina for the Voivodinians, with the same rights as the other regions and the same constitutional régime as is to be introduced elsewhere'.[2]

In 1934 talk of a 'Voivodina front' was fairly widespread. One gentleman told me that all the local Serb leaders were agreed upon it. The main point of the programme was that local taxation should be levied by and spent on the local inhabitants. Its advocates accepted, however, the monarchy and the common army, and were willing to contribute out of state taxation to the passive regions of Yugoslavia. I did not at the time feel that this movement was very strong. One must form one's judgements, not only by what is said on a given subject, but by the frequency and eagerness with which it is brought up; and by that standard the 'Voivodina front' was still embryonic. It seems, however, to have developed since. In the 1935 elections there was a large Serb vote against the Government and for Dr. Maček's list. In 1936, to judge from certain newspaper articles, the movement for federalization was growing increasingly persistent.

Thus the Serbs of the Voivodina—or some of them—have come the same circle as M. Pribičević's followers from Croatia. There is, however, little foundation for a genuine regionalist movement among them. They are too few, and too near Belgrade. One can imagine Yorkshire demanding federalism on the slogan 'away from London', but hardly Surrey. Actually, the separate local spirit of the Voivodina seems to be decaying since the change of frontiers. The Srpska Matica is no longer important now that there are the

---

[1] A. de Mousset, *Le Royaume serbe-croate-slovène* (Paris, 1926), p. 94.
[2] Pribičević, op. cit., p. 142.

museums in Belgrade; the local press is hardly required when the
Belgrade papers reach Novi Sad by breakfast-time. And since
there is absolutely no cultural, religious, or linguistic difference
between the Serbs of the Voivodina and those of Belgrade, there
is no bar to the former seeking their fortunes in the capital. Most
of their more able and energetic members are, in fact, drawn into
the larger national life, and are doing extremely well there; the
number of Serbs from the Voivodina holding high office in Serbia
to-day is remarkable, and probably exceeds that of the Serbs from
other parts of the kingdom now employed in the Voivodina. The
remainder, perhaps, are hardly capable of much initiative.

It is thus impossible to speak of a Serb problem in the Voivodina
in the sense in which there is a Croat or a Slovak problem, or even
a Roumanian question in Transylvania. The revolt, such as it is,
is against the character of the government, and would quickly die
away, apart from the chronic grumbling which is always to be
expected and must not be taken too seriously, if the methods of
Belgrade were, by some happy chance, reformed. It is not a
national question, much less a movement in favour of Hungary.
It has not even led the local Serbs to seek an understanding with
the minorities among whom they live.[1] Those members of the
minorities with whom I have spoken on the subject generally agree
that, while the Serbs from the Old Kingdom are less civilized in
their methods, they are also less chauvinistic. The few friendly
gestures made to the minorities since the War have come not
from Novi Sad but from Belgrade and have been more frequent
under the régime of the Democrats, and under the Dictatorship
itself, than during the terms of office of the Radical Party, to which
most of the Voivodinian Serbs belong. Few as are the crumbs
which fall to the Voivodina, it is the local Serbs who get the first
lick at them, and they show little inclination to share the dish with
their German and Magyar neighbours.

National feeling among the Serbs is, moreover, stiffened by the
dobrovoljci and colonists, who to-day form a not inconsiderable
element among them, and are the spoilt children of the Government, which has made many economic sacrifices for their sake and
allows them much liberty—in some respects even licence—in their
capacity of guardians of the gate. They are, as a class, fanatical and
tumultuous chauvinists, who would die rather than yield an inch of
soil to Hungary.

The remaining inhabitants of the Voivodina may be divided into

[1] Since writing these words I have been informed that the Serb leader of the
Voivodinian front now claims to have reached an understanding with the local
Magyars. If this maintains itself, it may, of course, prove a most hopeful
development for the whole Voivodina.

three classes: the non-Serbian Yugoslavs (viz. the Šokci and Bunyevci), the other Slavs (who, by a fiction accepted by both parties, are neither regarded nor regard themselves as minorities, but as part of the 'Staatsvolk'), and the minorities properly speaking. Between the position and the political feeling of all these there are many gradations.

The Šokci and Bunyevci have not had such a happy time as the Orthodox Serbs. They have certain grievances which they share with the minorities. To begin with, as one of them said to me simply, 'We object to theft and corruption, and we feel that we belong to the west and are being ruled now by Orientals'—words identical with those which the Croats so often use. They have suffered rather than profited by the land reform, since, although some of them received small allotments, their big communal properties were laid heavily under contribution for the benefit of the colonists and *dobrovoljci*. They have even educational grievances, although they do not constitute a linguistic minority, since in some of their centres, at least, the authorities have enforced upon them the use of the Cyrillic alphabet in the schools and in official intercourse.

Their religious susceptibilities, which are very tender, have been hurt in various ways. The laicization of the schools (to be described later) was much resented, particularly as many of their own teachers were dismissed and Serbs put in their places. Then they have suffered, perhaps more than any other peoples in Yugoslavia, from direct pressure against their religion. As we shall see presently, the religious question is not very acute in Yugoslavia. The Serb tends to regard religion as an unalterable attribute of nationality, and his instinct is less to assimilate than to discriminate—placing the non-Orthodox populations in a position of inferiority, but not attempting to convert them. This holds good in his relations both with the minorities and with the Croats and Slovenes; one of the few forms of persecution not practised in Croatia is the religious. But the Šokci and Bunyevci are in a peculiar position. They are admitted anomalies. Their religious tenets are those of the Croats, while their dialect and certain popular customs, folk-songs, &c., are more closely akin to those of the Serbs. The Serbs thus regard them as they regard the Macedonians, as Serbs *in posse*[1] and susceptible to assimilation, the chief outward sign of which would be conversion to the Orthodox Church, while the Croats claim them for their own. Something of a civil war goes on between the

[1] In 1866, however, their spokesman protested very vigorously against this appellation 'Catholic Serbs', insisting that they wished only to be regarded as 'Hungarian nationals of Dalmatian stock' (*nép-fajul dalmaták, nemzetül Magyar*), I. de Nagy, loc. cit.

claimants, in which the prospective prizes are the chief sufferers. There have been certain much resented instances of encroachments by the Orthodox Church in the Šokaz and Bunyevac districts: excessive building of Orthodox churches (for the benefit of the newly arrived and unpopular colonists), restrictions on the development of the Catholic organization, even half-forced conversions.

Nevertheless, the struggle, although a struggle it is, is already to-day essentially a family quarrel, an internal affair between the different branches of the Yugoslav people. This is true even of the religious question, since the former Magyar Roman Catholic hierarchy has been replaced almost entirely by Croats. The Bunyevac question has become a sort of variant on the Croat question, which means that the national problem has been solved in the Yugoslav sense. The Magyarone Party, which would welcome a return to Hungary, is confined to-day to the older generation and is naturally growing weaker year by year. The younger generation is overwhelmingly Yugoslav and rejects *a priori* the idea of returning to Hungary which, in their belief, would expose them to renewed Magyarization (I have not heard them discuss the possibility of receiving cultural autonomy within Hungary). Thus, although their position within the Yugoslav State is yet unsettled, though they have much to resent in that State, and express their resentment openly enough, yet they must be counted as partisans of the State in its ideal form and opponents of revision.

The strange, indeterminate position of the north Slavs (Slovaks and Ruthenes)[1] has already been mentioned. They have not been exempted from the uniform necessity of using Serb in official intercourse, nor from the ungenerous character of the minority school regulations to be described below; but the wind is tempered to them. They are allowed to use their language locally in oral communication with the authorities, and the Slovaks have been allowed to maintain a cultural society and a secondary school of their own, besides certain alterations in the régime enforced in the primary schools, and a satisfactory statute for their religion, for which they now possess an autocephalous Church, with bishop and general inspector. Their own leader (they have but one, who acts as chairman, secretary, or both to all their organizations, political, cultural, and economic) told me that his flock did not mind learning Serb, which, indeed, they had used even before the War as the local *lingua franca*, and learnt easily; they regard the present position, in fact, as facilitating a real cultural renaissance, easily to be reconciled with loyalty to the Yugoslav State.[2]

---

[1] There is also a considerable colony of White Russian émigrés, who have been treated with great generosity and are largely employed in minor official posts.
[2] A subsidiary cause of their content was, until recently, their extraordinary

I believe the same position to hold good of the local Ruthenes; all in all, the position of the non-Yugoslav Slavs thus appears to be satisfactory.

§ 6. YUGOSLAV MINORITY POLICY

We come now to the real minorities, admitted and treated as such—the Magyars, Suabians, Roumanians, and Magyarone Jews. The treatment of them, in general, is probably worse than that accorded to any other minorities with which this work deals. They have to undergo not only the severities under which all Yugoslav subjects have had to groan, but also quite special sufferings of their own; for the Yugoslav law and practice regarding minorities, as our description will show, is more ruthlessly illiberal than that of any other Successor State, outside Italy. If less is heard about the sufferings of the Voivodina than of Slovakia or Transylvania, this is due to a variety of causes, none of which reflect any particular credit on Yugoslavia: the relatively small area involved, its comparative unimportance to Hungary, who has not troubled to make much propaganda on the subject, the severity with which the authorities deal with persons suspected of making complaints to the outer world, and the cynical indifference with which they themselves receive such complaints, till these fall silent for very weariness.

Finally, Yugoslavia struck her blows at the minorities at the very outset, while Czechoslovakia and Roumania still hesitated. Thus some wounds have already cicatrized in the Voivodina which are still bleeding in Slovakia and Transylvania.

The chief mitigation which can be found lies in the fact that although individual exceptions, such as M. Pribičević, have appeared on the scenes, with often disastrous results, Belgrade is not, at heart, interested in the minority question. It is preoccupied with its main problem of adjusting the relations between the various branches of the Yugoslav race, and has had, as a rule, little thought to spare for anything else. Ignorance has spelt indifference, so that it would be difficult to rouse Serbian public opinion to a really consistent anti-minority campaign, such as occupies the thoughts of the more civilized nation of the Czechs. Many of the laws denounced by the minorities as oppressive (and rightly so, to

prosperity. These Slovaks are hop-growers, and after the War experienced an astonishing boom, so great that a single village boasted no less than fifty cars. The collapse of the boom brought with it a number of bitter complaints over the heavy taxation, and the Slovaks are said to have declared that 'they would do without festivals and banquets if they might have passports for Czecho-slovakia or America instead' (cit. *Nation und Staat*, Dec. 1928, p. 211). Nevertheless, they remain, so far as I could judge, docile and loyal supporters of Yugoslavia.

judge by their texts) are not aimed at them at all, but only at the
Croats and Slovenes, the minorities being simply ignored. Violent
and active persecution, where it occurs, is not usually perpetrated
by Government officials but by *četniki*, members of the 'Narodna
Obrana', and other juvenile desperadoes, who are, indeed, often
instigated and encouraged, and practically never punished, by
official circles. The more notorious Governmental exponents of
the iron hand have usually been sent, not to the Voivodina, but to
Macedonia or Montenegro.

In certain respects, moreover, the minority problem in the
Voivodina has been simpler than in either Transylvania or
Slovakia. The Serbs set themselves to achieve precisely the same
goal of complete national domination as the other new masters,
but they had less far to go.

As a nation, the Serbs before the War were by no means in such
a state of national inferiority as the Slovaks or the Roumanians.
Their peasants were largely freeholders, and occupied some of
the best land in the Voivodina. They boasted an old-established
and prosperous merchant class in many of the towns, and even
some rich landed proprietors. In the south there were a fair
number of Serbian officials. Economically and socially they stood
on much the same level as the local Germans and Roumanians.
The Magyars, indeed, possessed a richer upper class, but it was
not very numerous, and below it lay a very wide space until one
came to the majority of the local Magyars, most of whom were
labourers or dwarf-holders, far poorer, as a class, than the Serb
or German peasants. This frail Magyar top-layer melted almost
in an hour, largely by the action of the Magyars themselves, when
their officials migrated across the frontier to avoid taking the oath
of allegiance to Yugoslavia. The land reform destroyed most of
what remained. What remained behind was neither so economically
powerful nor politically so formidable as to call for any sustained
or systematic effort to cope with it.

Some of the minorities, too, have profited by considerations
similar to those which have guided both Czechoslovak and Roumanian policy. The Germans have, at certain periods, been allowed
very considerable cultural concessions, where it has seemed possible
to play them off by this means against the Magyars. The Jews have
been offered similar concessions to divorce them from the Magyars,
although treated with increased severity when the advances have
been repelled. Consideration for her ally has made Yugoslavia
from time to time don a velvet glove even in her treatment of the
Roumanians; only the Magyars, as the enemy *par excellence*, have
always had to meet the full brunt of every repressive measure.

But these concessions, where they have occurred, have been

incidental and often impermanent. It remains true that Yugo-slavia's treatment of her minorities has been harsh; and this added severity comes, as we said, on top of a régime exceptionally unen-lightened even in its handling of its own people.

§ 7. THE MINORITIES: POLITICAL AND ADMINISTRATIVE CONDITIONS

As regards political life, Yugoslavia's policy towards the minor-ities has been one of simple repression, on the whole uniformly applied, although the Germans have been treated a little less brusquely than the Magyars and Roumanians. During the elec-tions to the Constituent Assembly, the Germans and Magyars were not admitted to the voters' lists at all, under the pretext that, until the period laid down in the Peace Treaties for option had expired, it could not be said whether they were Yugoslav citizens or not. In 1922 all three minorities organized parties of their own. In the 1923 elections the Magyars were so terrorized by Serbian national-ists that they had to drop the idea of an independent candidature; but the Roumanians got a Deputy into the Skupština, and the Germans, who had drawn up a discreet programme loyal to the State and in detail not displeasing to the Radical Party, secured 7 mandates in the Voivodina, besides one in Slovenia.

In 1924, however, the German party, stung out of its calculated subservience to the Government by M. Pribičević's educational policy, committed the indiscretion of voting with the Opposition on the crucial question of the verification of the Croats' mandates. As it happened, their votes just tipped the scale against the Government. In rage, M. Pašić dissolved the parties of all three minorities (on which occasion some of the German leaders were assaulted with cudgels, revolvers, and even, in one or two cases, bombs). M. Davidović, who succeeded M. Pašić, allowed the parties to be reconstituted, but the pressure in the 1925 elections was so heavy that the representation of the Germans was reduced to five, while neither the Magyars nor the Roumanians secured a mandate.[1] In 1927 the Magyars made a compromise in one district with the Radicals, and in another with the Democrats, which allowed them to enter Parliament for the first time with three mandates, the Germans, who stood independently, securing six. In 1929, how-ever, all parties were again dissolved under the Dictatorship, and under the electoral laws issued since that date it has been im-possible for the minorities to put up lists of their own.

[1] According to the Magyars, nearly half their voters had even at that date not been registered, while many others (6,000 in Zenta alone) were struck off the rolls before the elections. Three members of the party executive were imprisoned a few days before the polling, following a charge (subsequently proved unfounded) of receiving foreign financial assistance.

The Germans were allowed one Senator and one (afterwards two) Deputies on the Government list, and the Magyars one Deputy. It is, however, clear that these are no more than spokesmen, or supplicants, who can state their case to the Government, for the latter to listen or not, as it pleases; neither can they indulge in any sort of real independence. The Magyar Deputy is denounced by the leaders of the original Magyar Party as a renegade and no true representative of his people. His attitude towards the State is certainly different from that of the official party leaders. I am less sure whether his more conciliatory policy is unwelcome to the peasants and labourers who form the great bulk of the Magyar minority, but obviously neither he nor any other minority's representative can speak in the least freely.

In local government the minorities have been equally powerless. There has, indeed, only been one period, of slightly over a year—1927 to January 1929—when any sort of representative local government has existed, and then the three Departments set up under the Vidov Dan Constitution were so arranged that the majority was always safely in Slavonic hands. In the communal elections of 1927, which were fairly free, a large number of Magyar and German representatives were elected; but an agitation promptly arose in local Serb circles, consequent on which the results of the elections, where favourable to the minorities, were largely annulled. The Prefect of the Bačka Department on his own responsibility annulled the mandates of all Magyar notaries in his Department, generally on the ground that they had not sufficiently mastered the language of the State. In 1928 there were in the whole Voivodina only 10 German and 6 Magyar village notaries, against 114 Slavs (nearly all Serbs).[1]

After 1929 the Voivodina was united with Northern Serbia in the Danube Banovina, thus ensuring a Serb majority,[2] and a return was made to the system which had prevailed until 1927, and all officials of local government, including villages, towns, and larger units, were appointed, the majority being Slavs. Thus the Banovina Council appointed in 1930 contained only 2 Magyar members; the City Council of Zenta, which is over 86 per cent. Magyar, had only 4 Magyar members out of 38; that of Petrovgrad (Veliki Bečkerek, Nagy Bečkerek), where the numbers of Serbs, Magyars, and Germans are about equal, had 2 Magyar members, 2 German, and the rest Yugoslav, &c. Communal elections were restored in 1933, but only those lists were passed as valid, the first 6 members of which in the communes, or all members in the case of municipalities,

[1] *Die Nationalitäten in den Staaten Europas*, p. 358. The Magyars were all dismissed in 1929.
[2] The Baránya was attached to the Save Banovina.

were able to read and write the language of State. The decision whether this condition is fulfilled is taken by higher authority. In any case, the notary is not elected but nominated. Similarly, under the municipal government Decree of September 15th, 1934, one-third of all Municipal Committees are nominated by the Ban, while the other two-thirds are elected, by open ballot, from parties founded on a basis of 'national unity'. The minorities can thus get representation, as in Parliament, only by standing on a 'national' list. In spite of this, it must be admitted that the new system brought about a real and substantial increase in the minority representation.[1]

In local as in central government Serbian is the only official language. An attempt by the Magyars in 1927, after the departmental elections, to obtain leave for the minority languages to be used equally with Serbo-Croat in the Bačka Department was rejected. In the communes, as in the larger bodies, all resolutions must be brought forward and minutes kept in Serb; although no similar rule is, clearly, enforced as regards the oral discussion, at least in the purely minority communes.

More galling, in practice, than this rule—since self-government has in any case played only a very small part in Yugoslav life—is the strict regulation whereby the sole language of administration is Serb. This applies throughout the entire Governmental hierarchy from the central Ministries in Belgrade down to the lowest instances. All official documents, notices, &c., are issued in Serb alone, and written communications to the authorities drawn up in any other language are simply thrown into the waste-paper basket, or at best returned to the sender. I have heard of cases in which communications from lawyers on behalf of clients have been returned, although written in Serb, because the paper used bore the lawyer's name and title in Magyar as well as Serb.[2] In the towns and larger villages, and in general, wherever the population is mixed, officials are sometimes actually forbidden to speak to the public in a minority language; cases are quoted where minority officials have been dismissed their posts for infringing this rule.[3] In some purely minority villages, oral communication in a minority

---

[1] I am officially informed that in 1935 the Serb Council included 13 Magyars and 4 Jews; that of Petrovgrad, 3 Germans, 4 Magyars, and 2 Jews; that of Vršac, 14 Germans; and that of Bela Crkva, 11 Germans—an undoubted improvement on the previous figures.

[2] Quoted in an account of the position of the Magyar minority which I must cite as 'Hungarian MS.', since it has not yet, so far as I know, been published. The author is a Magyar and strongly anti-Serb, and I have not used his information unless either I have been able to corroborate it, or my own experience has made it seem a priori probable. A petition to the League of Nations, dated 1935 and covering much the same ground, is quoted as 'Petition'.

[3] Hungarian MS.

language is allowed; but in others even this is forbidden, and villagers ignorant of Serb have to use interpreters.

In the Courts, defendants and witnesses are allowed to use their own language only if totally unacquainted with the language of State. All official proceedings are conducted, sentences promulgated, and records kept in the language of State only.

The language rule applies, of course, to public services such as posts and railways; nor will the reader be surprised to learn that Yugoslavia has followed the popular practice of Serbizing all local names, either by translating the original (if this was a Magyar or a German name) or by re-baptizing it boldly after some Serbian notability. Thus we get Pašičevo (a German village), Ninčičevo, and Pribičevičevo—the last name constituting a somewhat ironical comment on the mutability of human fortunes, since M. Pribičević, after whom it was proudly named, died in exile a few years later, a bitter foe to the régime. Street names, &c., are, of course, in Serb. Letters, under a decree of 1934, are not delivered if the old names are used in the addresses.

The insistence on the use of Serb in all public life has been made a pretext for excluding the minorities, almost without exception, from official careers. The higher posts have been filled from the first with Yugoslavs, chiefly Serbs from the Old Kingdom. A certain proportion of the railway employees, &c. (90 per cent. of whom were Magyars), were at first retained in their posts, even after they had refused to take the oath of allegiance (which in Yugoslavia, as elsewhere, was demanded before the territory had been legally transferred). The great majority of these were, however, dismissed as soon as Serb substitutes had been trained to take their places. The Vidov Dan Constitution actually made admission to public service for a Yugoslav citizen of nationality other than 'Serb-Croat-Slovene' conditional (unless by special exception) on ten years' residence in the Kingdom.[1] It is to-day very exceptional for a non-Yugoslav to be found in an official post, except in purely local administration, and practically unheard of for him to be appointed to one.[2] Pensions are now paid to the former Hungarian officials, but the final settlement was only reached in 1936, and many persons appear to have encountered extreme difficulties in making their claims good.[3]

[1] Art. 19.
[2] I am officially informed that 885 Germans, 632 Magyars, 276 Slovaks and Ruthenes, and 121 Czechs were employed in the Voivodina in 1937 by municipal and communal councils. Unhappily, my figures do not give the number of Yugoslavs so employed. There are said to be thirteen Germans, two Magyars, and one Jew employed in the office of the Banovina in Novi Sad. I personally only remember encountering two non-Yugoslav employees during my wanderings in the Voivodina, as against certainly several scores of Yugoslavs; but I was dealing chiefly with higher employees.
[3] *Hungarian MS.* See also *Die Nationalitäten in den Staaten Europas*, p. 367.

Unlike the other Successor States, Yugoslavia has even severely restricted the use of any other language than Serb in public, although non-official, life. Names and callings of shopkeepers, professional men, business firms, &c., goods in shop-windows, advertisements, the headed paper of businesses, &c., all have to be in Serb, and, in some places, in Cyrillic characters to boot (the use of Latin script underneath being sometimes, but not always, permitted).[1] The books of businesses must be kept in Serb, and in some cases practically all business correspondence. In one town the Prefect of Police ordered all shopkeepers to greet customers entering or leaving their shops in Serb. Only if the customer could speak no Serb whatever might the sale of the packet of soap or ribbons be conducted in Magyar.[2]

In cinemas only Serb captions may be used, &c.

A certain number of cases have occurred in which members of minorities have been threatened and even attacked by members of nationalist societies (with the tolerance of the authorities) for using their own language in the street or in public places such as cafés. The chief sufferers in these cases have been the Magyarone Jews. None of the outrages have (so far as I know) been so bad as the worst cases in Roumania or Italy, but that is the best that can be said for them.

All clubs, associations, &c., were 'Serbized' from the very outset, where they were not closed down altogether. Statutes must be drawn up, minutes kept, &c., in Serb alone. Concert programmes have to contain a proportion of Serb numbers; dances may not include more than one or two Hungarian national dances, &c. Sometimes even societies existing for the sole purpose of fostering minority culture, e.g. Magyar-reading circles, have been ordered to conduct their meetings in Serb, as though a society for the reading of the Welsh classics had been compelled to read and speak English only. An attempt has now been made (to which we shall return later) to regulate the question by leaving all general societies (with their accumulated capital) to the Serbs and founding quite specific minority cultural societies for the exclusive use of the minorities. It is, perhaps, hardly necessary to say that the Press, particularly the Magyar, stands under the strictest censorship.[3]

---

[1] The practice varies. In some places a surtax is imposed on Magyar or German signs: in some, the use of them is prohibited altogether; in others, it is free.

[2] *Hungarian MS.* These are, it is true, acts of individual officials and not sanctioned by law; but they have been very numerous, and some of the officials perpetrating them have held very high posts.

[3] The art of censorship varies curiously in the different Successor States. In Czechoslovakia, if a passage is censored, the paper has to appear with the offending columns left blank, thus displaying its shame. In Yugoslavia, on the

§ 8. THE MINORITIES: EDUCATIONAL AND CULTURAL QUESTIONS

Yugoslavia's cultural policy has been a compound of pure repression (with very occasional bursts of comparative enlightenment) and of the usual playing off of the non-irredentist against the irredentist minorities. Sometimes the one tendency has prevailed, sometimes the other. Immediately on entering into possession, she took over for herself practically the entire Magyar higher educational system, leaving only the elementary schools in the purely Magyar districts. The Roumanians were not even so well off as that, since their schools were simply taken over and the teachers ordered to learn Serb within a year. Seventy teachers and priests fled to Roumania and were replaced by Serbs, Russians, and Bulgars, so that for the time the Roumanian education in the Banat simply ceased to exist. Other Roumanian intellectuals were interned in Belgrade, or in their homes.[1]

The Germans, on the other hand, were at that time positively courted. The Magyar schools in German districts were hurriedly turned into German schools, and new German schools actually built in the Baránya. The gymnasium in Novi Vrbas, an originally German foundation which had afterwards been Magyarized, was re-Germanized, a second German private gymnasium was allowed in Vršac, and German parallel sections were established in the Serb gymnasia of Novi Sad, Pančevo, Bela Crkva, and Petrovgrad. While the Yugoslav troops were occupying Temesvár, a German was actually made civil governor of the district, and was promised a German university if the local Suabians would use their influence to secure the attribution of Temesvár to Yugoslavia.[2]

Something of a cultural renaissance began among the local Suabians, who, as we said, had been at the time 90 per cent. Magyarized. In June 1920 a 'Schwäbisch-Deutscher Kulturbund' was founded in Novi Sad and by 1924 had established 128 local groups in the Voivodina and Syrmia, with a total membership of 55,000. Both parties seemed satisfied, since the motto of the 'Kulturbund'—'Staatstreu und Volkstreu'—expressed the abandonment of the old Magyarone attitude in favour of active support of the Yugoslav State.

contrary, fresh matter has to be inserted, so that the reader shall not suspect that any disloyal sentiments could ever have been entertained; and that matter has to make sense of a sort. Thus the article is closed up and an account of a football match or a note on bee-keeping appears at the end. In Roumania the space has to be filled, but it does not matter how, so that a political article appears intersected with Mutt and Jeff strips, printed in any old order, often upside-down, and tantalizingly unfinished if the whole series is not required.

[1] V. Vărădean, 'Die Rumänen aus dem Jugoslavischen Banat', in *Glasul Minorități lor*, February 1930, p. 70.

[2] G. Grass, 'Das Schulwesen der Deutschen in Südslawien', in *Nation und Staat*, July–August 1928, p. 794.

The motives prompting this indulgence were, of course, purely political; in which connexion it must be remarked that, in so far as German culture has been protected in Yugoslavia, this has been the work of the Serbs alone, and has been absolutely confined to the Voivodina and Syrmia. The Slovenes, who have enjoyed *de facto* autonomy in their own districts since the War, have consistently striven to repress the German element there, and the Croats, although less violent, have been little more lenient. The question is really governed by the religious situation. In Croatia most of the Germans are Catholics, like the Croats, and as the two nations share also many cultural and historical traditions, linguistic assimilation also follows easily enough. In fact, the local Germans do not themselves strongly resist the assimilation which the Croats desire, since without it they can have no hope of an existence more spacious than that of a peasant.[1] It is therefore still proceeding fairly rapidly to-day. In the Voivodina, the religious difference between the Catholic or Protestant Germans and Magyars and the Orthodox Serbs forms a much wider gulf. The German will only naturally assimilate to the Magyar, and conversely the Serb does not regard any non-Orthodox as genuinely capable of assimilation. Thus, in the Voivodina, the only real alternative to a German with Magyar culture is a German with German culture, or else a totally uneducated German.

As soon as the immediate need for German support had passed, with the definitive settlement of the frontiers, the early complaisancy towards them vanished. In 1924, after the unfortunate *gaffe* of the German political party, Pribičević even suppressed the Kulturbund, and sequestrated its entire property, stating that the permission to found it had been 'a boon of which the Germans had proved themselves unworthy'. Its suppression was alleged to be 'also a measure of reprisal against the oppression of the Slovene minority in Carinthia'. Davidović cancelled his predecessor's action, but so many difficulties were put in the way of the Kulturbund that it was not able to resume work at all until 1927, and had only recovered a little of its lost ground when the proclamation of the dictatorship made it necessary to begin the whole story over again.

During this period also the Yugoslav scholastic legislation for the minorities took shape. The Vidov Dan Constitution merely stated, in this connexion, that 'racial and linguistic minorities will receive elementary education in their mother language under conditions to be laid down by law' (Art. 16, para. 13). For the time,

---

[1] In this connexion it is interesting that most of the German schools in Croatia, Slavonia, and Bosnia were opened under the 'Great Serbian' dictatorship. This policy was strongly resisted, especially by the Croat clergy.

however, owing to the difficulty of transacting business in the Skupština, the matter was left in the hands of successive Ministers of Education, who merely issued administrative decrees, and no law was enacted until December 5th, 1929, when the Dictatorial Government promulgated an Act which did little more than consolidate the earlier decrees. This Act has not since received any substantial modifications in principle. The Germans have, however, secured a few alleviations for themselves, while a special bilateral convention between Roumania and Yugoslavia, concluded in 1933 after years of fruitless negotiation, introduced a special régime for the Roumanians of the Yugoslav Banat in return for corresponding concessions to the Serb minority in the Roumanian Banat. Even this agreement did not alter the fundamentals of the Yugoslav system, which is most easily described as a whole, the modifications applying to different minorities being cited where they occur.

It may be observed that these laws apply also to the Slav minorities of the Voivodina (Slovaks, Ruthenes, &c.).

All education in Yugoslavia is, in principle, State education. In accordance with this principle, all minority schools in the Voivodina were taken over by the State, with their property, soon after the occupation, the teachers being declared to be State employees. It was provided at the time that existing private schools might be allowed to continue, but although Croat, Slovene, and Mohammedan schools in other parts of the kingdom received the benefit of this concession, no private or confessional minority school in the Voivodina was exempted under it, except a single German girls' burger school in Vršac. The 1929 Act again expressly prohibits the opening of new private schools, other than in quite exceptional circumstances.[1] Only the Roumanians are allowed under the Convention, if they wish, to open at their own expense private elementary schools, ranking as public schools, supervised by the State but with the examinations conducted, and certificates issued, by the Roumanian teachers. Thus, by a measure of very doubtful legality,[2] the chief minorities lost all their independence in educational matters, besides a great deal of valuable property.[3]

[1] e.g. on lighthouses, very small islands, or mountain observatories.

[2] When in 1934 Albania declared all her education to be State, the question whether this measure was compatible with her Minorities Declaration (which in this respect is identical with the Yugoslav Minorities Treaty) was laid before the Permanent Court of International Justice, which decided that she was not entitled to abolish the private schools (Advisory Opinion No. 64).

[3] The *Petition* gives a long list of the property in foundations, &c., simply seized and used either for Serb schools or for other purposes. It includes 20 Catholic Convents of one Order alone. In addition the Churches lost under the Agrarian Reform large estates, the proceeds of which had been used for the upkeep of schools.

Elementary education lasts for 8 years, but the schools are divided into two categories: lower (for the first 4 years) and higher (for the latter 4). In the latter, all instruction is given exclusively in Serb,[1] since Yugoslavia interprets her obligation under the Minority Treaty as applying only to the lower elementary schools.

In the latter, 'special sections' may be opened for the linguistic minorities where they reside in 'considerable numbers'. These are, for the Germans and Magyars, 30 per cent. (25 per cent. in exceptional cases), for the Roumanians under the Convention, 20 per cent.

Under the law, instructions in these 'sections' is given in the mother tongue, Serb being taught as a subject from the first class upward, while in the third and fourth years history and geography are also taught in Serb. In the Roumanian schools, the instruction in Serb begins only in the third year; a similar concession was granted to the Germans in 1931 but repealed in 1933. The instruction is always in Serb, i.e. with the Cyrillic alphabet, and many children spend their years mastering this alphabet without acquiring a word of Serb in the process.[2]

Kindergartens, under the law, are in Serb only, but the Roumanians are allowed kindergartens in their own language, and the Germans also obtained a similar concession in 1931. So far as I can gather, the Magyars have also a few kindergartens. In some places there are special 'preparatory classes' for minority children, but these are exclusively Serb and fulfil the purpose only of giving preliminary instruction in the Serb language.[3] In 1931 the Germans also obtained permission to organize courses for illiterates, under State control and on condition that they also gave instruction in the language of State.

Instruction in housekeeping, and apprentices' schools and lower special schools is exclusively Serb.

The syllabus in minority sections is the same as in the Serb schools. All teachers must know Serb perfectly (many minority teachers are said to have lost their posts on this score; but it may be with justification). Children of one minority language may not enter the school of another; if there are not enough children of one minority to justify their receiving a section of their own, they must attend the Yugoslav school (in any case, where both a Yugoslav

[1] In 1931 the Germans were allowed the concession that instruction in their schools should be in German for the first two years; but this was repealed in 1933.
[2] I was personally acquainted with a highly intelligent young Magyar mechanic in a garage in Belgrade who was just picking up Serb from his colleagues. He had read and written it at school for eight years without learning to understand one word of it.
[3] The *Hungarian MS.* describes these schools as compulsory, which, however, is officially denied; but it is curious that one of the concessions made to the Germans in 1931 was that these schools were not compulsory for them.

and a minority section exist, minority parents may always send their children to the Yugoslav section, but not vice versa). Jewish children, whatever their language, must attend the Serbian schools.

These provisions, which are similar to those in force in Roumania, are, of course, primarily directed against the Magyars in the Voivodina, and as such were rather welcomed by the local Germans, although in Slovenia they have been applied very severely against the Germans to the benefit of the Slovenes. They have, however, been utilized for a campaign of Slavization easily exceeding any Roumanization practised in Transylvania. In 1922 M. Pribičević issued a decree to the effect that the nationality of the child was determined by the authorities, who were to judge by his surname. Children with Slav names were forbidden to enter minority classes, and inquiries were often extended for some generations back (particularly in Slovenia) to see whether a Germanized or Magyarized name was not originally Slavonic.[1] In 1927 this rule was altered for the Voivodina (the amendment being extended to Slovenia in 1928) allowing children to be entered for minority schools 'according to their nationality, their habitual language and the declaration of their parents', and in 1931 the declaration of the parents was accepted—for the Germans but not for the Magyars—as the sufficient criterion; but in 1933 it was decreed that children of mixed marriages must enter Yugoslav schools if the father was of 'Yugoslav nationality', and the analysis of names was resumed on a considerable scale, to be abandoned once again in the autumn of 1936.[2] For Roumanian schools the declaration of the parents is accepted.

It is difficult to obtain statistics of schools, particularly since the Voivodina no longer constitutes an administrative unit. The Magyars possessed in 1934, according to official figures quoted by them, 132 parallel sections of elementary schools and 25 kindergartens,[3] as compared with the 645 elementary schools and 48 burger schools which were theirs before the War (the larger figure, of course, covering many schools established to Magyarize non-Magyar children). According to their own estimate, their present numbers would entitle them to 212 schools.[4] Yugoslav statistics

[1] In the Bačka an order was issued that children of mixed marriages were to be entered only in Yugoslav schools if either the father or the mother was a Yugoslav. (*Nation und Staat*, October 1927, p. 117.)

[2] *Danubian Review*, December 1936, p. 19.

[3] A Yugoslav official source gives me the figures for 1936, of 581 classes (= 170 sections?), 3 Magyar and mixed kindergartens.

[4] *Hungarian MS.* According to the *'Petition'*, the number has decreased since. Even children with Walloon, Italian, &c., names, descendants of old, long since assimilated settlers in the Banat, have been subjected to the analysis. They are sent, of course, to Serb schools, since no Walloon schools are available. An earlier order still decreed that children must enter Slav schools if their parents spoke a Slavonic tongue, even badly.

given me in 1934 claimed that there were then in Yugoslavia 154 German sections of elementary schools, with 580 classes, 38 kindergartens, and 6 burger schools. Five of the 6 burger schools were, however, closed in 1931, so these figures were already out of date. Some of the kindergartens are, moreover, really 'preparatory courses' teaching Serb only. On the other hand, the number of elementary schools has recently increased, and about three-quarters of the German children probably receive elementary instruction to-day in their mother tongue.[1] According to the same Yugoslav statistics, the Roumanians possessed 31 schools with 78 classes, and 4,807 pupils, which seems roughly the same proportion of pupils to total population as for the Germans.

A further grave deficiency is that the instruction even in the mother tongue is often given by Slav teachers who do not know the language properly.[2] This may not at first have been entirely the fault of the Yugoslavs since many Magyar and Roumanian teachers left the country voluntarily in the first days, and few local German teachers were available, owing to the Magyarization of their schools before the War. The situation, however, instead of improving subsequently, got steadily worse as the remaining teachers were retired, dismissed, or transferred to Macedonia, Montenegro, &c. No attempt was made to remedy the shortage until 1931, when the Germans got permission to start a private training college in Novi Vrbas for teaching in their elementary schools; the Roumanians were, under the Yugoslav-Roumanian Agreement, allowed a section in the training college at Vršac, and even the Magyars, after long negotiation, secured a single class of a section in a college in Belgrade. Progress seems, however, to have been very slow; for it was reported from German sources in December 1936 that although 33 German teachers had by that time become qualified, only one had been appointed to a post. According to official sources, 289 out of the 506 teachers in Magyar sections were Magyars.

The situation as regards secondary and higher education is less satisfactory still.

The authorities have always denied that the minorities possess any right to secondary education in their own language. The early concessions made to the Germans were cancelled by M. Pribičević in 1925, only the four lower classes in Vršac and Novi Vrbas being

[1] According to official statistics, the Germans possessed in 1936 766 classes (= about 192 sections) with 48,872 pupils and 675 teachers.

[2] *Die Nationalitäten in den Staaten Europas*, p. 347, quotes the case of the town of Ruma in Syrmia, where 1,232 German children are said to have had in the 'German' schools 6 German teachers and 24 Slavs, of whom 8 spoke German very badly and 9 not at all. In 1934 I was told that 'one-quarter of the teachers in the German schools spoke no German at all, one-quarter spoke it badly, and the other half was untrained'. The Magyars estimate that 'at least one-third' of the teachers in their schools are Slavs.

allowed to continue; and soon after, the German instruction in Vršac vanished also. The Act of 1929 provides only for secondary education in the 'language of State' and an Act of December 5th, 1931, lays down the same rule even for burger schools. Besides the training college and sections mentioned above, the Germans now possess only a private burger school for girls in Vršac (which they were allowed to start in 1933) and the gymnasium or half-gymnasium in Novi Vrbas; the Roumanians, parallel classes in the Vršac gymnasium; and the Magyars, parallel classes at two secondary schools: a 4-class gymnasium at Senta and an 8-class gymnasium at Subotica, in which, however, only the Magyar language and religion are taught in Magyar.[1]

The inadequacy of these provisions is enhanced by the fact that Yugoslavia makes it more difficult even than Roumania for a minority student to attend a high school abroad. The German and Magyar students thus depend exclusively on the Universities of Zagreb and Belgrade.

Finally, the tone of the instruction given is, according to the minorities, excessively nationalist in the Yugoslav sense, no consideration being paid to the special susceptibilities of the minorities. Requests by the Germans to use their own text-books have been refused. The provision of the 1931 Constitution that education must aim at inculcating the spirit of 'national unity', unexceptionable in itself, is often used as a pretext for denationalization. A particular grievance alleged by the Germans is that pressure is put on their children to join the 'Sokols', an institution which, admirable in many respects, is also specifically Slavonic in spirit and fundamentally unsuited to any other nationality.

It remains to describe the development of the general cultural life of the minorities. After the dissolution of the Kulturbund, a period of general pressure followed, under which all the minorities suffered. Under the Dictatorship the situation was at first even aggravated, as all associations had to re-submit their statutes for approval, which was often refused, and granted only after long delays.

Towards the Germans, indeed, Yugoslavia has recently shown a tendency (assuredly not unconnected with the increasing political rapprochement between Yugoslavia and Germany) to revert to the more liberal policy characteristic of 1919 and 1920. The Kulturbund, after a long wrangle over the question of the official language (during which it lost even some of the ground which it had gained since 1927) got its statutes re-approved in April 1931. Since that time it developed very rapidly indeed. It has a large head-quarters in Novi Sad and many branches (210 in December

[1] *Petition.*

1936). It organizes lectures, training courses, theatrical representations, and picture shows, has founded a great number of
popular libraries, issues several periodicals, and engages also in
various social activities, assistance to poverty-stricken communes,
labour exchanges, apprentices' courses, &c. Affiliated to it are an
association of German University students, a choral association,
an association of sports clubs, and a medical section. The organization of the Youth Groups is particularly active. In December 1936
there were no less than 142 of these. Thus an extremely vigorous
national life has developed which has largely made good the great
shortcomings of the official school policy.[1]

Incidentally, the organization has been able to expand its activities geographically since the reorganization of the country in 1929.
Syrmia is now included in the Banat of the Danube, and the
German villages there share in the work of the Kulturbund. It is
also slowly beginning to penetrate Slavonia, where a German
weekly paper is printed in Osjek. I was, however, informed that
the local Germans themselves do not welcome its activities there,
as tending to disturb their relations with the Croats.

It must be emphasized, once again, that this comparative toleration of German culture is confined to the Voivodina and its neighbouring territories. It has no counterpart in Slovenia, where the
hostility to the local Germans remains undiminished, and the
Slovene question naturally affects the feelings of both parties in
the Voivodina. Nor is the position idyllic, even in the Voivodina.
Cases are still common of arbitrary official prohibition of what
would appear, on the face of them, to be entirely harmless activities. Moreover, the school legislation has remained substantially
unchanged. Nevertheless, even the qualified cultural liberty
allowed the Germans has, as will be seen, had important effects
on the local political situation.

The Magyars have had a far more difficult time, owing perhaps
to faults on both sides. Yugoslavia is not anxious to see Magyar
culture or influence flourish, and is very quick to smell the political
rat behind every arras, while the Magyars undoubtedly find the
task of dissociating politics from culture as difficult as it is, to
them, unaccustomed. It is also true that the general cultural level
of the Magyars in the Voivodina was not high before the War.

The Dictatorial Government allowed them to open a Popular
Cultural Association, similar to that of the Germans, with head-
quarters in Veliki Bečkerek and permission to open branches in all

---

[1] According to the Yugoslav official document previously quoted, the Germans
possess in all 'more than 415 different cultural, recreative, intellectual and
humanitarian societies'; most of these are probably affiliated to the Kulturbund.
They also issue 26 newspapers.

towns and villages with Magyar populations. During the next two years a number of branches were opened, while a second association, the People's Circle of Subotica, also displayed much activity. There was promise of a real, if modest, development of local cultural life, whereby a Magyar of the Voivodina could at least hear a lecture in his own tongue, borrow a book from a library, and even see a play. The police, however, watched the associations jealously, and in the spring of 1934 the Ban of the Danube Banovina closed them both on the ground of alleged political activity. Long-drawn-out negotiations ensued, during which the cultural life of the Magyars vegetated dismally. Only in the autumn of 1936, when the Government, for the first time for many years, showed signs of a more liberal policy in cultural questions, particularly towards the Magyars, were the two associations allowed to re-open, and permission given for twelve more to be formed.

The Roumanians have a cultural association of their own—an unpretentious and struggling shrub over which the storms have passed which struck down the loftier trees.

A word must be added on the Church question which, from a situation which up to the War closely resembled that of Transylvania, has since developed quite differently. In the Hungarian Voivodina, as in Transylvania, the national life and cultural activities of the different nationalities were built up on their respective churches, the two branches of the Orthodox Church almost personifying the Serb and Roumanian nationalities, while the Roman Catholic Church, although it included Germans and Slavs as well as Magyars, was representative in chief of the Hungarian State and a strong Magyarizing influence.

By taking over the Confessional schools, with their property, Yugoslavia at one blow divested the Churches of most of their national-cultural importance, while the losses to which they were subjected under the land reform weakened them still further.[1] Their relationship with the State, as purely religious organizations, was regulated by a Law of Cults, the chief provisions of which are as follows:

No one cult in Yugoslavia enjoys a privileged position, and all are subordinate to the State. 'Recognized' cults (these are the Orthodox, Roman Catholic and Uniate, Islamic, Calvinist, Evangelic (German and Slovak), Old Catholic, and Israelite) constitute legal personalities, enjoy autonomy in the conduct of their own affairs,

[1] The *Petition* estimates the losses of the Reformed Church (the oldest of them all) at about 24 million dinars. The Orthodox Church itself, however, has also suffered considerably. When taking over church buildings for lay schools the civil authorities were, in theory, bound to pay rent, although they did not always do so. On the other hand, the payment of the teachers had often proved a heavy burden to the poorer churches and from this they were, of course, now released.

are competent to acquire, retain, and freely dispose of property of all kinds, within the limits of their respective Statutes and subject to the control of the State (one of the limitations being that their property must serve exclusively for church needs and not be used for any other purpose). They are entitled to levy for their own needs surtaxes on the State taxes, besides which they also receive subsidies from the State. Representatives of the Churches may not engage in any political activities or propaganda.

This law could not, of course, in itself divest the various Churches of their national character, but Yugoslavia has been remarkably successful in paralysing the minority Churches as national factors. The Protestant Churches of various denominations and the Israel-ites have formed national organizations without any constitutional link with any corresponding bodies outside Yugoslavia. In any case, these Churches are too small to constitute an important prob-lem. The Roman Catholic Church is a much more powerful body, but here, too, Yugoslavia has proved very successful. Under her Concordat with the Holy See, the boundaries of the dioceses have been remodelled to coincide with the State frontiers, and a Papal Nuncio resides at Belgrade, to whom the Roman Catholic bishops are directly responsible. They are thus removed from the in-fluences of Vienna and Budapest. More important still is the fact that Yugoslavia, unlike Roumania, is itself half a Catholic State, and in Croatia and Slovenia is able to draw on a large supply of national-ist, even fanatical clergy (for the Croat clergy had never been Magyarized as the Slovaks were). The Magyar bishops and clergy have gradually been replaced by Croats, so that to-day the Catholic Church in the Voivodina is a Yugoslav rather than a Magyar influence. The process has even gone so far that in some places Magyar and German children are unable to receive religious in-struction in their mother tongue, owing to the lack of Magyar-speaking priests (although elsewhere, it is true, one may still find a Magyar priest officiating in a mixed commune).[1] In this Yugo-slavia seems, as so often, to have overshot the mark, for the result has been rather to estrange the people from the Church than to reconcile them, through the Church, to Yugoslavia.

The only Church to-day not completely under the control of the State is the Roumanian Orthodox Church, which by special arrangement belongs to the Roumanian See at Timişoara.

There remains the question of the relationships between the various Churches, which is not wholly satisfactory. If the minority

---

[1] The position of the Protestant Church (which is two-thirds Magyar, one-third German) is worse still. Here there is great difficulty in getting pastors trained at all, since they are forbidden to attend the College in Hungary. In 1930, according to the *Petition*, 24 out of their 54 parishes had no pastor.

Churches have largely lost their national character, the same cannot be said of the Serbian Orthodox Church, which still regards itself in the Voivodina as the embodiment of Serbian national life. The rule against political activities is notoriously not enforced against the Orthodox bishops and priests, who pose as the champions of the State, while the State has in return granted the Orthodox Church many quiet favours, including what appears to be a disproportionate share of State subsidies.[1] The situation is, in fact, very similar to that in Transylvania, only, so far as I could judge, less acute. In some places there have been bitter complaints of the encroachments by the Orthodox Church; a case which has caused particular resentment is in Senta, where the Catholics have been prevented by the authorities from building a new church for which they had subscribed, and which they had even begun to build in 1914.[2]

In other places where I made inquiries, the local Orthodox Church was given a clean bill by the minorities.

'Forced conversions' have occurred, but they have been rare; but a law is said to have been promulgated in 1933 that children of mixed marriages must be brought up in the Orthodox faith alone.

§ 9. THE MINORITIES: ECONOMIC AND SOCIAL QUESTIONS

The economic readjustment has been less sensational and perhaps less painful than the corresponding process in Transylvania, for the reasons which have already been stated: the Serbs had less leeway to make up, the minorities fewer advantages to lose. In

[1] The following table shows (I) the number of adherents of each of the main creeds in Yugoslavia (according to the 1921 census); (II) the financial support (in dinars) accorded to each, under various headings, by the State in the 1929/30 budget; (III) the sums which would have been allocated had a strictly numerical proportion been observed; and (IV) the resultant + or − accruing to each Church.

	I.	II.	III.	IV.
Orthodox . .	5,602,227	61,561,613	47,600,455	+13,961,158
Roman Catholic and				
Uniate . .	4,776,845	35,612,363	40,320,782	− 4,708,419
Mohammedan .	1,337,637	19,983,954	11,390,391	+ 7,593,563
Protestant .	216,849	1,155,000	1,852,345	− 697,345
Israelite . .	64,204	1,131,220	542,399	+ 588,821
Old Catholic . .	. .	235,400	. .	. .
	. .	119,679,550	. .	. .

The grant to the Orthodox Church was made up of: (1) ordinary subsidy 46,312,613 D, (2) special contributions, 15,240,000 D. The position as regards the other Churches does not appear to have changed for the better since the above date.

[2] This particular question has, however, certain peculiarities too complicated to be stated here; but the case is not one of pure religious persecution.

essence, however, Yugoslavia has followed the same policy as Roumania in Transylvania or Czechoslovakia in Slovakia and still more obviously in Bohemia: to transfer the wealth of the country from the minorities to the majority. She has even carried this policy out more brutally than either of her allies.

In view of the agricultural character of the Voivodina, much the most important question in this respect is that of the land reform. The national purpose of this measure, as enacted in the Voivodina, has never been denied; for the Serb has at least the merit of frankness. Thus Dr. Sečerov, an ex-Secretary of State in the Ministry of Finance, wrote in a work published in 1930 that the real object of the reform was the destruction of the big landed proprietors in the Bačka, Banat, and Baránya, who were regarded as an 'a-national element'.[1] A typescript MS. given to me by the Press Section in Belgrade repeats this statement in almost the same words;[2] and I only refrain from quoting further evidence, because the point is generally admitted.

We may therefore take it that the reform was aimed directly at a class conceived to consist mainly of minorities who were made to suffer because they were minorities. The Serbian landed proprietors were not, indeed, entirely exempted; certain individuals, communes, and Church foundations suffered important losses. Nevertheless, official instructions have been preserved showing that in this respect also a degree, at least, of discrimination was intended,[3] and even the fact that some Yugoslav elements were involved does not affect the political purpose of the whole measure: the deliberate destruction of the big landowning class on the ground that it constituted an 'a-national element'.

But far more serious is the inequality in distribution, in which respect Yugoslavia has easily outdone Roumania or even Czechoslovakia. By order of the Government, no members of minorities were allowed even to buy land within a zone of 50 kilometres from the frontier without the consent of the Ministries of War and the Interior. In spite of careful inquiry on the spot, I failed to find

[1] Cit. *Die Nationalitäten in den Staaten Europas*, pp. 359–60.

[2] 'The big estates in the north had to be broken up on national as well as social grounds' and colonized from the interior 'in order to replace the national-politically unreliable element of the big landowners (who were mostly Magyars) by the particularly valuable colonist element and thus to set up an ethnical cordon against unfriendly Hungary'.

[3] The Hungarian *Petition* quotes two such orders, one from the Minister of Agrarian Reform, the other from a Chief of Section in the Ministry of the Interior. Both of these are of early date (1920 and 1921) and the policy may have been modified later; but it does not appear to have been quite abandoned. The *Hungarian MS.* quotes several cases of Serbs whose lands were spared; an official Yugoslav source, on the other hand, informs me that 'no single estate belonging to Yugoslavs, whether privately owned, Church or State, did not come under the Agrarian Reform'.

a single case in which such consent had been given, or any land granted to minorities at all, within or without the 50-kilometre zone.[1] On the contrary, it has often happened that Magyar peasants, who had bought land from communes, &c., out of their own savings have had the transfers cancelled and the fruit of their thrift and industry simply taken away and given to Serbs.[2] Thus the Magyar labourers and dwarf-holders who, as a class, needed land more urgently than any other section of the population, came away empty-handed. There are to-day probably anything between 80,000 and 120,000 landless agricultural labourers in the Voivodina, and some three-quarters of these are Magyars.[3]

The replacement of the landlords by the colonists has plunged this unhappy class into the deepest misery. Ironically enough, some of them now scrape a living by renting, unofficially and more or less illegally, the farms of *dobrovoljci* and colonists who are unable to cope with the local conditions.

Their position has been still further impaired, since the outbreak of the great agricultural crisis, by the systematic employment of Serbs and other Yugoslavs from the interior on such public works as are undertaken, and on harvest labour. Cases are even alleged in which private industries have been forced to dismiss their Magyar employees and employ Slavs instead.[4] A certain

[1] It was suggested to me that a few Germans had applied successfully for colonists' portions on the remote Albanian frontier and others had bought some land from estates in Slavonia. After leaving the Voivodina I heard, from a Hungarian source, of one village, said to be the only one, in which the local Magyars had received land. According to an official Yugoslav source, some Magyars were also able to buy land in Slavonia.

[2] Both the *Hungarian MS.* and the *Petition* quote cases of this kind. One case is also given in *Nation und Staat*, October 1927, p. 117.

[3] The *Danubian Review*, April 1936, p. 30, gives two figures in two consecutive notes. According to the first, 'official data record between 75 and 80 thousand landless agricultural labourers and natives in the Voivodina, the majority of whom are Hungarians'. The second quotes an estimate for 1932 by M. Savić, former Departmental Chief in the Ministry of Commerce, of about 120,000 landless labourers in the Danube Banovina, three-quarters of whom are Magyars. For the Government policy, cf. also a statement by M. Pavle Radić, Minister of Agrarian Reform in the Uzunović Cabinet of 1926, that 'the minority peasants and landless persons are not to benefit by the land distribution under the reform' (cf. *Petition*). I was also informed, by a Magyar in the Voivodina, that Magyar peasants had refrained from applying for land owing to threats from Budapest that if they did so, they would suffer for it when the revision came. This allegation has been very hotly denied by Hungarian sources, and I should not have recorded it had it not been repeated to me, when I inquired further, by a source I consider worthy of belief. Proof, in either direction, is impossible to-day. Any such threats cannot have been made in conspicuous fashion, or the Yugoslav propaganda would have made much play with them.

[4] *Danubian Review*, loc. cit. The *Hungarian MS.* also states that cases have occurred in which firms before receiving contracts have been forced to dismiss their minority employees. I have been officially informed that the allegations quoted above are without foundation; but I have myself read nationalist propaganda urging such steps; and no propaganda is allowed in Yugoslavia which is unpleasing to the Government.

number of them have found alternative employment in other parts of Yugoslavia, especially Belgrade, where national discrimination is not so strong. The Suabian maids and nurses, in particular, are a familiar and almost a cherished spectacle of the Belgrade streets, and some Suabian and Magyar masons and mechanics have found a new livelihood in the capital. There are said to be several thousand Magyars living in Belgrade to-day. There has also been some emigration to Macedonia, and waiters from the Voivodina are popular throughout Yugoslavia, owing to their courtly manners and wide linguistic attainments. The position of a large proportion of the Magyars remains, however, really desperate.

In other fields of economic life one hears exactly the same complaints in the Voivodina as in Transylvania. Minority undertakings have in some cases been 'nationalized', i.e. compelled to take on Serbian Directors, or to place a certain number of shares at the disposal of the Government. Credits are not granted to minority concerns, members of the minorities (although not taxed differently from the Serbs)[1] have to pay up their taxes promptly and in full, failing which their property is distrained on—whereas the light-heartedness with which the *dobrovoljci*, in particular, regard such obligations, and the indulgence shown them by the authorities are proverbial through the Voivodina. The minority banks were in any case impoverished by the collapse of their investments in Austro-Hungarian War Loan, &c. Owing to these difficulties, many of them have had to close down or to merge with Serb institutions.

The economic life of the minorities now centres chiefly round their co-operatives, and round small banks which devote themselves chiefly to operations connected with the local agriculture. The Germans have managed to develop these activities with reasonable success; they possess in Yugoslavia, according to official figures, 'more than 140 economic and financial societies, of which over 60 are banks, the remainder being organized on a co-operative basis. Their total capital is more than 100 million dinars.'[2] The Roumanians have 10 banking institutes which, according to the

---

[1] Except for the local taxes imposed in certain towns on shop names and signs, &c., written in Magyar. As regards credits, it is impossible to distinguish between the discrimination practised against the minorities, and that under which the whole Voivodina suffers. The *Petition* gives figures showing that in 1919–27 the Voivodina paid 24·07 per cent. of the total direct taxation of the kingdom, but only received 6 per cent. of the credits from the National Bank. For 1928 the figures were 25·72 per cent. and 6·5 per cent. They would probably be even more unfavourable if separate data were available for the Yugoslav and minority concerns in the Voivodina.

[2] From a type-written account of 'La Politique minoritaire en Yougoslavie', issued by the Press Section of the Yugoslav Foreign Office.

same source, 'entirely replace the co-operative institutions'. The Magyars are probably the worst off for national institutions, partly owing to the greater hostility reigning between them and the authorities, partly because they do not possess, and never have possessed, so large an independent peasant class. Their co-operative system originally depended on a head-quarters in Pest, which continued to support it until 1930; but in that year the Pest Institute withdrew its support, so that the Magyar co-operatives had collapsed under the weight of taxation,[1] while of their 168 banking institutions the majority had been crushed out of existence altogether, the small remainder having been 'nationalized' without exception.

§ 10. THE ECONOMIC PROBLEM

Not much need be said on the general economic position of the Voivodina. As we saw, its previous connexions lay all to the west and north, and it was then very favourably situated, possessed of assured markets and lying immediately on the lee side of a tariff wall which protected it from its most dangerous competitor.

Even if we leave aside as temporary phenomena such factors as the fall in production owing to the land reform, the disturbances through currency devaluation, &c., the change of frontiers and the break-up of the Austro-Hungarian Monarchy have undoubtedly proved disadvantageous. Markets abroad have no longer been safe or easy to find. Until 1924 there was no trade agreement between Yugoslavia and Hungary, and although for some years thereafter economic exchanges were quite brisk, the economic crisis brought about another abrupt reduction which later compensation agreements could only partly remedy. Trade has also been affected at times by the strained political relations between the two countries, and has always been made more difficult by the reluctance of Yugoslavia, in particular, to grant visas and give passports.

Better relations were maintained for some years with Austria, to which the Voivodina continued to export very largely. But Austria's efforts to make herself agriculturally self-supporting affected this trade considerably, and the Rome agreements of 1934 between Italy, Austria, and Hungary dealt it a further blow, since under these Austria diverted a large part of her imports from

---

[1] *Die Nationalitäten in den Staaten Europas*, p. 367. According to the *Petition*, 17 agricultural co-operatives survived, while 213 disappeared. This does not mean that the Magyar peasants are debarred from the co-operative movement, since many of them now belong to the Yugoslav Credit Co-operative, with its centre at Petrovgrad (Veliki Bečhereli). Co-operatives are not taxed if they belong to a recognized association; the old Hungarian system does not appear to have been 'recognized'.

Yugoslavia to Hungary. Czechoslovakia has never been a good customer to Yugoslavia, the 'Economic Little Entente' remaining more of a pious wish than a reality; and since she embarked on a deliberate and purposeful policy of autarky, in the interests of her own peasant proprietors, she has naturally been unable to take much of the surplus from the Voivodina. Roumania's structure is too similar to that of Yugoslavia for much trade to be conducted between the two.

Two countries outside the old Monarchy have done considerable trade with Yugoslavia, these being Italy and Germany. Italy, however, although occupying an extremely important place in Yugoslavia's foreign trading account, yet takes rather the products of the western half of the country. Her imports from the Voivodina were for a time affected by Signor Mussolini's 'battle of wheat' and, again, by the Rome Agreements.

Germany, on the other hand, has been a steady purchaser of the wheat, maize, and live stock of the Voivodina, especially since 1934,[1] and thanks to her, these products have always found their markets since the War.

Clearly, however, the welfare of the Voivodina must depend increasingly, as time passes, on its position within Yugoslavia. Hitherto the internal market has been comparatively unimportant. This is due in part to the forlorn state of communications[2] which, being itself partly a relic of Hungary's pre-War policy, may be expected to improve gradually; the bridges over the Save and Danube, only recently opened, must bring Belgrade several hours nearer. A more serious difficulty, however, is that inner Yugoslavia is itself an agricultural country which does not greatly need the produce of the Voivodina. There are, indeed, parts of it which cannot feed themselves, but most of these areas—Montenegro, the Lika, Herzegovina, and Dalmatia—are so desperately poor that neither can they import to cover their deficit; they simply go short. The industrialization which is beginning to take place in parts of Slovenia, Croatia, and Bosnia has not so far made any great difference; the workers earn such miserable wages that their purchasing power is negligible. Most of them are half peasants, whose families keep them in food, while the few pence which they earn go on salt, tobacco, and petroleum.

[1] Germany has taken, under the clearing agreements, much Voivodinian wheat which she has not herself consumed, but sold on to Holland for spot cash.
[2] In 1934 I was told in Vršac that the railways were so bad and so expensive that the local dealers preferred to take their goods 40 miles by road and then up the Danube by water. This may sound reasonable to English ears; but the usual local means of transport is the ox or buffalo wagon, which takes about 3 days to cover 40 miles, and the road a mere track through sand dunes, much of which I did on bottom gear, along the level, in the height of summer. I shudder to imagine it in wet weather.

So far, therefore, the Voivodina has remained the naturally richest agricultural area in an agricultural country, and its role has simply been that of a milch cow. The position is really more dismal if the heavier taxation which it now bears is justified by natural conditions than if it is discriminatory. In the latter case, a fit of wisdom in the Government might bring about a remedy; in the former, there is nothing to be done about it, until the whole country has reached a different stage of development.

Against this, it must be remarked that the local industries of the Voivodina, sheltered as they are to-day by the new tariff wall, have in many cases enjoyed considerable prosperity. There is clearly a future within Yugoslavia for the agricultural industry of the Voivodina; although the absence of non-agricultural raw materials must always leave it somewhat confined in scope.

Clearly the Voivodina does not present an economic problem anything like so difficult as Slovakia or Ruthenia. If the great economic unit of Austro-Hungary had to go, then it is hard to say whether it would ultimately find more difficulty in marketing its produce abroad as part of Hungary, or of Yugoslavia. As regards internal markets, if Yugoslavia were able to develop a denser population and a large consuming power, the Voivodina might fare better in Yugoslavia than in Hungary, while it is not essential to the economic structure of either country (perhaps Yugoslavia needs it the more of the two). For itself, it can exist under almost any régime. The change of frontiers has inflicted no irreparable damage on its inhabitants as it has, for example, on those of Ruthenia. They can live wherever they are placed; which is more than can be said for many of the peoples under our survey.

§ 11. POLITICAL FEELING AMONG THE MINORITIES

The political feelings of the Magyars are easy enough to describe. There is, so far as I could judge, no class of the population which is at all reconciled to Yugoslav rule. The chance of conciliating the peasants was missed when they were excluded from the benefit of the land reform, which, in fact, made the position of the hired labourer class far more difficult. The workers are too few to count greatly; and, in any case, Yugoslavia has not made any advances to them.

The leaders of the Hungarian party have always been correct in their official attitude—and, for that matter, in their utterances towards myself. Nevertheless, it is perfectly clear to any one not blind that the Magyar party never succeeded in changing its heart and becoming genuinely attached to Yugoslavia; nor can I see any reason why they should have done so.

In the 1931 'elections' a new leader—one M. Szántó—came forward with a programme of 'loyalty', on the strength of which the authorities allowed him to be elected on the Government list. The older Magyar leaders, without exception, refer to M. Szántó as a renegade, and a Jew at that, in the pay of the Government and without any following in the country. M. Szántó, on the other hand, maintains that he is as good a Magyar as any other; but he explained to me frankly that he thought the leaders of the official party mistaken. They were obviously in perpetual, barely concealed opposition to the State, and conceived their mission to consist in finding occasions for complaint against it at home and abroad. He himself accepted the State and worked to improve the lot of the Magyar minority within it on that basis; and he felt convinced that he could secure far more real benefits for his constituents by that method than by any other.

In this respect there is no doubt whatever that he is right. The needs and wishes of the poor labourers who make up the greater part of the Magyar minority are very modest. M. Szántó has certainly obtained much more for them than his predecessors ever did, including the rudiments (if they are no more) of a teachers' training college, and many minor local alleviations. Nor is it true that he has no following. I accompanied him on a tour of his constituency and received a very strong impression of the gratitude borne to him by these poor men, and ample proof that he had bettered their position in many small ways. Even the Yugoslav authorities are capable of coming, if not half-way, yet part of the way towards those who wish to meet them; and the ordinary peasant and labourer would much prefer to make the best of a bad job than to live in a state of perpetual feud with the authorities, who will always have the last word. The old Magyar leaders, in Yugoslavia as in Slovakia and the Crişana, have much to answer for. In some respects, as in the question of the land reforms, they have ignored or even injured the interests of most of their followers in defending those of a class, and they have kept alive a spirit of hostility by proclaiming their grievances to the outer world, in the hope of thus hastening on the day of revision, instead of seeking a remedy for them.

M. Szántó's attitude could, of course, be highly inconvenient to Hungary if the question of revision ever became practical politics; for it is his habit to assure the Government and the outside world of the loyalty and contentment of the Magyar minority. Clearly, Yugoslavia would use this as an argument against any territorial concession, and this is why she encourages M. Szántó in many ways.

I must therefore record my conviction that while nearly all the

Magyars of the Voivodina much prefer to be left in peace by all parties, and are profoundly grateful for any alleviations which a more conciliatory policy may get for them, yet in their hearts they find Yugoslav rule profoundly antipathetic. Were revision ever to become practical politics, M. Szántó's following would melt away like butter in the sun, and the great majority of the local Magyars would rally round the nationalist leaders. In this respect the new generation differs no whit from the old. Yugoslavia has not succeeded in Serbizing their hearts—nor, for that matter, their tongues. To bring about a true reconciliation, to imbue the hearts of the local Magyars with a genuine preference for Yugoslav rather than Hungarian rule, would need a long period of a very different government than Yugoslavia has yet known. The régime under which they have lived hitherto has been such as to make impossible even the beginnings of a reconciliation; it has, indeed, destroyed such sympathies as the Serbs had formerly enjoyed when Serbia was still a peasant democracy. Given a free choice, the vast majority of the Magyars of the Voivodina would, I am convinced, wish to return to Hungary.

Of the remaining minorities, the Jews have remained the most faithful to the Magyars. This is, perhaps, rather surprising, for, in contrast to Roumania, pre-War Serbia always lived on exemplary terms with her Jewish population, the great bulk of which are Sephardim, or Spanish Jews. Anti-Semitism in Serbia was, and is to this day, almost unknown, and the Jews in return have always been excellent Serbian patriots. The Jews of Serbia, led by the Chief Rabbi, have used all their influence to alter the attitude of their brothers in the Voivodina, but hitherto, so far as I could gather, with little success. Although encouragement from their fellow Jews and threats from Serbian nationalist organizations have been lavished upon them, most of them, particularly in their chief centre, Subotica, have continued to speak, feel, and act as Magyars.[1]

The result, incidentally, has been very unhappy for the Jews. The outbreaks and agitations against the so-called 'Judaeo-Magyars' have become in recent years hardly less violent in the Voivodina than in Transylvania. Deplorable excesses have occurred on several occasions. Naturally, however, these have had the contrary effect from that intended by their authors and have cemented the bond between the Jews and the Magyars.

The Germans are different. One need not pay too much heed

---

[1] See E. Prokopy, 'Wie die Juden der Vojwodina dem Ungartum entfremdet werden' in *Glasul Minoritaţilor*, January–February 1934, pp. 35 ff. My own observation fully bears out what M. Prokopy writes; also his conclusion that the various threats and complaints which he quotes 'amount to a testimonial that the local Jews, despite all obstacles and distress, remain attached to their Magyar mother tongue and Magyar culture'.

to their continual protestations of loyalty to the Yugoslav State, nor to their genuinely correct attitude. The Germans are no Catos, and could hardly, in their position, act otherwise.

They have, however, passed through a real transformation, analogous to that of the Suabians in Roumania. The process was slower to begin in Yugoslavia, and is still less complete, since Yugoslavia has tolerated less liberty, either cultural or political, than Roumania, even in the Voivodina, while the whole situation has always been poisoned by the open sore of German-Slovene relations in the north-west. Thus the number of Germans of the old generation who long remained, and remain, pro-Magyar at heart is still considerable.

Among the younger men, however, the national awakening which Yugoslavia had encouraged during the first years proved permanent. In 1933 an official representative of a changed outlook appeared on the scene in the person of one Herr Hasslinger, who headed an 'Erneuerungsbewegung' (Renewal Movement). Herr Hasslinger not only protested absolute and even vociferous loyalty to the Yugoslav State: he went so far as to reject even the idea of a minority political party, not to speak of an appeal to Geneva, saying that a minority could have no separate political or economic interests from the majority, but only separate national cultural interests.

The Yugoslav Government naturally countenanced and generously encouraged these theories. They encountered much opposition among the Suabians themselves, who believed that Herr Hasslinger's activities were prompted by pure personal ambition, and were detrimental to the local German cause, both as breaking up its unity and as encouraging the Government through their over-complaisance; for, they said, 'a minority leader should never say that he is satisfied'. In fact, Herr Hasslinger failed to depose the old leaders and seems to have vanished from the scene.

Nevertheless, an 'Erneuerungsbewegung' of a sort, emotional if not intellectual, has taken strong hold of the younger generation. The majority of them, even in the villages, are more or less Nazi in their sympathies, and although up to the end of 1936 the 'Erneuerer' (who had since found a new Führer) had not yet managed to get official control of the local German movement— had, indeed, suffered official defeat—yet the future seems to be with them. The gain is Yugoslavia's, the loss Hungary's. The Suabians of Yugoslavia complain bitterly enough of the shortcomings of Yugoslav rule; but in the main they feel not otherwise than their cousins across the Roumanian frontier. The cultural liberty which they enjoy is small enough, but at least it is more than Hungary permits. They are allowed to be Germans, and even to be Nazis, and they would not willingly sacrifice this licence for a return to Hungary where the Government still makes every effort to assimilate the non-Magyars and the Jewish press fans the flames against everything German. In fact Nazi theories, which place the preservation of 'Volkstum' above every other objective, are far more easily compatible with the Yugoslav idea of the State, which allows a minority to exist so long as it is powerless, than with the Hungarian, which is dominated by the idea of assimilation.

The Germans of Yugoslavia, like those of Roumania, are probably in for some years of very complete political confusion. Nor can we be sure that their militant spirit and often truculent manners will not end by involving them in many a conflict with the authorities. On balance, however, the intelligentsia must be counted as standing to-day for Yugoslavia rather than for Hungary on the revision issue, and the peasants may be relied on to follow their leaders.

The Roumanians are neutrals. They have little cause to love the Serbs, who until the conclusion of the 1933 Agreements treated them perhaps more harshly than they did the Magyars themselves. Yet by all their history and tradition, and above all by their religion, they stand nearer the Serbs (with whom they intermarry freely enough) than to the Magyars. They would be happiest if that part of the Banat in which they live could be joined to Roumania, but as regards the Hungarian-Roumanian dispute, as one of them said to me: 'the revision question is no concern of ours. We struggle for our human rights; where we get them is quite indifferent to us.'

§ 12. THE POSSIBILITIES OF REVISION

The development of political feeling among the different nationalities of the Voivodina has put a somewhat different complexion on the question of revision. In 1918, if we take as basis the 1910 statistics, probably not more than 35 per cent. of the population really wished to join Serbia; I compose this figure of all the Serbs, half the Bunyevci and Šokci, the majority of the 'other Slavs', and half of the 'others'. Close on 60 per cent. would probably have voted for remaining with Hungary; one may fairly make up this figure out of the Magyars, the Germans, the Jews, half the Šokci and Bunyevci, and a few others. I leave the Roumanians aside, as hostile to either solution.

It is true that this calculation takes the Magyars' figures for their own numbers at their face value; but the majority of the Magyar-speaking Slavs, Germans, and Jews included in the rubric felt Hungarian, if they were not genuine Magyars.

If for calculation of opinion to-day we take, as we must, the 1921 figures, it is the number of Serbs, and not of Magyars, that is suspiciously large. Immigration of colonists, *dobrovoljci*, and officials certainly accounts for part of the increase of 'Serbs', among whom, however, the Catholic Slavs are now also reckoned. The striking decrease of the Magyars is due partly to the emigration of refugees and optants,[1] partly to the changed attitude of some other nationalities, particularly the Germans and the Bunyevci, many of whom, especially of the latter, had been entered in the 1910 census as Magyar-speaking.[2]

Giving the Serbs practically the whole of their alleged figure, and adding nearly all the 'other Slavs', we get a figure of about 580,000 out of 1,380,000 or 42 per cent. who can be counted as definitely in favour of Yugoslavia, with perhaps 400,000 (the Magyars and a few others), or just under 30 per cent., as decidedly for Hungary. If the Germans, who still make up 24 per cent. of the local population, sided with Yugoslavia, that State would have an easy majority; if they sided with Hungary, Hungary would have just over 50 per cent. of the local votes. As we have said, given the present policies of the two states in national questions, the Suabian vote would go to Yugoslavia; but it must be emphasized that theirs is essentially a 'floating vote', and that an altered policy in Hungary towards her national minorities might bring about a complete reversal of the German attitude. A few years ago the same thing could have been said of the Bunyevci; to-day the assurance of cultural autonomy might still tempt a few of them back, but not, I think, many.

It may be remarked here that the old local spirit, which might once have led the population of all nationalities to welcome a federal arrangement such as might still prove the best solution for Transylvania, no longer exists in the Voivodina. The Magyars never possessed it; the latest-comers to the country (for, in spite of Hungary's thousand-year-old constitutional claim, the present Magyar population is only two hundred and fifty years old in the north, and under a hundred years old in the south), they regularly and even consciously represented the idea of the unitary Hungarian State against all regionalism. The Serbs have lost most of it in the fifteen years of their union with Serbia. The Germans retain it more fully than any other nationality, but even their mental horizon has grown far wider in recent years.

[1] These numbered about 35,000 between 1918 and the taking of the census. (*Glasul Minoritaţilor*, April–May 1932, p. 121.) The number has probably risen since to at least 45,000. There has also been a considerable Magyar emigration to Brazil.

[2] In each of the two chief Bunyevac centres the figure of 'Magyars' fell by some 50 per cent.: in Subotica from 55,587 to 27,730, and in Sombor from 10,078 to 5,105. In the Magyar town of Senta, on the other hand, it fell by 600 only, or about 3 per cent., and in the District of Senta it increased.

The situation as regards local revision has been altered both by the change of attitude of the Catholic Slavs and by the colonization. The former is probably the more important factor, for I doubt whether more than 25,000–30,000 persons can have been settled on the frontiers, and of these certainly not more than half are established and maintaining themselves by their own efforts.[1]

Even this, however, is not a negligible number; and, in addition, we must now calculate that most of the Bunyevci would probably vote for Yugoslavia to-day. According to the 1931 census, two of the three frontier districts of the Bačka showed a Yugoslav majority, only the eastern district still showing the Magyars in a large majority.

Even so, the Magyar element in the Northern Bačka and the North-Western Banat is very strong, and it should be possible to draw a line which, while leaving the main Serb centres in the south with Yugoslavia, would yet restore to Hungary many more Magyars than it sacrificed Slavs.

As regards the Darda Triangle the case for revision seems to me strong. It is true that the population immediately south of the frontier (and in part also north of it) is Slavonic; but the local Šokci who form the bulk of the indigenous Slavs have little national feeling, and they are in a minority. The 1910 (Hungarian) figures for the Triangle gave 20,937 Magyars, 14,770 Germans, 1,896 Croats, 6,436 Serbs, and 5,436 Šokci; the 1921 census showed 21,609 Yugoslavs, of whom 10,461 were Serbs, 13,973 Magyars, and 15,751 Germans; Pécs remains the more important market, although further from the apex of the Triangle than Osijek; and the Germans, young and old, with whom I was able to speak there, expressed a decided preference for Hungarian rule. The shifting beds of the Drave and the Danube do not seem very formidable (so far as a layman can judge) and the strategic argument smacks far too much of a compromise with force to leave one fully convinced either of its justice or its moderation.

[1] The Land Office in Novi Sad had under its charge in 1934 130 communes, with a total population of 9,671 families, 5,136 of whom were of local origin. 40 of the 130, with 6,800 houses, were new villages, something over half of which, say 4,000 families, were on the northern frontier. The Land Offices of Veliki Bečkerek and Vršac probably account together for about as many persons as that of Novi Sad.

FIUME

THE question of Fiume is the most absurd but the least acute of all those arising out of the dismemberment of Hungary. It may therefore be treated here very shortly.

Like the remaining towns of the east coast of the Adriatic, Fiume appears in the oldest records as a haunt of Illyrian pirates. It was conquered by Rome about 180 B.C. and Romanized. Afterwards it formed part of Charlemagne's Empire, and was subsequently under the overlordship, at times of the Patriarchs of Aquileia, at others, of the kings of Hungary. In or about 1465 it passed to the Emperor; was captured by Venice in 1503, but recovered by the Empire in 1511. In the division of 1522 it was assigned to Inner Austria, being the southernmost point on the Austrian coast; for immediately beyond the river of Fiume (Rijeka) began the Croatian coast. During all this period Venice was the undisputed Queen of the Adriatic, and succeeded in degrading all other ports in the neighbourhood to mere local importance. Early in the eighteenth century Charles VI and his councillors, particularly Prince Eugen, decided that it was essential for the Empire to possess an alternative port to Venice. It was a question of choosing not so much the best port as the least bad, for all the possible alternatives suffered under various disadvantages, with one great drawback common to all: the great difficulty of communications with the hinterland. Fiume was one of the first places considered—indeed, the Commercial Commission instituted at Graz in 1717 voted to create only one single free port, and that at Fiume, partly on account of its abundance of fresh water and the natural facilities of its harbour, partly for the curious reason that it was 'nearer to Naples'. Fiume was, however, rejected as difficult to defend when the neighbouring islands were in the possession of Venice; and after Aquileia and Drago had also been considered and rejected, the lot finally fell on Trieste as the main centre of Austrian trade; although Fiume was at the same time declared a Free Port and given the same privileges as Trieste.

In 1776 Maria Theresa, in response to the request of the inhabitants of Fiume themselves,[1] united Fiume with Hungary. It thus formed a tiny outlet for Hungary to the sea, between Austria on the one hand and Croatia on the other. The step was of

---

[1] 'Damals sind sie gescheiter gewesen', said an old gentlemen to me in Fiume in 1934.

enormous advantage to Hungary, which by this means acquired a means of escaping from the crushing preferential duties imposed in Austria against Hungarian produce. Owing, however, very largely to the bad communications, and to the hostility of Trieste and Venice, the trade of Fiume remained local for nearly a hundred years, during which it formed part of Napoleon's kingdom of Illyria from 1809 to 1814, of Austria 1814–22, of Hungary 1822–49, and of Croatia 1849–68. In the latter year the Compromise was negotiated between Hungary and Croatia, with the remarkable result that two different texts were reached. The Magyar version declares that Fiume is attached to Hungary as a *corpus separatum*, the conditions of its autonomy to be negotiated by agreement between Hungary, Croatia, and Fiume; the Croat text says simply that no agreement could be reached. The instrument was presented to the King and Emperor for signature with a Croat translation of the Magyar version pasted over the Croat text.[1]

In practice the town returned to Hungary as a *corpus separatum* and no attempt was made to negotiate the conditions. Croatia, however, did not abandon her legal standpoint, and two seats were kept vacant in the Croatian Diet for the Deputies of Fiume.

During the half-century 1868–1918 Fiume made very great progress. It had been a comparatively insignificant place—the population in 1851 numbered only 12,598. The port accommodation was primitive, and there was no communication, except by road, with the hinterland. Two factors made for its very rapid development. On the one hand Hungarian policy was firmly set on creating for Hungary an outlet independent of Austria; on the other, both Austria and Hungary were driven equally, by the protectionist tariff policy adopted by Germany after 1875, to enlarge their outlets in other directions. Plans for building the railway and for enlarging the harbour were set on foot immediately after the restoration of the Hungarian Constitution in 1867; and these were constantly adapted and enlarged at great expense to the Hungarian Government, which spent very large sums on the port and on subsidizing an Hungarian steamship line (subsidies were given also, on a smaller scale, to the sailing vessels). Special facilities were offered to goods exported or imported via Fiume; for although a tariff arrangement was in force for regulating the traffic equitably between Fiume and Trieste, this could be got round by a system of rebates. In fact the trade of Fiume increased very much more rapidly than that of Trieste, whose stagnation after 1869 was specifically attributed to the rise of Fiume.[2] Between 1871 and 1895 the trade of Fiume increased by 460 per

[1] Seton-Watson, *The Southern Slav Question*, p. 82.
[2] Tamaro, *Storia di Trieste*, p. 460.

cent. (bulk) and 524 per cent. (value), while the value of the trade of Trieste rose in the same period only by 26 per cent. In addition, a considerable industry was established in Fiume, notably a petroleum refinery, a naval construction works, and the Whitehead torpedo works. Fiume became a fine city, with magnificent public buildings, spacious streets and squares, a capacious harbour and storehouses, railway sidings, &c., on a lavish scale.

It must be pointed out that the rise of Fiume was not at the expense of Trieste alone, but also at that of the Croatian ports. The railways of Croatia, like those of Hungary proper, were controlled from Budapest, and were so planned that the only important railway line of Croatia was that leading from Zagreb via Ogulin to Fiume (a second line connected Fiume with Trieste via St. Peter am Karst), while the Croatian ports were without any railway communication whatever, and Dalmatia (under Austrian rule) possessed only a single narrow-gauge railway. Thus almost the whole maritime traffic of Hungary necessarily passed through Fiume, which was as important for Croatia as it was for Hungary proper.

The political question was always very important. When Hungary took Fiume over in 1868 it was almost entirely a Croat city; of the 12,599 inhabitants in 1851, 11,908 had been Slavs and 691 Italians. The population increased rapidly; in 1880 it was 20,981, in 1900 38,855, and in 1910 48,492. There was, of course, a certain influx of Magyars, whose numbers rose from 367 in 1881 to 6,493 in 1910—most of this increase being due to immigration of officials and of Magyarized Jewish merchants, although Magyarization may account for some small part of it. There was also a small population of German and other nationalities. The great feature was, however, the steady rise of the Italian element at the expense of the Croatian. The Croats, of course, inhabit the hinterland in solid masses, and even in the industrial suburb of Susak they continued to form some 85 per cent. of the population. Nevertheless, in Fiume, according to the census figures, they already constituted only 36 per cent. of the population in 1880 and in 1900 actually only 18 per cent., although by 1910 the figure had risen again to 25 per cent. (12,926). The Italians were estimated at 17,377 in 1900, and 24,212, or almost exactly 50 per cent. of the total, in 1910.

This remarkable change was due to the deliberate policy of Hungary, which saw no danger in the Italian element, but a great danger in the Croat, and therefore encouraged the former by every means at the expense of the latter. Italians were induced to immigrate from the neighbouring provinces, and were naturalized. The administration was Italianized, and all signs, posters, and inscriptions ordered to be written in Italian. Croat, on the other hand, was practically proscribed. In 1910 the 6,000 Magyars had 6 secondary schools, 2 burger schools, 2 professional schools, 2 elementary schools, and 2 kindergartens; the 24,000 Italians had 1 secondary school, 2 burger schools, 2 professional schools, 12 elementary schools, and 9 kindergartens, while the 13,000 Slavs had no schools whatever.

The decrease in the Croat and increase in the Italian element was not due to immigration alone. For centuries prior to the modern age Italian was the language of urban life, of trade, and of polite society along both shores of the Adriatic. Many a Slav, on rising in the world, adopted Italian manners and speech, and even Italianized his name. The greatest exponents of the Italianita of Fiume, as of Trieste, have been and are to-day men of Croat origin. Incidentally, most of the Croats of the coast are probably, by racial origin, Illyrians, whose ancestors were first Romanized, then Slavized. The distinction between the two nationalities is not easy to draw. In 1921 the leader of the Italian nationalist party bore the purely Slavonic name of Bellasich, while the Autonomist leader (who after his defeat took refuge in Yugoslav territory) was named Zanella.

For many decades the Magyar and Italian elements worked hand in hand, making common cause against the Croats. Only in the last fifteen years or so before the War was an attempt made to Magyarize the city. Pressure was placed on parents to send their children to Magyar schools, a knowledge of Magyar was required from officials, &c. The efforts were not very whole-hearted, and their intensity varied greatly according to the personality of the governor. In this period, however, a certain Italian irredentist movement grew up, although it was not strong, and was confined to the younger and more extreme elements. Politically, in 1914, the Italian irredentist movement had gained hold of perhaps 15 per cent. of the population. There was perhaps an equally strong Croatian or Yugoslav irredentism, while most of the population, including practically all the commercial classes, knew well where their interests lay: in the development of Fiume as an Hungarian port. It must be emphasized that the rise of Fiume was due to the special care of the Hungarian Government. Left to compete on equal terms with Trieste, Fiume could not have flourished as it did; while the city had not yet quite forgotten what it suffered from Venice in the days of her glory.

The attribution of Fiume to Italy after the War was the result of one of the strangest sequences of events which even 1919 witnessed, but those events are too well known to require re-telling in detail here. It may be recalled that in the Treaty of

London (May 4th, 1915) Italy did not claim Fiume, which was
intended to be the port of Croatia. Under the same Treaty,
however, Italy was due to receive Dalmatia. At the Peace Conference Wilson refused to recognize the Treaty of London as
binding on himself, and proposed to give Dalmatia to Yugoslavia,
leaving Fiume an international port within the Yugoslav customs
régime. Italy stuck to her demand for Dalmatia, and Orlando
now claimed Fiume also. It was over this question that the
Italian Delegation left the Conference. Meanwhile, the authorities
of the new Serb-Croat-Slovene State had taken up the standpoint
that in consequence of the severance of Croatia from Hungary,
Fiume had reverted to the *status quo ante* 1868 and become part
of Croatia. Croatian officials took charge of the administration,
and Serbian troops occupied the town on November 15th. They
were persuaded to withdraw on an assurance that no foreign
troops would enter Fiume for three days; in spite of which
assurance, Italian troops promptly disembarked, and the administration was taken over by Italians. Some French and British
troops arrived afterwards, but the Italians were always in charge.
While the Big Four in Paris were evolving a scheme for making
Fiume into an independent, demilitarized buffer state, d'Annunzio
made his famous coup on September 12th, 1919, establishing
himself as 'dictator'. Thereafter, the Italian *de facto* occupants
could never be dislodged, and year after year of confused and
miserable negotiation went on until, in January 1924, the arrangement now in force was reached, under which Fiume went to Italy
in absolute possession, with a strip of territory to the west which
gave it territorial continuity with Italy, placing the railway to
St. Peter–Trieste in its entirety in Italian territory, while Yugoslavia received the suburb of Susak, with Port Baros and the Delta,
and the railway to the hinterland. Yugoslavia also leased for fifty
years, without rights of exterritoriality, one of the three basins in
the main harbour of Fiume, with the adjoining quays and warehouses.

Of all the settlements made at the end of the War, few equal
and none, probably, surpass that of Fiume in utter futility. Fiume
is totally useless to Italy, the only benefit which she derives from
possession of it being the feeling that she is thereby annoying
and embarrassing Yugoslavia. It is true that the citizens of
Trieste, who are now also Italians, and even those of Venice,
benefit from the ruin of their rival. It is a fairly open secret that
d'Annunzio's escapade was largely financed from those two cities,
with no other purpose than to compass the commercial destruction
of Fiume. Fiume is, on the other hand, of great importance for
Yugoslavia. She has, indeed, extended her railway down to

Sebenico at great cost, but although it has developed considerably, neither Sebenico nor any other Croat or Dalmatian port is, or can be for many years yet, a serious commercial rival to Fiume. Hungary is, in a way, the greatest sufferer of all, since her access to her old port now depends entirely on the sufferance of Yugoslavia, both railways to Fiume running across Yugoslav territory; but this would have been the case even had Fiume been awarded to Yugoslavia, or made a free port.

During the years immediately after the War, and particularly during the period of d'Annunzio's escapade, traffic through Fiume and Susak alike practically stopped. Both places became like dead cities. Since that date the picture has changed. The commercial agreements made at the time of the settlement have worked fairly well, and traffic is revived. Inevitably, however, the traffic of Susak, with its thoroughly bad and inconvenient harbour—which has been somewhat enlarged, but the new quays can only be used during half the year—has grown, while that of Fiume proper has diminished heavily. Exact comparative figures are difficult to obtain from the Italian authorities, for reasons of policy, and from the Yugoslavs for reasons of slackness; but the following figures give some indication of the position:

1913
(Fiume and Susak)

Import				Tons
By rail .	.	.	.	1,314,780
By sea .	.	.	.	922,960
				2,237,740
Export				
By rail .	.	.	.	625,877
By sea .	.	.	.	1,173,883
				1,799,760

The corresponding figures for Trieste are as follows:

	1913	1930	1931	1932	1933
Import					
By rail . .	1,488,210	1,081,774	753,845	513,372	538,672
By sea . .	2,314,018	1,539,855	1,762,641	1,583,933	1,322,580
	3,802,228	2,621,629	2,516,486	2,097,305	1,861,252
Export					
By rail . .	1,209,336	970,421	1,136,060	825,148	678,774
By sea . .	1,135,712	737,851	607,873	488,678	479,298
	2,345,048	1,708,272	1,743,933	1,313,826	1,158,072

It will be seen that Fiume and Susak together have done rather better, by comparison with their pre-War record, than Trieste. This is, of course, only a proof of the necessity of Fiume for its

444 FIUME

hinterland, not of the advantage of giving Fiume to Italy; particularly since Yugoslavia is still the heaviest importer via Fiume.

To keep Fiume alive the Italian Government has made heavy sacrifices. Imports of all goods, except state monopolies, can be imported into Fiume free of all duty, if for local consumption.[1] Life in Fiume is thus exceptionally cheap, while the town also makes a considerable income by smuggling, as although the Customs officials in Istria are extremely alert, the nature of the ground is such that an active man can easily avoid the cordon. This concession costs the Italian Government over 30 million lire a year. Other subsidies also have been received from the Government. The petrol refining industry is still fairly prosperous, the crude oil being imported from Austria and refined in Fiume. The remaining industry appears to be stagnant, and unemployment is considerable. The figures for 1927, 1928, and 1929 (i.e. before the slump) were 1,806, 2,677, and 2,669 respectively.

The various raids, demonstrations, &c., of the post-War period were proclaimed as proof of the irrepressible longing of the population of Fiume to belong to Italy. In point of fact, in the only elections held under approximately free conditions (those of April 24th, 1921) the Italian Nationalists were heavily defeated by the Autonomists, who wished to preserve Fiume as a free city in the closest possible connexion with the hinterland. It is true that the population of Fiume has changed markedly since the War, and is now overwhelmingly Italian or Italianate. This is due less to immigration by Italians—although this has occurred, some rentiers being tempted by the low cost of living—than to the emigration of other elements. The population actually decreased by 8 per cent. between 1910 and 1924 (although it has since risen again slightly), partly owing to the repatriation of Hungarian officials, partly to the emigration of Croats owing to the disturbances and the difficult economic situation. Many of these Croats settled in Susak. Those who remained appear to have settled down, and I am informed that although the newspapers of Fiume and Susak indulge in mutual invective, the populations are peaceable enough. The frontier is not closed, and there are persons who cross it regularly daily or oftener, although in each case they have to present documents and get them stamped. Normally few difficulties are made, the chief trouble arising out of the desire of housewives in Fiume to take advantage of the still lower cost of living in Susak.

[1] A similar concession has been made to Zara, where even the Government monopolies are duty-free.

HUNGARY

§ 1. INTRODUCTION

ON turning to Hungary, we may pass over many of the questions which occupied us in the cases of her neighbours and successors. During the disturbed and altogether abnormal years which followed the War there were possibly certain tendencies, among some elements of the population, to prefer the supposed democratic atmosphere of the Successor States to the Red and White Terrors in Hungary; but all this is over now. There is practically no separatist feeling within Hungary to-day, among any social class of the Magyars, and, as we said before, little disagreement on the desirability of revision in Hungary's favour. The only political question which requires at all detailed consideration is, therefore, Hungary's present policy towards the minorities which the Treaty of Trianon left within her frontiers; and even that is important less for its present effects on the minorities themselves than for its bearing on the question of possible revision in the future.

§ 2. NATIONALITY POLICY

Hungary's nationality policy soon recovered from the temporary aberrations into which it had been led under Károlyi and Jászi. Those efforts to undo the work of nearly a century had, of course, come far too late. It had proved impossible even to begin negotiations with the Serbs and the Roumanians; the Slovaks were *de facto* united with the Czechs long before their statute was issued, the Ruthenes followed soon after, and the German autonomy remained a mere torso, which vanished almost unnoticed after the breakdown of the Commune and the re-introduction of the old order.

For a little while thereafter the Ministry of Nationalities was maintained under Professor Bleyer, whom we have mentioned as leader of the more moderate wing of those Hungarian Germans who had retained any national feelings whatever. The Ministry even produced, on January 7th, 1920, a new Draft Statute of Autonomy for Slovakia, which is of considerable historical interest as showing what concessions even the Hungary of the Restoration was prepared to make to preserve the allegiance of the Slovaks. Although an ingeniously argued accompanying report made it appear as though the ideas of the revolutionary period had been wholly abandoned, yet in fact the cardinal principle of 'national' representation was ceded, and the degree of autonomy projected was very considerable.[1]

Bleyer also drafted a new Nationalities Law, which also appeared on August 21st, 1919, as a Government Decree (M. 4044/M.E.). This gave the minorities the right to use their

[1] The report and the draft itself are reprinted in *Nation und Staat*, July 1929, pp. 703–7. Both are highly interesting. The report admits the existence of certain past grievances which must be remedied, notably the enforced use of the Magyar languages in schools and administration. The Slovaks must be given enough autonomy to content them, and in view of past events this must go beyond the Nationalities Law of 1868 (it is stated, incidentally, that the draft is the outcome of negotiations with the Slovak leaders and represents the minimum which they will accept). On the other hand, the national unity of Hungary must not be endangered, particularly as the Slovak Statute will form a precedent for the other nationalities. Jászi's ideas are repudiated as 'dangerous'; an 'Eastern Switzerland' and a federal republic are alike unacceptable, and the danger must under all circumstances be averted of allowing a number of *corpora separata* to grow up round the periphery of Hungary. The report claims of its own proposals that they escape this danger, merely adapting to national conditions the local autonomy traditional to Hungary. The competence of 'Slovensko' will be no greater than that of any other local area (at that time plans were on foot for a far-reaching administrative decentralization of Hungary).

The preamble to the draft Statute describes it as an agreement between the Hungarian State and the Slovak nation with the purpose of giving the latter unlimited possibilities of cultural development, self-government in all questions not touching the direct interest of the country as a whole, and due consideration for its economic needs. In matters not falling within the scope of the autonomy, proper consideration is to be paid to the special position of 'Slovensko' and the predominantly Slovak character of its population.

The territory of 'Slovensko' consists of the preponderantly Slovak areas of North Hungary. The autonomy applies to education, the Church, and social welfare (local institutions). Magyar must, however, be taught in all secondary schools, and Hungarian history and literature must be taught in Magyar. The minorities living together in 'considerable numbers' must receive instruction in their own mother tongue, but also learn Slovak. The language of administration and justice is Slovak, again with safeguards for the minorities, and the administration is responsible to the Slovak Government, but is to be decentralized as far as possible. Slovensko covers the costs of its own autonomous institutions, the State contributing in the same proportion as it does to the corresponding institutions in other parts of the country. There is a National Assembly, in which the minorities are represented, which has full power to legislate in all questions in which Slovensko is autonomous, subject only to the veto of the Central Government where its decisions conflict with laws of the State. There is a local Government, under a Governor elected by the Assembly, but a State official is appointed to control the working of the Government and co-ordinate the work of the autonomous and the State authorities. Slovensko is to have its due representation in the central Parliament; its own regiments and gendarmerie formations, its sub-directorates for post, telegraphs, and railways, and the personnel of the State railway and postal employees serving in Slovensko is to be recruited as far as possible from local nationalities. A Slovak Minister belongs to the Hungarian Government. He has to 'defend the local autonomy of Slovensko' and the national rights of the Slovaks living as minorities elsewhere in Hungary. He controls the execution of the Slovak autonomy and his approval is necessary for all Governmental dispositions touching the autonomous rights of Slovensko, or the national rights of Slovaks elsewhere, including the appointment of State officials inside Slovensko. Complaints regarding infringements of the above law are brought before a neutral Supreme Court; and the rights of Slovensko are also guaranteed in the Coronation Diploma.

mother tongue freely, even in the Hungarian Parliament. Any person was entitled to approach the legislative authorities, ministries, municipalities, communes, and all other instances in his own mother tongue and to receive an answer in the same language. Executive enactments were issued by the Ministries of the Interior, Education, Justice, and Commerce, and on December 13th, 1919, the Education Act was issued which provided that linguistic minorities should receive instruction in their own languages in all subjects if they could not speak Magyar, or if they understood Magyar, at least in religion, reading, writing, arithmetic, and certain other subjects. Where the numbers did not suffice for a school, a minority might have parallel classes, or if the numbers were smaller still, then some hours' instruction weekly in the mother tongue. Magyar was to be taught as a subject from the third year onward.

But the Slovak draft, of course, proved no more successful than any of its predecessors in its real and only object of buying the adherence of the nationalities to Hungary. The Treaty of Trianon inexorably lopped off from Hungary all the non-Magyar populations which could on any pretext be detached from it, leaving a central core which was nearly 90 per cent. Magyar-speaking.[1]

In these circumstances it seemed useless to continue a policy which had only been adopted with one purpose in view, and had signally failed to achieve it. More than this: Magyar opinion, conscious and unconscious, underwent a violent and perhaps a natural reaction to the old ideas and practices. It felt that concessions to the nationalities were not only futile but wrong in principle. Had not 1918 proved that the lessons drawn by Hungary after 1848 had been correct? If the nationalities had only been Magyarized they would never have been lost. The fault had thus lain, not in too much Magyarization, but in too little.

[1] The 1920 census gave the population of Hungary as follows:

Habitual language.	Number.	Per cent.	Of these, of Jewish religion.
Magyar . . .	7,147,053	89·6	450,526
German . . .	551,211	6·9	19,018
Slovak . . .	141,882	1·8	734
Roumanian . . .	23,760	0·3	142
Ruthene . . .	1,500	0·0	33
Croat . . .	36,858	0·5	292
Serb . . .	17,131	0·2	25
Others . . .	60,748	0·7	2,444
	7,980,143	100·00	473,214

The others included something over 23,000 Šokci, Bunyevci, &c., and over 6,000 Gypsies.

Voices were raised solemnly accusing past generations of slackness in their supreme national task.

At all events, there should be no repetition of the mistake. Even if it might be admitted that pre-War Hungary was incapable of Magyarizing the nationalities when they formed half the total population, at least the few remaining fragments could be absorbed once and for all. Trianon Hungary might be a poor thing, but it should be the Magyars' own.

Under the influence of these ideas, the Ministry of Nationalities was soon dissolved. The Minister of the Interior appointed three Commissaries, for the Germans, Slovaks, and Roumanians respectively, but their activities, never very great, soon became almost imperceptible.[1]

The new Nationalities Law and Education Act were never put into force, and the whole question remained unregulated until 1923, when two new orders appeared (Nos. 4800/1923 and 110478/1923). As regards the use of languages in justice and administration, &c., these measures re-enact, without important modification, the Hungarian Law of 1868, and thus resemble closely the Czechoslovak law, which is based on the same instrument. The official language of the State is Magyar. In the Commune, members of linguistic minorities can address the local officials orally in their mother tongue, and must be answered in the same language; and communal officials in minority districts must speak the local minority language. The Communal Council chooses its own language of business, minutes are kept in Magyar and also in the language of a 20 per cent. minority. Communications from Minority Communes to their own higher local authorities (County, &c.), or to the central authorities, may be in the minority language, but a translation in Magyar must be attached. In Municipal and County Councils any person may use his own language; minutes may be kept in a minority language also if 20 per cent. of the members desire.

Free use of minority languages in private intercourse is guaranteed.

As regards schools, the law provided that (a) in any commune containing an overwhelming proportion of the members of one linguistic minority the school committee and village council might, on the representations of the parents, decide to introduce, or (b) in a mixed commune, the parents or guardians of at least forty children belonging to one minority might ask for minority in-

---

[1] The Roumanian Commissioner died and was not replaced; the German resigned after a dispute with Professor Bleyer and was again not replaced. Their work has been taken over by rapporteurs attached to the Minorities Section of the Prime Minister's Office. The Slovak is still functioning within the limits imposed by decent reticence.

struction according to any one of the following three types, between which they were in theory free to choose:

A type: Instruction in the mother tongue, Magyar being taught as a subject;

B type: Instruction in the mother tongue in natural history, physics, chemistry, economics, drawing, and handcrafts; in the mother tongue and Magyar, in 'talking and thinking', reading, writing, arithmetic, and singing; and in Magyar in geography, history, civics, and physical culture;

C type: Instruction in Magyar, the minority language being taught as a subject; reading and writing in both languages.

No restriction was placed on the maintenance of schools by churches, associations, private persons, &c.

Under these Acts, the Germans possessed in 1928 forty-nine 'A' schools (nearly all of them in the Western districts, and survivals of the work of the Ministry of Nationalities), 98 'B' and 316 'C'.[1] The Slovaks had about 50 'B' and 'C' schools, the Roumanians (1931–2) 11.

In the summer of 1924 the German minority received permission to found a cultural association in Budapest, the 'Ungarländisch-Deutscher Volksbildungsverein', which became the centre and in a certain sense the representative body of the German minority. The Hungarian Government permitted and even supported it financially; on the other hand, it kept a control over its activities; the President had to be appointed by agreement with the Government, which also nominated half the members of the Executive Committee.

The Association, although far less vigorous than its counterpart in Roumania, was able to develop a certain activity. In the course of the next five or six years it founded 175 local groups in certain parts of the country. It also issued a weekly paper, the *Sonntagsblatt*, which represented the political views of its leaders.

The Slovaks possess only a purely cultural association, which issues a weekly paper in Slovak, a sort of blend of a parish magazine and Home Chat. The Serbs still own a religious foundation, the Thökölianum, which gives scholarships to Serb youths. None of the minorities possesses any separate economic organization.

The position had thus returned substantially to what it was before the War, except only that the Germans were the better off by their 'A' schools and by the foundation of the U.D.V. Even counting these, however, the separate national-cultural facilities afforded to the minorities in Hungary were probably less than those granted to the nationalities in any Successor State, Yugoslavia

[1] *Die Nationalitäten in den Staaten Europas*, p. 335.

Gg

not excepted. Of all the minority schools, only the German 'A' schools really deserved the name. The 'B' schools might pass at a pinch; but the 'C' schools (which, as we saw, far outnumbered the 'A' or 'B' type for some years) were 'minority' only by courtesy, and there were many non-Magyar communes in which not even a 'C' school was allowed to exist. It is true that the parents were in theory free to choose what type of school they would have for their children, but the 'parents' conferences' which had to make the choice were notoriously subjected to the strongest pressure from the local authorities and priests, who treated a vote for an 'A' school as tantamount to treason, and for a 'B' school as little better. The Catholic priests, indeed (and nearly all the German minority, as well as the Croats, Šokci, &c., are Catholics), proved more chauvinistic even than the lay-officials and often made it impossible for minority children to receive even religious instruction in their own tongue. There was no secondary education whatever, not to speak of higher education, in any non-Magyar language; not even a Teachers' Training College for the Germans.[1]

The head-quarters of the U.D.V. were under constant surveillance; its emissaries were closely watched when they visited the provinces. They were not allowed to penetrate at all into certain districts where it was believed that the population had already been Magyarized (though not securely); and in others, they were in constant danger of expulsion, if not arrest, and their activities so hedged about that in one place—to give an example—a lecture in German on the utilization of milk, which one of them had proposed to give to the local milk co-operative, was actually forbidden by the local authorities.[2] As for any separate political activity on a national basis, this was simply out of the question. There were Magyar political parties in Czechoslovakia and in Roumania and, for a time, in Yugoslavia, but there was, and is, no German party in Hungary. In other respects, too, the pressure on the minorities to denationalize was exceedingly strong. The practice of Magyarizing surnames continued unabated. A national society for that purpose was founded, its patrons, including the Habsburg Archduke Joseph, the Cardinal-Archbishop Seredi (who has himself practised what he preaches), three Protestant Bishops, and the Director-General of Posts. Its aim was announced in 1931 to be the Magyarization of 60,000–70,000 names

---

[1] Since 1927 there have, however, been courses in training colleges for students preparing for minority schools (8 for Germany, 2 each for Croats and Slovaks). There are also summer courses for teachers actually employed in minority schools. As regards the position of German secondary and higher education, it is important to remember that German language and literature are taught regularly as subjects in all Hungarian secondary schools and universities.

[2] *Nation und Staat*, February 1932, p. 332.

in a year, and the President of the Hungarian Railways and
M. Gömbös, then Honvéd (Defence) Minister, the later Minister
President, were singled out for especial praise as 'seeing to it
that the officials, officers and other persons subordinate to them
Magyarize their names'.[1] In 1933, by which time the movement
had grown more active still, the goal aimed at was no less than
100,000 names a year, a figure which was, indeed, fantastically out
of proportion to what was achieved or even what was seriously
attempted. It was reported that the process was almost complete
with the gendarmerie. The Minister of the Interior had requested
the Burgomaster of Budapest to draw the attention of his employees to the desirability of falling into line, the Director of the
State Railways had given his employees a certain date by which
to reply whether they would change their names. In other
Ministries and in many of the Counties and Municipalities similar
instructions and inquiries were taking place. The whole campaign
amounted to a hardly disguised compulsion exercised upon public
employees. The Supreme Court of Justice, to which the question
was taken on one occasion, decided, indeed, in favour of the person
defending his right to his original name, but this had little effect
on the action of the subordinate officials, or on that section of the
general public opinion which branded those who refused to submit
to the pressure as 'unpatriotic'.

It is true that not all Magyars approve of the Magyarization of
names. Many laugh at it, some actively dislike it. Moreover, even
where members of minorities have defied her wishes, Hungary
has honourably abstained from certain practices all too common
among her neighbours. By common consent, no discrimination is
practised against the most stubborn member of a minority in such
matters as taxation or civil (as distinct from political) justice.
Even in political questions, although the repression is severe, it
is orderly and unaccompanied by extra-legal excesses.

Finally, Hungary has been consistent. If she has pressed her
minorities, like no other Central European State, to abandon their
nationality, she has also offered them every legitimate inducement
to do so. Quick to punish, she is equally generous to reward.
Once a German, Slovak, or Croat accepts the Magyar national
ideal, every door is open to him. He may rise to the highest
position in State or Church and none will cast his non-Magyar
origin in his teeth, nor ask what name he bore before he doubled
its length and put a -y at the end of it. And with reason, for if
such inquiries once began, who knows where they would end? A
list of the ancestral family names of Hungary's leading men and
women would prove startling reading indeed.

[1] *Nation und Staat*, June 1931, pp. 108-9.

It must be emphasized that this attitude can have very great advantages for the minorities themselves. For the man who does not put his special national feeling above all other considerations, Hungary is the best country to live in of all the Successor States. And there are very many such, just as there are in the British Isles millions of persons of Irish, Scottish, or Welsh origin who have no desire whatever to spend their lives dozing in a Celtic twilight.

The question how far pressure to assimilate, such as is practised in Hungary, is preferable, from the minority point of view, to the discrimination which is commoner in some other States depends almost entirely on the outlook and the ambitions of the minorities themselves. And it is fair to recall that those minorities left to Hungary by the Treaty were, with a very few exceptions in outlying frontier districts, precisely those which in pre-War Hungary had welcomed the opportunities given them to merge themselves in the larger national life. It was thus perfectly well arguable that the laws and practices mentioned above were suited both to the needs and to the wishes of the minorities themselves. This could also be deduced from the character and attitude of the two men who were the acknowledged leaders of the German minority. Dr. Gustav Gratz, although he freely admitted, and where necessary emphasized, his German origin, was perhaps already more of a Magyar than a German. A conspicuous example of the lack of prejudice with which the Magyars have always welcomed adherents to their national cause, he had at one time actually been his country's Foreign Minister. He acted less as a German leader than as a mediator between the Germans and the Magyars.

Professor Bleyer, the real leader of the people, was more 'nationalbewusst', but he was of quite unimpeachable Hungarian patriotism. He had invariably defended Hungary's interests, to the extent of opposing the cession of the Burgenland, and of rejecting on principle the idea of an appeal to the League. His conception of the needs of the German minority was so modest that he regarded the growth of a German 'intelligentsia' in Hungary as detrimental to the national interests. He was against cultural autonomy for the Germans, and even disliked the 'A' schools, as going too far towards separatism.

Gratz and Bleyer between them managed for some years to maintain at least an outward appearance of harmony between the Magyars and their most important minority. Unhappily, Bleyer's endurance was at last exhausted by the pressure on the U.D.V. combined with the inadequacy of the minority schools, and, above all, the refusal of local authorities to carry out the existing laws (which, he always maintained, were liberal enough in theory).

For years he negotiated for greater liberty for the Verein, and for the transformation of the 'C' schools into 'B'. In 1927 Count Bethlen promised him that the U.D.V. should receive certain concessions, and that the 'C' schools should be turned into 'B' schools in the course of four or five years, being retained only in villages where there were too few children for parallel classes. While refusing Bleyer's request that the type of school should be decided on the basis of the census, not of the parents' decision, he offered that the school authorities should be advised to consult the parents again where the census returns suggested that the maintenance of a 'C' school was not justified. But further years went by; Count Bethlen left office; Count Károlyi came and went; General Gömbös arrived; and beyond the transformation of some of the schools[1] nothing was changed. Meanwhile, the resentment of the nationalist minorities, and of their cousins across the frontiers, was enhanced by the publication of the preliminary figures of the 1930 census, which showed that the German population of Hungary had sunk to 479,000, the Slovak to 104,000, the Croat to 28,000, the Roumanian to 16,000, the Serb to 7,000, the 'miscellaneous Yugoslavs' to 21,000, &c. At last Professor Bleyer decided to act, and during the Budget debate (the recognized occasion for the airing of grievances) of 1933 he made an exceedingly loyal and correct speech, setting forth the wishes of the German minority and asking for redress.

The result was an amazing outburst of fury on the part of the Magyar chauvinist Press and opinion. The best thing said in any quarter was that the speech was 'ill timed'; concessions had been 'just going to follow'. More generally, Bleyer was accused of being a 'Pan-German intriguer', a 'traitor', and many still less reputable things; his wife as well as himself was insulted; he had to fight a duel; and soon after died of something very like a broken heart.

The 'affaire Bleyer' proved, unhappily, a turning-point in the relations between Hungary and her German minority. The resentment was not on one side only. A large number of the Germans, including most of the younger generation, felt exceedingly bitter. For many of them, Bleyer himself had long been too moderate. They had disagreed with his condemnation of the 'A' schools and with his rejection of a German intelligentsia; they had thought him too complaisant in the face of many minor grievances. In view, however, of the great authority which he enjoyed, they had accepted his leadership. But if Hungary was to show herself so violently intolerant even towards a man so moderate, so deeply

[1] In 1933 the figures for the German schools were 40 'A' type, 191 'B', and 265 'C' with 90 kindergartens. (*Pester Lloyd*, June 6th, 1933.)

patriotic as Bleyer, then it seemed that every possibility of compromise had gone. Hungary, it appeared, would be content with
nothing less than complete, resistless Magyarization, and that
they could no longer accept. Like all the younger Germans
throughout Central and Eastern Europe, they were strongly
influenced by the new national feeling. They were impregnated,
as the generation of 1914 had never been, with the consciousness
of their 'Deutschtum' and the determination to preserve it.

The advent to power in Germany of National Socialism—in
itself perhaps a symptom rather than a cause of this new national
feeling—had naturally enormously strengthened and encouraged
the more radical wing among the Suabians. Some of the latter
had certainly been in touch with circles in Germany which had
begun to interest themselves vociferously in the question of
'Auslandsdeutschtum', and had drawn thence—if nothing else—
a new determination not to submit to Magyarization or to being
considered in any way a second-class element in the State. This
view was not necessarily incompatible with loyalty and even with
devotion to Hungary, but it was totally irreconcilable with the
current Magyar national policy, and hardly less so with the attitude
of Gratz and his followers.

The death of Bleyer, therefore, removed the chief restraining
element in the situation. For another year or so outward harmony
was still preserved, but the Radicals became increasingly impatient of the moderates, the moderates increasingly uneasy about
the Radicals. A prolonged internal and indeed subterranean
struggle went on within the U.D.V., and at last there came an
open split, or rather, a disintegration. The Government naturally
supported the moderates, and in 1935 the U.D.V. was 'purged'
of its more radical elements, Dr. Gratz remaining sole President,
while a priest of the name of Pintér, standing very near indeed to
official circles, came in as Secretary-General. The *Sonntagsblatt*
was suspended on a technicality, and reissued as the organ of the
moderate wing.

As a sop to the Radicals, the U.D.V. was allowed rather more
liberty of action; summer courses were instituted for the teachers
in the German schools (though a separate training-college was still
refused); and a definite promise was given regarding the 'C'
schools. This bore fruit in a new Order in Council of December 23rd, 1935, which, as regards the State schools, abolished the
'A', 'B', 'C' types in favour of a uniform type closely resembling
the old 'B' schools. The mother language itself, reading, writing,
arithmetic, composition, orthography, natural sciences, domestic
economy, hygiene, drawing, and handcrafts, were to be taught in
the mother tongue; the Magyar language, reading, writing, ortho-

graphy, geography, history, civics, singing, and physical instruction,[1] in Magyar. From the fourth to the sixth years, the chief
subjects taught in each language were to be repeated in the other.

These concessions were not, however, nearly enough to satisfy
the radical party,[2] who were also not willing to follow M. Pintér
as they had followed Professor Bleyer. The consequence was that
the German movement remained divided, the majority of the
younger men remaining in more or less open opposition, not only
to the Government, but also to their own official leaders.

Thus Hungary still finds herself haunted by the unlaid ghost
of the nationality problem. The demands of the most nationalist
Germans are, indeed, extremely moderate. They were summed
up by a recent writer as follows:

Solution of the question of schools, including kindergartens.
German Church Services for children.
A separate club for German University students.
Freedom of action for the U.D.V.
Application of the law regarding the use of minority languages
   in administration.
Cessation of the 'abuses connected with the Magyarization of
names'.
The possibility of applying to an impartial Court over minority
   questions.[3]

Corporate recognition as a 'nation' is not demanded; nor even
cultural autonomy, or a separate political party. There is little
that is Nazi about the programme, still less does it betray the
cloven hoof of irredentism. Indeed, apart from their genuine
attachment to Hungary, of which, from personal acquaintance with
several of the leaders, I am convinced, most of them realize that the
geographical situation of the greater part of the Hungarian
Germans entirely precludes irredentism for them.

[1] This refers to the 'Levente Organization', a sort of pre-military training.
The Germans have always accepted this in principle, but have asked, in vain,
to be allowed their own detachments. Cf. the Sokol question in Yugoslavia.

[2] The Hungarian Press represented the Act as a measure of great generosity.
One paper, referring to remarks of my own on Hungary's need to set an example
to the Successor States in the treatment of minorities, remarked that it fully
agreed with me; this had always been Hungary's policy, as was proved by the
new Act. However, the Act still puts the onus of asking for the school on the
Parents' Conferences, who have still to fear the pressure of the authorities; it
still fails to provide for an adequate supply of teachers; and above all it applies
only to the State Schools, which comprise only 19 per cent. of the whole. The
position of the Confessional Schools remains quite unaffected, while it is notorious that the chief pressure against the minorities has come less from the
Government than from the higher authorities of the Roman Catholic Church.
They have, however, been requested by the Minister of Education to fall into
line with the State schools, and are said to have agreed to do so. On the other
hand, complaints are already loud that even State authorities are sabotaging
the Act.

[3] *Nation und Staat*, February 1935, p. 326.

Nevertheless, in the eyes of the Magyar nationalists, who have been deeply frightened by the attitude of various circles in Germany, they are traitors. They are hampered by the authorities, vilified in the Press, outlawed in social life. When, in the 1935 elections, some of them stood for Parliament on the list of the Independent Small-Holders (although with the avowed object of representing the national as well as the economic interests of their constituents), the whole governmental machinery was brought into operation and their election prevented by scandalous methods. One of them was sentenced by a provincial court to three months' imprisonment for having publicly condemned the Magyarization of names. The higher court, on appeal, increased this sentence to five months' imprisonment and two years' loss of political rights; and the Supreme Court confirmed the sentence fully—an interesting commentary on the excuse which is often put forward, that the chauvinism is confined to provincial opinion and subordinate authorities. Actually, I have found very little difference between provincial opinion and that of the Budapest Ministries, including the highest quarters. The words of Ministers President are, indeed, more carefully weighed than those of the editors of local papers or the tin gods of local towns. Count Bethlen particularly, when he visited Berlin in the autumn of 1930, went out of his way to praise the German minority in Hungary as a valued element of the population and a channel through which sympathy for the German language and nature penetrated into Hungary. His great wish and object, he said, was the complete satisfaction of their cultural and linguistic desires. He repeated these sentiments in a declaration to the Hungarian Press, and again when, soon afterwards, he visited Vienna. The German minority was to play the part of a link between Hungary and the Germans. General Gömbös, too, in some of his numerous speeches (in which he was somewhat addicted to promising all things to all men) found heartening words for the brave Suabian peasants, whose blood flowed, indeed, so richly in his own veins. But neither Bethlen nor Gömbös made the nationalities any real concession while it was in his power to do so. And in this attitude they have certainly acted in accordance with the wishes of the great majority of Magyar opinion—far too moderately for a certain wing, which would have the traitors wiped out once and for all.

This attitude is prompted not only by general considerations—by the ingrained belief to which we have referred that no un-Magyarized citizen can be counted as safe—but also by a special complex towards Germany. The dominant feeling is perhaps not so much a fear that Germany, having swallowed up Austria, might lay claim to specific German-speaking areas in the Western

Counties (though horrid rumours, not all of them unfounded, have been circulated of a map showing the future Germany with frontiers reaching to Lake Balaton, and of Nazi agents circumperambulating the Western Counties),[1] as rather a general dread of German influence and domination. Joseph II is no less active a bug-a-boo than Adolph Hitler. These fears are, of course, sedulously fanned by the Jews, who edit and write the vast majority of the Press of Hungary.

One must sympathize with these fears, for Hungary has had good reason to dread German influence in the past. And yet, while sympathizing, one must still marvel that so very few Magyars understand the illogical character of their position. The most fanatical Magyarizers are at the same time the most active advocates of Treaty revision. One might have expected that, even apart from the question of revision in the future, the desire to protect the Magyar minorities beyond the frontiers would have led Hungary to follow a policy which entitled her to demand that the Successor States did likewise, viz. one of full encouragement of the separate national cultures of her minorities. Oddly enough, however, Hungary for years took little interest in the problem of minority protection. Its importance only began to dawn upon her when her confidence in the prospect of frontier revision in the near future began to wane. Even when she was forced to perceive that the new order could not be overthrown in a month or a year, the full truth of the proverb about the sauce for goose and gander did not penetrate the consciousness of 1 per cent. of the population. A distinction was drawn between the Magyar minorities, who represented an earlier stratum of population and a higher culture, and as such merited protection, and the non-Magyars, recent comers and boors at that, whose natural and proper fate was assimilation. Thus Magyarization was still justified in theory, as it was still practised.

For years the single influential voice heard to the contrary was that of M. Milotay, the famous Hungarian publicist. Quite recently, he has been joined by a few others, including Hungary's foremost modern historian, Professor Szekfű, who in a remarkable article urged that if the policy of identifying nationality with State was justified in any State, it was not in Hungary. Again, M. Ottlik published two articles in the same strain: 'Uj Hungária féle'[2] (*Magyar Szemle*, 1928), and 'Pax Hungarica' (*Nouvelle Revue*

---

[1] For examples of the literature issued in Germany and clearly of a nature to awaken the most lively apprehensions in Hungary, cf. C. von Loesch, *Deutsche Revolution* (Berlin, 1933); H. Steinacher, *Volkstum jenseits der Grenze* (Stuttgart, 1934); F. Lange, *Volksdeutsche Kartenskizzen* (Berlin, 1935).

[2] 'Towards a new Hungary.' Note the term 'Hungária', used in intentional contrast to the normal term 'Magyarország'. Cf. on this subject also the last section of Szekfű's book, *Három Nemzedék*.

de Hongrie, November 1934). But I doubt whether these ideas have yet begun perceptibly to influence either public opinion or Government policy. Both Count Bethlen and M. Eckhardt have recently found words of encouragement for the minorities; but then, Count Bethlen has left office, and M. Eckhardt has not yet been in it. Government policy, as we saw, has not altered beyond a little window-dressing, Catholic and public opinion has hardly changed at all.

Yet the question is clearly of fundamental importance in any consideration of the possibilities of treaty revision. The Successor States see this, if Hungary does not. This is why incidents like the Bleyer case do Hungary such immeasurable harm. There were in that case certain special circumstances. Bleyer, as a man, was unpopular, for reasons quite unconnected with his national policy, with the students who led part of the riotous scenes, which the Jewish Press took care to magnify in its anxiety to make a scarecrow of anything German. The incident was exaggerated far beyond its intrinsic importance, for the Magyar political leaders in all the Successor States, except Austria, have repeatedly suffered far worse things than were ever inflicted upon Bleyer, or upon the other national leaders of to-day in Hungary. Nevertheless, the fact remains that the Germans in the Successor States place the preservation of their *Deutschtum* so high that, unless Hungary alters her whole attitude, they will undoubtedly throw their weight against her if the frontiers ever come to be questioned; and the Successor States are handed, on a plate, the best argument against revision for which they could possibly hope.

It is true that Hungary, or some of her leaders at least, maintain that although the present 'unitary' policy is suitable for Trianon Hungary it could be different if the frontiers were revised. Thus Count Bethlen declared publicly in 1933 that the minorities restored to Hungary would enjoy complete autonomy, and that Hungary would even submit to an international guarantee in this respect. The Bleyer draft of 1920 may perhaps be taken as earnest of what Hungary might in such circumstances be prepared to offer. But hitherto the minorities have been inclined to answer that a foretaste of deeds would be better than words. Nor are they sure that Count Bethlen represents all Hungarian opinion. For example, an article published in 1932 in the *Pesti Hírlap*, a nationalist paper of low intellectual level and wide circulation, preaches cultural liberty in the Greater Hungary to be established after revision 'for all minorities except the Daco-Roumans, Yugoslavs, and Pan-Germans who refuse to give up their national community with their co-nationals beyond the frontiers'.[1] When

[1] Cf. *Nation und Staat*, May 1932, p. 972.

one considers how readily the slightest resistance to Magyarization is denounced as 'Pan-Germanism', 'Pan-Slavism', 'Daco-Roumanism', &c., the wish of the prospective minorities for very sure guarantees is not difficult to understand.

The Jewish question in Hungary is quite different from that of any other minority. The Jews want exactly what the Magyar demands of a 'nationality': the fullest possible assimilation. Nothing pleases the Hungarian Jew so much as to be taken for a pure-blooded Magyar; no one carries the Magyar mentality to such extremes as the Magyarized Jew. The differences that arise between the two nationalities are due, not to the same causes as separate Magyar from German, but rather to an occasional reluctance of the Magyar himself to accept quite fully precisely this one recruit: to the instinctive anti-Semitism latent in every non-Semitic race among whom Jews live in large numbers. Now and again this feeling flares up and expresses itself in action; but hitherto the phase has always passed, and the curiously intimate *mariage de convenance* has been renewed.

Immediately after the overthrow of the Commune, many of whose leaders had been Jews, there was a very bad outbreak of anti-Semitism, during which bands led by army officers, members of high society, and active politicians committed some of the worst excesses that have taken place in Central Europe since the War; certainly the worst anti-Semitic excesses. The outbreaks, however, gradually died away, although isolated instances occurred for years after the main 'White Terror' had been liquidated. They have not recurred since. Great fears were entertained when General Gömbös became Prime Minister, since during the Terror he had been one of the most notorious Jew-baiters. But he disavowed his past, promised to treat the Jews with toleration, and kept his word.

There has, indeed, been no country in Europe containing so high a proportion of Jews which has suffered them so gladly. It is fortunate for each that their qualities are so nicely complementary. The Magyar is the ruler and the administrator, the Jew the business man and intellectual. Thus a sort of unwritten compromise has been reached by which the Magyar supplies the administrative landowning and land-cultivating class, while the Jews manage the business, the shops, and most of the free professions. The Magyar tolerates the Jew, the Jew supports the Magyar.

In point of fact, since business has proved far more lucrative than landowning, the Jew has had the better of the bargain, and he has had the sense to realize this and not to press his claims too hard. There has only been one open conflict since the White Terror ended. Hungary in 1920 passed a law, notoriously aimed at the

Jews, which restricted the numbers of students of each race and
nationality admitted to the Universities to a figure proportionate
to the number of Hungarian citizens of that race or nationality.
The West-European Jews appealed to the League and the law was
revised, although more in name than in fact. The 'numerus clausus'
was not, and has not been, repealed in reality, although it is not
strictly applied, so that the Jews are allowed a number of students
which is below their real requirements, but about double their strict
national quota. Characteristically, the Hungarian Jews did not join
in the appeal but asked, and got, from the Hungarian Supreme
Court, a ruling that they did not constitute a separate nationality.

This incident might perhaps be regarded as a by-product of the
White Terror, and its liquidation as marking the end of a chapter.
Since that time all has been peace, as regards official actions, and
the sincere attachment of the Hungarian Jews to their country is
not to be doubted. If it is impossible to describe the Jewish
question in Hungary as completely solved, this is because of
certain symptoms which have appeared in recent years, dangerously
resembling what has occurred in Roumania. As in that country,
there is a large plethora of unemployed 'academical youth'.
University education is not, indeed, so cheap in Hungary, nor is
it nearly so easy for a peasant's son to achieve it. On the other
hand, there are innumerable impoverished middle-class families,
including the many thousands of refugee State employees from
the Successor States. In spite of every effort the Government
cannot find posts in the State services for all these young men, and
they are now beginning to knock on the doors of the business
houses—to find the desired jobs held by Jews. Further, Germany
is near enough to Hungary for its ideas to prove infectious, and
various small National Socialist parties with specifically anti-
Semitic programmes have been founded. These were taken rather
lightly by Hungarian public opinion for several years; but that
they took themselves more seriously was shown by the extraordinary outburst in the spring of 1937 when, it appears, some of
them really planned a *coup d'état* on 'Nazi' lines. This was duly
and energetically suppressed. Far-seeing Jews were much more
deeply disquieted when the Government set afoot discreet inquiries to certain business houses, &c., as to the possibility of
limiting the number of Jewish employees. There are certainly
some Jews who regard as a serious possibility a new outbreak of
economic anti-Semitism. Up to date this has not occurred, and it
is still fair to give Hungary high marks for her treatment of the
Jews and to emphasize the attachment of the Jews to Hungary—
adding in parenthesis that they do much to inflame the situation
with respect to the other minorities, particularly the German.

§ 3. THE ECONOMIC PROBLEM

As has been seen, the War found Hungary in the middle of a process of development which was being conducted on very definite and carefully planned lines. The purpose was to create at least a partially self-sufficient planned national economy within the frontiers of the then kingdom. The periphery, with its mineral deposits, forests, and water-power, was to supply the raw materials and to contain those industries which, by their nature, were best situated in the vicinity of their raw material and their power supply; Budapest was to be the site of the finishing and luxury industries, as well as the centre of administration and finance; while the great plains of Central Hungary provided the agricultural produce which, until this period of development began, had been Hungary's traditional source of wealth.

The Peace Treaty, roughly speaking, took from Hungary all the periphery, leaving her with Budapest and most of the chief agricultural districts. In other words, the principal loss in material resources was in the raw materials required by the manufacturing industry. Hungary lost 84 per cent. of her forests,[1] approximately the same proportion of her iron-ore, and all the copper and nearly all the other non-ferrous metal-ores such as lead, zinc, bauxite, and manganese; all the salt also was lost. Over 70 per cent. of her lignite remained, but nearly 90 per cent. of the water-power was alienated. On the other hand, while the total area left to her was 32·7 per cent. of the former figure, she retained 57 per cent. of the arable land, including 45·7 per cent. (1911–15 averages) of the land under wheat, 62·9 per cent. of that under rye, 47·3 per cent. of that under barley, and 39·1 per cent. of that under potatoes. Hungary has now the highest percentage of arable land of any country in Europe except Denmark.

So far as stock-breeding is concerned, Hungary was left at the end of 1918 with rather less than a third of the cattle she possessed in 1911, about half the pigs and horses, but only just over a quarter of the sheep; further losses resulted from the Roumanian invasion of 1919. The Treaty left Hungary somewhat deficient in fodder. Only 35 per cent. of the area formerly under maize remained, and 37·2 per cent. of the land under clover, though 62·6 per cent. of the land under turnips, and 58·8 per cent. of that under vetch and 56·5 per cent. of that under lucerne was left. It should be added that about 70 per cent. of the vineyards formerly owned by Hungary remained to her under the Treaty.

While the settlement took away most of the industrial raw

[1] For these statistics, see Dr. Ladislaus Buday, *Dismembered Hungary* (Budapest, 1922). Cf. *Justice for Hungary*, pp. 253 ff.

materials, it left Hungary with a disproportionate share of the industrial plant. Nearly half of the undertakings remained, and nearly half of the workers formerly employed. Thus the new Hungary was more highly industrialized than the old; in the latter, according to the 1910 census, 64·5 per cent. of the population had been engaged in agriculture, fishing, and forestry, and 23·6 per cent. in mining, industry, trade, and transport, while in 1920, in the new Hungary, the figures were 55·8 per cent. and 30·1 per cent. respectively. The losses fell, of course, very unevenly on the different industries. For example, 91 per cent. of the quarries were lost, 89 per cent. of the saw-mills, 73 per cent. of the cotton-mills, 68 per cent. of the glass-works, and 60 per cent. of the iron- and steel-works. On the other hand, 82 per cent. of the machine industries, 75 per cent. of the clothing industry, and 58 per cent. of the food-stuffs industries—mainly flour-mills— remained.

It is true that in many cases where Hungary lost important industries, she lost also the raw materials which they required. But the general effect was to leave Hungary wholly, or almost wholly, devoid of a number of essential industries, while burdened with a number of factories which either, as in the case of the machine and most of the finishing industries, were now forced to depend on imported raw materials or, as with the flour-milling and other agricultural industries, had been built up to supply not only the old Hungary but Austria as well.[1]

The loss of material resources by no means completed the list of economic and financial losses which Hungary suffered through

---

[1] Pasvolsky, *Economic Nationalization of the Danubian States*, gives the following figures for 1923:

	Productive capacity of undertakings expressed as a percentage of those of pre-War Hungary in 1913.	Raw materials available in post-War Hungary, expressed as a percentage of those available for pre-War Hungary in 1913.
Machinery . . .	82	42
Food products . .	58	44
Leather . . .	58	48
Glass and stone . .	58	40
Metallurgy . . .	50	10
Textiles . . .	41	15
Chemicals . . .	40	30
Paper	20	12

Similarly, only 30 per cent of the flour-milling industry of Budapest (the largest in the world after that of Minneapolis) could be utilized in 1925, owing to the lack of grain, which formerly came from the southern territories now separated from Hungary.

the Peace Settlement.[1] These further losses are naturally of a far less tangible nature; to ask what they were is, in effect, to ask what would be the economic position of the new Hungary if the territorial redistribution had not taken place. In the nature of the case such a question is not one to which there can be any precise answer. One thing, however, is clear: that no attempt to answer it would be intelligible without some account of Hungary's economic and financial development since the War.

The declaration of the republic, the Bela Kun episode, the Roumanian invasion, and the attempt thereafter to restore some sort of order, all put a very serious strain on Hungary's national finances, which were already suffering from four years of war. In addition, the State had also to assist, by pensions and otherwise, the 330,000 Hungarians who had been living in territory now under foreign rule and who had either been expelled from their homes or had migrated voluntarily to Hungary.[2] A further extraordinary liability imposed on the national finances arose out of the agrarian reform, moderate though this measure was when compared with those effected in the neighbouring countries, which began in 1921. Moreover, the Treaty of Trianon had declared (Article 180) that the unspecified cost of reparations should be 'the first charge upon all the assets and resources of Hungary'. This provision made it impossible for Hungary to meet these exceptional expenses by borrowing abroad even if foreign markets had been able and willing to absorb a loan sufficiently large in the years before 1923.

The State was therefore compelled to resort to inflation, a process which did not cease until the reconstruction loan was issued in the summer of 1924. The external value of the Austro-Hungarian krone had already depreciated as the result of war financing from a gold parity of 20·26 cents (United States old gold parity) to about 7 cents in November 1918. During 1919 a separate currency, the Hungarian krone, was created and in the following year Hungary received her share of the assets, mainly gold, of the central bank of the Empire, the Austro-Hungarian bank. But in spite of this, depreciation proceeded apace and prices rose, since the Government was forced to print notes in order to meet its liabilities. By the middle of 1924 the external value of the krone was little more than 0·001 United States cents, about one-twenty-thousandth of its gold parity. It is noteworthy, however,

---

[1] E.g. an important direct loss to Hungary's balance of payments arose from the great diminution in the amount of remittances from emigrants, most of whom came from the parts of Hungary lost to her under the Treaty.

[2] The civil service had also been reorganized shortly before the War, as a result of which the number of civil servants coming into the pension list has increased steadily during recent years.

that the depreciation of the Austrian krone was considerably more rapid until the Austrian currency was stabilized in 1922, an indication that the potential economic strength of Hungary was considered to be greater than that of Austria.[1]

The restoration of normal economic conditions in a period of both political and economic chaos was, of course, almost out of the question. Nevertheless, considerable progress was made in some directions even before reconstruction was placed in the hands of the League. Conditions in the Successor States were almost equally chaotic, and they had not yet been able to loosen their economic ties with Hungary in response to the requirements of nationalistic policies. Moreover, the redistribution of land carried out after the War by Czechoslovakia, Roumania, and Yugoslavia had seriously reduced their agricultural production, while the much less drastic reform carried out by Hungary[2] had not the same effects. In the case of maize there was even an increase of production. Thus the Successor States were still compelled to rely for a large part of their agricultural raw materials on Hungary, whose exports increased from the equivalent of 190·6 to 392·2 million pengö between 1920 and 1923, no less than 70·6 per cent. of the total in the latter year going to Austria, Czechoslovakia, Roumania, and Yugoslavia. Imports, which rose from 484·1 to 625·7 million pengö between 1920 and 1922, fell to 490·7 million in 1923, but in that year some 63 per cent. of the total came from the above four States. The difference of value between imports and exports was made good partly by services and partly by relief credits from the Allied Powers.

In the manufacturing industry, however, the position was worse. The central problem of re-equipping the industrial system for the new and now greatly restricted home market, and eliminating superfluous plant, was seriously complicated by the difficulty of importing raw materials at a time when the currency was depreciating and the import surplus was at an abnormally high level; and since the new frontiers had cut off Hungary's periphery from her centre, the great majority of the raw materials needed by her factories now had to be imported. This problem was left almost untouched in the first few years after the War. Meantime, budgets were unbalanced, deficits could be met only

[1] A full discussion of Hungary's monetary history from 1918 to 1924 is contained in vol. ii of *European Currency and Finance*, a report prepared in 1925 for the Commission of Gold and Silver Enquiry of the United States Senate, pp. 103–24.

[2] In all, a little over 1,000,000 yokes of agricultural land were distributed, something less than 700,000 yokes of which went in dwarf holdings to persons who had previously been landless. Over 45 per cent. of the agricultural land of Hungary still consists of holdings of over 100 yokes, and 30 per cent. of properties of 1,000 yokes and over.

by inflation, and the currency was steadily depreciating. It was clear that external assistance was required if any solution was to be found. That help was provided through the League of Nations reconstruction scheme, negotiations for which began in April 1923.[1] In briefest form, the outlines of this scheme were as follows: reparation payments, except for deliveries of coal, were suspended until 1926, after which the average annual payment, for twenty years, was to be 10 million gold crowns. The Reparations Commission lifted the first charge on Hungary's assets and revenues. An independent bank of issue was established and financial reforms carried through, the League providing a Commissioner-General to supervise the reforms; and a foreign adviser was appointed to the bank of issue. A loan of 250 million gold crowns was issued in July 1924 in London (which took up £7,902,700), New York, Milan, Zürich, Amsterdam, Stockholm, Prague, and a small tranche, in Budapest. The krone was stabilized and a new currency, the pengö, introduced in July 1925.[2] The budget was balanced, and the whole programme of reconstruction completed well within the prescribed date, June 30th, 1926.

It now at last became possible for Hungarians to face the wider problems of reconstruction: the discovery and conquest of new markets for Hungarian exports, the rationalization of industry, and in general the adjustment of the new Hungary's economy to the new conditions. Outside Hungary, particularly in London and New York, the success of reconstruction gave confidence to the investing public, and to bankers whose connexions with Hungary had often reached far back into the past, but who had naturally been deterred by the chaotic conditions hitherto prevailing. In other words Hungary was ready to adjust herself to the new economic conditions just at the stage when foreign capital was ready with the finance without which such a readjustment would have been impossible. The result of this conjunction of circumstances was that after the reconstruction loan was issued, Hungary enjoyed five years of comparative prosperity.

During all this period foreign capital was entering the country on a large scale. It was estimated by Dr. de Schober[3] that between 1924 and 1929 the nominal amount of long-term foreign capital

---

[1] For a detailed history of the financial reconstruction of Hungary undertaken by the League of Nations, see R.I.I.A., *Survey of International Affairs, 1924*, pp. 423-37.

[2] The parity of the pengö was fixed at 27·82506 to the £. Early in 1924, when the reconstruction scheme was threatened by a temporary refusal of the United States to participate in the loan, the Bank of England had advanced £4,000,000 to the State Note Institute on condition that the Hungarian currency would eventually be stabilized on a sterling basis. (Article by Dr. Alexander Popovics, *The Economist*, December 20th, 1930.)

[3] *The Economist*, December 20th, 1930.

invested in Hungary, including the League loan, was not less than £50 million gold,[1] of which about £20 million came from the United States and £19 million from Great Britain. Some £12 million was taken up by local authorities such as the Counties, the municipalities, especially Budapest, and the communes; and used mostly for public utility purposes. A further £15 million was laid out in agricultural mortgages and applied partly to financing purchases of stock and plant required as a result of the land reform, partly to improving agricultural production and to replacing losses incurred during and immediately after the War. About £5·6 million was invested in industry, notably in the construction of a power-station near Bánhida to supply Budapest, which was financed in Great Britain. Lastly, nearly £4 million was invested in urban real estate. Equally important, perhaps, was the large volume of foreign short-term credit, estimated by Dr. de Schober in 1930 at about £18 million,[2] which was made available to Hungarian banks, mainly by the British, American, Swiss, French, and Dutch banking systems.

Thanks largely to these short-term credits, Hungary achieved an almost spectacular success in foreign trade during these years. The value of exports rose from 667 million pengö in 1924 to 1,038 in 1929; that of imports from 815 million in 1924 to 1,183 million in 1928. The value of imports still habitually exceeded that of exports, largely owing to the considerable imports of capital then taking place and to the growth of industrialization; but invisible exports also increased substantially during these years, particularly the net income from the transit trade, and the remittances from emigrants. These items, of course, tended to lessen the deficit, though it certainly remained a deficit.

Hungary's foreign trade in this period continued to be based, roughly speaking, on the exchange of her agricultural products for manufactured articles. More than half her exports were classified as food and drink; more than half her imports as finished goods. Semi-manufactured imports accounted for about 40 per cent. of the total; manufactured exports for only a fifth. Quantitative changes as compared with the previous period are impossible to determine; the principal qualitative change, it would seem, was, as regards exports, that less agricultural produce went to Slovakia owing to the increase of agricultural production in Czechoslovakia. The old trade in manufactured exports to Transylvania and Croatia-Slavonia (particularly agricultural machinery) did not disappear, for the corresponding manufacturing industries in Roumania and

[1] It would seem that the amount was rather larger, since the figure apparently allows for amortization effected between the two dates.
[2] Other estimates put the figures considerably higher.

Yugoslavia were not yet able to compete. Qualitative changes in imports were considerable. Timber, chiefly from Transylvania, and most of the non-ferrous metals all had to be imported.

When allowance is made for Czechoslovakia's agricultural policy and for the far less important policy of industrialization in Roumania and Yugoslavia, Hungary's trade in the years 1924–9 suffered less than might have been expected. More than half her foreign trade was still with the Successor States; in 1928, 63·6 per cent. of her exports went to Austria, Czechoslovakia, Roumania, and Yugoslavia, which countries accounted for 51·7 per cent. of Hungary's imports in that year. About a tenth of Hungary's exports went to Germany in this period; about a fifth of her imports came from that country. A growing market was found in Italy for Hungarian exports, possibly owing to the political connexion; and the percentage of exports rose from 6 in 1924 to nearly 13 in 1930. Trade with Western Europe was on a small scale, but tended to increase; and a noteworthy beginning was made in the attempt to find markets for Hungarian products overseas.

Meanwhile the position of the producing farmers was not unfavourable. Agricultural prices, if not rising, were at any rate maintained at a high level; and capital, ultimately provided by foreign banks, was available for improving production, though interest rates were high. Production did in fact increase considerably in most of the more important crops. Thus the annual average production of wheat from 1926 to 1930 was no less than 22·3 million quintals, as compared with 16·2 million in the preceding five years, and 20 million from 1911 to 1915.[1] Similarly the average production of maize was 16·3 million quintals during 1926 to 1930 as compared with 15·1 million quintals during 1911 to 1915, though it reached 17·9 million from 1921 to 1925. The production of barley, rye, oats, and potatoes also improved considerably from 1926 to 1930 when compared with the preceding five years, though it did not attain to the levels of the years 1911 to 1915. This is true also of sugar-beet, the average annual production of which rose from 9·8 million quintals during 1921 to 1925 to 14·8 million in 1926 to 1930. Vine growers also did well, although rather less satisfactory results were obtained in stock-breeding.

The solution attempted for the manufacturing industry was to achieve the greatest possible degree of industrial self-sufficiency. This, in turn, involved the introduction of a protective tariff. Whether this policy was deliberate[2] or not there was much that could be pleaded in justification. Since the War the density of

[1] Post-War territory.
[2] This view is maintained by Gustav Graz. The policy is ascribed by him to Count Bethlen, who came into office in April 1921. See 'Die Wirtschaft Ungarns, 1919–1934', in *Zeitschrift für Politik*, vol. xxiv (1935), p. 96.

population had increased considerably, the outlet of emigration was rapidly disappearing, and further industrialization seemed the only answer, failing a really radical agrarian reform.[1] Moreover, some use had to be found for the existing industrial plant. Lastly, to manufacture in Hungary what had previously been imported would lead to a considerable (and, at this time, very necessary) saving in foreign exchange. What is surprising is that more serious resistance was not encountered from the agricultural interests, for to exclude the manufactures of Austria and Czechoslovakia would encourage these States, it might be thought, to exclude Hungary's agricultural products. However, they appear to have agreed to industrial protection on condition that similar protection was accorded to their own products, and in 1924 protection was introduced.

The rapid progress of industry during these years was not due to protection alone. The banks, which, in Hungary as in most of Central Europe, owned most of the larger industries, passed on many of the credits which they were receiving from abroad to industry as working capital. In other cases, the receipt of credits released other of the bankers' funds for this purpose. All in all, industry experienced little difficulty on the financial side. Moreover, the level of wages was comparatively low. Thus, remarkable success was achieved in this period, for the comparative prosperity of agriculture stimulated internal consumption, while the surplus production could still be exported to Roumania and Yugoslavia as was seen above. The progress made can be judged from the following table:

Value of Industrial Production

	(*In million pengö.*)	
	1913	*1928*
Food and drink . . .	807	1,106
Textiles	95	378
Iron and metals . . .	293	317
Machinery	262	236
Chemicals	144	202
Others	303	608
Total	1,904	2,847

It is true that the progress was not uniform. It is doubtful, for example, whether the milling industry has ever been employed at anything like capacity since the War. But in general the progress was considerable, particularly in the textile industry. Between

[1] The number of entirely landless agricultural labourers was estimated by one authority in 1933 at over 2,000,000; that of dwarf-holders whose holdings were insufficient to support themselves and their families, at nearly 1,000,000. See C. A. Macartney, *Hungary* (*Modern World Series*, London, 1934), p. 245.

1920 and 1929 the number of cotton spindles rose from 30,000 to 243,000, and of woollen spindles from 6,000 to 69,000.

The budgetary equilibrium introduced by the reconstruction programme was maintained throughout these years, and the first deficit did not occur until the fiscal year 1930–1. Ordinary expenditure rose considerably—from 728 million pengö in 1925/6 to 965 million in 1928/9—but revenue was increased *pari passu*. No serious difficulty was experienced in collecting taxes, although so far as can be judged the *per capita* level of taxation was higher in Hungary than in the other Successor States. Lastly it may be mentioned that Hungary's liability on reparations account was definitely settled after The Hague Conference of 1930. In addition to the sum mentioned above,[1] Hungary undertook to pay an annual sum of 13·5 million kronen from 1944 to 1966; and the lien on her assets was finally rescinded. The so-called optant question[2] also was settled in 1930.

The outward aspect of the position towards the end of this period may be summed up somewhat as follows. The currency had been stabilized and order reintroduced into the national finances. Foreign trade had increased considerably. Prices were at a high level, and the farmers, whose production had recovered to the pre-War level, had enjoyed some years of prosperity. In industry, the desire to achieve self-sufficiency had led to something like boom conditions. A superficial observer might have supposed that Hungary had succeeded in establishing an economic *modus vivendi* within the limits of the Treaty of Trianon.

By the end of 1929 the foundations upon which this apparent recovery had been built up were, one by one, beginning to collapse. Since the middle of 1929 the trend of world agricultural prices had been downward, and was rapidly acquiring momentum. In Hungary, the index of wholesale prices fell from 100 in 1929 to 78·5 in 1931. Foreign, particularly American, capital was by no means so easy or so cheap to obtain, though both in 1930 and in 1931 the Treasury managed to negotiate two considerable short-term credits abroad for the purpose of balancing budgets whose equilibrium had been disturbed by the growing agricultural depression. But the foreign debt was now very heavy; the total annual charge for amortization and interest had reached some 300 million pengö,[3] and even in Hungary doubts were beginning to be

[1] See p. 465.
[2] Viz. the question of compensation to be paid by the Successor States to Hungarian nationals expropriated by them as a result of agrarian reform.
[3] Special report by the Financial Committee of the League on the Financial Position of Hungary, October 24th, 1931, p. 8. Of the countries taking part in the Stresa Conference of 1932 (Austria, Bulgaria, Czechoslovakia, Greece, Hungary, Poland, and Yugoslavia) Hungary had the largest *per capita* foreign debt, viz. 432 Swiss francs per head. The next highest was Greece, with 378

expressed[1] as to the desirability of increasing the strain on the balance of payments by further borrowing abroad. Meanwhile, in the autumn of 1930 the desire of Czechoslovakia to extend her agricultural production led to the denouncing of the commercial agreement between that country and Hungary; and to a violent fall in Hungary's trade with Czechoslovakia, formerly one of her best customers.[2] Then came the failure of the Oesterreichische Credit-Anstalt in May 1931—a disastrous blow; for not only had the financial organization of Hungary been closely connected with that of Austria, but the event dispelled any confidence which might have remained in Central Europe as a whole. Finally, the collapse of the German banking system in July 1931 led to a financial and economic crisis of the first order in Hungary itself.

It is not possible to enter into the details of the crisis of 1931–3 or to describe all the various developments which led to the subsequent partial recovery. Certain aspects of the crisis must, however, be carefully examined if a correct conclusion as to Hungary's present position is to be obtained.

The crisis of the summer of 1931 was primarily financial. Beginning outside Hungary, it hit that country very severely owing to its overborrowed condition. The foreign debt charges could be met only by further borrowing or by converting the surplus of merchandise imports into a surplus of exports, for the net invisible exports were negligible by comparison. The former alternative being out of the question, the latter had to be attempted. But Hungary's exports, being predominantly agricultural, had greatly diminished in value; and markets, such as Czechoslovakia, were, one by one, being restricted. Therefore, although an export surplus was achieved, for the first time since the War, in 1930, the total value of the trade had so fallen that the surplus was of little real value.

	Value in million pengö.			Volume in million quintals.	
	Imports.	Exports.	Import (−) or export (+) surplus.	Imports.	Exports.
1928	1,183·3	803·3	− 380·0	66·3	21·7
1929	1,063·7	1,038·5	− 25·2	67·1	27·5
1930	823·3	911·7	+ 88·4	48·9	22·9
1931	539·4	570·4	+ 31·0	33·5	18·8

Swiss francs per head, the lowest Bulgaria, with 118 Swiss francs per head. (League of Nations: Commission of Enquiry for European Union: *Report of the Stresa Conference for the Economic Restoration of Central and Eastern Europe* [1932, vii, 11], p. 7).

[1] Cf. article by Dr. Béla de Imrédy in *The Economist*, December 20th, 1930.

[2] Exports to Czechoslovakia fell from 154·7 million pengö in 1930 (or 17·0 per cent. of Hungary's total exports) to 23·8 million pengö (or 4·2 per cent. of the total) in 1931.

Realization that the service of the foreign debt could not be met if these conditions continued led to the withdrawal of foreign capital from Hungary in the spring and summer of 1931, and, in Hungary itself, to a flight from the currency,[1] which the classical expedients, such as the raising of the bank-rate,[2] were quite unable to prevent. The situation came to a head when the German banking system broke down in July; when Germany imposed a bank holiday, Hungary followed suit, and when the Hungarian banks reopened, it was under a régime of rigid restrictions on the transfer of money abroad. These measures enabled the Government to allay the immediate fears of the population as to the stability of the currency, though the stability was of a most artificial nature. In August the principal short-term creditors agreed not to withdraw any more of their credits, to which decision they have since adhered; a formal standstill agreement with the principal short-term creditors was signed in January 1932, and has since been periodically renewed. In December 1931 a moratorium was imposed on the transfer of foreign currency on the entire medium and long-term debt, public and private. The Reconstruction Loan only was excepted from this provision.[3]

The internal situation called for more active remedies. The increase of public expenditure since 1924 had been substantial, but as the income of the farmers decreased owing to the fall of prices, revenue shrank. Expenditure could not be rapidly compressed, and a heavy deficit was realized in 1930–1. The situation was examined by the League in October 1931, and Hungary undertook to reduce expenditure, to restrict internal borrowing, and to install a resident representative of the League until financial stability should be assured. A period of deflation began.

The effect of the crisis on the agricultural population was perhaps the most serious. Long after the financial and budgetary crisis had been settled, in principle at any rate, world prices continued to fall. In Hungary, the index of wholesale prices (1929 = 100) dropped from 78·5 in 1931 to 76 in 1932 and to 62·7 in 1933, and the average price at which wheat was exported in 1932 was hardly more than 9 pengö per quintal, as against 32 pengö per quintal in 1926. Moreover, the restriction of foreign

[1] In spite of a credit from the Reichsbank in the spring of 1931 amounting to $5 million and a further credit from the Bank for International Settlements of $21 millions and £1 million, the gold and foreign exchange holding of the National Bank fell from nearly 200 million pengö at the end of 1930 to about 120 million by the end of June 1931.

[2] The bank-rate was raised to 9 per cent. in September 1931.

[3] Sufficient funds were in the hands of the Trustees of this loan to pay the full interest in foreign currency up to July 1933. Since that date, up to the time of writing, half the interest due has been transferred in foreign currency.

markets for Hungarian agricultural produce continued; in 1932 Austria began to limit very severely her imports from Hungary. The effects of these developments upon Hungarian agriculture were catastrophic. On the one hand there was an enormous fall in the purchasing power of the farmers.[1] On the other there was a serious decrease in efficiency, the incentive to which was quickly disappearing.[2] A considerable decrease in yield resulted. Of the six principal crops (wheat, maize, barley, rye, oats, potatoes) the average yield of maize and barley only was higher during the years 1931–5 than in the preceding five years. The yield of potatoes fell from an average of 71 quintals per hectare in 1926–30 to 56·6 quintals per hectare in 1931–5.

The benefit to Hungary of the good harvest of 1931 and the excellent harvest of 1932 was thus greatly reduced, and the Government had to come to the assistance of the farmer. But the State's attempts to support prices, in particular those of wheat, had little real effect on the position, while involving the taxpayer in heavy losses.[3] Greater results were achieved as regards agricultural debt. The farmers had borrowed heavily, usually on mortgage, when prices were high, and were now quite unable to meet their charges. The carrying out of contracts would have involved wholesale dispossession and serious social disorder. The principle of the Government's policy, formulated in a series of provisional measures from 1932 to 1933, was that foreclosure should be suspended provided current interest was met at a reduced rate; in some cases the State took over part of the debt. A settlement was not finally reached until October 1935.[4] This settlement, though less radical than those effected in neighbouring countries, imposed a heavy burden both on the creditors and the State. No estimate of the

---

[1] The West European finds it hard to imagine the complete absence of money in the country-side of Central and East Europe during the worst of the crisis. In whole villages of Hungary not 20 pengö in cash were to be found; everything was conducted on a barter basis, drinks in the public house being paid for by potatoes, the weekly shave by a dinner a month, and so on. The Government itself was forced at one time to accept taxes in the form of wheat.

[2] Between 1925 and 1928 the number of tractors in use rose from 1,188 to 4,000. In a report for the years 1930–2, the British Commercial Secretary at Budapest stated (Great Britain: Department of Overseas Trade: *Report on Economic Conditions in Hungary 1930–1932*) that 'owing to the great fall in the prices of agricultural produce, not only has the purchase of tractors entirely ceased, but the use of them has also been discontinued, and several thousands of them are lying idle all over the country'. The same was true of threshing machinery. Similarly, 1·9 million quintals of artificial fertilizers were used in 1928, but less than a sixth of this figure in 1933 (ibid., *1933*).

[3] The methods by which the State attempted to support wheat prices is described by the Representative in Hungary of the League Finance Committee, Mr. Royall Tyler, in his first report (p. 7), for the fourth quarter of 1931, and his third report (p. 8), for the second quarter of 1932.

[4] The details are given in Mr. Royall Tyler's 16th report (for the third quarter of 1935), pp. 9–10.

total of liabilities assumed by the State can be given, but in
Mr. Royall Tyler's opinion[1] they 'reach the limit at present
[October 1935] possible without incurring serious danger'.

On industry the effect of the crisis was nearly as catastrophic.
The fall in agricultural purchasing power made it almost impossible
to sell many products to the farmers, particularly as the price of
manufactured articles naturally fell more slowly than that of agricultural produce, in spite of the efforts of the Government to
support the latter. The scarcity of foreign exchange restricted the
purchase of raw materials, at best, to the barest necessities. Exports were greatly reduced owing to the import restrictions abroad.
Lastly, many of the more important concerns had been financed,
through Hungarian banks, by foreign capital which was no longer
available. Consequently, during 1931 and 1932 production in
many branches came almost to a standstill. The undertakings producing capital goods, iron and steel, machinery, and chemicals,
were hardest hit; for instance, in 1932 only about 100 threshing
machines were exported in all, as compared with an export of
about 1,500 to the Balkan States alone in normal years. The
milling industry also, which, as was seen, suffered seriously from
the Treaty, was gravely affected, for grain supplies from the Balkan
States ceased almost entirely, and the flour milled in Budapest fell
to 150,000 tons as compared with about 800,000 tons before the
War. On the other hand, the necessity to restrict imports undoubtedly stimulated the tendency already noted towards self-
sufficiency. Even in the worst years of the crisis there were
branches of industry which benefited from this development. The
textile industry, for example, began during these years to manufacture yarns which had formerly been imported.

In 1933 a gradual recovery began. The farmer was helped by
the gradual rise in wholesale prices. Industrial activity, stimulated
by the need to reduce imports, increased greatly. Foreign trade
also improved considerably, and the balance of payments benefited
by the development of an important tourist traffic. The budget
was favourably affected by the general increase of activity, and
deficits were substantially reduced. The foreign creditor alone—
up to the time of writing—was not permitted to share in this
improvement.

The improvement in the position of the farmers was due partly
to the relief afforded by the State to agricultural debtors, but even
more to the rise in prices. The index of wholesale prices, which
includes those of a number of not strictly agricultural products,
rose from a low level of 62·7 (1929 = 100) in 1933 to 74·1 in 1935,

[1] Ibid., p. 10.

and stood at 73·6 in 1936; the rise in the price of agricultural produce can be seen from the following figures:[1]

	Wheat. (per 100 Kg.)	Live Cattle. (Middling quality) per Kg.	Calves. (per Kg.)	Pigs. (per Kg.)
	pengö.	pengö.	pengö.	pengö.
Jan. 31, 1932 .	12·53	0·50	0·86	0·85
Dec. 31, 1932 .	12·80	0·62	0·70	0·87
,, 1933 .	7·15	0·54	0·79	0·77
,, 1934 .	16·73	0·49	0·78	0·80
,, 1935 .	18·45	0·50	0·88	0·95
,, 1936 .	20·10	0·79	1·16	1·14

Moreover, while the difficulties of exporting agricultural produce
to the Successor States did not decrease, a market was found in
Germany for a considerable proportion of Hungary's agricultural
goods, the sale of which was financed by a clearing agreement.
Thus, though the basic principles of Hungary's agricultural system
remained unchanged since 1931, the value of agricultural production increased from 860·2 million pengö in 1933 to 1,109·8 million
pengö in 1935. The figure in 1936 was probably even higher,
though not as high as that for 1929, viz. 1,819·2 million pengö.[2]

This recovery in agriculture, combined with the drive towards
self-sufficiency, led also to an industrial recovery. The index of
industrial activity stood at 127·4 (1929 = 100) in the third quarter
of 1936 as compared with 114 in the corresponding quarter of
1935, and averages of 97·5, 83·9, and 76·9 for the years 1934, 1933,
and 1932 respectively. Production in several important sections of
manufacturing industry towards the end of 1936 was close to
capacity; and new plant was being built. For the textile industry
alone, the index of activity (1929 = 100) stood at 138 in the third
quarter of 1936, as compared with 106·7 in the third quarter of
1935, and averages of 123·1 for the whole year 1935, 129·4 for 1934,
115·6 for 1933, but only 85·1 for 1931. These figures suggest that
the desired end, viz. the achievement of the maximum of industrial
self-sufficiency, has been brought appreciably nearer during the
last few years. This conclusion is supported by the fact that Hungary's imports of manufactured goods have fallen considerably in
the last few years, while imports of raw materials and semi-
manufactured goods have increased. From 1926 to 1930, 52·1 per
cent. on the average of Hungary's imports were manufactured
goods and only 40·7 per cent. raw materials and semi-manufactured
goods. In 1935 the percentage of manufactured goods was 37·1,

[1] Quarterly reports of Mr. Royall Tyler.
[2] These figures are given by the Hungarian Statistical Office and the annual
Die Volkswirtschaft Ungarns, issued by Dr. Georg Kemény, Dr. Mark Mitnitzky,
and Josef Vágó.

that of raw materials and semi-manufactured goods 47·8. Industrial self-sufficiency could, of course, be carried a stage farther if Hungary were to attempt to manufacture substitutes for the raw materials which she lacks. Of this there has so far been no sign, and there is probably not sufficient capital in the country to finance such an experiment, which would be costly in the extreme.

Since the worst year, 1933 for imports (312·6 million pengö), and 1932 for exports (334·5 million pengö), the value of Hungary's foreign trade has steadily improved. In 1936 imports were valued at 433·5 and exports at 509 million pengö. These figures do not bear comparison with those for the period 1924–30, and the volume of imports in 1936 was still less than half that of 1929, though the volume of exports was 20·7 million quintals as compared with 27·5 million in 1929. The export surplus, however, has been maintained every year since 1929.

Changes in the distribution of Hungary's trade are perhaps more remarkable. The proportion of Hungary's exports to the Successor States has continued to decrease from 57·2 per cent. of the total in 1929 to 31·3 per cent. in 1935. In the latter year only 43·6 per cent. of her imports came from these States, as compared with 48·8 per cent. in 1929. Germany, acting through her clearing agreement, has become Hungary's best customer. Exports to that country in 1935 were 23·9 per cent. of the total as against 11·7 per cent. in 1929, though imports from Germany have increased much less. Partly as the result of the Rome Pact of 1934 and of Hungary's refusal to participate in sanctions, exports to Italy have been maintained at about 13 per cent. of the total. Lastly, trade with Great Britain has greatly increased. Exports to Great Britain, only 3·6 per cent. of the total in 1929, rose to 8·1 per cent. in 1935, and were probably even higher in 1936; the percentage of imports increased from 2·8 per cent. in 1929 to 5·1 per cent. in 1935. Of the structural changes in Hungary's trade the most important, the decrease in imports of manufactured goods and the increase in those of raw materials, have already been noted. There was a complementary change in the structure of exports; manufactured exports rose from 19·4 per cent. of the total, on the average, in 1926–30, to 29·9 per cent. in 1935; exports of food and drink fell from 52·2 per cent. to 44·9 per cent.

The increase in Hungary's foreign trade since 1933, and particularly in the export surplus, did not necessarily relieve the exchange position, since over three-quarters of Hungary's trade is conducted through clearing agreements, as the result of which a favourable balance cannot be converted into free exchange.[1] The

[1] It must not be forgotten that the improvement shown by the actual figures of trade under the clearing agreements is often of an essentially artificial nature. For

only country whose trade with Hungary yields an appreciable export surplus of free exchange is now Great Britain.[1] The depreciation of the pengö since 1931 is a further factor which should be borne in mind in considering Hungary's foreign trade. Since December 1935 this depreciation has been officially recognized by the authorities to the extent of $33\frac{1}{3}$ per cent., for the National Bank now pays a premium of 50 per cent. for free currencies such as sterling and the dollar, though, in order to avoid the consequent increase in the payments of pengö required by the foreign debt, the pengö has not been formally devalued by $33\frac{1}{3}$ per cent.

The exchange position, nevertheless, undeniably improved after 1931. The exchange restrictions were considerably simplified, although not relaxed, and the gold and foreign exchange holding of the National Bank (valued at the old parity rate of the pengö) rose from 90·2 million pengö on June 30th, 1934, to 126 million pengö on December 31st, 1936.[2] Moreover, the increasing tourist trade has brought in substantial sums in foreign exchange. The foreign debt has decreased considerably, owing largely to the devaluation or depreciation of nearly all the currencies in which the debt is expressed, and also to the willingness of foreign creditors to take repayment at a loss by selling their pengö cheap to Hungarian exporters and foreign tourists. Thus the foreign funded debt of the State fell from 1,315 million pengö at the end of June 1931 to 800 million pengö at the end of December 1936.[3] Similarly, the debts subject to the standstill agreement on Hungary's short-term debts to foreign banks were only about 320 million pengö[4] in the middle of June 1936 (before the devaluations of September 1936), though the figure must have been at least twice as high in June 1931.[5]

Yet up to the time of writing the arrangements arrived at in the winter of 1931–2 for dealing with the foreign debt have remained

example, if Germany were to return to a free exchange system it is doubtful whether she could continue to take such large quantities of Hungary's exports; and the fact that Italy is importing large quantities of Hungarian goods (at artificially high prices) is due chiefly to political considerations. A further problem arising out of trade through the clearing agreements is that there is often great difficulty in providing suitable imports into Hungary, e.g. in return for exports to Germany.

[1] The balance in favour of Hungary has increased from £171,000 in 1930 to £1,739,000 in 1936.

[2] This was partly due to the purchase during 1935 of gold in the hands of the public.

[3] Special Report of the Financial Committee to the Council of the League, October 1931, p. 5; Mr. Royall Tyler's 21st report (fourth quarter of 1936), p. 6.

[4] Mr. Royall Tyler's 19th report (second quarter of 1936), p. 14.

[5] Cf. Special Report of the Financial Committee to the Council of the League, October 1931, p. 20.

in force without any material change. On all the long- and short-term debts, other than the League loan of 1924, little or no interest has been transferred since 1932 and amortization has been entirely suspended. This position is not primarily due to the current budgetary situation of the State. In 1936, for example, there was a noteworthy increase in revenue, and the relation of revenue to expenditure was more favourable than it had been for several years past, though it is true that, owing to the suspension of transfer and to various other factors, the floating debt has increased from 402 to 720 million pengö between the end of September 1931 and of June 1936.[1] Similarly the position of other borrowers has noticeably improved; farmers have done better, industrial concerns have increased their profits; the banking position has benefited; and there has been no major failure since 1929.

So far as Hungary was concerned, the three principal manifestations of the crisis of 1931 were the restrictions imposed on her chief markets, the fall of prices, and the impossibility of a further recourse to foreign capital. By the beginning of 1937 it might reasonably be said that Hungary had made some progress towards adjusting herself to these new conditions. But it is the opinion of Mr. Royall Tyler that the recent figures 'must be taken to represent more or less what Hungary, in present circumstances, can make out of foreign trade, the actual amount of exports year by year, of course, depending much on the harvest. Unless markets are reopened, it appears unlikely that she will be able greatly to increase her sales abroad or her export surplus.'[2] Thus certain very definite limits are set to the extent of recovery. Inside these limits there were signs in the early part of 1937 that recovery had progressed nearly as far as it could. Further progress would seem to be dependent upon a restoration of the world conditions which prevailed before 1931; and it may be added that such progress will inevitably require further imports of foreign capital.

In the light of subsequent events it is difficult to avoid the conclusion that the equilibrium apparently achieved in the economic system between 1924 and 1930 was due to the large volume of foreign capital entering the country in those years. But it is most important to remember the assumptions on which this money was lent. Of these the most weighty was that no fundamental alterations would take place in the structure of Hungary's foreign trade, particularly with the Successor States. This assumption was by

---

[1] The State pays part of the service of the foreign debt in pengö which it then reborrows. The steady increase in the floating debt which results is, of course, a real weakness.

[2] 21st report (fourth quarter of 1936), p. 11.

no means unjustifiable. For even in 1930, as was seen, Hungary was still to some extent fulfilling her old function of exporting agricultural produce in exchange for the raw materials of the provinces she lost after the War, and if this position had not changed, Hungary's capacity to pay would now be materially different from what it is. The other important assumption relates to the level of prices, for clearly it was unjustifiable for Hungary to borrow abroad on such a scale if the prices of her chief exports were not to remain at or about the level at which they stood during the borrowing years. On these suppositions it might reasonably have been maintained that Hungary's foreign borrowing during these years was merely a preliminary transaction necessary to set the economic system on its feet until such time as Hungary had accumulated sufficient working capital of her own.

These assumptions have, however, been proved false. There has, after all, been a fundamental change in the structure of Hungary's trade. Moreover, the progress of agricultural production in Czechoslovakia and Austria, and, to a lesser degree, of industrialization in Roumania and Yugoslavia, suggest that the change is permanent, and that the old position, even as it was before 1930, will in the present circumstances be most difficult to recover. For this reason, if prices rise to the level of 1929, the effect on Hungary's economic system will be far less than would otherwise have been the case. It is not suggested that for these reasons Hungary's foreign debt will never be repaid; on the contrary, as was seen above, the position of the foreign creditor was probably more favourable in the early part of 1937 than it had been since 1931. What is suggested is that the foreign borrowings of 1924–30 did not, as it was hoped at the time, provide a permanent solution for the difficulties imposed on Hungary by the Peace Treaty, but merely enabled their solution to be postponed.

In the meantime, however, those difficulties have been increased, as was seen, through the restrictions on Hungarian foreign trade which have since been imposed by the Successor States. So far this is an ample justification for the policy of industrialization at present being pursued. But even now Hungary is, in certain cases, manufacturing more industrial products than she can herself consume. As industrialization is extended, this surplus will increase, and will be limited only by Hungary's lack of raw materials. Thus it may be anticipated that in addition to marketing her agricultural surplus, the difficulty of which is more likely to increase than to decrease, Hungary may shortly be faced with the problem of finding foreign buyers for a growing surplus of manufactured goods as well, since an increase in industrial production will not diminish the necessity to export, owing to the need to import industrial raw materials. It cannot be denied that these difficulties arise directly or indirectly from the Peace Treaty, in so far as it enabled Hungary's peripheral provinces to be included in the separate tariff areas of the Successor States. The questions so raised have yet to be answered. It is in answering them that Hungary's fundamental economic problem consists.

NOTE

Since the above section was written, Hungary has attempted to reach a comprehensive settlement of the foreign debt question with her foreign creditors, and agreement was reached in July 1937 as to the future service on many of the more important categories of Hungary's foreign debt. In each case provision was made for a resumption of payments in foreign exchange, whereas up to this stage Hungary had paid in pengö for all except the League Loan; and the settlements were for a period of at least three years, instead of being on a year-to-year basis, as had hitherto been the case. With regard to the $7\frac{1}{2}$ per cent. League Loan, a proposal was put forward for a permanent settlement, viz. that the interest payable should be $4\frac{1}{2}$ per cent., in place of the $3\frac{3}{4}$ per cent. paid since 1932, and that the loan should be redeemed by the operation of an annual sinking fund of 1 per cent. This proposal the bondholders' representatives recommended the bondholders to accept. On an issue of Hungarian Treasury bills, of which £1,770,000 were outstanding, mostly in London, the Government offered to pay 3 per cent. in sterling during the next three years (half in interest and half in redemption), as compared with a payment of only $1\frac{1}{2}$ per cent. interest in pengö in the preceding year. A further offer was made in respect of the long-term bonded debt other than that of the State, which chiefly covers the debt of the municipalities, ecclesiastical bodies, and certain private bodies. On this class of debt between $1\frac{1}{2}$ per cent. and $1\frac{3}{4}$ per cent. is to be paid in foreign exchange during the next three years in interest, although since 1931 no interest or amortization had been paid in foreign exchange at all. Finally, a new standstill agreement was initialled by the short-term banking creditors providing for payment in foreign exchange, instead of in pengö as hitherto. The agreement is to remain in force conditionally for three years; 1 per cent. is to be paid in interest and $4\frac{1}{4}$ per cent. in capital repayment per annum. At the time of writing, negotiations are in progress with regard to the State long-term foreign debts.

CONCLUSIONS

THE overwhelming majority of public opinion in Hungary remains profoundly convinced of the injustice of the Treaty of Trianon, and persistent in demanding revision of its terms. This demand is by no means confined, as is sometimes suggested, to a small band of 'feudal' magnates to whom the partition of Hungary and the measures introduced by the Successor States have meant the end of a position of almost regal wealth and power; nor even to the larger middle class whose careers as administrators and teachers in the non-Magyar districts are now closed to them. The voices of those who have suffered direct material losses are, perhaps, loudest in the chorus of complaint. The poor are less vocal; they have never been encouraged to talk much, anyway, and they may even regret the extreme vigour with which the revision campaign is prosecuted as exacerbating, on the one hand, relations between Hungary and her neighbours, and providing, on the other, too easy an opportunity for diverting attention from social problems within the country. But those Magyars who actually oppose the idea of treaty revision are few indeed: a mere handful of political extremists (many of them in exile to-day) who so hated the social structure of Hungary, despaired so utterly of reform, that to destroy it they were willing to see the country itself destroyed. The vast majority of their countrymen, of every political tendency, feel otherwise. The maintenance of Hungarian integrity was upheld with equal fervour, although by very different methods, by all four Governments—Conservative, Liberal-Socialist, Communist, and Conservative again—which ruled in Budapest in 1918–19; and by no one more pertinaciously than by Bela Kun, the little Jewish pseudo-journalist and Communist leader from Transylvania; and all four Governments, on this question if on no other, had behind them the vast majority of their country. To-day the demand for revision of the Treaty is voiced, and sincerely, by all classes of Hungarian society, from the big landowners through the officials and business men down to the workers and peasants. And the feeling in this respect shows small signs of diminishing. After the first few years had elapsed, when the gaping wounds made by the dismemberment had been bandaged—the refugees established in new houses, the businesses re-orientated, the first and most painful reforms (whether deserving that name or no) carried through in the Successor States—a certain appeasement or resignation was apparent, due in large measure to the economic prosperity brought about by a great influx of foreign loan capital; in part also to a feeling of sheer helplessness in the face of the overwhelming force represented by the upholders of the *status quo*. Then came the terrible economic depression which gripped Central Europe after 1929, the enfeeblement of the League of Nations, the rise of Germany, the encouragement given to Hungarian aspirations by Italy; and at once the smouldering embers burst into flame again.

Granted the premiss that the Treaty was mistaken and unjust, then the demand for revision can hardly be dismissed, as it is by some of Hungary's neighbours, as mere war-mongering. Even if the Millerand letter was only meant to refer to details of frontier rectifications, yet the Treaty of Trianon itself provides for a possibility of its own revision on a wider scale in Article XIX of the League Covenant, which stands at its head.

And the relevancy of the idea of justice to the Treaty has never been denied. The Allies may have been under no technical obligation to apply the 'Fourteen Points' to Hungary, as they were to Germany, but their moral obligation has never been contested to apply these Points, and in general the principles enunciated by Wilson in his various speeches, most conveniently summed up in his phrase: 'the guiding principle of justice to all peoples and nationalities'. Indeed, what they maintained in their discussions with Hungary at Trianon was that although they might be dictating, they were dictating justice; it was precisely justice that required the dismemberment of Hungary and even the details of the frontier settlements.

And the beneficiaries of the treaty themselves adopt exactly the same attitude. Here and there a conscience may be queasy about some particularly generous local concession, but, as regards the broad lines of the Treaty and practically all its details, Hungary's neighbours are no less sincere, no less passionate in their belief in the justice of their acquisitions, than Hungary in the injustice. They would not thank the investigator who dismissed their right as merely one of might.

Between two such opposite views on the merits of what was done at Trianon, who shall be bold enough to judge? Particularly as no definition of justice in international affairs has ever been given, or is ever likely to be given. One may imagine it *in vacuo*; but take any question of practical politics, and a dozen considerations arise, each commanding respect, each in flat contradiction to some other which appears equally weighty.

It must, in the first instance, be emphasized that, except to some extent as regards the Austrian frontier, the Treaty was not a negotiated, but a dictated one. Hungary was not even invited to

Trianon until the Allies had made up their minds, and the mass of maps, historical essays, and statistics which her delegates brought with them represented, from the point of view of the Conference, so much waste labour. The single concession which they elicited was the 'Millerand Letter', which amounted to very little. It was clearly meant to apply only to details of frontier adjustment; and although Hungary built great hopes on it, and tried to utilize it for much larger purposes, such expectations were clearly doomed from the outset to disappointment.[1]

The fact that the peace was imposed and not negotiated would not necessarily make it unfair, since one can well suppose that a wise and impartial outside authority might have reached a just settlement more easily than could be obtained by the wearisome argument of claim and counter-claim. But in truth, the circumstances in which the Treaty was drawn up were not conducive to the application of ideal justice. Hungary had been manœuvred, and in part had manœuvred herself, into the most unfavourable situation that can well be imagined. Although, as we have said, the territorial clauses of the Treaty were not confessedly punitive, there was yet undoubtedly a feeling at the Peace Conference that the ex-enemy States represented Powers of Evil, to restrain which was a moral duty on humanity. Hungary had to bear her full share of this odium for her part responsibility in the original declaration of war and her subsequent unwavering conduct of it; the more so as Count Tisza never made public his original opposition to the ultimatum, and his later stipulations. Károlyi's efforts to reverse the position in October 1918, although sincere and well-meant, were quite incredibly naïve; not only the Serbs and Roumanians, but the Czechs also had long since got the ear of the Entente. It was far too late. President Wilson preached the necessity of democracy, but when Károlyi tried to follow his advice he was insulted for his pains by the French general commanding in Belgrade. Indeed, Hungary could do nothing right now. Each step of hers led her deeper into the slough. The Liberal-Socialist experiments in disbanding the old army and organizing a new force on democratic lines only led to chaos and weakness, and allowed Hungary's neighbours to press forward into her territory. While she could never have organized a successful resistance to the whole treaty, as Turkey did, yet it is quite possible that had she been possessed of efficient and determined military forces at the end of

---

[1] It is even sometimes suggested that but for the hopes which Hungary reposed in this letter, she would have refused to sign the Treaty. I cannot, however, believe that at that stage in events she could have refused her signature. It may be regrettable that M. Millerand used such high-flown language, lending itself so easily to false interpretations, but I cannot believe that the course of history was influenced thereby.

1918, she might have made considerably better terms for herself. When at last she did undertake a more active resistance, it was highly unfortunate for her that this should have been done in the name of the Third International. The help which Moscow had promised never came, and the Western Powers were only frightened by the spectre of Bolshevism and strengthened in their resolve to exorcise it. Finally, when the reaction came, it came again in such form as to give an easy handle to Hungary's enemies.

The net result of all her efforts was thus to leave her branded with the mark of war-guilt, doubly aggravated by the imputations of Bolshevism and reaction; whereas of her four neighbours and principal prospective beneficiaries, three were safely ensconced on the side of both victory and moral superiority.

True, it was not Hungary's neighbours, but the Western Powers which drafted the Peace terms. But they, too, had been fighting for long years against Hungary, or against her allies, and their representatives, being human, were inevitably influenced by war psychology. Few of them could escape a natural presumption against Hungary which was enhanced by the fact that they had been for years, and were again during the decisive weeks of the Peace Conference, exclusively in touch with her enemies. They took their decisions alone, but first they asked Czechoslovakia, Roumania, and Yugoslavia to state their cases. They had themselves to supply any counter-case required; and they would have been more than human indeed if, in the circumstances, they had proved themselves very efficient devil's advocates.

Nor were they even altogether free to exercise this function. Although the Treaty of Bucharest was put aside as invalid, the presumption remained and was never questioned that Transylvania, at least, belonged to Roumania of prescriptive right. It was only frontier details that had to be settled, and the point of rejecting the treaty was only to rebut Roumania's claims to Magyar territory beyond the ethnographic line, and in the Banat. Similarly, the great decision of principle as regards the Slovaks had been taken long before, and promises publicly held out to the Yugoslavs also. Wilson's answer to the Andrássy note that 'the Czechoslovaks and Yugoslavs must themselves be judges of what will satisfy them' constituted a very far-reaching commitment indeed. It was no less important that France had already decided, in the main, her future policy in South-Eastern Europe, which was the strengthening of the three States which subsequently formed the Little Entente; so that the French delegation—perhaps the most active and influential of all in these questions—hardly even pretended to be neutral.

And finally, there was the decisive consideration that in some cases before the negotiations began, in almost all by the time they were complete, Hungary's neighbours were in *de facto* political and military control of the areas which they meant to appropriate. As a writer of great authority has frankly admitted,[1] a *fait accompli* had thus been created which the Peace Conference could not undo if it would. The Successor States might be persuaded or pressed into withdrawing from a few frontier positions, but anything so far-reaching as a plebiscite, which Hungary demanded for the occupied areas, would have been worse than useless, because the beneficiaries would simply not have given up their spoils, and there was no one to force them to do so.

It can, then, hardly be denied that the scales were weighted against Hungary; and she can fairly complain that she was, at least, unlucky in the way the decisions went. As regards the main question, whether justice demanded that she should be dismembered into a number of national States, one may in fairness recall that the Allies were setting aside, with hardly a thought, considerations of legitimacy and historic right by which an earlier generation than our own set great store. The idea that so-called 'national determination' should automatically override these other claims in the name of justice is, after all, a thoroughly revolutionary one, which had never before been applied so extensively. And although we are accustomed to believe that Europe was settled on this basis in 1919 and 1920, yet the Allies never even suggested that it should be applied to their own territory, and President Wilson himself, its great prophet, hesitated to recognize diplomatically the Baltic States which, in application of the principle, had separated themselves from Russia, on the ground that to do so could involve ingratitude to an ally. If Hungary had not been in the enemy camp, her historic claims would scarcely have been ignored so cavalierly as they were. Possibly, indeed, the partition of Hungary would never have taken place in such wholesale fashion had the Partition of Poland, a century earlier, not provided Germany and Austria with an Achilles' Heel apiece and had not the Russian revolution eased the consciences of the Allies in this respect.

In different circumstances, again, more weight might easily have been attached to one plea by Hungary: that many of the non-Magyars were of recent origin, immigrants and 'guests', to whom she had given shelter, who could not fairly claim the same consideration for their national claims as an indigenous nationality. Hungary somewhat marred her own point by over-insisting on it and by exaggerating its applicability; but it has assuredly some substance.

Far more important, however, was the assumption of the Allies

[1] Temperley, 'How the Hungarian Frontiers were Drawn' (in *Foreign Affairs*, April 1928), p. 435.

that so far as possible *all* non-Magyar peoples ought to be freed from the Magyar yoke. The suggestion that the majority of the Slovaks, for example, might not want to be delivered from Hungary at all was clearly never taken seriously. If the existence of a Magyarone party among them was admitted, their members were regarded as renegades. The nationalist point of view was felt to be the only natural and proper one.

Thus the doctrine of self-determination was used to detach not only the Roumanians and Serbs from Hungary, but also the Slovaks and the Bunyevci. And more: although the position of the Ruthenes, who were not being given a national State of their own, was obviously different, they were yet attributed to Czechoslovakia as a more 'natural' connexion for them than the Hungarian. But the assumption was carried farther still: it was supposed that the 'neutral' or 'third-party' minorities, such as the Germans in Northern, Eastern, and Southern Hungary ought also to be reckoned in the non-Magyar camp. Thus in the Voivodina, for example, the Germans were added to the Serbs, and it was found that the Magyars were in a minority; whereas if the Germans had been added to the Magyars, it would have been the Serbs whose claim might have appeared thin. There was obviously a general belief, quite sincerely held, that the Magyar rule was something quite particularly oppressive and, above all, unnatural. It was felt that the new national States were automatically justified, and that even where it was necessary to attribute minorities to them, this did little harm, because they were more democratic and socially more advanced than Hungary. Moreover, it was believed that the Minority Treaties which the Successor States were being required to sign would give adequate protection.

The way to test how feeling really stood among the peoples concerned would have been by plebiscites. Hungary demanded this at the time, and her grievance that the request was refused, already strong on the face of it, was made to look far stronger still when, in the one instance in which a plebiscite was allowed to her (in Sopron), it went in her favour. I personally should hesitate to use the analogy of the Sopron plebiscite, because I know that it was not fairly taken, and do not know whether the abuses determined the result. But the demand in general was a fair one. The popular 'declarations' in Turčiansky Svätý Martin, Prešov, and Novi Sad were clearly not representative expressions of opinion by the whole of the populations concerned, even though they did represent the views of certain sections. The real reason why the Allies could not insist on plebiscites was, as we have seen, quite a different one.

The truth was that national feeling was not nearly so advanced among the 'nationalities' of Hungary as the Peace Conference was

made to believe. Besides the Magyars themselves, only the Croats
and the Roumanians had really strongly developed national consciousness. That of the Serbs, once active, was in decline; that of
the Slovaks was confined to a handful of intellectuals, while a far
larger number of educated Slovaks went into the other camp and
became enthusiastic Hungarians. This was even more true of the
Ruthenes and the minor Yugoslavs, and of all the Germans except
the Transylvanian Saxons. And even among those who did not
actively 'Magyarize', there were many who would have been fully
content with the integral application of the Nationalities Law, if
they could only have obtained it. The automatic identification of
the point of view of the nationalist leaders with that of the whole
nationality was probably the gravest injustice, and the most far-
reaching in its effects, of all inflicted upon Hungary.

If, therefore, the principle of self-determination had been
genuinely applied in 1919, it is most probable that Transylvania
would have voted for union with Roumania, but that a majority
among the Slovaks and Ruthenes would have asked to remain
within Hungary, with a measure of self-government on the lines
of the Ruthene Statute. Croatia-Slavonia would, of course, have
joined Yugoslavia, and the Serbs of the Voivodina would have
wished to do so also; but, taking all the nationalities of the
Voivodina together, Hungary would probably have got a clear
majority. In the northern Burgenland the vote would most likely
have gone to Hungary; in the south, to Austria.

But, once the main decision was taken, the determination of the
frontier in detail was also done in a manner most unfavourable to
Hungary. As we have said, there were very many cases in which
economic, strategic, and ethnographic considerations conflicted.
In practically every case (except that of Austria) the ethnographic
claims of Hungary's neighbours were done the very fullest justice;
only quite absurd demands, just as that for the Slav Corridor
through West Hungary, were rejected. There was, as we said, a
patent desire to leave as few non-Magyars as possible in Hungary.
But where the Successor States (again excepting Austria) asked for
territory not ethnographically theirs, on economic or strategic
grounds, then the fact that Magyars had to be sacrificed to these
necessities counted for little. Thus Czechoslovakia, to guard her
communications and her economic interests, was given a wide strip
of Magyar plain; Roumania again had the benefit of the doubt, in
the interests of her communications, Yugoslavia could hardly
suggest that the Northern Bačka and the Baránya were necessary
for her on economic grounds, but she asked for them as strategic
necessities, and got away with it. Incidentally, it is clear that
strategic considerations weighed more in the decision regarding

Ruthenia than ever appeared at the time. There is, on the other hand, practically no instance where Hungary received any important concession from Czechoslovakia, Roumania, or Yugoslavia on any of these grounds. The cumulative effect of all these decisions was, again, to create a situation genuinely unjust to Hungary. The number of Magyar 'frontier minorities' left to the three main Successor States far exceeded that of their own nationals left just inside the frontiers of Hungary; their strategical positions were much the stronger; their economic interests far better safeguarded. The scales were weighed in matters of detail, as when the broader question was considered.

§ 2. THE POSITION IN 1937

Looking back to-day it is easy to find fault with the work done at Paris and to sympathize with Hungary's contention that much grievous injustice was done to her. Yet it would be unprofitable to dwell only on the past. If we are to consider to-day the possibilities and the justification of revision, we must do so in the light of conditions as they are now, not as they were twenty years ago.

For much has changed since the treaty was concluded. It was, as we saw, probably true then that many of Hungary's nationalities were still in that passive attitude which she required of them and which France, for example, asks of her minorities to-day: reserving national feeling, as it were, for the home circle, but acquiescing in the supremacy of the dominant nation and ready, even anxious, to merge in it so soon as there was any question of public life, or, indeed, of any wider social activities. But to-day this old-fashioned outlook has practically vanished. It survives among many of the Jews in all the Successor States; but, among the other nationalities, only among certain rather backward peasant communities. It is most widespread among the minorities left in Hungary herself, where most of the Slovaks, nearly all the Southern Slavs, and a few of the Germans still hold to it. Outside Hungary, one finds it among the Croats of the Burgenland, and here and there elsewhere, as among the Ruthenes of the Voivodina. But in general it is rapidly giving way to a more modern outlook.

It has melted like summer snow among those nationalities who have tasted power, in the shape of the Roumanians, the Serbs, and the Slovaks. All of these races are now strongly and aggressively nationalist, with a nationalism which is now inseparable from political ambitions. Nor can we deny a similar feeling to the Ruthenes, even though its exact future direction is still uncertain. Hardly less striking has been the growth of a new nationalism among the Germans, beginning with those of Hungary's neighbours but

including to-day—a belated but most important phenomenon—
the younger generation within her own frontiers.

Not every Slovak or German, much less every Ruthene, is,
indeed, a nationalist to-day; but each of these nationalities has
now developed its class of leaders, its official, commercial, and
intellectual bourgeoisie, its administrators, teachers, bankers, industrialists, from whom the new ideas will spread downward and
outward into the masses. Their nationalism is thus a 'fait acquis'
which our generation will not see changed except to grow stronger
still. Nothing could now eliminate it short of such wholesale
measures as the Habsburgs carried out in Bohemia during the
Counter-Reformation.

Thus if, by waving an enchanter's wand, we were to put back
the frontiers of 1918, we should by no means be restoring the situation as it then existed within them. The Magyars would find a
determined mass as large as their own, divided, indeed, geographically and belonging to many nationalities, but in almost
every case determined to resist further assimilation, to develop
their own national cultures, and to have and hold a large amount
of political self-government.

And not only would the nationalities be in themselves far more
exacting in their wishes and far better able to press for them, but
they would also be in a much more powerful position inter-
nationally. No one can reasonably doubt that Yugoslavia and
Roumania have come to stay as fully sovereign states. Both of
them are already very different from the Serbia and the Roumania
of the nineteenth and even the early twentieth centuries, when they
were small and inexperienced States, Roumania being, in addition,
condemned to discretion by her Alliance with the Dual Monarchy.
The support which they could give to the Serbs and Roumanians
within Hungary would be on a very different scale from what they
could afford before the War, and the attraction which they would
exercise would assuredly be steady and powerful.

We must ask, too, whether, in imagining a restoration of the
frontiers of Hungary, we are supposing also the reconstitution of
Austria. Such an event hardly seems probable; but, without it,
Hungary would be deprived of a support which, as we have shown,
was immensely valuable to her national policy during the half-
century after 1868—without which, indeed, in the opinion of many
of her own leaders, she could not even have attempted that policy.
Further, failing the reconstruction of Austria, and unless, alternatively, Germany were to engulf the Historic Lands of Czechoslovakia, we must reckon with the Czechs exercising (on the
Slovaks) an attraction comparable, if not quite equal, to that of
Serbia and Roumania on their own respective kinsmen.

Obviously, the general development of national feeling and the changes which this has brought about outside Hungary's former frontiers, as well as inside them, have transformed the whole position fundamentally. The 'thirty million Magyar kingdom' has vanished for ever into Cloud-Cuckoo-Land. Even if the old frontiers were restored, Hungary could never again hope to Magyarize the chief nationalities, nor is it at all likely that she could even content them with an integral application of the Nationalities Law.

It is true that Hungary herself does not imagine that she could revert to the conditions or to the policy of 1914. Besides renouncing Croatia-Slavonia altogether, she seems inclined to-day to envisage leaving Transylvania in some sort of independent position; and for the other areas inhabited by non-Magyars she asks, not their unconditional return to herself, but only plebiscites among the peoples concerned. She has also stated, through Count Bethlen, that, if these areas were restored to her, she would grant their inhabitants 'national' autonomy, for which she would be prepared to accept an international guarantee.

While paying tribute to the fairness of this request (which is not the less reasonable in principle for the immense practical difficulties which it would entail), I yet feel bound to say that so long as the map of Europe remains otherwise unchanged in its essential outlines: so long, that is, as the independent national States of Roumania, Yugoslavia, Czechoslovakia, and Austria exist (or, in default of Austria, any German State covering the present Austrian territory), I cannot easily conceive of the Slovaks, Roumanians, Yugoslavs, and Burgenland Germans voting for a return to Hungary under any terms whatever. However wrong the Treaty of Trianon may have been, the developments of the past twenty years have now supplied a post-dated justification of its main principle of dismemberment of Hungary; and so long as the national States in question are able to maintain themselves, no conscientious man could possibly recommend the 'integral' restitution of Hungary.

It is another question whether the frontiers of the new States ought to be regarded as intangible. Hungarian opinion, as we saw, protested not only against the larger principle of the dismemberment of Hungary, but also against the way in which it was carried out in detail. It argues that if the principle of national determinism is to be adopted, it ought at least to be applied equally; and demands the unconditional return, without plebiscite, of that string of predominantly Magyar territory, contiguous to the frontier, which runs round a large part of her new boundaries: which would give her back, according to Hungary's own figures (based on the 1910 census) at any rate 800,000 odd Magyars from Slovakia, at the sacrifice of only 60,000 Slovaks, and over 400,000

Magyars from Roumania, at the expense, again, of 60,000 Roumanians.

As regards this claim, events have brought no such change as they have in the larger question. The figures given above of course flatter the position of the Magyars to-day, since emigration of their officials and other optants and immigration of new officials, business men, and colonists from other parts of the Successor States have brought about certain changes in the populations of the border areas; to which must be added, of course, the effects of 'de-Magyarization'—whether justified and natural or not, need not concern us here. This process has, however, chiefly affected 'third-party' minorities, notably Jews and Suabians. It is only in Slovakia that it has had any important effect on the numerical relationship between the Magyars and the principal nationals. Where, therefore, an area, particularly a rural area, was genuinely Magyar in 1914 it is usually Magyar to-day also. I cannot feel that excessive attention ought to be paid to the new colonists, in view of the difficulty which most of them have experienced in making good, and the artificial nature of the whole process. Their governments have usually paid out large sums to establish them; it would cost them little more to reverse the process.

Hungary's claim to the preponderantly Magyar areas contiguous to her frontiers is even stronger to-day than it was in 1919, in one important respect. She can no longer fairly be regarded as the sole villain of the nationality drama. This does not mean that all States treat their minorities equally badly. Czechoslovakia deserves credit for the comparative liberality of her policy. But experience has now shown us that when a state commits itself to a national policy, the position of the minorities is bound to become extremely difficult, at best. Good intentions will not suffice, for they may have to yield before the force of circumstance, as is shown, again, by the case of Czechoslovakia (with relation to her recent emergency legislation). We also see to-day that the League Minority Treaties did not afford the protection and compensation that was hoped.

All the States concerned, and not only Hungary, have adopted national policies. In all, the minorities have suffered more or less severely, and, as I have indicated in the separate sections, I believe it true to say that in them all, even in Czechoslovakia, the majority of the local Magyars would wish to return to Hungary.

Social considerations are rather more complicated. Here, again, we have learned to our cost that Hungary is not the only sinner. She remains in some respect the most oligarchic of all the States with which we are concerned, as Czechoslovakia is undoubtedly the most democratic. The awful examples of Yugoslavia and Italy since the War should, however, warn us of the danger of giving nations differential treatment according to their alleged degree of civilization or even to their past records.

Given the form of the national State, which is of its very essence so deeply inimical to national minorities, and especially to those related to races living immediately across a frontier, peace and justice are probably best served by reducing the number at least of such frontier minorities as far as possible. This principle should, I believe, be applied wherever the question lies between Magyars on the one hand and Slovaks, Western Germans, Roumanians, and Serbs on the other. Since practically all the doubtful points were given against Hungary in 1919, an even-handed application of this principle would result in considerable modifications in her favour to-day.

It remains, of course, impossible to draw the frontiers so as to coincide absolutely with the ethnographical line. In certain areas considerations of economic viability remain so strong that they are bound to be given first place. But even these can be often reduced more than might at first be suspected by special arrangements such as servitudes over railway lines, free zones, &c. In certain districts these have been attempted and have worked reasonably well.

As for strategic frontiers, I think that they should be adopted only in quite special cases, and for preference only in order to defend a weak state against a strong one, not, as in the Voivodina, vice versa. As a rule they are the least defensible of all claims.

Where the ethnographical principle must be modified, it would seem fairer to try to balance out the numbers of the two minorities on each side of the frontier as evenly as possible.

In the various special sections of this book I have mentioned the places where such frontier rectification seems to me easiest and fairest. I can claim no infallibility for my own proposals. It was not possible for me to go all along the frontier, nor all along the ethnic line, nor to investigate the economic connexions, much less the strategic importance of every border area. I can do no more here than suggest that in principle, if the system of the national State is to be preserved, the frontier ought to follow as nearly as possible the ethnic line between the Magyars and the Germans (in the west), Slovaks, Roumanians, and Serbs; and that where this line cannot be followed, the advantages and the minorities ought to be balanced as equally as possible.

In any case, whether revision is effected in Hungary's favour, or whether the frontiers are left as they are to-day, an attempt ought to be made to expand and reinforce the system of minority protection. Experience has shown that it is only in exceptional cases that a minority contiguous to its own national State will ever be truly content to live as a minority under alien rule. Nevertheless, good

minority legislation and administration, although it cannot compensate for severance from the mother country, can at least do
much to mitigate the distress of that position.

A different situation arises where large numbers of third-party
minorities are involved. These are naturally far more dispassionate
than the principal nationals or minorities; they are not moved by
the feeling which makes a Magyar or Serb declare that he would
rather be in Hungary, or in Serbia, even though he might there
be materially, culturally, and administratively worse off than in his
own national State. One finds, indeed, some relics of this feeling
(in favour of Hungary) among certain of the Magyarized Jews of
the Successor States; but it is dying out among the younger generation of Jews, and among the other large dispersed minority, the
Germans, it has already vanished almost entirely. The Germans
and many of the Jews are perfectly prepared to put themselves up
to the highest bidder.

With minorities of this type, it *is* possible, and necessary, to
differentiate between the policies adopted towards them by the
different States: not in order to praise or blame motives, but
simply to estimate results. As regards the Jews, the position, as
we have shown, is various and obscure, with a general leaning
(except perhaps in Czechoslovakia) in favour of Hungary. But as
regards the Germans, who are more numerous still, one must say
frankly that, of all the States concerned, Hungary has been the
most unwise in her behaviour. She has not been the most oppressive—on the contrary, in many respects she has been more liberal
than any of her neighbours; but she has been the least ready to
meet the present German point of view. She has many excuses,
since the older generation of her own Germans have disavowed
their children, but the fact remains that the present generation of
Germans in the Danube valley insists above all things on the right
to maintain, foster, and confess its 'Deutschtum'; and Hungary
allows that right more grudgingly than any other Successor State.

On that ground, the Germans in the Successor States are, on the
whole, opposed to a return to Hungary. If, therefore, one had to
settle the fate of districts where they are strong, e.g. the Bačka and
the Banat, on the basis of the supposed wishes of the population,
without the help of a plebiscite, one would have to count them as
being on the side of Yugoslavia and Roumania respectively and
leave the areas accordingly under their present dispensation.

The Germans are not in the slightest degree attached to either
the Serbs or the Roumanians (still less to the Czechs); if Hungary
offered them more favourable terms, they would immediately
accept them and change their allegiance once more with the utmost
cheerfulness. They would, however, require to be assured that

Hungary's overtures were sincere and likely to prove permanent, and Hungary's past record and present policy have not encouraged that belief. Hungary is, of course, herself in a dilemma, because to increase her German population in the south-east and the east would mean to reinforce both the numbers and the national spirit of what she already possesses in the centre and west; and she is not at all certain that this would not lead to an irredentist movement in her western Counties, and perhaps to the eventual loss of fresh territory to a *gleichgeschaltet* Austria. That, however, is, as we say, her look-out.

The fact remains that, in large parts of what used to be South-eastern Hungary, the Germans to-day hold the local balance between the Magyars and the Serbs and Roumanians respectively. If Hungary chose to adopt such a policy as would tempt the Germans to wish to return to her, there would be a good case for restoring the areas in which Germans and Magyars together hold a clear majority over Serbs or Roumanians.

Up to a few years ago the Šokci, Bunyevci, and 'Wends' of the Prekomurje might fairly have been counted as third-party minorities. To-day they, with the Slovaks of the Voivodina, ought probably to be reckoned with the Yugoslavs. There remains, however, the case of the Ruthenes, who cannot at present be attached to any national State of their own. The true reasons for giving Ruthenia to Czechoslovakia were strategic, whereas the economic argument for restoring it to Hungary, in the interests of all parties, is exceedingly strong. While recognizing, therefore, the good work which Czechoslovakia has done in that country, contrasting as it does most favourably with what Hungary did and left undone before the War, and recognizing also that considerations of 'Weltpolitik' must be given exceptional weight in this area, I have yet written that in my opinion the interests of the local population would be better served if it were restored to Hungary. In order, however, to prevent national, social, and economic injustice, it would have to be given a very wide degree of autonomy, based, perhaps, on the draft worked out in 1918 but brought up to date in the light of later experience and placed, as Count Bethlen himself suggested, under an effective international guarantee. If this were not done, complaints would at once arise again, and those who recommended the change would regret their action.

The 'lesser revision' on lines something like these would, I believe, be only equitable. It accepts the principle of Hungary's dismemberment on national lines and seeks only to draw the consequences without favour to either party. I believe, too, that it would remove a considerable number of the acute causes of friction in the Danube valley to-day. It would not seriously diminish either

Yugoslavia or Roumania; and I think it possible that Hungary herself might in time come to accept it as a final solution as far as these two countries are concerned. Even to-day, as often in the past, the Magyars and Serbs have often inclined, as it were *malgré eux* and in the intervals of acute controversy, towards friendship; and it is not at all impossible that if Roumania treated her Magyar population wisely she might make of it a bridge for establishing a similar friendly relationship with Hungary.

There remains, however, the case of Slovakia, which is far more difficult. One cannot fairly suggest that no local concessions should be given to Hungary at the expense of Slovakia. Czechoslovakia was treated fully as generously, in points of detail, as either of her two allies. Yet the concessions were in a way more necessary to her and even local readjustment might seriously endanger her.

The fact is, of course, that while Yugoslavia and Roumania, in spite of their internal difficulties, are really solidly founded blocs which can stand a good deal of chipping, Czechoslovakia is a fine but delicate structure, which a little pressure here or there might shake very badly. It has too many danger-points, too many vital necessities. Since the Historic Lands contain one German for every two Czechs, the Slovaks are vital to enable the Czechs to preserve their dominant position; the strip of plain in the south is vital, for economic reasons and to make communications possible; Ruthenia is vital to enable the structure thus built up to keep in touch with its allies; and so on. And in the minds of many, Czechoslovakia herself is vital to the balance of European power.

So long as Czechoslovakia exists, and so long as we accept the system of the national State in the Danube valley, then we must say of the Slovaks what has been said of the Serbs and the Roumanians: that it would be contrary to the principle of self-determination to hand them back to Hungary to-day. One can only propose local readjustments, leaving the main position as it stands now.

It is, however, much less easy to imagine Hungary resting permanently content with such minor changes in the north, than in the east or the south. For the historic, economic, and also the spiritual connexions between Northern and Central Hungary were in the past always far closer than those between the centre and the remote and exposed east and south. The severance of those connexions has inflicted upon her a real blow from which it seems doubtful—on economic grounds, if none other—whether she can ever entirely recover.

We are thus faced with two requirements which cannot possibly be reconciled on the basis of the national State; and although it may appear utopian and unpractical to suggest it, I am convinced that the only true solution for the problem of Slovakia, as indeed for that of the Historic Lands of the Czechoslovak Republic, for Transylvania, and ultimately for the whole Middle Danube Basin, lies in the abandonment, by all concerned, of this unlucky attempt to make a single nation dominate an area inhabited by so many different nationalities.

It is an attempt that has never once proved successful. During the earlier period of Hungary's history, as we showed, conditions were widely different, and the ideas of modern nationalism were unknown. Then followed the age of the Habsburgs, when Hungary, although *de jure* independent, was *de facto* bound hand and foot. A hundred years ago began the movement which evolved into the attempt by the Magyars to create of Hungary a *Magyar* national State. Looking back we may say that in this or that particular she was unlucky, that, given more time, she might have made more progress. But the conditions were actually more favourable than not, and the fact remains that she failed. The Treaty of Trianon is proof thereof.

Thus it is true to say that up to 1918 a national State in the modern sense of the word never existed in the Danube basin; the attempt to create one only led to disrupture of the old political unity. The natural deduction would be that this form of State is unfitted to local conditions, and therefore not destined to endure. The history of events since 1919 seems to me only to have confirmed that lesson. The Successor States have the advantage over Hungary of blocs of their majority peoples (or peoples able to fulfil that role) outside the areas which they have received at Hungary's expense; but within those areas only Austria among them has very many fewer minorities, relatively to the total population, than Hungary had herself. Practically all these minorities are discontented with their position, and must always remain so, so long as they are treated as minorities in both the numerical and the moral sense. A solution which is repudiated by so large a proportion of the peoples concerned has few of the marks of permanency.

Those who believe in the principle of the present order, without being blind to its defects, yet hope that by extending and improving the system of minority protection, and by removing tariff barriers and similar obstacles to free intercourse, the frontiers could be so 'spiritualized' as to become invisible. I should be the last to deny the advisability of better minority protection, which is one of the most urgent needs of to-day, and ought to be a first object of consideration, whether the frontiers are modified or left intact. But it is useless blinking the fact that no minority protection yet devised has prevented any State from doing with its minorities precisely as it wished. The only real check hitherto has been such intrinsic strength as some individual minority may have possessed.

The most elaborate improvement of the League machinery will hardly alter this position very greatly. As for economic co-operation, this, if it ever comes, will be a consequence and not a cause of political appeasement. Political considerations have hitherto invariably outweighed economic. Hitherto, far from becoming invisible, the frontiers have grown more and more formidable during the past twenty years.

The only permanent solution of the problem of the Danube basin lies in the adoption of complete national equality among its inhabitants—the transformation of the area into a true 'Eastern Switzerland' in which every nationality alike can find national liberty and a national home. If this principle once prevails, it may truly be argued that it does not particularly matter where the frontiers are drawn. If, in spite of this, I still hanker after seeing a unified territory re-established corresponding more closely to that of the old Hungary, this is because of geographical and economic considerations. Some parts of the old Hungary have fared better than others since 1919; a few corners may actually have gained by their altered position. But, broadly speaking, the old Hungary did form a natural unit which seemed to possess an inherent strength lacking in some of its successors, and a State established within those boundaries, but on a better political basis, should be able to secure for its inhabitants a higher standard of living than the new formations based on ethnographical considerations.

The old Hungary certainly commanded very strong centripetal forces, of one kind or another. It has shown in the past a very remarkable coherence which cannot be altogether fortuitous. There were centrifugal forces too, notably that of nationality, which became so strong that in 1919 all else had to give way before it. Yet I cannot but regard the present solution as one of despair. I believe that the forces making for unity will ultimately prove so strong that a way will be found to adjust the relationships between the different nationalities in such manner that they will find it not merely possible to live together, but impossible to do otherwise. I think that it can fairly be said of Hungary what Palácky said of Austria in 1848: that if she did not exist it would be necessary to invent her.

INDEX

PRINTED IN GREAT BRITAIN AT THE UNIVERSITY PRESS, OXFORD
BY JOHN JOHNSON, PRINTER TO THE UNIVERSITY

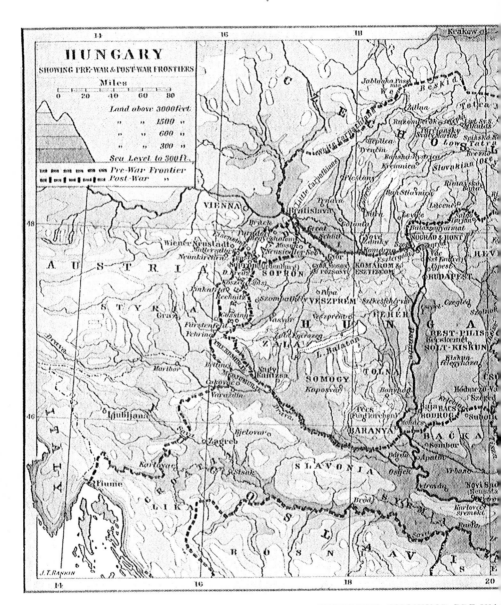

HUNGARY, SHOWING PRE-WA[R]

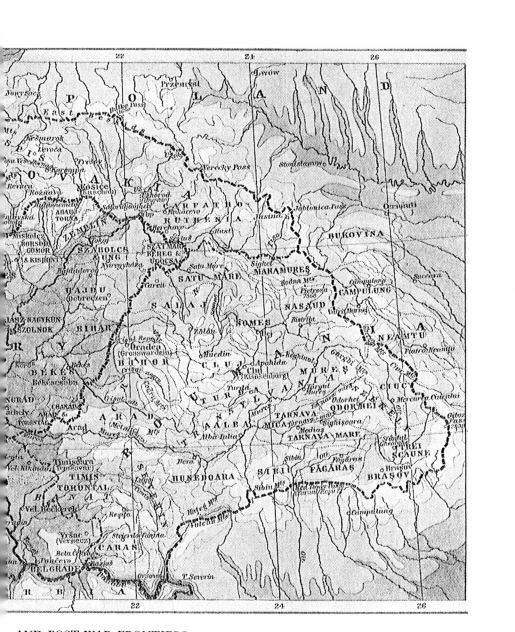

AND POST-WAR FRONTIERS